# THE TROUBLE WITH CANADA
# ...STILL!

# THE TROUBLE WITH CANADA ...STILL!

## A CITIZEN SPEAKS OUT

## WILLIAM D. GAIRDNER

Toronto and New York
www.bpsbooks.com

First published in 2010 by Key Porter Books, Toronto

Published in 2011 by
BPS Books
Toronto and New York
www.bpsbooks.com
A division of Bastian Publishing Services Ltd.

ISBN 967-1-926645-67-4

Cataloguing-in-Publication Data available from Library and Archives Canada.


Cover design: Sonya V. Thursby
Cover image: Veer
Text design and typesetting: Alison Carr

*For my family*
*and all who cherish*
*freedom and responsibility*

# TABLE OF CONTENTS

# ACKNOWLEDGEMENTS

There are many people to whom I owe the deepest gratitude for helping me shape this book. First and foremost are my wife, family, and friends, who so often, even when they found themselves unfairly captive to my concerns of the moment, willingly served as sounding board and critic for many of the ideas expressed here.

Many others have assisted by way of direct research, tax calculations and charts, fact-finding, editorial comment, or, most often, with counter-arguments in open discussion that helped with the discernments essential to any such enterprise. I thank most sincerely: Niels Veldhuis, Milagros Palacios, Nadeem Esmail, Martin Collacott, James Bissett, John Thompson, Kevin Gaudet, Derek Fildebrandt, Janet Ajzenstat, Ian Gentles, Rory Leishman, Gwen Landolt, Diane Watts, Rainer Knopff, Chris Sarlo, Tom Flanagan, Ken Kristjanson, Salim Mansur, John von Heyking, Jean-Luc Migué, Richard Bastien, André Carrel, and Brian Day.

My gratitude to the staff of Key Porter Books of Toronto for their confidence in undertaking the first edition of this anniversary edition of the book, especially for the enthusiasm and intellectual interest of executive editor Jonathan Schmidt, the careful copy editing by Liba Berry, the insights and energy of Tom Best, VP Marketing, and the efforts of publicist Katherine Wilson. My thanks as well to the intrepid warriors of BPS Books for publishing the paperback edition.

# PREFACE TO THE 2010 EDITION

When I began this revised and updated version some twenty years after the original, I was a little surprised that my feelings and motives were no less strong than in 1990. For a writer, the revision process after such a long period is an adventure because it forces an encounter between the facts then, and the facts now, the author then, and the author now. So I confess to a certain curiosity because many of the facts of our national life have changed, and so have I. More time, deeper reading, and more thinking about the trouble with Canada meant I was going to have to argue a little with the person I was in 1990.

## THE FIRST WARNINGS: WHEN I VOTED FOR TRUDEAU

My first sense there was trouble with Canada began during the Trudeau era (1968–1984) when I saw this fine country falling into the clutches of what I was quite certain were sweet-sounding but inherently destructive political, economic, and social policies. Until then, I was a completely non-political person who had actually voted once for the bright-sounding man with the rose in his lapel. I always admired Trudeau's strength of character, political savvy, passion, and decisiveness. In retrospect, I still do. But my instinct told me he was instigating a one-man regime change for the worse in the country I knew and loved. In all the most important political, economic, social, and legal aspects of Canadian life he was turning the country upside down. And by what right? Political and legislative change of the ordinary sort is one thing; that can be reversed by a free people. But changes to the fundamental moral, legal, economic, and even linguistic foundations and understandings of an entire people ought to require more than a slim majority in Parliament.

So, entirely new feelings began to arise, along with a pervasive sense of helplessness. For how do you fight back when the political parties among which we must choose are so identical in their thinking? No party back then was complaining—or has since complained—about the sudden transformation of Canada from a free, common law–based constitutional democracy in which *the will of the people as voiced in Parliament was "supreme,"* into a new, constitutionally mandated welfare state far too often directed by the rule of unelected judges who cannot be removed by any power in the land.[1] Trudeau plopped his Canadian Charter of Rights and Freedoms on top of us in 1982, and it states (sec. 52) that to the extent that any (existing or future) law of Canada is "inconsistent" with the Charter, it is "of no force or effect." As I saw it, with the stroke of his pen, the will of the Canadian people was subjected forevermore to an alien form of entrenched, judge-dictated Statism. This book is one man's best effort to lay bare the details of this regime change and to suggest ways to reverse it and regain our true freedoms and rights.

This is not a book about Trudeau. But I am very critical of Trudeau and his socialist fellow-travellers of that time, for I saw him then, and still do, rather as Tolstoy saw Napoleon. The dictator, he said, was an actor in the tide of time, a man riding inside the carriage of history, holding ribbons that he thought were the reins. In the same vein, and with lots of personal flourish, Trudeau was a kind of flamboyant actor on the stage of Canadian history, reading his lines and cues from a script written mostly by influential French social planners of the seventeenth century and forward. So although Trudeau often comes under attack in this book, its main thrust is not personal. Rather, it is a critique of an entire style of continental rationalism of which his whole life—his lifelong motto was "Reason before Passion"—was an expression. I argue that even though this style of rational social planning gave rise to a politics alien to our founding ideals and to our roots in British liberty, he nevertheless almost single-handedly managed to impose it on an entire nation, and for that we continue to pay the price detailed in this book.

## WESTERN COMMUNISM GONE
## (NOW ON DISPLAY ONLY IN TAX-FUNDED UNIVERSITIES)

In the twenty years since 1990, in many unexpected ways, Canada and the world have changed a lot. As if in an impossible dream, we witnessed the astonishingly rapid demise of international communism and the Soviet bloc, the crumbling of the Berlin Wall, the end of "the Evil Empire." Many of us hoped this would be a final and definitive lesson to the West that socialism doesn't work, except in heaven where you don't need it, and in hell where you already have it. But we can see now that the Evil Empire served a beneficial purpose, too. It was America's—and the West's—definitive ideological enemy, and by dint of sheer opposition it provoked us to hang on to the fragments and tatters of our founding belief in liberty. But there has not been a totalitarian "enemy on the Left" for some time now against which to contrast and defend those beliefs. And with the ascension of Barack Obama to the U.S. presidency—an office that a tyranny-fearing American founder, in a wonderfully memorable expression, condemned as "the fetus of Monarchy"—we are at this very moment watching our once freedom-loving neighbours charge full steam into the arms of the State.

This still feels rather strange to anyone who recalls that in the aftermath of World War II, to call someone "a socialist"—let alone "a Red," or "a communist," or "a pinko"—was tantamount to the worst of insults, both in Canada and the United States. After all, people such as my godfather, who died at twenty-two when his Spitfire was shot down south of Paris with a 500-pound bomb on board, were convinced they were fighting to prevent the spread of Statism, whether national socialist (Nazism), or international socialist (communism). But now the word "socialist" has come into common parlance as a normal and acceptable descriptive term for ... what *we* have become. I am certain if my god-father could return to see what we have done with the freedoms for which he gave his life, he would say he died in vain.

## WORLD WAR IV AND THE CLASH OF CIVILIZATIONS

The other major change is still very much with us. The burning images of the Twin Towers collapsing and people leaping to their death from melting windows—the shock of 9/11 and the threat of Islamist jihad—have caused some astute observers to say: "Wake up!" For in the eyes of many experts, just as the Cold War was in reality a protracted World War III, 9/11 announced the commencement of World War IV. It is but a recent expression of a centuries-long advance-and-retreat between Christendom (the now-secularized "West") and Islam that has finally manifested in our backyard.

## WHAT ABOUT A BOOK?

It was pretty clear that by 1990 a lot of citizens had fundamental objections to, and felt tremendous frustration over, Canada's regime change, primarily because until the now-defunct Reform Party arose there was not a single political party to which they could turn in protest. All were embracing some form of Statism. The whole country seemed to have undergone a kind of historical amnesia, forgetting our root beliefs in limited government, our many safeguards—constitutional, legal, and cultural—against political tyranny, our long, bloodied, and halting history from Magna Carta forward in defence of British liberty. In the end, a single vote seemed useless as a protest. But might the country be brought to its senses by a book explaining the trouble with Canada?

The story I wanted to tell was, and still is, aimed at all concerned citizens searching for answers to our troubles. Once empowered with a little knowledge of the political and moral contradictions and paradoxes of the turn we had just taken, would we, could we reverse our course? In this respect I departed from the general view that we are a calm, compromising, pragmatic people. I have always felt that this notion is a self-congratulation that to our national detriment might very well camouflage a spiritual dullness and a certain lack of intellectual and moral vigour. I hoped that a tell-it-like-it-is book—a cavalry charge from an unexpected quarter—would stir us from our slumber.

At the twentieth anniversary of this book there is a broader and deeper story to tell. The bones of the story, so to speak, are the same. But a lot of the muscle and sinew is very new. This book is broader and deeper than the original and in addition to the fresh facts, the numbers, the objectively measurable signs and symptoms of our national course, it probes the most significant moral questions that ought never to have slipped our consciousness for so long.

I remain convinced that any whole truth sincerely expressed will eventually find its readers, despite how severely that truth is initially suppressed or discouraged by those whom it makes uncomfortable.

We still live in a free country.

But it is mostly books that keep it free.

# INTRODUCTION

On the whole, Canada is a great place to live. It's beautiful, wealthy, politically stable (unless engaged in a bogus referendum on Quebec separation), does not make war, and is rarely subject to natural disasters. What more could we hope for? What we see on the surface is a healthy, harmonious picture.

But despite their outward appearances, countries, like biological organisms, bear within themselves the seeds of their own health or decay. We admire a woman's beauty spot until one day we learn it has turned cancerous. Same spot. But a very different judgment. Just so, and despite external appearances, there is within all countries a constant, ever-present struggle between the political, economic, and cultural forces that lead to strength, and those that lead to weakness. Canada still seems a very healthy nation as compared to many others, and there are very few other countries in which I would care to live. But all nations rise, maintain for a while, then enter a long decline. None has ever escaped this historical truth, and it is the job of the writer to spy—if he can—the forces of success or decline invisibly at work. This book is written for all Canadians concerned about the next generation, a plea to remember, to recognize, to defend, and, where possible, to return to the core political, economic, and moral values that made Canada so strong in the first place.

Alas, what we increasingly see is a flight from commonly held values altogether, about which very few seem bothered. Morality, indeed, the entire notion of objective truth, has been relativized and privatized to such an extent that we no longer conceive of truth in any common public sense.[1] We don't care how others live as long as they don't harm us personally. When it comes to whether or not their individual behaviour reflects poorly on us all, demeans our society, corrodes our sense of nationhood and civic pride, sets a terrible example for youth, or is shameful in itself and therefore an insult to community standards . . . we don't ask. We're all travelling solo like passengers on a ship with no particular course, just "a-blowin' in the wind." Very few bother to ask where we came from, or where we are headed. If we seek direction at all, it's usually from the hip science of the day (mostly picked up from newspapers), or perhaps from something we saw on the Internet, or the evening news. As for the eternal issues of human life? We are by now quite accustomed to waiting for judges to tell us what is right and wrong (with relief that we no longer have to bother our own heads about such things. Phew!). In this respect, many of us have simply surrendered the fundamental responsibility all free citizens ought to feel to play a role, large or small, in directing the course of their common life. Instead, a lazy, misplaced respect for "experts" overrules our best natural instincts and judgments. And hey, as long as what you do doesn't harm me, who cares?

Without the social bonding that arises naturally from common vision and purpose, however, daily life becomes increasingly a war of all against all. Looking out for Number One. Then the rules of the game change very rapidly. We change from a well-formed society sharing a general and deeply felt—even if unarticulated—agreement about the good things we honour and want conserved, and the bad things we simply will not put up with, into a mere collection of taxpayers who have abandoned all effort to sustain a common life. We will still quickly form into self-interested groups for merely pragmatic reasons of personal advantage, money, or power. But in general our society, once considered a kind of well-functioning molecule, so to speak, seems fragmented into its constituent particles, or atomized. We seem increasingly to be self-regarding individuals wandering around on the deck with only our differences or diversity to celebrate, yet oh so ready to be "outraged," to demonstrate publicly, to protest or defend, only if our personal interests are threatened. Do we any longer share a common higher vision?

## THE DYNAMICS OF THE POLITICAL SANDWICH

Here is a handy metaphor that will recur in this book, and that I believe is of utmost importance.

All free nations (distinctly not unfree ones) may be visualized as forming a kind of three-layered structure, a political sandwich, so to speak, each layer distinguished by its form of control.

At the top is *the State*, the only layer with a monopoly on force. Its form of control is coercion and power, and it is therefore authoritarian by definition.

In the middle is *civil society*, a community of countless voluntarily formed human associations such as families, clubs, sports teams, corporations, churches, charities, and so on, which has no monopoly on force and so must rely for cohesion and control on the various forms of moral authority it naturally generates by means of religion, parental instruction and obligation, employment contracts, rules of conduct, the natural leadership of the highly esteemed, and so on. This authority is voluntarily accepted by members of society who choose to live, work, and play within such groupings, or it is rejected at a price. But for adults at least, social and moral authority is never coercive because no one is forced by law to join or to leave a family, a church, a team, a university, a charity, or a company, and so on, except for misconduct, malfeasance, terms of contract, and the like.

At the bottom is the mass of *autonomous individuals* whose natural form of control (or lack thereof) is self-control.

As we go forward, I will be speaking more about the natural tendency of the coercive State at the top to undermine and weaken the freely formed middle layer of civil society so as to garner the allegiance of and achieve increased control over the millions of autonomous individuals in the bottom layer. It does this by taxing citizens at increasingly heavy rates over time, and with the funds substituting sweet-sounding government goods and services for as many as possible of those goods and services that the members of civil society once provided for, or offered voluntarily to, or sold to, each other. In this way, over time, the regulatory, or welfare, or cradle-to-grave Nanny State substitutes itself for civil society as the origin of human security and happiness.

## WHAT INTERESTS THE POLITICIANS

The socialist, modern liberal, or Statist (in modern political history, at least), tends to be most interested in capturing control of the top layer.

The conservative tends to concentrate on conserving the vitality, solidarity, and freedom from excessive government of the middle layer. He strives to block takeover by the State from the top, and all weakening of the natural social and moral bonds of civil society due to increasing pressure of individualism that arises from the bottom.

The libertarian tends to deplore the authoritarianism of the top layer, distrusts the moral and social authority that is an emergent property of the middle layer, and celebrates only the freedom of the autonomous individual at the bottom.

The concern of the conservative, then—it is also my own—is that the best and only proven protection for the freedom of individuals is the social bonding that is natural to, that is, in fact, a spontaneous property of the middle layer in which individuals are formed in the first place. In other words, individuals do not "enter" society at any time, as if by contract, from outside it. They are created within healthy societies that serve both as the enabling and restraining forces of human character. Individuals, however, no matter how well formed, are powerless to resist the state by themselves. But millions of them, freely bonded by a common allegiance to the myriad voluntary associations of civil society, especially when united against Statist values, can easily do so.

That is why conservatives, from ancient times to the present (again, I am not talking about any so-called "conservative" political party now, for many of these have betrayed this very point), although they have never denied the value of individual liberty, insist that the rights, claims, and institutions of civil society (that middle layer) constitute *a set of real relations greater than the sum of the individuals that comprise them.* Society, in other words, is not just some abstraction. It comprises real concrete relations that are prior in importance to, and that cannot be derived solely from, the existence of mere individuals.

Once having arrived at this understanding of the political dynamic, everything then comes down to the central question it is the pleasurable burden of this book to address. Namely, do we wish to be a nation guided by a philosophy of free and responsible individuals working with each other in home, in village, in civil society, and in the larger community of the nation to reconstitute and defend such free and commonly valued ends? Or, must we abandon all such vision and therefore any possible common ends and turn over ever more of the responsibility for the direction of our lives and our once-free society to the regulating State?

## PLUNDER BY ALL POLITICAL PARTIES

Alas, the latter choice seems to be winning out, and it is leaving a scandalous trail! For the first hundred years after our founding in 1867 until Trudeau came along in 1968, we Canadians more or less thrived by living well within our means. We all understand that it is essential to give government enough money to perform its basic public duties. But for much of that period this was done without any need for an income tax. Zero. Indeed, it is a surprise to learn that for most of human history, while taxes on trade, tariffs, and so on were considered to be morally acceptable, a tax on labour was considered utterly reprehensible, and the language used to describe the condition of a people forced to pay such a tax was the language of slavery. Here is the British-American revolutionist Josiah Quincy in 1774, protesting the mere *idea* of taxing human labour. For in such a regime, he cried out, "And I speak it with grief—I speak it with anguish—I speak it with shame—I speak it with indignation—we are slaves! The most abject sort of slaves!" For most of the long history of the English-speaking people, at least, an income tax was always considered a form of slavery-once-removed! For anyone will agree that if government confiscates 100 percent of your income, you are a slave. Just so, our own founders would have argued that any tax that takes half the fruit of your labour by force, every year of your life, makes you half-a-slave-once-removed. We have indeed changed! But, how? And, why?

## HOW BAD IS THE PLUNDER?

If we want a foolproof indicator of the degree to which a people is financially, if not physically, enslaved to the State, we just need an accurate picture of the annual total of all visible and hidden direct taxes paid, expressed as a percentage of Gross Domestic Product (GDP). Chapter 7, "Canada at a Glance," gives this sobering overview. When we add to this sorry picture the *total* national debt, which includes all federal, provincial, municipal, and Crown corporation debt, as well as all unfunded liabilities (promises by governments to fulfill its future obligations), we get a picture of the extent to which government obligates even future generations of unborn citizens to pay for our profligate current consumption. Canada's national debt waits like a vulture to pick meat from the bones of citizens yet to be born.

For those interested in the numbers, the short story is that all three levels of government in Canada had accumulated some $791.2 billion in direct debt by 2008. This was down a little from the $800.4 billion in 2001, but way up from the $533 billion of 1991—the year after the first edition of this book was published. In addition to this burden, there are today more than $2.4 trillion in total (unfunded) government liabilities (promises to pay in the form of future obligations such as Medicare and Old Age Security). The so-called "stimulus" spending triggered in 2010 is estimated to balloon this net direct debt by another $50-plus billion very soon, and billions more every year until . . . who knows when? As of 2008 all this debt resulted in $75,942 owing in eventual taxes by every citizen—every man, woman, and child—in Canada, or over $150,211 for every taxpayer, or over $385,000 per family of four with only one taxpayer. In view of the rapid demographic change in Canada due to fewer children being born, and a rapidly aging population, it is pretty clear that Canada's various levels of government are making promises they cannot keep. Those who want a quick picture of Canada's federal debt should visit www.debtclock.ca and watch the meter running. At $53,000 per minute, by the time I have finished typing this Introduction, in only *two hours*, Canada will have accrued millions more in debt! At this rate, we accumulate $135 million in new debt liability per day.

## OUR FOUNDERS' MESSAGE WAS: "HANDS OFF!"

There is a long history of expert opinion, from the ancient writer Polybius, to Montesquieu and Burke (our founders were familiar with all of them), to the effect that no system that had a democratic element could work in a large country, because people cannot be expected to care about the shenanigans of legislators thousands of miles away with whom they can never meet nor shake by the collar. So the powers of government would have to be divided between central, or general, functions that concern the whole nation, and local matters that concern only each region. Then, Canada would need a constitution that would bar central government from meddling in too many local affairs, and that had the additional advantage of enabling each province to manage its own local budgets, culture, schooling, health care, and the like. This was especially important to Quebec, the only province with a French-Catholic majority, a French culture, and a heritage of French "code law" (much more about that in chapter 1). In general, we created a system of British liberty that sent the message "Hands off!" to excessive central government control from thousands of miles away over the lives of individuals in their local communities. Indeed, it was one of our French-Canadian founders, Sir Etienne-Paschal Taché, who proclaimed in a loud voice, "The last cannon which is shot on this continent in defence of

Great Britain will be fired by the hand of a French Canadian." How stirring!

From the start, Canadians were rightly suspicious of all democratic mob rule, of "strong democracy" by which the 51 percent think they have a right to oppress the 49 percent. The horrors of the "democratic" French Revolution were still alive in memory, and the Americans in their "republic" (and despite their own safeguards against too much democracy) were tearing each other to pieces south of the border in a democratic fratricide.

That is why our softer democratic element (elections only for the House of Commons and the provincial legislatures) is "representative," and not direct, and why our senators are appointed (rather than elected), for they represent regions, rather than electors. From the start we granted a more important role to central government than did our American neighbours, who began with a stronger revulsion for government tyranny. To make a federal system, however, like them we divided powers between central and local governments in our Constitution (the BNA Act, 1867). But to want a *strong* central government does not mean we ever wanted a *BIG*—correction, a *HUGE* central government. We also wanted *to prevent the tyranny of Statism*. For example, our original Constitution forbade provinces to borrow beyond their own means, or credit. And there were measures designed to prevent central government from invading, overpowering, or otherwise controlling local affairs by means of fiscal bribery, or by ignoring the constitutional division of powers separating a list of specific *provincial* duties and functions from a list of specific *general* (or what we now call "federal") government duties. All our founders wanted *to prevent big government from infantilizing its own citizens.*

But the idea that has replaced this founding ideal is quite otherwise. I call it "coercive humanitarianism." We have moved from a notion of what I owe and must do, to what I am owed and must have. From providing for myself and those to whom I have obligations, to ensuring I get by law from others what I think I deserve. From giving, to getting.

Given this situation, we must ask, how can such a problem—a national moral illness, really—be cured? My answer is that we must first clearly understand the illness (Part One of this book) before considering the possible cures (in Part Two).

## ARE WE CREATING TOOLS OF SUCCESS, OR DECLINE?

A main argument of the book is that once the negative effects of the "Popular Illusions" are surmounted, there will naturally arise from any society that energetically promotes the "Freedom System" I describe, a definable set of values and institutions, which, once effectively put in place and supported with the right cultural attitudes, will produce responsible freedom and adequate wealth almost anywhere on earth. Of course, having the tools is one thing. Using them and sustaining the right culture and the right laws to properly maintain them is another.

For more than a century and a half in the Western democracies, these tools—dependent as they are on liberty (especially economic liberty)—have been under attack by those who promote what I call a "Handicap System," under which liberty is suppressed by egalitarian Statism. This reaction has always been easy to see in the works and writings of the international socialist movement, and for most of the twentieth century was far more radical than what we have seen in Canada. Here, adverse reactions to the tools of freedom and wealth creation range from simple failure to defend them, to unwitting support for radical policies by otherwise well-intentioned people unaware of the ideological consequences of their own thinking, to well-orchestrated efforts to lobby for outright socialist programs and legislative measures intentionally destructive of our nation's success. In many cases, as we shall see, Canadian governments have actually bankrolled radical groups openly aiming to overturn our traditional way of life. How can this be?

## THE LEFT-RIGHT PENDULUM ... IS MOVING LEFTWARD

It must be observed that even though the old right-left pendulum continues to swing in many nations (from liberal to conservative, democrat to republican, and back again, under whatever catchy labels), the general direction, the pendulum itself, whether at the moment moving left or right, tends to move evermore leftward, to more Statism. This is true even of Canada's most "conservative" parties. For example, in the past any truly conservative party would have detested the mere idea of a state controlling personal health care, rationing it, or regulating it, of anonymous bureaucrats sneaking peeks at your private doctor-patient records without your permission, and so on. But neither the Reform Party when it existed, nor the current Conservative party of Canada has ever dared object openly to socialized medicine. Not even close. Neither will any of them touch truly conservative social or moral issues with a ten-foot pole. I mean to say that even members of conservative parties are for the most part only "fiscal conservatives," and are otherwise in many respects leftist and Statist themselves. The Conservative prime minister Brian Mulroney, for example, outspent even the socialist Pierre Trudeau. And in retrospect, it seems bizarre that everywhere in the world, as an insightful contemporary author has put it, what we mostly see is *more democracy, but less freedom*.[2] In other words, more Statism, and more official means to punish transgressions of State orthodoxy. Now, isn't that a paradox? Democracies—political systems that were supposed to ensure more freedom and political control *by* the people—are, in fact, increasingly regulating our lives and shutting freedom down. A good test of this assertion would be to ask anyone this question: "Can you name a single country in modern history that, as measured by the size of its tax burden, has reduced the size and influence of the State." Then listen to the silence.

## CANADA AT A GLANCE

In "Canada at a Glance" we will see charts showing graphically exactly what has happened to Canada over the span of many decades. With respect to such things as national wealth and debt, personal income and taxation, and other such vital matters, readers will be able to see where we stand today as compared to the nation we once were, and also where we stand among nations of the world. A nation irresponsible in its economic behaviour can be compared to an irresponsible family, corporation, or individual. The difference is that when these latter go bankrupt, they have to close their doors, immediately mend their ways, and start over. But a nation can go bankrupt with the doors open simply by taxing its citizens at ever higher rates and by printing money. Canada still looks pretty responsible when compared to many other nations. But the signs of trouble are here and have been present for some time, visible to those prepared to see them. Canada has no room to move. We have only massive debt; no surpluses. So, if the illness isn't treated properly and there happens to be a real crisis, Canada could get very sick.

## THE ISSUES

Part Two of the book deals with the issues at a much deeper level than in the original edition, digging far below the surface to find the truth camouflaged by our many ideological confusions. For this section, the reader had best be sitting down. Examined are a strange welfare system that hands out money not only to the poor, but also dollops of it to the middle class and the rich; a leaky immigration system so badly run that it has been changing the country from within without anyone's expressed permission; a mediocre medical system that rations health care and has even threatened jail for trying to spend your own money to get better private care (not even the communist countries did that!); a foreign-aid fiasco where a lot of our money ends up in the hands of the international war machine, or of terrorists, or is used to buy weapons for despots; a radical feminism that undermines our deepest family traditions and that has so afflicted our society that we have now become anti-male; a multiculturalism and diversity program that by definition erodes our unity and our founding heritage; a criminal justice system that is dangerously lenient and that over the years has released thousands of violent offenders into society, even though we know almost to a certainty how many of them will re-offend, or even kill again; and many other disturbing subjects that are dividing our nation, and that have become "transactions of decline" in terms of nation-building.

It is my objective to show that these issues are real-world expressions of the confused philosophical and ideological tensions highlighted in part one. So the aim will be to question these policies sharply, and to suggest—no, to insist—that all Canadians should take a more active role in deciding what the common vision—the course, direction, and life of our nation—ought to be, and in ensuring that our public policies reflect that vision. But no one can make a sincere judgment as to how the issues of our national life ought to play out until they have made a concerted effort to inform themselves on the reasoning (or lack thereof) by which they are justified. Why, exactly, are we doing something this way instead of that way?

Enter the role of the writer. I make no claim in this book to have presented all possible sides of every issue. That would be a daunting task. Besides, the positions of those whose views I strongly oppose are available in almost any Canadian newspaper on a daily basis. What I have tried to do instead is to present the troubles, the strong arguments against them, and then the alternatives that I think could prevent us from going over the cliff toward which I believe we are headed in one policy area after another.

Mention should also be made of the fact that this book, unlike the first edition, contains a number of "Snapshots" which are intended to serve as windows onto the special facts or arguments provoked by the corresponding text. They make it easier for readers to mentally summarize various situations.

There are a lot of fireworks in this book, and I certainly don't expect everyone to agree with all the views expressed. However, if a sincere effort is made to face the bald facts and sincere arguments set out here, readers will better understand the great majority of silenced Canadians who are upset with, even appalled by, what has been done to their country.

# PART ONE
## THROUGH THE LOOKING GLASS

# 1: CANADA'S REGIME CHANGE

*The two great things that all men aim at in any free government*
*are liberty and permanency . . . there is not on the face of the earth*
*a freer people than the inhabitants of these colonies.*
—Thomas D'Arcy McGee, Legislative Assembly of Canada, February 9, 1865

*Self-reliance is the best means of education in politics as in anything else.*
*If our rulers are sent us from England or Ottawa we will always lack*
*self-reliance . . . "Rely on yourselves" is the cry of the people of England.*
—Francis Barnard, Legislative Council of British Columbia, March 21, 1870

## FREEDOM, VIRTUE, AND AUTHORITY

The central fact of the nation for the past half century is the transformation, or (to use a current term) the "regime change," that began in the mid-1960s and continues to shape our way of life. Bound to it, like electrons rotating around a nucleus, is a cluster of historical, political, social, economic, and even sexual realities it will be the aim of this chapter to explore. At first it may seem bizarre to suggest connections between things so disparate as the nation's constitution, its sexual attitudes, and something like the national debt, but by the end the connections should be very clear. Before looking in detail at exactly where we are, however, let's take a look at how we got here in the first place.

The deepest political question facing any nation has to do with its choice of system, or style of government. How should we work out the problems of *freedom, virtue,* and *authority*? What are the limits of freedom? What is the nature of the social good, the virtue for which we strive? How much or how little should these matters be controlled by the State? These questions are of timeless and universal concern to all people, and the way in which they are answered by the nation and by individuals dictates the framework within which we exercise power over each other, earn our living, use our manners, punish our criminals, and otherwise build our lives. As it happens, the answers to these questions have been deployed in two opposing patterns throughout the Western world, and Canada has been a laboratory for both.

## TWO OPPOSING PATTERNS OF GOVERNMENT

The roots of these patterns, or styles, may be traced to ancient times, but their more recent modern expressions are to be found in the French and Anglo-Scottish Enlightenments of the mid- to late-eighteenth century, and forward.[1] Because both styles found a home in Canada, it is extremely important for us to understand the difference between the "French" and the "English" visions, for they were at war on our soil before the birth of our nation, and have been in legal, linguistic, cultural, and constitutional tension in Canada ever since. I will be arguing that we may think of Canada's regime change as "The Revenge of Montcalm," because although the English won the territorial battle in 1759, the French won the constitutional war in 1982.[2]

The terms "French" and "English" are more than just convenient labels, for these two very different methods of social and political organization found their earliest homes and most complete theoretical expressions in France and England. The first has its modern origin in the so-called "rationalist" mentality of the influential French philosopher René Descartes (1596–1650). The second is rooted in the anti-rational "organic" theories having to do with spontaneous social and economic organization that were worked out by the English (and the Scots). As a visitor to France or England I could not choose between my affections for either place; but I know under which style of government, law, and freedom I distinctly prefer to live. The crucial difference between these two styles comes down to their opposing views of civilization. For the French school, civilization has always been raw material to be fashioned according to the rational plans of political philosophers. For the English school, civilization is an inheritance from wise predecessors, a product of centuries of trial and error, a tender growth rooted in ancient custom and tradition and not to be discarded lightly for any dream-world utopian plan.

### The "French Style"

The French style has distant Roman origins, but as practiced by modern governments it has become a prototype for bureaucratic Statism and is chiefly concerned with rationalized power. Rooted in the belief that the lowly masses need to be looked after, controlled, and raised up by their betters, this style results in an effort to create order and keep anarchy at bay by ensuring that an elite political class is maintained with the instinct and authority to instruct the people in social virtue. In modern France, for example, would-be politicians and civil servants are trained at special political schools.[3]

This is a top-down "managerial" (*dirigiste*) concept of society that rests on a utopian vision bent on social perfection—by force, if necessary. It is not a vision aiming for virtue, independence, and freedom in individual citizens. Rather, as it has a low view of human beings, it aims for social perfection and assumes that once this is properly engineered by a corps of trained political elites, all citizens will get used to their improved life, will conform, and will live happily under its tutelage. It is a style "shot through with romantic visions of a new political community in which all previous religions would be replaced with a new civic religion: the religion of rationalist humanism," and its passion is for "the universal regeneration of mankind."[4] The French Revolution was its political consequence, the Terror and the guillotine—killing off non-conforming citizens—its natural and bloody end, as it must be for all fanatically egalitarian regimes.

Jean-Jacques Rousseau laid the theoretical framework for this "democracy of the One" (my phrase) under which the will of each citizen is mystically absorbed into a virtuous single "General Will" (une volonté générale) that must then be "interpreted" by political leaders. Its simplest formulation can be seen in Rousseau's educational novel Émile, in which he urged all free individuals to "transport the I into the common unity, with the result that each individual believes himself no longer one but a part of the unity and no longer feels except within the whole." Although I am not certain he ever deeply understood the dangers inherent in the concept of a General Will, Canada's former prime minister Pierre Trudeau used the phrase repeatedly in his own work.[5] Someone has said "an institution, like a country, is the shadow of a man," and I argue that Canada is living in a shadow.

The most vicious recent forms of national striving for Rousseau's General Will were, of course, the National Socialist (Nazi) movement in Germany, the fascist movement in Italy, and the international socialist movement called communism. Each in its own way fancied itself to be a more pure form of "democracy" than anything theretofore attempted, and each relied on, and received, massive public support.[6] The astonishing rate at which the communist Evil Empire crumbled—of which there was barely a hint when work on the first edition of this book began in 1988—is vindication of the book's argument that taken to its extreme, this style of controlling freedom and making society virtuous must eventually turn against its own citizens and, as history has shown, may be murderous beyond belief.

In its softer forms, as in Canada, it tends radically to depress the wealth-creating instincts of the people by removing incentives for personal and family advancement, and at the extreme, substitutes for those instincts a pervasive dependency on the State, a labyrinth of regulation and taxation of commercial and social life, a fear of authority, a fear of speaking one's mind against the prevailing orthodoxies,[7] and a general clamouring for influence and bureaucratic power. After all, in such a system most of us would rather govern than be governed. Scholars such as Paul A. Rahe in Soft Despotism, Democracy's Drift, calls this style "the French disease"[8] or, less harshly, "the tutelary state." In this book it is called, simply, "Statism."

### A "Top-down" or "Handicap System"

The idea of coercing equality is not new in human history. In ancient Greek mythology, when Procrustes, the wicked son of Poseidon, saw that many of the travellers who came to his home did not fit his bed, he determined to make them fit either by stretching them on a rack or by cutting off their feet. The myth points to the well-known ideological imperative of this style, which is to operate on a coercive "handicap" theory of government whereby the strong or the "privileged"—or most often simply the most successful—must be handicapped in the hope of equalizing all. We shall see that such a method ends up handicapping the entire society, for more forced equality always requires more government, and absolute equality requires absolute government. In 1989, we were witnesses to an extraordinary display of popular reaction to this top-down phenomenon in the *glasnost* of the U.S.S.R. and the hunger strikes and nationwide demands for freedom in East Germany, Poland, and the Baltic States—and to its cruelty when the top-down system prevails utterly, as in the tragic oppression of freedom fighters at China's Tiananmen Square in June of that year.

Accordingly, and due to the necessary distinction between guiding elites and the people, such States inevitably create two kinds of law. They have the law of the land, most often set out in an idealistic and very abstractly worded national code. And they also have what the French call *droit administratif*, or administrative law, which is a set of special immunities and protections from the law of the land for all government officials and administrative officers. Typically, in the French style, officials of government are *above the law* for otherwise illegal acts done in the performance of their duties.[9] The language police in Quebec and in Canada at large, our Orwellian human rights commissioners, our pay equity police, affirmative action police, and many more such controllers are just a few examples.

### The "English Style"

The term "English style" is used not because the English are inherently better people, but because from the creation of Magna Carta in 1225, to the development of a system of parliamentary sovereignty in the seventeenth century, to the invention of dividing, checking, and balancing State power, they were the first to entrench in common law clear and concrete legal *means of action* for the protection of individual freedoms and property against abuses of power.[10] To this day, the ordinary English Habeas Corpus Acts protect free individuals from arbitrary State action, and as the great English legal scholar A.V. Dicey put it, they "are for practical purposes worth a hundred [abstract] constitutional articles guaranteeing individual liberty." That is because mere high-sounding legal principles, abstract statements or opinions about basic rights as if they were things conferred from on high, may be interpreted this way on Monday by one judge, and that way on Wednesday by another. Or, they may simply be removed by the stroke of a pen. But practical legal means that have existed as enforceable rights for centuries, and are to be found firmly embedded in hundreds of actual case-law precedents and in actual legal documents, contracts, deeds, and licences all over the land, can only be removed by invading every office, filing cabinet, business, and private home and vault. That is, by a total revolution.

In sum, under the French style individual rights are *deductions* drawn from the abstract principles of the constitution. A charter may declare proudly that we have a right to "freedom," but a judge is required to deduce what that word means. The meaning deduced may be arbitrary, and dependent only on the opinion of the judge. In the English style, in sharp contrast, the principles of the constitution are *inductions*, or generalizations based upon centuries of actual concrete decisions pronounced by courts as to the rights of given individuals that have then become precedents for the law of the land. The French judge wrestles with an abstract concept of "freedom." The English judge tries to decide if when someone parked his car in front of your driveway your real (not abstract) freedom was diminished. In the English system, concrete decisions based on real facts like blocking someone else's driveway and recorded in law cannot be altered by the arbitrary opinions or feelings of a judge because the fact determined was that the guy either blocked your driveway, or he didn't. And that becomes a precedent for deciding the meaning of freedom in all future driveway-blocking cases. Such real freedoms are not easily suspended because they are not dependent on judges' feelings or political leanings, but rather on fixed and final court facts, decisions, and settlements deemed reasonable.

From 1867 until 1982, Canada relied on the English style. Then came our regime change to the French style. The shadow. So, in Canada's 1982 Charter of Rights and Freedoms, what do we find written at the top, as Part One, as if our inherited freedoms and rights were suddenly transformed into a gift from government? These words:

> The Canadian Charter of Rights and Freedoms *guarantees* the rights and freedoms set out in it subject only to such reasonable limits prescribed by law as can be demonstrably justified in a free and democratic society [emphasis mine].

Most people are reassured by the notion that something is guaranteed by government. But in the English system, such a sentence is an insult to the prevailing tradition—our tradition! Your tradition! For as I say, English liberty is not a thing invented, defined, and conferred by the State. So how can it be guaranteed or produced by a State? It cannot.

Important legal elements of the English style have been traced to the thirteenth century, where we find that even then, England as a whole was different from the rest of Europe, primarily because "a central and basic feature of English social structure has for long been the stress on the rights and privileges of the individual as against the wider group or the state."[11] The English people have always valued free will, individual rights and responsibilities for one's deeds, individual and political liberty, and economic freedom and property rights with all the contractual and legal protections attached thereto. The dominant feature of this style is not *power*, but *liberty*. From a purely pragmatic point of view, the English realized very early that the simplest, least expensive, most tolerable, and most likely way to ensure a virtuous society (to have well-behaved, in contrast to badly behaved, citizens) was to think of each individual as a kind of free agent, adding to or subtracting from the moral fabric of society under a common set of rules, equal for all. Religion was clearly essential to such a vision as morality's source, and so morality, too, was considered a bottom-up phenomenon guided by a standard of personal conduct derived from God and the natural moral law.

With this respect for individual agency came the idea that the role of government is not to control the people and manage society or individual morality, but to create an environment in which each citizen, subject to the same rules, will self-control. Suffice it to say that such moral agents function best in a politically decentralized and free society in which the fullest expression can be given to personal and family needs, free enterprise, private property, and local interests. Moral and social authority under this method is obtained through the strength of family, church, town, and hundreds of other spontaneously organized voluntary social groups, each with its own constraining rights, obligations, and traditions. Such a nation is less interventionist, is non-managerial, non-egalitarian, and promotes political and economic freedom under limited government. *Canada was constituted as this very kind of nation in 1867.* The two quotations at the head of this chapter give a clear indication of the liberty spirit of those times in Canada, and any economic atlas of the world will show that the freest and wealthiest nations on earth are those that have recognized and incorporated this style to some degree.

### The Bottom-up "Freedom System"

The English style may be thought of as a bottom-up system, a local order that is not imposed, but arises spontaneously from the actions of millions of individuals exercising freedom and responsibility under a "rule of law" that protects and applies to all equally, with *no exceptions for governors or the governed.* We are as likely to see a prime minister or a president or other high officials dragged up on the carpet as an ordinary person. Natural differences in gender, skill, intelligence, effort, talent, and ingenuity are expected to flourish, and self-fulfillment through striving for excellence is rewarded. This in turn results in a spontaneous "Freedom System" that permeates society simply because rules of just conduct and rewards of many kinds are the natural objective of free human striving.[12]

Such a Freedom System is always in deadly conflict with the sort of Handicap System we find in all egalitarian societies, however, for the two have utterly different goals: the former to allow free expression of differential excellence, the latter to hide and equalize differences. And so wherever they are forced to coexist, bizarre and unnatural political, economic, and cultural "transactions of decline" will always occur (think of them as the ideological skewing of reality to make things fit an official orthodoxy, just as Procrustes cut off the feet of his guests to make them fit his bed). In the end, many of these transactions will be perceived as unjust and perverse, and will—*must*—manifest in a gradually demoralized and timid people and in bizarre legal struggles over which abstract right trumps another.

## CANADA: THE STYLES CLASH

As it happened, these two rival systems coexisted at the birth of the Canadian nation. England was enjoying the fruits of parliamentary democracy during the Victorian period, while France was suffering the aftermath of revolutionary and imperial despotism and a succession of fragile governments.[13] English stability and productivity were the reason a majority of Canadians until recent times believed fervently that the British-derived political, economic, legal, and cultural institutions of Canada were of inestimable value and should not be undermined. Their sentiments were summed up by the English historian Paul Johnson:

> Virtually all the ideas, knowledge, techniques and institutions around which the world revolves came from the European theatre and its ocean offshoots; many of them quite explicitly from England, which was the principal matrix of modern society. Moreover, the West is still the chief repository of free institutions; and these alone, in the long run, guarantee progress in ideas and inventions. Powerful societies are rising elsewhere, not by virtue of their rejection of western world habits but by their success in imitating them ... The sober and unpopular truth is that whatever hope there is for mankind—at least in the foreseeable future— lies in the ingenuity and the civilized standards of the West, above all in those western elements permeated by English ideas and traditions. To deny this is to surrender to fashionable cant and humbug.[14]

## "LEGAL ORIGINS" SCHOLARSHIP AND THE "FRENCH DEVIATION"

Since the early 1990s, there has developed a lively international scholarship examining the historical consequences that different legal traditions have on the success of nations. Called "Legal Origins" studies for short, the terminology used in this field to describe the two most clearly contrasted systems in modern history is the British common law and the French civil law systems. These labels correspond to my own preferred labels, "bottom-up" and "top-down," or the "English" and "French" styles. In an important survey paper written for the World Bank in 2003, scholars Thorsten Beck and Ross Levine summarized the interesting historical background as follows:

The origin of European law was Roman, of a kind that evolved on a case-by-case basis, just like the English common law to which it gave root. But when the sixth-century emperor Justinian became concerned about the evolving "checkerboard" of legal doctrines, he attempted to unify and codify the law. Whereas Roman lawyers had always proceeded by developing legal principles from real human experience and then upholding them as concrete legal principles beyond the reach of individuals or the State, Justinian attempted to reverse this tradition by placing the will of the emperor and the State above the law. Termed the "Justinian deviation," this was an attempt *to dictate what is legal from abstract principles and theory*, rather than to derive enduring principles from actual human experience.

Justinian failed, however, and Roman tradition prevailed. Many since have attempted their own Justinian deviations, however, and in modern history the French emperor Napoleon Bonaparte—"the people's Monarch"—was the most successful because "codification under Napoleon supported the unification and strengthening of the state."[15] What drove Napoleon was the powerful French emphasis on logic and "reason," combined with Rousseau's mystical emphasis on the General Will (as described above). Accordingly, and like Justinian, "Napoleon sought a code that was so clear, complete, and coherent that there would be no need for judges to deliberate publicly about which laws, customs, or past experiences apply to new, evolving situations."[16] This resulted in a more rigid legal formalism in all countries linked with France, and so much so that modern attempts to do what Justinian did are now commonly described as a "French Deviation."

The French complaint about the English system was made memorable by Voltaire, who, on a visit to England, complained of the local variations in English common law by exclaiming: "When you travel in this kingdom, you change legal systems as often as you change horses!" This variation in English common law was just as offensive to Canada's prime minister Pierre Trudeau, who publicly mocked our English "checkerboard federalism."

The English legal tradition has been opposed to all Statist legal schemes for a good reason, however: it evolved from the resolution of actual human disputes, and thus English courts for centuries have rested on the conviction that "the life of the law has not been logic: it has been experience."[17] You could not invent a slogan more opposed to the French Deviation.

An underlying theme of this entire book is that although Canada has been a home for centuries to both common law and code law styles, the latter was—until 1982—confined to Quebec. Then, in the manner of a Napoleonic martinet, Pierre Trudeau more or less imposed the French Deviation on Canada as a constitutional regime change that was alien to our ancient and very English way of life.

The Snapshot that follows summarizes a few of the sharp legal, institutional, and economic disparities that scholars have attributed to these opposed traditions.

# SNAPSHOT
The Differences between Common Law and Code Law Countries

| Item | British Origin "Common Law" Countries | French Origin "Code Law" Countries |
|---|---|---|
| Role of State & the Courts | Courts separate from the State | State placed above courts, which are within the State |
| Character of The Law | Concrete, evolving tradition from case-law precedents. Britain rejected the idea of Code Law as a revolt against English legal experience | Abstract, procedural, formal. Code Law was "new" law meant to replace old Common-Law. and to be immutable (this was Napoleon's objective) |
| Focus of Law | Obsessed with facts of each case, tends to admit case law as basis of legal interpretation | Obsessed with logical principles of codified law. Cases do not change the legal code |
| Legal theme | "The Life of the law is experience" | "The Life of the law is logic" |
| Law is Shaped | by actual court decisions | by legal doctrine |
| Attitude to private property rights | Common law rooted in defence of property rights against State power (Rest of Canada) | Code law rooted in defence of State rights against property rights (e.g., in Quebec) |
| Power & finance | Tends to de-centralize State power, supports free finance & contract rights, & larger firms | Tends to centralize State power. Wary of free finance and contract rights. More smaller firms |
| Financial Development | Larger stock markets, active initial public offerings, high levels of bank credit, (Protestant roots tend to develop freer credit markets) | Smaller stock markets, less active initial public offerings, lower levels of bank credit, (Catholic roots tend to inhibit credit and lending) |
| Information Disclosure, Liability Rules & Creditor rights | Very strong rules, and thus enforcement of private contracts. Strong creditor rights | Weaker rules and poorer enforcement of private contracts and creditor rights |
| Long-Term Economic Growth | Higher growth in all Common-Law countries and their former colonies | Lower long-term growth in Code law countries and their former colonies |

Source: Thorsten Beck and Ross Levine, "Legal Institutions and Financial Development," prepared for the World Bank under the title "Handbook of New Institutional Economics," World Bank Policy Research Working Paper 3136, September 2003. It may be found at www.nber.org/papers/W10417.

## HOW QUEBEC HAS BECOME THE MOST STATIST REGIME IN NORTH AMERICA

The next Snapshot contrasts the social and economic realities that have flowed from these distinctions as manifested in Quebec, contrasted with Canada as a whole (the Rest of Canada—or ROC). The paradox (and irony) of the story buried in these numbers is that the French-style code law (our Charter) under which all Canadians now live has produced the well-known ancient tension of *Imperium in imperio* (power within power) in Canada, felt most strongly by ... the province of Quebec. And how has Quebec reacted? By the strangest of ironies: it has relied on our English constitutional and legal heritage—our British liberties—to build its own French-style provincial welfare state ... inside what has become, since 1982, a much larger French-style Canadian welfare state.

The realities of the historical "bidding war" between Quebec and Ottawa so well detailed by Brian Crowley in *Fearful Symmetry* are clearly laid out there for all to see.[18] However, an economic bidding war is to be found in all States, especially federal ones, whenever a significant minority of the population unified by distinct historical, cultural, or economic motives has enough population and power to vote as a block and hence to "swing" a national election. Of course, all Canada's provinces continue to play the bidding war insofar as they are able. But it has resulted in massive and disproportionate economic transfers from Canada to Quebec in a kind of loyalty bribery (one small example: Quebec received 85 percent of all Canada Day celebration funding in 2008).

The larger truth, however, is that Quebec has always had the option to use the billions received in transfer payments over the past century to create the freest and most powerful economic jurisdiction for its size in North America. Instead, it has used those monies to build the most Statist regime in North America. So the most fundamental question to be answered is this: Why has Canada lurched leftward, and Quebec even more so? The answer must be found in the deeper philosophical, moral, and legal forces and changes in Canadian and Quebec history.[19]

---

## SNAPSHOT
Quebec: a Welfare State within a Welfare State

| Item | Province of Quebec | ROC (Rest of Canada) |
|---|---|---|
| Percent Canadian Population | 1966—29 %<br>2009—23.2 % | — |
| Provincial Expenditures as % of Provincial GDP* | 28% (2008) | 20% (Ontario) |
| Economic Freedom (2006) of 10 provinces and 50 American states** | 10th prov. (least free) & last of 50 States | Ontario 2nd-freest prov 47th among States |

| | | |
|---|---|---|
| GDP growth 1981–2006 (inflation adjusted) | 77.6% increase | (ROC) 109.9% increase |
| Unionization*** Public + Private (2003) | 37.4% | 27%—Ontario |
| Subsidies to Businesses 1990–2005 | 40–50% of all Canadian business subsidies are in Quebec | |
| % Workers on Employment Insurance | 80% of all unemployed in Quebec (& Atlantic provinces) | 33% of all unemployed in ROC |
| Single people on welfare**** | 21.4% (2000) Quebec has the highest social assistance rate of all provinces | |
| % francophones in Canadian civil service****** | 32% of all Canadian civil service jobs | 40% of all civil service jobs in the Ottawa region |
| % of 71,290 Federal "bilingual positions" held by: (2009) | First language francophones: 63% | First language anglophones: 37% |
| Share of Federal Transfers of $14.8 Bill. (2008) | To Quebec alone 56.7% ($8.4 Bill) | To six other "have-not" provinces 43.3% ($6.5 bill) |
| Common Law families | 44% | 16% (2006) |
| Suicide 1991–2000 | 30.7 per 100,000 (5th highest rate in the world) Prior to 1975 suicide was lowest in Quebec | 16.7 per 100,000 Ontario/ BC/Alberta |
| Abortion | 41.3 per 1,000 pregnancies | Ontario 26.5 per 1,000 |

* Denis Saint-Martin, Director of European Union Centre of Excellence, Université de Montréal/McGill University, at www.carleton.ca/eropecluster. Saint-Martin's article. "Quebec's Social Model: a Case or Europeanization Outside Europe?" makes the case for Quebec as a European welfare state within Canada.
** From J. Gwartney, R. Lawson, W. Easterly, *Economic Freedom of the World, Annual Report*, The Fraser Institute, Vancouver, 2006. Data and definitions available at www. freetheworld.com.
*** Figures from part of chapter 9, Gérard Bélanger, *Economie du Québec, Mythes et Réalité* (Montreal: Varia, 2007).
**** Brian Crowley, *Fearful Symmetry* (Toronto: Key Porter, 2009). This was a helpful source for much of the data for this Snapshot; see also the work of Jean-Luc Miqué, *Étatisme et Déclin du Québec* (Montreal: Les Éditions Varia, 1998).
***** Calculations by economist Jean-Luc Miqué, by email to this author, October 10, 2009.
****** Marie-Eve Hudon, "Official Languages in the Public Service from 1973 to the Present" (Ottawa: Library of Parliament, 2000), p. 20. Cited in Crowley, above.

In my view this Snapshot gives a picture of a dying society. The French Deviation is worming away at Quebec, and also at ROC. How did it happen? How did Canada's original classical liberalism—that fierce love of liberty and self-reliance expressed in the quotations at the head of this chapter—become Statism?

## HOW DID LIBERALISM BECOME STATISM?

Perhaps the most common political feeling in all the colonies of the New World was that with their religious and civil liberties protected in a well-ordered society, individuals left alone by a government that set the same rules for all would rise or fall by their own efforts. Importantly, this was a political philosophy consistent with the underlying Judeo-Christian notion of individual moral agency (the belief that individual humans can freely form a moral society). This stirring notion was originally made popular by proponents of "liberalism," the root meaning of which is from the Latin *liber*, meaning "free." There was resistance, not to government per se, but to *excessive* government, and so we ended up with a BNA Act that forbade central government from intruding on specified local matters. All New World settlers were moved by two ideals: liberty and moral perfection. Most of them began as religious idealists in spiritual revolt against a corrupt world, and for them all, the most obvious and dangerous form of tyranny was government, for which "corruption" was a synonym. The New World was to be their new Eden.

By the middle of the nineteenth century, however, as materialism and secularism encroached upon and weakened these religious and community bonds, people saw the terrible uses so many made of their freedoms. Many prospered, but some did not manage their freedom very well and became dissolute and dependent on society. The grand notion of liberty and moral agency was not producing the perfect world. So almost imperceptibly, by the middle of the twentieth century, and vastly accelerated since the mid-1960s, all the political parties of our nation slowly turned their backs on liberty and embraced the twin philosophies of *Statism* and *egalitarianism*, neither of which had ever before in the long history of the English people played more than a transitory role.

At this time the notion made famous by Karl Marx in the *Communist Manifesto* that human misery is a result of class oppression of workers by capitalists was prevalent. Even those who couldn't accept Marxism's most utopian and paranoid nonsense, however, nevertheless could immediately see the political usefulness of the new envy-based reality that Marx had by then made so popular. It boiled down to the notion that "my misery is not my fault. It is the fault of 'the system'!" Almost immediately, as it were, our once freedom-loving politicians saw that stimulation of a general public envy was a potent means to power. So the language of freedom and "opportunity" began slowly to change to the language of social and economic "rights." These new rights would then be asserted as claims against a State set up and expected to satisfy them.

At this point our newly minted "liberal" Statists had to insist that everyone has the *right* to the same social and economic *results* in life, regardless of any differences in social condition, degree of effort, moral qualities, or good or bad personal habits or decisions. Equality now had to be "substantive" (everyone has a right to the same substances, or quality of life), and the State was to be its most powerful instrument.

Canada was about to opt for its own brand of constitutional socialism.

The Snapshot below gives a sense of what was going through the mind of the man who engineered this regime change for Canada.

## SNAPSHOT
What Pierre Trudeau Said

- "I believe in the necessity of state control to maximize the liberty and welfare of all" (1958).
- "We have a great deal to learn from the Soviet Union" (1971).
- In London England, January 13, 1969, Trudeau was asked by British students: "What society would you like to make Canada?" To which he replied: "Labour party socialist—or *Cuban socialism or Chinese socialism*—socialism from each according to his means."
- In his 2010 biography of Trudeau, *Just Watch Me*, author John English recounts how, after the loss of funding due to the Soviet withdrawal from Cuba, Fidel Castro sought Trudeau's advice on how to liberalize Cuba's rigid socialist system. But . . . Trudeau (the "liberal"!) advised Castro against liberalization.
- "All the ideological thrusts are for *centralization*" (1950).
- "[Nationalists] will one day come to realize that they will only be able to make the transition from the past to the future *by means of social radicalism*" (1956).
- "We haven't been able to make it work, the free market system. The government is going to have to take a larger role in running institutions . . . It means there is going to be not less authority in our lives, but perhaps more" (CTV year-end interview, 1975).
- "Every reasonable person now recognizes *the duty of the federal government to manage the country's economy* in the interest of all its people and all its regions" (1975).
- "It doesn't matter where the immigrants come from" (March 15, 1979, in Vancouver).

- "There is no official [Canadian] culture" (October 8, 1971, speech to the House of Commons).
- "We have spun the wheel . . . but the observer, who is on the deck and smoking his pipe, or drinking his tea . . . doesn't realize it, but perhaps he will find himself *disembarking at a different island than the one he thought he was sailing for*" (1969).

Sources: Quotations are as cited in David Somerville, *Trudeau Revealed* (Toronto: BMG Publishing, 1978), or from other sources and media, as indicated. All italics are mine.

## HOW CANADA OPTED FOR "LIBERTARIAN SOCIALISM"

As it happened, as he had a French-Canadian father and a Scottish mother, Trudeau embodied the French and English styles described above in his very person. Canadian scholars burn a lot of energy debating whether Trudeau was a socialist or a libertarian and assume the two are contradictory. For he famously said that "the State has no place in the bedrooms of the nation." But he also entrenched coast-to-coast radical equalization policies in his Charter. Here was a man very comfortable with multiple mistresses, with legislating homosexual rights, and who, even as prime minister, did not mind taking off his clothes and sunbathing nude in mixed company.[20] He was a flamboyant libertarian who imposed the most controlling and expensive Statist regime on Canada in its history.

So was he a socialist or a libertarian?

My answer: he was a "*libertarian socialist*," and we Canadians all now live under his libertarian socialist regime. But how? How can this circle be squared? These philosophies are opposites, aren't they? Not really. Not if the two labels are applied to different things. Think of what is individual, private, and physical: your body. Then think of what is public and general: a service like health care, or education, or a language right. Trudeau's Charter combined and enabled these two conflicting styles by encouraging the separation of the private body from the public body. He was a libertarian in that he believed matters of the private body are no one else's business. But when it came to goods he felt we all deserve from the State . . . ? Why, then a powerful system for providing, equalizing, and controlling access to such goods must be set up, and this would be done through fiscal bribery of Canada's provinces, territories, and regions; that is, through shared-cost programs or grants financed by much higher levels of taxation and unconscionable borrowing. But what kind of socialism was it? What kind of libertarianism?

## HIS SOCIALIST CONVICTION

Trudeau was trying, as mentioned, to spin the wheel slowly so that without realizing the change of direction, Canadians would find themselves disembarking at a different island than the one they thought they were sailing for. Fundamentally, on the public level, all that he did was clearly and resolutely substitute the French Statist style for the English liberty style at every opportunity. By the time he was finished, Canada had changed from a fiscally stable, low-debt, reasonably free, only mildly socialized nation under limited government, to one bending under huge public debt, highly managerial, and much more thoroughly socialist in its fiscal and social commitments. In his first book, *Federalism and the French Canadians*—a manifesto of sorts—Trudeau clearly outlined this plan for Canada. At the time, most leftists argued that socialism could not successfully be planted in a nation such as ours with an existing federal system because the powers of governance in such nations are already divided between central and local jurisdictions, and this division of powers is entrenched forever in their constitutions. So the general conclusion was that Canada was not, and never would be, a candidate for socialism. But Trudeau disagreed. He spoke admiringly of "that superb strategist, Mao Tse-Tung" who argued that "planting socialism" in various regional strongholds was "the very best thing." Accordingly, Trudeau developed the argument that systems such as Canada's, contrary to the advice of all the theorists, can indeed be made socialist, and that our British-style federal system "must be welcomed as a valuable tool *which permits dynamic parties to plant socialist governments in certain provinces, from which the seeds of radicalism can slowly spread.*"[21]

## HIS LIBERTARIAN CONVICTION

Trudeau probably wrote as much about individual rights as about socialism, and most scholars, and the public in general, continue to believe these two political philosophies are in clear contradiction. Certainly, in their party platforms, socialists and libertarians are sworn enemies. But as mentioned, Trudeau's genius was to combine these contraries by splitting their domains between what is inside our skin and what is outside it: private body and public body; person and *polis*.

He was throwing the Canadian people a bone by reducing the larger realm of freedom to which they had been accustomed to their persons and bodies. But all the "public" freedoms having to do with economics and trade, private property, education, provision of health care, welfare, and so on, would fall under Statist regulation. He knew that if he left us as unfettered and as free as possible with respect to most of our personal bodily activities and pleasures, we would be lulled into believing we were still free in *all* our former ways. But those—the patchwork of common law freedoms—were precisely the ones he despised: the bottom-up political, economic, and legislative realities essential to the creation of the British style that produced our quite intentional checkerboard federalism. And he despised the people who created or defended such freedoms as well. To him, Canada's parliamentarians were "just nobodies," and "a crummy lot" (this, he uttered publicly in 1969). In short, the entire British style was a reality that stood in the way of his French-style plan for Statism. So the system had to be changed. Trudeau was Canada's Procrustes, doing his utmost to make a one-size-fits-all political bed for Canadian citizens.

His libertarian ethic, which says that liberty means doing whatever you want as long as you don't harm anyone else, was absorbed from typical English individualist thinking that was radicalized by John Stuart Mill in his canonical booklet *On Liberty* (1859). It is called Mill's "Harm Principle," and it so neatly articulated Mill's simplistic argument for the *privatization of morality* that it has by now become the standard reasoning in defence of personal moral autonomy all over the Western world. Prior to Mill, throughout our long Judeo-Christian tradition, morality—codes of right and wrong behaviour—had always been considered a community good. Moral standards reflected common religious and community standards. The metaphor was that we all conduct our lives within a common moral bubble wherein by means of conviction, belief, and debate, we sustain a common set of shalls and shall-nots that defines us morally . . . who we are. Mill argued instead that we each ought to live within our own private self-defined moral bubble, and be concerned for others only if we bump into them. Then we just apologize, or negotiate a solution to any harm done.

Mill failed to see that if you are completely alone in the universe it is true that you can do whatever you want, and call it "morality" if you like. But because there are no other human beings in existence and you cannot therefore help or harm anyone else, you can also call it Winnie-the-Pooh, or anything else you wish. However, as soon as someone else exists in addition to yourself, you must take into consideration whether your actions will help them, or harm them, now, or in the future, directly or indirectly. Suddenly, what was a personal and private act, becomes public, and thus falls under the term "morality," rightly considered. In his person and in his politics, Trudeau combined two conflicting styles: the personal libertarianism articulated by Mill and the Statism of Rousseau.

## SOCIALISM AND THE SEXUALIZATION OF THE MASSES

Modern Statists soon see that the people will easily accept an amazing degree of political, economic, and attitudinal control—and taxation—in exchange for greater private and personal freedom from a traditional morality increasingly caricatured as the old slave master. That is why it seems almost an equation worming its way through all modern democracies that as real freedoms are diminished, sexual freedom increases. That is also why so much of modern democratic discourse centres on the rights and pleasures of the physical body, as distinct from former eras when it centred on political freedom and rights, and on the freedom of the spirit.

Consider how many of the radical egalitarian claims made in the name of democracy have to do with the body: abortion rights, homosexual rights, contraception rights, single-parent rights, transgender rights, cohabitation rights, in vitro rights, and so on. We could say that the primary site for democratic dispute in modern times has shifted from conscience, to body, from morality to personal appetite, from very public debates over general moral rectitude, to personal will and sexual desires.

Conclusion: The people tend not to complain about the historical losses of their political and economic freedoms, or of being controlled even in their speech and inner attitudes, as long as they get complete sexual and personal bodily freedoms as a substitute. We no longer crave an *escape* from the body (the objective of so many in the past who saw human beings as slaves to their own appetites), but rather the opposite—*immersion* in its functions and pleasures as a democratic right. Accordingly, the past century has been witness to a perfect correlation between rising taxation, government regulation, and citizen dependency, paralleled by increasingly open sexual expression and claims of "sovereignty" over the body. The old spiritual ecstasy in contemplation of transcendent spiritual meaning (an ultimate meaning higher than, and beyond the reach of, the State), is a goner. Instead, we may think of the sexualized democratic State as a political entity *that strives through the offer of substitute physical ecstasy to incorporate transcendence into itself.* That is to say, by means of a generalized and open sexualization of the masses (which must include a vigorous moral and legal attack on the former restrictive biologically based natural sexual order as "discriminatory" and "anti-democratic"), the democracies of the West have sought to resolve the great political problem of the missing moral and spiritual transcendence in secular societies. This was a move that entailed a certain loss of our real freedoms.

## HAVE WE RETURNED TO OUR PRE-CONFEDERATION STATUS?

At the time Canada's regime change was being engineered, there was no single political party opposed to the strongman rejigging of an entire nation's historical rights and ways. There was lots of government advertising for Trudeau's program, special discussion groups, TV debates, and so on. But unlike countries such as Australia, Switzerland, and many American states where popular consent is mandated for constitutional changes, Canada had—still has—no such provision. I submit, therefore, that despite all the official bluster, there was no fully informed popular understanding or consent for such radical change. Suddenly, the law-making activities of Canada's legislators, who are sent to Ottawa to express the will of the whole people to whom they are responsible, were henceforward to be subordinated to, and constrained by, a remarkably egalitarian Charter (notwithstanding the ironies of extremely inegalitarian reverse discrimination it contains) and by the opinions of unelected judges responsible to no one, who would be asked to interpret what it meant. This in turn meant that what would matter most in future would not be who the people sent to Parliament to express *their* will (representatives who at least could be removed in the next election), but *which judges* would be put on a bench from which they could not be removed, there to express their personal will as law, if they so desired.

For this citizen, at least, this meant that Canadians, citizens of a nation that had fought for a very long time prior to 1867 to wrest "responsible government" on the British model from the controlling hands of alien legislators and judges in England, were now being shoved—shovelled?—back into their pre-Confederation condition. In short, after a mere 115 years of existence as a self-reliant people exercising responsible government, we surrendered the supreme authority over our own lawmakers and handed it back to judges we could not remove. Suddenly, with the stroke of Trudeau's pen, we—he—replaced *parliamentary* sovereignty with *judicial* sovereignty.

Trudeau imagined himself to be a man of the people, an elite "Legislator" (to use Rousseau's term) to whom the people would relate directly. So to him, Parliament was simply an irrational institution that was in his way. Indeed, he declared with a fierce pride that his new French-style code law would be *stripping Canada's legislatures of their oppressive powers.*[22] He detested what was to him the scandalous fact that people he considered "nobodies," and a "crummy lot," could make or unmake their own laws as they wished. So it's true he stripped the people of their powers. He stripped us all. That's what the Charter did, and continues to do, simply because, as mentioned, nobody knows what the Charter is supposed to mean. So once again, as in the days prior to Confederation, we have to ask judges to give us our law—except this time around they happen to be sitting in Canada, instead of in England. All this, and far more, happened in the space of sixteen years of Trudeau's reign.

For all this, there has been a real cost that can be measured in dollars and cents.

## THE NATIONAL-DEBT PRISON

Predictably, in order to finance such utopian schemes, it was Trudeau, as we shall see, who after opening the ideological door, also opened the floodgates of irresponsible deficit spending to pay for the most astonishing and rapid period of growth in government staffing and spending in Canadian history. We will soon see that on a per capita basis, this may have been the most astonishing non-wartime expansion of government power of any free nation in history. He inherited a total national debt of $18 billion from our entire first hundred years of Confederation in 1968, and raised it to $200 billion (fully 46 percent of GDP) by 1984, his final year in office. In 1984–85, his most profligate year, his government spent fully 51 percent more than it took in. Below is a graphic illustration of our regime change in dollars and cents. Trudeau cannot be blamed for all of this, of course. But he established our Statist deficit-spending trend, and in the sense that we are now incapable of paying off our national federal debt, *Canada has never recovered.* He was followed by a number of prime ministers who continued this reckless habit. By 2008 (and expressed in 2008 dollars since 1968), Canada had spent $1.5 trillion in *interest payments alone* on our total federal debt, with little to show for it today except the principle amount of the debt. Here is the historical picture since Confederation, with projections to account for future "stimulus-spending" deficits. It is true that we got something in the form of government services for some of this money. But much of it was used to grow government itself, for consumption, for "equalization," and for infrastructure we could not afford and still have not paid for. A basic truth of such graphs is that total national debt is a clear measure of the degree of Statism present.

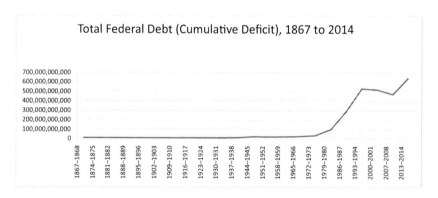

Source: Derek Fildebrandt, Canadian Taxpayers' Federation (March 11, 2010).

Perhaps the greatest irony of such irresponsible spending in the name of equality, however, is this: there has never been a socialist state in history more "equal" politically or economically than our free Western societies. Commenting on this fact when the USSR, the world's most catastrophic test case for socialism was still in existence, Harvard's Barrington Moore Jr. wrote that although the determinants of inequality are different—economic in free societies, and political in unfree ones, "there is as much inequality in the Soviet Union as the United States ... the same holds true for China." However, he failed to mention the small matter that more than tips the scales in favour of free societies: in addition to their inequalities, those two socialist states in total murdered some 80 to 100 million of their own legal citizens.[23] Statism can be very bad for your health.

## THE CALL FOR "MORE DEMOCRACY"

In the measure that the power of the top-down State intrudes into everyday life, public moral consensus starts to decay, and trust in political leaders to fragment. Then, delegated sovereignty begins to seem alienating. Elected representatives become more unresponsive to the people, or their laws are defeated by unelected judges, or both. At this point we start to hear calls for a little more "direct democracy," or "people power." Not surprisingly, it is usually the rise of the tax-hungry and wasteful Nanny State that spurs the call for more direct citizen input. That is what happened to me.

In fact, this book was originally such a reaction, and in it I recommended various instruments of direct democracy because I was certain the traditional way of life of the Canadian people was being betrayed against their true will. We needed "citizen initiatives" such as the Swiss have used for a long time to pass laws directly and bypass a Parliament that refuses to do our will; we needed referendums to give national consent on profound constitutional changes; and we needed "recall," an instrument used to fire politicians who lie or cheat or radically betray promises to those who elected them. Today I am less certain such measures would improve much, and they might even make things worse, because I think the culture is more fragmented than ever. (More on this in the last chapter.)

I am still persuaded, however, that over matters so fundamental as a root-and-branch change of an entire nation—especially with respect to its core community morality, its political institutions or constitution, its basic system of law, its language rights, or its ethnicity—*all citizens must be deemed in principle to have a personal stake*. In this respect, I think Canada's all-but-forced regime change from a nation in full exercise of its historical English rights and liberties, into a radical welfare state steered by the political ambitions of a single powerful man in the space of two decades (roughly mid-1960s to 1984), while constitutionally legitimate, was morally illegitimate. Indeed, fully *one-quarter of Canada's citizens*—7 million citizens living in the province of Quebec—refused consent, and one million aboriginal Canadians were never asked.

Even worse, when he came back from the dead for his 1980 election campaign, Trudeau intentionally misled the people of Canada (especially those of Quebec) by strategically eliminating all talk of the constitutional changes he was planning. Indeed, his election strategists urged *"that he keep silent on the constitution*—the issue that he had insisted on stressing [in his losing campaign] the previous May."[24] So, when, on the night of May 16, 1980, during his speech to a hushed crowd in Montreal's Paul Sauvé Arena, he said he wanted to "take action to renew the constitution," virtually every Quebecer present assumed he meant action to guarantee Quebec's provincial powers and the distinct society status within Canada it craved. Instead, he was plotting to suppress their hopes forever in favour of his national socialist dream. In effect, he lied point-blank to the very people to whom he was appealing for support. He also lied to himself as he reluctantly betrayed and reversed his own principle of "Reason before Passion," for he had finally accepted his handlers' advice that political success comes from manipulation of the people's emotions, and not from reason.[25] With tears in their eyes, they gave him a standing ovation. But it was a fraud: *the radical regime change he was gunning for was never put on the public table,* either by him or by the Liberal party. He knew very well that if he had told the people truthfully what he intended, he would never have been elected. What I am calling for is a reasoned reassessment of these corrosive facts and of the immorality of the Handicap System under which we now live, and thus, plainly speaking, for a reactionary politics.

There is a silenced majority of Canadians deeply upset by these changes who feel that because all our political parties are now Statist in orientation, they only rarely see their deepest values reflected in ordinary media, by courts, or by government. They are discouraged at the number of special interest groups and projects they are forced to support through tax dollars (such as the $1.3 billion spent since 1973 on radical feminist causes: see chapter 10). A silenced people will not march in the street every time they see something they don't like. Neither have they the time to become experts in fields such as political economy. But they know what they think and feel: they're fed up, cynical, and worst of all, they're totally distrustful of the political process—a dangerous climate for any democracy because it leads to cocooning and dropping out.

The various terms explored so far—the French versus English styles, the top-down versus bottom-up tension, the Freedom System versus the Handicap System, common law versus code law—all of these paired terms are an attempt to set out a basic philosophical context in which policy can be considered in Canada. In effect, whenever someone offers a political opinion, you have only to decipher which of these two conflicting options for social governance is being promoted, and then the opinion falls more easily into place. The clash of these two styles has been the constant theme—everywhere felt, if not everywhere seen—of Canada's struggle to govern itself and establish its institutions ever since the Battle of the Plains of Abraham in 1759. One of the impediments to a clear focus on the nature of this ongoing struggle is the existence of what I call the "popular illusions," and it is to these we now turn.

# 2: EIGHT POPULAR ILLUSIONS
## OBSTACLES TO CLEAR THINKING

*Our contemporaries are constantly excited by two conflicting passions:
they want to be led, and they wish to remain free . . . They devise a sole,
tutelary and all-powerful form of government, but elected by the people.
They combine the principle of centralization and that of popular
sovereignty; this gives them a respite: they console themselves for being
in tutelage by the reflection that they have chosen their own guardians.*
—Alexis de Tocqueville, *Democracy in America*, 1840

### IDEOLOGY IS DESTINY

The popular illusions described below in a sense embody the unofficial *counter-ideology* of our society, and if they are at a long, steady, and unchallenged variance with our founding ideology, they will prevail. Policy will then be based on them.

In what follows, each illusion is described as a popular belief without foundation, running counter to some original core principle of the nation. Each in its own way, these illusions play a role in substituting the Statist style for the liberty-based way of forming a nation. All of them are discernible in the ordinary experiences of everyday life and can be discovered with minimal effort in any daily newspaper. Once you are aware of them, they can be easily spotted—the way a horticulturalist identifies common weeds—in the ideological garden of our country. If you believe that ideas (when we are thinking clearly) and assumptions (when we are acting, but not necessarily thinking) shape government policy, then you will surely agree that it is of the utmost importance for a society to get its ideas and assumptions right—to have an appropriate ideology. By "ideology" I mean *a structure of interdependent ideas that serves as a basis for the formation of government policy.*

In such matters, however, Canadians are largely an inarticulate people, and this leaves us exposed, if not to immediate political disaster then to gradual social and moral gridlock, so to speak. That's because in daily life we tend to rely on too many assumptions that are in conflict with each other, or that contradict themselves. Earlier I spoke of our nation as a ship with no course. But as the folk saying goes: If you don't know where you're going, you'll end up somewhere else! My continuing argument will be that if Canadians do not equip themselves to see clearly how political ideologies work, however inarticulate these may be, they will be vulnerable to the processes of decline, and ripe victims of political expediency. Unless we master and direct our own destiny, future generations will read how it mastered us. In this respect, *ideology is destiny.*

## THE FREE-LUNCH ILLUSION
*(How the government's sleight of hand fools us into believing it really has money of its own.)*

There is a widespread and unfortunate illusion afoot that the government has its *own* money, that what we get from government is "free." But I always tell my children: "Nothing is free. It's prepaid!" Too few citizens understand that government *has no money of its own*, that the only money government can possibly have (except for the sale of a few services, licences, and the like that we pay government to provide, and then pay to receive) is obtained through appropriation, and comes from only three sources: government either *takes* the money from us (creating a tax burden), or it *borrows* it from us or from foreigners (creating a debt burden), or it *prints* money for itself (creating an inflation burden). In this sense, the game of government, once it goes beyond establishing and enforcing the rules for a level playing field, is truly a zero-sum game. *What it gives to some, it must first take from others.*

This point can be illustrated to students, or your own children, simply and dramatically. The lesson begins this way. First arrange for two students (Mary and John) to come to class with ten one-dollar coins representing their annual income. Then tell the whole class that you will represent government (you want them to see how it works). Ask both students what they feel is the most important thing government ought to provide.

Mary will say something like, "I think a good government ought to provide police and free daycare." John will say something like, "I believe every Canadian should be guaranteed free health care and a pension."

Then ask each to come to the front of the class with their money. Hold up your empty hands (to show that government starts with no money) and ask Mary to give you five dollars. Put three in your pocket (the cost of government), and hand two to John, saying, "Here's your health care."

Then take five from John, pocket three, and hand two to Mary, saying, "Here's your free daycare." Repeat the process to "fund" Mary's free police and John's "free" pension. They will each end up with four dollars, and a firm lesson in government. (You will end up with six from each.)

Properly executed, this will be the most memorable and effective political education of their young lives, for they will quickly see that government money is an illusion; that the government's power and influence increase only because of the wealth it takes from the people; and that we are duped by the free-lunch mentality. Most of all, they will realize that by demanding a free service from government they are really demanding it from their neighbours, and when the latter do the same, it is being taken from them.

Since, by definition, government services are anywhere from 10 to 150 percent less efficient than the same services rendered privately (see chapter 5 for the figures on this), the net productivity result is always a loss. But here's the real moral rub: *No government can confer a benefit upon one person or group without penalizing another.* What it gives to one, it must first get from another. Even if it prints money for itself, it is virtually taking money from future generations who must pay for the hidden tax of inflation. That's an iron law of economics. The social welfare state is therefore a great fiction, by which everyone tries to live at the expense of everyone else.

## THE FIXED-PIE ILLUSION

*(How misunderstandings about the process of wealth creation lead to resentment of success.)*
When thinking about *government*, it is correct to label it a fixed-pie or a zerosum game. Even when government succeeds in "priming" or "stimulating" an activity that might not otherwise have been started, or to save an enterprise from bankruptcy (like the American and Canadian car industries after the sub-prime meltdown), it is impossible to do this in a cost-efficient way because "stimulus" money must first be taken from efficient taxpayers (they have money) to "prime" the inefficient activities of others (who do not have money), which means the economic power of some will be suppressed to improve the economic power of others. It's a vote-buying scheme.

As for government "enterprises" such as Crown corporations? They discourage true commercial efficiency and entrepreneurial risk and reward because they are political, bureaucratic entities that lack a basis for economic calculation. Debt that would have bankrupted inefficient private operators is often forgiven and excluded from the reported financial "success" of the operation. In short, there may be some good economic or even policy reasons for some state enterprises, and these have played an important role in the development of Canada from the start. However, whether an operation is run by government or private interests, it is subject to the same laws of economics, and if the return on investment is there for government, then it's certainly there for private operators, who are at least risking their own funds, and not the public's. The world of the so-called private sector is just the opposite of government. First, it's misnamed. It should be called the "productive" sector, for this is its most beneficial feature. Properly considered, all successful entrepreneurial processes worldwide are *growth* processes, in which the economic pie is not fixed. It gets larger all the time because new wealth and value are continuously being generated.

So to think of the productive world in fixed-pie terms—which is how people in the Middle Ages thought about all commercial activity—is wrong. If your neighbour gets wealthier than you, it doesn't mean that he or she has taken wealth you otherwise might have had. The same applies to the economic activity of nations.

Despite calamitous misunderstandings about how growth is achieved, the modern world-trend is growth: slow, but ever upward. The productive pie is increasing in size almost everywhere. In his 1987 book, *Passage to a Human World*, Max Singer, of the Hudson Institute, wrote that by World Bank calculations the percentage of the world's nations living in poverty will have fallen from 50 percent in 1960 to 16 percent by 2008.[1] That was a pretty close estimate: the August 26, 2008 "Poverty Update of the World Bank" has this to say: "Poverty has been declining at the rate of about one percentage point a year, from 52 percent of the developing world's population in 1981 to 25 percent in 2005. This is no small achievement, given that the number of poor fell by 500 million in this period." In a January 2008 online discussion for Hudson, Singer wrote that "by the end of this century, when China and India will have become wealthy, probably three-fourths of the world will live in wealthy countries."[2]

The fact is that even very low but steady annual growth can produce tremendous results. England ruled the modern world after a steady average annual growth of only 2 percent over a hundred-year period. So the answer to wealth creation is steady annual growth so that investible capital increases. The formula for calculating this phenomenon is: 72, divided by the average rate of growth, which equals the time needed to double net wealth. For example, with a growth factor of 2 percent per annum, a nation could double its net wealth in $72 / 2 = 36$ years. Not bad! Of course, net growth means a bigger pie for all concerned—including the government (unless, like the Swiss, we limit government spending by legislation). *However, if we don't grow, government may still grow!* It can do this because it knows that *deficits are just deferred taxes.* Whereas private enterprise can grow by increasing productivity and through savings, government can grow only by *taking more of our wealth by force.* Even if, having found that it cannot squeeze out more in taxes without causing a public reaction, it borrows from other sources, and then we or our descendants still have to pay the debt back through still more taxes. So remember this the next time someone tries to fool you with the fixed-pie argument. It's true for all governments and tends to be true for socialist states because their system creates a dampening effect on wealth production—but it's not true for free societies in which all boats go up on a rising tide. The secret to successful wealth production is to create the wealth-producing machine (see chapter 4) while being sure to limit government's ability to paralyze it at the same time. To do the former without the latter is an invitation to tax penury.

## THE RIGHTS ILLUSION

*(How rights become claims against the State for specific goods.)*
There is rampant public confusion about "rights." So let us explore the meaning of this term for a few moments. The traditional, or classical, concept of rights as understood in all the countries born of England refers to certain specific rights as set out and protected by common law, and also to a general right of individual freedom. Such specific rights as freedom of thought and speech, private property, association, and the like are often labelled "negative rights" because they protect our right *not* to be interfered with. The general right of freedom under our system means you have a right to do *anything you wish* as long as you do not break the law. That is quite different from a state where law is so arbitrary and the people accordingly so frightened they correctly fear they can do *only what is permitted*, and only in the way permitted.

Another traditional conception of rights is so-called "natural rights." For example, the American Declaration of Independence of 1776 speaks of an "inalienable right" to "life, liberty, and the pursuit of happiness." The term "inalienable" means these things are considered rights that cannot be taken away by any moral or legal right of others, and are part of what we are by virtue of the plain fact that we're human beings. Canada's Charter of Rights and Freedoms lists such standard rights said to be equal for all, but they are all subject to limitation according to what is "reasonable" in "a free and democratic society." In Canada, the courts have usurped the right of Parliament to declare what "reasonable" means. (More to come on that insidious process later.) But neither the American Declaration nor the Canadian Charter say anything about duties, or the rights of the community, or what should be done when new rights are invented by courts that collide with other rights.

Of course, anyone who thinks about the term "rights" can figure out that much of what I have just said is wish fulfillment, if not blarney, simply because we can *say*, or *declare*, we have all sorts of rights. But if we cannot protect ourselves against harm by others, or by the State itself, a right means nothing at all. Same for freedom. *We have as much freedom, and as many kinds of rights, as can be protected or enforced* by the customary laws of the land, and that is the only guarantee of them. Ever. It sounds good, but does not help much to say that a right is "inalienable." That is just an expression of the emotional value you place on that right. And the sorry truth is that certain rights once considered inalienable—for example, the property right, or the right to free speech—can weaken or strengthen according to the times, and according to the political views of judges, as they have in modern Canada and America.

When I was a boy in the 1950s, someone caught breaking into your home in the night was very likely to get himself (I bow to PC) or herself shot, or at the least would go to jail for a very long time. So there wasn't much break and enter back then. The maximum punishment today for break and enter in

Canada's Criminal Code is still life imprisonment. But judicial respect for the sacred right of private property is so low now that many homeowners or shopkeepers have themselves been sent to jail for pointing a gun in self-defence at, or even just for badly beating up, a scary thief breaking into their home or stealing from their store.

In the same vein, Canada's Human Rights Commissions (HRCs) have had a field day trying and fining people just for speaking their minds. Usually they are after so-called hate crimes, and I'm sure no one could ever count the number of those that have occurred in the form of hateful and hurtful actions against others. But these HRCs are not after hateful actions. They are trying people just for speech (spoken or written) considered normal by the speakers. For example, devoted Christians following their own religious teachings are obligated to teach publicly and to their students and children that homosexuality is a sin, or at the least an objective disorder of the soul. And yet even though we are still a Christian nation (according to our 2001 census, about 77 percent say they are Christian), some HRCs have tried and fined Canadians for expressing these beliefs in public. This is an example of a collision between the right of free speech (and thought) and the right of religious belief.

My main concern, however, is that recently the term "rights" has been transformed into one with a very different—and dangerous—new meaning. Today, when we say that someone has a "right" to something, we typically mean that a person has an enforceable claim to *a specific good, service, money, or privilege* to be obtained from another person, a corporation or from the State. Such rights are called "substantive" or "positive" rights because the person declaring them wants much more than to be left alone. He or she wants something specific and tangible to be provided.

I submit that this radical change—so common now in all welfare states—is a net subtraction from the moral quality of our national life. Why should this be so? Simply because as a free person with the protected right to walk where you wish, think, speak out and so on, within the law, *you are undertaking these actions yourself.* No one is being forced to *do* anything for you. Others are simply being *restrained* from preventing you from doing these things for yourself. That arrangement is a healthy situation for any society. But increasingly since the mid-twentieth century this noble idea has deteriorated into the perverse notion that a right is also a *claim* against others for something to be supplied by them. By now this has led to a wholesale "rights fever" in Canada and in many other nations, so that instead of upholding and protecting a right to *freedom* from government by restricting its intrusive activities, we have encouraged exactly these intrusions. Some will say that this is how we get from liberty to fraternity. But on that score we must take a lesson from wiser folks. When, in 1850, the French statesman Alphonse de Lamartine said that his countryman Frédéric Bastiat's philosophy of government was inferior because it guaranteed only *liberty*, while Lamartine's system included *fraternity*, Bastiat replied: "The second half of your program will destroy the first!"

That is exactly what is happening in Canada today. The law, as an instrument of justice, has been perverted into an instrument of injustice—an instrument not of protection, but of egalitarian coercion (often disguised in humanitarian garb), generating our rights fever. Why, I have even heard someone argue that he had a "right" to be married! I pointed out, to his embarrassment, that if he had a right to be married, then someone else had an *obligation* to marry him, for a moment's reflection reveals that these are *reciprocal* notions. Just so, all modern positive rights considered as claims against the State for goods and services are really claims against other citizens, now or in the future. (Remember: the State has no money of its own.) The government of the day just happens to be the broker who takes a sizable commission for arranging all this feasting on each other.

Somehow, as dependence on Statism has increased, an immoral chain reaction has been established, which looks like this:

WANTS  >  NEEDS  >  RIGHTS  >  CLAIMS

First, a *private* "want" is voiced. Next, it is described as a *public* "need." Then a *legal* "right" is asserted as a *moral* "claim" against society (the rest of us). One look at the Universal Declaration of Human Rights, largely drafted by a Canadian, John Humphrey, who taught law at McGill University, and was honoured on December 10, 1988, on the fortieth anniversary of the declaration, you will feel good all over. Who wouldn't? It reads like a cornucopia of the good life—especially articles 24 to 30, which basically say that everyone on earth has a right to a very nice, secure, and enjoyable life. There is little imaginable to which the individual does not have a "right," most of it to be provided "free" (that is the language in the declaration). And all these wonderful goods, services, and benefits are to flow from the simple *declaration* of these rights. But this is a misleading fantasy which ought never to have confused the provision of equal *protections* by the State (so that we can gain these things ourselves) with the *provision* of goods and services *by* the State.

Future historians will say the modern welfare states of the worlds gobbled themselves right up by falling for such an illusion, because to the extent that such generalized claims for goods to be provided by others are successful, the private sphere of individual and social responsibility is diminished, liberty is defeated by enforced fraternity, and the wealth of the nation is redirected toward yet another unproductive transaction of decline.

# THE DISCRIMINATION ILLUSION

*(About our national fear of preferences.)*

There is an unfortunate but telling anecdote about a man who goes to the Canadian Broadcasting Corporation to be interviewed for a job as a radio announcer. Half an hour later, he emerges, downcast, to meet his friend, who says: "What's wrong? Didn't you get the job?" The applicant replies: "N-n-n-o. Th-they d-d-didn't h-hire m-m-me b-b-because I'm b-b-black!" (substitute: Chinese, Pakistani, male or female, Christian, Muslim, whatever).

Of course, anyone would feel sorry for this fellow, who obviously applied for the wrong job. But the telling feature of the story lies in the way it illustrates the discrimination illusion. That is, it clearly separates the difference between acts that should be called a *negative prejudice* (which prejudges something negatively before all the facts are known) and those that are simply normal discriminating actions, or preferences. The first kind are mindless generalizations based on limited experience or on "stereotypes," which are intended to harm in thought or action others of whom we unjustly disapprove.

On the other hand, many stereotypes are positive and extremely helpful because they spare us a lot of grief. I like the humorous example the well-known U.S. economist Walter Williams uses about a man walking in the jungle who hears a lion roar. Well, rest assured, it was only his preconception, or stereotype, about the behaviour of lions that spared him his life as he jumped into a tree before ever seeing the lion! In the CBC story told above, the hiring supervisor rightly discriminated against stutterers, about whom he held a stereotype: all stutterers stutter, and they're no damn good on radio.

A general problem in our present society is the confusion between negative and positive prejudice and preference—a confusion that is damaging because it vulgarizes meaningful distinctions by equating them with hurtful ones. Indeed, I should mention a pang of sorrow that the very verb "discriminate" once referred to a skill we all hoped to see emerge in our children. Not long ago, to say that so-and-so was "a discriminating person," or made "discriminating judgments," was a high compliment indeed. In judging the actions of others we would often say, "You have failed to discriminate between (this and that), you still don't get it!"

But once again, feel-good human rights activists, affirmative action do-gooders and high school counsellors with wacky degrees in "self-esteem" teaching have imposed on us a certain moral terror that makes us afraid to make our ordinary preferences known, and that snuffs out our good judgments along with some of the bad ones. But if the idea behind this is to rid society of bigots, it can't be done by driving useful distinctions underground. Bigots love such confusion. This problem needs more distinctions, not fewer. When Walter Williams says he fully intends to discriminate in taking a black wife (because he has black parents, wants black kids, and thinks black is beautiful), well, he's dead serious, and rightly so. But can you imagine a white Canadian saying publicly that he fully intends to discriminate in taking a white wife? Why, he'd probably be hauled before the Human Rights Commission in record time.

If Canadians don't want to become a nation of sheep, they must learn to distinguish between statements and acts of negative prejudice, and normal and positive discriminating acts; between actions the intention of which is to avoid or to harm others, and those that arise from simple observation or personal experience. I remember being at a wedding once where a lot of women welled up with tears during the speeches. Afterward I said, "You women sure cry easily." One of the women, by reflex, said, "That is soooo *sexist!*" I replied, "It's not sexist if it's true. It's just an observation."

But what I have called the egalitarian-Statist mentality, so eager to erase all legitimate differences, has cowed us into either immediate mental erasure of our normal discriminating thoughts and preferences, or into making only positive remarks about others, which amounts to a childish and servile form of insincerity and false flattery. It's a form of public lying. Worst of all, such a philosophy suffusing any society has the effect of suppressing bad as well as good and useful distinctions (oops, I mean, discriminations).

The second crucial consequence of the discrimination illusion is the confusion between *cause* and *effect*. We have been brainwashed into seeing discrimination where none exists. For example, it is true that, statistically speaking, all Canadian women as a group earn somewhere around 60 to 70 percent of the income of all men as a group (2008 figure). The conclusion of the uninformed is that therefore women are discriminated against in Canada's workforce, due to a glass ceiling. However, just a little scrutiny reveals how misleading this illusion is. For The fact is that *most* women and *most* men get married. When they do so, *most* women quit their full-time jobs, take part-time jobs, or reduce their work hours to raise families (the figures are presented in chapter 10). *Most* men, on the other hand, quickly worry about how they are possibly going to support that family, pay for a home, education, and so on. So they take better jobs, go for promotion, work harder and longer, or may even take two jobs. The result? As a group, the total wages of all married women drop, while the total wages of all married men rise. If all you do is compare the two groups without taking into account this phenomenon of personal choice, or preference, on the part of married men and women, you will indeed find a large average difference. However, this is a reflection not of discrimination, but of life choices that are obscured by statistical aggregation.

Interestingly, bachelors in all age groups show average wages about 60 percent of married men's for the same reason: no family to support. But guess what? Never-married women and never-married men in Canada, at all ages, earn the very same wages, and where small differences exist, they tend to favour women. So the differences we see are real and understandable, but

THE TROUBLE WITH CANADA ... STILL! 57

they are a result of preferences. They do not result from negative discrimination. This is a typical example of the discrimination illusion at work. Inevitably, advocacy groups have exploited the public confusion between cause and effect that underlies many policy matters like this. It's a bit like assuming that because drownings and ice-cream sales are highest in August, ice cream causes drowning. Canadians should challenge irresponsible allegations of discrimination aggressively before yielding to intimidation.

## THE EQUALITY ILLUSION
*(How the idea of equality is a logically impossible dream.)*
When I was a child, it struck me as peculiar that whenever the whole school was required to run a foot race, the general result was always the same: the few fast and strong ones always finished up front somewhere, followed by a growing crowd of runners, which then tapered off into a few stragglers at the end. When we went to watch a regional championship, the pattern was the same. And it held true even for the Olympic Games. In other words, no matter how narrowly defined the band of measurement, the spread of differences or abilities always showed the same pattern.

However, I also felt it a truism that no two things are the same, that everything is in flux and, as the Greek philosopher Heraclitus said, "You cannot step into the same stream twice." Little by little, the conflict between these two observations grew in my mind until I realized that although everything in the universe might be *different* from every other thing, the *patterns* formed by large numbers of events or things, the laws governing them, might be quite predictable, whether those different things were incomes, seashells, intelligence, or physical skills. Later in life, I discovered what statisticians call the "normal curve," called a "bell curve" because when sketched, it looks like a bell: few at the bottom, most in the middle, few at the top. It was the pattern of the foot race, on paper. Some universal law must be at work! I immediately drew several jarring conclusions:

• If the law holds, then people can never be "equal" in anything.
• To seek equality, or sameness in things, is necessarily an illusion—an elusive quest.
• Subdivisions of measurement, provided the sample group is large enough, and there is no "sample bias," will always produce the same normal curve.
• Therefore, regardless of how objectively good or bad something may actually be, some people must always be at the bottom, many in the middle, and some at the top of no matter what we are measuring.

Neither does the unit of measurement matter. The 100-metre race, for example, was first measured in fifths of a second, then tenths, and now hundredths—sometimes even thousandths. But with a large enough sample, we always get our normal curve. The "law of variations," which predicts this "normal curve" behaviour of large groups (but not of individuals), is at work, and therefore, to the extent that measurement is meaningful, *equality is impossible*.

Now, how does this fact of life affect social policy? Very simply, it strongly reinforces the idea that *liberty* and *equality* will always be mutually exclusive, if by equality we mean (and this is what social engineers mean) striving for equal social results or outcomes (whether in wages, material resources, or intelligence). It means that modern social policy, in striving for State-enforced equality, is striving for an unattainable goal. It means that once, say, subsistence level is reached by everyone in a population, there will still be "poverty" if we are measuring it in statistical variation only. Indeed, the poor in Canada are defined "distributionally" in this way, so that by definition they will always be here, even if the lowest income group were to earn $100,000 per year. In fact, despite massive efforts to "redistribute" income in Canada since 1951, the per-quintile share of income (income received by the population divided into five groups from lowest to highest) has held steady as a rock over time. According to Statistics Canada, "This means that although each group's income has increased substantially, there's been no movement toward greater equality between the groups." Later in this book I will explain why the phrase "toward greater equality" is biased and presumptive wording that assumes all citizens should have equal incomes. But why? No one expects an apprentice to make as much as a skilled artisan, or a young executive to make the same as one with fifty years' experience, or a clerk to make as much as the president. More on this later. For now it is sufficient to remark on the misleading fact that because we define the poor distributionally in this way, if Canada through some entrepreneurial boom were to have, say, a thousand more millionaires tomorrow, this would automatically mean we would have far more poor!

## THE DETERMINIST ILLUSION

*(How we are encouraged to blame our environment for everything.)*

People have argued since the dawn of recorded history over the issue of *determinism* and *free will*. These are dry-sounding terms, but anyone used to the history of ideas will always detect this debate overtly or covertly at work in all civilizations. Are we the result of causes we cannot alter, or are we masters of our own destinies? Aristotle and Plato, all their students since, and all Christian theologians have worried about this question. You might even say it is the core issue of modern philosophy.

It is crucial for any society to resolve the debate over determinism and free will effectively because social policy is developed as a result of the changing outcome of this debate over time. It is of the utmost importance that any society decide—no, *declare*—whether we are free agents or whether we are determined by our social circumstances, our personal history, and so on. Since personal actions have consequences, no society can render justice if it cannot decide who is responsible for individual actions: to whom, to what party, to what institution, to what *cause* should consequences be allocated? Is the drunk a drunk because his father was? (Then how about his brother, who is *not* a drunk because his father was?) Is the criminal guilty and to be fully punished or will the defence win the case by saying, "It was true, my lord, that he held the gun, but history pulled the trigger"?

So there it is. The whole determinism–free will debate turns on the matter of the just allocation of consequences. And it so happens that whole civilizations have risen and fallen, depending on how this matter got settled. One thesis of this book is that the Statist mentality actively pushes public opinion in the direction of determinism, while a liberty ethic does the opposite. The former seeks to allocate consequences to the social environment (examples are our soft-headed criminal justice system, and the writings of most behaviourists and sociologists); the latter to the individual (the Protestant work ethic, all religions, positive thinking, the human potential movement, and so on). For most societies, most of the time, this is an ongoing debate. Young, dominant cultures tend to be aggressive and achievement oriented, and allocate consequences individually (the best examples are the United States and Canada until the mid-twentieth century). But as cultures age, one of the weakening agents is the gradual shunting of this allocation to the environment (fate, a bad upbringing, etc.), or to other social groups (class warfare, the soak-the-rich mentality), or to the factional warring of political interest groups (the Left, or the Right, is leading us to perdition).

My personal twist on the whole matter is that this decline cannot be avoided unless the determinist illusion is settled by first realizing that the debate is circular, and that it must be set aside in favour of the following propositions:

Proposition 1: Human affairs in relation to the environment are, in fact, hopelessly intertwined, and as good a logical (not moral) argument can be made for one side as for the other. It is as easy to argue that life consists of infinite free possibilities as it is to argue that because every effect has a cause, life is determined in its every minute aspect. For this reason, no scientist or philosopher will ever "logically" settle the debate to everyone's satisfaction. But it may be settled morally. Therefore,

Proposition 2: Even if science were to prove, logically and irrefutably, that our lives are determined, we would simply have to ignore this conclusion. Why? First, because there is for every consequence a chain of causes that is, for all practical purposes, infinite. Second, any society that intends to be moral (freedom is a necessary precondition for moral life) must make a fundamental decision to opt for free will in order to conduct its affairs. In short, human moral—and therefore, social—life is not possible without clear support for the individual allocation of consequences. So there you have it. There is a high correlation between the freedom of an entire society and its insistence on free will and individual responsibility, just as there is a high correlation between the lack of freedom in a society and its insistence on determinism, or social, or class, or "systemic" causality. The first kind of society will insist you pay for your own actions. The second will excuse you morally and condemn you to "re-education" or state therapy, and make others pay.

My concern for Canada—for the West—is that we have forgotten this bit of truth, to our great peril, and this has loosed upon us the "psychology of excuse." Through this, we will slowly become a dispirited people, blaming our history, our genes, our families, our social class, the rich, the bureaucrat, the privileged, illness, mental torment, some food we ate, and so on for our condition. There is a murder case in which the defence lawyer won acquittal using the now-famous "Twinkie defence" (Twinkies are a snack cake). He claimed that his client had consumed a whole bag of Twinkies and was sugar-overloaded, and therefore not responsible for the murder of his victim! When whole societies start falling for things like the Twinkie defence, or let a murderer go free because he claims he was "sleepwalking" (he may have been, but for goodness' sake, lock him up!), or allow cases like a liability suit against a beer company because the plaintiff drank too much of the company's product before his car accident—when such things occur without public outrage, the foundations of an ordered society cannot hold much longer. For, when individual responsibility crumbles, lawyers get rich, but society crumbles.

The fundamental problem arises from our failure to distinguish between physical states or feelings, and moral actions. After all, two people may be in exactly the same lifelong turmoil or pain, so that both may wish to kill someone. But the decision of one to go jogging, or to a therapist to cope with this urge, and of the other to murder, is a moral decision, not a physical one. The "psychology of excuse" is just one outward manifestation of this transfer of responsibility from the individual to the "environment" in a self-consuming "war of all against all."

The concept of fairness based on individual responsibility that has always lain at the root of our civilization may not be a perfect principle, but it is so far the fairest discovered, for it allocates consequences accurately, based on an identifiable perpetrator. It refuses to look beyond this to physical determinants precisely because this would lead to a chain of excuses and destroy the general moral tenor of society. After all, it is not a great leap from blaming other individuals, to blaming our family life, to blaming our genes, to blaming society in general, to having no society left at all. We must disabuse ourselves—and our legislators of these illusions, and bring back *caveat emptor* (buyer beware) in all things.

# THE POVERTY ILLUSION

*(How we have destroyed the meaning of "truly needy.")*

It is difficult to discuss "poverty" when you have always been well off—and the vast majority of living Canadians, compared with most in the world, have always been "well off." In 2007, the average top marginal tax rate was $80,699. If we use that as our cut-off we could argue that any Canadian earning over this amount annually may be officially classified as "rich" for taxation purposes (about 7.4 percent of all tax filers).

Despite this, there is a poverty illusion which is, I fear, promoted with particular enthusiasm and carelessness by modern Statists. For example, we are commonly asked to accept the idea that the poor are a fixed class of people to whom we ought to be transferring more wealth. The wealth is supposed to "cure" their poverty (if you think of it as an illness) or at least provide them with a dignified reclassification (if you think statistically).

Now, I cannot remember ever seeing a newspaper article in Canada seriously questioning the idea of "poverty," let alone asking what the term *means*. No wonder. Agencies working to end poverty use leaky definitions. Here is a popular definition from the website of the World Bank: "Poverty is hunger. Poverty is lack of shelter. Poverty is being sick and not being able to see a doctor. Poverty is not having access to school and not knowing how to read. Poverty is not having a job, is fear for the future, living one day at a time. Poverty is losing a child to illness brought about by unclean water. Poverty is powerlessness, lack of representation and freedom."

We may be excused for thinking some of these are catch-all terms specifically Western in their focus (school, reading, no job, fear of the future, one day at a time, powerlessness, lack of representation, lack of freedom). A bit of general reading in this area, however, will suffice to persuade the average person that there is a good deal of chicanery afoot, for it turns out that very little is known about poverty, and even less is agreed upon (despite the harmonious, almost beatific confidence of the media in their own views on this subject). And so we, the public, are quite vulnerable to being told anything a propagandizing journalist may want us to hear. The poverty illusion in Canada says:

- Poverty is defined by the presence or absence of material resources.
- We have a class called the poor.
- They suffer because they have fewer material resources (money, goods) than those who are not poor.
- If we don't give them a handout, their condition will worsen.

But we need a clear perspective and sharper insight on this matter. Not that we should ever lose our capacity for sympathy with the truly needy. Far from it. We need more of this quality in our materialistic world, and, as we shall see later in this book, Canadians, as compared, say, to those we assume to be greedy capitalistic Americans, and despite our self-flattery in this respect, are not a very generous people. Actually, we are about half as generous per capita as Americans (and in terms of philanthropy, they are the most generous people on earth).

But let us at least attempt to avoid being witless victims of poverty propaganda. Let us protect ourselves against being browbeaten into shelling out for a trumped-up abstraction, an illusion. What, if anything, do we know about poverty? In chapter 8 this topic is examined in some depth. But for the sake of clarifying the poverty illusion here, I draw chiefly from Charles Murray's two classic books, *Losing Ground* and *In Pursuit of Happiness and Good Government.*[3] First, Murray dispels the poverty-equals-misery illusion. He tells us that the main objective of human beings the world over is the "pursuit of happiness," which everyone more or less reduces to: a "justified satisfaction" with one's life. Second, he says that in order to pursue happiness, we have to satisfy certain basic needs, as outlined by Abraham Maslow in his famous hierarchy of needs model. First we need food, shelter, and clothing; then we go after security, then love, and so on; and ultimately, we pursue "self-actualization" (at least in the West). Third, he points out that the first, or "subsistence," level is the cut-off point for happiness. People the world over report great unhappiness if they fall below this point. But almost the moment they exceed this point, their self-reported happiness skyrockets—and is not appreciably increased by greater amounts of money or things.

Murray's analysis is revolutionary because he has had the boldness to extricate the idea of happiness from the solely material framework in which it has been confined for more than two hundred years. He also gives us a clear idea of how difficult it is to determine who makes up the class called the poor. He points out that even poverty experts have an awful time deciding what they mean, or how a poverty-line income is to be calculated (defined in most of the world, but not in Canada, as three times the amount of annual income needed for an adequate diet). Here's why. He is speaking of the United States, but his comments, summarized below, provide a valuable general message.

1.  Poverty measures are insensitive to local differences in the cost of living; for example, between expensive big cities and inexpensive rural areas or small towns.
2.  They do not capture the "non-monetary differences in quality of life." For example, how much money would it take to persuade a poverty-level city family to move to the sticks, and vice versa?
3.  The definition of poverty is too relative. As long ago as 1940, when government was lamenting poverty in Harlem, New York, Harlem already "had a per capita income that would have placed it fifth among the countries of the world!"

4.  No one can definitively decide on rather crucial matters, such as: Should we be counting individuals or families when defining poverty? Much of the world considers it natural to count the total family unit. Is a student over eighteen living at home "poor"? Is a working woman who stops going out to work to raise a family "poor"? No attempt is made to explain these differences.

5.  Even worse—how much money do the poor really have (as opposed to how much they officially say they have)? It is well known that even legal income is often wildly underreported.

6.  What about the "cash-only, please" underground and the "contra" economy? Figures suggest that from 20 to 75 percent of the income of the poor is underground.

7.  Finally, Murray tells us that "as of 1980, the many overlapping and in-kind benefit programs had made it possible for almost anyone [in the United States] to place himself above the poverty threshold."[4]

Here I report on two significant articles that appeared when I was first writing this chapter that ought at least to unseat the prevalent opinion that the poor is a fixed class of human beings. First, the internationally respected magazine the *Economist* (August 6, 1988), reporting on conclusions from the latest poverty studies, wrote that "although 13% of Americans are officially poor, an American has under a 1% danger of staying long among them, provided she or he does three things: *completes high school, stays more than a year in a first job even if at minimum wage, gets and stays married*" [italics mine]. (The *Economist* refers to many of the poor who cannot manage these three things as "self-manufactured.") Next, from *National Review* (October 1988) came the following:

A University of Michigan study that tracked the year-to-year economic vicissitudes of five thousand American families found that only 48.5 per cent of the families who were among the wealthiest 20 per cent in 1971 were still there in 1978; 3.5% of them had fallen into the lowest 20% bracket. Conversely, 44.5% of the families in the poorest fifth in 1971 were no longer there seven years later. Six per cent had actually risen all the way to the highest fifth ...!

And ... in 2010 we have the Economic Mobility Project, an American initiative devoted to measuring "the ability to climb up or fall down the economic ladder within a lifetime or across generations." And we learn: two-thirds of Americans have higher real incomes than their parents; children born into the lowest-income quintile are more likely to surpass their parents' incomes than children from any other income group; and astonishingly, as adults almost 60 percent of those born into the bottom level have moved up, and about 60 percent of those born into the top level have moved down. Uneducated black and white children do not do as well on these measures, nor do women; both groups experience more downward mobility, blacks more precipitously than whites; family background matters a great deal, as does education; but between blacks and whites who finish four years of college, there is no racial gap in mobility—both groups have high upward mobility.

All of which suggests a few conclusions about the poverty illusion. Above subsistence level, "poverty" is a rather subjective and very *relative* concept; official definitions and statistics are grossly unreliable; and even when we can pin down who the poor are, they are generally not the same people year after year (except, as is so often the case, when government is paying them to stay that way). I am also somewhat distrustful of poverty studies in general for the reason that so much wealth in Western democracies, especially at the level of the trades, is "cash-only, please." In Canada, the underground economy has been estimated at anywhere from $50 to $100 billion per year. Governments get some notion of this amount through analysis of tax returns as compared to welfare payments. But when poverty rates are based on partial incomes, the results must be tenuous.

## THE SOAK-THE-RICH ILLUSION
*(The real shock is that the rich don't have as much as we like to think.)*
I have come to believe that the governments of welfare states like ours, which soon realize that they cannot get much money from the rich, promote the idea of "progressive" (punitive), "soak-the-rich" tax rates in order to create strong feelings of public envy, thus persuading them to "accept complacently a burden of government expenditure and taxation that they would not otherwise tolerate."[5] In other words, the welfare state encourages public envy and resentment in order to divert attention from its plundering of the middle class. If we can be persuaded that the State is going to soak the rich, its hand can slip deeper into the pockets of the middle class, and below, where the *real* tax money lies. This is the conclusion arrived at once you realize that there aren't very many rich people in Canada and they don't have as much income as we believe. When you stop to think about how much power and coercion are exercised under the banner of the illusion that wealth will be taken from the rich and redistributed to the poor, the truth comes as a great shock (as it does for any middle-class citizen who votes for a candidate because he or she promises to soak the rich, and then discovers: "We *are* the rich!").

Truth is that in 2007, the top 30 percent of families earned 60 percent of all income and paid almost 66 percent of all taxes. They indeed bear most of Canada's tax burden. But who belongs to this illustrious group called the rich? A Canadian family in 2007 was counted as rich—in the top 30 percent of families—when its total cash income reached $81,501. The average income of all families earning more than that was $143,179. The message here is that those who advocate soaking the rich to finance the welfare state . . . are already doing so! But I don't think many families at this entry level consider themselves to be rich. How rich is rich?

If we use the $80,000 figure as our cut-off, and argue (as a fanatical Statist) that all incomes above that amount should be confiscated at a 100 percent rate and redistributed equally to all those earning less than $80,000, what happens? In the tax year 2005, exactly 1,697,290 persons (7.4 percent of all taxpayers) filed personal income tax returns reporting income of $80,000 or more. The total reported was $257 billion. If the state had taxed away *all* the income of taxpayers earning more than $80,000, the total additional tax revenue for 2005 would have been $54.9 billion higher than it actually was. Redistribution of this entire amount to the 21.3 million taxpayers with incomes less than the $80,000 cut-off would have gained them $2,582 each—on average, about 9.7 percent more that year. But only once.[6] For, with such a drastic move, all the rich would have been wiped out, along with their businesses and the jobs they created. However, because many spouses, children, and dependants do not submit returns, this amount, if sprinkled to all citizens below the cut-off, would probably amount to less than $1,000 each.

So much for soaking the rich, for the philosophy of progressive taxation, and for the redistribution that this is supposed to accomplish. Even a casual study of the matter suggests an elaborate shell game, wherein, by the maintenance of such illusions, the people are being forced to part with ever more of the fruits of their labour. What a sorry picture is produced! For the forty-five years from 1961 to 2007, here are the increases in the costs of the most basic items essential for decent human life compared to the rise in taxation in the same period—food: 505 percent; clothing: 455 percent; Consumer Price Index: 610 percent; shelter: 1,063 percent; cash income: 1, 230 percent; and . . . drum-roll, please . . . taxes: a whopping 1,704 percent! However, you buy that house or condo (shelter) only once in a blue moon, but you pay that 1,704 percent tax item every year.

People continue to think their government is soaking the rich and paying the poor. But in too many respects they are really soaking each other to pay each other while the new class of bureaucrats and politicians act as highly paid managers of this elaborate performance, raking off a large commission at all three levels of government in the process. To describe this, economist Filip Palda speaks of "churned transfers," by which he means government transfer payments that leave citizens no better off—perhaps even worse off—than they would have been if they had simply received an equivalent tax cut, for "money is taxed out of a citizen's pocket, filtered through a government bureaucracy, and funnelled back into that same citizen's pocket. The tax and subsidy misdirect the individual's economic efforts, and so create a deadweight loss."[7] Palda estimates between 15 and 49 percent of Canada's government spending might be fairly described as churning.

I fear that we will never reverse this drive to ever-larger government until all the popular illusions become unpopular. This will happen only through public resolve to return to the traditional sense of freedom and responsibility that beats at the heart of a truly free society, the complex, interwoven aspects of which will be covered next.

# 3: DEMOCRATIC CAPITALISM
## BREAKING THE CHAINS OF
## ECONOMIC STAGNATION

*Social forms are constructs of the human spirit.*
—Michael Novak, *The Spirit of Democratic Capitalism*

*The laws of the market are nothing less than the
laws of democracy applied to economics.*
—Alain Peyrefitte, *The Trouble With France*

Let us begin by noting that capitalism, roughly understood as mutually ben-eficial trade between individuals, tribes, guilds, corporations, or any other entities, such as states, is a human universal. Where not suppressed, it will flourish, and where supported by the right legal and regulatory framework— that is, where it is protected by laws in favour of freedom of contract, and outlawing fraud—where it exists as a dependable system, it will boost wealth creation enormously.

The word "democratic" is attached here simply because the enormous in-crease in global wealth of the past two centuries has been accompanied by an increase in the number of more or less democratic regimes. I say more or less because this massive increase in wealth has also made possible far more lucra-tive tax harvesting by modern democratic states, which have used it to become more Statist, or welfarist, in their orientation. In short, greater wealth has fuelled far more regulatory regimes to the extent that we have today more democracy in name, but less freedom in reality. More wealth has enabled everyone to do more of what they do best: businesses to grow business, and governments to grow the State. Needless to say, there is a complicated structural contradiction between these two trends. States may vary in their control of economic freedoms from simply serving as night watchmen to becoming state capitalists owning and regulating the most important formerly free enterprises. France, for exam-ple, has long played a role in its large hybrid state-governed "private" enterprises. U.S. president Barack Obama is agitating for unprecedented new state control of major American financial and manufacturing sectors.

Nevertheless, the two words belong together because modern democratic capitalism is a bottom-up rather than a top-down system in which wealth crea-tion is only possible because people get what they want in exchange for their money. Any business owner knows that if you please consumers, you will suc-ceed; if not, someone else will do so, and you will go out of business. The whole system is driven from below by the masses, the *demos* (this Greek root word for democracy means "people").

William Easterly, one of the world's most interesting foreign aid experts, writes in *The White Man's Burden*: "Democracy is a bottom-up system that rewards local, specialized knowledge in a similar way to free markets. In a de-mocracy the squeaky wheel gets the grease."[1] Indeed, he shows an extremely positive relationship between degree of democracy and level of income in the nations of the world—the more democratic, the higher the per-capita income. I should also mention here the extraordinary growth in the number of more or less democratic regimes over the past century.

On this note, readers may enjoy following the arguments of Professor Rudy Rummel of the University of Hawaii who has made major contributions to the study of "democide"—the tendency of non-democratic regimes to slaughter their own people. The figures are horrific, and they show clearly that Statism is very bad for your health![2] Rummel has also constructed a "democ-racy clock" that tracks the conversion of nations to democracy since 1900 (you can see the clock at http://www.hawaii.edu/powerkills/DP.CLOCK.HTM). Rummel concludes that democracies simply do not make war on each other; the more two nations are democratic, the less their mutual violence. Democracies also have by far the least internal violence and virtually no demo-cide. And we must add to this that democracies are the wealthiest nations of the world. These facts are so astonishing we need to ask how they came to be. As it turns out, the evolution of the English bottom-up style—what I have called the Freedom System, has been long, and not without difficulties. Let us step back in time, not merely to refresh our memories of the past, but also to recognize how very much of the past is still with us.

## EARLY CAPITALISM

Capitalism did not begin to appear as a distinct economic system until the end of the Middle Ages in Europe, during the greater part of which feudalism pre-vailed. In terms of power relationships and the dominance of one class over another, feudalism could be defined as an arrangement whereby vassals ex-changed their labour and their freedom for the right to work the lord's land, from the produce of which they paid him a portion as a tax. They also owed him military service in the event of war, and he owed them protection from invaders and other enemies. Such was their "contract." (We will see that many of the economic policies that rigidified medieval society and helped to keep it poor are never far from our doorstep. In Statist-type nations, where the focus is on regulatory control of life, they return repeatedly with only slightly different names.)[3]

Capitalism was straining to be born during this period in Europe, especially in England, but could not fully emerge for a number of reasons: feudal life was overwhelmingly agricultural; economic and political authority were not yet separate (the lord was both); custom and law determined the terms of exchange according to which a "just price" had to be paid for something purchased and a "just wage" paid to labour (wages were set by political decree, not by the market, which is exactly what has returned in our minimum wage and so-called pay equity legislation today). Contributing to this extreme rigidity were the absence of free exchange, minimal use of money (goods were bartered for other goods), and the fact that the authorities (especially the Catholic church) considered supply and demand irrelevant to daily life. Most important, the church forbade the charging of interest, which was considered immoral because it constituted material gain without visible work. Islam continues this custom. A linguistic vestige remains in our own use of the phrase "unearned income" to refer to investment income. It is an attitude that reveals a misunderstanding of the "work" done by capital when it is lent at risk. Clever merchants in such regimes avoided the interest sanction by using "discounted bills of exchange." That is, they were allowed to lend someone a sum, say, $90, in exchange for a note guaranteeing a fixed future repayment of $100. The difference was considered their insurance against the possibility of default. This was a fascinating and clever invention and one of the crucial tools of wealth creation during the early stages of the development of capitalism. It was also an early example of commercial inventiveness in the face of man-made obstacles.

Largely as a result of such creative use of lending instruments, capitalism developed rapidly and spontaneously, especially in England where economic rigidity was less pronounced than on the European continent. There, it took until the nineteenth century to achieve the same degree of political and economic freedom acquired by the English more than two centuries earlier.

## "CAPITALISM" AND WHAT IT MEANS

Formed from the Latin root *caput*, meaning "head," "capital" originally referred purely to capital stocks of money and funds carrying interest. But in retrospect, the term *"caput"* is especially suitable as the root for "capitalism" because its most powerful contribution to humankind has come not from its emphasis on the material production of wealth, but on the products of the head: the intelligence, organization, innovation, and cultural and spiritual values that have made such wealth production possible. In recognition of this, we have very recently coined the term "human capital." Hong Kong, for example, one of the wealthiest spots on earth per capita, has zero material wealth or resources. But it has a lot of people with smart heads, trading freely, relatively unencumbered by regulation. Unfortunately, the remarkable development of capitalism was given a bad name by its opponents—especially by Karl Marx, in his book *Capital* (1867)—and it has never lost the negative connotation he gave the word.

But the term is also imprecise, for the fact is, all nations of the world, no matter what their type of political system, employ capital. The telling question is to what degree that capital is employed by free individuals, or by the State on their behalf. In the first, and I believe best, case, free people employ it on their own behalf. In the second (the case in all highly Statist nations), it is employed *for* them by politicians who think they know best what is good for others— and, not incidentally, for themselves as they rake off a sizable commission for their controlling activities!

The distinctive feature of true democratic capitalism (as distinct from despotic capitalism), wherever it is employed successfully, is not that it uses capital, but that it is inextricably linked with human freedom and the institutions of freedom. That is why Statists have always disliked capitalism. They can't stand the idea that free people with only personal interests will be controlling the ultimate economic outcomes of the nation with no overarching plan. The idea that there will be a hundred pairs of shoes among which to choose, instead of one best pair made by government and available to all in some five-year plan (as the Soviets used to call these things) offends them deeply as irrational. True enough. And that is its beauty. Manufacturers of shoes are not trying to please the government, they are trying to please consumers of shoes. And when the system is free, it is competitive, and so the consumer can always find the least expensive or the most expensive pair, as desired.

So rightly speaking, capitalism—free economic rights and activities—is part of the Freedom System because at bottom it is truly about freedom, and though it has managed to survive in despotic surroundings for brief periods, it cannot function for long without freedom and it is manifestly a "system." As early as 1776, in his groundbreaking book *The Wealth of Nations*, Adam Smith called this phenomenon the "natural system of liberty." Two hundred years later, 1976 Nobel laureate Milton Friedman wrote *Capitalism and Freedom* to illustrate the power of this connection between freedom and wealth creation. Another work readers will enjoy and that influenced this writer is Michael Novak's moving book *The Spirit of Democratic Capitalism.*[4] Further to this, a recent anthropological study of fifteen societies reported in *Science* (March 18, 2010) concluded that capitalism makes us kinder people. The study found that the likelihood that people would "play fair" with strangers (or punish them for not playing fair) increased with the degree to which they were integrated into markets and participated in a world religion.

## A MORAL IMPERATIVE FOR OUR TIME

One of the telling points Novak makes in a book rich with insights is that while throughout history moral people have always felt a sense of altruism, a responsibility to help the needy, that feeling has always been accompanied by a sense of frustration. Famines were the rule. Wealth seemed elusive except for the few. Misery has been the lot of two-thirds of humankind. But what I call the "tools of freedom and wealth creation"—and despite what seems to be their tendency to self-destruct on occasion, as during the 2008 sub-prime lending crisis—have never been so clearly understood as they are today. And because they are now available to us, human beings have a new moral obligation to ensure that the principles from which such tools are derived are spread as far afield as possible. Novak's vision is that, once and for all, human material suffering can be ended if we have but the will. What was once only wishful thinking is now within our grasp because *we now know how to create wealth.*

Since the first edition of this book was published, the Western world has had an unexpected opportunity to watch what happens when West meets East, so to speak. That is to say, when a civilization such as our own that has learned how to use such tools attempts to export them to civilizations that may not welcome them as we assume they will, such as Iraq and Afghanistan. Despite the attempts of some of these people—natural traders all—to import our ways, we see them daily encountering resistance from their own centuries-old clerical, legal, and moral systems. To an extent, despite the existence of the Internet and such, they are stuck in the Middle Ages, as we once were, and cannot get out unless they adapt our tools to their way of life. Indeed, much of this book will touch upon the many ways in which the tools of freedom and wealth creation are stifled in our own Canadian society due to assumptions born in the Middle Ages. But first, let us look at the positive effects created in the world by the very first and most famous burst of wealth in human history, now called the Industrial Revolution, which is continuing to this day as a general modernization and technological revolution.

## THE INDUSTRIAL REVOLUTION, CHILD LABOUR, AND SLAVE LABOUR

Modern opponents of democratic capitalism, loosely characterized today as the Left (they are not all conveniently confined to a particular party), are not hard pressed to find horror stories they are pleased to quote regarding the evils, indignities, and social dislocations created by the Industrial Revolution. There are whole libraries of documents on this grim and still-controversial subject. Child labour, unsanitary conditions, long hard hours of back-breaking work, and early death are on the not-always-unbiased record. In fact, such abuses have been on the record for most of human history and, in much of the world, according to the Anti-Slavery Society, still exist.[5] The Industrial Revolution, it turns out, accelerated and multiplied not only the process of wealth creation, but also enough social difficulties to require reforms. But while no right-minded person would today consider the working conditions of those times desirable, our indignant criticisms are softened when we stop to remember that for the vast majority of the poor in the early industrial age were a measurable improvement on their alternatives—most commonly starvation, begging, or crime.

As for child labour, it has almost always been their own parents who willingly sent children to work in factories, mines, and sweatshops because such families needed the money. Home life for the poor at the dawn of industrialization was, for the most part, a sordid experience. But even a well-known critic of the period, Dr. Peter Gaskell, who himself opposed child labour, wrote that "the employment of children in factories ought not to be looked upon as an evil, till the present moral and domestic habits of the population are completely reorganized. So long as home education is not found for them, and they are left to live as savages, they are to some extent better situated when engaged in light labour, and the labour generally is light which falls to their share."[6]

Although mostly absent in wealthy nations today, in much of the world child labour, and various forms of child as well as adult slave labour, are still widely used, for to outlaw them would bring real hardship and therefore resistance from the people. I am persuaded that the only way to end true child labour for the millions of the poor caught up in it (as distinct from casual child labour performed by the children of the well-off) is through a combination of legislation and economic activism leading to increased national wealth. Legislation alone has never succeeded.

As for slavery in Canada . . . is this a joke? Not quite. A little booklet entitled *Slavery and Freedom in Niagara*, by author Michael Power of Welland, Ontario, surprised me and got me going on this subject. In school we learn only that Canada-the-good served as a kind of Holy Land for persecuted slaves who escaped from a barbaric United States. But this has created an unjustified belief in our moral superiority. Below is a Snapshot on Canada's role in real slavery.

---

## SNAPSHOT
Slavery in Canada—What?

Around the year 1780 there were about 4,000 blacks living in the Canadian British colonies, of whom about 1,800 were slaves. Canada's first anti-slavery law (of sorts), of July 9, 1793, did not exactly outlaw slavery. It was called An Act to Prevent the Future Introduction of Slaves. In other words, slavery would remain legal, but no more slaves could be imported to Canada.

In pioneer Canada, slave owning was widespread among the emerging political and social elites of Upper Canada. Peter Russell, Matthew Elliot, and many other distinguished men who sat on the Legislative Council of Upper Canada each owned dozens of slaves. Most sought to protect their right to own slaves by arguing that a slave was legally owned property, and the right to own property was fundamental to all free societies. Courts that took away legally owned slaves could then take away land, or homes, and tyranny would reign. Canadian farmers asked: Who will compensate us for our freed slaves, and the lost benefits from slave labour? Many settlers were Loyalists who came here because government had promised them cheap land on the condition they clear it, and their slaves were purchased specifically for that purpose. The government had lured them. Was the government now going to ruin them?

An irony of the history of slavery in Canada is that many individual U.S. states (Delaware, Michigan, Rhode Island, and Connecticut) had banned slavery outright twenty years before Canada prohibited (only) the future importation of slaves. So the state of Michigan became an instant haven for slaves escaping from Upper Canada. Canadian slave owners complained bitterly, imploring Canada's Lieutenant-Governor to stop what was in effect a reverse underground railroad. He refused.

## A DISTORTED RECORD

Vast amounts of energy have been spent by generations of critics to characterize the Industrial Revolution as a time of exploitation by cruel and greedy capitalists. But this criticism is misdirected. What was unique about the Industrial Revolution was not that it was based on self-interest, but that at long last there had been combined with this self-interest, for the first time in human history, a set of definable, repeatable, transposable political and economic techniques that had the spontaneous effect of benefiting large masses of people. It may have been caused by the self-interest of capitalists, but it was successful only because that self-interest was inherently other-directed; for capitalism could not possibly have succeeded unless it gave large masses of people exactly what they wanted, of the right quality, in the right quantity, and at the right price. As Adam Smith pointed out, the revolution succeeded in providing silk stockings not for princesses, who had always had them, but for the common folk, who had never had them—and at a cheaper and cheaper price.

It remains one of the mysteries of human life why so many have spent so much energy to vilify the first event in history that succeeded in dragging humankind up by its bootstraps from the millennia of slavery and poverty that had theretofore been its lot. Indeed,

the invention of the market economy in Great Britain and the United States more profoundly revolutionized the world between 1800 and the present than any other single force. After five millennia of blundering, human beings finally figured out how wealth may be produced in a sustained, systematic way. In Great Britain, real wages doubled between 1800 and 1850, and doubled again between 1850 and 1900. Since the population of Great Britain quadrupled in size, this represented a 1600 percent increase within one century.[7]

In addition, mortality rates dropped sharply, the price of manufactured goods plummeted, life expectancy jumped, and unemployment was never greater than 8 percent. I don't think much more needs to be said to suggest that the standard view most of us have imbibed has been the weak-kneed version fed to us by critics who have not bothered to research the facts themselves. Someone who has is Ludwig von Mises (teacher of Friedrich Hayek, the 1974 Nobel economist), who tells us:

> The truth is that economic conditions were highly unsatisfactory on the eve of the Industrial Revolution ... The factories freed the authorities and the ruling landed aristocracy from an embarrassing problem that had grown too large for them. They provided sustenance for the masses of paupers. They emptied the poor houses, the workhouses, and the prisons. They converted starving beggars into self-supporting breadwinners. The factory owners did not have the power to compel anybody to take a factory job. They could only hire people who were ready to work for the wages offered to them. Low as these wage rates were, they were nonetheless much more than these paupers could earn in any other field open to them. It is a distortion of the facts to say that the factories carried off the housewives from the nurseries and the kitchens and the children from their play. These women had nothing to cook with, and to feed their children. These children were destitute and starving. Their only refuge was the factory. It saved them, in the strict sense of the term, from death by starvation.[8]

Enough said. I do not wish to suggest that there were no rascals in such times. There certainly were. There was an adequate share of business rascals, government rascals, and all other sorts. There always have been and there always will be. But the final lesson of the Industrial Revolution is that the rich indeed got richer, but so did the enormous middle classes and the poor. Canada itself is an example of this. Per-quintile shares of total income here have not changed in the past century, yet real income (adjusted for inflation) for all the quintiles has multiplied many times over. Indeed, one of the few things on which economists of all stripes agree is that a rising GDP is the best cure for poverty (that is, for real poverty based on a measure of the adequacy of basic needs, and not on a measure of personal income relative to the incomes of others).

## THE MODERNIZATION EFFECT

Exhaustive research has been done on so many aspects of capitalism and industrialization that a consensus has emerged that it is almost impossible to separate the effects of democratic capitalism from the effects of what is now called "modernization." In other words, over the past two and a half centuries, there has been a modernization effect that has spread—is still rapidly spreading—at different rates over the entire world, almost regardless of the political ideology controlling any particular country.

Whether a country is socialist, a dictatorship, or a democracy of some kind, there are certain common dislocating social effects of modernization, and it is wrong simply to blame these on the political system. Rather, they are effects of scientific discoveries and technological inventions on modern culture in general, and they will occur wherever such modernization is introduced.

It is also clear today—and this was forcefully spelled out by Peter Berger in his book *The Capitalist Revolution*—that democratic capitalism, the free-market system in general, and the tools and institutions of wealth creation it developed have had a powerful accelerating effect on modernization. In other words, the rate of modernization is powerfully increased if democratic capitalism is also present. As Berger put it, "Capitalism provides the optimal context for the productive power of modern technology."[9] I would add that it also provides most of the ideas and inventions.

If you want to see the effect of modernization in a country without democratic capitalism, you have only to visit the socialist nations of the world. Despite the fact that they, too, use capital, they tend to exhibit what Swedish economist Sven Rydenfelt has called "a pattern for failure" in his ominously prophetic book by that title,[10] which examines just how socialist economies set about undermining their own wealth-creating potential. The standard response to this revelation is that the distribution of wealth in socialist nations is "fairer," so it doesn't matter if as a whole their economies are not more robust, and that it is legitimate to surrender some freedom for more equality. But we will see later that this argument does not hold up. The socialist nations are no more fair than democratic capitalist ones, and from a pure equality-of-income point of view the socialist nations do no better than the democratic capitalist nations. Not only do they do no better than us, they do no better at a far lower level of per capita wealth. If anyone doubts this claim, they need only examine the life in any former satellite of the USSR, or live in Cuba or North Korea for a while.

The next chapter will survey the actual tools of freedom and wealth creation, both conceptual and practical, without which it is unlikely that any nation will be able to develop a sustainable tradition of wealth and progress.

# 4: THE FREEDOM SYSTEM
## HOW IT WORKS

*A man owns two cows. Under communism, the government confiscates both cows, and sells him back some of the milk. Under socialism, the government takes one of his cows and gives it to his neighbour. Under democratic capitalism, he gets to sell one of the cows, and buy a bull.*
—Anonymous

Over the past two or three centuries we have been undergoing a transition, or "passage," from an inhuman, poverty-stricken world to a more humane and wealthy world.[1] At the turn of this century there were only a handful of wealthy countries. But by 1988, there were more than thirty-five. In that year, futurist Max Singer maintained that by 2008 more than 15 percent of the world's people would be living in wealthy countries (defined as having an average longevity of seventy-two years, and three-fourths of all children finishing high school). He overestimated a bit, but he was very close. In every such nation wealth has been the means to higher ends: new expectations for health care, education, nutrition, quality of work, professionalism, transportation, and communications, the sum total of which raises the general standard of living for all to levels never before achieved.

In view of this, nothing is more surprising to an observer of democratic capitalism than the discovery that this most powerful system of wealth production has never really had a prophet, nor a simple document or manifesto of the kind important to all other social and political revolutions and movements. What is even more surprising is that while an important function of the educational system in most nations of the world is to ensure that the young appreciate and defend core national values, it doesn't work that way for us. If anything, democratic capitalism is often presented as a malign alienating force in society by teachers who do not understand it and who have no direct personal experience of the way it works. In other words, we live under a system that struggles to survive within a society that begrudgingly accepts its benefits. At the worst, our universities are overpopulated with people the British philosopher Roger Scruton describes as "oikophobes" (*oikos* is Greek for "home"), which is to say, people who hate their own national home. The core of the so-called postmodern movement, a university-generated phenomenon that is just now wearing down, was at bottom a West-hating intellectual movement.

Indeed, the very system upon which our success depends seems to generate its own internal enemies and often funds their activities. The only way such a self-annihilating trend can be reversed will be through a commitment on the part of a majority of citizens to more deeply understand and then thoroughly promote the principles, tools, and institutions responsible for our historical strength. This is likely to be a long and daunting task, as Statists in the West have long since captured the majority of media and the faculties of our universities.[2] Even the so-called conservative political parties in most Western democracies are far from committed to what I describe as our Freedom System. Nevertheless, I embark now on its defence with three crucial points to be observed first.

## WEALTH IS NOT NATURAL, BUT CREATED

To be blunt, nothing has economic value unless someone is willing to pay for it, a point made clear with a simple question: Does a large vein of pure gold that is completely inaccessible five miles beneath the ground have any economic value? Most people would say: Not as long as it stays in the ground. In fact, if in trying to mine it we spend more than we can sell it for, it has a negative value. At best, we can say it has only potential value until a method is created to extract it from the ground at a cost less than its market price.

Obviously, none of us would bother to do the back-breaking work to get gold out of the ground if doing so cost *exactly* the same as the yield from the sale of the gold. We would do so only if we were relatively certain that after paying for equipment, wages, rents, utilities, taxes, and so on, we would be left with *more* value than the sum of all our direct expenses and could still expect to replace worn-out machinery, put some money aside for recessions, strikes, and so on. It is this margin of revenue over expenses, normally called profits, which is so misunderstood by the opponents of democratic capitalism, who think everything ought to be done on a not-for-profit basis. But without the possibility of gaining this marginal excess of income over expenses, no business, and no individual, can do anything but stagnate or decline economically.

Furthermore, no country, regardless of its natural resources, has any wealth at all until one person creates or produces a product or service another is willing to buy. It all boils down to getting the gold out of the ground, smelted, and on the shelf, or the car out of the factory and into the showroom. As Julian Simon has pointed out, "the ultimate resource" is not natural at all, for it doesn't matter what a nation has in the ground if it doesn't care or doesn't know how to get it out, or if no one wants to buy it.[3] At best, we can only say that a nation has potential wealth. Japan is not rich in natural resources. Neither does Switzerland grow chocolate. Neither did Taiwan, a tiny beleaguered island of immigrant Chinese, 1/250ᵗʰ the size of mainland China, ever have great resources; yet it outproduced mainland China economically until the 1970s, despite the latter's size and population of one billion people. The lesson in this is that all countries are potentially very rich in human capital: innovation, the entrepreneurial spirit, the work ethic, the individual desire to succeed, and other such complex human factors are what form the most important part of any system of wealth creation.

Finally, history has provided us with an enormous and dramatic continent-sized human experiment to prove convincingly a main contention of this book: countries that recognize and use the tools of freedom and wealth creation will be better off than those that do not. I am referring to the experiment of the North and South American continents. Even though they were discovered by Europeans in the same historical period and, arguably, have comparable natural resources, it is only the North that has fully developed those resources, both natural and human, so as to give it a pre-eminent economic position in the world. Why is this so? Very simply, because the North Americans got the system right. They implemented and further developed the ideas and institutions discussed here. The historical result of this experiment is that whereas Canada and the United States are at the very top of the economic success charts on a per capita GDP basis, no South American nation placed in the top twenty-five in the world in 1988. By 2007, the World Bank placed the United States 10ᵗʰ, and Canada 15ᵗʰ. The highest-ranking South American nation was Chile at 42ⁿᵈ, beaten by the small Caribbean islands of St. Kitts and Nevis at 41ˢᵗ.

## "THE NATURAL SYSTEM OF LIBERTY"

When Adam Smith thus characterized democratic capitalism, he did so with the understanding that no system of political economy would ever be perfect. But above all, he felt, let it be natural. The entire subject of his innovative book on the causes of the wealth of nations explains how this natural system works. He liked it, not because he felt it was at all times high-minded (what system is?), but *because* it worked. And he reasoned that it worked because it was natural. Most important, the unintended beneficial consequence of this natural system of liberty is that it serves the common good of the greatest number of people, and does so by forming a spontaneous order that is based on voluntary exchange, free from coercion. A key factor, therefore, in the success of the tools of freedom and wealth creation is that they are not top-down tools imposed by government planners or intellectuals. They are natural, bottom-up tools that have evolved from centuries of trial and error, and that survive best in free nations because they are naturally successful and benefit all who use them. So the use of the word "system" here does not imply a consciously created or imposed set of regulations or methods. Just the opposite. The "system" arises spontaneously as an emergent property from the human actions of free people who develop it and use it as naturally as they use their own language, in the creation of which none of them has played a conscious role.

Government has only one legitimate role to play in this: to create and protect an institutional and legal climate in which the system can flourish with justice. This role—one government has vastly exceeded today, as we shall soon see—is like that of a referee who regulates and adjudicates a game but does not intend to play it.

## A CLEVER SPLITTING OF THE SYSTEMS

Finally, a key feature of the complex natural system we are discussing is that it works best when its three most important areas of influence—political, economic, and cultural—are kept apart. Perhaps one of the greatest achievements of democratic capitalism during its emergence—or rather, its escape—from the rigidity of the medieval feudal system, was the splitting apart of these three spheres of influence (which had been controlled up to that point by a central authority) and their divided but interdependent flowering as a pluralistic system. One of the greatest threats to wealth production under democratic capitalism today is the threat of abandoning that pluralism and returning to a modern form of feudal stagnation by driving these three realms together again under egalitarian Statism. Talk in many circles now is of emergent "liberal fascism" in America,[4] the most powerful economic engine in the world, under Barack Obama's administration, by which is meant the tendency for the State to set itself up as provider of life's essential needs and to overregulate, to own, and/or to operate former private sector entities. If so, this will be a new form of medieval control imposed not by religious authorities, but by those who have made a religion of the secular State.

## THE POLITICAL TOOLS
### Individual Freedom and Responsibility

It would be difficult to find anything more important to the development of democratic capitalism than the long, primarily British tradition of individual freedom and responsibility, many versions of which have sustained the free world since its beginning. The origins of this tradition are now fairly well known,[5] and in a world context it is clear that the idea of relying on individual freedom and personal responsibility as the moral bedrock of a nation was and remains an extremely radical and powerful idea, one which has always been— must be—in direct and irreconcilable conflict with Statism of any kind.

I should mention here, however, that by emphasizing the British tradition of individual freedom I am not suggesting that such persons wanted nothing to do with others. Far from it. Whether in England or the many British colonies, people who thrived on this tradition did plenty of social bonding, as I like to call it. Many of them were deeply religious and understood that we need freedom less to do what we want than to do what we ought. And doing what we ought usually meant partaking freely in deeply meaningful associations such as family, church, charities, enterprises, clubs, and so on. The real emphasis of British liberty, in other words, was not a distancing of individuals from each other, but a distancing of the solid communities they chose to form from intrusive government, or the State.[6]

Part and parcel of this philosophy is the deemed right of everyone to do anything that is not prohibited by the law. In other words, its underlying assumption is that our freedom is a right or condition won through our historical experience, and is not something granted to us by any government (since we have it already), nor can it be taken away by decree (though it can be made ineffective by legislation, or so limited by law as to be practically nonexistent). In short, human freedom precedes the existence of the State. It is an integral part of the human condition, and as such is basic to our humanity, because without freedom, the act of choosing right from wrong is impossible, and therefore a moral society is impossible. It is this rigorous chain of interdependent ideas—from freedom, to choice, to responsibility, to a moral society—that constitutes our foundation.

### Freedom to Associate or to Disassociate

An essential adjunct of individual freedom is the right to associate with, or disassociate from, others. Obviously, this is a moral right inherent in the meaning of democratic capitalism, and to override it by law, for the purposes of social engineering, is plainly coercive. Unionism is a case in point. No one could oppose the right of free individuals to associate to form unions. But objections can be made when governments grant unions coercive powers that force individuals to support them. So-called forced union dues, which require workers to pay dues to a union at their place of work even if they refuse to join, are just one such immoral force in society, as are union regulations that make it extremely difficult for workers to dissolve a union once it has been established. A country's workers cannot be said to be truly free until they have the right to join or quit union membership at will, free of coercion from the union itself, or from government regulation forcing them to pay dues. In contrast to Canada, in the United States, "right to work" laws protect workers from mandatory union membership, or mandatory dues payment, and unions there are correspondingly weaker.

### The Right to Own and Enjoy Private Property

Why is the concept of private property so important to the free world? After all, as long as we have a right to use things, why should we care if we own them? But unless we own them, despite our best intentions, we simply do not care as much about the condition of things we use. That is likely why so many public buildings, university hallways, subway stations, and the like have an unloved and often grubby feel about them. We could even say that when people spend effort on something they own, it's as if the effort is stored up or invested in the objects cared for. Private family garden plots in the former Soviet Union, which totalled only 3 percent of all cultivated land there, produced an astonishing 27 percent of that country's total farm output.[7] This also explains why virtually all commune experiments eventually transform into property-based organizations, or fail outright.

The next reason for the importance of private property follows from the first. If we are forbidden to own a thing, then in the unlikely event it is improved by our work, we still cannot sell it for more than it was originally worth. In other words, without the right to own things, we have no enduring means or incentive to acquire greater wealth for ourselves or our children. The fundamental engine of wealth production depends on the voluntary exchange of goods and services between two or more parties, all of whom consider themselves better off after the exchange than before. Without the concept and right of property ownership, and voluntary exchange, secure economic growth is not possible.

A natural outgrowth of the right to private property is therefore the idea of contracting between free individuals. It is easy to see just how these first two building blocks of wealth creation—freedom (in this case, to make contracts) and property—form a structure, in the sense that neither one means much without the other and would crumble without it. What is the point of having a right to own property—books, shoes, a home, or anything whatsoever that could be considered "ours"—if we cannot freely decide what to do with them?

This understanding is the reason so many Canadians were upset when this ancient and hallowed common law right to own private property was intentionally left out of Canada's Charter in 1982 by Trudeau and all the first ministers. They left it out because the most socialist of them all, NDP leader Ed Broadbent, insisted they do so as his price for signing. He worried that a right to private property would hamper the government's ability to expropriate private property. Precisely. If Trudeau had not been so socialist himself, he would never have agreed.

Often criticized as the advantage of the rich over the poor, owned property is really the last bastion of protection for everyone from the long arm of the State. If even the poorest citizen has a right to own property and this right is protected by law, then even the State will have difficulty wresting property from that individual. And if the State cannot easily take property from individuals, it cannot easily make them do its will. With property rights protected by law, however, a single citizen can defy the whole government. All Statists are keenly aware of this fact of life. That is why the very first thing an outright Statist government will do is try to strip people of property through punitive or even total taxation, and by nationalizing or minutely regulating all industries, especially banks, manufacturers, and communications media.

At the extreme, when property rights are weak in law, masses of people can easily be relocated to areas of the country in which the State wants them to live. But when property rights are strong, this cannot be done easily. In nations without such rights, such as the former Soviet Union, Cuba, Romania, Tanzania, and Ethiopia, this was done regularly to millions of ordinary citizens. In Tanzania, Julius Nyerere, an avowed socialist, who at first foreswore coercion, tried to persuade millions of his people into collective communities with incentives. But only 20 percent responded. So when his plan had obviously failed, he forced the peasants to relocate to his *Ujamaa* communes. Thirteen million people—then equal to half the population of Canada—were driven crying and wailing from their ancestral lands and homes, powerless to resist because they had no legally protected property rights. To ensure the success of his plan, Nyerere then resorted to burning millions of their ancestral homes. The horrific cruelty and the failure inherent in such schemes are exposed in fascinating detail by Professor James C. Scott of Yale University in *Seeing Like a State: How Certain Schemes to Improve the Human Condition Have Failed.*[8] To Nyerere's oppressions in Tanzania he devotes a whole chapter. What did Canada do? In *The Northern Magus*, Richard Gwyn describes Pierre Trudeau's admiration for his friend Nyerere (and for the dictator Fidel Castro, another friend). Under Trudeau, millions of dollars in Canadian foreign aid were sent to Tanzania to help with this cruel forced "resettlement." Just prior to publication of the first edition of this book, in a stunning about-face, the chief economist of the Soviet Union called for the legalization of private property to end "decades of State exploitation of workers" (*Toronto Star*, October 4, 1989).

## THE PRIVATE CORPORATION: A MIGHTY ENGINE OF WEALTH CREATION

The idea of the free corporation is a young one.[9] In medieval times, the king or lord owned everything, including enterprises, in that he granted groups wishing to enter into a commercial venture a "concession" that required a "royalty," or payment to the king, and in the beginning, corporations required "charters" from the Crown to operate, often as monopoly businesses. But by the seventeenth century charters were eventually replaced by "general laws of incorporation" recognizing that people had already found a multitude of ways to do business by forming partnerships, trusts, and other similar contractual arrangements. During this long evolution the State ceased to be a grantor of corporate privileges, and became merely a registrar, with a few refereeing powers. By then corporations had certain essential features: they are considered to be a person or "entity" under the law, separate from their owners. Thus they can sue and be sued, just as a person can. They also have the privilege of limited liability, so that shareholders are liable only to the extent of their interest in the company. And finally, they have by law a perpetual life, which is to say that they have the legal right to continue beyond the death of the owner(s). As such, a corporation essentially mirrors the idea of the free and responsible individual, except that its liability can be limited by law.

But all countries have not discovered this essential tool of wealth creation. It took the former Soviet Union fully three centuries longer than the English to finally emerge from their medieval commercial situation and grant Soviet families the right to form private corporations. It meant that the Soviets were finally recognizing one of the basic tools of wealth creation, and its superiority to centrally planned economies. I wrote the following words in the first edition of this book in late 1989, just before the Iron Curtain fell:

> This change may well prove to be the thin end of the wedge for the Soviets, simply because free enterprise cannot be truly free without the right to private property, individual freedom, contractual rights, and all the inevitable cultural attitudes that accompany these traditions. For these are the tools of liberty, and they are hell-bent on a collision course with the whole idea of the centralized State, which only understands the tools of power.

At bottom, it is really the energy, flexibility, and innovative power of limited corporations that is the engine of production in the free world. They serve the economies of free nations as a kind of testing ground for ideas that make economic sense. On this score, hundreds of thousands of private corporations and individuals bear the risks of failure, for it is a little-known fact that about 40 percent of all new corporations fail every year. The ones that make it reap the rewards of success, and in this manner, millions of corporations spread over more millions of individuals a total economic risk that would otherwise fall only upon the State and therefore on the taxpayers. If we were assigned the task of teaching some new country how to create wealth, one of our most essential tools would be the development of the private corporation.

## THE CONCEPT OF LIMITED GOVERNMENT

The complete absence of government results in anarchy and barbarism; total government results in slavery. The history of humankind's efforts to avoid both extremes has resulted in every possible combination in between. But a historical scorecard would show that the dominant pattern for most civilizations has been heavy-handed, top-down government control, by which the few exercise nearly total power over the many. Even most "democracies" end up as de facto oligarchies. And while it is true that all governments are inherently top-down because there is no government without governors, the ultimate question concerns the source of effective sovereignty: Does political power originate with and flow up from the sovereign people, or down from sovereign governors?

The modern, basically Anglo-American-Canadian realization that civilizations could achieve more by *reducing, dividing, and checking* the power and influence of government is unique in modern history. Yet we live at a time when this unique experiment is being threatened everywhere by the new barbarians of Statism. A simple indicator of growing Statism is total government spending expressed as a percentage of GDP. By 1992, Canada's level was 53 percent! Happily, this alarmed a lot of people, and so new austerity programs, combined with a long stretch of high economic growth, caused this relative percentage to fall over the next decade and a half so that by 2007 the figure was just under 39 percent. Despite such fluctuations, however, the overall historical trend of expenditures in all democratic countries is ever upward. It is almost impossible to name a single democracy today that has a smaller government as measured by the ratio of total government expenditures to GDP than it did a generation or two ago. We have much more democracy, but much less freedom. Most shameful of all, it seems a truism now that the Western democracies have simply never learned how to control the growth of big government.

In order to help us discern the extent of top-down control, Freedom House makes an annual practice of ranking the world's nations by their "degree of freedom."[10] There has been amazing progress in the sense that in 1989 there were only 69 "electoral democracies" in the world. But by 2008, there were 119. Despite that designation, however (there are a number of unfree democracies), only 89 of the world's nations (46 percent) were judged to be "free." Canada is in the highest rank. A surprising number of South American nations fare poorly.

Unfortunately, what the ranking does not show is the slow movement toward or away from freedom *within* nations such as our own; which is to say, it neglects the extent to which central governments can betray their own founding constitutional principles either by abuse of the law when it is considered an instrument for social engineering, or by spending powers that bribe regions with conditional grants in order to control them from the top. The Canadian and American federations have extensive experience of both forms of anti-constitutional Statism.

For me, a good starting point to think about government is Henry Thoreau's observation: "That government is best which governs least." Here is a brief list of the defensible basic functions of a limited government:

- The defence of the people against external enemies and internal threats— force or fraud against persons and property.
- The maintenance of some meaningful and effective democratic element in government so that sovereignty flows upward from the people.

• Protection of the people's political, economic, constitutional, and common law rights, freedoms, and traditions through the establishment of rules of just conduct, equal for all, accompanied by a rule of law for public conduct and the adjudication of disputes. In such a system, courts are expected to apply the law, but are barred utterly from making law.

Those wearied by the growth in the power and influence of government at all levels will read this list and weep. For the distance we have travelled from this noble standard is indicative of far more than the power lust of politicians and the indifference of the people. It fairly cries out the terrible loss of confidence in our own moral capacities as a free people, the loss of our old fierce will to order and govern our own lives freely, together, and locally. Plainly and simply, we have lost the fearless courage of our forefathers, who would have objected violently to the impudence of paid bureaucrats telling them how to live. I enjoy the story about when Thoreau went to jail for refusing to pay a small tax he considered unjust. He was visited by Ralph Waldo Emerson who approached his cell and said, "What are you doing in there?" Thoreau replied: "What are you doing out there!"

## REPRESENTATIVE PARLIAMENTARY DEMOCRACY

A system in which freely elected representatives of the people make laws in a parliamentary setting against the check of a loyal Opposition is another crucial tool of wealth creation. This type of democracy developed more or less alongside modern capitalism, both as other-directed systems intended to respond to the wishes of citizens—to the people as voters communicating their thoughts to representatives, and to consumers buying, or refusing to buy, goods and services. A democracy that does not respond to voters becomes a tyranny; an enterprise that does not respond to consumers goes bankrupt. We Canadians all but invented the further concept of responsible government, which says that the prime minister and his cabinet are responsible to the legislature of the people, and cannot act as if independent of that responsibility.

And yet, in the last quarter of the twentieth century, we witnessed the creation by our government of a new constitution specifically designed to engender and encourage government interference with our free democratic-capitalist system in order to achieve national social welfare goals. It is true that much of this was already in practice long before Trudeau and the first ministers made it a national ideal. But in doing so they set in stone a political philosophy that is best described as a revolution against our own founding principles. Indeed, there is weighty legal argument that "the federal spending powers" insofar as they intrude into our provinces have always been illegal.[11] These powers are deployed in the form of "conditional" as well as "unconditional" federal grants that seduce provinces into conformity with national programs that end up controlling things that are by law exclusively under provincial jurisdiction. The top-down practice of bribing Canadians into socialism in this way is, arguably, unconstitutional, and therefore illegal. But it continues. Canada remains a nation that has become a welfare state against its own constitutional prohibition of exactly that.

For there is no avoiding the truth that any redistribution of tax dollars taken from all the people to have-not provinces, or fiscal bribery enabling central control of a program under local provincial jurisdiction, is by fiat *also an extension of central power* over the provinces to which no one has ever expressly given consent. It is also a direct *transfer of power away from the electorate to elites*, and as such ought to alarm any thinking Canadian. These transfers extend the power of the central State into matters such as health care, family allowances, grants to universities, and hospital insurance, to name but a few. They are tantamount to a kind of administrative federalism that contradicts the intentions of our founders, the written law of the Constitution, and the definitive legal precedents concerning federal-provincial jurisdictions established in the law of Canada. Our federal government should either withdraw from all such areas of spending or seek a constitutional amendment supported by a referendum to legitimize this currently outlaw behaviour.

## ECONOMIC FREEDOM TO CONTRACT

The first and most important economic freedom is the right to contract fully with another person on any legal and mutually agreeable terms. Trading your old bicycle for your neighbour's old ladder is a form of contract, which can work only if each party first checks out the goods and then agrees to the exchange. Once you accept his ladder and he takes your bicycle, there is "a meeting of the minds," as lawyers say, and a contract has been consummated without recourse, should either change his or her mind. The principle of *caveat emptor* is at the basis of such an exchange, as is the principle of fair value received.

We are only now beginning to realize that all economic value is *subjective*, in the important sense that it is based on free choice and personal contractual responsibility. It is not only ludicrous for government simply to *declare* that something such as a job has a bureaucratically determined economic value (as dictated by minimum wage laws or pay equity laws) or a lease for your apartment (rent control), but worse than this, it is a measurable and distinct interference with the two key partners to a contract. The new third party to such contracts (the government) will generally produce a degradation of this relationship because its method is based on coercion and the least knowledge of the three parties. In this sense, such interference is immoral, because if one of the two true economic partners decides to withdraw, as when a discouraged developer decides to get out of the rent control game and invest money somewhere else, the tenant who relied on the government to help him is left with no apartment to live in at all. Similarly, when the shirtmaker must close up shop because so-called pay equity legislation (so misunderstood, and to be explained in a later chapter) has forced her out of the market, the government is unlikely to hire the now-jobless workers. Instead, it will shift that burden to the hapless taxpayers through an unemployment insurance program, which has all but degenerated into another form of welfare.

A further deleterious effect of ever-present government is that Canada is rapidly becoming an ever-more litigious society. Today, an individual of sound mind and body over twenty-one years of age can find so many ways to wriggle out of the most straightforward contractual commitment, and there are so many judges and lawyers out there waiting to help with this, that the whole idea of a simple contract between consenting adults has become almost a joke—if it were not so serious! As a result, there are as many interpretations of a fair contract as there are lawyers to write them, and judges to judge them. This is, clearly, a burdensome situation for any business and for society as a whole, since most such legal work is not economically productive. When one's word is no longer accepted as one's bond, where cleverness is measured by legal tricks, and honesty is cheapened, we are on the way down.

## THE USE OF MONEY

Most of us never stop to consider the strange properties of money because we are so used to it. But the development of money as a general instrument of exchange has been crucial to our system. In ancient and medieval times, exchange was often achieved primarily by barter. Under the barter system, trade was restricted to one person's desire for the goods of another. I would gladly trade you my saw for your dinner plates. But if I needed only six dinner plates and I felt my saw was worth twelve plates, the likelihood of a trade was diminished. What to do? As often as not, I would end up taking a few items thrown into the deal that I didn't really want and then would be faced with the job of trading those with someone else, and so on. Trading was burdensome because it was restricted by the problems of inventory, distribution, and spoiling.

But money changed all that. Its use as an instrument of exchange meant each party was freed from the restrictions of barter. It also meant that whereas a man could not accumulate, say, a large quantity of perishable goods in exchange for something he owned, he could accumulate any amount of money, which was easy to store. Before the widespread use of money, trade was cumbersomely restricted to the immediate usage value of the items traded. But with the advent of money, usage value didn't matter as much anymore. Money could be exchanged for anything. From this point forward, things acquired an exchange value, that took the place of their usage value in the minds of both parties. This subtle transformation has troubled all socialist thinkers, especially Marxists, ever since. In the next chapter this will be dealt with more fully, but anyone who wishes to understand the primary reason for the socialist/Marxist antagonism to capital accumulation need only look to this usage versus exchange value conflict. In an excellent work, Professor Don Lavoie tells us that classical Marxism, the ultimate form of socialism, had as its serious aim the complete abolition of the use of money, as well, of course, as that of markets, prices, and property.[12] But as Georg Simmel argued many years ago, "the development of the capitalist money economy went hand in hand with the liberation of the individual—or, perhaps one could say more accurately, *with a whole set of liberations of the individual.*"[13] Ironically, it was the very abstract and universal quality of money that socialists hated so much that in fact freed humankind from bondage to material things. Examples abound of immigrants to the West who arrived devoid of assets, save for their native wit and readiness to work. The money they earned and saved enabled them to buy the property or things they wanted and to climb in status in a way that once and for all broke the heavy chains of class and material bondage. We must therefore be struck by a contradiction: socialists who say they despise private property and money, and who claim it is their mission to help the poor, have never acknowledged that more than any other single physical reality, it was the universal exchange qualities of money that finally freed the common man from things, and from masters.

But the ultimate reason money is such a dreaded threat to socialism is that the daily buy-and-sell choices made by millions of individual citizens constitute a form of dollar democracy that makes tyrannical State control of individuals and the economy almost impossible. In other words, money, every dollar, is a means by which the people themselves vote on national economic policy outcomes on a daily basis. This drives Statists absolutely crazy. They understand that *rational central economic control is inversely proportional to the volume of money controlled by the free choices of the people.* In a country like our own, where the total tax burden on the average income has in recent times reached 50 percent, the government has effectively appropriated half of that freedom. But if money in the hands of free individuals is threatening to Statists, pooled money is even more so.

## THE INVENTION OF DEPOSIT BANKING

Once money became popular as an instrument of exchange, and individuals and corporations began to collect sums larger than what they needed for daily transactions, the problem arose of what to do with the excess money. Without banks, people hid surplus money under the mattress. But money that was merely stored at home could be lost or stolen, so people looked for a safe place not only to store it, but to put it to work earning interest for them. Commercial deposit banking arose as a free-market solution to this dual problem of providing both security and earning power for the savings of the people (originally in the form of gold, later in currency).

Today deposit banking is a formidable tool of wealth creation because the very process of depositing (buying) and lending (selling) money generates an increase in the money supply. This increase is then loaned out for further investment, which creates more wealth and thus more deposits, which are in turn loaned out, and so on. In other words, deposit banking creates an upward spiral of new wealth in a process that is central to any nation's economic well-being.

If we imagine Bank A with initial holdings of $1,000,000, we can see the upward spiral. Bank A, as required by law, holds back a portion in reserves (for convenience, we'll say 20 percent), and lends out the rest. These borrowers in turn deposit at their own banks (Bank B) where, if their ventures are successful, they will deposit even more. Bank B in turn lends out its money to still others, who deposit these smaller amounts in their banks (Bank C), and so on, in a long chain reaction:

| BANK A | BANK B | BANK C |
|---|---|---|
| (1)  $1,000,000 (initial capital) | $800,000 | $640,000, etc. |
| (2)  Reserve: $200,000 | 160,000 | 130,000 |
| (3)  lent out: $800,000 | 640,000 | 510,000 |
| (3)  = amounts available for loans to individual customers of each bank | | |

So there it is: by the facility of deposit banking, after a reserve is maintained by law as security against deposits, the balance is loaned out to create new wealth. So long as the flow of deposits and loans is predictable, reserves maintained, and loans secured, the system works. After the loans and cheques written on them have travelled to only two other banks (the process could in principle continue to many others, each smaller in scale than the one before), the original $1,000,000 has become $1,950,000! (If readers are wondering where the banks get the money they start with or new money to accommodate growth, the simplified answer is: they get it from the nation's central bank, and they give the central bank a note in return.)

Leaving aside for the moment some valid criticisms of the entire banking system, we can see that compared with leaving our savings under the mattress, deposit banking is a powerful tool of wealth creation. We can easily imagine how nations that either do not have such a system or are bent on government control of all banking functions vastly reduce the entrepreneurial use of money and are prone to stagnate financially.

In Western society, the new wealth created by the banking system can be used by entrepreneurs to the benefit of their communities. But a standard method of accounting is required so that traders will not confuse financial apples with oranges. Such a system accurately tracks the creation of new wealth—or losses—in any financial entity.

## DOUBLE-ENTRY BOOKKEEPING

The development of double-entry bookkeeping was an important tool of wealth creation that enabled buyers and sellers to track the integrity of financial entities in a way that isolated each one from all others. The idea of determining assets and balancing them against liabilities at all times meant not only that each engine of production could be studied as such for greater efficiency, but also that it could now be bought or sold on universally understood terms. The important balancing feature for all corporations in comparing total assets with total liabilities became the value of the shareholder's equity, and the rise or fall in this value was now easily quantifiable. By this means, the market value of an enterprise could be reliably determined.

The ability to construct a historical record of value in this way (and for that matter, the simple ability to determine profit and loss in a universal accounting language) is essential to wealth creation. Combined with the free-market price system, it provides business owners and economists with an objective basis for determining value. The foundation of this value, under our Freedom System, is decision-makers to whom cumulative deficits, profits, or losses will be precisely allocated in accordance with the individualist principle of responsibility. In socialist systems this ability to assign value and determine profit and loss does not—and cannot—exist because their wage and price controls and manufacturing decisions are coerced, not freely made. In this sense, their economic values are artificial because for them supply and demand operate not through clear economic signals, but through confused political dictates. The real cost of one pair of socialist-manufactured boots could be a thousand dollars. But no one can really say. Their financial planners are therefore faced with an irrational balancing of assets and liabilities based on political considerations—such as meeting a five-year plan—rather than on objective measures of value. As a worker from the former Soviet system put it: "They pretended to pay us, and we pretended to work." Everyone fudged and lied. You can't run a business for very long without real numbers, nor can a country's finances be controlled for long without them—indeed, they cannot even be known. So much for the condition of the numbers. What about the condition of the workers under these two systems, and how are they affected by the revolution called the division of labour?

## THE DIVISION OF LABOUR

This is one of those extraordinary themes of history that has served as a political watershed for half of humankind. As the Industrial Revolution developed increasingly specialized and machine-based forms of production, early socialist thinkers such as Henri Saint-Simon and Karl Marx strongly felt that the spectacle of workers doing the same mindless task all day, just one part of a larger, more complex assembly process, was dehumanizing. Socialist opponents of free enterprise still think so. Obviously there was some truth in this. I've done such work myself, and didn't like it much. But what Marx failed to acknowledge was that the division of labour was, and remains, one of our most basic methods to increase productivity.

We tend to believe that new wealth is a result of people's working harder today than in the past. But this is not necessarily so. In fact, it would be very difficult to match the workmanship and labour of, say, medieval craftsmen, who had very high standards, and worked about twice as long per week as we do. Rather, what has caused our fabulous increases in wealth is the new savings/ new investment/new machinery cycle, combined with the division of labour. Contrary to Marx, division of labour—except in totalitarian countries—is not exploitive but freely assumed. It depends on contract, as do most financial arrangements, whereby a worker sells skills on a labour market, trying to get the highest price possible, and an employer buys labour for the lowest price possible. The fair wage—like the fair price—is just what both parties agree on. What else could it be? Such contract labour is a marvellous invention of the free world because the worker gets a fixed return with low risk, and the freedom to bid up the wage, while the employer may increase his or her return by accepting more risk. Ultimately, of course, all wage and price levels are determined, not by owners of capital, or of economic entities, or by workers, but by all the consumers who make the final decision to buy or not to buy the commodities produced. This is dollar democracy at its best. In an effort to bring the labourer the highest wage, the owner the highest return, and the consumer the lowest price and highest-quality product, labour tended naturally to get divided.

This division springs from a natural human tendency, or law, not of history—as Marx thought—but of conservation of energy. Two workers going out to cut wood, for instance, could each cut and carry wood home. But it is more likely they will agree that one will cut and one carry, or both will cut and then both carry. Their labour will be divided in the interests of efficiency. A more dramatic example is that whereas one worker might build a car in two years, a thousand with all their different skills can build thousands of cars in two years. Fundamentally, one of the oldest divisions of labour in history, one much reviled by feminists today, is the division between the work of men and women, whereby in the greater part of the world the men agree to provide and protect, and the women to nurture and process. Whether it is fashionable to say so or not, this simple and very specialized gender division of labour whereby a reproductive family performs as an economic unit is still the world's common engine of national wealth production, and remains so to this day.

Those with socialist leanings object that the division of labour is tedious and dehumanizing because the worker is cut off, or "alienated," from the natural end result of the work. The person installing car bumpers may never see the end product: the finished car. It may well be tedious and unpleasant work. But most basic human labour, whether in a rice paddy or a factory, is tedious. But at least in a free nation, those who dislike such work can save what they are able and leave for other work, or they can group together and start their own business. In a free society, where individual circumstances are not determined by regulation or State direction, a high degree of mobility is afforded to everyone, especially to those who innovate and take risks.

Of course, division of labour according to skill means that some people will receive higher wages than others. The Left is fond of arguing that where wages are low by Western standards, workers are exploited. But this is an invalid complaint. For no worker in a free society is forced to do the work freely offered. Unless a gun is held to the head of an employee, forcing him or her to accept the conditions and pay offered, there can be no "exploitation." In fact, the use of this term, in the absence of such force, is sloppy. For no employer is under any obligation, financial or moral, to offer more in wages than the least required for someone to accept the job offered. It is a truism that most people who shop seek out the best they can find for the lowest price. Buying labour is no different. And the quickest and most foolproof test of whether or not a wage is "enough" is its acceptance by the employee, who can always refuse, and then the employer must either raise the wage, find another taker, or close up shop. If there is no other work available, it is not a legitimate criticism to say that the employee is exploited because there was "no choice," for before the employer brought the job to market, there was no job at all. In many situations in the world, the only alternative is starvation, compared to which any kind of wage is a blessing. This calls to mind situations in which multinational companies employ Third World labour for rock-bottom wages. We can deplore this all we like, but the wages *will not* go up until the employees refuse to work for the going rate, and the wages *cannot* go up if higher wages raise the price of the final product so high that no one can afford it. Between these two crucial and free decisions (to buy and sell labour, and to buy and sell the product of that labour) lies the wealth-creating process itself. In a free society, individual choice does not always mean we will be able to change the world we see in our own favour, but it does mean that we are always free to choose for ourselves the best of the available alternatives, and take the sometimes unpredictable consequences.

## INSURANCE

Throughout its history, commercial life has been shot through with risks which, if great enough, can prevent transactions from taking place. In the long run, lots of financial transactions amount to a form of sophisticated high-stakes gambling in a game with few rules and lots of unpredictables, where fortunes are made and lost at the margin. For those who stand to win or lose their enterprise, it all comes down to "risk and return," regardless of the amount at stake. Most people involved in risky transactions therefore look for a means of avoiding, transferring, or spreading their risk. One of the most important tools of wealth creation has therefore been the invention and subsequent evolution of insurance to spread risks sufficiently to enable ventures both physically and financially dangerous to be undertaken.

Certain forms of insurance such as marine insurance have been available since ancient times, and were designed to protect against physical loss or danger. The insurer would receive a huge premium from the insured if a voyage was successful, and nothing at all if it failed. But this was too risky for most, and was therefore left to specialists. Over time, therefore, general insurance evolved to cover all sorts of ordinary merchant risks, enabling the merchant-marine business to attract investors who would otherwise have been too cautious to enter such a risky market. This, in turn, created capital flows previously unavailable, and at one stroke took away from the adventurers some of the risk of loss and provided enormous injections of new investment into commercial ventures once considered hazardous. The beauty of such a sophisticated insurance technique, in which small investors felt safe, had a parallel among the insurers themselves, who co-insured with other insurance companies or with pools of investors unconnected with the venture itself, in order to further spread their own risk.

## FREE MARKETS AND JOINT STOCK COMPANIES

A natural extension of insurance and co-insurance strategies, which spread risk to non-participants in financial ventures, was the evolution of joint-stock companies, which in effect spread risk—and reward—to a multiplicity of *owners*. No one really could have foreseen the phenomenal rise in popularity of joint-stock companies that has taken place over the past two centuries, another in the long list of flexible financial instruments based on individual freedom and private property rights. The most conspicuous and creative feature of such companies is that they are able to raise money for expansion through the issue of various classes of debentures or shares, some with preferences as to the receipt of dividends, redemption, or convertibility, and in addition offer the protection of limited liability.

When the history of the evolution of democratic capitalism is finally written, the joint-stock company will be recognized as one of its proudest institutions, a device that spurred wealth creation in the West and spread that wealth to large masses of people at the same time. To the chagrin of socialist ideologues, this effective tool of free enterprise has even succeeded in creating a more "progressive" allocation of wealth to the people than any single political scheme to achieve the same end. A recent and dramatic example of this sharing of real wealth with the people was former prime minister Margaret Thatcher's program of privatization in Great Britain. This program, unlike most, aimed not to sell public corporations to private ones—a mere transfer of assets from a government corporation to a private corporation—but to sell off the majority of shares to a broadly based mixture of workers, management, and the general public, thus achieving a truly progressive spreading of real wealth to shareholders who really did "own a piece of the action," as the saying goes. When Petro-Canada was launched, it was primarily public, and the federal government fatuously declared it was "ours." But that was a lie. Petro-Canada was never ours because individual Canadians never personally owned shares the way that individual Brits owned shares in British Airways. For when you own something, you can sell it, and we had nothing to sell. All we really owned of Petro-Canada was its debt, which the government knew very well it could force us to service by raising our taxes.

Another way to look at things is to say that while the government triple-taxes, or triple-handicaps, us (through personal, corporate, and consumption taxes), democratic capitalism triple-bonuses us (through salaries received, dividends earned, and equity gained on any shares owned).

## THE CULTURAL TOOLS

As a young boy, I asked my father what a dead person was like, and he answered: "Like a house with nobody home." Just so, all the political and economic tools discussed so far are of incalculable importance to the success of democratic capitalism. But unless they are vivified by the living will of the people to sustain the ideas and values that shaped those tools, they are like a house with nobody home, a mere empty structure. So when I speak of "cultural tools," this has little to do with our preferences in literature or music. I am using the term in a very broad sense to capture the whole set of ideals, morals, principles, concepts, and traditions that sustains any unified nation or people. For the real threat to civilization arises from the simple fact that laws are made by mere mortals and are therefore changeable. If good values drift to bad, though the noblest legal institutions remain in place, the worst villainies may be carried out in their name.

British historian Paul Johnson's insightful book *Modern Times: The History of the World from the Twenties to the Eighties* eloquently demonstrates this point. In it, he traces the history of despotism in the twentieth century and shows clearly how, if the will of the people to protect their freedoms is absent, those with a greater will can pervert even the strongest institutions of free societies and turn them to their own destructive purposes. "It is a commonplace," writes Johnson, "that men are excessively ruthless and cruel not as a rule out of avowed malice but from outraged righteousness. How much more is this true of legally constituted states, invested with all the seeming moral authority of parliaments and congresses and courts of justice! The destructive capacity of the individual, however vicious, is small; of the State, however well-intentioned, almost limitless. Expand the State and that destructive capacity necessarily expands too."[14]

He shows in detail how Germany under Hitler suffered this very sequence of events, as did the Soviets, all the Eastern bloc nations they subjugated, the Italians, the Chinese, the Tanzanians, the North Vietnamese and Cambodians, and so many others in the twentieth century who were destroyed, pillaged, starved, or murdered mostly in battles between and within what Churchill called "the mighty educated states." Be careful, is the message.

At present, Canada, like the United States, is in the long process of endangering its very existence as a free nation at the hands of successive governments that have wilfully undermined core values and traditions and replaced them with a set of alien values from the Statist tradition. In a system such as our own, this process can be stopped only by the people, and only then when the people have realized what is happening, and then have elected leaders to express their will to conserve what is valuable. This book is an attempt to tell them.

But modern Canada is ruled by the people (their representatives) mostly in name. In fact, we are led by a government and bureaucratic oligarchy that for a few generations has propagated values alien to the long-term interests of the Canadian people. It does this either by camouflaging its agenda or by simply proceeding in opposition to, or without much regard to, the expressed will of the people. Any comparison of government action with national poll results will illustrate this point. The people want capital punishment for especially heinous crimes? The government bans it, and rapists and killers are back on the street in twenty-five years or less. The people want lower taxes? The government raises them. The people want to reduce the size of government and the national debt? The government borrows more. (As of this writing, the newspaper reported that the budget *deficit* for 2010 may be more than $56 billion!) The people do not want official (forced) bilingualism? The government forces it on them (though Quebec, to its credit, declines). The people want to slow immigration and to favour traditional stock? The government increases the flow, and disregards country of origin. The people want a better climate for free enterprise? The government vastly increases the regulation of business. The people have never, not once, agreed that a healthy child that is no danger to its mother's life could by law be aborted right up to the point of natural birth? The government is so frightened of losing the feminist and leftist vote it cannot bring itself to pass a law protecting our most vulnerable citizens. Canadians have never approved of gay marriage. Nevertheless our government (in contrast to the French government which has adamantly rejected gay marriage) declines to protect natural family formation as the best place for children and passes a law saying that "any two persons" can join in (a mockery of) marriage. We were the first nation in history to declare as a matter of State policy that it is acceptable for a child to be raised without a mother or a father in his or her home. And this is government by the people, for the people? This list goes on and on.

One reason government gets away with this so easily is that the people are no longer sure what values they cherish, so they cannot speak out with one voice. The importance of individual freedom, responsibility, family, free enterprise, hard work, self-reliance, local government, good manners, personal success, and so on are no longer emphasized in our schools; and on television, on radio, and in the daily newspapers—everywhere—are replaced by their opposite: the popular illusions discussed in chapter 2.

## PERSONHOOD

"Personhood" is an awkward word for an important concept. Each of us is not *merely* an individual unit, but more profoundly, a *person* in the sense that we are "an originating agency of insight and choice."[15] In this very important sense, the values of a free nation cannot simply be handed down from on high, but must be created daily in the hearts and minds of the people who freely choose them, defend them, and propagate them.

But this concept of what it means to be a full person is utterly alien, even actively repressed, as a threat to communal life in many societies, and in socialist political theory is constantly under attack as "rampant individualism." That is because the whole idea of actively fulfilling oneself as an individual person is "designed to frustrate the totalitarian impulse."[16] Just so, at the heart of all socialist/Statist systems you will always find a strong philosophical and political effort to eradicate the idea of the individual, or the person-as-value-creator, from the thinking of the people. Nobel laureate Friedrich Hayek summed this up nicely in *The Counter-Revolution of Science*: "Consistently pursued Statism must lead to a system in which all members of society become merely instruments of the single directing mind and in which all the spontaneous social forces to which the growth of the mind is due are destroyed." This form of attack on personhood and on the idea of individual conscience first took definite form in the early nineteenth century, most notably through the work of two Frenchmen, Henri Saint-Simon, and his student and collaborator, Auguste Comte, both of whom had strong socialist-authoritarian views. It was Saint-Simon who saw "more clearly than most socialists after him that the organization of society for a common purpose, which is fundamental to all socialist systems, is incompatible with individual freedom."[17] Earlier I made the point that the French style is in direct conflict with our traditional British liberty, and that it has nevertheless made inroads by infecting—that is the right word—such influential British thinkers as J.S. Mill. He had a lifelong habit of turning intellectuals he admired into personal saints, and all but worshipped at the shrine of Auguste Comte. Mill's thought was in turn a direct influence on what I have called the "libertarian-socialism" under which we now live. At root, it is the many possibilities of personhood that supply the foundation for all other social institutions of free societies. With this one cultural value in place, a society is ready for the bottom-up system of government. Without it, a society is ripe for the top-down authoritarian formation so typical of Statist systems of all stripes.[18] If the first protection against tyranny is love and respect for individuals and their creative and ever-evolving personhood, the second is the veneration of the family as cradle and shelter for the growth of individuals.

## THE FAMILY

"Blood is thicker than water," we were told as children. And sure enough, the same brother or sister who enraged us could, if suddenly attacked by an outsider, spark in us the strongest passions of courage, love, and protection. The family is a natural presence in our lives, and especially when we are children it is the absolute centre of our world. As adults, we have a crucial moral responsibility for the strengthening or weakening of this institution, whether we wish it or not. How we build or destroy our own families, and how we defend the institutions set up to protect them, multiplied by millions of Canadians, will determine the stuff and fibre of the family for generations to come. If the most fundamental *political* building block of democratic capitalism is the individual and personhood, the most fundamental *social* unit is the family, which nurtures and creates this reality. Practically speaking, however, we could reverse this order, and say that the family is first, for it is in the bosom of the family that the crucial values, disciplines, and standards of individual behaviour are formed and transmitted from generation to generation. In the same way that private money is a threat to the economic theory and policy of the homogenizing socialist State, so the traditional family is a threat to all efforts to inculcate Statist values and standards in the people.[19] This was well observed by the Soviet writer Igor Shafarevich in *The Socialist Phenomenon*, where he wrote that "at least three components of the socialist ideal—the abolition of private property, the abolition of the family, and socialist equality—may be deduced from a single principle: the suppression of individuality." This phenomenon is at work in all socialist revolutions, kibbutzim, communes, and similar experiments. I will always remember a scene from the chilling movie *The Killing Fields*, in which the communist Khmer Rouge are holding a "re-education" class for villagers. A young child is told to come forward to a drawing on the blackboard of a mother, father, and kids ... and rub out the linked hands of the whole family. That was a filmic emblem of a totalitarianism that saw the private family as anti-State.

This eradication of the idea of the family is not limited to times of war, but has been occurring in peacetime in many Western nations, led by Sweden where Statist/egalitarian social policies are more widespread than in Canada (though we are gaining fast). Young architects from Sweden's Directorate of National Planning, for instance, try to mould collective feeling through architecture. One of them, Jan Stromdahl, says, "The political climate helps us . . . I am interested in collective living and want to see it spread . . . By removing amenities from the home and moving them into communal premises, you can force people to live communally . . . Once they see the advantages of the new kind of life, they will want to change." And one of his professors at the directorate tells us that the "environment has to be planned so that the family situation can be corrected. Children have to be socialized at an early age, in order to eradicate the social [family] heritage." Roland Huntford, author of *The New Totalitarians*, was among the first to blow the whistle, warning us that "it is an acknowledged aim of Social Democratic ideologists (and others) in Sweden to break up the traditional family, because it fosters individuality and because it fosters class distinction and social disability."[20] Huntford tells of a social scientist writing for the Swedish Institute (a promoter of quasi-official Swedish views), who declared under the heading "The Family Is Not Sacred": "I should like to abolish the family as a means of earning a livelihood, let adults be economically independent of each other and give society a large share of responsibility for its children . . . In such a society we could very well do without marriage as a legal entity."

At least the Swedes have the merit of openly declaring their political and ideological agenda! In States like Canada, however, where ideological thinking is no less present but a lot less codified and lucid, the State does not dare to attack the family *explicitly*. Astonishingly, it may promote the idea of "the family" or of "families" in words, while providing funds to special interest groups to de-emphasize the naturalness of the heterosexual family. On this note, and as an example of how rapidly Canada has been speeding toward a radical restructuring of its own traditions, I should mention that in 1990 I said publicly that one day soon Canada would have homosexual marriage, for which I was mocked as an extremist. Now it is here.

But to continue, such radicalizing states also tend to promote staggeringly expensive State daycare programs as a "right" for all women (regardless of income, and without regard to the real financial burden on taxpayers or of government care on the minds and hearts of the nation's children); or they offer extensive State support for single parents, the most disastrous model for which was the American Aid to Families with Dependent Children (renamed since) which even left-wing politicians now agree served as an incentive program that lured poor (mostly black) women out of their parents' homes to have babies without husbands (if they married, they lost income support). Finally, there is the deadly equation: more government = more taxes = the necessity for two incomes. Politicians seem impervious to the basic and time-honoured economic lesson:

if you subsidize something (like illegitimacy or laziness) you get more of it—that's basic reward-and-punishment theory. At any rate, government programs have the effect of directly or indirectly undermining the traditional family by subsidizing dependence on the State instead of on our families.

Citizens who have any doubts about this wraparound totalitarian direction of Canadian Statism need only go to the website Service Canada: People helping people (www.servicecanada.gc.ca) to see the latest transmogrification of compassionate conservatism (never thought I'd see the day). Once there, click on "Life Events" and wait for it: you will be treated to offers of government assistance in such categories as: "Having a baby," "Managing your debt," "Getting married," and "Getting divorced," and ah, yes, the Nanny State will even spring to your side in the event of "Losing your wallet." As economist William Watson wrote when deploring this trend: "With Service Canada this big and informative, who needs a family?"

The success of groups that have lobbied for government policies destructive to the family unit is perplexing, for to speak only in terms of economic success, it is clear that the traditional procreative marriage and family is an enormously effective spur to economic growth and wealth creation for the entire nation, and on every imaginable social and physical scale married people do better than others. They have fewer emotional problems, less disease,[21] and make far more money than singles. And yet, in his book *Men and Marriage*, George Gilder writes of the sad state of government policy in the United States, that "everywhere in America unemployment, illegitimacy, divorce, and separation find fuller favour in the laws of the land than does raising children in an intact family."[22] We have reached a similar stage in Canada.

## PLURALISM OR AUTHORITARIANISM?

Only when we have established a clear rationale for the importance of individuals and the families that nurture them can we ask what kind of society is best suited to their growth. The choices available to us range from societies that are more or less open, to those that are more or less closed. "Openness" refers to a political system according to which individuals are largely self-governing. It implies tolerance, or pluralism—that is, openness to a huge variety of alternatives and differences coexisting under a general rule of law. General rules of law—the only sort that parliaments were originally meant to pass—encourage and permit the flowering of natural differences and are typical of open societies. But closed, or authoritarian, societies go far beyond this to create "imperative" laws of the social-engineering, reverse-discrimination variety, in an effort to equalize the results, or outcomes, of their societies. But I always argue: it is far preferable to have more freedom, more social mobility, and less equality than to have less freedom, more social rigidity, and more equality. Never forget: the most "equal" society possible, not counting the guards, is to be found at your local jail.

We can see now how all these cultural values should tie together. Individuals are basically trusted to govern themselves according to a common set of rules, within which their individual differences are allowed and expected to flourish. Families are openly promoted and protected as society's most important moral-cultural institution for nurturing this flowering. Because we acknowledge that humankind is inherently capable of tyranny, checks and balances are set up to prevent any one group from monopolizing power.[23] And finally, preference is necessarily declared for a pluralistic, open society, stressing freedom, the natural expression of talents, and co-operation between its self-governing parts. This sounds to me very much like the classical liberalism to be found at the origin of this country.

All this considered, it is apparent that ideological systems are structural, in the sense that the ideas that form them are linked, and support each other, like a building. Attacks on the foundation, or too much substitution of parts that don't belong, may eventually bring the whole thing down. Democratic capitalism, and all forms of socialism, are very different buildings based on different principles. They can't be mixed without trouble.

A tidy metaphor for this is two children each building a playhouse from sets of plastic blocks built on different interlocking principles, one called Lego, and the other Duplo. As many parents will know, these two types of blocks cannot be fitted together because each has its own structural system, or integrity. It so happens that political-economic systems have the same kind of internal integrity, which must at all costs be protected. But the bureaucrats who try to build with them don't know that, and they tinker around for the longest time mixing the two kinds of blocks. They may succeed in getting the house off the ground, but only by gluing, Scotch-taping, or balancing one piece against the other. In the end, this ideological and structural confusion succumbs to its inherent instability, and can be held together only by constant surveillance, coercion, and force. That is, by bureaucrats, supervisors, commissions, by—let's face it—labour police, pay police, rent police, liquor police, language police, and the many other people with police powers such societies require in order to be propped up and kept running, all financed by us and our neighbours.

After making it successful, I sold my first business because government was telling me whom I had to hire (affirmative action officers visited us), what I had to pay them (pay equity officers demanding to see payrolls and forcing nonsensical job evaluations on us), and was even dictating the maximum price I was allowed to charge for my product (it had become a price-regulated industry). One day I even had a visit from a government worker who arrived with a dry-bulb thermometer and told me that a tenant had complained about being cold. She was a woman who, unbeknownst to him, insisted on wearing skimpy dresses in winter. Her officemate, to the contrary, complained about being too hot. He said I had to keep my building between so-and-so temperature, or I would be fined. So I told him to get out, declined to renew the woman's lease, and eventually sold my business. Gone. And good riddance.

## THE FREEDOM SYSTEM

Inherent in a system that encourages the flowering of individual differences and the free expression of our humanity under the rule of law is the idea of rewarding excellence. While everything described in this chapter is a specific tool of freedom and wealth creation within what I call a Freedom System, the actual idea of rewarding people for excellence is nowhere carved in marble. It is cultural, in the sense that it has been carried for generations in the hearts and minds of the people of free nations. For them, rewards, or the lack thereof, are intuitively linked to the idea of personal and family success or failure. Once the rules are set, everyone has to play by them. Infractions are punished; success is rewarded. Such societies have been borne forward on the intuitive belief that any conception of reward or punishment other than one indelibly linked to personal responsibility is morally unworkable; that a society that encourages the blaming of our circumstances for a lack of success becomes morally bankrupt.

Once a society chooses to swallow the determinist illusion it is doomed. There is really no one to blame for failures except our history, "the system," or each other. The rights illusion takes over. When a society reaches this point, it becomes overly litigious, cranking out more lawyers, accountants, and court settlements instead of more buildings, factories, and higher-quality products. Furthermore, even though some may not think it fair, the idea of individual responsibility is an all-or-nothing principle. It cannot be applied to some people, or groups, and not to others—for there would be no end to the no-fault claims. So on a broad political scale, whole nations may be typified by where they stand with this type of behaviour as they struggle to balance justice, mercy, and liberty. If we spread an economic atlas of the world before us, we will see that the wealthiest nations have Freedom Systems imbedded in them from bottom to top (tyrannical nations have them at the top, but never below), and that the poorest—at least in the West—are often outright tyrannical or "redistributionist." These latter often take property in the form of land, assets, and tax plunder from those who are productive, rake off their commission, and then, so that they can stay in power, give what's left to those who are not very productive. In less tyrannical social welfare states, a huge commission is still skimmed off from the tax harvest for the bureaucratic establishment, which grows apace. Ironically, this commission, rent, or fee amounts to a perverse sort of Freedom System in the form of secure jobs, salaries, and special privileges for those who are inventing and administering the Handicap System. Their idea is that the stronger you are, the bigger the load you carry. This leads logically to the penalizing of excellence, tax evasion and myriad loopholes, underground or black market economies, and to the skewing of natural human values once rooted in work and merit.

Obviously, there is an inherent conflict between the Freedom System and the Handicap System, and alas, in Canada we have increasingly de-emphasized the freedom and emphasized handicapping. This can be seen in daily life right from school athletic programs that tend to emphasize co-operative mediocrity, to instituting quotas which, by their nature overlook excellence, to major government affirmative action programs, which use the force of law to discriminate officially. The first and still most notorious North American test of such reverse discrimination was the *Bakke* case in California, in which a white student everyone admitted was better qualified for medical school was turned down in favour of a black student because there were not enough blacks to fill the ethnic quota for the program. It turned out that the favoured black student had scored very low on the same test on which Allan Bakke had scored over 90 percent. Bakke sued the university, and won. A short time later, the U.S. Supreme Court in the famous *Weber* case upheld the principle of racial quotas. It was as if Martin Luther King had never made his famous speech! It was a case of the Handicap System beating out the Freedom System, and it resulted in society's getting a lower-quality product than it would otherwise have obtained. If you were a patient with an operable brain tumour, which doctor would you prefer? I suspect you wouldn't care what colour the doctor was, as long as he or she was the best. Quota thinking, however, generally results in transactions of decline because standards are lowered, tests made easier, and quality reduced everywhere. In the end, quotas (whether racial, or gender based, or intelligence based, doesn't matter) will produce a cynical populace that learns to expect tokenism and a double moral standard that accepts mediocrity in some, but pretends that it's excellence. The result? You may be granted a Ph.D., but did you really earn it? The cynicism that flows from affirmative action does favours to no one. Our politicians are cynical, too. They know that many of their programs are transactions of decline—but why should they care, if we are stupid enough to pay them in votes for such programs?

The lesson to be learned is that there must be a structural alignment between a country's underlying political-economic philosophy and its Freedom System, or else it will eventually fail. It will most certainly fail if that system— that misalignment—is based explicitly on handicapping (as in the former U.S.S.R.) or, less dramatic, but no less fatal (Canada beware) if there is an inherent conflict between the moral and political philosophy that made the nation strong in the first place and the subsequent imposition of a philosophy intended to engineer a "fairer," but coerced, result.

## ECONOMIC ACTIVISM AND THE IDEA OF PROGRESS

It comes as a surprise to learn that the ancients, particularly the Greeks and Romans who so influenced the Western world, had a generally fatalistic and cyclical notion of history. The idea of "progress" that we toss around so lightly would have seemed alien to them, for they imagined the universe around them as a circle of recurring phenomena, in which the life and death of people, the seasons, and all worldly events succeeded each other in a noble, but endless and interlocking, round, governed by the powers of their gods and the special ceremonies of their societies.

This world view was—and remains in many cultures—a primordial response to the awesome power of nature, which held such dominion over human beings and their world, and served as a mythical and religious fortification against the threat of ceaseless change. At any rate, such a world view led to material pessimism and economic stagnation, for the thought of hoping for progress, in the sense of change for the better, was contrary to everything such cultures held sacred. Here, for example, are a few lines from *The Consolation of Philosophy*, written in AD 524 by a famous Roman named Boethius. It was a work that influenced every learned person's attitude toward wealth creation (among other important things) from its publication until the end of the Renaissance a thousand years later. Lady Philosophy, one of his characters, in what is in effect a teaching dialogue with Boethius, is talking about wealth, and tells him that

if all the money in the world were acquired by one man, everyone else would be penniless. The sound of a voice can be given equally to many hearers, but money cannot be distributed among many persons without impoverishing those who give it up. Riches, then, are miserable and troublesome: they cannot be acquired by some without loss to others.[24]

This is what we today call "zero-sum" such as we saw in the fixed-pie illusion—the idea that economic wealth is fixed in size, and therefore no one can gain without hurting someone else. While such an attitude might seem remote from us, we should not be fooled. It is very much present in many countries today, and although we say we believe in progress, this envy-based notion is manifest in our own society.

The way in which Christianity participated in this stagnation is well known, so that whereas today it is not unusual to find devout Christians at peace with the values of capitalism, this has not always been so. Indeed, in the original of this book, I included a chapter on pulpit socialism because the Catholic church in particular was then far more wary of the tools of freedom and wealth creation than it seems to be now.

As it happened, there existed a fierce tension between traders and the Christian church for centuries before the Reformation, for the church preached against material wealth, riches, pricing for profit, and in particular the charging of interest on money loaned. In medieval times, this static idea of history was not outwardly different in its effects on society from that of ancient times, but the combination of Christian beliefs, a static world view, and feudal control of all aspects of society was particularly deadening. This effect, visible in modern socialism, inevitably results in what has been called the rigidification, or the militarization, of society. (Each was assigned a role in the economic and social structure. A microcosm of this effect today can be seen in "featherbedding," or making a paying job out of nothing much, as often happens in government institutions and union shops.) This rigidity is only slowly broken down, and then primarily by the concentrated effects of economic freedom.

Historically, the idea of progress seemed to take hold of our imagination during and after the Reformation, in which so many forces in society struggled against government and church authority and finally broke free, achieving that all-important separation of the political, economic, and cultural realms. Then it was precisely the joining together of the belief in progress with the dominant values of a Christian society that gave a final and still-accelerating burst of energy to the creation of wealth. In other words, once Christians began to believe that the creation of wealth was an acceptable activity, things really began to take off. The result of this crucially important attitudinal change to a belief in progress was first grasped, as Novak reminds us, by Max Weber in his seminal essay "The Protestant Ethic and the Spirit of Capitalism," and belief in the possibility of progress (of all kinds) through economic activism is now seen as the one crucial factor without which a nation simply cannot successfully raise itself from poverty to wealth.

Examples abound, but here's a personal anecdote. I had a friend who invested heavily in a silver mine in South America (in a region where the static world view still permeated economic life). He calculated everything except the attitude of the people toward work and progress. He failed, lost a lot of money, and came home. The reason, he explained, was that he knew all the workers in his little town earned only ten dollars per week. So he would pay them twenty to work his mine. The result? They came to work on Monday very happy indeed. He immediately imagined his future success. But on Wednesday at noon everyone went home. Horrified, he discovered that in their view nothing much could be changed with more money, they were happy with what they had, and if he was going to pay double, they were going to work half. He never succeeded in changing something so fundamental. The lesson is that our attitude toward progress is a reflection of our attitude toward mutability in general: whether we want to alter our condition as part of an evolving, improving world, or settle for repeating an endless round of materially unproductive (but in themselves perhaps quite satisfying) activities.

## THE PRODUCTIVE POWER OF FAITH

I am using the word "faith" in both its religious and general sense because long after a culture has openly ceased to centre itself on religious or spiritual ideals, its life continues to unfold from them, although often in a quite distorted form. Such roots run deep, having grown in the same soil for millennia. So this section is not about churches or organized religion. It is about faith (albeit shaky) and the spiritual attitudes (however distorted) that serve as the source of the majority of our actions and, in a world untethered, still manage to keep us together because we are drawing from a kind of moral surplus of the past. It is possible that the success of democratic capitalism *requires* such soil in order to be ultimately successful. Even though the success of the "four little dragons" of the Far East, as Hong Kong, South Korea, Singapore, and Taiwan are called, might appear to refute this, because they never shared our cultural heritage, they were all formed on Western institutions in their modern period, before which they were exceedingly backward nations. There are also some interesting parallels between Eastern spiritual asceticism and Western Calvinism, which to some extent may account for the East's easy digestion of the economic activism of the West. Weber labelled this aspect of Western thought "inner-world asceticism," in part to explain how those basing their ideals on (Calvinistic) Protestantism went about "earning" goodness.

One of the most interesting requirements of any faith before economic activism can be successful relates to the people's view of the nature of God and His presence in the material world. Notwithstanding its recent economic successes, India is a country that for millennia has rested on the belief that God is everywhere present in the material world, and so we see a reluctance to manipulate that world to material advantage. If you believe that God is present in every blade of grass, or tree, or housefly, you do not harm the grass, cut the tree, or kill the fly easily. This belief is called "immanentism" by theologians, and cultures in which it is found believe that God is everywhere present (is immanent), or indwelling, a part of the entire universe. Such cultures (like those of many of our own North American Indian peoples) in which this belief is strong tend to remain static economically, in part for this reason. They are content with spiritual wealth, and economic activism threatens the foundation of that spirituality virtually by disturbing the order of God's world. The economic lethargy this encourages is further accentuated if such people also hold beliefs such as reincarnation, or other forms of fatalism that basically teach them they have no control over their destiny.

Although there is also a distinct tradition of immanentism in the West, it is by and large secondary to our common conception of God and how He may be regarded. We tell our children in Sunday school that "God knows everything," but not that He is part of the chair we sit in or the beef we eat. Even the prayers of Christian children are imagined by them to be a sort of magical telegraph system to God, who is "in heaven," and who will answer our prayers through symbols (they hope), or (if they are very good) directly. For the Judeo-Christian tradition has evolved from a notion of a God who is everywhere felt, but nowhere seen. He is what the ancients called a "*Deus absconditus*," or a not-present God. (Jews believe the Messiah is yet to come, many Christians that he has come, and will come again.) Essentially, we communicate with Him through prayer, and we get to *know* Him not directly, as, for example, an Indian knows his God, but indirectly, through revelation. Ours is a religion of conversion, in which we strive to know God, and then (if at all) experience Him in a sudden spiritual manifestation. (Converts say they are "born again.")

An advantageous feature of such a faith is that it does not implicitly prohibit us from exercising our will upon the material world for our own betterment (environmentalists might say our own ruination). In fact, we have worked out our everyday theology in such a way that we say God expects us to use the world for such betterment and, by extension, for the betterment of others (see Matthew, parable of the talents, 25:14–30). Such a conclusion has not been arrived at easily, and having evolved over two thousand years has resulted in a commingling of the creative energies of Western man with the natural resources of the earth (the "subdue the earth" theme) in such a way that our actions feel consistent with our faith. Thus we believe we labour in a direct or indirect sense *for* our God, and not against His will. A fascinating example of this hangs on the wall of a business friend's home. His family, devoutly Christian, develops large office buildings. On the wall is a picture of one of their forty-storey towers, and superimposed on the photograph is an image of Jesus. I was stunned by the picture because of the way it so neatly summed up the idea of working for God. The difference between the Indian view in which God actually is expressed in the inviolable tree or plant before us, and the Christian view in which we *transform* such material things to His glory, means everything if you are thinking about economic activism. It's tougher for those who find God already there before they even think of economic activity. But we don't. So we make offerings to Him with the work of our hands, hoping to please Him. You can make the point—difficult to sustain—that this has led to a rape of the environment or, conversely, that it has nourished and fed millions of people who would otherwise have starved, as they are doing daily in many countries without such beliefs in economic activism.

The reason why Christianity ties in to the promotion of competition is that although it is very interested in "community," it is particularly interested in the moral worthiness of individuals. This has enormous importance for understanding social policy in the West. For worthiness is not, as under socialist regimes, decided by an elite, or imposed, or only material in nature. In fact, unlike the socialist tradition, the Christian tradition denies the possibility of true community without a focus on individuality. Why? Because Christian values are consonant with the ideas discussed in chapter 1 of this book: that each of us must act as a moral agent in life, and that a truly moral society must be formed from the bottom up, not the top down. This conviction is embodied in the Christian notion of "subsidiarity"—the ideal stating that all human problems must be solved by those concerned at the lowest level first, and help sought from higher levels of the State only in the case of failure, and by agreement. Our original system of federalism dividing constitutional powers, as stipulated in our BNA Act, 1867, was a reflection of this very ideal. I argue it has since been betrayed.

Most radical of all, perhaps, it was Christianity that first created what Rousseau complained of as the "two heads of the eagle" (of sovereignty). It makes a radical split between Caesar and God, the earthly and the heavenly kingdoms. Indeed, it is the case that without the two heads—the spiritual head pushing back the State head—the latter would long since have subjugated all of us. Thus, to speak less theologically, a society of free individuals, each coming to moral fulfillment, then supports a full community of similar individuals who are held together not by some coercive, Statist ideal and the fear this implies, but by an uplifting common faith in a strong community of values individually and freely upheld. This is the link through Western Christian faith to the idea of competitive self-improvement as the true ground for the creative individual. Even Karl Marx, the most hardened enemy of capitalism, realized that "political democracy is Christian in nature because man in it—not man in general but each man separately—is considered a sovereign and supreme being."[25]

Finally, all this is intimately associated with the Christian idea of fallibility, or sin, and the consequent search for future betterment. (Whether or not this is an accurate reflection of these theological grounds is another matter.) Cultures that do not believe in future betterment simply do not believe in the future. They believe in an ever-recurring present. Some of them don't even have a word for the future.[26] But we do, and this, combined with a deep desire to better ourselves as we strive toward that future, provides us with an enormously powerful motive for economic activism. (That some Christians believe in predestination, or some Eastern religions that we are already perfect, does not affect this powerful cultural force in the West.) This is quite a different form of optimism from that found in the minds of socialists, for it finds its expression in concrete personal achievements, in real, as compared to abstract utopian, concepts.

One final point on the effect of faith on economic activism is the matter of self-denial. To the extent that no nation can accumulate capital for investment and productive expansion without savings, and that savings are a result of spending less than we bring in, wealth comes about in part through our willingness to postpone present gratification for future gains. This is in pointed contrast to the socialist idea that capitalism thrives on greed for profits. For it is only profits that can produce savings, as all else is consumed by expenses. And only savings put aside from corporate or personal profits can supply individuals or corporations protection against emergencies, funds for research and development, or the many other tangible benefits of a successful operation. When the economic activities of entire cultures are informed by such an attitude, the result is an extremely powerful cultural tool of wealth creation that is threatened by State-imposed disincentives, in particular by social programs that remove the incentives to work, earn, and save.

In the next chapter we will turn to what I have called the "socialist reaction" to democratic capitalism, or the Handicap System, which has its own structural integrity, and thus is enormously dangerous to freedom and democratic capitalism. Paradoxically, the latter, which is successful wherever it has been tried, has millions of practitioners. But it has been close to an ideological failure. Socialism, on the other hand, has been an ideological success, but a practical failure wherever it has been imposed. But this has not prevented utopian thinkers from promoting it vigorously, for their standard response to revelations about this failure is that it has never been properly tried. Ironically that is a secular-theological response because they are comparing the present to an as-yet-unrealized perfection, or heaven on earth. So we must keep in mind that in the next chapter we will be comparing a system with a practical, measurable, proven record, as described here, to one which in the minds of its own proponents is imaginary, or utopian, in character, and therefore not falsifiable.

# 5: THE HANDICAP SYSTEM
## THE SOCIALIST REACTION TO
## DEMOCRATIC CAPITALISM

*If you're not a socialist by the time you're twenty,*
*you haven't got a heart; If you're still a socialist by the time*
*you're forty, you haven't got any brains!*
—old European saying

*[W]e are in the danger of over-government; that we are suffering from*
*the too-great extension of the functions of the State . . . In my opinion we*
*are moving towards socialism. We are moving through the mist; nearer*
*and nearer with every bit of government ownership and government*
*regulation, nearer and nearer through the mist to the edge of the abyss*
*over which our civilization may be precipitated to its final catastrophe.*
—Stephen Leacock, 1924[1]

*The trouble with socialism is that eventually you*
*run out of other people's money.*
—former British prime minister Margaret Thatcher, 1976

Of the various forms of Statist thinking, the one that ought to concern us most deeply is socialism. This is because its whole founding purpose—*the specific, openly stated intention of all honest socialists*, whether revolutionary Marxists or peace-loving dreamers—is to *replace* democratic capitalism with a better, more "just" system of social and economic organization. This has been the ongoing, worldwide struggle of socialists for the past 150-odd years, and is the expressed intent of Canada's New Democratic Party (NDP), and of the Socialist International.[2]

## WHAT DO WE NEED TO KNOW ABOUT SOCIALISM?
There are only four questions anyone living in a democratic-capitalist society ought to be able to answer in order to understand the workings of the system that was specifically designed to replace our own:

- Where has socialism come from?
- Why do socialists complain about our society?
- What are the solutions socialism offers?
- Why is it that socialism doesn't work?

## Where Has Socialism Come From?

To begin, there is an endless variety of socialist views out there, many of which are intellectually interesting in their own right and therefore tend to supply a lot of academics with full-time work. However, although all forms of socialism differ in the *means* they choose, they tend to agree on the *goal* of striving for a better social and economic system than the one that exists in democratic-capitalist countries. But no one has ever created a better system than our own. On Remembrance Day, 1947, Winston Churchill rose in the House of Commons and said wisely, "Democracy is the worst form of government—except all those other forms that have been tried from time to time." It is this utter absence of an attractive real-world alternative that marks all forms of socialism as utopian. They are only able to complain about our system as compared to a utopian one they insist is possible in the future. Somewhere. Down the road. Financed by others (bring your chequebook). And so it goes. To me, this flimsy basis for social change is the next thing to religious fanaticism and is therefore most dangerous. In fact, many scholars suggest that socialism, in this time of declining religious faith, is just a secular mirror of the otherworldly spirituality found in all religions. So my aim here is to arm my readers against the natural enemy of their traditional values and institutions. To do this, I will have to simplify a good deal.

The term "socialism" as used here will therefore include its other variants, such as "Marxism," "democratic socialism," and "communism," a generalization for which there is much precedent. As the influential political economist Joseph Schumpeter wrote in his widely praised book *Capitalism, Socialism and Democracy*, "I have not separately defined collectivism or communism . . . but if I had to use them I should make them synonymous with socialism."[3] And this is echoed more recently by one of the world's most lucid writers on political economy, Thomas Sowell, who says, "In the late years of their lives, Marx and Engels used the terms 'socialism' and 'communism' interchangeably . . ."[4] The difference between these two terms, as G.D.H. Cole, chairman of the Fabian Society, pointed out in 1941, "is one of tactics and strategy, rather than objective."[5] In short, the difference is mostly one of degree. Communists want the same things as socialists, but they are prepared to get them by more violent and revolutionary means. A convenient distinction useful to Canadians who until very recently have been so wary of using the word "socialism" to describe even their own manifestly socialist programs is that the only real difference between the "social welfare state" (the gentler term) which is distinguished by a thorough regulation of society, and socialism proper, is that the latter is careful not only to control, but also to own, all property.

But just so that we don't get stopped on such fine points, and on the grounds that you can get as badly burned by a campfire as a bonfire, the position I have taken in this book is that *there is a gradation of ideas*, from simple, everyday notions of social justice that make everyone feel warm all over, such as "Everyone should be treated equally," to more complex plans to bring about social justice through socialist dictatorship or even outright revolution.

I am not suggesting that we will ever succumb to authoritarian, one-party socialism such as is normal for all communist states, past and present. But we can easily end up with the same dispiriting mess whenever multiple parties agree on a policy like socialized medicine, or the fraudulent pretend-legal use of Human Rights Commissions to control public attitudes and discourse. They may of course actually agree in principle on such things. But too often they agree only for sleazy party gain, or because they are too frightened to resist a policy that is flagrantly Statist and oppressive of human freedom (such as socialized medicine or HRCs). What we have in Canada today looks something like loose multi-party socialism. In such a case, the people have no serious alternative on offer, and they live as if under one socialist party. To have no political options is in a sense to be disenfranchised. Strangely, our official socialist party, the NDP, still avoids the word "socialism" like the plague, even though its own manuals, as we shall see, are filled with socialist talk of a smarmy Marxist nature. Bob Rae, until he became premier of Ontario, actually refused to call himself a socialist in public, despite the fact that his party was a paid-up member of the Socialist International. Our former federal NDP leader Ed Broadbent was for a time one of that organization's vice-presidents. A dinosaur locked in a memory box.

## THE ORIGINS OF SOCIALISM

*When radical leaders over the last 2,500 years have sought to enforce equality of results, their prescriptions were usually predictable: redistribution of property; cancellation of debts; incentives to bring out the vote and increase political participation among the poor; stigmatizing of the wealthy, whether through the extreme measure of ostracism or the more mundane forced liturgies; use of the court system to even the playing field by targeting the more prominent citizens; radical growth in government and government employment; the use of state employees as defenders of the egalitarian faith; bread-and-circus entitlements; inflation of the currency and greater national debt to lessen the power of accumulated capital; and radical sloganeering about reactionary enemies of the new state.*
—Victor Davis Hanson, 2009

It seems that almost everything can be traced to the dawn of recorded history, and socialism is no exception. After all, citizens have always been rightly concerned that their societies should be just and well ordered. And, of course, Christianity itself (like many other religions) supplies us with plenty of concern for the meek of the earth. Warnings against the accumulation of wealth abound in parables about the difficult time any rich man will have getting into the kingdom of heaven.

But modern socialism only emerged as a direct alternative to democratic capitalism during the success of, and I'm sure mainly because of, the social dislocations and "inequalities" created by the Industrial Revolution. Just before this, around the time of the French Revolution (1789–1803), there were many social theorists who were outraged by what they saw as centuries of privilege, feudalism, aristocracy, and government tyranny.

Socialism was a call for social justice for the masses that intended not (like Marxism) to get rid of the State altogether, but, on the contrary, to use the coercive power of the State to guarantee social justice. This decision by socialists to use state coercion to achieve their goals is one of the most telling features of this political movement. It has resulted in a paradox that haunts socialists to this day, because it was the coupling of a religious type of utopian ambition, with the use of force to achieve social goals (which I have termed "coercive humanitarianism"), that has been devastating for humanity. In short, the very core method of socialism raises the fundamental moral question: How can you achieve justice by unjust means? You don't need a Ph.D. to know that you can't. But this is the pact with the devil that socialists of all stripes have made. They have agreed among themselves to use the force of law, not to *protect* us from State tyranny, but to *promote* their own dream-world goals, which can be brought about only through legal tyrannies, small and large. What they all agree on is that *it is legitimate to sacrifice freedom for equality.* This entire book is in utter disagreement with that objective.

## THE ROOTS OF THE FRENCH STYLE

The most influential early socialist thinker was surely Henri Saint-Simon (1760–1825), the first to lay the intellectual foundations of the French style of government outlined in chapter 1. It was primarily under Saint-Simon's influence that the ideal of establishing a just society for all, free of the evils of the past, quickly became perverted into the ideal of "setting up an elite for the rational *control* of society."[6] Fancying themselves empowered by the authority of rationalism, logic, and the scientific method, Saint-Simon and his followers had a pervasive fear of the dangers they felt were inherent in free societies and competitive free markets. Free enterprise struck them as irrational, out of control, and driven only by individual and corporate greed. They didn't see that the capitalist who tries to please only himself fails, whereas the one who pleases others, succeeds; that democratic capitalism is other-directed before being self-directed. (You could even make the argument that capitalism, far from being greedy, works best when it is a form of grovelling servitude to the wants of others.) At any rate, to replace capitalism, he "sought to institute a complete monopolization of economic activity under a unified plan."[7] In effect, "it was the chief exporters of the Saint-Simonian system ... not Karl Marx [who had no theory of wealth creation] who first clearly articulated the goal of a comprehensively planned society: a hierarchical organization of the whole world's industries into 'a vast workshop, labouring under a common impulse to achieve a common goal.'"[8] This is beehive thinking at its best. For it was Saint-Simon who "saw more clearly than most socialists after him that the organization of society for a common purpose, which is fundamental to all socialist systems, is incompatible with human freedom and requires the existence of a spiritual (meaning political) power which can 'choose the direction to which the national forces are to be applied.'"[9] By this, Saint-Simon meant that such societies would need an elite, educated class to steer their destiny. We read in the last chapter a comment on the *énarques*—the highly trained class of technocrats who run modern France from the top. Welcome to Ottawa, the idea of pervasive central government, and the regime change imposed by our 1982 Constitution designed precisely to permit and encourage government to engineer social and economic outcomes.

The growth in government required to bring about such social engineering is staggering, and an early alarm that signalled just such a binge was sounded for Canada in a 1983 book entitled *Governments Under Stress*, by Colin Campbell, who surveyed many governments and many world leaders, but had a field day when he got to Trudeau and his colleagues. Trudeau, he informed us, built an administrative monstrosity, replete with twice the per capita number of advisers than used in the U.S. and five times the number in the U.K. Further, between 1975 and 1979, in proportion to our size, he put Canada through "perhaps the most furtive expansion of central agencies the world has yet experienced."[10] He did this by creating new government agencies like the Federal-Provincial Relations Office, the Office of the Comptroller General, and the Ministries of State for Economic and Regional Development and for Social Development. That's just one indication of where Saint-Simonian centralist thinking leads. Although Canada's population between 1910 and 1984 only tripled, the number of federal civil servants alone swelled from 20,000 to a staggering 284,000, or fourteen times the 1910 total. And that trend has not stopped.

As of 2005, the number of Canadians *paid directly by government*[11] was:

- Federal gov't without military:        284,900
- Provincial and territorial gov'ts:     349,280
- Local governments                      371,710
- Health and social services             755,920
- Universities and colleges              308,900
- Local school boards                    550,610
- Military                                85,710

  ---------

- Total                                2,707,010

Not to be forgotten (for the English socialists were far from idle when Saint-Simon was at work), across the channel another well-known promoter of Statism, Robert Owen, was busy advocating "a national system for the formation of character."[12] But whether English, French, or German socialists, the conclusion historians have reached is that "by about 1840 Saint-Simonian ideas had ceased to be the property of a particular school and had come to form the basis of all socialist movements."[13] Polish historian Leszek Kolakowski referred this archetypal formulator of the French disease as "the real founder of modern theoretical socialism," and the great historian Elie Halévy called him "the great precursor" of Marxism. Even John Stuart Mill said that he "sowed the seeds of nearly all socialist tendencies which have since spread so widely in France."[14] Mill in his later life himself had a powerful hand in spreading them in England and her colonies.

Whenever we hear a Trudeau, a Bob Rae, a Jack Layton, or a Michael Ignatieff whining about the desperate need for a "national industrial strategy," we are just hearing echoes of the Saint-Simonian ideal and the French model. In our government's insistence on so many constitutionally promoted affirmative action programs, we are hearing echoes of Robert Owen's desire for "a national system for the formation of character." Trudeau, just like Owen, spoke of "the need to develop new values, and even change our institutions." This is an example of the elite socialist's top-down, dial-a-culture mentality in full flight. They remind me of a close relative who, having returned all revved up from a "human potential" seminar, announced that he and his wife had carefully drawn up a "code of personal conduct" for their family and it was now posted on the refrigerator door. You should have seen his face when I asked him, "What's wrong with the Ten Commandments?"

## GRADUALISM

Although very little of what passes for social policy in Canada can be said to have the sort of clear ideological foundation attributable to socialism proper, a summary glance at the underlying aim of true socialism will certainly help us to spot its weaker, but no less damaging, cousin here in Canada (and in our U.S. neighbour). For the most part such objectives are achieved through a process political theorists call "gradualism." In this slice-by-slice technique, the salami of freedom is reduced to nothing over time. The method took its name from the Roman general Quintus Fabius Maximus, who harassed his opponents mercilessly, but never joined them in all-out battle. The socialist Fabian Society in Britain adopted this strategy as a matter of principle in its effort to permeate existing institutions with such thinking, thus hoping to achieve socialism without revolution. Wherever gradualism is at work, there is no marching, no manifesto. Instead, objectives are achieved through such things as a pervasive bias toward Statism in the media (and the universities), often achieved simply by neglecting the other side of the story as "not newsworthy." An example is the experiences of Canadian journalists Ezra Levant and Mark Steyn, and of *Maclean's* magazine, dragged as they were before the martinets of the moment under threat of heavy fines and other punishments, with no ordinary legal recourse against these inquisitions. As for my own experiences with inadequately educated media critics seeking to shut down free argument? Too numerous to mention.

Such top-down control and regulatory objectives are achieved through highly vocal (and State-funded) interest group influence, through strategic political placements, and not least through government grants for all sorts of radical groups and individuals. For example, there has always been lots of money for the three hundred or more strident radical feminist groups in Canada, doled out by the Status of Women office in Ottawa to the tune of multimillions per year (see the total in chapter 10: over half a billion dollars doled out since 1973); but barely a thin dime for conservative pro-family groups like REAL Women, which, after endless refusals, finally secured a grant for $21,000 in 1989—and had only asked to see if it would be forthcoming. This latter group is entirely self-supporting. For a book-length examination of how radical Statism so gradually but deeply infects every aspect of a once-traditional society, from schools, to media, to family law, to the courts and even international law, I humbly recommend *The War Against the Family* as a follow-up to this book. Better be sitting down. It illustrates insidious radical gradualism at work; nice, well-intentioned, effective, and utterly dangerous to our civilization.[15]

## UTOPIA: THE IMAGINARY GOAL

All socialist doctrine is united in expressing dissatisfaction with the existing social order and is pervaded by a near-religious desire for an ideal future society. They are, in effect, political religions. In this sense, socialists have an advantage over everyone else. Completely enamoured of an attractive ideal society of the mind, they are at liberty to complain about everything that falls short of this ideal—which everything must do. Until the end of 1989, the most unreported fact of our era was the slow death of socialism. But this does not bother them. Far from being disappointed, they reply that it hasn't really been tried yet, and get renewed conviction from its failure. Such people are termed "teleological," or abstract-goal-oriented thinkers, and they share a utopian, or dream-world mentality in that, like astrologers and parapsychologists, they are attracted to doctrines that are unfalsifiable. You can't beat them with the present facts, for they will plead the future. The very last words of NDP leader Ed Broadbent before he resigned were: "Utopia must be our guide" (*Globe and Mail*, Sept. 29, 1989). If you walk around with a three-cornered hat and your forearm under your jacket lapel like Napoleon, you will likely get treated for mental delusion. But if you walk around spending taxpayers' money on a never-before-seen social ideal that is a fantasy in your head, you can run a political party.

What Broadbent said was a quote that fell into my lap while writing this chapter, and it was but a Canadian echo of the core communist theme as admitted to *Time* magazine by a Soviet general after the collapse of the Soviet Union who, when asked to explain what the Soviets were trying to achieve by oppressing and murdering an estimated 50 million of their own legal citizens over a seventy-year period, answered: "*The Kingdom of God on earth—or Communism, as we call it—before the third Millennium.*"[16]

A natural question from the curious might be: What is the true source of a utopian spirit so strong that believers are willing to oppress, incarcerate, and murder millions of their own unbelieving citizens to realize their dream world?

My answer would be that the original egalitarian dream of the West is rooted in the story of the Garden of Eden before the Fall. Then, humans were assumed to be perfect. All were good, all were equal, and all property was shared equally. Even as early as the Middle Ages, spiritual egalitarians were longing to create again this lost Eden, a world in which there would be no *meum* and *teum*, as the Latin saying went. No mine, and thine.

All the modern radical utopian movements of the Western world are in this sense secular, or political, religions, which is to say, religions without God. Without God, human beings have to assume the role of God. And because as secularists they have lost all belief in the possibility of an other-worldly kingdom of heaven, they become desperate to create one here, on earth. Then, because transcendent moral standards go out the window with God, they soon argue that any means is justified to achieve their utopian ends. In short, the spirit of religion may be gone, but the hard-wired desire for a perfect world remains.[17]

# WHAT IS THE SOCIALIST COMPLAINT?
## They Don't Like Individualism or Free Markets

All socialists find the philosophy of individual freedom abhorrent and the idea of a "community of individuals" a contradiction in terms. Individualism of the "enlightened self-interest" variety found in the tradition of classical liberalism they think of as simple, naked greed. The idea of the individual as a moral agent forging a community of freely upheld values (that did not originate with the State) they see as creating moral chaos, a ship with no rudder, or rather a flotilla of ships with no chart.

They prefer instead a centrally controlled agenda of political, economic, and moral values designed to permeate society under the stewardship of an elite. If the elite can't reach its goals by moral persuasion, then it may use the courts, which are said to be "balancing" the rights they pretend to guarantee, to achieve their declared goals. The *droit administratif* mentioned in earlier chapters is a key tool of all such regimes: one rule for the people; another for their masters.

The socialist doesn't understand that the sought-after *community* of values can be morally authentic only if it's freely formed in a bottom-up fashion and upheld by individuals behaving as responsible moral agents, both individually and socially within the myriad voluntary associations of civil society to which they gladly bond themselves.

In contrast, the socialist sees the free market as an extension of all that is loathsome in personal liberty and "selfish" individualism—a free-for-all of competing material desires that can only result in wasted resources and lead to the sort of "business cycle" expansions and contractions that socialists believe are typical of an inefficient economy. Indeed, despite the fact that the 2008 subprime mortgage crisis was for the most part a failure of government regulators who themselves only years prior had encouraged the financial industry to engage in government-insured "affirmative action lending," the spectre of a greedy and selfish capitalist Wall Street was postured as the sole guilty party. All Statists deftly sidestepped the possibility that the greatest cause of warped economic cycles, as we now suspect, has always been interventionist government policy.

Economists such as the Chicago fresh-water school, as they are called (because they work near Lake Michigan), maintain convincingly that government policies can never react to market crises in time to solve market problems. Only individuals, especially those at risk—whether for a paycheque or for a corporate debt—and intimately involved in market transactions, can do that. With rare exceptions, government efforts to "correct" market conditions are inevitably bureaucratic transactions made for political, not economic, reasons, which therefore send faulty signals to buyers and sellers, and thus function as salt in the otherwise minor wounds of an economy that is normally self-healing. Finally, government planning, with its powers proportionate to the wealth taken from the people, will always suppress the effects of what I have called the "dollar democracy" freedoms exercised by the people.

## Socialists Don't Like Real Social Justice

Fundamentally, all socialists are united in believing that present social arrangements are inegalitarian. Some people are born rich; some are born poor. Socialists delight in saying with a cynical smile that under our system of maximum liberty (rather than maximum equality) "the rich and the poor alike are free to sleep under park benches." They will generally argue that the conditions of our lives are for the most part not of our own doing, that wealth tends to end up in the hands of too few, and therefore the State should play a strong and permanent role in redistributing it. They are careful to ignore the fact that, with the exception of the very top level of earners, whom we reward handsomely for their expertise and for taking the risks they do, democratic-capitalist societies have a record for wealth distribution as good as or better than that of any socialist nation in history. Nor do they consider it important that the wealth created under democratic capitalism is freely exchanged between sellers and buyers, whether individual or corporate, and that it is individual consumers who gladly make certain people wealthy simply by eagerly purchasing what they have to offer. None of the people who made Oprah Winfrey, or Microsoft's Bill Gates, or Céline Dion, or Lance Armstrong, or the shareholders of so many companies very wealthy did more than buy a book, some software, a concert ticket, a bicycle, or any of a million other moderately priced things . . . in very large numbers.

Importantly, the lack-of-justice charge of socialists is often very moving because we are all, without exception, in general sympathy with the truly needy. The crucial point, however, is that the liberty solution to this dilemma is to acknowledge openly that although life may not be inherently *fair* in the sense that we are not all born into the same conditions, nor do we have anything like the same skills or capacities—let us at least be *free*! Simply put, democratic capitalists believe it is impossible—both logically and practically—to achieve greater equality or fairness by stifling, or possibly even destroying, the very tools of freedom and wealth creation that have lifted multitudes up by their own bootstraps everywhere they have been put to use. The problem does not have to do with equality only, but with general social well-being. It helps no one to have a completely equal but wretchedly poor society. But it helps everyone to have a well-to-do, if less equal, society, in which the poor, relatively speaking, are far better off than in a wretchedly equal society. I argue that freedom and equality are asymptotic, which means contraries, and the more you have of one, the less you will have of the other—by definition.

The reason for this depressing emphasis of socialists on equality and the redistribution of wealth is that, not surprisingly, no socialist has ever produced a workable theory of wealth creation. Marx didn't have one.[18] Saint-Simon certainly didn't. No Canadian socialist has one either. There isn't one in existence because it can't be done. That is why we will always and only hear socialists talk about how to redistribute wealth, but never about how to create it.

This sad truth leads us to the conclusion that all forms of socialism are little more than vast parasitical schemes for the forced redistribution of the freely created wealth of some, to others deemed worthy, by the class of elites administering the redistribution after taking their considerable commission.

## THE ECONOMIC TOOLS OF SOCIALISM

### Central Planning

In 1975, as if prompted directly by his intellectual predecessor Saint-Simon—or perhaps by his bosom buddy Fidel Castro—and at a time when Canada enjoyed a standard of living among the highest in the world, we heard with astonishment our own prime minster Pierre Trudeau say: "We haven't been able to make it work, the free market system. The government is going to have to take a larger role in running institutions . . . It means there is going to be not less authority in our lives, but perhaps more" (CTV year-end interview, 1975).

There you have it. For those sensitive to the subject, this speech might as well have come through a loud-hailer from the Socialist International. The primary socialist solution to what they regard as the "dog-eats-dog" chaos of the free market is comprehensive State planning (or "State-eats-all-dogs"). The socialist desires a society that will produce only what government bureaucrats decide people "genuinely" need, instead of what a strong or wealthy producer informs them (through advertising and the like) has been made for them in the hope they will buy it, just to make his company richer. It's the *motive* for commercial activity that so irks the socialist: the fact that people freely buy for what the socialist considers artificial reasons (such as vanity, acquisitiveness, power, status, personal hobbies), instead of for reasons that conform to the State's vision of the social good (eliminating inefficiencies, equalizing the goods of all, etc.).

But more to the point, socialists consider all economic activity to be amenable to "rational planning," an ambition we will soon see is very naive. Despite this, the idea of rational central economic planning is attractive to dreamworlders and intellectuals, mostly due to the promise of rational efficiency implied in the notion of matching production precisely to consumption and, by extension, of leaving advertising (the lure to false needs) and even profits (the payoff for greed) out of the picture. Curiously, socialists never ask themselves: Why other than for altruism would anyone work themselves to the bone, invest, take risks, and so on, without profits as a reward? Or, how any enterprise could survive without a rational margin earned over real costs—the profit—to finance research, innovation, and renewal. Of course, some people will produce things, sometimes at very high levels, for short periods of time, under the influence of moral suasion or revolutionary zeal, especially when lured with promises and dreams of a future utopia. But such euphoric schemes are usually very short-lived.

The only other method that results in a lot of effort expended without material reward is labour under the threat of force. (Most socialist, and certainly all totalitarian, systems end up falling back on this after the moral suasion wears thin.) If you add up all the Statist systems the world has ever known, this stacks up as the world's most popular method for getting work done. It is effective in armies and prisons, and is the method relied upon in State "production quotas" and five-year plans such as were seen in all the Eastern bloc nations in the twentieth century. But the result, as the Russian people used to say, is that "they pretended to pay us, and we pretended to work!" They made mountains of quota-produced government shoes that no one wanted to wear.

Again, socialists are united in their desire to redistribute society's wealth so that all have equal resources at their command. That's how the vaunted fairness is to be arrived at. We must all start the poker game of life with the same hand. But they do not say much about the *differences* between us after the game has begun. They cope with any emergent differences by constantly reshuffling and redistributing the deck as soon as anyone gets ahead—which, of course, ruins the game. If men get ahead of women, richer ahead of poorer, stronger ahead of weaker, hard workers ahead of lazy ones, or the educated ahead of the uneducated, that's the government's signal that it's time for a reshuffle. In general terms, the reshuffling technique boils down to handicapping those who are ahead in whatever the race might be.

Despite its obvious failures worldwide, socialists still plug away at the idea of central planning, an ideological necessity in which they are trapped by virtue of their primary beliefs. The cure for any attraction to this idea is to read a compelling survey of this economic and social disaster, such as Sven Rydenfelt's *A Pattern for Failure*. And if you want a more detailed, complex, and fascinating treatment, try the work discussed earlier, Professor Don Lavoie's *National Economic Planning: What Is Left?*

## Ownership of the Means of Production

All truly socialist societies insist that because the root of the modern capitalist evil is private property—*meum* and *teum*—especially properties that produce wealth such as factories and other large concerns through which they assert that money ends up in the hands of the few—such concerns must be owned by the State, not by individuals. By their logic, it all makes sense. Ignoring the crucial role of profits in the production process, they prefer to set up "non-profit" agencies, for which the burdensome taxes levied to cover administrative and regulatory costs are a form of profit-taking by another name that allows the State to expand.

Trudeau and his cohorts pushed for the nationalization and regulation of major sectors. President Obama has done the same in the United States. Canada's energy production was almost destroyed through Trudeau's disastrous National Energy Program (NEP)—estimated to have cost the nation about $15 billion directly and between $100 and $200 billion in lost entrepreneurial activity—and investment in general was stifled through his counterproductive Foreign Investment Review Agency (FIRA). He established hundreds of other agencies, commissions, and Crown corporations, all designed to control Canada more centrally. Subsequent governments have since learned that capitalism is like a huge bull and, rather than killing it, socialists should hitch their wagon to it. Accordingly, since 1988, many of these programs have been abolished, and many Crown corporations privatized, even such national symbols as Air Canada.[19]

As the pendulum swings from socialism or its ilk to democratic capitalism or its ilk, the Canadian people are swung through repeated rounds of institutional change, enormous confusion and cost, social strife, and perplexity, all because they have never paused to evaluate their own ideological ground, their national founding belief system (as outlined in this book) and truly declared their preference. If we had all been more alert, we would have recognized Trudeau's policies as libertarian-socialist. His intent was to create the illusion of personal freedom while at the same time taking more of the so-called means of production or, for that matter, anything of social or economic importance, out of the hands of individuals and corporations and turning it over to the control of the State, while taxing us more to pay for these transactions of decline. It was all part of the French style critiqued here. On March 5, 2010, at a Eurocopter company, President Nicolas Sarkozy of France announced: "The state is going to profoundly review *its role as shareholder in the big industrial companies.*" He said the state would from now on have two representatives in all companies with state shares, and the bosses of those companies would have to meet twice a year with government to discuss strategies, investments, and results. This is just smiling French Statism at work. Let the fudging begin!

**Tax Freedom Day**
In practical economic terms egalitarian reshuffling is achieved through so-called "progressive" taxation, meaning: as you work progressively harder, take progressively larger risks, and earn progressively more money from people who freely pay for your products or services, the State progressively takes more of it away from you. In Canada today, if you calculate the *total incidence of all taxes* on individuals from all three levels of government, you will arrive at what is called Tax Freedom Day. This is the first day in the calendar year that the average taxpayer finally stops working 100 percent for government, and begins working for him- or herself and family.[20] It fell on June 6 in 2009—fully *two months* later than in 1961. In the United States, for 2009 it

fell on April 13. Although this date fluctuates a little, and in both Canada and the U.S. was a little earlier in 2009 than in some previous years, this fluctuation is often only due to recessionary periods because when there is less income there is a smaller tax harvest. But everyone should be seriously alarmed at the inexorable march forward of this date (remember: we had no income tax at all before 1917).

No one keeps track of the enormous cost of this pernicious scheme, which, incidentally, consumes billions of dollars supporting civil servants at all three levels of government. When I was working on the first edition of this book, John Raymond reported on the disturbing result of the redistributionist mentality as outlined in the Burns Fry Economic Outlook (*Globe and Mail*, August 26, 1988): "Federal expenditures on various social programs totaled almost 60 billion dollars this year, representing 60% of non-interest expenditures" of our federal government. Of this enormous amount of money (Canada's GNP in 1987 was $537 billion), "less than 17 billion will go to the poor." And here's the corker: Raymond said "if you exclude the six billion dollars that the government contributes to welfare, *76% of social spending will go to middle and higher income Canadians*" [italics mine]. What? That's precisely the "churning" activity of Statism I have mentioned: we are soaking each other, to pay each other.

## THE POLITICAL TOOLS
### Interventionism: the Militarization of Society
From everything we have said, it follows that in order to achieve its objectives, the socialist-style State must resort to programmatic regulatory intervention on a regular basis (hence, a kind of "militarization" of society). Such States tend to use national *economic* interventions such as wage and price controls, rent controls, minimum wage controls, agricultural marketing boards, and thousands of other specific controls on free enterprise, in the form of regulations, bylaws, licences, taxes, threats of fines, and so on. Then there are *political* interventions such as energy programs, affirmative action programs, quotas, and pay equity programs, bilingual programs, medicare programs, and a host of regional-parity measures designed to equalize parts of the country that are inherently—and will always be—unequal. Then there are the ubiquitous cultural and moral interventions designed to align the people's behaviour and attitudes with State-approved ethnic, sexual, linguistic, and mostly unworkable cultural ideals such as the "great Canadian mosaic"—unworkable not because Canadians are not tolerant, which they seem to be, but because these programs promote foreignness and the celebration of identity differences among Canadians. The socialist-style State is proud to intervene, and even considers itself to have a social and moral duty to do so, as it strives to enforce the equal distribution of money, property, and the political and moral orthodoxies of the day.

It is hard for us to understand that modern free societies were not originally set up to intervene in this fashion. In fact, they were set up by classical liberals precisely to *prevent* such interventionist meddling in the lives of citizens. For this reason, one of our philosophical godfathers, John Locke, made it very clear that in a free state the power of the legislative body should be limited to the passing of laws as *general rules of just conduct equally applicable to all citizens.* We would all do well to memorize that phrase and measure our society against it at every opportunity.

### Welfare and Universality

Socialism is nothing if it does not help the poor and the downtrodden, for then it would be a failure even in its own eyes. In a prosperous society such as our own, socialists are thus driven to define ever-greater classes of the people as "needy." In other words, socialism needs the poor in order to survive as an ideology, and so it takes pains to avoid all absolute standards of need, preferring relative ones, as we shall see in a later chapter. Suffice it to say for now that without the continuous generation of more and more novel social welfare classifications and programs, even its most ardent promoters would have to question its naked use of power to extract the wealth of producers for so many indefensible purposes. For it is clear that modern socialism needs a welfare system far more than society needs socialism. More debilitating is the fact that socialists shrink from admitting that coercion underlies their morality. Hence socialism—especially in well-off nations, is driven to seek ever more novel moral justifications for its programs (because there are fewer and fewer economic ones), and one of these is the notion of universality. This is the idea that because distinctions between rich and poor, capable and incapable, lazy and industrious, bright and stupid, motivated and unmotivated, honourable and dishonourable, worthy and unworthy, are deemed odious, welfare must go to all members of groups or classes of citizens deemed deserving. For example, we get talk of a right of all women to universal government daycare, without distinctions to be made between a Rosedale mom in a fur coat with a tennis racquet under the arm, and a truly needy poor mother. This program was pushed aggressively by "conservative" prime minister Brian Mulroney as "a sacred trust"—words meant as a dart to the heart of the hapless taxpayers he wanted to dun for the billions necessary to make such a cockamamie idea work. When he did this, I wrote a letter to him: "You are too Pink. If you don't get more Blue, you won't see any more of my Green!"

Remember that socialism strives to create equality where none would naturally exist. So all mothers will have access to daycare without regard to their need or wealth, and the wealth of the families that look after their own children was to be generously taxed to provide daycare for those that don't. It is always possible to define and needs-test those who are truly needy. But Statists shun this because such an act would "deprive the needy of their dignity."

But what kind of dignity is left when we promote taking something by force from others as a right? And what kind of country takes taxes from all, to render a service to all, regardless of real need? Answer? A country bent on making everyone dependent in some way on the State.

Canada has a lot of "sacred trust" ideas floating around, and we will see graphically, in chapter 7, that sacred trusts have a way of turning into a "sacred bankruptcy," and that the guaranteed social security the State is supposed to be providing rests on financial quicksand. Governments attempt to deal with this by reneging on promises: through so-called clawback programs (such as my Old Age Security); de-listing formerly funded services (dropping medical services we used to get "free"); and eventually by raising the age of retirement or discounting promised pensions—all desperate measures to undo the initial absurdity. For now, we merely need to know that welfare and universality are two ideological concepts—intellectual necessities, so to speak—of any socialist program, which can be and have been put in place by political parties of all stripes. And thus, as the Fabians say, does socialism "permeate" our institutions.

## THE CULTURAL TOOLS OF SOCIALISM
A matter of obvious importance to all Statist regimes is some form of control and direction of their orthodoxies via cultural expression. Statist regimes insist on such as a national public broadcaster (the CBC) and national culture bureaucracies that control what other broadcasters are permitted to air (the Canadian Radio-television Telecommunications Commission [CRTC]). Codes for acceptable speech, thought, and content permeate such organizations and hence filter what the people are allowed to hear and see. With respect to common decency and community moral and artistic standards, some of this is desirable. But State funding and control of arts, culture, and media lead to far greater dangers, and inevitably, all organizations touched by regulation and control of attitude and speech must come to heel. They mostly do this by tailoring their programming in the form of grant-seeking behaviour to fit the official orthodoxies.

Here's a sobering revelation from author John Metcalf, who was well-known when all this got started, and once sat on a Canada Council jury. Commenting on the culture in Canada in the 1980s, he complained that "the big commercial publishing houses are subsidized. The smaller literary presses are subsidized. The still smaller regional presses are subsidized. The writers are subsidized. The literary critics are subsidized. Translation is subsidized. Publicity is subsidized. Distribution is subsidized. More bizarre than perhaps anything else, the Writers' Union of Canada is subsidized."[21] In Metcalf's view—and my own—"the acceptance of subsidy means that consciously or unconsciously the writer is joining the state's enterprise. However arm's length the relationship, *the writer [play, movie, art show, whatever] is entering into a partnership with the State*" [italics mine]. And, of course, when it comes to the

State's motive in offering money gifts to artists, Canada's motive is the same as that of any other social welfare state. The money is not given to promote literature. It is given "to promote *Canadian* literature, books which the government vainly hopes will foster a greater sense of national unity and will forge a national identity." The artist becomes a tool of policy.

When the original of this book was published, I told Jack Stoddart (then president of Stoddart Publishing), himself a liberal, that there was no way in hell I was going to have the typical "thank-you" for federal and provincial government funding *that appears in all Canadian books printed*, in a book called *The Trouble With Canada*. I told him that if he needed money to subsidize the cost of publishing my book, I would be happy to give it to him myself. He didn't ask for it. And to this day, I think the original of this book printed by Stoddart in 1990 is still the only Canadian book published in recent decades by a mainstream publisher without government support. That was a small victory for freedom from the State. But I regret to say that the ten books I have published since all have an obedient thank-you printed on the fly-leaf because my publishers just wore me down with whining about how they could not succeed without government money. You will find the same blurb in this book. Other than self-publishing, there is no way out. Trapped. Surrounded. Defeated.

What Metcalf had to say about literary culture holds for every other cultural activity in Canada, too, because most of it is an instrument of the State's effort to aggrandize its own activities as cultural caretaker and to create what it hopes will be seen as a highly visible justification for putting its hand so deeply into the pockets of the people. But what our artists really need, as Metcalf insists, is "to be free from culture," so that they can be free from the State. Literature and the other arts must be taken back from the State and given back to citizens. The new editor of this book penned in here: "That would be great if your citizens gave a damn, Bill. But they don't." To which I answered: "If you are right and they don't give a damn, then why are taxpayers forking over money to produce books about which they don't give a damn?" My argument is that citizens who want culture should pay for it themselves. There is something deeply odious about seeing so many well-heeled patrons at places such as Roy Thomson Hall in Toronto or at equivalent venues elsewhere in this country enjoying high culture made possible in large measure by taxes plundered from ordinary people from Victoria, B.C., to St. John's, Newfoundland. What this really means is that even the noblest souls can be purchased—and it turns out that there are thousands of them. Just for fun, go to www.writersunion.ca and watch the logos for various government funding agencies pop up. The Writers' Union of Canada in 2009 had 1,700 members, and I suspect all their books are subsidized ... by such as the readers of this book. The Public Lending Right system also now pays out annually over $10,000,000 to 16,000 Canadians authors for having their books available to readers in public libraries. I receive over $2,000 per year for this "right." I accept it on the pitiful reasoning that I have already paid a lot in taxes to a government that is now giving a little of it back to me under this program. I confess to a certain sense of corruption in accepting it. But that is precisely the micro-mechanics of the general Statist immorality about which I am complaining throughout this book. How does one escape? A clean refusal to accept is obvious. But then you are letting the corrupter benefit more than would be the case if you at least take some of it back. It's a horrible circle.

## FAULTY THEORY, FAULTY EXECUTION

### The Knowledge Problem

In a remarkable book on this subject, Don Lavoie lays out in unimpeachable detail the reasons why "comprehensive national economic planning" can't work. I will be drawing heavily from his important third chapter, entitled "The Knowledge Problem," which I think ought to be required reading for all federal and provincial finance ministers. The only thing better than this would be to require all government workers and all leftist intellectuals to own and operate a corner store for a year. Then watch the country come to its senses!

Lavoie's basic thesis is that central economic planning and regulation can never be successful because it is impossible for a central planner to have a command of all the incredibly detailed and intricate "knowledge" (as distinct from the "data") necessary for such a plan. What he calls the "knowledge problem" refers to the fact that "a central planning board, even when well-intentioned, would lack the knowledge to combine resources in a manner that is economic enough to sustain modern technology."

### The Chess Game

One image Lavoie uses to drive this point home is based on the game of chess. In a thought experiment, he asks us to imagine teams of thousands of chess players at a competition. What would happen, he asks, if a coach suddenly asked all players to move their same piece at the same time? Of course, it would be chaos. Every game of chess, just like every market exchange, is different, and though the rules are the same for all players, it's a competitive transaction with infinite possibilities. *Only the players* are in a position to know best what their next move should be because only they can complete the game by taking the hundreds of calculated risks necessary to win. The analogy is a good one because each citizen, *operating under fixed rules of just conduct, equal for all*—our standard for good government—surely must know his or her own situation most closely, has a personal interest at heart, and wins or loses each of life's manifold games accordingly.

### Prices Are Key Signals

Importantly, after making sound arguments for complexity, Lavoie then argues that "the function that prices play in a market is a cognitive one. It is to reduce for each decision-maker the otherwise overwhelming number of technologically feasible ways of producing things, to the relatively much smaller number that appear to be economic—that is, to those that appear to more than repay their costs."[22] Any political, merely data-based decision—such as: "all players must now move the queen"—that intervenes or interferes with actual buyers and sellers therefore will never clarify, and can only confuse such knowledge-based signals.

### Knowledge Versus Data

As he reveals the underlying fallacy of central planning, Lavoie stresses that *data* and *knowledge* are not the same thing. The assumption that mountains of data loaded into our computers constitute knowledge is a booby trap. It does not, and cannot, for

> the truly relevant "data" that a planning organization would need . . . resides deeply embedded in and dispersed among the separate minds of millions of people. In the relevant sense of the term, the data do not exist. The knowledge relevant for economic decision-making exists in a dispersed form that cannot be fully extracted by any single agent in society.

In short, "the Market is the source of that knowledge which rational activity requires; it is thus indispensable." Such subjective knowledge, he adds, "is inextricably connected to the knowing subject and crucially dependent on the subject's values and beliefs. . . ." This, of course, is particularly true in the fields of business, and economics, where so much of judgment, after the facts are gathered, is based on experience and intuition. This is an observation that ties in directly with the whole bottom-up nature of free contractual activity under democratic capitalism, in which the mass of the people (rather than some elite), all operating under the same set of rules, is considered the cradle of social and economic intelligence, generating and sustaining values spontaneously in billions of daily transactions. And so it is that even the more modest efforts to guide or steer markets toward particular outcomes (as agricultural marketing boards attempt to do) "are really blind and dangerous obstructions of the very source of that knowledge which is essential to rational economic decision-making." Such interventions inevitably end up subsidizing inefficiencies and penalizing excellence, thus dampening growth and vitality (although such protectionist measure may indeed secure needed votes).

### Articulate Versus Inarticulate Knowledge

A further difficulty which we have conveniently hidden from ourselves is that a lot of the important knowledge we hold is completely inarticulate. That is to say, we know it, but we don't know how we know it. Riding a bicycle is a good example of this because even very small children can perform this complex act with no articulate knowledge of *how* it is possible (indeed, the physics describing how a bicycle stays vertical once in motion is very complex). Language is another worldwide example of inarticulate knowledge. All of us can make ourselves understood perfectly well in our native language without needing any special education, and without having a clue as to the complexities of the phonological, syntactical, or grammatical systems that make a language intelligible.

### True Knowledge Depends on "Wholes"

Drawing from philosophers Alfred North Whitehead, Friedrich Hayek, and Gilbert Ryle, Lavoie reminds us that all inarticulate knowledge relies on circular, or intuitive, judgments about "wholes" grasped intuitively and often in advance of any decision, that form an ever-present, subtly shifting basis for our knowledge of the world. It's not that we don't need individual facts, and maybe lots of them. Rather, it means that information about the facts alone is not very helpful. How could a bureaucrat in some central-planning office, for example, with no means of tapping into an enormous and widespread network of inarticulate and intuitive knowledge held in so many heads make the right decisions to benefit all? Bereft of such knowledge, this is simply impossible. So the bureaucrat does what any one of us would do in the same situation: he or she makes not an *economic* decision, but a *political* one that looks good, and normally and naturally one that will also advance the personal career of the bureaucrat and the life of the bureaucracy. (On this note, here's a challenge: name a single important bureaucrat in any modern democracy who has ever approached a boss and asked for a smaller budget and fewer staff.)

### The Principle of Mass Communication

If the most important knowledge is inarticulate, how then is it communicated? Here, Lavoie compares human mass communication to that of ants, termites, and bees, for there are striking similarities. Ants, after all, build complex communities and accomplish tasks no single ant could perform alone. Yet *there is no master ant*, no Statist ant smarter than all the rest, directing them. On the contrary, there is a "spontaneous order" of a kind quite common in the biological world, whereby we see an "ordered pattern that emerges without being the product of anyone's deliberate design but only as an unplanned outcome of the mutual adjustment of its parts." This Lavoie terms "a higher level order that evolves out of a furious turmoil of lower level disorder." (This only apparent disorder is the free-market activity that planners and Statists dislike so much—because they don't understand it). Such spontaneous orders are now often described as "emergent properties," which is another way of saying that the whole is more than the sum of its parts.

For such communication to work, insects use chemical substances called pheromones to send each other signals. To achieve the same kind of spontaneous economic order, humans use prices, and, Lavoie says, "for either of these processes to work, information not only has to be sifted out of pheromone or price signals but must also be injected into them. These signals carry only as much knowledge as has been imparted to them as an outcome of the rivalrous multidirectional tugging taking place among competing individuals."

The key point in this complex but common-sense argument is that to try to turn the material factors of production into a regulated common national property, which is what Marx and, after him, all Statists—Trudeau famously in Canada, and Obama currently in America—attempt to do "would be to deprive the economy of its main source of economic knowledge." And that's the key reason from economic theory, as mentioned, why socialism has never worked, except in heaven where you don't need it, and in hell where you already have it.

## COST, EFFICIENCY, AND TRANSACTIONS OF DECLINE
### Socialism Costs Twice as Much

In a refreshing little pamphlet entitled *Friedman on Galbraith*,[23] Nobel laureate Milton Friedman maintained that "there is a sort of empirical generalization that it costs the State twice as much to do anything as it costs private enterprise, whatever it is."[24] His studies were among the first to put what many had suspected so bluntly, and the ratio discovered held for everything examined. He cited U.S. studies "on the productivity in handling accounts of people in the governmental social security system and in the private insurance system and private commercial insurance agencies." As he put it, "Lo and behold, the ratio of productivity was 2:1." The same ratio held for private versus public fire departments, and schools: "In schools there is no doubt that there is at least a 2:1 difference." That is, if you divide total costs of schooling by total students in the public and private systems, you find that private schooling is approximately half as expensive (when governments report per capita costs of public schooling, they generally omit land costs, borrowing costs, debt costs, amortization, and many other costs that private schools must face).

More recently, Anthony Fell, former chairman of RBC Capital Markets reported (*National Post*, May 28, 2009) that in 1997 a World Bank study of sixty privatized companies in eighteen nations found that the privatized companies increased output by 27 percent and profitability by 45 percent. A University of British Columbia study of Canadian Crown corporations privatized between 1985 and 1996 showed the same dramatic results. One of the most dramatic stories is about CN Rail, which was a union-controlled public basket case costing taxpayers millions of dollars every year. It is now a private company with a market cap of $22 billion and is the first or second most efficient railway system in North America. One dollar invested in CN the day it went private is now worth

$10. A Conference Board of Canada study released in June 2009 argued that productivity has surged in Canada's transportation sector due to privatization, deregulation, and increased competition, with gains up to 200 to 400 percent in many industries so affected. An individual who was trying to buy CN Route (CN's public trucking division) in the late 1980s told me privately that CN Route was spending more money *every year* on the maintenance of its fleet than the cost to replace the entire fleet with brand-new vehicles!

**How Does Socialism Fare Internationally?**
If we ask how socialism fares internationally as a practical system of political, economic, and cultural production, we find repeated examples of failure. Swedish economist Sven Rydenfelt's examples of agricultural costs and his productivity comparisons between socialist and private systems have staggering implications. In the view of many such economists, when push comes to shove, the best rule of thumb is how well each system can provide for its people materially and morally. Will they be full-bellied, secure, and free, or hungry, frightened, and half slaves? Listen to Rydenfelt's view:

- "In all poor countries, the peasants constitute up to 90 percent of the population."
- "With few exceptions the regimes in these poor countries pursue socialist policies."
- "The socialist countries of the world are, as a rule, *unable to feed their own people*. An economic-political system with such a fundamental deficiency must be inefficient and, in the long run, dangerous."[25]

In a later chapter on foreign aid, we will see just how much hard-earned Canadian money is thrown prodigally at such regimes by Canada's government. For now, here's what Rydenfelt tells us about the efficiency of what was once the world's largest experiment in socialism, the former U.S.S.R. It is rather dramatic.

In the United States, a mere 3 to 4 percent of the population is involved in agricultural production, while 23 percent of the Soviet people were so involved. However, U.S. farmers "produce substantial surpluses for export, while in the Soviet Union approximately *one-third* of the food supply [was] either imported *or produced on private plots which were not included in Soviet agricultural Statistics*." The ostrich mentality implied in this horrendous Soviet inability to feed its own people was, and remains, simply inconceivable to us, but it illustrates how ideological fervour can be a mind trap for any nation, once a monolithic morality is built upon it and a complete infrastructure of lives and careers becomes dependent upon it. Everyone looks the other way.

The Soviet private garden plots were the best—and most embarrassing—example of this. Because of anti–private property legal restrictions, the average size of such private gardens was only a third of an acre (.02 hectare), yet with 35 million of these, representing only 3 percent of total Soviet cropland (the rest was farmed communally by the state, in a form of wage slavery), these tiny private peasant gardens turned out fully 27 percent of total Soviet agricultural production annually! It is fascinating but sad to see in operation what amounts to a duplication of the medieval feudal system of output whereby the serfs, who owed homage to the State instead of to a feudal lord, were virtually paying him in slave labour on communal farms, then turning any leftover energies to private production. This pattern of failure is typical of all such regimes (Romania, Ethiopia, Cuba follow suit), wherein the output of the peasants is milked dry to support the urban elite that feeds on their energies. Rydenfelt quotes history's best authority, V.I. Lenin: "If the workers and peasants do not wish to accept socialism, our reply will be: Why waste words when we can apply force?" This is a blunt form of what I call the "coercive humanitarianism" of which we can see perhaps more well-meaning, but no less immoral, forms in all social welfare states. Canada's form is enforced from the top via the courts using our Charter of Rights and Freedoms as an enabling document.

What Rydenfelt argued so convincingly from the world's experience in trying to feed itself over the centuries is that there is a direct positive correlation between the degree of freedom permitted to private entrepreneurs and the level of national agricultural output. He saw then that the direct result of this worldwide experiment in self-nourishment was that "the United States is the greatest exporter of food—in the early 1980s it exported 55 percent of all food sold on the world market—while the other, the Soviet Union, [was] the world's greatest importer of food." Now the United States is still the world's major food producer, and the Soviet Union is gone.

**Economic Efficiency**
The primary reason for socialist inefficiency is the problem of "economic calculation," which boils down to common sense. If no basic unit of value in the form of prices is allowed in the political-economic system, then economic calculation will be impossible. Since hard-core socialist theory repudiates the value of private commercial activity and attempts to steer an economy with political measures, it loses its basis of economic calculation. It substitutes a political value for an economic one. The very first principle of Canada's socialist party, the NDP, is:

> That Production Shall Be for Use, Not Profit
> Economic Activity will be directed to meeting the social and individual needs of the people. It is the aim of the New Democratic Party to modify and *control the operations of great productive organizations* ... [to] ensure that economic production will be directed primarily to *meeting the economic and social needs of the people* and not to the profits

of private enterprise . . . The powers and responsibilities of all levels of government, federal, provincial, and municipal, will be invoked to carry the plan to a successful conclusion (federal NDP convention, 1963, T.1.2) [italics mine].

Close study of this seemingly humane paragraph will produce a shudder of anxiety in anyone who has ever studied economics, the dreadful and deadly track record of socialism, or tried to run even the smallest business. When the NDP says it will "direct" economic activity, it means *it will force people to do its will.* When it says the powers of all three levels of government will be "invoked," it means that it will create an army of bureaucrats, regulators, and inspectors *who will have virtual police powers over private citizens and their enterprises* (rent police, pay police, wage police, affirmative action police, recycling police, pay equity police, language police, and more). Well, I don't much like using the word "police" to describe these people. But every other word just camouflages their true powers. They are not merely "inspecting" or "reporting": they are actually enforcing and punishing. But what does "directing" an economy mean?

It means socialists would have to create an anti-world to succeed in their goals—which is precisely what they have tried to do at every attempt. The consequence is that although both the free-society capitalist and the coercive socialist both want "the greatest good for the greatest number," the former wants it to emerge as a spontaneous result of "the natural system of liberty," without the need to stoop to the immorality of coercive humanitarianism. The latter wants to direct it from the top by means of force. Same goals. Very different means. The former wants a good social and economic result to flower naturally under a rule of law. Socialists want to force the flower, but kill it in the forcing—and the well-being of everyone declines as a result.

### Socialism Generates "Transactions of Decline"
Successful economic activity has its own tools and internal logic and will be a success or failure according to the use of those tools and compliance with the logic. It so happens that most of us have been taught to think of economic activity as a *national* phenomenon. But Toronto's own Jane Jacobs, in an absorbing book entitled *Cities and the Wealth of Nations*, convincingly argues that the process of wealth creation has little to do with the lines on the map that confine the nation, but a great deal to do with the economic and trading relationships within and between cities, the basic engines of wealth production.

In her most important chapter, "Transactions of Decline," we learn why successful empires (and I argue that Canada is now—post 1982—constituted as an official, if loose, internal socialist empire) "become too poor to sustain the very costs of empire." In a nutshell, it is because once cities become strong and wealthy, they enter into too many political, economic, and social policies that amount to transactions of decline in which the wealth created by a productive part of the empire, or nation, is siphoned off to support a weaker, unproductive part. If you like, this is how they cope with the regional strife generated by envy. This is the price such empires or nations pay to sustain their unity. Welcome to the modern empire of Ottawa. Behold, our national strategy to achieve unity by appeasing poorer regions.

The most prevalent transactions of decline in history, however, have been military spending to support far-flung empires; Canada has so far been spared this sink hole. But virtually all large nations—especially federal ones—have internal "empires," constituted by relations between their major cities and their "hinterlands," or supply regions. For these, the second-most prevalent transactions of decline are welfare and regional-support policies, and in our race to create the perfect social-welfare state we have become masters of this kind of transaction. In fact, as far as I know, we are the only country in history that has declared regional equality a constitutional objective. But, as Jacobs warns: "Welfare programs [that aim] to bring standards of living and services in poor regions into line with those of prospering city regions unfortunately also work out as transactions of decline. If they are unremitting, they too drain city earnings unremittingly. If they are at all generous, then if anything they are even more voracious feeders on cities than military programs."[26]

Further, she writes, in countries like Canada, it is "the hundreds of varieties of national insurance, welfare benefits, and special grants and subsidies that are now distributed" that push us into decline. But even "agricultural price supports and other agricultural subsidies are analogous to welfare programs in drawing upon city regional economies to support poorer regions." So how does this result in decline? Very simply. For it is not as if these transfer payments add to national wealth, for the "goods and services the subsidies buy turn up, just as military goods and services do, at destinations which don't and can't replace imports with local production. Nor does receiving subsidies—unearned imports—help them become capable of doing so. Not being earned, these do nothing to promote versatility at producing in subsidized economies."[27]

In short, such social-egalitarian manoeuvres are sumps of wasted money that merely buy time for central governments and create mounting debt which they are ever harder pressed to service, let alone repay, as the claims of the non-producers mount and the dollars from producers dwindle relative to these claims. This is especially true if there develops a demographic shift such as we are now experiencing, in which the ratio of young producers who pay the taxes, to older people who claim the benefits, alters swiftly. Such debt then must be serviced by the inflationary governmental practice of increasing the money supply faster than the productive capacity of the nation, by further long-term borrowing, and often by currency adjustments—in general, by forcing future generations to pay for our present consumption. Once again: deficits are just deferred taxes. So all these methods are what I have called *the tools of wealth destruction*, and they are inherent in that slow, downward-spiralling process. In fact, if you were asked to destroy a free-world economy slowly and deliberately, these are the very tools you would invent. To make Canada's situation worse, Jacobs warns that "large nations plagued with active or latent separatist movements use subsidies to contain restiveness and discontents"—this is what Crowley called "the bidding war"—and that "subsidies, precisely because they are transactions of decline, are economic time-bombs."[28]

The Western world has witnessed the destruction wrought by many such time bombs in the decline of the Turkish, Spanish, Portuguese, French, British, Soviet, and now, it seems, American—and perhaps Canada's "internal" empire—all bled of revenues to finance expansion, war, welfare, and regional equality; all by depressing "volatile intercity trade in favour of city trade with inert economies."[29]

Canada, we can see, is constitutionally primed for a difficult trip into the future. Choosing my words carefully, I would say that rarely has a wealthy nation so cheerfully, so un-self-critically, with so little learned from the past and such scant concern for the future and for the loss of personal freedom, so smugly launched itself on such a wide-ranging orgy of transactions of decline in the name of justice and equality.

## A BRIEF LOOK AT SWEDEN

Inevitably, when defending socialism, its proponents cite Sweden as a model socialist state. For Trudeau, while minister of justice under Lester Pearson (1967–1968), Sweden was the middle way between Soviet communism and American capitalism. It is usually the only case of a "successful" socialist State that anyone dares to cite, although, strictly speaking, it is not truly socialist. It is a social welfare state. Indeed, it is what I call a "tripartite State" such as Canada is close to becoming (if we are not already there). These are States in which one-third of taxpayers work for government, one-third of the people depend for some serious portion of income on government, and one-third of taxpayers produce the wealth. At this stage, in any democracy where getting votes is the name of the game, the first two parts will always combine for policies that rob the third, and then the game is over, and decline must become steeper, and automatic.

In his book *Disturbing the Nest*, David Popenoe revealed comprehensively to the West for the first time the impact of the social welfare state on society and particularly on the natural family. Prior to World War II, Sweden was a highly conservative, religious, and traditionalist nation. But social engineers, led by Gunnar Myrdal and his wife, Alva, became determined to convert their country into a model secular socialist State, by means of "regulation backed by compulsion."[30] Popenoe detailed the result.

Sweden has become highly atheistic, and is the Western world's most apartment-oriented society. Swedish social policy has focused not on the family, but on the autonomous individual. Sometimes mistakenly called "individualism," this is really "autonomism," mostly expressed as a subsidized, equalized economic independence and self-satisfaction. For such a State can easily control single persons once it lists them all as individuals on its computers. But families, which are ever shifting and which create a private, inward nuclear loyalty, are harder to influence or control. Thus, Sweden has developed social and tax policies specifically designed to break down the nuclear family into constituent individuals. The key to this was the abolition of the family split-income tax in favour of an individual tax for all workers, whether in families or not. The new rule was that all citizens must be self-supporting (and thus individually taxable).

Despite this emphasis, and perhaps predictably, Sweden became the first Western nation to have the majority of its voters dependent in some way on public funds—and thus beholden to the hand that feeds. Sweden was also the first Western nation in which the marriage rate crashed to the lowest in the industrialized world; nearly half of all children born in Sweden in the mid-1980s were to unmarried parents, and by 2006 it was 55.5 percent. About 36 percent of all Swedish marriages ended in divorce and the breakup rate for cohabiting couples with one child was even then three times that of married couples, giving it the highest "family dissolution" rate among advanced societies. By the mid-1980s, Sweden already had the smallest average household size and the highest percentage of single-person households in the Western world. Some 33 percent of households contained only one person—that figure was 63 percent in Stockholm. Along with the decline of family life, marriage, child-bearing, and the generally alienating age stratification of Swedish society has come a sharp decline in volunteerism and private charity.

Even more bizarrely, many Swedes now soak each other to pay each other. In a recent study of public finance, Sherwin Rosen comments that the Swedes "have nationalized the family, and commercialized the private household," adding that in most countries the vast majority of services people provide to each other are furnished privately, by households, off the record, so to speak. But "in Sweden, a great number of women are paid *to look after the children of those women who are employed in the public sector caring for the parents of the women who are watching over their children!*" In what is clearly an understatement, Rosen adds that this cannot be a net contribution to productive activity.[31]

Here is a peek at some cross-national statistics showing Canada, the United States, France, and Sweden on some crucial family trends from the 1990s to the mid-to-late 2000s. Such international statistics take years to gather, so these are quite fresh. You can see that all are more or less trending to the Swedish example. The figures are selected from David Popenoe's Rutgers University National Marriage Project at www.marriage.rutgers.edu, where readers will find much more of interest, with copious research references.

## SNAPSHOT
Cross-National Family Breakdown
1990s to mid-to-late 2000s

| Country | 1990s | Mid-2000s | |
|---|---|---|---|
| *Lone-Parent Families as a Percentage of All Families with Children* | | | |
| Canada | 1996 22.3 | 2006 29.1 | |
| USA | 1996 28.3 | 2006 27.8 | |
| France | 1990 14.5 | 2001 18.0 | |
| Sweden | 1990 18.0 | 2006 24.5 | |
| *Number of Marriages per 1,000 unmarried women over 15* | | | |
| Canada | 1995 34.0 | 2006 22.2 | |
| USA | 1995 50.8 | 2005 40.7 | |
| France | 1994 22.3 | 2005 20.8 | |
| Sweden | 1994 17.2 | 2005 20.0 | |
| *Percentage of Births to Unmarried Women* | | | |
| Canada | 1995 30.5 | 2005 25.6 | |
| USA | 1996 32.4 | 2006 38.5 | |
| France | 1996 39.9 | 2006 50.5 | |
| Sweden | 1996 53.9 | 2006 55.5 | |
| [Author's note: high rates of abortion may account for the falling Canadian number. Abortion is far more restricted in other nations of the world.] | | | |
| *Percentage of Children in Lone-Parent Families* | | | |
| Canada | 2000 21.3 | 2005 22.5 | +5.6 % |
| USA | 1996 25.4 | 2004 26.4 | +3.9 % |
| France | 1991 8.9 | 2001 13.3 | +49.4 % |
| Sweden | 1999 21.0 | 2005 21.3 | +1.4 % |

If such numbers hold for the future, only about 60 percent of Swedish women will *ever* marry, compared to about 83 percent of American women who will do so. Contrast this with the 1950s when marriage rates for women in both nations were in the mid 90 percent range. Today, about 28 percent of all Swedish couples are cohabiting, compared to 8 percent of American couples. In both countries, the risk of couple dissolution is several times higher for cohabiting couples than for married couples. A key factor in American family breakdown (despite the fact of the most sex-ed material in history pumped into the schools) is teen pregnancy. In America in 2002 the rate was forty-three babies per thousand girls aged fifteen to nineteen, but in Sweden that number was only . . . three.

A fact seldom mentioned in assessing the figures for the United States, however, is that there are three main ethnicities there: white, black (about 13 percent) and Hispanic (about 13 percent). Mixing them all together paints a false picture of how each is doing. But there is a lot of research available that breaks things down by race and, sadly, the gap is especially unfavourable to blacks. About 75 percent of black births by 2008 are out of wedlock, compared to about 25 percent of white births. Hispanics tend to fall in between, with about 50 percent of births out of wedlock. That has been a disaster for the American black family, 85 percent of which were living as intact families in the 1950s.

But whatever the ultimate reasons, any thoughtful person examining these numbers would conclude that these general trends are not good for children—the most defenceless party in this picture. Having said this, Popenoe points out that while Sweden shows the most disastrous picture in terms of marriage rates and births to unmarried women, it is nevertheless a very child-friendly society: all married couples with children must wait six months before a divorce is final (Canada and the United States make no distinction in ease of divorce for couples with children, or without). Abortion is forbidden in Sweden after the eighteenth week of pregnancy (in Canada, abortion is allowed up to the moment of birth; same in all but three U.S. states). Anonymous sperm donation is forbidden in Sweden, and in vitro fertilization allowed only if the woman is in a legal marriage or marriage-like relationship.

A closer look at Sweden, however, will draw the conclusion that whereas individuals there are marriage negative, so to speak, and have withdrawn from tradition in this respect, the State—which has promoted and subsidized this marriage-stripping ethos, has taken on the role of überparent. Sweden is child-friendly only because the State has set things up to accommodate a *public national life with children, by ideological preference to a private family life.* The hard fact remains that in Sweden as in all other countries in which this kind of marriage stripping via Statism has occurred, the incidence of serious life problems among children from broken homes is two to three times higher than elsewhere. It is truly the world's first Nanny State: autonomist to the core, strictly and minutely regulated, with very high taxation, an official hostility to religion and private life, and very marriage and private family averse.

The reason for including this comparative bit on Sweden is that Canada has been following the Swedish model for decades. This is a model which has not arisen voluntarily from "the people" either there or here. Rather, it has been articulated and implemented by radical social engineers via an intentional policy manipulation and transformation of traditional private and family life so detailed, pervasive, and insidious as to be almost invisible. It has come about by "regulation backed by compulsion."

We may consider ourselves forewarned, but not forearmed.

# 6: THE POLITICAL PARTIES
## WHERE THEY ONCE STOOD—WHERE THEY STAND NOW—AND WHERE YOU STAND

Nothing quite equals the naked confusion seen in the eyes of otherwise competent people when asked on what political philosophy their preferred political party *really* stands; what were, and are, its underlying principles, beliefs, and standards (as distinct from its election promises of the day)? Such conversation openers are usually unproductive and lead to hostility. Embarrassment is followed by double-talk, followed by a hasty change of subject or retreat to a very emotional comparison of political personalities. To further complicate matters, political contests in all the Western democracies have become a media event, Hollywoodized, and sound-bitten, with public awareness of underlying ideological motives sadly ignored. It is through such neglect that we leave ourselves exposed to the emotional manipulations by parties and media in a daily drama that usually hides underlying longer-term motives.

Most of us have been trained by this course of events to see what I call "prostitution politics" as the norm. We relate to the parties the way a customer relates to a call girl. We arrive at an intersection, and there is an attractive prostitute on each of the other three corners—say, an NDP, a Liberal, and a Conservative. Determined to get the most for our money we quickly discover that each prostitute will energetically compete with the others to promise the most. The decision is not too difficult. We have already decided to go with the one who promises the most for our money.

This story—and our final choice—changes considerably, however, if we arrive at the corner seeking not only a good time, but also a good life partner. Suddenly, in addition to our interest in sex, we want to know about long-term conduct, morals, principles, character, and all such matters that distinguish the good from the bad, the temporary from the durable, the true from the false, and so on. In short, our questions, and the answers we expect, are now very different. Well, "you get what you ask for," as they say.

We recklessly vote for programs we are told are "free" without remembering that nothing in life is free, without regard to the burden our choices may place on our children's futures, to the kind of nation we ought to be building, or to the many freedoms we've surrendered without a struggle, and so on. So they've got us trained. Or to be fairer, we've got each other trained.

But a political prostitute won't start behaving like a good spouse until we ask different kinds of questions, making it known that we expect answers of a certain quality—or we're not interested. The only way this will be possible is if the electorate knows what *principles* the parties claim to stand for and can then connect the wild *promises* they make to their underlying political philosophy, or as a betrayal of same. Are they just putting a wet finger to the wind of political expediency, or are they steering a course in keeping with their own principles, regardless of the wind? Are we getting more Band-Aids or a cure? Of course, practical circumstances often require compromises with respect to final choices of any party or leader—especially if the party does not have a majority. But to make a practical compromise of the moment because one is handcuffed (say, with a minority government) and so cannot truly fight, is a very different matter from losing one's declared ideals entirely or betraying one's own foundational principles. The aim of this chapter is to help readers compare the "classical" aims of our main political parties and then contrast them with their modern behaviour.

## THE CLASSICAL LIBERAL

What is called "classical," or "true," liberalism emerged with force near the end of the eighteenth century, after a period now called the Enlightenment, which was characterized by a high enthusiasm for science, reason, and the possibility of finding ultimate solutions to the problems of organizing human societies. This original liberalism declared with passion that a just society free from oppression could be established on the basis of respect for individual liberty. The defence of this liberty required surrounding the individual with a number of so-called "natural rights" and beliefs that would have to be guaranteed in law, such as property rights, privacy, free association, free speech, voting rights, economic rights such as outlined in chapter 4, and so on. In a nutshell, the classical liberal venerated *the morality of individual responsibility, under limited government with equal opportunity and just rules of conduct for all under a rule of law.* No exceptions. This was primarily an English ideal, though one much admired and communicated clearly to later generations of the English-speaking people by European writers such as Montesquieu, and in Canada's own tradition by many admiring French-Canadian politicians at Canada's founding. This was the central political ideal that shaped Western civilization or the "free world," and which is now so sadly under attack mostly within these same nations (more than from tensions between them). Used as a test of political freedom, this standard will generally expose everything from petty to major tyranny.

Below, under "The Modern Liberal," we shall see how deformed this original and noble liberal standard has become, unbeknownst even to most so-called liberals who do not realize that "one of the more extraordinary developments in the intellectual history of the twentieth century [has been] a profound change in the meaning of liberalism."[1] Somehow, in the rational search for equal *opportunity* and justice for all, the moving standards of the original classical liberal—which so many in the West have died defending—were submerged by a new kind of liberal who has eagerly joined hands with the State, not to ensure freedom and equal *opportunity* for all, but through "progressive" social engineering to *coerce* and extract from the body politic the equal *results* these new liberals began craving. Somehow, the ideal of liberty got bumped, and replaced with the ideal of equality. The classical liberal of the past, so passionate for freedom, would have declared this despicable beyond belief.

## THE CLASSICAL CONSERVATIVE

The classical, or "true," conservative is optimistic about human beings, but far less optimistic about human government. Although individual freedom, private property, free enterprise, and related matters are valued perhaps even more than by the classical liberal, the classical conservative *objects to the idea that human societies should be engineered at all, in any event certainly not according to abstract theories forced upon people by utopian intellectuals.* In a striking observation, G.K. Chesterton once remarked that a crazy person is "someone who has lost everything except his reason." At first, this statement sounds a little odd because we are trained to identify what is right, with reason. But what Chesterton meant was that a crazy person may still be able to add 2 + 2, or tell the difference between a car and a goat, or memorize part of the telephone book. We say such people are crazy mostly because they have lost the human glue that holds society together: good manners, fellow feeling, a belief in right and wrong, charitable emotion, and so on. A normal human being who sees a child drowning in an ice-cold pond will jump in to save the child. But a crazy person who has lost such instincts and habits and has only his or her reason left will say, "It's not reasonable to jump into icy water. You could drown, too!" And of course, that is true.

So, following, among others, the enormous influence of Edmund Burke whose important work *Reflections on the Revolution in France* (1790) powerfully moved the best minds of half the world against radical excesses, the conservative argues forcefully that when relying on reason alone, without the traditional cautions of custom, manners, and morals, people will tend to reason themselves into tyrannical political and moral policies to justify imposing their personal notions about human perfectibility on others. For the true conservative, however, civilization can never be dialed up on a planner's computer or outlined in a manifesto (or a Charter). Rather, it is like a tree of great age, with deep, invisible roots. Revolution, or for that matter, any sudden, unwise change in social policy, will cut us away from those roots, leaving dead leaf and branch, but no civilization. History, of course, has proved him quite correct. The liberal view that humans are basically born good and that human reason will eventually produce a society of "material and cultural achievement" must be tempered by a deeper truth: that we are all a mixture of angel and devil, that final perfection is impossible (therefore, watch out for the silver-tongued promises of social engineers), and that over the centuries we have developed hundreds of necessarily imperfect but satisfactory political, economic, and cultural institutions and traditions that have served civilization tolerably well up until now.

A true conservative believes deeply that a social and moral "tradition" that has worked tolerably well for a long time is really just another word for virtue (manners and morals) become a habit. These habits we once described admiringly as positive "prejudices" in the sense that all civilized people would correctly prejudge a situation so that social behaviour was ordered, rather than chaotic. When we teach our children when and how to say thank-you, we are instilling an automatic prejudice in the conservative sense. Any society that sets out to destroy such fundamental habits is immediately faced with the upsetting task of reinventing civilization on a daily basis, but without benefit of the stored wisdom of the past, of political and cultural ways so old and venerable that they speak as if with the authority of the collective unconscious and therefore ought to be "conserved."

Due to a profound respect for such teachings and because experience shows that human planners, especially governments, have a way of mucking up most things they try, the conservative is especially skeptical of abstract theories of human improvement: there must be a brake on imprudent enthusiasm for changing society for the better, in the absence of any solid evidence that it *can* be changed for the better. For the conservative, civilization is not a matter of politics, or of social policy, as today's radicals are so fond of assuming, but rather a matter of practical *customs, manners, and morals*. These are the foundation stones of a functioning and free civil society. As for a better world? The conservative has always insisted that if everyone would strive to cultivate the classical conservative virtues, so-called social problems would largely take care of themselves. What virtues? Those born, nourished, and to be conserved in the oldest human institutions of marriage, family, church, local community, social relationships, intimate friendship, daily work, laws of private property, free mutual contract, and so on. Such virtues may be tempered by reason, *but reason cannot create them.* Neither can they be created by government, nor simply conferred or forced upon a people via a constitutional shopping list in a top-down fashion.

The conservative is not against *prudent* change. Nor does he or she wish simply to preserve the status quo at all costs. The chief concern is over rash and imprudent change. So, the theme is: "If it ain't broke, don't fix it." For tampering could make it worse. The reason? Because the abstract thinker does not see the roots. Only the tree. If you cut the tree, it will die. So the conservative says, because much of what is important is invisible to us, like those roots, let's not be so conceited as to think we can reinvent the whole system of humanity in a day. Above all, Burke felt, let us avoid and reject like the plague all abstract, merely theoretical solutions to human woes as insufficient reasons to smash existing institutions and restructure entire societies. For such ideas spring not from experience, or from real human sympathy, but *from the cold calculation of those who would use the force of the State to force others to live in their dream world.* In other words, they spring from false sympathy. From the dangerous infatuations of the radical intellect with his or her own ideas. Burke aimed his barbs especially at levellers of the type so prevalent today, whom he considered to have hardened hearts "nearer to the cold malignity of a wicked spirit than to the frailty and passion of a man." The word "progressive" used in connection with conservatism he would have found an abomination invented by idealistic politicians suffering from a civilizational deficit. Again, lest the reader believe this to mean conservatives are against progress in the sense of basic political, material, or scientific advances, this is not so. Their objection is to the use of the word "progressive" to imply that our present arrangements are unsatisfactory, not as compared with *an existing and proven better method*, but as compared with a theoretical fantasy in the name of which progressives are prepared to sacrifice living, breathing, workable relationships and institutions. History shows that such idealists are too often quite willing to sacrifice living, breathing human beings—often millions of them—to their abstract ideals.[2]

So above all, Burke upheld a belief in traditional natural law, in *the necessity of a moral order that transcends mere men and their governments*, without which they would eventually devour themselves in struggles for power, like mad dogs— or mad radicals. He wanted people to affiliate with and bond to a free civil society conducting itself under natural law, as their best protection against State power. This natural law, stating that we must do good and avoid evil, we can sum up as "the commands of right reason that follow nature for the common good." So here we have right reason (we must try to save a drowning child) not wrong reason (forget it, that water is ice cold!) commanding us to follow nature for the good (of ourselves and our civilization), and not for the bad (say, giving in to a natural desire to kill a bad person), and all for the common good (and not just for our individual good).

Perhaps the best-ever description of the evils of regimes that "level" all natural distinctions and differences comes from the mouth of Shakespeare's Ulysses in his play *Troilus and Cressida*. We are there warned that the end result of all egalitarian regimes, is that once they are set up,

Then everything includes itself in power,
Power into will, will into appetite,
And appetite (an universal wolf,
So doubly-seconded with will and power),
Must make perforce an universal prey,
And last, eat up himself.

"Eat up himself." That is exactly what happened in the most levelling "democratic" event in modern history, the French Revolution, when Robespierre and his radical friends were beheaded by their own revolutionary disciples ... who had become even more radical than they.

## THE CLASSICAL SOCIALIST

Of all the views, classical socialism, which got off the theoretical ground in the middle of the nineteenth century, was obviously the most radical, for it set out to replace the private "bourgeois" capitalist social and political order with one based on entirely different values. Simply put, whether in its *revolutionary* Marxist form, or in its softer social welfare form such as we now live under, classical socialism sought to create a *new society* in which property and the means of producing wealth were either owned by the State, or at the very least, controlled by the State, rather than by individuals and corporations. Socialists wanted to transfer the affections found in all natural human social bonding, from the myriad voluntary associations of civil society such as family, club, team, charity, church, to the State itself. It does this with the help of heavy taxation, comprehensive regulation, and public funding of government goods and services as substitutes for those things that were once supplied by people for each other. In doing this, they hoped to eradicate all economic and social differences between individuals and classes. Most important, in their social utopia the production of all goods and services would be managed, not by free people with private personal, family, and corporate motives, but *by the State aiming at political and economic utopia.*

The former communist nations were the more extreme type in which governments owned everything and tried to direct productive output to public ends with one failed five-year plan after another. The national socialist (Nazi) system in Germany did not seek to actually own very much, but it controlled productive enterprises by regulation, taxation, and quotas dictating production for the State, and in these ways directed them as effectively as if they were owned outright. They were called national socialists because they repudiated the "international" socialism of communists. They wanted a purely German (or Italian) national socialism, not something run by those they considered ignorant uncivilized Ruskies. Soft-socialist welfare states such as Canada achieve the same national socialist aims by owning and directing a great many tax-funded Crown corporations, by internal trade regulation, by progressive income, capital gains, and wealth taxation, and most of all, by so-called shared-cost spending by which Ottawa bribes the provinces to follow federal regulation of their internal programs in exchange for money from Ottawa. I don't want to overuse the term or suggest anything evil (merely very devious and coercive) when I say that this makes it a truly made-in-Canada national socialism.

Arising, as it did, substantially in reaction to the enormous increase in wealth and the consequent social dislocations caused by the Industrial Revolution, classical socialism was, in the eyes of many observers, merely a secular manifestation of the ideals of a weakened Christianity. As faith in God and the afterlife weakened, it would be replaced by faith in human beings and their governments. The heavenly kingdom to come would be an earthly kingdom created in the here and now by socialists. Thus is socialism a reflection not of a practical, but of a theoretical and dangerously utopian urge.

All three of these classical positions can be thought of as conflicting answers to the question: What moral order is required to produce a good society? Classical liberalism rests its case on freedom and the individual's ability to decide how best to live, within the context of rules of just conduct equal for all. The classical conservative is wary that despite this laudable standard, the liberal will, in the absence of a profound respect for the institutions, traditions, and moral habits of a civilized order, be misled by the frail candle of abstract reason when taken as a beacon. Then enter the planners who succumb to the lure of shallow and, by definition, inadequate rationalism, to the changeable findings of social science, and to the temptations to use state power, forcing, and in the extreme, killing, others to produce the perfect society. Finally, the classical socialist attacks the entire philosophical and moral basis of both these orders, preferring to ground the good society not in the moral choices of the free private individual, nor in the freely chosen customs and standards of a civil society, but in the deliberations of a centralized State which has an egalitarian and authoritarian concept of the common social and economic good as its motive—a motive it insists is superior to those of any private individual, any society, or any religious morality.

What, then, *restrains* the individual under each of these systems?

Under classical liberalism, the individual is restrained by the rules of just conduct, which must be the same and enforced for all without exception (like the rules of the road), or the justice inherent in them is lost. Under classical conservatism, the individual is further restrained by the impressive weight of custom, tradition, and the venerable institutions of civilized life, all tempered by reference to a common transcendent moral standard (most often a religious morality). This is the weight and force of what G.K. Chesterton described as "the democracy of the dead": the societies in which we live include the wisdom of our ancestors. Under classical socialism, all of these values are rejected in favour of restraint by a unitary and necessarily all-intrusive State that seeks with its monopoly on power to fulfill its vision of a just and egalitarian world, *whether the people want it or not.*

What has happened to the modern counterparts of these positions?

Against objections I can hear in advance, I will attempt to outline where the present choice among political parties lies with reference to the standards of the classical past, and also within the context of previous chapters of this book. In a general sense, it is important to know what kind of world our party of choice is creating for us and for our children. For example, which parties are pushing us toward more socialism? Which are insisting on more political and economic freedom? Which want a more severe Handicap System?

## THE MODERN LIBERAL

Canada's modern "liberal" party has little to do with classical liberalism and its proud and passionate defence of individual liberty *against* the State. In our universities we may find a few vestiges of this ideal, but as explained in an earlier chapter, for Canada's "Liberal" party and the American "Democratic" party, that original focus on liberty has long since given way to the promotion of Statism. This wholesale switch in the original anti-Statist position of liberals took a mere century to bring about and in Canada was vastly accelerated by Pierre Trudeau and his "liberal"—especially French-Canadian—colleagues: Serge Joyal, Jean Chrétien, Marc Lalonde, Monique Bégin, Jean Marchand, Gérard Pelletier, and many others who are on the public record as striving to bring about a more highly centralized State in Canada. My point is that what has been referred to in this book as the French deviation has been a result deliberately engineered and imposed by government, especially by Canada's federal Liberal party, and this has included a lot of fellow-travelling from modern "progressive conservatives," and of course with the fawning support of the NDP, our socialist party of record.

One of the first warnings to Canadians of this shocking phenomenon was Peter Brimelow's *The Patriot Game*, which minutely documented the sellout of English Canada to the French style of government and to the modern liberal dream of a centrally controlled, multicultural, regionally balanced nation sustained by bizarrely lopsided financial and emotional nourishment of French-English relations, and by enormous constitutionally mandated interregional transfer payments to all provinces and territories (especially to buy off Quebec). He shows how, with unmatched ambition, the Liberals under Trudeau embarked on their quest for more power in 1968 and were eventually to amass a "concentration of federal government employees in Ottawa [proportionately] three times as large as that in Washington, D.C.," to help them.[3] Unnoticed by most English-speaking liberals, Canada's Liberal party drifted—no, charged— toward socialism in all but name, dragging Canada after it. At warp speed, classical liberalism was abandoned by the parties and social groups that originally espoused it, in favour of the more interventionist mixed-economy complex of attitudes describing itself as social democracy.

The six isms upon which the Liberal party has based its political life since 1968 are: centralism, elitism, official bilingualism, multiculturalism, egalitarianism, and nationalism. The first two take care of the Liberals' political, economic, and cultural vision of a socialist or (for the squeamish) a social welfare govern-ance. The other isms, to which more could be added, are essentially like the marketing arm of this political philosophy, the new orthodoxy presented to the people as a national unifying program, dependent on all the normal fanfare, federal spending, transfer payments, and other control devices such programs require to be successful.

In speaking of nationalism as a form of radicalism, Brimelow forcefully reminds us that all such isms are "essentially a cover for a hidden agenda of unlimited social engineering concerned not with the liberties of the past, but with a newly-controlled future, not with patriotism, but with power." What this means is that in one of the most stunning and as yet publicly unconfessed reversals in modern political history, the classical liberal movement (not only in Canada, but also in Britain and the United States) from which so much of what was good in Canada's founding and in Western civilization—our most fundamental political, governmental, cultural, and legal institutions and liber-ties, our very political and social lifeblood—has been unceremoniously shown the door. We will never get these back unless we take them back.

Meanwhile, the modern liberal is in a very strong position because, as explained earlier, modern liberalism has cleverly adopted libertarianism with respect to the private body, sexuality, and other "personal" moral issues, and has combined these with socialism with respect to all matters considered public. The resulting libertarian-socialism is a uniquely modern liberal blend that appeals to a lot of people. It is by now Canadian political orthodoxy. In this way, modern liberalism has incorporated into itself what might otherwise have divided it.

## THE MODERN CONSERVATIVE

The modern conservative is embarrassed by reality. One observation will do to illustrate: any mandated government medicare program (remember, in Canada there have been threats of heavy fines and/or a jail term for daring to offer private medical care options to public care) is a profoundly Statist program. Yet no single "conservative" leader in Canada has ever dared to oppose it. Not a word. And I submit it is a contradiction in logic to describe any party that supports such a program as conservative. Perhaps "gutless conservative" would be more apt. That is why I say the modern conservative is an ostrich, uncertain philosophically of what he or she stands for, or against. For a long time, in a stroke of pure prostitution politics, the ridiculous label "progressive" was attached to the party name. For those with classical conservative instincts this was a great disgrace, because a true conservative is far more concerned with conserving what is tried-and-true than with any notion of "progress" for its own sake (after all, it's easy to see that progress may in fact be a regress). After all, nothing new under the sun has been invented with respect to basic human values, nor ever will be. This means that *to go forward, we may need first to go back*: to reclaim and defend the institutions, moral values, and habits of thought that have always been central to human thriving (and to Canada as it was originally confederated). The fundamental things, such as the need for honour, truth, decency, care for family and neighbours, hard work, living within one's means (individually and as a nation), and so on, have been known for millennia. The problem, therefore, is: How should we properly order society in order to revive and then conserve these things?

Although conservative prime minister Brian Mulroney seemed often to ignore the foundations of conservatism, he took some important steps to dismantle the state in Canada ... while taking others to ensure its longevity. Immediately after he came to power with a huge majority, he proceeded to confuse every true conservative in the country, vying with liberals for much of the same turf. He soon became one of our biggest-spending prime ministers ever, racking up huge deficits his first term, and then in the next election losing every one of his seats but two. On the way, however, he did introduce a number of "conservative" measures. He dismantled Trudeau's disastrous National Energy Program, which was "one of the most far-reaching revolutionary policies ever to have emerged from a Canadian Government."[4] It had driven half the nation's oil rigs south of the border in what business columnist Peter Cook called "the biggest exodus of capital in Canadian history" (*Globe and Mail*, November 5, 1987). With the same motive (of reversing another of Trudeau's socialist schemes), Mulroney ended the damage caused by the Foreign Investment Review Agency (FIRA) which had resolutely discouraged international investment in Canada. In his most successful initiative, he managed to sign the Free Trade Agreement with the United States, the world's largest and richest trading nation (80 percent of Canada's foreign trade is with the U.S.). But his riskiest bid for glory was his failed attempt to heal the wounds in Canada's constitution-making endeavour. He wanted to "bring Quebec in" because Trudeau had so meanly "left Quebec out" of the repatriation process. So Mulroney cobbled together the Meech Lake Accord. Though badly flawed, this deal did attempt, among other things, to decentralize power in favour of more local decision making. It was an attempt to reverse Trudeau's constitutional changes. It failed because Trudeau successfully attacked it, Premier Clyde Wells of Newfoundland rejected it, and Canadians rightly saw it as giving too many favours to Quebec (not incidentally, Mulroney's home province, and one essential to his election). It betrayed a fundamental principle of English constitutional thought: We must all live under *the same law*. No special favours. No *droit administratif*. No special labels. No "distinct" societies, or other such playing around with the terms of Confederation. Clearly, no future prime minister will ever make *that* mistake again.

Yet, in November 2006, Prime Minister Stephen Harper also declared in Parliament "that this House recognize(s) that the Québécois form a nation within a united Canada." Okay, so Quebec is distinct, but only *within Canada* (and by deduction, not without Canada). He cleverly threw Quebec a bone—but with a long leash attached. As for Harper's conservatism? I believe he is personally deeply conservative, and that he hates the handcuffs. But he has yet to shake them off, and so he has chosen the pragmatic route of compromising his core principles in an attempt to get a majority, failing which, he will probably resign and go play hockey. Prior to the 2009 market meltdown there was no significant cutback in government spending, and then he embraced the copycat Keynesian idea of a stimulus package, even as French president Nicolas Sarkozy boasted about this trend, stating that the sub-prime crisis had "put the French model back in fashion." There was the president of France himself, touting what I have called the French style. As a result, Canada will have another massive deficit in 2011 of $49.12 billion to follow the projected deficit of 2010 of $54 billion. Clearly, Canada's total debt of almost $600 billion—a burden cranked up for the first time ever outside of wartime by Pierre Trudeau—is still with us and may *never* be paid off.

Despite the handcuffs, however, Harper has: withdrawn public funding from offensive films and TV shows; built up the military; extended home-budget relief for children's sports and the like; strengthened Canada's Arctic sovereignty; and toughened immigration procedures. This latter is especially so with his *Discover Canada: The Rights and Responsibilities of Citizenship* booklet, in which, among other things, he warns newcomers that "Canada's openness and generosity do not extend to barbaric cultural practices that tolerate spousal abuse, 'honour killings,' female genital mutilation, or other gender-based violence. Those guilty of these crimes are severely punished under Canada's criminal laws." Bravo. This is one of the first instances in living memory of a prime minister stressing citizen responsibilities, rather than rights. About time. He has also armed our border guards; has abolished our feminist-dominated Court Challenges Program; has legislated $1,200 tax relief for families and abolished the liberals' government daycare idea; has raised the age of sexual consent from fourteen to sixteen; has called for tougher criminal laws, and an end to lenient sentencing and automatic early parole for non-violent crimes (after serving only one-sixth of a sentence!); has opposed legalization of marijuana; has allowed income splitting for retired couples. And . . . at long last has ended the abortive (at $2 billion, fully 1,000 percent over budget) long-gun registry that criminalized honest citizens while proving utterly ineffectual at nabbing criminals with their illegal handguns. Smart. Careful. Not overly bold.

Yet.

## IS "DEMOCRACY" CONSERVATIVE?

But where does this leave Canadian conservatism? Most Canadians still remember Preston Manning and the Reform Party of Canada as an attempt to push back the liberal welfare state with grassroots popular democracy. Now, this was confusing because popular democracy can easily result in a majority oppressing the minority, and so it is not really "conservative." True conservatives throughout history have always been leery of democracy (and of mob rule) for this very reason. If they welcome democracy as a legitimizing force in government, it is always as only a filtered or restrained democratic element directed to legislate for the good of the whole people, and not merely for the small number of constituents in each small part of the country. Indeed, in many "democracies" on the British model, elected representatives are specifically forbidden to take instructions from voters on the grounds that once elected, they must consider the good of all the people, and not just their own electors. At bottom, Preston Manning's Reform Party was intended mostly to use the voice of the people (especially people in the West) to push back the socialism imposed on all Canada by the Centre-East.

As mentioned earlier, the original of this book sprang from the same motive. Because so much new Canadian legislation at the time seemed to be against the will of the people, as every reliable poll was indicating; or because it was so obviously an outrageous and arbitrary invention of the courts, people protest was in the air. Both the Reform Party and this book were spontaneous protests against the heavy hand of a growing Statism, and at the time some direct democracy seemed like the only way to fight back. There was no other.

Reform fought the good fight and had its day, and for a time was an important opposition party. But it was inevitably sucked in to the leftist-centrist vortex because Official Opposition was not enough. Preston Manning wanted to be prime minister. This same vortex of liberal orthodoxy has sucked in Stephen Harper, who knows very well that in a left-of-centre country he can only stay in power by staying in ideological handcuffs. And that is because he knows . . . "It's the culture, stupid" (and yes, it's also "the stupid culture"). Manning gambled, and this writer gambled, that if given the opportunity and the tools, the Canadian people would push back the Statist orthodoxy that has been the defining feature of modern power in Canada for almost half a century. But that was not to be. It may never be, because . . . conservatism in the Western democracies has become divided against itself.

## SPLIT CONSERVATIVES

Conservatives, even if they admit to such a philosophy, are quick to specify that they are either a "fiscal" or a "social" conservative. Now, what can these terms possibly mean? Someone who says "*I'm a fiscal conservative*" is a person who is declaring against big government and in favour of free enterprise, lower taxes, private property, private and corporate contractual rights, and the like. But at the same time this phrase sends a message that they are in favour of maximum individual freedom, that abortion is a woman's right, that they don't care about homosexual marriage (because it doesn't affect them personally), and believe neither society nor the State has any right to dictate personal morality. When this person thinks about the rights of the individual and how these are to be balanced against the rights of society (even if he or she concedes there are such rights, that society is far more than an abstraction), the tendency is to judge the issue at hand in favour of the individual.

Now, if we had to locate the single most important distinction between the true conservative and the classical liberal, it would be this: When balancing the rights of individuals against those of civil society, the conservative argues that except for obvious individual oppressions, society must be preserved and prevail. That conclusion is upheld because the true conservative believes deeply that the individual is a product of a well-formed society, and not the reverse: a well-formed society creates and nurtures free and responsible individuals; individuals do not spring forth this way from whole cloth, and then create society. The second conclusion is that the natural rights of society (and what we sometimes call the common good) must prevail in any contest with the rights of mere individuals. In short, society cannot ignore, but must insist on, its own reasonable long-term priority over the individual, precisely to ensure the common good. This is why I say a fiscal conservative who holds the opposite view is no conservative at all, but rather, is a libertarian (about which, more below).

Accordingly, someone who says "*I'm a social conservative*" is a person who may share "fiscal conservative" views about taxation, smaller government, deregulation, and so on, but in addition holds that the rights of a free and well-formed civil society are in all the most important social and moral respects *prior* in importance to the rights of individuals. This person will argue that the killing of any human life is wrong and the weakest human life of all requires the strongest protection; that marriage is a natural procreative institution aimed at the creation and protection of children (and this is the only reason States ought to be involved in protecting or privileging married people. Hence, homosexuality ought never to be normalized or privileged); that pornography commercializes and brutalizes our most sacred intimacies, fosters crime, and has systemic spill-over effects on the young and on society at large that extend far beyond the privacy of individual users, and this demeans us all. And so on. Which is to say that all true conservatives are "social" by nature because although their political philosophy holds high the value of individual rights, it grants priority to the customary rights and obligations of society and its venerable institutions, and above all to human community. In doing so, the conservative makes a singular distinction. In keeping with the metaphor of the political sandwich described previously: the conservative is opposed to oppressive and intrusive Statism from the top, but also to radical "me first" individualism that intrudes from the bottom to corrode community bonds. What the conservative cherishes and strives to "conserve" is a flourishing and free "organic" civil society—the middle part of the political sandwich—that serves as a barrier and the only real protection for the human person against both these extremes: collectivization from the top, and atomization of society from the bottom. Alas, for the modern conservative, no combination of these two elements—fiscal and social—is available as a blend to counter the powerful libertarian-socialism that now dominates the public square. Modern conservatives live in a house divided.

## THE MODERN SOCIALIST

Canada's New Democratic Party is Canada's national socialist party of record (though Canada's national form of socialism has been mostly designed and institutionalized by "liberals"). Of the three federal parties, the NDP has had the least to lose by attempting to remain ideologically pure. Nevertheless, it has cheated in the sense that it has resolutely disguised the truly radical nature of its ideology and objectives by downplaying its hard-core socialist roots. Indeed, until very recently a Canadian would never hear an NDPer use the word "socialist" in public. What are the party's objectives? We hardly need to ask. As mentioned, the NDP is a registered member of the worldwide organization for socialists called the Socialist International (see www.socialistinternational.org) and its former leader Ed Broadbent was, at one time, a vice-president of that organization. Enough has been said in chapter 5 about the objectives of social-ism as a political philosophy. However, I strongly suggest that anyone who wishes to understand the true heart of the NDP as originally constituted in Canada ought to read through the early resolutions of that party, predictably subtitled "Taking the Future On."[5]

In those more than 265 pages can be found detailed party resolutions of the most radical nature on every conceivable social, economic, and cultural subject. Almost without exception, they seek to resolve each and every nation-al, community, or personal problem of the Canadian people through the use of State power. Almost without exception, they call for more tax dollars, more redistribution of wealth, more agencies, commissions, inspectors, Crown corporations, and all the paraphernalia they drag along with them. The NDP has been resolute in its call for "planning" to achieve its "*new society*" (federal convention, 1977); its aim is "to modify and control the operations of the great productive organizations" (1963). It is "proud to be part of that great world-wide movement of democratic socialist parties" (the Socialist International) that has the goal of providing "an egalitarian society" (1983); NDP/socialists "believe in planning" and "reject the capitalist theory" regarding supply and demand, and they wish "the transfer of title of large enterprises to the state" (1983); they also want every "affirmative action" policy conceivable, unilateral disarmament of the West (including withdrawal from NATO), total "universal-ity" of all conceivable social services, equality of incomes, and banishment of corporate competition (1977). In short, the NDP "will not rest content until we have achieved a democratic socialist Canada" (1983).

All this speaks for itself, and there is no need to elaborate on the rampant philosophical confusion, especially the contradictory coupling of "democracy" with "socialism," which ought to embarrass any astute person. For true democracy is a bottom-up form of government, while true socialism is top-down. They cannot be reconciled. In summary, one's jaw simply drops at the utopian yearning for perfection on earth in every NDP resolution and, not least, the constant recommendations to use State power to coerce some Canadians to produce this dream (via aggressive tax harvesting by government) for others. Never mind that nowhere in the NDP strategy is there any mention of what I have called the "tools of freedom and wealth creation." The NDP simply assumes that freedom and wealth will always be here, just as children believe that money grows on trees.

This brief summary of the modern parties and their positions should serve to explain why so many Canadians are frustrated at the true lack of a distinctive choice in Canadian politics. What kind of choice is before us when the leaders of our two largest and ostensibly different parties are merely vying or colluding with each other to spend all our money and borrow billions more (remember, deficits = deferred taxation), while the third wants the government to run everything on wealth the people couldn't possibly produce under such a system—a conclusion driven home by a simple study of the miserable productive capacities of all socialist nations of the world. Hence, our frustration. Hence, our unheeded cry for a clearer choice.

## WHERE HAS THE YEARNING FOR FREEDOM GONE?

Here's a proposition: Our three modern parties have so trampled upon the classic individual freedoms and wise restraints on governmental power that made great nations possible—that made Canada possible—and have so tightly joined their coercive purposes to the powers of the State, that all three parties, lacking any truly principled ethical standard that could control the abuses of government itself, are now simply vying for a greater or lesser right to engineer society. The result of this lack of principles, in which the only race left is for more power over our freedoms and wealth, is the reduction of political warfare to promises and personalities. Exactly what we see in the press every day. Prostitution politics.

So if someone were to ask me where our time-honoured concern for freedom has gone, I would say, underground for some fifty-odd years now, and showing its head today mostly in libertarian political theory. A capsule summary of libertarian thought is presented here, not to suggest it is the answer to all our prayers (it definitely is not), but that it is the answer to the question: Where has our venerable concern for freedom gone? The modern Liberal party no longer discusses the topic at all, and certainly has not formed its policies on the principle of liberty versus Statism (its classical starting point) for more than a hundred years. And let us not be fooled. The "freedoms" Trudeau and the liberals brought us with their Charter of Rights and Freedoms were all French-style abstract and judge-defined freedoms, distinctly not established English ones. Indeed, Trudeau made certain (in Section 52) that our founding conception of "British liberty" was to be legally subordinated to the code law he favoured. Just so, we are now wrapped in the chains of judicially dictated and controlled (and therefore judicially alterable) "freedoms and rights," all of which are "balanced," one against the other, by judges who cannot be removed and who hold sway in their ermine robes. So if you enjoy the philosophy and writings of the original classical liberals, you will find much to enjoy in modern libertarian works.

## THE LIBERTARIAN ALTERNATIVE

What is a libertarian? Someone who holds *that the only good reason for one person's interfering with the freedom of another is self-protection.* That's the bottom line. Anything that exceeds that standard is coercion and therefore inadmissible. For many of us that is a thrilling moral standard and one with the weight of a lot of thinkers like John Locke (*Second Treatise*, 1690) and John Stuart Mill (*On Liberty*, 1859). But libert*arianism* should not be confused with libert*inism.* The latter has to do with adoring the delights of the flesh. The former has to do with adoring freedom and the personal responsibility that goes with it. Therefore, libertarians in general are against centralized, interventionist government in the political, economic, or moral-cultural lives of the people. They are in strong support of equality before the law, but abhor any use of State power to coerce equal social outcomes. When I wrote the words above, I was excited by, but did not as yet see, all the dangers even of the libertarian position. I am still, to some extent, a libertarian in economics, but more a follower of the great conservative thinker Edmund Burke[6] in social and moral matters. The dangers of libertarianism I outline below. But I don't want to overlook its strengths.

The bulk of political writing today on the subject of freedom and State power has come from the pens of writers with libertarian sympathies in works such as Robert Nozick's *Anarchy, State, and Utopia*; Richard Epstein's *Takings: Private Property and the Power of Eminent Domain*; Charles Murray in *Losing Ground*, and David Boaz, *A Primer on Libertarianism*. Of course, there are also the works of the great Austrian writers and sympathizers such as Friedrich Hayek in *The Road to Serfdom*, and Ludwig von Mises in his *Socialism*, and in wellknown works like Milton Friedman's *Capitalism and Freedom*, and James M. Buchanan's *Limits of Liberty*. This is not a crowd of idle intellectuals, for Hayek, Friedman, and Buchanan have all won the Nobel Prize in economics.

If asked what is wrong with libertarian thought, I would say mainly only one thing: it ignores "the small patriotisms" that the conservative Burke thought were so important as instruments of local authority, such as find expression in the relationships between parent and child, teacher and pupil, elder and junior, supervisor and employee, master and apprentice, priest and congregation, and so on. It ignores the "traditions are virtues become habits" theme. Not that libertarians refute these sources of local authority, it's just that they regard them as matters of personal choice and would likely find the world (for them, at least) just as good without them or with other freely chosen institutions. Like the classical liberals before them, who went about their business pursuing individual freedom, this leaves libertarians exposed to the mob rule of the majority as it goes about its business of pursuing power. For in the sense, as Burke warned, that all that is necessary for evil to triumph is for good people to do nothing, libertarianism is socially a basket case. That's because good people doing nothing is enough for evil to triumph, but it is not enough for the good to triumph. For a true conservative, the good is not defined by temporal hopes and dreams; it is defined by reference to a transcendent moral standard of timeless and enduring moral values, the natural law, the most venerable of our customs, traditions, and institutions that we cannot hope to create on the spot, and which form the core of a free civil society.

A libertarian would respond to this complaint by saying that the "good" is a matter for individual decision; it is not pre-established by the State (or by society, or by a church). Many agree with that. The difficulty is that unless you have some shared prior notion of the good, of high moral values, and put in place institutions, laws, and customs to protect them, individual actions are based on mere personal or sectarian desire. If your definition of the good is only individual and temporal, then the moment those who believe in it die off, wiped out by a real or moral plague, the good has no social progeny, no social or cultural artefact, no "infrastructure" that continues beyond individual believers, no enduring roots. And without roots, there is no tree. That's the conservative's complaint about libertarianism, a philosophy that seems to work best in a world of educated individuals who already have a strong personal sense of responsibility. The party tends to attract such as members and candidates. It falters in the imperfect world of ordinary humankind who will tend to drift if their community is not rooted in a set of established moral values and social and political traditions defended as such. So to summarize, for a libertarian the individual is prior to civil society. For a true conservative, however, the common good of civil society, and the need for its preservation, are prior in importance to the wants of any mere individual. In this, the true conservative stands alone, aiming to preserve and protect a free civil society against the ambition of the socialist planner at the top who seeks to control society for Statist ends, but also against the radical individualist at the bottom who tends to defend mostly the aims of free and autonomous individuals, but has not much to say or to defend about civil society.

Below is a Snapshot that may interest readers who want to position themselves with respect to Canada's modern political parties.

## SNAPSHOT
The Political Parties

| | Modern Liberal | Modern Conservative | Socialist/NDP | Libertarian |
|---|---|---|---|---|
| Freedom | Freedom is only as defined by judges under charters. Likes central control. Equality trumps freedom | Emphasizes role of individual, but freedom limited by responsibility & social duties | Secondary to social outcomes. Wants social equality, freedom from class & economic oppression | Unlimited except by prohibitive law. Equality a non-issue |
| Role of Courts | Prefers judicial sovereignty to parliamentary sovereignty. Role of courts is to "correct" democracy by improving legislation | Parliamentary sovereignty is preferred, and rule of law. Judges should not make law. That is the role of legislators | Whether by judges or legislators, law must be directed to socialist policies and rights | Courts should enforce same rule of law for all and stop trying to engineer social outcomes |
| Role of Democracy | Under suspicion because "the people" are not sufficiently "liberal" | Role of the people should be defended via parliament & balanced federalism | "Social democracy" must trump liberal (individualist) democracy and rights | It's just a system and only as good as the degree of liberty it promotes |
| Role of State | Very pro-Statist, welfare-Statist, centralist for all public goods | Prefers local gov't to central. But is also Statist on social programs (b/c so politically attractive) | State must direct social & economic life. But recently willing to use capitalism for socialist ends | Very anti-state. Best gov't is least gov't. |

| | | | | |
|---|---|---|---|---|
| Role of Welfare | Seeks welfare to allow flourishing of all (giving equal fish to all) | Prefers private charities (and teaching to fish, not giving fish) but also mired in welfare programs | Welfare and universal social benefits are a right, not a privilege | Free individuals should fend for themselves. Private charity is only real charity |
| Role of Society & Family | "Progressive" universal programs used to compete with society's checkerboard care | Seeks to preserve support role of civil society. Sees State programs as intrusive (but uses them) | Seeks to equalize all family and social services | It is what it is |
| Taxation | More tax needed to grow state functions & regulation | Confused, speaks against taxation, but is big spender | Higher taxation will provide more social equality | Most taxes are legal plunder |
| Public Debt | Debt okay to achieve public services | Says it's wrong but incurs debt b/c people want both lower taxes *and* more benefits | Public debt is an investment in future generations | Robbery, just deferred taxation of future generations |
| Social Institutions | Exclusionist, too private & privileged, so regulates them | Caves in to modern liberal view (except for social conservative wing) | Seeks to universalize and tax-fund all social benefits | As you wish, but don't tell me what to do |
| Economic Freedom | Prefers public priorities to private ones, subsidizes all takers, tends to overregulation | Tends to privatize, prefers free enterprise to regulation, but also very Statist | Wants public enterprises, more regulation of wages and prices, more pro-labour laws | Wants free enterprise & private property in all things |
| Morality | Secular values, rights, & moral decisions left to courts to decide. Mostly choice based. Libertarian for personal things, socialist for public services | Upholds private moral & religious beliefs (except social cons. who fight for public morality). No longer defends public moral standards | State social and moral decisions define morality. Moral rights defined and "balanced" by courts | Morality = maximum freedom |

| | | | | |
|---|---|---|---|---|
| *Role of Religion* | A private matter. State has secular values only. Bans religion from public square | Defends religious rights but also separates from public square. Defends role of religion in moral life of society | Separation of Church and State. Secular material and social goals primary | Religion is just a personal thing |
| *Marriage, gay rights* | Homosexual marriage legalized, proudly sanctioned as a "right" | Reluctantly has gone along with gay marriage. Social cons consider it a disorder of the soul | Defends equal marriage benefits for all, easy divorce, universal tax-funded daycare | Sex, marriage, family matters private & not business of the State |
| *Abortion* | Defended as a personal choice. Unborn child not recognized as a person until "born alive" | Privately against abortion on demand, but silent on the law. Social cons wing adamantly against all abortion | Defends a woman's "right" to abort unborn human life and State funding of abortion | Abortion a personal judgment |
| *Medicare* | a universal right to state-funded care. Bans private options for basic care | Accepts universal State care, but also wants many private options available | Bans all private care; wants "free" medicare for all | Should have free market for all medical care. Get the state out of it |

# 7: CANADA AT A GLANCE
## THE GRAPHIC DETAILS

Enough of theory. The simple purpose of this chapter is to give readers an objective graphic overview of the trouble with Canada to complement the first six, more theoretical chapters, and at the same time serve as a basic reference point before heading into the more emotional issues of Part Two. Close study and reflection on these charts will repay the reader by meshing the political, economic, and social arguments in the first six chapters with the real-world consequences of the regime change Canada has experienced over recent decades.

It's very difficult for most people to determine this course. One day, we get a presumably factual report on the national debt, or the poverty level, or the personal tax rates, from one "expert"; and the next, a variation or outright disagreement from another. After a while, there is understandable cynicism and distrust in "the numbers"—especially if they are generated by governments trying to protect their reputation. In addition to such political motivation there are lots of good reasons for confusion. For example, even though governmental, academic, and think-tank organizations try to coordinate with each other, they often use different databases; some use calendar, some fiscal years; some publish in constant dollars, some in current; they use different base years to calculate trends; they have different definitions for their terms, and different countries often include different items in their reports. Enough said. There is a lot of quicksand out there. Some of these numbers (like the total national debt) are changing so fast you almost need a new chart every week. Even so, the charts that follow will give readers a grasp of where Canada was, and where it is now.

A word on sources. For the charts in this chapter I have relied almost exclusively on the fine work of two people: Niels Veldhuis, M.A., director of Fiscal Studies at the Fraser Institute, and his colleague Milagros Palacios, M.Sc., senior economist. Derek Fildebrandt of the Canadian Taxpayers Federation has also been helpful in supplying two revealing charts. These organizations, along with a number of other Canadian think tanks interested in freedom and free markets such as the C.D. Howe Institute and the Frontier Centre for Public Policy have been instrumental in alerting Canadians to the dangers of Statism for a long time. In the past half century Canada has become a markedly less free country, for many of the reasons explained in this book. But it still tolerates many private institutions without which Canadians would be far less likely to know the whole truth.

## The Comments

These charts are more or less self-explanatory. However, I have made a brief comment following each. These comments are mine alone, and are not to be understood as connected in any way with the institutions or persons that assisted in the preparation of the charts.

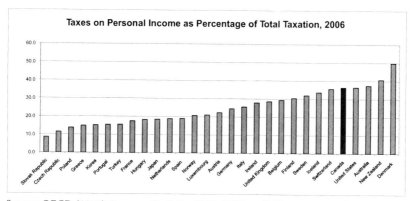

Source: OECD (2008), Revenue Statistics 1965–2007, available at www.oecd.org.

Comment: This chart tells us to what extent personal work is burdened by taxation—a lot. Income taxes imposed on Canadians as a percentage of all national taxation are at a rate close to the highest in the developed world.

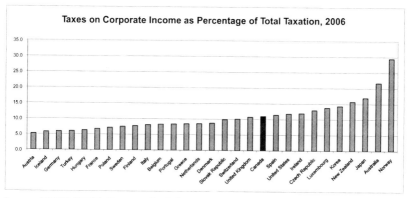

Source: OECD (2008), Revenue Statistics 1965–2007, available at www.oecd.org.

Comment: Any corporation must maintain a decent profit margin (income remaining after all expenses) to stay in business. When governments decide to tax corporations, the tax is an expense to the business, and this reduces profits. A corporation must then raise the price of its goods and services to maintain profit margins in order to yield a viable return. When it does so, the tax is effectively passed on to consumers in the increased price. Conclusion: A "corporate" tax is really just another hidden consumer tax.

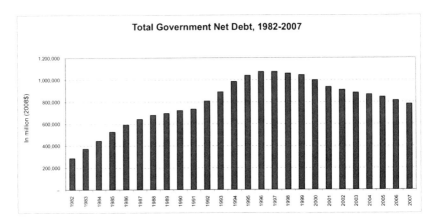

Source: Statistics Canada (2009), CANSIM Table 385-0014.

Note: Includes all levels of government: federal, provincial, and local. Data for the consolidated federal, provincial, and territorial governments are as at March 31, and the local government data are as at the end of the fiscal year closest to December 31 of the previous year.

Comment: This is a shocking picture—in constant 2008 dollars—that only looks better than in the late 1990s because it has been coming down. It had to be brought down through spending controls because had it continued, Canada would have been declared high-risk or bankrupt by the international finance community. A contention of this book is that when the Liberals under Trudeau made Canada a debt-ridden nation for the first time ever outside of wartime, they began a trend that may never be reversed. In 1993, Canada had a deficit of $38 billion, and the same year borrowed $39 billion to pay interest on our total debt. So essentially all the money borrowed in 1993 was used to pay interest on past borrowing. The grand total of all interest payments on Canadian federal debt only, since 1961, is just over $1.5 trillion (in 2008 dollars).

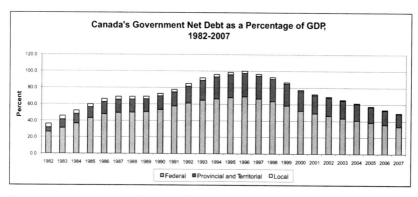

Source: Statistics Canada (2009), CANSIM Table 385-0014; calculations by authors.

Note: Includes all levels of government: federal, provincial, and local. Data for the consolidated, federal, provincial, and territorial governments are as at March 31, and the local government data are as at the end of the fiscal year closest to December 31 of the previous year.

Comment: So we touched almost 100 percent in 1996, and now are at a far better level. That is mostly because our GDP is so much higher that it makes the debt level look better, which, relatively, it is. Charts below will show the Canadian debt level per capita, by family, and by prime minister. But a better *relative* debt level is still a massive debt. Why should Canada have any national debt?

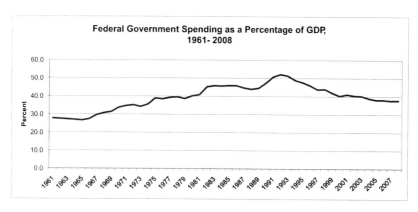

Sources: Statistics Canada (2008), Canadian Economic Observer: Historical Statistical Supplement, Catalogue 11-210-XWB, Issue 2007/08 (July), Table 3, available at http:// www.statcan.gc.ca/bsolc/olc-cel/olc-cel?lang=eng&catno=11-210-X; Statistics Canada (2009), Canadian Economic Observer (March), Available at http://www.statcan.gc.ca/ pub/11-010-x/2009003/tables-tableaux-eng.htm; calculations by authors.

Comment: The trend from 1961 onward was ominous, and after 1993 was reversed. Until the sub-prime crash, beginning in 2008 the higher GDP made our spending look better by disguising its rate of increase. But Canada's federal deficit, with spending now around the 38 percent of GDP level, is projected to be $53.8 *billion* in 2009–10, and $49.2 billion 2010–11. So this chart will tick up once again. For comparison, U.S. spending as a share of GDP has been around the 21 to 22 percent level since 1970. It shot to over 27 percent with President Obama's first budget, and is projected to average around 23 percent until 2019.

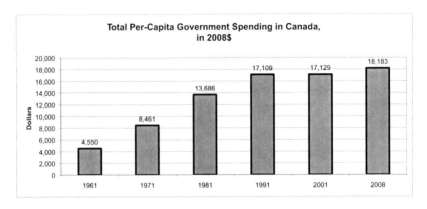

Sources: Statistics Canada (2008), Canadian Economic Observer: Historical Statistical Supplement, Catalogue 11-210-XWB, Issue 2007/08 (July), Table 3, available at http://www.statcan.gc.ca/bsolc/olc-cel/olc-cel?lang=eng&catno=11-210-X; Statistics Canada (2009), Canadian Economic Observer (March), available at http://www.statcan.gc.ca/pub/11-010-x/2009003/tables-tableaux-eng.htm; Statistics Canada (2009), Provincial Economic Accounts; Statistics Canada (various issues), the Consumer Price Index, Catalogue No. 62-001-XWE; calculations by authors.

Comment: this chart is in constant 2008 dollars, so we are comparing apples to apples, and it is for federal spending only. Thus we can easily see the impact of the relentless growth of federal government on each citizen. This load is far greater if considered as carried only by taxpayers, rather than per capita by all citizens.

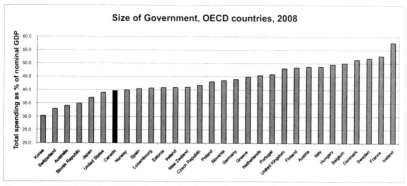

Size of Government, OECD countries, 2008

Source: OECD (2009), OECD Economic Outlook 85 (June), available at http://www.oecd.org/document/61/0,3343,en_2649_34573_2483901_1_1_1_1,00.html.

Note: Data refer to the general government sector, which is a consolidation of accounts for the central, state, and local governments plus social security.

Comment: As mentioned throughout, Canada has undergone a regime change that has validated egalitarian socialism and pointed us away from where Switzerland is now, and where we once were, to where Sweden is now on this chart. Unless we take action to reverse this trend, that is our future.

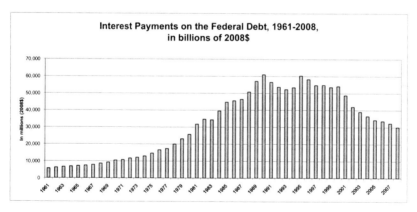

Interest Payments on the Federal Debt, 1961-2008, in billions of 2008$

Sources: Statistics Canada (2008), Canadian Economic Observer: Historical Statistical Supplement, Catalogue 11-210-XWB, Issue 2007/08 (July), Table 3. Available at http://www.statcan.gc.ca/bsolc/olc-cel/olc-cel?lang=eng&catno=11-210-X; Statistics Canada (2009), Canadian Economic Observer (March). Available at http://www.statcan.gc.ca/pub/11-010-x/2009003/tables-tableaux-eng.htm; calculations by authors.

Comment: If Canada had managed itself properly and governed with balanced budgets for all these years, all this money in interest, as well as the principle amounts borrowed, would have been saved and put to work in Canada. Outside of a temporary national crisis such as war, there is no reason for a national government to spend more than it takes in. For a country is no different than an individual or a family: like squirrels, you should put away some of the nuts when you have them, for the bad times. A person, a family, or a country living well within its means should have surpluses to tide it over in a crisis. We don't. So when the sub-prime financial crisis hit, we fell into deficit spending once again. It is hard to avoid the conclusion that all this money has been used to buy votes—but the people have not protested.

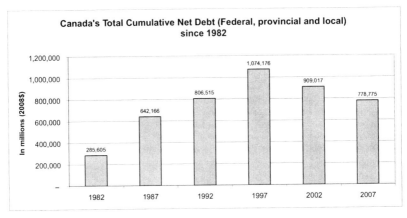

Source: Statistics Canada (2009), CANSIM Table 385-0014; calculations by authors. Note: Includes all levels of government: federal, provincial, and local. Data for the consolidated, federal, provincial, and territorial governments are as at March 31, and the local government data are as at the end of the fiscal year closest to December 31 of the previous year.

Comment: Though better now, we had over $1 trillion in total debt in 1997! Below, we will see what this means for individuals and their families. This sorry picture does not include the substantial unfunded liabilities of Canada's governments in the form of promises to pay future pensions, medical care, welfare, etc. These sums push the real 2007 total over $2.4 trillion.

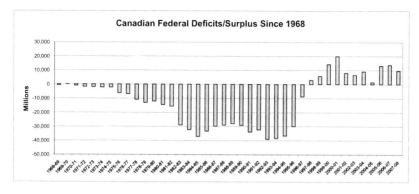

Source: Canada, Department of Finance (2000 and 2009). Fiscal Reference Tables. Available at http://www.fin.gc.ca/pub/frt-trf/index-eng.asp.

Note: Due to a break in the series following the introduction of full accrual accounting, data from 1983–84 onward are not directly comparable with earlier years.

Comment: Here is the history: improvement around the turn of the millennium; back into deep deficits with the "stimulus" spending of 2009–10. This chart illustrates well the fact that nations that carry high structural debt put themselves and their citizens in a kind of debt prison from which they may never escape. The reason? They have no room to tax citizens more heavily (already at the upper end of income confiscation), and no reserves to withstand crises. So they must fall into heavy borrowing once again.

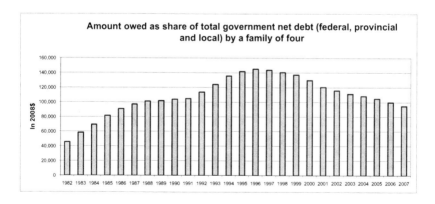

Source: Statistics Canada (2009), CANSIM Table 385-0014; Statistics Canada (2008), Quarterly Demographic Estimates, Vol. 22, no. 4, Catalogue No. 91-002-XWE, available at www.statcan.gc.ca; calculations by authors.

Comment: this makes it apparent that a young person with a spouse and two kids will be carrying (as eventual tax load) almost $100,000 in national debt incurred by predecessors, mostly for historical consumption and debt service that had little to do with those currently forced to pay. (For the individual amount, just divide by four.) If these amounts had been mostly for more permanent transgenerational things like roads, bridges, and the like—so-called infrastructure—there would be an argument it is an investment in the future. But even then, such an investment should be financed from current accounts, and not from transgenerational borrowing (debt offloaded to future generations). It is immoral to force the unborn to pay for our current consumption, and even (if to a lesser degree) for the many questionable more permanent things. Example: Canadians are still paying for the $1 billion cost of the Montreal Olympic stadium of 1976. To what extent are government projects paid for with debt financing in fact monuments to political opportunism pawned off as public benefits?

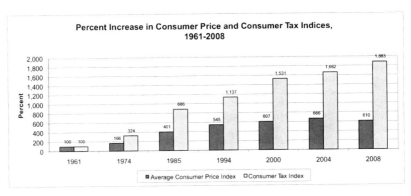

Source: Palacios and Veldhuis (2009), Taxes versus the Necessities of Life: The Canadian Consumer Tax Index, 2009, Fraser Alert (March), available at www.fraserinstitute.org.

Comment: This chart ought to embarrass any politician of whatever stripe, as nothing explains the difference in the percent increase between the CPI and the CTI other than the growth of government. Lest we forget: more taxation = more power over your life and freedom. In 2008, the CPI actually went down, but taxation continued to rise.

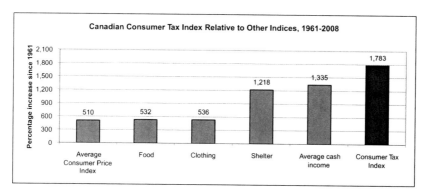

Source: Palacios and Veldhuis (2009), Taxes versus the Necessities of Life: The Canadian Consumer Tax Index, 2009, Fraser Alert (March), available at www.fraserinstitute.org.

Comment: Another embarrassing display: the State reaching ever more deeply into the pockets of hard-working citizens.

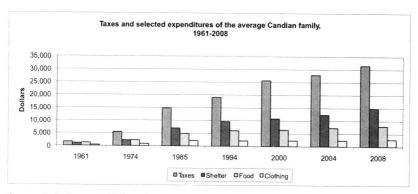

Source: Palacios and Veldhuis (2009), Taxes versus the Necessities of Life: The Canadian Consumer Tax Index, 2009, Fraser Alert (March), available at www.fraserinstitute.org.

Comment: How did we ever create a nation in which the biggest expense by far for a family is . . . taxes—double anything else? Taxes! Just pause to reflect on the difference in the situation in 1961 and 2008. These were very different worlds indeed, and Canada's regime change from a free to a Statist country is reflected here.

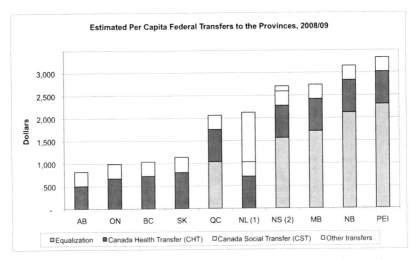

Source: Canada, Department of Finance (2009), Federal Support to Provinces and Territories, available at http://www.fin.gc.ca/fedprov/mtp-eng.asp; Statistics Canada (2008), Quarterly Demographic Estimates, Vol. 22, no. 4, Catalogue No. 91-002-XWE, available at www.statcan.gc.ca; calculations by authors.

Notes:
(1) The 2005 Offshore Accord included an upfront payment of $2 billion in 2004–05. The amounts reported here include notional allocations from the 2005 Accord and cash amounts from the 1985 Accord.
(2) The 2005 Offshore Accord included an upfront payment of $830 million in 2004–05. The amounts reported here include notional allocations from the 2005 Accord and cash amounts from the 1986 Accord.

Comment: This chart shows the extent to which tax money is being taken from all and then spread to all in the great equalization game. Recent reports show that many of the have-not provinces of Canada (in 2010–11, P.E.I, NS, NB, Quebec, Ontario, and Manitoba received $14.4 billion from the four "have" provinces) actually provide better services to their citizens than the have provinces (in terms of nurses per capita, lower average cost of university education, and so on). This is an indicator of how welfare states inevitably become mired in "transactions of decline" that drain their most successful people and regions (see "Unequal Services," *National Post*, February 25, 2010, p. A4).

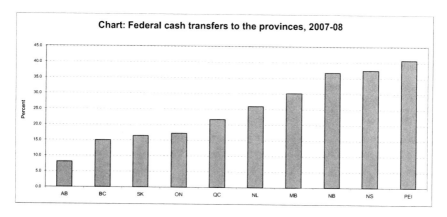

Chart: Federal cash transfers to the provinces, 2007-08

Source: The Fraser Institute, 2009.

Comment: This chart is a measure of the dependency of provinces on the federal government.

Canada's Debt Load by Prime Minister, adjusted for inflation

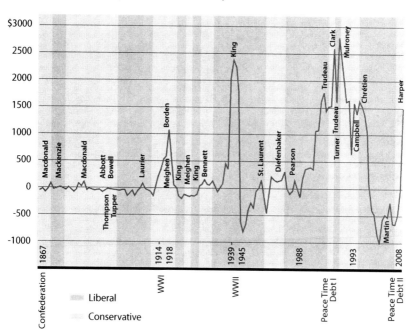

Source: Derek Fildebrandt, National Research Director, Canadian Taxpayers' Federation (November 2009).

Comment: This chart shows the inflation-adjusted, contribution per capita in annual deficits or surpluses, of the government of each prime minister from Confederation to the present. Outside of wartime, Canada avoided structural deficits until Trudeau's regime change of 1968. Note: this chart shows federal deficits/surpluses only. It does not show provincial or municipal deficits, nor any unfunded liabilities of government. Note that a Liberal PM, Jean Chrétien, actually lowered this per capita annual deficit load considerably. However, it remains the fact that post–World War II Canadian governments, whether liberal or conservative, have not been able to reverse the Canadian debt trend significantly since the Trudeau era.

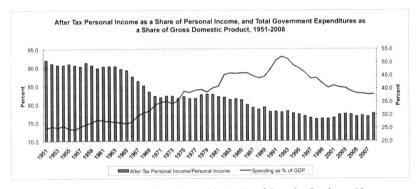

Sources: Statistics Canada (1999), Historical Statistics of Canada, Catalogue No. 11-516-XWE, available at http://www.statcan.gc.ca/bsolc/olc-cel/olc-cel?catno=11-516-X&lang=eng; Statistics Canada (2008), Canadian Economic Observer: Historical Statistical Supplement, Catalogue 11-210-XWB, Issue 2007/08 (July), Table 3, available at http://www.statcan.gc.ca/bsolc/olc-cel/olc-cel?lang=eng&catno=11-210-X; Statistics Canada (2009), Canadian Economic Observer (March), available at http://www.statcan. gc.ca/pub/11-010-x/2009003/tables-tableaux-eng.htm; calculations by authors.

Note: Includes all three levels of government: federal, provincial, and local.

Comment: This is surely the most dramatic of all the charts because it shows a direct inverse relationship between what is left in your pocket after each year of work, and the presence of government in your life. You can see the big change happening around 1968 when Canada's regime change first got under way, to be legitimized by the Charter in 1982. The rate of decline in spending as a percentage of GDP has been due partly to alarm in the international financial community at Canada's growing structural debt: "Canada: Get your house in order"—but truth to say, the percent decline looks better than it might have because of the boom economy of the decade ending in 2007.

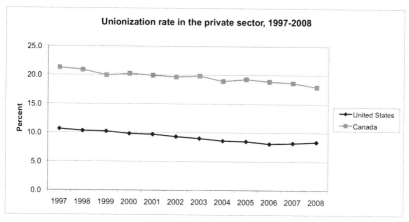

Source: Statistics Canada (2009), Labour Force Survey; Hirsch, Barry, and David MacPherson (2009), Union Membership and Coverage Database from the CPS, available at http://www.unionstats.com/

Comment: Nothing to say, except I think the decline is a good thing, and that the difference in productivity rates between Canada and the United States is partly explained by this chart.

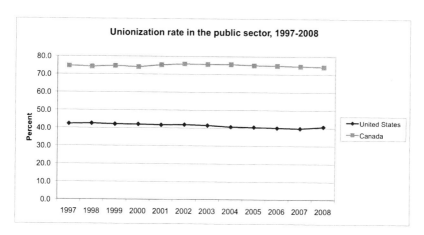

Source: Statistics Canada (2009), Labour Force Survey; Hirsch, Barry, and David MacPherson (2009), Union Membership and Coverage Database from the CPS, available at http://www.unionstats.com/

Comment: In the last chapter, I recommend the banning of the right to strike for all public unions on the grounds that such a right is in flagrantly contradicts the term "public servant." There should be no legal right to withhold services from people who are forced to pay your wages.

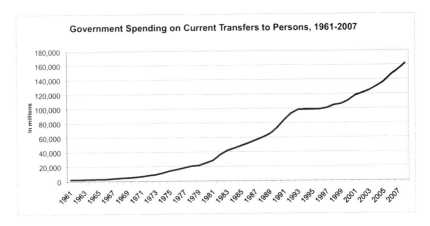

Government Spending on Current Transfers to Persons, 1961-2007

Sources: Statistics Canada (2008), Canadian Economic Observer: Historical Statistical Supplement, Catalogue 11-210-XWB, Issue 2007/08 (July), Table 3, available at http://www.statcan.gc.ca/bsolc/olc-cel/olc-cel?lang=eng&catno=11-210-X; Statistics Canada (2009), Canadian Economic Observer (March), available at http://www.statcan.gc.ca/pub/11-010-x/2009003/tables-tableaux-eng.htm; Statistics Canada (2009), Provincial Economic Accounts; Statistics Canada (various issues), Consumer Price Index, Catalogue No. 62-001-XWE; calculations by authors.

Comment: Again—in $billions you can see the uptick starting around 1968 when Canada began its regime change, one that has continued apace ever since.

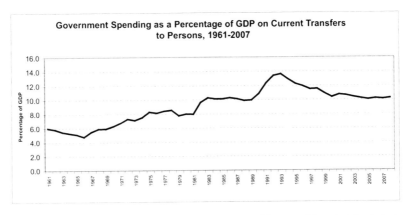

Government Spending as a Percentage of GDP on Current Transfers to Persons, 1961-2007

Sources: Statistics Canada (2008), Canadian Economic Observer: Historical Statistical Supplement, Catalogue 11-210-XWB, Issue 2007/08 (July), Table 3, Available at http://www.statcan.gc.ca/bsolc/olc-cel/olc-cel?lang=eng&catno=11-210-X; Statistics Canada (2009), Canadian Economic Observer (March), Available at http://www.statcan.gc.ca/pub/11-010-x/2009003/tables-tableaux-eng.htm; Statistics Canada (2009), Provincial Economic Accounts; Statistics Canada (various issues), The Consumer Price Index, Catalogue No. 62-001-XWE; Calculations by authors.

Comment: Again, a recent downward trend because debt was at crisis levels by 1993. But overall, the trend has been upward, and it will rise again when accounting for stimulus borrowing is included.

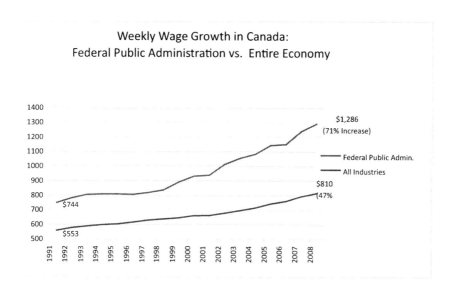

Weekly Wage Growth in Canada:
Federal Public Administration vs. Entire Economy

Comment: In 1991, federal public servants* enjoyed a "pay premium" of 34 percent compared to the average weekly wage earned by individuals working in other occupations. In other words, the average federal public servant was paid 34 percent more than the average worker in the economy for the same category of work. Since that time, wages have grown across the economy, but federal public servants have seen their wages rise at a much more rapid rate. In 2008, the average participant in the Canadian workforce earned $810 per week, an increase of 47 percent from 1991 levels. But the average federal public servant's weekly wage had swelled to $1,286, a whopping 71 percent increase from 1991 levels. As a result of this rapid pay escalation for federal public servants, their "pay premium" jumped from 34 percent in 1991, to 59 percent in 2008. If the rate of wage growth in the public sector had been held to the level of wage growth in the rest of the economy since 1991, the cost of public administration in Canada by 2008 would have been reduced by $2.5 billion a year. Repeated for each year since 1990, that would have saved Canada some $20 billion or more. Conclusion: Public sector wages must be brought into line with private sector wage growth as quickly as possible.

---

* The term "public servant" as used here refers specifically to public administration workers. These workers are defined by Statistics Canada as those: "primarily engaged in activities of a governmental nature, that is, the enactment and

judicial interpretation of laws and their pursuant regulations, and the administration of programs based on them." Source: Frontier Centre for Public Policy, October 8, 2009. [Minor editing for space by this author.]

## Total Debt Interest by Prime Minister

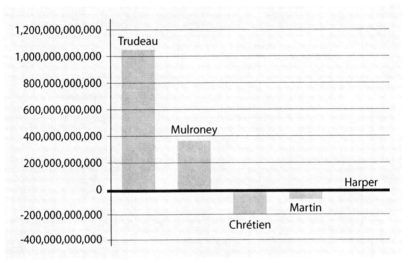

Source: Derek Fildebrandt, Canadian Taxpayers Federation, 2010.

Comment: This chart is a rough picture of the total public debt interest paid by Canada on its cumulative federal debt under each of these prime ministers, from the beginning to the end of their terms in office, and carried forward until 2014–15. The year-over-year *change* in "public debt charges" for each year for each prime minister was adjusted for inflation and then added back to each prior year's total. Upon their leaving office, the interest of their final year in office was added to itself for every year thereafter. This is a simplified representation of debt-interest charges that does not include variables such as the exact rates at which bonds were sold, or thereafter the exact amounts paid in subsequent years, and various other factors. This should be considered an *estimate* of the impact of each prime minister's deficit or surplus over this time period.

The amounts calculated, and left as a fiscal burden or benefit to the people, are as follows:

| | |
|---|---|
| Trudeau: $1,020,969,832,206 | Yes . . . that's over $1 trillion in interest payments over 42 years |
| Mulroney: $366,716,246,735 | Almost $367 billion for Mulroney over 26 years |
| Chrétien: -$176,323,026,684 | Yes, this Liberal PM has saved Canadians $176 billion in interest |
| Martin: -$64,830,138,200 | Another Liberal PM has saved Canadians almost $65 billion in interest |
| Harper: $4,712,810,470 | Back in the red again (however, this number is so small it barely registers on the graph). |

# PART TWO

## THE SHAPE WE'RE IN

# INTRODUCTION

The whole purpose of Part One was to focus on the underlying causes of the trouble with Canada, constantly keeping in mind the intelligent, interested non-specialist who will likely never have the time to explore these matters in depth, but who, intuitively dissatisfied with Canada's direction in the recent past, craves answers. I have tried to present as clearly as possible the background of the major ideological forces at work—often unperceived—in our country, and also to develop certain conceptual tools in the form of ideas and terms that help to communicate the subject.

Among those developed are concepts such as the "French" versus "English" style of governance, captured in the "top-down"/"bottom-up" distinction; the "popular illusions" that arise when a whole society goes off its moral course; the underlying philosophy and virtue of democratic capitalism as a "Freedom System"; the socialist reaction to it as a "Handicap System," complete with its "transactions of decline"; and the differences between classical and modern liberals, conservatives, and socialists. Following this, a variety of charts and profiles of opinion and fact on Canada have been presented to illustrate the real political and economic effects of our misdirected policies. In short, it has throughout been my intention to provide a foundation of concepts and language useful to the reader in the effort to understand the forces at work in the direction of our society.

Other than in books like this one, which are of necessity somewhat philosophical in tone, the way in which most people think about policy—and the philosophy from which it arises (however incoherent)—is by taking concrete positions on the issues. In the balance of this book, therefore, I will be discussing a number of issues—all currently of great concern to Canadians (if column inches in our newspapers are any measure) and will try to show how the assumptions underlying these issues arise from and are directly linked to the clash of ideologies that historically have torn at the fabric of Canadian life.

# 8: THE GREAT WELFARE RIP-OFF
## SOAKING EVERYONE, TO PAY EVERYONE

*A decent society provides*
*A ladder up which all may climb,*
*And a net beneath which none may fall.*
—old saying

*The waste is distressing, but it is the least of the evils of the*
*paternalistic programs that have grown to such massive size. Their*
*major evil is their effect on the fabric of our society. They weaken the*
*family; reduce the incentive to work, save, and innovate; reduce the*
*accumulation of capital; and limit our freedom. These are the*
*fundamental standards by which they should be judged.*
—Milton and Rose Friedman, *Free to Choose*, 1980

It is considered bad form to debunk welfare. Taboo. You risk immediate classification as a cold and heartless person. Or, perversely—in view of the fact that everyone is striving to be well off—your remarks are disqualified if you *are* well off. How could you possibly understand? So periodically we wake up to more news about how, despite Canada's economic well-being, we are failing because "5 million live in poverty"—or some such absurdity.[1]

Sixteen percent of all Canadians? Very unlikely, we think. But who are we to say? So at best we mutter disbelief to a close friend. But the chances of indulging in a full discussion on welfare or poverty in Canada are very slim for a very good reason: very few ordinary citizens *know* anything about welfare, poverty, or the needy, for the simple reason that very little is known, and what *is* known the ordinary person learns about from journalists or academics who usually support the growth of the State and are by and large shockingly uncritical.

So this chapter seeks, not to debunk poverty, but phony poverty, as a corrosive deception that clouds our understanding of the real thing, and therefore blocks the normal humanitarian feelings for the true charity that almost all human beings stand ready to provide. In this respect, nothing is quite so dangerous to an individual, a nation, or even to the poor themselves as the blind acceptance of a "condition" that many of us suspect has been largely defined by social policy experts on the government's payroll, then used as a cudgel to beat us all into a sense of collective guilt, robbing most of us of money, and the truly needy of self-reliance. How guilty, how responsible should we feel?

It depends. It depends on the truth. And even then we need to ask: Whose truth? By whose definitions? And even if true by their definitions, are the definitions good ones? Are they reasonable? Policy experts ideologically sensitive to this field will already have had indigestion by the time they've read this far. And well they should. What is going on is a scandal.

## THE WELFARE BOOM: HOW A "HAND UP" BECAME A "HANDOUT"

There is nothing more emblematic of the Handicap System outlined earlier than "social assistance," welfare, and other myriad redistribution programs that strive to fulfill the old Marxist slogan "From each according to his ability, to each according to his need." In Canada, in 2008, the federal government took a lot of money out of each province in taxes, then skimmed off a sizable commission to pay for arranging all this—how much it is impossible to discover—then sent back fully 24.9 percent on average of each province's income. The province that received the least was Alberta at 8 percent, and the most, P.E.I. at 40.7 percent. Obviously, Canada continues to play the role of Handicapper General in the old socialist-redistribution game rather vigorously. In an earlier chapter I mentioned the bizarre finding that many of the have-not provinces are actually better off than those provinces that fork over to help them!

How has this happened?

First of all, it wasn't always this way, either in the United States or in Canada, where the patterns have more or less followed those of our southern neighbour. In the United States, for reasons peculiar to its development, social problems and the social policy response to them occurred more radically and earlier than here: despite all the mythology about a rampantly individualist America, they were Statists long before us. And in this sense, the American experience has served as a huge social experiment we would do well to watch more closely. In the welfare department at least, America is a patient with a more advanced form of the same disease from which we suffer. This means we have had the opportunity of seeing the future before it arrives and of returning to good health at a lesser cost by changing the course of treatment. But instead we behave as if nothing is wrong, and wallow happily in justifications to support our sacred trusts, the universality of our social programs, and the like. But Americans passed this point a while back. Major critiques of their social policy scandal such as Milton Friedman's *Free to Choose*, George Gilder's *Wealth and Poverty*, and especially Charles Murray's two major works, *Losing Ground* and *In Pursuit of Happiness and Good Government*, unsettled the American welfare establishment. These were serious academic and, more important, moral examinations of what Western democracies have wrought with their altered sense of charity. There are few comparable major works published by Canadian authors—most of whom complain that government is not giving—or we are not getting—enough. Few, if any, ever challenge the moral basis of the social welfare state and its policies. One who does, and very ably, is Canadian professor Chris Sarlo, whose work on poverty I will discuss shortly. At any rate, both in the United States and Canada, the historical change in welfare thinking unfolds as follows.

Throughout the nineteenth century, until the early part of the twentieth, the normal conception of welfare held by most people, including by the poor themselves, was that welfare was a reward for indolence; that if given a free lunch, so to speak, most ordinary folk would choose to keep taking it and would prefer not to work. Sustained long enough, this practice would lead to whole generations of indolent people. This attitude persisted through World War II until about 1950. The reigning philosophy then was that *the needy ought to have a temporary hand up, but in no circumstances a long-term handout*. The hand up soon lets go, forcing them to climb the rest of the way on their own. The handout creates financial rewards for not climbing. Murray tells us that even President Franklin Roosevelt, who is often blamed for creating the welfare state in America through his New Deal programs, only intended his Unemployment Insurance, Old Age Security, Workmen's Compensation, and the worst of these—AFDC (Aid to Families with Dependent Children, but since renamed)—to assist *the truly needy*.

In Canada, it was the Marsh Report of 1943 that created the blueprint for the country's social welfare state. Its first serious recommendation was the extension of welfare benefits then paid to foster mothers for the care of orphans, to *all* mothers caring for their own children in their homes, well off or not. This was an example of social entropy at work as Canada moved toward sameness and loss of distinction (even though our reason for helping orphans is crucially different from any motive for helping the natural children of intact families).

In the early 1960s, when confronted with news of growing poverty in America (sensationalist news, based on very questionable assumptions, it now turns out), President John F. Kennedy, in the full flush of postwar economic growth, changed the name of the game. He made impassioned speeches saying that it was not enough for the government to give *temporary* help to the needy. It now must take *an active continuing role* in helping them. With this new attitude, the paternalistic State was assuming moral responsibility for the condition of the poor and needy—conditions previously assumed to be their own responsibility. The hand up (and then you're on your own) had become a handout (we'll help as long as you ask). Society was suddenly sliced up into two classes: no longer the responsible and the irresponsible, but *the responsible* and *the faultless*. Suddenly, poverty was *no one's* fault. Henceforth, it was declared "structural," the fault of "the system." In fact, Canada's National Council of Welfare[2] calls it "system-induced"—a perfect example of the determinist illusion gone rampant.

In Canada, this very change was echoed in the 1960 policy conference of the federal Liberal party, held in Kingston, Ontario, in which universality policies were given broad support. In the United States, under President Lyndon Johnson's Great Society programs, so much money was thrown at welfare and the needy that the Department of Health, Education and Welfare alone had a total budget greater than the GNP of most of the world's countries! During the 1970s in the United States—a trend followed obediently by Canada—"the forty-four major welfare programs grew two and a half times as fast as GNP and three times as fast as wages."[3] Concurrently in Canada, Prime Minister Pierre Trudeau and his Liberal party embarked on the most centralized social welfare experiment ever seen in our history, moving the nation from a condition in which government was more or less balancing its budgets to one in which at one point it was *spending close to 50 percent more than it took in annually*. He did this by creating a top-heavy elitist bureaucracy, raising taxes out of all proportion to other living costs, and by borrowing irresponsibly (no intent or plan to ever retreat from debt), thus committing future generations to pay for his internal empire. Alas, an overspending trend was established that was subsequently followed even by "conservative" governments—because they saw they could get away with it.

But no State can survive for long on such a basis. It turns out that, as in other socialist nations, much of this increase in social spending has resulted in the kinds of "shifting, diffusing, equalizing, concealing, shuffling, smoothing, evading, relegating and collectivizing the real risks and costs of economic change"[4] that are certain to desensitize any economy. Which is unfortunate, for just about the only thing on which poverty experts agree is that the higher the GNP, the lower the real poverty levels. In other words, we can get rid of real poverty by raising GNP—and this is the most compelling case for sticking with the Freedom System. I believe that in Canada, through a combination of private charity, good neighbours, and *some* government programs, but especially through our economic growth, we've all but eliminated real, or absolute poverty. But it's impossible, both in principle and in theory, to eliminate relative poverty because it's "distributional" in nature. Indeed, and bizarrely, we will see that Canada has a poverty-calculation system that produces higher numbers of poor . . . if we become wealthier! This chapter seeks to help Canadians avoid being taken in by such a policy sleight of hand, the disturbing consequences of which will be revealed more fully in the analysis to come. We need to understand what real poverty is—and is not—so that the natural charitable and generous instincts of the citizenry do not descend, led by bureaucratic dupery, into cynicism.

# HOW EQUAL "OPPORTUNITY" CHANGED TO EQUAL "OUTCOME"

The financial and moral cost of this disastrous shift in moral responsibility and self-reliance, from our tradition of personal freedom and responsibility for self and family, to a new ethic placing blame on "the system," has been nothing short of catastrophic. It is designed to foster resentment and dependence at every turn because it specifically positions the State as an agency able to provide equal outcomes for all. We shall see below that this is itself a bogus objective because not all, but almost all, economic inequality in free societies is a result of natural age, experience, and skill differentials, and not of discrimination or oppression. At any rate, once we jump on the envy bandwagon, the people become polarized. Like iron filings drawn to magnets, the country divides into those who produce and want to protect what they have earned, and those who want to share by right (and so, by force) in what the former have produced. In this respect, the shift from the idea of a State set up to provide and protect equal *opportunity*, to one that is expected to provide equal *outcomes*, or results, has been decisive, and has resulted in what the insurance industry calls a "moral hazard." George Gilder summed up the misguided policy effects as follows:

"The moral hazards of current programs are clear. Unemployment compensation promotes unemployment. Aid for families with dependent children . . . makes more families dependent and fatherless. Disability insurance in all its multiple forms encourages the promotion of small ills into temporary disabilities and partial disabilities into total and permanent ones. Social security payments may discourage concern for the aged and dissolve the links between generations . . . All means-tested programs . . . promote the value of being "poor" (the credentials of poverty), and thus perpetuate poverty."[5]

As if to point out the ingrained nature of this moral shift, members of the American National Welfare Rights Organization meeting in 1967 "were not demonstrating so much for jobs as for *the right to long-term, unfettered, generous charity.*"[6] These were demands by the reasonably well-off to soak their neighbours. It relied on the reverse-discrimination provisions of a newly fabricated (judge-made) "found" law to do so.[7] After this moral shift took place, hardly anyone argued that it was fundamentally wrong to take tax dollars from one worker whose paycheque, the government had decided, was too large, and give them to another worker whose paycheque, the government had decided, was too small. Ten years earlier, hardly anyone would have argued that it was right.[8]

What were some of the most deleterious effects of this elite-initiated shift in the social and moral fabric of society? The most harmful was the removal of the moral distinctions that previously had always been in place between independence and dependence, between the hard-working, honest poor, and the lazy, shiftless, dishonest poor, resulting in what Murray aptly terms "the homogenization of the poor." But the truth is that North America was built by poor people, or children of the poor, very few of whom ever *stayed* poor. And there had never been a distinct line between them and others that anyone could define. Most important, those at the bottom had their own sense of social status (dignified poor versus scummy poor) and of the many clear distinctions within that status (hard-working versus lazy). In her definitive study *The Idea of Poverty*, Gertrude Himmelfarb emphasized the importance of such distinctions, telling us that "more recently, it has been recognized that such moral concepts were an important part of the social reality for people of all classes and persuasions . . . Respectability [was] just as much a fact of life for the poor."[9]

In fact, many of the so-called poor—especially farmers—viewed themselves as "the backbone of the nation and on a considerably higher moral plane than the effete rich."[10] Those of low income were the ones who knew best the differences between the good poor and the bad, the slovenly and the hardworking, the responsible and the irresponsible, the caring and the uncaring; in short, between those who planned and worked hard for a better future for their families, and those who didn't. If they happened to fall into the net, they were aware of a complex, interrelating set of moral boundaries, sanctions, and spurs to success that inherently constituted "the ladder up which all may climb." But in one short stroke, we removed the ladder and started feeding and paying the poor to stay in the net: welfare was becoming a very attractive long-term alternative to a low-paying job. If you were poor, an alcoholic, uneducated, unemployed, or pregnant (or all those things), there would be a program for you. But if you were willing to take any job to make your own way in the world, were disciplined, respected your elders, worked hard to get ahead, kept your job, and stayed out of trouble and away from drugs and loose sex—it would be hard to qualify. From then onward, the twisted logic of the whole business was predetermined. Social policy thinking became like the snake that tries to eat its own tail. Experts began to argue that since the condition of the poor wasn't their fault, the State had to set about liberalizing eligibility standards to get rid of the stigma of welfare and preserve the dignity of the poor (something of which our self-respecting immigrant poor had never, theretofore, been deprived).

In this very same way, Canada's National Council of Welfare deplores any effort to distinguish between the "deserving" and the "undeserving" poor.[11] Murray sums up this new attitude tidily: "Because the system is to blame, all people on welfare are equally deserving of being given a hand . . . There was no longer a mechanism for stamping someone unworthy. On the contrary, *many of the social-service programs required as a condition of eligibility that the participants be failures.*"[12]

In what looks like a policy objective to create a new class of victims the state succeeded admirably. In the space of a few generations it completely eliminated ordinary—let's call it "success-morality"—from the lives of millions of people whom it began classifying as both failed and faultless. The State was investing in failure rather than success.

But the people are not stupid.

## THE ELITE WISDOM AND THE POPULAR WISDOM

Again and again, in *Losing Ground*, Murray shows how the elite wisdom of social scientists and policymakers is wrongheaded, and how the premises on which the popular wisdom is based is right on the mark. In fact, the second half of his sobering book shows clearly that "social policy since 1964 has ignored these premises and it has thereby created much of the mess we are in."[13] What are the premises of the popular wisdom, the *vox populi?*

Premise 1: People respond to incentives and disincentives. Sticks and carrots work.

Premise 2: People are not inherently hard-working or moral. In the absence of countervailing influences, people will avoid work and be amoral.

Premise 3: People must be held responsible for their actions. Whether they are responsible in some ultimate philosophical or biochemical sense cannot be the issue if society is to function.

Instead of heeding this wisdom, we have chased after the Statist ideal. And what have we created with it? The *Canada Year Book* 2008 (an annual summary of government policy results and motives) assures us that "Canada's social security system ensures that all Canadians have at least a minimum of resources available to meet their basic needs, and essential services to maintain their well-being."[14] In 2005–2006, the median government transfer to unattached individuals (and to those in families of two or more) was $3,500. In that year, an astonishing 7.9 million families (88 percent) and 3.8 million individuals (83 percent) received government transfers of some substantial kind.[15] In that year, some $183 billion taxpayers' dollars were taken by all levels of government from some citizens, and used to fund hundreds of interlocking social services programs for other citizens (often the same ones!). The *Year Book* mentions many of these programs, and alludes to many more—federal, provincial, and local. And yet there is no hint or certainty given as to who the truly needy are or precisely how recipients are being helped. In other words, monitoring and public reporting of results is minimal. This is despite the fact that we have been borrowing heavily for decades to cover cost overruns and are still doing so. It's hard to believe, but total consolidated (all three levels) government debt was fully 100 percent of GDP in 1996, a year Canada spent $62 billion on debt service alone. By 2007 things were "better," but our total debt was still at 50 percent of GDP. The federal portion alone in 2008 was at $476.9 billion and was piling up at the rate of $53,000 per minute! Check that debt meter again, at www.debtclock.ca. About 14 percent of all government spending in Canada (all three levels) is on

social assistance, the majority of which goes to "the poor." But the really important question remains to be answered: Who *are* the poor?

## THE POVERTY SCANDAL: WHO ARE THEY?

There is plenty of information about the poor in Canada that we are asked to
accept at face value, most of it prepared by sympathetic journalists, academics,
and other "poverty warriors" whose motives are impure, to say the least, because they stand to gain something in terms of income, job security, career
advancement or prestige by ensuring that Canada always has a class called "the
poor." And the story they tell always seems to be the same: there are more poor
than ever before; they are getting poorer as the rest of us get richer; Canada is
increasingly populated by the poor; our society is failing in its responsibility to
make them not-poor. But is this true? It is important to ask ourselves exactly
who the poor are, and therefore whom we should be helping (failing which,
any sane person would be justified in calling us heartless). But surely it is just
as important to ask whom we should *not* be helping because their claims to be
poor are tenuous, if not bogus. In order to increase our sensitivity to these
questions, let us try to answer the quiz that follows.

---

## SNAPSHOT
Our Attitude Toward Poverty

To which of the following persons would you give assistance if you could?
("Poor" here means someone defined as having a reported income below the
"Low Income Cut-off" [LICO] used by the Canadian government to define the
poor.)

1.  A poor person, with four kids, suddenly struck with a terrible disease.
2.  A poor, severely disabled person.
3.  A poor person struck by natural disaster such as a house fire, no insurance.
4.  A poor, elderly person with no income.
5.  A poor person who refuses to take good work offered (feels it is beneath
    him or her, or doesn't like "that kind of work").
6.  A person ranked as poor because he or she did not declare all income (like
    many other Canadians!).
7.  A poor person who continually commits petty crimes, is slovenly, untrust-
    worthy, etc.
8.  A poor person who makes good money selling his or her house or land.
9.  A poor person who has low reported income, but receives a sizable
    inheritance.
10. A poor person who has low income, but lives on an owned farm, grows

most of his or her own food, has no rent or mortgage, and decent retirement savings.

11. A twenty-year-old student in school full-time living on money from parents.
12. A poor woman who continues to have more children because she qualifies for more welfare support with each.

I am willing to bet that most people would feel a readiness to help the first four people on this list, with some qualifications, perhaps, but few, if any, of the remainder. And yet, provided the annual *reported income* of each of these people was below the "low income cut-off" (LICO) point established by the National Council of Welfare, *all of them would have been included* in the 3.3 million Canadians whom this council stated were living in poverty in 1988, just before the first edition of this book came out. That same year, an independent citizens group called the Canadian Council on Social Development (CCSD), using its own method of calculation, said that about 26 percent of all Canadians—5 million—were poor. Five million! For most sensible Canadians this smelled a lot like somebody was "lying for justice," and this made such claims easy to dismiss at the risk of also dismissing more genuine claims (assuming we can find out how these are determined). More recently, the National Council of Welfare's figure for 2006 was 3.4 million people, or 10.5 percent of Canadians, while the CCSD estimate for 2004 was 3.5 million, or 11.2 percent. The latter organization adds that between 1999 and 2004, "approximately 4.5 million Canadians experienced poverty for at least one year."

## MEASURING POVERTY

There are two common "indirect" measures of poverty used in Canada, and one for the United States. All three are indirect methods because they consider income level as a proxy for real poverty, but they are not directly connected to the cost of life's basic necessities.

For Canada, the LICO is most commonly used by Statistics Canada, and by virtually all other groups involved in the poverty lobby, and so it has acquired a quasi-official status even though Statistics Canada has repeatedly stated that "the underlying difficulty is that poverty is a question of social consensus, defined for a given point in time and in the context of a given country. *Decisions on what defines poverty are subjective and ultimately arbitrary.*"[16] Wow. That sure set the alarm bells ringing!

To its credit, Statistics Canada has stated it is well aware that its measures "are low income and not poverty measures" and that such cut-offs do not take into account such things as personal or family wealth, access to subsidized goods and services, age, future earnings potential, and the like. But this does not stop those who have something to gain from high poverty estimates from so using them. Here are some brief definitions:

*The LICO measure of poverty:*
The LICO is an income threshold below which a family is expected to spend 20 percentage points more than the average family on food, shelter, and clothing. Such a family is considered to be in "straitened circumstances" or of "low income." Using a base year of 1992, it was determined that in 2008 the average Canadian family actually spent 43 percent of after-tax income on these three items, and so the LICO for 2008 was 63 percent (adjusted for inflation, region, and family size). There is no explanation available as to why 20 percent is added, rather than, say, 10 percent, or 30 percent. This appears to be an arbitrary percentage.

When using LICO, Statistics Canada typically estimates that on average about 15 percent of the Canadian population is of low income. In 2008, the LICO for a family of four in an urban community of 30,000 to 100,000 people was set at an after-tax cash income of $29,013 in current dollars.

*The CCSD measure of poverty:*
This Low Income Measure (LIM) is the most popular measure internationally, and is equal to one-half of the "median" annual national income for a family of three, adjusted for family size (the difference between an "average" and a "median" measure, however, is quite significant. In a gradual series, which spikes up sharply, as do national incomes near the top, a median measure will always provide a lower number than will an average. An example is given in the note).[17]

*The American measure of poverty:*
The "Orshansky" method sets a poverty line equivalent to the cost of a nutritious "economy" diet, multiplied by three. So, if a nutritious economy diet costs a family, say, $800 per month ($9,600 per year), the poverty line would be $28,800.

The same year that the two Canadian organizations mentioned above made their estimates (they were apart by 1.7 million—a factor of 50 percent), Professor Christopher Sarlo, a Canadian expert on poverty definition and calculation, whose excellent work has informed much of this section, wrote that using the "basic needs," or necessities-of-life approach, "just under 1 million Canadians, or about 4 percent of the population were poor in 1988."[18]

Now, there is obviously a huge gap between saying, "There are 5 million poor" and "Just under 1 million Canadians." One or the other of these statements must surely be trivializing poverty, either by grossly exaggerating its presence, or its absence. Reading on may help us decide which is the case. Of course, most hard-working, proud Canadians find it extremely upsetting to hear that Canada has any poor at all—especially any poor children—and especially after so many billions in tax money are taken from them to resolve exactly this sort of social problem in the first place. But until they try to answer a quiz such as the one on page 188, they don't really think much about the *kinds* of poor, or about the missing moral and economic distinctions they most definitely feel ought to be preserved before we take billions of dollars from some, and hand them over to others, only to get . . . more poverty.

My bet is that after thinking about the widely varying definitions of poverty in use, our charitable feelings begin to shift a little. Especially when we learn that for LICO calculations, gambling wins and losses, capital gains or losses, lump-sum inheritances, receipts from the sale of a home or other property, personal belongings, income tax refunds, loans received or repaid, lump-sum settlements of insurance policies, income-in-kind, and subsidized goods and services (much used by the elderly, who loom large in the ranks of the poor as defined) *are all excluded.* The LICO also ignores wealth held by individuals who own their own homes: in 1980, some 44.1 percent of all those counted as poor Canadians owned their own homes, and 90 percent of employment insurance (EI) recipients in Newfoundland owned their own homes. Ten years later, about 18 percent of those counted as living below LICO, but who owned their own homes, were mortgage free. Now, a mortgage-free home can be used as collateral for borrowing to buy things like . . . food and clothing (rather than, say, taking handouts from other taxpayers). So we can see how the moral context surrounding poverty in Canada can get a little complicated (if not upsetting).

There is more. The LICO also ignores something crucial: the life-cycle aspect of people's income-earning experience. We all earn much less when we are young, and when we are old, but our poverty definitions ignore the rapid increase in earnings by the young, as well as the sudden income decline associated with aging. More disturbing is this question: Why, every year, are about 500,000 students who have incomes below $12,000, counted as poor? Obviously, they have low income because they are being supported by their parents. But once they graduate, they progress to become members of Canada's highest income-earning class for life. This is precisely the sort of count that outrages people and hardens them against charitable feeling.

Again, what about the fact that although of low *income*, the average *wealth*—their total assets comprising property and investments—of those over sixty-five who are counted as below the poverty line is five and a half times their annual income. In 1988, more than half a million Canadian seniors' households were counted as poor, even though 250,000 of them owned their own homes, 90 percent of them mortgage free. There are a lot of struggling younger householders, not counted as poor, who would love to be mortgage free.

Further to this, we get a bit of a surprise when we ask, "What are the general characteristics of poor households in Canada?" Sarlo gives Statistics

Canada information informing us that in 1991 families that were defined as poor by the National Council of Welfare had the following characteristics: 99.6 percent had flush toilets (any lacking them were in rural areas); 99.1 percent had refrigerators; about 50 percent had automatic clothes washers and dryers; almost 50 percent had freezers; 97 percent had telephones; 97 percent had radios; 97 percent had colour TVs; 34 percent had VCRs; 67 percent had cable TV; and 53 percent had at least one automobile.

By now most readers have become a little suspicious and are wondering why our governments and our various poverty agencies are using definitions that are so loose and relative, instead of a more absolute measure.

## THE DIFFERENCE BETWEEN "RELATIVE" AND "ABSOLUTE" POVERTY CALCULATIONS

Much of Sarlo's work has been dedicated to persuading poverty experts that the standard methods for estimating poverty—especially the LICO—are too relative and accordingly lead to a gross exaggeration of the number of poor in Canada: calculations based on relative or absolute poverty measures can produce differences in the order of millions of people.

Even more damning for the LICO system, however, are the following bizarre but logically inevitable conclusions it produces:

1) More national wealth will mean . . . more poor!

If you use LICO to calculate the number of poor, you end up in a situation where, as mentioned, if there are suddenly a greater number of wealthy people in Canada—say, one hundred more millionaires next year—there will, by this definition, automatically be a few hundred thousand more poor . . . even though the objective condition of the poor has not changed. In other words, if real incomes were to double, or even triple, over time, enabling all to have far more purchasing power, but with no change in the distribution of wealth, the proportion of poor in the population would remain unchanged.

2) Those objectively poor will be defined as . . . not poor.

If used in a country where everyone is objectively very poor in terms of lacking basic needs such as food, shelter, and clothing, a relative calculation will show that such a country has almost no poor, because no one has a high income relative to which they can be measured as poor. So, *in the poorest society we can imagine, there would be no poor?* Clearly, the LICO is a failed method for measuring poverty. Further, if we were to use the CCSD measure for a very poor country—half the average income (where average is bare survival)—the definition would have everyone dead!

3) The poor are created by the definition itself.

Once we decide to use a relative-poverty definition, it is meaningless to think of ever eliminating poverty, for you cannot eliminate something created by the definition itself.

The conclusion to which a reasonable person is forced by these facts is that Canada's definition of poverty has little to do with real poverty (a lack of life's basic essentials) and is, in fact, a measure of *income inequality* falsely presented as poverty. If income inequality is the right standard, then, compared to, say, Wayne Gretzky or Oprah Winfrey, almost everyone in the world would be counted as poor.

Neither should we fail to notice that income inequality has little to do with *wealth*, for the reason that a person can be very wealthy (own a home, a car, a boat, stocks, a cottage, etc.), but arrange to have very little actual cash income. Indeed, smart people try to arrange their financial affairs in just such a way to avoid excessive income taxation. Note also that I have not bothered to mention that poverty warriors only count *reported* income. The cash-and-barter underground economy in Canada has been variously estimated at 5 to 8 percent of GDP, or to be conservative, somewhere between $50 and $100 billion annually. So we know there is a significant black market of unreported income in Canada, and we also know that the poor are involved, because when governments compare welfare outlays to the reported incomes of poor families, they find that underreporting (noted by Statscan) is about 20 percent for employment insurance cases, and about 40 percent for cases of social assistance. That's a whopper.

## WHAT ABOUT COMFORT POVERTY?

Of course, there are many poverty activists who argue sincerely that relative poverty is, in fact, the best measure to use because poverty to them is as much "psychological" as physical. They insist that the traditional notions about basic needs are "Victorian" and "mean-spirited" because people who fall behind others in the race of life, even when they have all the basic necessities, do not enjoy a "decent" standard of living and so ought to be classified as living in poverty. Further, they say that because no one owns the resources of the planet, everyone has a right to share in the wealth of society equally; and that share ought to be linked to what anyone may reasonably be expected to enjoy in terms of social well-being.

This argument has a certain moral force, and it adds an entire social needs layer (the right to have vacations, birthday parties for their children, people over for dinner, etc.) to the basic needs argument outlined below. In other words, this lobby maintains that poverty is *properly defined* as income inequality, rather than according to fulfillment of basic needs. But above, we saw what a morass of confusion such a definition generates, and this seems to be inescapable.

In addition, there is the concern that as a whole society gets wealthier, poverty lobbyists are driven to rely on ever-softer definitions of poverty in order to feed their lobby. In short, poverty lobbyists *need* a class called "the poor," and will rejig their definitions accordingly. But the ordinary person, even many of the poor themselves, rest their case for defining poverty on the fulfillment of basic human needs; always have, and always will.

## THE ALTERNATIVE—RESTORE THE
## BASIC NEEDS APPROACH

As Sarlo maintains, most people the world over have always considered real (as distinct from social) poverty to be a matter of a genuine deprivation of life's basic needs, and he argues persuasively that "by including as 'poor' those who are merely 'relatively less well off' we do a great disservice to the genuinely deprived."[19] In addition, *we repel the most charitable instincts of caring citizens*, and thus do a disservice to the entire cause of helping the truly needy. So the most important motive for getting our definition right is that we can then get our morality right. On this score, and like most other citizens, Sarlo would not be opposed to some additional measure of economic or social "comfort" beyond the basic needs. But that is a very different thing from an assessment of true poverty, for as he puts it, most people would agree that "not having alcohol, tobacco, a one week holiday at a cottage and costly recreation does not make one poor."[20]

Here is Sarlo's description of what constitutes the basic needs of human life, the world over, for all time, and in most places—at least in the developed world. He is quick to point out that these necessities are absolute with respect to type (such as food, shelter, clothing), but relative with respect to quality and kind (basic shelter in Canada may mean a rented apartment, in Somalia a decent mud hut, in the High Arctic, a good igloo). Here are the basic needs based on Canadian standards of acceptability: a variety of popular, nutritious foods purchased at grocery stores that fulfill the complete balance and energy requirements according to the Canada Food Guide; apartment rental accommodation with the number of rooms appropriate to family size and with the full complement of essential furnishings, necessary household supplies and a telephone; clothing, which is purchased new, appropriate to the season, and with replacement rates assuming normal wear and laundering; and a full range of regular, preventative, and emergency health care including personal hygiene, dental and vision care. Finally, essential transportation linking one's shelter to [the procurement] of other basic needs must be included even though not itself a basic physical necessity. The sum of the costs of these items for families of given size constitutes a basic needs poverty line.[21]

To this list Sarlo later added "other basic needs" such as apartment insurance, laundry expenses, public transportation or vehicle costs, personal-care items, out-of-pocket health care, and miscellaneous items such as photocopying, stamps, library cards, and the like.

Because we are talking about Canada, and not a truly poor place on earth such as Bangladesh, this description of poverty would very likely constitute "poverty plus" to a lot of people in the world. But that is another discussion (see Snapshot on comparative poverty measures, below).

Using the above descriptions for calculation, Sarlo presented the following table for 1988. The difference in results is pretty clear:

|  | *CCSD* | *LICO* | *Sarlo's Basic Needs* |
|---|---|---|---|
| Poverty Line ($ income) | $26,941 | $22, 371 | $13, 140 |
| Canadian Poverty Rate (percent) | 15.4 | 10.1 | 2.5 |
| Number of Poor Families | 226,262 | 172,115 | 43,292 |

(For comparison purposes, these families were assumed to reside in a community of 100,000 to 500,000 persons. Transportation in this definition means whatever means of getting about is required to obtain the other necessities.)

With the exception of a telephone, he remarks that his basic needs method would have held good to define the poor "even 200 years ago." One could quibble with even this list, of course, because it is easy to imagine a contented minimalist, or a priest, or a student living by choice in a major city without a telephone, or a television, or much furniture, and without caring much about having regular shampoo or toothpaste, or ever bothering to see a doctor, and yet whom we would not consider poor.

The important point, however, is that Sarlo has thrown down the gauntlet as an appeal for honesty in definition, and on behalf of all the people who pay the shot. Us. In an email communication to this author describing his 2008 effort to define poverty in Canada,[22] Sarlo wrote:

"I really like this piece because I do several important things: provide the latest update on poverty rates; challenge relativists using their own words that clearly contradict their idea of poverty; challenge the Canadian government on poverty measurement and poverty alleviation based on their own public commitments; and also challenge Statistics Canada to look at and improve the quality of the data that we all use to measure poverty and inequality."

To this we must say: Bravo! This search for a standard of truth in defining poverty took a lot of courage in an ideologically pro-poverty environment.

What is clear from the most recent assessment efforts is that poverty rates in Canada have declined rapidly over the past decades from about 12 percent of the population in 1969 to about 3 percent by 1974, and then by some measures they have slowly drifted upward—especially child poverty—to about 4.5 percent by 2005. But by other measures they have drifted downward. The available data are simply too mixed and confusing to provide any sharper conclusions, other than to say that poverty in Canada seems to have settled in at somewhere around the 3 to 5 percent level depending on which methods and data are relied upon.

What follows below is my own comparison between what I would take to be real, anguishing poverty, Sarlo's basic needs, and the LICO relative measure.

## SNAPSHOT
On Poverty

| | Real Poverty | Sarlo's Basic Needs Poverty | Relative Poverty (LICO) |
|---|---|---|---|
| *Food* | Catch as catch can. Minimal daily calories. Often misses meals. Two meals per day = lucky. Spotty nutrition, some malnutrition, food banks, and begging | Full range of popular nutritious foods re: Canada Food Guide, no food banks or begging, three meals/day | Spends adjusted 43 percent of income on the three basics of food, clothing and shelter (has 57 percent of income left over for other purchases) |
| *Housing* | Living free with friends and/or relatives, works for rent, has few rooms, or shares room(s) with others | Rents apartment with rooms appropriate to family size, has household insurance | Many own condo/home which has appropriate rooms for family size, and home insurance |
| *Clothing* | Same old clothes always second-hand learns to sew, launder by self, inadequate for winter, mostly donated clothing | All clothing purchased new, appropriate to season, laundered, replaces with new, pays for laundry | As for basic needs + other affordables from 61.5 percent of income, laundry machines, buys/replaces clothes new |
| *Furnishings/ Accessories* | No owned furniture, no phone, no regular supplies | Owns all essential household furnishings new, all new supplies, has phone | As for basic needs + other affordables, bought new |
| *Health Care* | As prepaid by government, cannot afford any out-of-pocket care or preventative care, dental and eye care only as provided by gov't | Full range of regular preventative, and emergency health care and personal hygiene items & dental and eye care and out-of-pocket health care | As for basic needs + other affordables for personal care and out-of-pocket health care |
| *Transportation* | Walks everywhere, occasional public transit, or hitches rides | Has vehicle or sufficient for public transit | May own personal vehicle or pays full public transit |
| *Miscellaneous* | No extras, gets these free from others or goes without | Can afford photocopying, stamps, library cards, etc. | Can afford photocopying, stamps, library cards, etc. |

# THE DIFFERENCE BETWEEN EQUALITY AND EQUITY

The question of equality is deep and dangerous—it upsets a lot of people because they equate equality with justice, and therefore with rights of one kind or another (take your pick). But if asked, these same people usually cannot define the difference between "equality" and "equity" without a little pondering.

By "equality" we tend to mean "everyone must be treated the same," or all must receive the same shares of or value in something or other. For example, in a democracy today we say everyone (even prisoners) must have an equal vote—one person one vote. And in countries derived from the English way of life, we say that all must be treated equally under the law. As parents, we are very careful to "treat our children equally" in family life and in our wills.

But "equity" is another matter. It has more to do with what is *deserved* than with what is *equal*, and therefore with a very different notion of justice about which we can get just as worked up. For example, when it comes to distributing shares of a company to owners, we don't do it on the basis of equality, but of equity. That is, we do it on the basis of cash equity (cash invested), or so-called "sweat" equity (crucial work or concepts contributed). And we pay employees according to what is deserved for the different jobs they are doing, not by some measure of equality.

Even so, while it is true in a modern democracy that all citizens have an equal vote, no one is fooled into believing that this is equitable, because they know that the vote of a deranged prisoner is probably worth a lot less than the vote of a very wise and responsible citizen. Indeed, in Britain until the early twentieth century, many educated people had the right to "plural" votes—as many as six each—for that very reason. And when it comes to things like our last will and testament, we may change the shares or amount going to a child who has morally wronged us or others, or cut them out entirely, and we would defend this passionately, not as "equal," but as "equitable"; we would say they got what they bloody well deserved, and no more.

So equality has to do with the mathematical and often artificial attribution of equal proportions, or rights, or amounts, on the (I think often false) assumption that all entities under consideration are exactly the same.

Equity, in contrast, has to do with the just, but unequal, attribution of benefits or rewards or responsibilities. Examples include: welfare (we give it to the poor, not to the rich); obligations (adults have legal and moral obligations, children do not have); material rewards (we give more pay to those who contribute more, or have more skill, or brighter ideas); allocation of responsibility (we expect more from those in positions of authority). In other words, equity always points to what is naturally deserved or expected in the circumstances, which in the ordinary course of life may be altered by age, biology, gender, moral justice, skill level, intelligence, and other similar factors.

## EQUALITY HAS REPLACED EQUITY

Accordingly, I propose here a theory of modern civilization to the effect that over the course of the past two or three centuries there has been a relentless effort that has been growing in intensity in all the Western democracies to replace the time-honoured moral principle of equity with the political principle of equality. Which is to say that there has been a slow but steady levelling tendency aimed at eradicating the natural differences between human beings and their social and biological circumstances, such that equalization has replaced just deserts; sameness has replaced difference; a demand for equality has replaced a demand for equity.

This is the root source of so many modern affirmative action policies (meant to compensate for racial, gender, socioeconomic, or intelligence differences deemed to be a result of social inequalities or injustices). Another visible manifestation of the equality drive has been the attack on privilege and exclusion of all kinds in the interests of engineering a wholly imaginary equal society. So, male members of a golf club, say, find themselves under attack because they have a men's-only barroom (though no one presently bothers to protest women's-only clubs, or women's facilities that provide lounge chairs in their washrooms to ease monthly cramps, or pregnancy fatigue, nor do they complain when women are not required to lift the same loads as men, nor to run as fast as men in full battle dress, and so on). Nevertheless, more equality is the trend.

Whence comes this trend? A short answer is that we are witnesses to, and agents of, the flourishing of a very ancient religious myth of human equality as it was presumed to exist in the Garden of Eden prior to the Fall. Modern democracies are busy promoting a secular version of this as a dream world of human perfection as they imagine it must have been before we became fallen, or bad. We imagine that in this perfect dream world people were once equal in all ways (before social and economic oppression, class differences, rich and poor, private property, and so on), and that back then we all enjoyed the fruits of the earth in common. This was the theme song of international communism, as it is today of the growing "international ethics" movement (if for different reasons).[23]

So even though in this secular dream world God and religion are long gone (chased out of the democratic public square), the thesis is that the moral and cerebral wiring of the Western (Judeo-Christian) world has remained the same. This is called the "secularization thesis" (not my term) and it is the strongest explanatory framework for the modern egalitarian myth now controlling so much national social policy in the post-Christian West. It deserves the name of myth because even though no such human society has ever been seen in all of history, it is the wholly imaginary assumption against which our political, economic, and social life is now measured. And this is why, whenever there are discussions of what constitutes "a just society," these two terms—equality and

THE TROUBLE WITH CANADA ... STILL! 199

equity—are so often confused (sometimes quite intentionally if there is political advantage on offer).

For example, people tend to react with a sense of deep injustice when they see the table below because it shows that the per-quintile *shares of income in Canada have remained amazingly stable for almost fifty years.* Is this not outrageous? Hasn't Canada been transferring gazillions of dollars from one Canadian to another for the same half century, precisely to make incomes more "equal"? So then, how come the top fifth has as much after-tax income as the bottom three-fifths put together? After so much frantic redistribution in the sacred name of equality, why are the shares of income uncannily the same, year after year?

Distribution of Total Canadian Income by Percentage
by Household Quintile shares—1951–1999[24]

|      | Bottom | Second | Middle | Fourth | Top   |
|------|--------|--------|--------|--------|-------|
| 1951 | 4.4    | 11.2   | 18.3   | 23.3   | 42.8  |
| 1975 | 4.0    | 10.6   | 17.6   | 25.1   | 42.6  |
| 1999 | 5.45   | 11.0   | 16.80  | 22.88  | 43.87 |

Indeed, when social activists (who want everyone to be more "equal" in income) see this table, they all but weep over the lack of "equality," and immediately insist it is hard evidence of a lack of "progress," adding how "unfair" the capitalist "system" is.

However, these same critics, if pressed, would not likely say that a young worker ought to be paid the same as an older, more experienced worker, or that a plumber ought to be paid the same as an aeronautical engineer, or a student the same as a professor. No, they would say: that would not be "equitable," or "fair." In short, these two standards remain in tension and conflict in our civilization. We want things to be equal, but also fair, even though (to be fair), many things must be, and are understandably, and quite naturally, indeed ought to be, unequal. In fact, even the most radical social activist would scream "unfair!" if told that to establish true social equality, his or her paycheque at sixty-five years of age will have to be the same as the paycheque received by all twenty-year-olds, or that when that individual is promoted to a managerial position, that paycheque must be the same as when he or she was an incoming labourer. Just so, as it turns out, almost all the differences in per-quintile shares of income in Canada (and in most other countries) are a result of real differences in skill and age throughout the life cycle. The bottom quintile in Canada, for example, almost entirely comprises retirees (many of whom, as we saw, tend to have sufficient wealth, but low income).

And then, if we go further with a mind experiment and imagine that all citizens earn exactly the same total *lifetime* income, it doesn't take a lot of figuring to realize they earn different amounts at different ages and skill levels, and so their earnings would be counted in each quintile accordingly, as they travel through the cycle. In other words, as long as society comprises large numbers of people of different ages, skill levels, aptitudes and experience, the life-cycle pattern of earnings we see in the table will always be the same. It is written, as they say.

So it seems that a society that is sufficiently free to permit income differences and mobility based on equitable rewards for age, experience, and skill *will always fail on the equality scale.* Which is another way of saying that it is only if all workers were of the same age, experience, and skill level at all times that all incomes could ever be equal. But only then.

A conclusion? In the name of a foggy-headed equality myth, dreamworlders have constructed an elaborate ideal of a fair and just society, even though *no case has ever been satisfactorily made that society would be morally, economically, or productively better if incomes were the same for everyone.* The larger complaint about the unfairness of the entire capitalist system is also weak, because the very same life-cycle shares of income hold steady as a rock even among public sector employees within capitalist societies, and also within all socialist States.

## INTERNATIONAL REDISTRIBUTION

So much for the effect of income redistribution policies *within* Canada. Is there any evidence that democratic capitalist nations have income distributions worse than the hard-core socialist nations? None. So wrote Harvard University's Barrington Moore Jr. in his now-classic *Authority and Inequality Under Capitalism and Socialism*: "Though the determinants of the position on the ladder are different, mainly economic in the USA and mainly political in the USSR, the distance from the bottom rung to the top one turns out to be about the same in both cases."[25] As two upset reviewers of this excellent little book said of Moore's conclusion, "We should understand just how jarring [this conclusion] is. One of the great, generally unchallenged, 'laws' of social sciences is that centrally-planned economies trade freedom for equality, an exchange many American academics are willing to make . . . The implication is that while Capitalism is better at producing wealth, Socialism is better at distributing it . . . Not only do most social scientists accept the existence of this trade-off, they virtually never subject it to even moderately systematic examination." In other words, egalitarian nations are no more "equal" in incomes, nor in any other sense, than the free nations of the world. And so, these authors conclude: *"The traditional notion that freedom is exchanged for equality under socialism has no basis in fact."*[26]

Moore shows what an intellectually dishonest, rickety mess this is, and concludes that *there simply is no particular relationship between political systems and equality*—although, again, there is a very strong (84 percent) correlation between having better income at all levels and GNP. Sadly for much of the world, says Moore, the only way socialism can survive is by encouraging scarcity. This is what gives it its authority, for *"the power to ration is the power to rule."* Canadians take note! Moore stresses, finally, the fact that although there is much talk about the national and international power of corporations, this is chaff, mere idle chatter and propaganda, for the power they exert in no way resembles the massive authority that socialist officials can exert over the livings and lives of millions of subjects.

So much for "redistribution" as an excuse for those who promote Statism. Less bread, but more legislative and regulatory—as well as real—barbed wire seems to be the rule. These facts, these truths of history, rightly dissolve most of the flimsy egalitarian arguments used to overturn society in the name of a new Garden of Eden.

## THE COMING NIT IDEA—WATCH OUT!

Canada, in its despair over the moral-hazard effects of welfare that I've been describing, has flirted from time to time with the negative income tax idea (NIT), or what we innocently call a "basic income supplement." That's a fancy expression for a graduated subsidy, by which recipients would receive a cash payment to bring them up to a specified income level. Theoretically, this would replace all other benefits, as well as the considerable load of bureaucracy that comes along with it. What toying with this idea amounts to is a recognition by governments that welfare doesn't work—"so let's just give them the money!"

This idea gained great credence when it suddenly got support from Milton Friedman in his book *Capitalism and Freedom*, in 1962. He calculated that if you took all the money that the welfare system costs the United States and sprinkled it among the poor and the needy, each would receive about [on today's terms] $50,000 annually! So, the thinking went, why not just *give* them the money? Of course, it's not that simple. Nevertheless, Canada has periodically flirted with this idea. But before leaping into another abyss, we would be well advised to consider the now-famous SIME/DIME experiment conducted to test precisely this idea.

The Seattle (and Denver) Income Maintenance Experiment of 1971–1978 —called SIME/DIME for short—was the creation of an enthusiastic union between modern social policy researchers and idealistic government bureaucrats from the U.S. Office of Economic Opportunity (OEO) in the mid-1960s. No study since has come close to this one in scope or detail. The agency's sole and express purpose in creating the experiment was to *prove* that the only way to win the war on poverty was to use some form of Guaranteed Income

Supplement. "Somehow, *proof* must be established that a guaranteed income would not cause people to reduce their work effort, get married less often, divorce more quickly, or any of the other things that the popular wisdom said it would cause them to do."[27] Charles Murray wrote that the OEO's proof "took the form of the most ambitious social-science experiment in history. No other even comes close to its combination of size, expense, length, and detail of analysis." The study used 8,700 people as subjects, and lasted ten years. (A planned twenty-year sub-sample was cancelled in 1980.) One hundred research articles were published from the data, and it cost many millions of dollars. As Murray put it, "The proponents of the NIT in the Johnson administration were out to slay the folk-beliefs that welfare makes people shiftless. The NIT, properly redesigned, would provide work incentives and get people off the welfare rolls."

The experiment took large low-income groups in Seattle and Denver and told half of each group that they would be guaranteed no less than the official poverty-level income if they couldn't earn it. The other half was on its own and would receive no benefits or guarantees whatsoever. What was the result? Here's a summary.

1.  The guaranteed income group reduced their work effort "by 9 percent for husbands and by 20 percent for wives." These reductions were mostly caused by dropping out of the workforce altogether. Analysts said this was a particular disaster because it was often the wives who could lift families out of poverty.
2.  Even more disastrous: the hours of work per week put in by young males not yet heads of families was reduced by 43 percent! Just when they should be preparing for family life, they dropped out of the race. Even when these people married, their work effort was still down 33 percent.
3.  Periods of unemployment claimed by members of the experiment who lost their jobs were lengthened by 27 percent for husbands, 42 percent for wives, and 60 percent for single female heads of families.
4.  The dissolution of marriage was far higher for all those receiving the guaranteed income payments than for those who did not.

The economist Martin Anderson, using elaborate and detailed analysis of the NIT experiment, estimated that if the NIT were applied nationally, it would, on an average-case basis, result in a 60 percent reduction in national work effort. Further, the work reduction observed was over and above reductions already experienced as a result of existing welfare programs. In short, "the NIT experiment made a shambles of the expectations of its sponsors. But at the same time it was being conducted, the disincentives it would later demonstrate were being woven into the fabric of the welfare system."

The mere idea that Canada's social engineers would ever *consider* such a scheme—which they do periodically—in the face of such a volume of conscientious proof that it can't possibly work, is a mark of gross moral and intellectual incompetence.

This chapter has examined some of the facts, arguments, moral bases, and misconceptions surrounding Canada's welfare system. As a service to readers who may be wondering how much room Canada has to play fast and loose with more social spending, I present the sobering Snapshot below.

Canada's *total direct debt* (federal, provincial, and local) has been referred to elsewhere in this book. As of 2008 it amounted to $23,651 for each and every citizen; and for each family of four (in 2008 dollars) was $94,605. That is the amount that government will eventually have to extract from each of us. It is called "government debt." Strictly speaking, however, as government has no money of its own, there is no such thing as "government debt." It is always personal debt (again, corporations "pay" taxes, too. But they get the money they need to pay all their expenses, including their taxes, from consumers).

On top of all this, Canadian governments have made promises to provide various future benefits and programs (such as Old Age Security—OAS, "free" medicare, and the Canada Pension Plan—CPP, as discussed above) that have never been properly funded. They are PAYGO schemes, funded from current tax revenues. The original justification was that a lot of younger workers could easily fund a smaller number of retirees. But whereas in 1965 only 7.7 percent of Canadians were over sixty-five, by 2040, that figure will be 26.5 percent. The State will really have to soak the young to meet these promises, or renege on the promises by delisting certain medical services, by further clawing back OAS payments, by reducing pension promises, and by extending the age of retirement. Watch for it.

In closing, I give a brief summary of the total current unfunded liability of Canadian government that will have to be settled by taking more of your money . . . to give some of it back to you.

---

## SNAPSHOT
Canada's Direct Debt and Unfunded Liabilities
$150,200—For Every Man, Woman, and Child (as of 2009)

Total Consolidated Government Liabilities as of 2004–05
These liabilities include direct debt, debt guarantees, contingent liabilities, contractual commitments, and program obligations (OAS, medicare, CPP, Workers Compensation, and pensions). Here is the breakdown in detail, in millions (so add *six zeroes* to each of the numbers below, to arrive at the $billion—or $trillion—amounts):

| | Contingent Liabilities | | | |
|---|---|---|---|---|
| | Direct Debt | Debt Guarantees | Contractual Commitments | Program Obligations | Total Government Liabilities |
| Canada (All-inclusive) | 791,191 | 128,793 | 184,427 | 1,324,896 | 2,429,307 |
| | | | | | So about $2.4 trillion |

The $1,324.9 billion shown above as "program obligations" includes the unfunded liabilities of CPP, OAS, and medicare. The breakdown for each of these unfunded liabilities is as follows:

| Fiscal Year | CPP | OAS | Medicare | Total |
|---|---|---|---|---|
| 2000 | 443.0 | 279.3 | 301.5 | 1,023.8 |
| 2001 | 466.1 | 299.2 | 323.0 | 1,088.4 |
| 2002 | 507.5 | 315.9 | 331.1 | 1,154.5 |
| 2003 | 516.3 | 337.8 | 347.0 | 1,201.1 |
| 2004 | 538.4 | 355.7 | 364.0 | 1,258.1 |
| % Increase 2000–2004 | 21.6 | 27.3 | 20.7 | 22.9 |

To this total ($1,258.1 billion) must be added a further $66.8 billion for federal pension plan benefits, Workers Compensation, and QPP (Quebec Pension Plan) liabilities, to arrive at a total program obligation for Canada of $1,324,896,000,000 (roughly $1.3 trillion).

Summing these amounts produces a deferred tax liability of $150,000 for every Canadian citizen.

(Breakdown supplied by Milagros Palacios, Senior Research Economist, Fraser Institute)

## WHAT IS TO BE DONE?

We have gotten ourselves into an awful mess, and there is probably only one way out of it:

1.   As a society, we must recognize and promote the hard truth that the only certain and self-respecting escape from poverty comes through hard work,

and (an unfortunate truth) the poor often have to work harder than any-one else if they expect to escape—not less hard.

2. Scrap the entire unwieldy, morally depressing mess of welfare programs and the bureaucracy that sustains them. Scrap them slowly, and humanely, but scrap them. As Murray advises: "Leave the working-age person with no recourse whatsoever except the job market, family members, friends, and public or private locally-funded services. It is the Alexandrian solu-tion: cut the knot, for there is no way to untie it."

3. Provide only emergency and in-kind assistance to the able-bodied of work-ing age. Some suggestions to improve EI would be: 1) lower EI payments to 50 percent from the 55 to 60 percent now paid, to a maximum of $400 per week; or, put all EI recipients on a decreasing-payments scale from 80 percent to 30 percent at the thirtieth week of unemployment, etc.

4. Use "workfare" for the able-bodied of working age who want help from the State (Canadians have often said in polls that *welfare recipients should be made to work*). Try "educafare": if you want EI, you have to attend edu-cational-upgrade classes, and job-search classes. Ensure that personal net wealth is checked out (any inheritance, ownership of home, savings, etc.) prior to giving other people's money to anyone.

5. Murray again: provide "billions for equal opportunity, not one cent for equal outcome, because government cannot identify the worthy, but it can protect a society in which the worthy can identify themselves."

6. Establish hard criteria to define the helpless and truly needy of society, and means tests to guarantee the public that their money is not wasted. Make them feel good about helping the "truly needy" (but only when and after their own families, friends, and communities have failed them). This ensures that the important moral pressures that two generations of wel-fare warriors have worked hard to eliminate will come roaring back, and stay in place, keeping the State and its egalitarian ideology out of the lives of the people.

7. Accept the fact of life that in a society built on individual freedom and responsibility there is no way to remove the stigma of welfare (the only way such a stigma can be removed is if those who take something free from society in some way repay it); rather, ensure that society vigorously promotes the surefire ways to avoid welfare: hard work, staying on the job, better education, and strong family roots. Ensure that welfare is the last thing for which anyone tries to "qualify." The *Economist* once reported that anyone who: keeps a first job for at least one year, gets a high school educa-tion, and gets married, has a less than 1 percent chance of staying poor.

8. We must publicly reject the whole misleading promise—the lie—of Statism and its false confidence in economic equality as a panacea for society's ills. That is an unachievable, top-down lie promoted mostly to

bolster government itself, and not as a justification for justice, as is often claimed. On the contrary, we must focus on the Freedom System as described in this book, with all the available tools of wealth creation, thus forcing up GNP and real purchasing power for all. We do not want a society in which everyone is made "equal" by government force, intrusion, wraparound micro-legislation, mind control of public and private attitudes, and official reverse discrimination. Rather, we want a society in which everyone is free to be what they wish, but without guarantees, in an environment of maximum opportunity under the same rule of law. Once this formula is properly promoted, increases in real wealth will automatically dissolve absolute poverty. Relative poverty can never be eliminated because we create it by our definitions.

# 9: FOREIGN AID
## HOW MUCH? TO WHOM? AND WHY?

*When the World Bank thinks it is financing
an electric power station, it is really financing a brothel.*
—Paul Rosenstein-Rodin, deputy-director, World Bank, 1947

*There is less freedom in many African countries today than
there was in the much-maligned colonial period.*
—Archbishop Desmond Tutu, 1988

*It comes as a surprise to the layman, but not at all to the experts,
that food aid arriving in Bangladesh and many other places
isn't used to feed the poor. Governments typically sell the food
on local markets and use the proceeds however they choose.*
—*Wall Street Journal*, 1988

*Between 1970 and 1998, when aid flows were at their peak
[US $15 billion per year], poverty in Africa rose from
11 percent to a staggering 66 percent.*
—Dambisa Moyo, *Dead Aid: Why Aid Is Not Working*, 2009

The moment we hear the words "Third World," a distinct image leaps to mind—normally of an emaciated black child, with swollen belly and haunting eyes, crawling with flies—that evokes universal pity. This image causes a moral wincing in most of us, which, if we allow ourselves to think about it a lot, makes daily life difficult. After all, what in the name of heaven can justify such pitiable anguish in the life of a small child? What is *really* going on in these countries, anyway?

This chapter is the result of my effort to find out. In this regard, I will be discussing the matter of indirect government-to-government foreign aid, not the many direct types of humanitarian assistance offered by caring individuals or citizen groups. The latter has been more or less ongoing for generations, and much of it takes place privately between free organizations of the West, and individuals, families, citizen organizations, and church groups in foreign nations. At the least, there is some hope that the private package or money you send personally will arrive in the intended recipient's hands. I encourage as much of that hands-on direct aid, person-to-person, group-to-group as possible.

But government-to-government "foreign aid" is another matter. This has to do with large sums of money *transferred between the governments* of nations, either directly or through a variety of subsidiary or international organizations, either as conditional or unconditional loans or grants of one kind or another. By its very nature, it is political and ideological in nature, and the citizens of many donor countries have been duped into believing all is well. It is not.

There is a distressing scenario to explain why, even though Canada still carries a total national direct debt (federal, provincial, and local) of just under $800 billion—and therefore some $94,000 per family (of four) that will eventually have to be extracted in taxes—hard-working Canadians continue to cough up around $3 billion annually for foreign aid. Most probably believe that they are feeding starving little children. In some cases that may be true and Canada may indeed have a decent record in delivering this sort of foreign aid. My intent is not just to take aim at Canada, but at the overall big picture of Western foreign aid, which does not look so good. Indeed, many contemporary experts, as we shall see, increasingly believe that "foreign aid" may actually be "foreign harm," that *by its very nature, foreign aid may actually generate poverty in Third World countries.* What? How could so much intended help be actual harm? Well, I suppose we can all think of stories of individuals who get dependent on handouts, or kids so spoiled by Mommy and Daddy they lose the will to make it on their own. Countries are not much different.

So perhaps we should begin with some basic questions, such as: What is the reason for this immense international transfer of wealth from the so-called First World to the Third World—over $2 trillion since the 1970s—over half of which has been given to sub-Saharan Africa in that period either in grants (just given away), or as conditional or "tied" aid—which means such things as: "shape up," or, "buy X from us" and we'll give you the money—or else loaned at very low interest rates with repayment often, and usually, forgiven. Perhaps we should begin be asking: What *is* the Third World, anyway?

## THE UNITED NATIONS: AN INSTRUMENT FOR THE REDISTRIBUTION OF THE WORLD'S WEALTH?

*Step One*: When the United Nations was created at the end of World War II its ostensible purpose was to preserve world peace. It was set up specifically as a political organization, not an economic one. But through its democratic voting structure—one nation, one vote—it was soon apparent who would be running the show (although not financing it). Of those that initially joined the UN, well more than half were what we today call Third World nations, and such nations now form a large majority bloc of the 192 member nations (of 245 countries in the world).

*Step Two*: By the time of the 1964 meeting of the United Nations Committee on Trade and Development (UNCTAD 1), such nations had already hit upon the idea of forming a kind of international begging union and calling themselves the Third World. This was in distinction to the First, or free, world, and the Second, or totalitarian world of the communists (now defunct, but for Cuba, North Korea, Laos, China, and Vietnam). In order to make this concept believable, this newly formed group had to develop a coherent begging ideology to get what they wanted from the other two "Worlds." Basically, what they mostly wanted was money, and a few peculiar rights.

*Step Three*: Leaning heavily on arguments and ideas derived from Marxism-Leninism, and to some degree from then-popular British socialists, here in essence is what they declared, through a variety of UN documents released in the 1960s and 1970s, initially by a group called the Group of 77 (still in existence with the same name, but currently it consists of 130 countries).[1] These nations were virtually the insiders at all the UNCTAD meetings. Here is what the Third World (later to renickname itself the "South") claimed:

- When the rich get rich, the poor get poorer. (This is essentially the fixed-pie illusion operating internationally.)
- The wealth of the rich is the result of exploitation of the poor nations. (This is the determinist illusion at work.)
- The rich world owes the Third World "restitution"—it must pay for its exploitation, past and present. The rich world is guilty as charged. (In this, we recognize the soak-the-rich illusion.)
- A "New International Economic Order" is required (called the NIEO, for short). The role of the NIEO is *to ensure that the world's wealth is equally distributed*. (This is the equality illusion rearing its head.)
- Such restitution is not a matter of *charity*, it is a matter of *right*. The Third World has a legitimate claim on the wealth of the rest of the world. (Here, operating at the international level, is the rights illusion.)

We saw this same—and very successful—ideological effort of the left to convert charity into a right in matters of domestic welfare policy in the last chapter. Below is an excerpt from a speech by Julius Nyerere, former dictator of Tanzania, and an elegant spokesman for international begging, which in one breath sums up this NIEO thinking.[2] The cleverness in his remarks springs from the fact that no one would wish to argue with his motive—the eradication of poverty—but he uses it here to sell his larger redistributionist idea for "African Socialism," one that permitted him to force his personal utopian vision inhumanely on the lives of millions of his own unwilling peasants:

"In one world, as in one state, as I am rich because you are poor and I am poor because you are rich, transfer of wealth from rich to poor is a matter of right; it is not an appropriate matter for charity. The objective must be the eradication of poverty and the establishment of a minimum standard of living for all people. This will involve its converse, a ceiling on wealth for individuals and nations, as well as deliberate action to transfer resources from the rich to the poor within and across national boundaries."[3]

In this vision he fancies himself as one among other international intellectual policemen governing a world in which incomes are *extracted* from others, rather than *earned* by oneself; in which "everybody, everywhere is entitled to a substantial income regardless of economic performance."[4] This is but an international version of the same tired and discredited Marxist dogma that we still hear muttered by socialist academics in our universities: "From each according to his ability, to each according to his need." In their eyes, "formal equality" in a free society, under a rule of law that is the same for all, is insufficient because the result of true freedom is that because some are hard workers, and some lazy, some bright and some stupid, some honest and some crooks, we end up with too many social and economic differences between citizens and regions. Too much inequality, in their eyes. And so they call upon the state to impose so-called "substantive equality" to make people and regions more equal in material terms. But for this to succeed there must be different laws for different people, classes, and regions, and this always requires replacing the rule of law with the arbitrary rule of men, and the imposition of widespread reverse discrimination—what I have called the Handicap System.

Such has been the evolution of the ideology of the so-called Third World. Study it carefully, for by now it is the entrenched game plan designed to take many dollars out of your pocket and your children's pockets for a long time to come. Shortly we will ask how many dollars, to which countries, and for what purposes. Before doing so, we should consider how astounding is the Western blindness to the fact that although "the NIEO is the entrenched instrument of an ideological assault on the West . . . well designed to engender guilt feelings among Western intelligentsia, [it] has never really been answered by the West. No major political leader in a Western country has raised his voice to present a case for the free societies or to emphatically reject the barrage of accusations. Minor politicians daring a rejoinder suffer verbal abuse in the media for 'their insensitivity.'"[5]

Professor Karl Brunner made this comment before the advent of Prime Minister Margaret Thatcher, President Ronald Reagan, and, importantly, Jeanne Kirkpatrick, former U.S. ambassador to the United Nations, all of whom carried the critical torch to the Third World. Kirkpatrick's bold defence of Western principles of freedom and free trade was starkly unlike the whining of Canada's former ambassador to the UN, Stephen Lewis, who quickly made one with the South. Lewis was at the time on the international hustings urging us to "write off African debt" (*Toronto Star*, April 2, 1988). His personal aim was "to persuade Western governments to increase the amount of aid given to these nations." The same article mentioned as an aside that Canada had already forgiven nearly $700 million in sub-Saharan debt to that date.

Looks like Lewis got what he wanted. In the thirty years between 1978 and 2008 Canada has forgiven a whopping $1.3 billion in foreign debt. Part of the debt-relief motive currently is the widespread notion that it is Third World foreign debt that is starving little children. Indeed, some of these countries are so poorly run (and so dependent on foreign aid) that they spend more each year to service their foreign aid debt than they receive in new foreign aid. So the ongoing subtext is the sly implication that this whole mess is the fault of the world's wealthy nations (for expecting to be repaid). Indeed, the new International Ethics movement mentioned earlier argues passionately that all citizens of the world have "a negative duty" not to harm others through their monetary, trade, and lending policies. In other words, if it can be shown that others are indirectly harmed due to a policy that may be of benefit to ourselves, but which has nothing directly to do with them, the guilty party is nevertheless all those—you and me—who benefit from the policy, because we all have a duty not to harm others, directly or indirectly.

My complaint about this form of argument is as follows. While it may certainly be true that some people elsewhere in the world are harmed by exclusion from a policy (say, they cannot qualify for credit at my bank, so they can't get a loan; or, I don't let them join my trading group because I suspect they cannot pay me), the argument suggesting that therefore their poverty is my fault fails to consider the many ways in which these same people directly as well as indirectly benefit from positive policies and economic programs. Examples are the Internet, road and bridge construction, cellphone networks, rail lines, computer technology, clean-well technology, miracle medicines, microlending, and so on. The point is that if you want to tally direct and indirect harm, you must also tally direct and indirect benefits. At any rate, what galls about the guilt-inducing negative-duty charge is that our media are not angry at the leaders of these nations for their gross irresponsibility, their diversion of aid money, their instigations of genocide or civil wars, or their fancy lifestyles in the midst of their own starving people. We hear none of this. No. They are angry at us for not being more generous still, and then have the audacity to blame millions of pitiful indirect foreign deaths on us. Too much twisted logic and yellow journalism for me.

So what is the ordinary Canadian to think of this Third World business? I am going to draw first from the internationally respected scholar the late Sir Peter Bauer of the London School of Economics for an answer. He was among the first prominent poverty analysts to supply us with a well-researched, cool-headed analysis of the lamentable and weak-kneed posture adopted by Western democracies in the face of what far too often looks like the Third World's incredible incompetence, rapacious greed, and pandemic corruption.[6] In a head-to-head debate, he would have demolished international aid beggars like Stephen Lewis rather handsomely. Here's why.

## THE "THIRD WORLD" IS A MYTH

First of all, there is no such thing as the "Third World." This term was invented by a collection of nations that have only one thing in common—a hunger for large doses of free aid from the productive West. Which is to say that if all nations of the world are ranked by per capita income from highest to lowest, there is no clear dividing line between the "rich" countries of the First World—also called the "North"—and those of the Third World—still often called the "South." (In his latter days in power, Pierre Trudeau had a boutique intellectual interest in the so-called North-South dialogue.) But the fact is that many very large upper-class groups and societies within what are called Third World nations are demonstrably wealthier than many large lower-class groups within Western nations. In brief, the Third World concept cannot be defended on economic grounds because it is not an economic concept at all. It is a purely political idea invented the better to take advantage of the ready availability of foreign aid, much of which seems proffered to alleviate "the white man's burden" (the title of a fine book on this whole mess by William Easterly, reviewed below).

## THE THIRD WORLD IS EXTREMELY HOSTILE TO THE WEST

Second, Bauer maintains that "the distinctive features of the official ideology of the Third World are: pronounced and often bitter hostility to the West, the market system, and the [classical] liberal economic order; virulent allegations of Western exploitation as the cause of Third World poverty; and an insistence on large-scale international redistribution of income and on their right to expropriate politically powerless groups." And, of course, this ideological platform is generally supported by Western media.

## THE ELITISM OF EGALITARIANS

*Nyerere's approach devastated much of postcolonial Africa.*
—*Forbes* magazine, 1999

The "powerless groups" mentioned above are such as the five million or more peasants Tanzania's noble-sounding Julius Nyerere, then the socialist darling of black Africa (and of Western university leftists), forced to relocate into his failed experimental commune villages (called *Ujamaa*). To be fair, he was a charismatic dictator who wanted Tanzania to be free of all international begging, and he was convinced this could be achieved by the creation of a self-reliant "African Socialism" rooted in traditional African communalism. Although, typical of all dream-worlders, who deplored the private family entrepreneurship of independent farmers working only for themselves, he initially wanted this uprooting done without violence. But when he failed to persuade them, he "put the entire machinery of the State behind compulsory, universal villagization."[7] With police powers he simply forced millions of people to relocate far from their ancestral homes to work on government-planned communal farms. To prevent them from returning whence they came, he then ordered their original homes burned to the ground, depriving these poor people of their basic rights and property in the name of his unworkable (and, I might add, very radically leftist Western) vision. This was coercive humanitarianism on an international scale. Through the NIEO, he solicited support for this right at the UN, and the Western nations—almost all of which were giving him money— were silent on the immorality and bloody cruelty of these measures. In his 1988 report, Canada's Auditor General, Kenneth Dye, complained that Canada helped "train farmers" for Nyerere's whacko project to the tune of $13 million . . . but had no idea as to the results. But such "large-scale maltreatment of many millions of politically ineffective or defenceless people is commonplace in the Third World. The maltreatment includes expropriations, expulsion, or even massacre and is tolerated, encouraged, or supported by governments prominent and articulate in the United Nations."[8] Canada is one of these.

Statists everywhere, and throughout history, it seems, and notwithstanding all their talk about human dignity, communalism, and equality of the people, follow the same course. First comes the abstract dream-world ideal to be set up for the benefit of all equally. Then comes the effort to persuade the people to break with their local customs and traditions and adhere to the latest State "plan." But the people resist because they do not trust government and do not want to give up what they know and love for something only bookworm intellectuals are so certain will be better for them. So then comes the force. At first the methods used are carrots and sticks. Benefits are promised for compliance, and heavy taxation introduced for resisters. If there is continued resistance, a turning point is reached. Then the "equality" approach is abandoned, and we see elitist judgments substituted for those of the people because planners are convinced they know best what is good for the people, whose consciousness has not been "raised" as yet. So at this point, in a passionate belief that the glorious ends he imagines for the people justify any means to push them there, the Statist begins to include physical coercion. Nyerere and his henchmen were certain their communal *Ujamaa* ends justified the means . . . so, what is a little home-burning, or killing, when paradise looms? As it happened, Nyerere's modern planned village in Tanzania was "a point by point negation of existing rural practice" that offended every ancient African principle of kinship, home building and settling, shifting cultivation, pastoralism, sharecropping, lineage authority, and the pleasures of free and independent small scattered settlements.[9] Canada assisted in this grotesque experiment.

Canada has had what CIDA describes as "a long history of development co-operation" with Tanzania that began in the 1960s when Nyerere was an international hero of the Left. The CIDA folks have always been mostly sympathetic leftists themselves, and so we can be pretty certain they were right there wining and dining him too, eager to throw other people's money at him. Strange this: Here was an African intellectual, trained by radicals in the universities of the West (master of arts, University of Edinburgh), trying to plant the failed Statist ideals of the Swiss Rousseau, of the British socialists, and even of China's despotic Mao Tse-tung . . . in the jungle? CIDA says that "between 2003 and 2007, [it] contributed more than $70 million to Tanzania's education plan." Well and good. I fervently hope that my forced contribution resulted in some needy children learning to read. But I still don't get it. Why can't Tanzania sell one of its tanks or jet fighters, and buy books and hire teachers to help its own children? See below for what happened to Nyerere and his dream world.

## SNAPSHOT
Why Communalism Can't Work

1. The foundational ideal is that all individuals and families should surrender their private ambitions for the common good because private work is selfish, whereas common work is altruistic. In the beginning, "equality" is the core value.

2. Practically speaking, it is assumed that when stage one is achieved and all are working together for a common goal, machinery and costs will be lower because all work will be coordinated: ten families in a co-operative won't need ten tractors, and so on. Each stage of work will be coordinated for real need, rather than for profits, resulting in less cost and less waste, therefore more production and wealth for all.

3. So communal work begins, and as long as moral suasion is high, all do in fact co-operate and the "plan" seems to work. For a while. But soon the obvious problems of different workers' attitudes, skill levels, work output, personal capacities, and different care of tools and machinery, and so on, raises its head.

4. Workers begin to notice that because all the equipment is now held in common, it is not looked after with care and pride as it used to be because

no one stands to lose personally. So machinery and tools break down. But as they belong to no one in particular, no one can be blamed. So repairs and costs for new tools musts be spread to all equally. At this point . . . more equality begins to look a little unfair. Some are being asked to pay for the carelessness of others.

5. Soon, workers begin to notice that while they always used to work very hard and loved it because they and their families got ahead in life, not all workers are that way. Some are definitely slower than others, show up later, produce less, don't tidy up as well after work, and grumble continuously about how hard the work is.

6. The initial communal euphoria is beginning to wear thin, and the stronger and better workers are now resenting the fact that they are working twice as hard as others for the same reward. They begin to see that lazy workers have discovered they can "profit" from the system as "free riders," simply by doing less. Suddenly, things no longer look "equal."

7. So, at this point, "equity" raises its head and workers begin to insist that equity (what is deserved) is a more fair and rational standard than equality (sharing equally).

8. By now, the plan is heading for moral and economic collapse. Some people start to recommend breaking up the commune and going back to private work and care of self and family. If the people are lucky, things simply revert slowly to normal traditional ways, the ideological wounds are licked all round, excuses are made, losses counted, and people go their own way, a little wiser. However, if the whole plan has been coercive from the start, the government's planners start fining people, passing production quotas, and so on. In the end, they bring out their machine guns to force the desired result, and forced communalism continues until it rots from the inside out, as it did in the U.S.S.R. The lesson learned? Equity works better than equality.

## THERE IS NO ECONOMIC ARGUMENT FOR FOREIGN AID

Capital transfers to Third World nations are largely wasted. Here's why. Any capital project either shows a good return on investment, or it doesn't. Such a project either creates wealth, or consumes it. It is always a net plus or a net minus to somebody. If it is a net plus, and this can be shown in financial pro formas, it will have no trouble attracting capital from the private financial markets of the world. Aid is not needed. If it is a net minus, then it consumes capital on an ongoing basis—it is just another "show project," an economic sump draining productive dollars from the nation. Of course, we could argue that without aid a particular project might never be built. But in this case, the contribution of aid cannot exceed the avoided cost of investible funds. In short,

Third World nations benefit only from the avoided cost of borrowing—a minuscule advantage of "aid" over privately raised capital.

At worst—and most often—"official wealth transfers increase the resources and power of recipient governments compared with the rest of society . . . [and thus] enhance the hold of governments over their subjects, and promote the politicization of life."[10] Foreign aid allows such governments to forestall turning to more productive measures; keeps unproductive ways going longer than normal; allows governments to continue to oppress productive minority segments of the population, to restrict the inflow of foreign capital, enterprise, and skills, and to continue with economic controls, price-fixing, and other policies that restrict any possible flowering of initiative. For Tanzania in 1980, aid was 18.1 percent of GNP, 106.8 percent of tax receipts, and 152.8 percent of its export earnings! Tanzania was at that point a non-country economically, dependent, disabled, and diabolical in its human rights policies, like many other Third World countries, complete with their fleets of chauffeured Mercedes-Benz cars for big shots. Honest, hard-working Canadians were taxed more to give Tanzania $26.8 million in foreign aid in 1987. Twenty years later (2006–2007), we gave Tanzania $49.4 million. But in the same year, Tanzania spent $162 million on arms and military expenditures (see Snapshot on military spending below). Not sure anyone knows how much of our money went to bombs and airplanes.

## FOREIGN AID DOES NOT RELIEVE POVERTY

As Peter Bauer has pointed out, "Foreign Aid does not in fact go to the pitiable figures we see on aid posters, in aid advertisements, and in other aid propaganda in the media. It goes to the governments, that is, to the rulers, and the policies of the rulers who receive aid are sometimes directly responsible for the conditions such as those depicted."[11] Unfortunately, Western aid money often aggravates the condition of the poor, not the reverse, for several reasons. It allows Third World leaders and despots to continue with fanciful socialization projects that amount to vast transactions of decline. It subsidizes such nations for remaining in their pitiable condition by creating a whole class of aid professionals, politicians, and bureaucrats whose vested interests lie not in ending poverty, but in ensuring their own continued well-being—*which can continue only as long as poverty remains.* It provides such people with huge show projects with which to impress and subjugate their people, but does not produce economic wealth. In short, the same phenomenon is brought about by international transfer payments to unproductive nations, as is brought about by internal transfer payments to Canada's own internal empire of unproductive regions: they reward people for remaining unproductive, and for staying in unproductive places.

But this is a fool's paradise. Nations that cannot feed their own children do not need fancy show projects stuck in the jungle, they do not need international airlines they cannot maintain or fly themselves, and which the locals certainly cannot afford to use, ever. Worst of all, virtually all these countries maintain very large and expensive military forces and spend lavishly on arms— *about one-fifth or more of the entire world's annual armaments expenditure is by struggling Third World nations*. See the Snapshot below for Canada's involvement in this sham. Finally, there are many rich people in Third World nations, the rulers of which, "while demanding external donations in the name of international redistribution, are not particularly interested in domestic policies to help the poor."[12] Aid, in fact, enables governments to pursue even extremely damaging policies for years on end because the inflow of funds conceals from the population the effect of such policies. For example, without direct monetary assistance from the West, dictator Nyerere would not as easily have been able to proceed with his large-scale forced collectivization of peasants. If Canadian tax dollars assisted him in this inhumane project, do we not bear a moral responsibility for the terribly sad and dislocating experience of the surviving poor of Tanzania?

## FOREIGN AID CANNOT HELP THE WEST

A favourite theme of aid workers is that foreign aid is helpful to the West (creates allies, markets for our products, etc.). But this is not so. We cannot say that by giving our dollars to others, to enable them to buy back our products (as with tied aid), we are further ahead. Rather, foreign aid stifles entrepreneurship, creates unemployment in both donor and recipient nations, diminishes the volume of investible funds in the donor countries, and perpetuates anti-enterprise policies in both donor and recipient nations. If aid made these people themselves productive of wealth, that would be a different matter. But it doesn't. In fact, just like welfare at home, *foreign aid subsidizes the condition for which it is given*. It is a handsome reward for remaining in that condition. In the first edition of this book, I wrote that foreign aid will "Newfoundlandize" the Third World. Though today that statement is just a little unfair to Newfoundland, because although in 1988 fully half Newfoundland's income was "aid" from Ottawa, by 2008 this had improved to 25.9 percent. Now, it is Prince Edward Island that takes the most aid from Ottawa of all Canadian provinces, at 40.7 percent (with Nova Scotia and New Brunswick not far behind). It's a merry-go-round.

## FOREIGN AID IS NOT RESTITUTION FOR EXPLOITATION

Here's another red herring, for "the notion that Western prosperity has been achieved at the expense of the Third World is a variant of the familiar misconception that the incomes of prosperous people have been extracted from the less well-off." In other words, it's a variant of the fixed-pie illusion. In Bauer's famous letter to *Commentary* rebuking U.S. senator Daniel Patrick Moynihan for a few misconceptions, he rebuts this idea as follows: "Contacts established by the West have been the principal instruments of material progress throughout the Third World. For instance, all the foundations and ingredients of modern social and economic life were brought to sub-Saharan Africa by Westerners, mostly during the colonial period."[13]

And from Karl Brunner: ". . . far from the West having caused the poverty in the Third World, contact with the West has been the principal agent of progress there."[14]

From sewers, to the telegraph, to shipping, to railroads, to electricity, to the computer, to the telephone and cellphones, to all modern production technology, to agricultural methods, to ordinary engineering construction, to medicine, to pesticide control of crop blight, to satellite communications and the Internet—you name it, the West took it there. Malaya had no rubber, nor India tea, until the British took them these things. Bauer shows convincingly that the wealth of Third World nations is directly related to their past or present contact with the West, not the reverse, as is so often claimed. Some will argue that the West took them rubber and tea all right, but then exploited labour there to grow these crops. But once again—and leaving slavery out of it on the grounds that just about everyone, black, brown, yellow, and white has been involved in that nefarious practice (and some black and Arab nations still are, as is India)—"exploitation," in the absence of force, is philosophically a sloppy concept. Low wages? Perhaps. Hard work? For sure. But compared with no jobs at all, or destitution, or hard work for no pay, this is a boon. And the record shows that almost all nations that were colonized by the West are now better off (all North America, Australia, Hong Kong, and many of the former African and Asian colonies), whereas the countries that were never colonized, such as Tibet, Ethiopia, Afghanistan, Iraq, Nepal, and Liberia, are still wallowing in developmental backwaters.

## FOREIGN AID WILL NOT MAKE THE THIRD WORLD AMBITIOUS

Many labour under the impression that material progress of the kind experienced by the West is merely a matter of resources, or hardware. But the truth is the opposite. It is the software of civilizations—the human capital—that creates material progress, with which any amount of hardware can be easily purchased. Ambition, willingness to work very hard, to sacrifice for family and children, to save for the future, and, above all, the desire to make progress in the sense of improving one's own world, are the key factors. At the heart of such a cultural matrix there must always be present that most important ingredient— the entrepreneurial process. This must include what I called "the tools of freedom and wealth creation," including especially a sufficient number of innovative, far-seeing, risk-oriented individuals who virtually utilize the capital saved by all those working to create new capital ventures—and thereby new employment, products, services, and so on, in a material upward spiral of growth in GDP that eventually benefits all. Money thrown at a society without such tools is worse than wasted. At least if it were merely wasted, no harm would be done except the loss of capital pools for the donors. But instead, as we have seen, its insidious effect is to train whole societies to depend on it, and thus further handicap them. Bauer underlines this phenomenon: "Economic achievement depends on people's attitudes, motivations, mores, and political arrangements. In many countries the prevailing personal, social and political determinants are uncongenial to material progress: witness the preference for a contemplative life, opposition to paid work by women and widespread torpor and fatalism in certain countries."[15] Further, he adds: "The poorest groups in the Third World tend to be materially unambitious. Official handouts to improve their economic conditions will have to be continued indefinitely if the beneficiaries are not to relapse into their original poverty. Poor people can therefore be turned into paupers. Whole societies can be pauperized in this way."[16]

Examples cited by Bauer closer to home are the Navaho Indians of the United States and the people of Micronesia, who are so heavily aided that a U.S. government economist reports that "any kind of work here, is very hard."[17] Canada also keeps whole tribes of First Nations people in a form of domestic race-based apartheid, dependent on handouts. The Snapshot at the end of this chapter illustrates the dreadful social realities of Canada's aboriginal people, to whom the federal government alone transfers $6 to $8 billion every year (no one knows the exact amount, much of which is transferred from hundreds of other government agencies), and yet *whose social conditions and behaviours are far worse than those of many countries to which we give foreign aid*. Bauer adds examples of Third World nations where soil and climate are suitable for multiple crops, but only one is grown. No one wants to do the extra work. If you wanted to set up a diabolically clever program to detrain people—to make them unlearn whatever cultural habits and beliefs got them at least this far along—you couldn't do better than with a foreign aid program.

## HOW MUCH MONEY DOES CANADA SPEND IN FOREIGN AID, AND ON WHOM?

Canada had a history of a century of fiscal responsibility until the Trudeau years (1968–1984), during which we began running enormous annual deficits, the full impact of which can be seen in the charts in chapter 7. Things improved after the peak borrowing year of 1992, and we lowered our total national debt (federal, provincial, and local) from the over $1 trillion mark, to the $791 billion we carried by 2008. It is surely a great mystery to most that despite this enormous debt—and we have projected annual deficits in the order of $53 billion to be added to this total once our stimulus spending is under way—that Canada continues to *borrow* money, which it then turns around and *gives* away (or lends at cheap rates, then forgives) to Third World nations, obviously in the confident assumption that we and our children will be happy to pay off such debts in the future.

If, like many Canadians, you feel that Canada should at least get its own financial house in order before giving our money away to others; or if, like many, you think that even then, such charity is a private matter and government should not be giving away the money of citizens it has not consulted, to countries with offensive political, economic, cultural, and human rights practices; or if you believe that if we can't stop giving it away, then let's at least give it only to countries in sympathy with our own values and dedicated to helping themselves—if you believe any one or all of these things, you are very much out of step with Canada's foreign aid policy (which is also, of necessity, its foreign policy).

## WHAT ABOUT "FLIGHT CAPITAL"?

A lot of aid money sent into Third World countries ends up in the private hands of corrupt officials and is sent back out to be invested in Western markets. Aid money in, investment capital out? Canadians are suckered into sending borrowed Canadian money to Third World countries that don't have enough confidence to invest at home. Here are a few snippets on the flight-capital situation, all in U.S. dollars, from the 1980s until today.

- International bankers think flight capital totals "about $250 billion annually—about two-thirds of Latin America's debt." During its years of debt crisis, Mexico smuggled out an estimated $84 billion—a figure that rivals that country's $100 billion foreign debt. Venezuelans, with a foreign debt of $32 billion, shipped out $58 billion (*Globe and Mail*, May 1, 1989).
- *Die Welt* reported (January 28, 1989) that Brazil and Mexico together sent out as much as $10 billion, as much as the two countries had to find to service their foreign debt. Former Mexican president José Lopez Portillo became a "dollar-billionaire" in this fashion (*Die Welt*, March 4, 1989).
- In a study of nine developing countries (to which Canada shipped about $92 million in aid in 1987), international economics expert Michael P. Dooley estimated these same countries shipped out about $100 billion in flight capital.
- And in 2009, in Dambisa Moyo's *Dead Aid*, we read this shocking statement: "At least US $10 billion—nearly half of Africa's [2003] foreign aid receipts—departs Africa every year" (p. x).

Here are a few selected countries among hundreds that Canada helps with your money. You be the judge of the correctness of this strange notion of charity.

| | INDIA 1986–1987 | 2007 |
|---|---|---|
| AMOUNT GIVEN | $170.96 million | $19.9 million |
| MILITARY SPENDING | US$9.648 billion | US$24.7 billion |

Canada has recently phased out many of its India programs. And while it is true that India has many poor, it also has a great many rich, and many in between, and so anyone giving money to India would surely want to question its internal national priorities. It is disturbing to know (or worse, to see) so many Indians starving in the streets, even though India has the largest livestock population in the world. It has 57 percent of the world's buffalo population and 16 percent of the world's entire cattle population—over 187 million head. India also has one of the world's best-equipped armies. Its armed forces total greater than 1.32 million combat-ready men, and their military equipment includes 3,978 tanks and 900 high-tech combat jet aircraft. Six of its air force squadrons of strike fighters are armed with nuclear bombs. Couldn't India sell a few of these tanks and fighter aircraft, and feed its own poor, instead of coming to us for handouts?

Further, India employs a widespread form of slavery known as "tied," or "bonded," labour. This is labour—sometimes lifelong—supplied by extremely poor, low-caste Indians who have made the mistake of borrowing a few rupees from landowners or factory owners who then oblige them to repay it in work. The ignorant workers never really learn how much they owe, and the owners keep them in bondage by charging them back for all sorts of things (shovels, rent, water, interest, medicine, a mat to sleep on) so that their debt can never be repaid. There are an estimated 20 million bonded labourers in the world, and many millions of these semi-slaves are in India. These debts can be transferred from one generation to another, so that children are literally born into the debt slavery of their parents. Yet, when Indians treat their untouchables poorly, there is mostly world silence, even though "something like 105 million Indians remain untouchables and are regarded by the rest of society as inherently inferior. They are probably the largest oppressed minority in the world. Untouchable men are even forbidden from shaping their moustaches upwards—the act would signify an intolerable self-assertion."[18]

Further still, India is a major human rights violator, which should disqualify any country for aid. As for its "Third World" status? The *Globe and Mail* Report on Business of January 1987 reported that by then, post-colonial India had "moved beyond textile and steel mills and railways to climb to tenth place in the ranks of industrialized nations. Its engineering industries are world class. It has sent homemade satellites into orbit on Indian-designed rockets. And last year it commissioned its first fully indigenous nuclear reactor." India is also the twenty-sixth largest producer and exporter of military arms in the world, and the number one importer of arms ($2.3 billion in 2008). In view of such expertise and obvious wealth, perhaps India should be giving *Canada* foreign aid. All this is upsetting, to say the least, and Canada and its government ought to be ashamed. Indian poverty must be solved by changes in India's own attitudes and a reallocation of its internal priorities and resources, and this shameless begging for funds from Canada and other Western nations must be stopped.

|  | *ETHIOPIA* | |
|  | *1988* | *2007* |
| AMOUNT GIVEN | $55.3 million | $83 million |
| MILITARY SPENDING | US$420 million | US$262 million |

Like many Third World nations enchanted with socialist theory—usually picked up at Harvard or Yale or the London School of Economics by wealthy graduate students who then return home to "solve" their nations' problems— Ethiopia suffered through a Marxist regime from 1974 to the overthrow of dictator Mengistu Haile Mariam in May 1991. Mengistu tortured and executed thousand of his political enemies, and during that period indulged in an extremely repressive forced collectivization of poor peasants.

Peter Worthington, then a columnist for the *Financial Post*, visited Ethiopia and took photographs of the operation. Stacked against the wall were a number of 50-kilogram sacks of flour marked "CIDA—Gift of Canada." The refugees said it was normal for the Ethiopian army to grab and use such aid supplies. Other foreign aid, such as scarce cooking oil, they said, was being sold by the government at $3.50 a gallon, also to help finance the army. By the end of 1987, Canada had given more than $65 million in aid to Ethiopia—$27 million of it in food (how much of it actually reached the hungry?). According to Worthington, there was widespread unhappiness among the people of Ethiopia that Canada was helping the oppressor government.

## REPUBLIC OF SOUTH AFRICA

| | 1988 | 2007 |
|---|---|---|
| AMOUNT GIVEN | $7.83 million (1989 budget) | $9.9 million |
| MILITARY SPENDING | US$2.3 billion (1986) | US$3.9 billion |

Canada was embroiled for many years in a foreign-policy war against South African Europeans, which it conducted with haughty self-righteousness. I understand why people disliked apartheid. It was race- and blood-based, nasty and brutish. But it paled in comparison with the human rights infractions and tribal slaughters—remember Rwanda!—in so many African nations, almost all of which have been embroiled in internal and transborder racial warfare and persecution against other blacks, Chinese, Jews, "coloureds," you name it. This appears to be Africa's major sport, and I don't like any of it. But what I disliked more was Canada's holier-than-thou attitude in giving financial "aid" to all the frontline states, "aid" that even Zimbabwe's thuggish Robert Mugabe told newsmen would take various forms, including "military training." Mugabe said that "he had received a commitment on military aid from Prime Minister Brian Mulroney during a private meeting between the two" in New York City in late September (*Globe and Mail*, October 4, 1988).

Were we crazy? Journalist Eric Margolis wrote: "I met with a senior officer of the Zimbabwean army. He told me that Zimbabwe's general staff considers the border with South Africa to be the nation's only *safe* border" (*Toronto Sun*, October 6, 1988). In short, "Zimbabwe has troops poised on all its borders with its *black* neighbors—but not against South Africa, from which *there is absolutely no military threat.*"

So why the selective morality from Canadians?

Why do we send even a penny to a nation that spends $3.9 billion annually on bombs and airplanes, soldiers and warships?

## RECENT CRITIQUES

A reasonable question a reader might raise concerning this chapter is: "What does this have to do with Canada?" The answer is that as long as Canadians are forced to spend billions of their hard-earned dollars in foreign aid on other countries, they have a right to know, indeed, a duty to find out, what their money is used for. I think private foreign voluntary aid generated by individuals, corporations, churches, and charities is a fine thing. What follows is a summary of recent critiques of government-to-government foreign aid only. I am not suggesting nothing good comes from some kinds of foreign aid. I am saying that in general the overall result is shocking.

Books about foreign aid, pro and con, continue to spin off the presses of the world. But there seems to be a common theme of late: it isn't working; it has never worked; and it can't work, for reasons we are finally (maybe) beginning to understand. Below are some thoughts drawn from Dambisa Moyo's *Dead Aid*, Paul Collier's *The Bottom Billion*, and William Easterly's *The White Man's Burden*.[19] All lively. All very critical. All hopeful there is a better way.

Moyo is a highly educated African from Zambia with a Ph.D. from Oxford. Just the stuff for TV and lecture circuit sound bites. Her *Dead Aid* more than fills the bill. She asks why the majority of sub-Saharan African nations "flounder in a seemingly never-ending cycle of corruption, disease, poverty, and aid-dependency" despite the transfer from the rich countries to Africa of $1 trillion "development" dollars over the past fifty years. Her answer—blunt and shocking—is that they are that way *because of foreign aid*. Aid, she protests, "has been, and continues to be, an unmitigated political, economic, and humanitarian disaster for most parts of the developing world."

As an aside on this very note, in February 2007, Canada's Senate Committee on Foreign Affairs issued an impressive and exhaustive examination of Canada's role in Africa entitled "Overcoming 40 Years of Failure: A New Road-Map for Sub-Saharan Africa." Many of the recommendations parallel the suggestions in this chapter. The report can be found at http://www.parl.gc.ca/39/1/parlbus/commbus/senate/com-e/fore-e/rep-e/repafrifeb07-e.htm#_Toc158951655. Here is the Senate's chart showing the decline in sub-Saharan Africa, which has been a bottomless pit for the world's aid dollars for half a century:

## Sub-Saharan Africa's Share of Global Economic Activity (per capita): 1965-2004

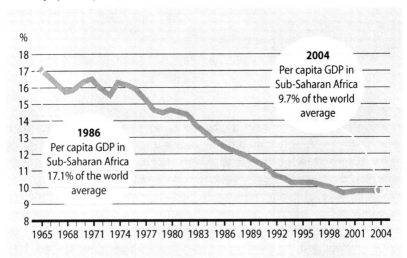

Source: World Bank

But Moyo does see progress—half of forty-eight sub-Saharan nations now hold regular elections, and sixteen of them have functioning stock markets—but writes that Africa's real per capita income today is lower than it was in the 1970s, and by 2015 sub-Saharan Africa will account for one-third of all world poverty. She argues that there is no difference between grants and loans because the latter are always at well below market lending rates, and are usually forgiven anyway.

The 1990s brought what was for Africa the novel stress of liberal-democratic "governance"—an attempt to create institutions of government and civil society (rule of law, property rights, contract rights, etc.) that are quite common to the West, but, alas, not to Africa. Moyo calls this "the donor's final refuge." Despite this all-out democracy push, however, Africa today still has eleven fully autocratic regimes. Indeed, the recently formed Canadian Center for Democracy has complained that CIDA seems prepared to focus a majority of its financial assistance on twenty-five countries, despite the fact that Freedom House, an organization that tracks and ranks the freedom of nations, has identified nineteen of them as "dictatorships" or as "unfree" and very corrupt nations.

By 1992, Africa was getting $17 billion every year in what Moyo describes as "glamour aid" (since reduced to $12 billion per year due to "donor fatigue"). Countries were trying to outdo each other at the white-guilt pity party. But corruption grew as the West continued to "prop up a swathe of pathological and downright dangerous dictators," such as Amin, Seko, Mengistu, and Doe. The competition among these leaders "to be more brutal to their people, more spendthrift, more indifferent to their country's needs than their neighbours were, was matched only by the willingness of international donors to give them money to realize their dreams."

Zaire's Mobutu Sese Seko absconded with $5 billion. Roughly the same amount was stolen from Nigeria by President Sani Abachi (and placed in Swiss bank accounts). Jean-Bedel Bokassa's "coronation" as emperor of the Central African Empire cost $22 million. Nigeria was ranked the most corrupt nation on earth in 1996. And . . . there are estimates that almost half of Africa's foreign aid dollars are sent out of Africa every year! Moyo cites a World Bank study to the effect that "as much as 85 percent of aid flows *were used for purposes other than that for which they were initially intended,* very often diverted to unproductive, if not grotesque ventures." On March 11, 2010, the UN Security Council reported that as much as half of all food aid sent for the people of Somalia is either diverted to corrupt contractors, radical Islamists, and local UN reps, or simply stolen.

But all the latest schemes have failed miserably. And Moyo doesn't believe that downloading Western democratic institutions on people who are not ready for them is necessarily the answer, either, the recent history suggesting that "democracy can hamper development" if conditions are not ripe. In that case, she prefers "a decisive benevolent dictator" to push through reforms that warring factions in an untried democratic system without a liberal heritage of debate simply cannot manage to bring about. For Moyo, it is economic growth that brings about the conditions for democracy, rather than the other way around ... and "the one thing economic growth does not need, is aid."[20]

But Moyo is not daunted, and proposes a range of market and civil law strategies to end or reverse the situation, from micro-financing, to new trade rules for business and markets that read like a primer from Adam Smith. I leave it to readers to reach into her book for these. But the overall message is pretty clear and depressing: aid is "the silent killer of growth" because it discourages local investment and saving, reduces public spending, becomes a substitute for tax revenue, creates massive and crippling dependency in the recipient nation, and feeds corruption. In a memorable image, a British official complained that Kenya's corrupt ministers were eating like gluttons "and vomiting on the shoes of the foreign donors." Perhaps most discouraging is the fact that aid culture creates dependency in the donor nations as well.

The World Bank has 10,000 employees, the IMF some 2,500, UN agencies 5,000, and there are at least 25,000 employees of registered NGOs. Moyo estimates that around 500,000 aid professionals are in the worldwide business of making sure billions of dollars keep flowing into their "aid portfolios," adding that "their livelihoods depend on it." A good sign for the truths in her book is that the world's most leftist aid buff, Harvard's Jeffrey Sachs, finds her ideas to be "absolutely pernicious, and could lead to the deaths of millions of people." The rock star Bob Geldof and many other aid boosters are ganging up on her.

Paul Collier's *The Bottom Billion* has sold over fifty thousand copies and made a mark because his work points to a kind of statistical sociology of poverty. He argues that there has been too much aid concentration on the five billion people in the world who for some time now have actually been moving out of poverty, though at different rates. The intentionally scary part of his book is the detail about the bottom billion who are diverging from the rest of us and falling into deeper stagnation, poverty, and despair.

The fascinating aspect of this book lies in Collier's concentration on the characteristics of the failed versus the successful nations that doom them to become and to stay poor, or to rise up. His message to the developed and developing world is that the bottom billion are sinking as fast as the rest are succeeding, and so we need to do something over the next couple of decades to reverse this trend or pay the serious consequences of facing a billion people on the planet who have formed "a ghetto of misery and discontent" that will be increasingly impossible for a comfortable world to tolerate.

Collier positions himself and his solutions in between left and right, scolding each side for their stale remedies. In the end, however, he wants ever more aid money, so that gives us a hint of where he is coming from, as they say. But contrary to the socialist-hugging Left who dislike militarism and "hate capitalism," he argues that positive international military interventions (to block civil riots and unrest), combined with free trade, and market economies with all the tools and institutions necessary for this are essential to growth and success. Contrary to the Right, he argues that their global growth cure ("all ships go up in a rising tide"), while it indeed works for most of the world, is too simplistic for the bottom billion who have found themselves in a variety of "traps," and are "stuck at the bottom." This remark is aimed at such as Moyo (above) and Easterly (below).

The four traps are: the conflict trap (repeated revolution, or coups); the natural resources trap (natural commodity wealth that is a disincentive to create wealth, a lure for rebels to capture the supply of it, and bait for corruption); the trap of being landlocked with bad neighbours; and the trap of bad governance in a small country.

About 980 million of the world's people are stuck in one or more of these traps, 70 percent of them in Africa, and the rest are such as Haiti, Bolivia, Laos, Cambodia, North Korea, and so on (some fifty-eight countries in total). In them, life expectancy is fifty years (while sixty-seven elsewhere); 14 percent of children die before their first birthday (4 percent elsewhere); 36 percent of children suffer long-term malnutrition (20 percent elsewhere).

By 1990, the bottom billion were diverging from the rest of the world at the astonishing rate of 5 percent per year. Collier says we need to think of them as a billion people "stuck in a train that is slowly rolling backward downhill." A powerful image, that. Then, speaking against the prevailing far-left orientation of most academics and aid workers, he warns that we need to figure out how to make these countries grow, and that "they will not grow by turning them into Cuba."

More ominously, he warns that "a cesspool of misery next to a world of growing prosperity *is both terrible for those in the cesspool and dangerous for those who live next to it.*" He means the rest of us, adding that "some citizens of the rich world are going to die as a result of chaos in the bottom billion," due to the export of diseases, epidemics, and terrorism. Collier's observations, all based on statistical aggregations, are riveting:

- Seventy-three percent of people in the bottom billion "have recently been through a civil war, or are in one."
- Halve the starting income of a country, and you double the risk of civil war.
- A typical low-income country faces a 14 percent risk of civil war in any five-year period.
- Each percentage point added to the growth rate knocks off a percentage point from this risk.

- The resource trap? Dependency on oil, diamonds, and the like substantially increase the risk of civil war. Collier tells of rebel leader Laurent Kabila of Zaire marching cross-country to seize the government, who said that "all you need is $10,000 and a satellite phone." By the time he got to the capital, he had struck deals worth $500,000 with resource-extraction companies—enough to fund his army of disaffected teenagers, most of whom saw the coup as the best way to get rich quickly.
- Resources for diaspora communities have also fuelled rebel movements in many countries.
- The Tamil Tigers "got money from Tamils in Canada; the bomb that killed or injured more than 1,400 people in Sri Lanka's capital city, Colombo, in 1996, was paid for from a Canadian bank account."
- Aid can make civil unrest much more likely because young disaffected men with everything to gain want "the payoff to power," and are more than willing to rape, maim, and kill for it.
- A typical seven-year war leaves a country 15 percent poorer than when it started.
- Thirty-eight percent of the people in the bottom billion live in landlocked countries with bad neighbours—overwhelmingly an African problem. In contrast, Switzerland and Austria are also landlocked, but very successful because they do so much trade with good neighbours (many of whom have coastal transportation to offer). But the 38 percent have bad neighbours to whom they are "hostage" either because there is little or no trade with them (nothing to trade), or they are at war with each other, or a genocide is under way, or they have collapsed economically, or all of these things. Not one of these landlocked countries has ever made it to middle-income status.
- By 1990, almost 40 percent of Africa's private wealth was held abroad ("voting with their wallets").

Collier's proposals for reversing all this are a mixture of hope and, I think, illusion. First, he wants international aid workers to switch the world focus from the middle to the bottom billion (where so few aid workers are active now), from sexy Rio de Janeiro, to miserable Bangui. He also wants the guilt-ridden Western aid workers on the left to stop thinking that the countries of the bottom billion are "there to pioneer experiments in socialism." Canada—take heed! He urges that despite their anti-capitalist biases, the Left has to "learn to love growth."

As for the Right, they have to "move on from the notion of aid as part of the problem—as welfare payments for scroungers and crooks" (though he certainly details a lot of that). He wants the Right to understand that some countries are "stuck" in the traps he describes, and that mantras about free markets are just

too simple for them. He then prescribes proactive international military interventions (for regime change) to stabilize failed nations and forestall war; and a
handful of new "laws and charters" to guide the conduct of nations with respect
to: the extraction and management of natural resources; banking and investment (please, Switzerland, stop hiding the fortunes of corrupt Africans); for the
proper installation of democracy; for the budget transparency of nations; for
post-conflict management; and for ending rich-country and poor-country
trade barriers.

In closing, he says that the "clarion call for the right" is William Easterly's
*The White Man's Burden*, which he says is correct to mock the delusions of the
aid lobby, but that it exaggerates the downside. I read the latter book before
Collier's, and it still seems the most sensible to me because the "laws and charters" Collier wants would necessitate a whole new top-down level of international planners, government, and courts to help the bottom billion.

Easterly has different, and more attractive, suggestions that begin with a single
memorable question and contrast: Why, despite the US$2.3 trillion spent on
foreign aid over the past five decades could the world's aid establishment not
manage to get 12-cent medicines or four-dollar bed nets to the world's poor to
stop five million deaths from malaria, while on a single day in 2005 the economies of Britain and America managed to deliver nine million copies of the
Harry Potter book to eager fans? It is heartbreaking, he writes, that "global
society has evolved a highly efficient way to get entertainment to rich adults
and children, while it can't get 12-cent medicine to dying poor children."

Now, that statement, that contrast, drives right to the heart of his book:
"Planners," he insists, are rewarded for creating top-down utopian schemes to
"help" the poor, with little accountability for on-the-ground results, while
"Searchers" are like entrepreneurs in a market system looking for what individual poor people actually want. Planners create top-down global blueprints,
usually of the utopian, one-size-fits-all type; Searchers adapt to local conditions
with piecemeal, bottom-up solutions. Easterly's ideas appealed immediately
because on so many fronts he is recommending that we encourage foreign
countries to develop a bottom-up approach that echoes in most details the
"tools of freedom and wealth creation" that were recommended for Canada in
chapter 4 of this book twenty years ago. In a sense, the original of *The Trouble
with Canada* was a foreign aid manual addressing Canada's self-colonized internal empire. Everywhere, it contrasted the two most prevalent "solutions" to
how we ought to live and work together: "utopian top-down social engineering" or "piecemeal bottom-up reform." So I was delighted to see that Easterly
opposes by the same labels the disastrous French top-down planning approach
sanctified by the likes of Jean-Jacques Rousseau, to the English bottom-up
piecemeal approach recommended by such as the Englishman Edmund Burke.

He then illustrates the amazing difference by contrasting the catastrophic, embarrassing, and grotesquely expensive failures of the world's foreign aid planners with the amazing results of such as the Gang of Four—the miraculous self-help success of Hong Kong, Singapore, Korea, and Taiwan in raising themselves "from third world to first over the last four decades" through a diligent use of the tools of freedom and wealth creation. He invites "idealists, activists, development workers of the world" to gaze on them in amazement, because "you have nothing to lose but your utopian chains." What a breath of fresh air that is!

Easterly roundly scolds the aid establishment for its conventional "Poverty trap/Big Push" thinking, typical of which is the focus of the UN Millennium Project[21] requiring the raising of even more foreign aid dollars, when such aid has been found to fund mostly consumption rather than investment, and so "has zero effect on growth." Canada has committed to providing more than $5 billion per year by 2010.[22] Easterly's shocking charts show a steep inverse correlation between aid and growth, and also between aid and democracy: more aid means less of both. In short, more aid means more poverty! As antidote, he writes that the free market is already an available and "universally useful system," and one of humanity's most underrated inventions is the "unrestricted right to produce, buy, and sell." Any country that succeeds in creating a citizenry and a culture that adopts all the tools of freedom and wealth creation, protection for private property rights and persons, legal title, citizen trust, rule of law, free trade, etc., will not need the help of the West because "market instincts are hard-wired into human nature," and they "create opportunities for anyone to get rich by borrowing and investing." Okay, he means in combination with all the other necessary features of what I have called a Freedom System. For "there is hope once you give up the Planner's ambition of universally imposing a free market from the top-down," and embrace the "confusing welter of bottom-up social institutions and norms essential for markets."

Easterly's sharp distinction between the operation of French-style, *civil code–law* nations, and English-style, *common law* nations supports the rendering of that important distinction in the recent history of Canada as described in the first chapter of this book. A series of studies, he writes—one of them cited in chapter 1—compares development in countries with an English common law tradition to those with a French civil law tradition. The latter system is codified in abstract principles at the top and attempts to deal with reality without bottom-up feedback from the real world, and hence has trouble adapting to quickly changing situations. In contrast, the former is based on actual cases from which legal and economic principles are only afterward derived. He adds that, ironically, France herself is more flexible at top-down adaptation than her colonies—and for this book that would include Quebec. The theory that Quebec is a faltering welfare state within a larger welfare state is bolstered by the Snapshot in chapter 1 showing the poorer performance of Quebec compared to the rest of Canada.

Overall, we end this chapter with a vindication of the bottom-up Freedom System for Canada, and the conviction that it ought to be a foreign aid recipe for all other countries (and our own provinces!) struggling under a top-down system because, as Easterly warns, "Any state that is powerful enough to protect citizens against predators is powerful enough to be a predator itself."

## SNAPSHOT
Canadian Foreign Aid

Here is a list of some of the countries to which Canadian taxpayers gave almost a third of CIDA's annual $3 billion budget for foreign aid in 2006–2007.

Contrasted with this is the amount these same countries spent, in the same year, on weapons and military expenditures.

Paul Collier, in *The Bottom Billion*, estimates that "something around 40 percent of Africa's military spending is financed by aid . . . the militaries of the bottom billion are running an extortion racket and our aid programs are the victim."

| Recipient Countries | Amount Given 2006–2007 (In current Can$) Source: CIDA | Weapons and Military Expenditures 2007 (unless noted) (In constant 2005 US$, rounded) Source: Stockholm Int'l Peace Research Inst. |
|---|---|---|
| China | $37.2 million | $63.6 billion |
| India | $19.9 million | $24.7 billion |
| Brazil | $9.0 million | $15.5 billion |
| Pakistan | $25.3 million | $4.2 billion |
| South Africa | $9.9 million | $3.9 billion |
| Mexico | $5.0 million | $3.9 billion |
| Egypt | $16.1 million | $2.6 billion ('08) |
| Morocco | $10.0 million | $2.4 billion ('08) |
| Argentina | $860,000 million | $2.1 billion |
| Vietnam | $29.2 million | $1.3 billion |
| Sudan | $133.8 million | $1.3 billion |
| Nigeria | $21.0 million | $1.2 billion |

| | | |
|---|---|---|
| Philippines | $24.5 million | $1.0 billion |
| Lebanon | $17.6 million | $1.0 billion |
| Jordan | $6.9 million | $937 million |
| Bangladesh | $64.7 million | $767 million |
| Kenya | $32.4 million | $348 million |
| Ethiopia | $83.0 million | $262 million |
| Uganda | $20.3 million | $237 million |
| Tanzania | $49.4 million | $162 million |
| Zambia | $18.0 million | $165 million ('08) |
| Zimbabwe | $85.0 million | $107 million |
| Jamaica | $3.9 million | $65.6 million |
| Nicaragua | $7.7 million | $35.2 million |
| | **Total Canada Gave to These Countries: Can$730.6 million** | **Total Military Spending by These Countries: US$131.8 billion** |

## CANADA'S SECRET APARTHEID SYSTEM

Since the last quarter of the nineteenth century, the Canadian government has maintained a race-based apartheid system of Native reserves. Its general features include: federal legislation that legally controls the blood-based local separation of natives and whites; the financing and legal establishment of reserves exclusively for natives; indirect rule by chiefs and tribal councils (recently augmented by a third layer of native government, native police forces, etc.); reserve programs controlled by white bureaucrats (though now many include native administrators); racial separation through the encouragement of native social and cultural institutions; government tolerance of blood-based residential criteria policed by natives living on reserves (all natives with the correct amount of native blood, only, can be card-carrying members, etc.).

Originally, native people were herded into these reserves by the Canadian government because they were dying out. This voluntary apartheid system was originally intended to protect Canada's native people from the worst effects of white civilization. In many respects it has done so. The native population of Canada is now 3.8 percent of our population, and is our most fertile group. Nevertheless, it is a population in deep trouble, as the Snapshot below illustrates. It remains a mystery why so many Canadians who expressed outrage at South African apartheid, a system that legislated tribal, blood-based homelands, do not blink an eye at Canada's own system of apartheid. That difference is likely because the South African system was obligatory, whereas Canada's is voluntary. Nevertheless . . .

When young people tell me they are going to Africa to help the poor in some foreign aid project, I often explain that many native people in Canada are doing worse than Africans, live in a genteel apartheid system here in Canada, and need their help. But it does not register. They do not think the High Arctic or northern Saskatchewan is as romantic a place to work as an African village in Kenya.

Finally, one could argue that a good way to test the claims of socialist theory would be to set up an apartheid-style reserve system for a formerly free people where billions are spent every year to maintain them free of charge, then check out the results a hundred years later. Below is the shameful result of this test in Canada. I close my overview of foreign aid with the thought that we need a Peace Corps (or some such initiative) to address this "foreign aid" problem on our own soil.

## SNAPSHOT
Canada's Dirty Little Secret

| Item | Registered Indians (Items 1–7 excl. Quebec) | Rest of Canada (Items 1–7 excl. NF & LB) |
|---|---|---|
| 1) Life Expectancy | | |
| Men | 71.0 yrs (2005) | 77.0 (2005) |
| Women | 76.5 yrs (2005) | 82.5 (2000) |
| 2) Births per 1,000 women | (1999) | (1997) |
| age 15–19: | 106.3 | 19.9 |
| age 20–24: | 173.7 | 64.2 |
| age 25–29 | 131.7 | 104.1 |
| age 30–34 | 73.2 | 84.9 |
| 3) Heavy drinking | 26.1 percent | 16.1 percent |
| 4) Obesity | 22.8 percent | 14.1 percent |
| 5) Smokers | 62 percent (1997) | 23 percent (2000) |
| 6) Suicide Deaths per 100,000 | 27.9 (1999) | 13.2 |
| (Suicide constitutes 38 percent of all on-reserve native deaths for ages 10–19; and 23 percent of all deaths for ages 20–44. Figures exclude Quebec) | | |
| 7) Diabetes For ages 45–64 | 19 percent | 4.3 percent |

| Education | 66 percent of children on reserves will not graduate from high school. "More likely to go to jail than to graduate."[#] | ROC figure is 10.9 percent dropout rate (2002) |
|---|---|---|
| Aboriginals sentenced to jail (2007–2008) | 24 percent of all admissions to jails (though only 3.8 percent of pop.); anywhere from 35 percent to 80 percent of inmates in western provinces | |
| Aboriginal offender | 68 percent Indian, 34 percent Metis, 4 percent Inuit | |
| Criminal offences¨ all incidents Rate per 100,000 | N.W.T—47,561 Nunavut—36,806 | ROC—7,424 (2007) |
| All crimes of violence Rate per 100,000 | N.W.T—6,547 Nunavut—7,816 | ROC—931 |
| Violent crime by Indians (Correctional Services Canada—2004) | | |
| Homicide: | 28 percent | |
| Serious assault: | 39 percent | |
| Sexual assault Rate per 100,000 | N.W.T—406 Nunavut—667 | ROC—64 |
| Percent classified as "high-risk" on admission to prison | Inuit—85 percent Indian—73 percent Metis—68 percent | |
| Percent of above groups with gang affiliation | 1997—14 percent 2004—23 percent | |
| Likelihood of re-offending | Almost three times non-aboriginal rate | |
| Main causes of death Ages 15–44 | Violence and accidents, of which 50 percent are alcohol-related. This group 3 x as likely to die as result of violence as non-aboriginals | |
| Urban children under 6 in poverty¨¨¨ | 80 percent | |
| Income disparity with non-aboriginal peers[##] | | |

| On reserve: | 50 percent lower | |
|---|---|---|
| Off reserve: | 23–38 percent lower | |
| Children under 15 in lone-parent homes (large urban areas) | 46 percent | Non-aboriginal urban children—18 percent |
| Child and teen prostitutes who are aboriginal[###] | close to 90 percent | |

Main sources: Tom Flanagan, *First Nations? Second Thoughts*, 2nd ed. (Montreal-Kingston: McGill-Queen's University Press, 2008); and John Richards, "Why the Gap in Health Outcomes?" Chapter 3 in *Creating Choices: Rethinking Aboriginal Policy* (Toronto: C.D. Howe Institute, 2006). And Statscan: http://www.statcan.gc.ca/pub/81-004-x/2005004/8984-eng.htm.
Other sources:
[#] http://www.ccsd.ca/cpsd/ccsd/c_ab.htm
[*] http://www.statcan.gc.ca/daily-quotidien/090721/dq090721b-eng.htm
[**] http://www40.statcan.gc.ca/101/cst01/legal04d-eng.htm
[***] Canadian Senate Hearing, http://www.parl.gc.ca/37/2/parlbus/commbus/senate/com-e/abor-e/rep-e/repfinoct03part2-e.htm#1.6percent20percent20Exitingpercent20Gangpercent20Life
[##] Sharon Proudfoot, "Aboriginals 'astoundingly poorer' than other ethnic minorities: Study," *Canwest News*, March 30, 2009.
[###] cited in Michael Harris, *Con Game*, p. 83.

## WHAT IS TO BE DONE?

1. Stop giving all government-to-government aid. Encourage citizens to get involved in personal, corporate, and aid via charitable organizations. One of the messages of this chapter is that so-called foreign aid may actually be foreign harm.

2. Start balancing our national budget, and retire our own horrendous national debt. Perhaps ask China for a forgivable foreign aid loan of a mere $1 trillion for this purpose—as we cannot seem to escape our own fiscal gluttony. A joke. Sort of.

3. Once our own problems are solved, and we are paying our own way, let's encourage individuals to give true humanitarian aid, but only when our government can prove that such aid is without question going to individuals, families, and communities in need. This can be encouraged by allowing the same tax deductions as for domestic charity.

4. Even then, Canadians must carefully distinguish between giving a hand up, and a handout. Nations that refuse to help themselves, or persist in fatalism, or whose ideology is bent pell-mell on burying ours (such as Marxist-Leninist or other socialist nations), must be encouraged to

change before we will help them. If they want to learn, we can teach them how to fish.

5.  Don't encourage aid to any country involved in war unless we want to fight that war, which is a decision for the nation, not for ministers of external affairs, or feminists at CIDA.

6.  Don't encourage aid to any country that denies a minimum of civil and human rights to its citizens while spending on large military budgets.

7.  If we are going to play conscience of the world, then let us do so even-handedly. Let us ensure that our own minorities have equal protection of their rights. Quebec's English minority, for example, does not have such protection, and the condition of our native people, as we have seen, is a national disgrace.[23] Then, if it makes us feel good to preach morals to others, let us be bold enough to do so evenly, to all concerned. Selective morality is reprehensible. For example, there were generations of Soviet and Eastern bloc repressions, genocides, and mass murders about which Canada's political scientists, media, and other do-gooders were and are still ominously silent. We rightly express a national indignation over horrors such as the Nazi Holocaust, but we have never spoken as a nation against the even larger horrors and exterminations suffered upon innocent human beings by the Soviet communist system. We should.

# 10: RADICAL FEMINISM
## ATTACKING TRADITIONAL SOCIETY

*It will be plain that the first condition for the liberation
of the wife is to bring the whole female sex into public
industry, and that this in turn demands the abolition of the
monogamous family as the economic unit of society.*
—Friedrich Engels, The Origin of the Family,
Private Property, and the State, 1884

*You see, we want a whole transformation of
society in the most revolutionary way.*
—Louise Dulude, former president, National Action
Committee on the Status of Women, 1987

*The end of the institution of marriage is a necessary
condition for the liberation of women. Therefore it is important
for us to encourage women to leave their husbands . . .*
—US "Declaration of Feminism," November 1971

*My goal in life is to change the entire social and economic structure
of Western civilization, to make it a feminized world.*
—from obituary notice for activist Marilyn French (National Post, May 7, 2009)

Perhaps I should begin by pointing out that there have always been "feminists"
around. There were female protest movements in ancient Rome where women
tired of homemaking would insist on their right to fight in battle "just like
men"—and even to do this bare-breasted if they wished. Most men would
likely agree that the mere sight of a pack of half-naked women rushing toward
them in battle would be a very effective deterrent to warfare.

At any rate, then as now, discussions of feminism can get overheated, so I
want to clearly distinguish my topic—*radical* feminism—from the ordinary
concern of reasonable men and women to be fair-minded with respect to the
sexes. Most women who think of themselves as feminists today simply mean
they believe that fairness, or equality, ought to be applied evenly to men and

women in our society, unless there exists a good reason for differential treatment. For in some cases women have advantages over men, and they don't want to lose them. Couches in women's washrooms, job exemptions from lifting heavy objects, immunity from military conscription, lots of special legal dispensations and biases in favour of separated or divorced women and mothers, and so on, are just a few examples. Of course, these they describe as "justified" or positive discrimination. And so do I.

But I also like to temper the whole issue of the war of the sexes by saying that there are many ways in which men have always been, and continue to be, treated unequally (some of them reasonable). So woe betide us if men ever manifest the same lack of confidence in themselves as women have done for the past few decades and start a worldwide "masculinist" movement. They would have lots of fodder.

For example, men carry a disproportionate "death burden" in society. They die much younger than women do; there is a "life gap" favouring women all over the world. They are also vastly more often the victims of violent crime than are women. They also suffer outright discrimination in wartime: over 120,000 Canadian men have been killed in battle, 150 in Afghanistan as of this writing; and a handful of women, of which three in Afghanistan. Men also suffer an unfair anti-emotional bias, and a stereotype-burden: we say "men can take it"—so listen, don't even *think* about crying, eh? Society also unfairly expects men (not women) to compete financially for their entire lives, and face scorn and failure if they can't hack it. Boys begin to feel this expectation in a big way when they are about fifteen. They don't have the same safe harbour, default option of homemaking and child-rearing as women do. Men also suffer a considerable child-custody bias, and an alimony bias in favour of women: the wife has to be a raving suicidal maniac for them to get custody of their own kids. Fathers are also often jailed for non-payment of child support and alimony, but never women. Most painfully, men suffer a grievous abortion/child-support bias: they have no legal say whatsoever in decisions over the life or death of their own children in the womb if a woman wants to abort them, but if she alone decides to keep them, the father is legally forced to pay support until the children are eighteen. Men also suffer a prison-term bias, receiving far longer sentences than female criminals for the same crimes. They also suffer a strip-search bias; female-to-male strip searches are allowed, but not the reverse. As for the death penalty? Men in all countries are far more likely than females to receive a death penalty for the same crimes. Male punishment in life begins early, for even as very young children, boys at home or in school are punished more often, and more severely, than girls.

Enough. I don't want to whine (frowned upon in a male). I just wanted to set the record straight by saying that life is chockablock with biases and discriminations, some of them reasonable, some of them unreasonable. It's just that a soft-minded and gullible public has let feminists get away with the "poor me" ploy as if, despite the fact modern Western females are the wealthiest, best-educated, most privileged class of women in world history, they were some kind of oppressed class of domestic slaves.

Radical feminism has gone even beyond this charge, however, and anyone who studies it in depth will soon see that in its most alarming form it is a program for the complete restructuring of society through government-funded social engineering of an insidious and unnatural kind. These angry people are not interested in equal *opportunities* for women; they want equal *outcomes*, or results, even if these have to be *forced* on everyone by the powers of the State; and even if men and women, left to their own free devices, would never choose such outcomes. Indeed, once dissected, every ill of socialism can be found in radical feminist practice: in its reliance on all the popular illusions described in this book; in its dependence on coercive power; in its ignorance of the basics of economics; and in its angry psychology of resentment. On its own, in other words, radical feminism would be a tempest in a teapot. But with the power of the State, the courts, and millions in public funding, it has caused profound social and moral dislocation. Lest anyone think this is chicken-feed funding, here is a shocking Snapshot showing total feminist funding in Canada since 1973.

---

## SNAPSHOT
$1.3 to $1.5 Billion Taxpayers' Dollars Spent on Feminist Programs

In 1973, Trudeau's government established the Women's Program. Administered by Status of Women Canada, it is a program that has sprinkled millions of dollars annually to hundreds of feminist groups who aggressively promote the feminist agenda by such things as complaining to the United Nations about Canada's alleged poor "gender equality" record; lobbying the Canadian government for universal daycare and for increased female participation in the labour force; agitating for quotas to get more women into Parliament; advocating for legalization of prostitution and the sex trade, and so on. The clear bias of this program from the start has been the notion that all women are a disadvantaged underclass, both in Canada and in the world at large. Accordingly, almost every single initiative and group supported by this $1.3 billion since 1973 has been radically leftist in orientation, whether concerned with foreign aid for abortion, tax policy, international trade, child custody laws, transgenderism, the redefinition of marriage, or other such matters. In fact, it is almost impossible to find any normal (non-radical) women's concern, activity, or ambition during this period that has been funded by Canada's Women's Program. On the contrary: more than a billion dollars of taxpayers' money has been used by both Liberal and Conservative governments to enable the pursuit of radical leftist objectives that are clearly opposed to the mainstream interests of Canadian women as a whole. The amounts shown here were all obtained by REAL Women of Canada from government sources, and the relevant websites are listed below.

- Status of Women Funding total from 1999 to 2009: $240,289,000
  This sum includes the payment by the Women's Program to feminist groups for these years. However, a fair estimate is that if amounts from years prior to 1999 (not currently available) were included, this amount would be double—or almost a half-billion dollars.
- Women's Program funding total from 1973 to 2009: $294,345,020
- Total of Canada's "foreign aid" funding to establish "gender equality" in other countries from 1999 to 2006: $792,800,000

In 1981, Canada ratified the United Nations Convention on the Elimination of All Forms of Discrimination Against Women (CEDAW). This treaty is used by a feminist-dominated UN Treaty-Monitoring Committee to promote an international feminist agenda that includes things that are not explicit in the treaty, such as the tax funding of abortion and the legalization of prostitution. Canada's Women's Program also funds a women's group called the Feminist Alliance for International Action (FAFIA), which is an alliance of many other government-funded women's groups dedicated to using Canadian taxpayers' money to spread feminist ideology both here and abroad. Since 1999 this group has received $1.8 million. For what? To pressure Canada's federal government to meet its CEDAW commitments. FAFIA is staffed by tax-funded professional feminists who rotate from one government-funded feminist organization to another. Status of Women, Foreign Affairs, and FAFIA regularly co-operate to train and fund delegates whose objective is to promote Canada's radical feminist agenda at the United Nations, even though Canadian taxpayers and Canadian women as a whole have never identified with, nor expressed support for, this agenda, whether at home or abroad. Indeed, they have more often than not opposed it.

Source: Public Accounts Canada http://epe.lac-bac.gc.ca/100/201/301/public_accounts_can/index.html
Status of Women Canada is currently funded through Canadian Heritage.
Source: Status of Women Canada, for the Standing Committee on the Status of Women's First Report which lists funding for every year since 1973: http://www2.parl.gc.ca/HousePublications/Publication.aspx?DocId=1622471&Language=E&Mode=1&Parl=38&Ses=1
Source: Canadian International Development Agency (CIDA) web site http://www.acdi-cida.gc.ca/acdi-cida/ACDI-CIDA.nsf/eng/JUD-31195111-KF2

Citizens of the future will be hard put to explain why government has so lavishly funded a feminist movement that has persistently mounted *a fundamental attack on the whole idea of a free society as it has painfully evolved over the past five centuries,* from principle to practice. We will look back at our crumbling walls and wonder: How did we so blithely allow the Trojan horse of radical feminism within our gates? Of course, sometimes moderate feminism can be just as dangerous as the radical form, because it alters social structures without this expressed intention. But whether the trigger is pulled by a sleepwalker or a revolutionary, the same explosive damage is done. Those of us who cherish the core values that have made this nation strong—freedom, family, free enterprise, individual responsibility, reward for effort, rule of law, and so on—must learn to recognize the very different values and tactics of those who are determined to destroy these core values, however unwittingly. In particular, we must learn not to be seduced by the gossamer language in which such aims are couched.

## UNDOING THE SUCCESSES OF THE PAST

In response to the widespread employment of women and children in factories that was threatening family life during the nineteenth century, social reformers fought hard to establish what was called a "family wage" sufficient to raise a family of five.[1] It was a policy created to protect men with families from unemployment. They would always be given preference over male or female singles in the search for jobs because the social aim was to get children out of the workplace and into the home for proper care and schooling. Once it became established, the family wage—or "living wage," as it was sometimes called—was seen as a social contract fortifying the family, therefore all of society, and therefore the entire nation. Single women (or men who did not intend to found a family) vying for the jobs of men who had to support wives and children were quite normally seen as a direct threat to the general welfare of society, and maybe greedy, to boot, because with no children or spouse to support, why did they want to, why should they, be paid more than their life situation required? For this reason, women were regularly denied jobs, passed over, or even demoted or let go in favour of a male family-wage earner. After World War II, women hired during wartime were let go in droves for this very reason—they held jobs needed by men returning from war. Everyone understood this reasoning.

What an irony that just after more than a century spent consolidating and protecting the central role of the family in society and the importance of investing *personal* parental care in our children, we are now assiduously breaking all this apart, lobbying for both parents to work outside the home, and for universal, free (tax-funded) and, by definition, *impersonal* government daycare. In the recent past, society chose family and children over individual material wealth: so we grew as a nation by natural increase. Now we are choosing individual wealth over family formation and children: so we are not replacing ourselves. Then, reformers struggled to help women and children get off the streets, out of the factories, and back into the home so that children could be properly raised and educated. Today's reformers have been busy stigmatizing stay-at-home wives and trying to drive women into the marketplace once again. The only thing common to the two sets of reformers is the use of State power to do this.

Not long ago a commonly held view was that it was not just money that brought social stature, as we tend to think so narrowly today, but a combination of the virtues for which rich and poor alike strove, the path to which was most often pointed out by the women of society. But modern women, thanks to sexual "liberation," have yielded the high moral ground they once controlled. The good-better-best range of manners and morals that infused their world has been replaced by a general, feel-good, whatever-turns-you-on ethic. They may have wanted down from their pedestal, but that pedestal was also an altar at which men, however quixotically, worshipped. Having stepped down, however, they must now play on the same field as men. For this, alas, they are ill-suited, owing to their generally lesser offensive-aggression (which is not the same as the domestic *control* at which they tend to excel), and to the competitive handicap to which their biology leads—the natural desire to have and to care for their own offspring. Everyone knows, of course, that some women are just as defensively aggressive as men, or more so (especially when defending their children and families), and that men *can* look after children; but most men are unwilling, and cannot carry them, bear them, or suckle them. Of course, in a free society any couple that wants to reverse such natural customs is utterly free to try, and for some this may be preferable. And if heads and hearts were interchangeable, an absolutely equal sharing of outside work (at least the banal, repetitive kind) might make something like that possible. But they are not.

So the traditional familial division of labour has always had a purpose: simple efficiency. It is an arrangement that has enabled societies great and small to do the important work of ensuring their own continuation. What the important nineteenth-century social arrangement did so clearly was to consolidate the idea of marriage, family, and the crucial importance of superior child-rearing *normally available only from parents (or relatives)*.[2] The inevitable result of this was to make men *dependent* on women for sex, family, and children—and women on men for physical protection and financial support. This implicit and universal sexual-social contract of humanity has always specified that men will *provide and protect*, while women will *process and nurture*. The man finds and brings home the food and protects family from enemies; the woman cooks the food and suckles the babies. Both sexes were seen to need each other equally, if differently. Women always knew they could bring men to heel by withholding what men wanted most. Men, in turn, could bring women to heel by threatening to withhold support and protection. In order to prevent the wanton occurrence of the latter—especially during a woman's child-rearing phase when she was naturally handicapped in terms of competitive wage-earning power—there were always extremely strong social and legal sanctions upholding marital vows, parental responsibility, and child support.

A key element in this division of labour was a general acknowledgment of the obvious fact that men and women are naturally and universally different in many, many ways (see "Brain Sex," below). In short, "men are not better than women and women are not better than men; men and women differ."[3] I would add that women and men are each in their own natural way, and in general, better at some things, and worse at others. Most women raise babies a lot better than men, and most men are better fighters than women. Much better. Everyone acknowledges such universal truths. However, in their effort to escape their own biology, it is these very differences that rile feminists so, because they correctly see that *unless they can prove that men and women are the same*, they haven't got a case. Either men and women are naturally different, and these differences manifest themselves naturally in different values and life choices; or they are born exactly the same, and the different social outcomes are a result of oppression and discrimination. No sensible person has ever believed this feminist storyline, and so in considerable desperation feminists recently have adopted the lightweight so-called "postmodern" view that all human gender is "constructed," or a product of the mind. This is a manifestly inadequate view of human reality that has traction only in university courses on gender politics. So by way of staying focused only on what can be discussed reasonably, let's take a closer look at the feminist case for sameness, keeping in mind that the main reason for exploring this in depth is to test the ideological grounds for the feminist attack on traditional society.

## THE FEMINIST REACTION

> *Feminist theory . . . is passionate and Salvationist in a similar way to Marxism, new religious movements, and occult enthusiasms: all of them know in advance not only the conclusions they will arrive at but the appropriate attitude toward those conclusions. Academically, it is mostly unsophisticated. A little light generalizing work is followed by polysyllabic decoration and some spray-on indignation.*
> —Kenneth Minogue, *Times Literary Supplement*, June 7, 1991

The modern feminist reaction to the pro-family arrangement outlined above gathered steam throughout the early part of the twentieth century, accelerated by the experience of two world wars in which so many women were put to work out of the home. It was also reinforced by a growing worldwide egalitarianism expressed in various collectivist movements—fascism and communism—

themselves the contributory causes of those wars. Along with this came the vastly increased wealth of all free Western nations, which meant in turn the possibility of historically unprecedented tax harvesting, and therefore the possibility of ever-larger governments, huge, as never before seen. This in turn meant that more and more government services for "the people" could be dreamed up and actually delivered on a massive scale as never before imagined, in the hope of votes to be gained. For such States—all now less-free "democratic" states—the greatest competitor for citizen loyalty was (and remains) voluntary civil society and its mainspring, the private natural family. This in turn meant that governments vying for votes had what has turned out to be a socially destructive motive to compete for citizen allegiance, against the inward pull of civil society and the family. New tax-funded "free" services were the State's weapon of choice and became widely offered as replacements for those things families and their communities had always voluntarily arranged to provide for themselves. Soon local clubs, associations and art guilds and the like faded in importance, to be replaced by government-subsidized recreational, cultural, and social equivalents. Citizens were initially offered the big programs such as social security and unemployment protection, but before long they were offered everything from kiddie soccer to flower arranging, to courses in personal and business finance, to beginner guitar and dance courses—all state-funded or subsidized. In order to provide such things "equally," the State had to begin an "atomization" of society by changing the historical focus on the family unit, to a new focus on autonomous individuals. In this manner, without regard for any private or economic or circumstantial family differences, the State was re-engineering the former State/society relationship into a new State/individual one. For this to succeed, civil society and the natural family as its foundation had to be weakened in influence, and when it came to the rising ideological imperative of "equality," this meant that biological gender as the deciding factor in family formation and sex-role differentiation had to be neutralized. The public schools and education ministries of the State would do that job. Enter modern feminism as an arm of the autonomizing State. That is the general background for the corrosive forces worming away at all modern societies.

More specifically, the rise of feminism in the twentieth century was directly linked to the Marxist anti-capitalist movement through Simone de Beauvoir's influential book *The Second Sex*—basically a treatment of the condition of women. There was much of originality in it, but she herself volunteered that its underlying philosophy was derived largely from the work of her philandering companion, Jean-Paul Sartre. In it, de Beauvoir was militantly anti-capitalist, anti-property, anti-marriage, and anti-family. She admired the Soviet model of society, of all things: "Marriage was to be based on a free agreement that the spouses could break at will; maternity was to be voluntary; pregnancy leaves were to be paid for by the state, which would assume charge of the children. . . ."[4] Much of that has indeed come to pass. She was talking about Soviet society as her ideal, but it might as well have been about Canada, 2010, because that is still our radical feminist song. De Beauvoir was succeeded by serious North American feminist writers like Kate Millet, Betty Friedan, and Gloria Steinem, most of whom shared her admiration for socialism under one name or another, which "can be considered virtually a further distinguishing mark of feminism."[5] These second-wave feminists were in turn succeeded by a virtual army of postmodern feminists whose turgid works are still visible on any bookstore shelf devoted to their ever-more-creative forms of envy-and-oppression theory. But it doesn't matter. When it comes to putting a finger on just what feminism's basic beliefs are, we can encapsulate the philosopher Michael Levin's four points (his words in quotes) as follows. Feminists believe:

1.  That "men and women are the same"—anatomical differences apart. [This is a version of the equality illusion at work, and a lot of recent science on sex differences blows that argument right out of the water—see "Brain Sex," below].
2.  That "men unfairly occupy positions of dominance" because they have been raised in the myth that boys are more aggressive than girls, and have been taught mastery, while girls have been taught people skills instead [a version of the determinist illusion]. Without this stereotyping, all "leadership would be equally divided between the sexes."
3.  "Traditional femininity is a suffocating and pathological response" to women's restricted lives and must be abandoned. Everyone must reject the idea that sex has any significant effect on one's nature.
4.  All the above changes "will require the complete transformation of society." [The principal tool here is the rights illusion. See the quote by Dulude at the head of this chapter].

## DO THE FEMINIST ASSUMPTIONS HOLD UP?

In order to do their work of attacking a traditional, biologically based natural society, radical feminists have had to argue "there are no innate differences" between men and women. Accordingly, and on this—as I shall show, false— assumption, they have pushed for (and won) various pay equity statutes, and state-funded abortion-on-demand laws, and continue to argue that state-funded daycare is a right. All these claims and the programs linked to them are seriously flawed. The rest of this chapter shows why.

A major shot across the bow attacking the "no biological differences" claim—the foundation stone of all feminist theory—was an early report on the assumption of male-female sameness by Eleanor Maccoby and Carol Jacklin, two feminist psychologists from prestigious Stanford University, published in their exhaustive two-volume work *The Psychology of Sex Differences.*[6]

These two social scientists set out to survey the entire field of studies on psychological sex differences, under the assumption there were none. But what they learned was that clear and important differences exist between boys and girls *even before birth*. There are wide, and universal, differences across whole ranges of physical sensitivity, illness, perception, learning, tactility, language, spatial abilities, pain threshold, and on and on. Of course, there are great similarities, too. But significant differences are detected in all areas studied, through the various stages of development. This would not surprise most parents, for as Levin humorously reminds us, "Any veteran of adolescence and parenthood still able to believe that boys and girls are born alike has already withstood more evidence than any laboratory can provide." The best-known difference is the general superior female ability with language, and general superior male ability with mathematics and spatial relations—both noticed early and continuously throughout life. (My own case is quite the opposite.) But the most important difference, one I am sure Maccoby and Jacklin hoped they would not find, but certainly did, was in "aggression." In their chapter on "power relationships," here is what they report: "It is time to consider whether the sex difference in aggression has a biological foundation. We contend that it does":

1. "Males are more aggressive than females in all human societies for which evidence is available."
2. The sex differences are found early in life, at a time when there is no evidence that differential socialization pressures have been brought to bear by adults to "shape" aggression differently in the two sexes.
3. Similar sex differences are found in man and subhuman primates.
4. Aggression is related to levels of sex hormones, and can be changed by experimental administrations of these hormones.

For anyone who seriously considers the whole subject of male-female sex differences, this early and sweeping survey must be conclusive, especially because these authors were working hard to *discount* male/female differences in the scientific literature. Quite clearly, *there are no grounds whatsoever for the pivotal feminist claim that males and females are fundamentally the same*, and "the accessibility of the immense volume of material on sex difference makes the continued respectability of feminism no less than a scandal."[7]

Even though most sensible people can see that boys and girls, and men and women have always behaved differently, and normally desire different kinds of lives, many modern social scientists and ideologues caught up in the feminist egalitarian myth have resisted this truth. So strong was this resistance that by the 1960s radical feminists actually *set out to change biology*, mostly by ignoring it entirely, disputing its findings, or attempting to reverse male and female behaviours through social conditioning. As biologist Glenn Wilson emphasizes, they were interested not in what *is* but in what they felt *ought to be*. If boys are too aggressive, let's punish aggression. If girls are not aggressive enough, let's reward aggression. My own high school, formerly a boys-only school, is now coed and boasts of teaching boys and girls "against the grain." In a 2008 school brochure, teachers and parents were urged to make sure that boys and girls "spend time in activities that they may not be 'hardwired' to choose of their own accord." I think that "make sure," means "force them." The underlying faith of such teachers is—has to be—the strange belief that boys and girls start life exactly the same and that all human differences are therefore "socially con-structed." Most honest social scientists thinking in this strange way end up dis-covering that their egalitarian ideals have biased their research results.

In the past twenty years, however, much more, and more in-depth scien-tific work has been done on sex differences of all sorts, much of it with the help of modern technology, and I have summarized many of these studies in *The Book of Absolutes* under the rubric "Brain Sex."[8] The scientific evidence in sup-port of innate, natural, and universal male-female differences must now be considered overwhelming and conclusive. However, because many of these differences are matters of degree, it helps to think of overlapping circles when imagining such things. In other words, science has found that although a large number of skills and behaviours are shared between the sexes, the averages for each sex are distinctly non-aligned. This means we can never say all men or all women do so and so or behave in such and such a way. But we may say that "on average," they do. Suffice it to say for now, however, and merely to whet the appetite, that such brain-sex differences—most of them universal and cross-cultural (in all societies studied to date)—are presumed to have a biological basis, whether hormonal or brain-based, but usually both. Patterns found show clear differences in such things as: levels of sense awareness, verbal abili-ties, math abilities, spatial abilities (both imagined and actual), throwing and targeting skills, fine-motor skills, rotational and directional skills, skills in games like chess (spatial emphasis) and Scrabble (verbal emphasis), problem-solving psychology, and more.

## BRAIN SEX

*Boys and girls are as different above the neck as they are below.*
—Anonymous

Until around the 1970s most of this argument was conducted as a verbal nature-nurture slugfest. Words, and *lots* of statistics. But since then it has been fought—and won—in favour of clear biological differences—with CAT and PET scanners, MRI machines, and electron microscopes. These and many other combinations of extraordinary technology and biochemistry have revealed irrefutably that various parts of the brains of men and women are *structurally* different and, even where they are the same, they often *function* very differently in fascinating ways when performing the same tasks. Such findings soon began causing sex-difference researchers to recant their previous faith in the "blank slate" idea of the mind (the idea that we begin life with a mind like a blank slate on which life will write) and to admit it is no longer tenable to believe that males and females are born with the same behavioural dispositions.

This is a lay book for the general reader, so I do not want to burden this chapter with proofs. Those interested are encouraged to see my notes for some references,[9] or to search the Internet under topics such as "cognitive sciences," "sex and cognition," and the "psychology of sex differences." Here is a brief summary of what the reader will find:

- A great number of studies show that male and female babies behave differently in the womb (movements, heart rates, etc.) and also moments after birth (give different attention and have different intensity of reaction to the same objects, sounds, and tactile sensations).
- Infant girls—but not infant boys—distinguish a baby's cry from other general sounds. Male babies prefer objects to people, females the reverse.
- Girls develop language, fluency, and verbal memory earlier than boys and process such information faster, a difference observed by all researchers.
- Girls are less rule-bound and boys more so. Boys need rules to tell whether they are winning or not. Their preadolescent play is often such rank-related play.
- From birth, boys are more aggressive, competitive, and self-assertive than girls (perhaps the most common finding, worldwide). Even when one-year-old babies are separated from their mothers and their toys by a fence-like barrier, the girls tend to stay in the middle and cry for help, while the boys tend to cluster at the ends of the barrier, trying to find a way out.
- Human cognitive patterns and their related brain organization are apparently permanently influenced by physiological events that take place by the fourth fetal month.
- At the University of Pennsylvania's School of Medicine, a combination of PET scans and high-resolution MRI technology used to study brain metabolism has shown that *even at rest*, doing nothing in particular, there were male-female differences in brain metabolism in seventeen different brain areas.
- Beginning at puberty, men are more prone to physical violence (most crime is committed by males between the ages of fifteen and twenty-five), and women are more prone to emotional volatility. In the same period, men show more confidence, concentration, and ambition, whereas women show more social sensitivity and interest in relationships. About

85 percent of all crimes are committed by males, and there are specific, universal sex differences in the styles, types of victim, and post-crime behaviours of male and female perpetrators of violent crimes.

- Boys are better than girls on a variety of spatial skills. This advantage is cross-cultural and is practically universal in males. The spatial-skill sex difference becomes quite marked after puberty and is even observed in animals.

- Women are superior to men at certain tasks requiring memory for the location of objects, and at many language tasks.

So it seems that from birth males tend to strive harder than females to reach the top of any power hierarchy they encounter, and they create their own hierarchies to reach the top if none exist. Boys are usually more aggressive, more Machiavellian in their pursuit of power, and crueller and more willing to hurt others than girls. Studies abound showing that men the world over tend to devalue, if not despise, victims—especially their own—whereas women tend to take pity on them. Nothing in this male attitude is particularly admirable, but that's the way it is. This was driven home to me by a television documentary of a World War II concentration camp entered by Russian soldiers. The commentator remarked that many of the soldiers not only stole from the women prisoners, but raped them as well. Now, these women were the most emaciated imaginable, some close to death. With sadness and disgust it hit home that no woman could possibly find a man in that condition sexually arousing, or wish to degrade him so. With that thought, my awareness of the chasm that exists between the physical and moral lives of males and females struck home even harder. And let us not forget that throughout history, and even though lots of women do such things too, it is the men who have been prone to abandon children, murder them, bayonet them in war, rape them, take them into slavery, and so on. The truly great crimes of history have been perpetrated by men—I think of countless tyrants, especially the modern ones such as Stalin, Hitler, Lenin, Pol Pot, Mao, and their like, who wrought cruelties of a kind and scope that beggar the imagination. And let us never forget: they were all utopian socialists. In this prototypical sense only, radical feminism (striving for aggressive control of social outcomes) is a very male undertaking.

Anthropological studies universally verify the reality of male aggression and hardness, *which can be induced in any female, human or primate, by the simple administration of male hormones.* Anyone who has had occasion to mix with athletes on steroids has known this for years. Both male and female athletes take only *male* hormones, for an obvious reason—to enhance power and aggressiveness. Contrarily, *female* hormones administered to long-term violent criminals succeed in pacifying them. Of course, aggressiveness is highly valued in societies the world over, and so men tend to be rewarded for this kind of behaviour. In other words, learning plays an important secondary role, but not a primary one. Anthropological and biological studies confirm that through hormones, men in general are rendered more aggressive, exploratory, volatile, competitive and dominant, more visual, abstract, and impulsive, more muscular, appetitive, and tall . . . less nurturant, moral, domestic, stable, and peaceful, less auditory, verbal, and sympathetic, less durable, healthy, and dependable, less balanced . . . more compulsive sexually and less secure. Within their own sex, males are more inclined to affiliate upwards—toward authority—and less inclined to affiliate downwards—toward children and toward the weak and needy.[10]

As a natural result of this, there is no society in the world in which true matriarchy has ever existed, or is in any way emerging today. Fascinatingly, the beginning of all these differences is right in the womb. For we all begin life as females, biologically. We become male only if the Y chromosome is present, and sufficient male hormones then act upon our early development. Maleness *is* biological difference—there is nothing "constructed" about it. Even genetic girls, accidentally exposed to male hormones, consistently reject most of the attempts of the culture to feminize them.[11] Enough said. What are we to make of all this? Very simply, that men monopolize leadership positions because they try harder to get them does not mean that men always deserve these positions or that men do a better job in them than women would if they became leaders. The only sense in which male dominance is "right" is that it expresses the free choices of individual men to strive for positions of power and the free choices of individual women to do other things.[12]

My addendum to this is that *aggressiveness* and *control* are two very different things. In external structures, like armies, or businesses, the former generally leads to the latter; but in interpersonal relationships, not necessarily so. Everyone can think of couples in which the male is more aggressive, but the female controls the relationship and the tenor of the family. Women tend to be just as aggressive as men defensively, when fighting for their loved ones or some deep-rooted belief, but are universally less aggressive than men offensively. Recall the great line from *My Big Fat Greek Wedding*: Husband: "The husband is the head of the family." Wife: "Yes, my dear, but the wife, she is the neck."

## WHAT ARE THE EFFECTS OF INNATE SEX DIFFERENCES ON SOCIETY?

Briefly put, they can be devastating—unless society sets itself to control them, as it did in the nineteenth century. Alas, we have long since sowed the wind of sexual egalitarianism, and we are reaping the whirlwind. For, as George Gilder poignantly argues in *Men and Marriage*, the unconstrained public philosophy of males the world over, to the great detriment of society, tends to focus on *immediate gratification*. Single young men are a distinct hazard to society and its procreative health for the following reasons. They vastly prefer hit-and-run

sex. They are wildly more aggressive than females. Although single men represent a percentage in the low teens (and falling) of the population over the age
of fourteen, they commit nearly 90 percent of major and violent crimes. They
drink more, have more—and more serious—car accidents than women or
married men. Young bachelors are twenty-two times more likely to be committed for mental disease—and ten times more likely to go to hospital for
chronic diseases than married men. Single men are convicted of rape five times
more often than married men; they have almost double the mortality rate of
married men, and three times that of single women, from all causes.

Because homosexuality is overwhelmingly a "hit-and-run" phenomenon
for males (distinctly not so for females), and suits their predilection for immediate—and often anonymous—gratification, such homosexuality is in accord
with the sexual nature of males and thrives when male/female role distinctions
are suppressed. Cultures that want to guard against the threat of homosexuality must therefore drive a cultural wedge down hard between maleness and
femaleness, for it is no simple coincidence that homosexuality is flourishing in
a time of feminism. They go together like the two sides of a coin. Just so, the
attempt of the State to neutralize male and female differences is manifest in its
parallel effort to "normalize" homosexuality, marketing it to us in its agencies
and schools as a "value-free" matter of sexual "orientation." In such matters,
the State is promoting and financing the elimination of meaningful and socially
useful differences. Of course, homosexuality is much more than an orientation; it is also an ideology, and today, there is a whole feminist school promoting homosexuality as liberation from men, marriage, and traditional society,
and true feminism as lesbianism. In its heyday, the January 1988 newsletter of
the U.S. National Organization for Women (NOW), we read: "The simple fact
is that *every woman must be willing to be identified as a lesbian to be fully feminist.*"
Some make the weak argument that heterosexuality is also ideological. But that
is a manifestly absurd argument blind to the biological facts and truth of
human nature in human history.

The real truth is that this whole matter of sexual liberation—which is code
for liberation from natural biological propensities—has backfired. Men have
benefited sexually in the short term, but certainly not in the long. Women have
lost in both because they have surrendered the one sure means of control they
had over men, the one sure method that enabled them to have children, provide
for them, protect them, and nurture them *personally* at the same time—all paid
for by doting males—if they so desired. Now, in some despair, millions of abandoned mothers are turning to the patriarchal State for sustenance. But of course,
States can only be such a father either by employing women in huge numbers
(80 percent of low-paid public service clerical staff in all Western social democracies are women), or by taking the tax money the increasing number of low-
income female-headed families requires from singles, and from fathers and

252 10: RADICAL FEMINISM

mothers in intact families. Even worse, as Gilder explains, feminism, by default, has allowed men to create a system of serial polygamy—one in which the stronger (wealthier, more successful) men can enjoy many partners. But a woman loses out in the sense that for the purposes of child-bearing, her chances of locating a strong husband are biologically confined to a few fleeting years of her life. If she waits too long to marry, the strong males her own age get taken in a rapidly peaking, concave-sided pyramid of diminishing choices. Worse still, in societies that choose both to neutralize natural sex differences and to permit "liberated" sex, the homosexual under-culture always vies for normality with the core culture, attacks traditional values, and recruits otherwise procreative (and usually younger) males. In other words, "polygyny produces homosexuality."[13] It does this both by liberalizing the sexual choices for strong males (thus destroying the equal apportionment of possible mates) and, in its feminist guise, by setting the female ethos against the male ethos, thus encouraging sexual resentment between men and women. This, in turn, leads to less marriage, something seen immediately in Sweden when it took the lead by enthusiastically embracing sexual liberation. Sweden's marriage rate between 1966 and 1973 did a freefall to around 50 percent of its former level; more people began living alone (more than 63 percent of the residents of Stockholm now live alone); and divorce, or "couple dissolution," as the Swedes call it, rose drastically.[14] Multiple mates? Easy sex? Multiple mistresses? Homosexuality? Easy divorce and cohabitation? A booming pornography industry? All these inevitably undermine heterosexual monogamy, which is unfortunate, because "monogamy is designed to minimize the effect of sexual inequalities—to prevent the powerful of either sex from disrupting the familial order . . . any sexual revolution, therefore, will tend to liberate more men than women."[15]

It is for this reason that "the crucial process of civilization is the subordination of male sexual impulses and biology to the long-term horizons of female sexuality."[16] Gilder convincingly argues that because of the male-female hormonal difference in biology, *society basically must be set up to tame men and their barbaric proclivities.* For without the long-range reproductive goals of women, men would be content to fight, enjoy their lust, wander, make war, compete, and strive for power, glory, and dominance. In his view, in terms of the larger purposes of human civilization that depend utterly on sufficient procreation, successful child nurture, and strong families, males in general are inferior sexually to women, who because of their biology control the entirety of the sexual and procreative order (or disorder) of human life. In fact, males are in this sense only neither sexually nor morally *equal* to females, and therefore "the man must be *made* equal by society." That is, men rely for personal meaning and success on the socially purposive roles created for them by their culture. Thus is the contract struck between men and women whereby he *provides and protects*, she *processes and nurtures*. Again, a woman who wants to try all four of these things, or switch it all around, is free to try (at least, in a free society this is true). But most, the world over, do not—because the system works. What this means is that men, lacking in the distinctiveness and biological determinateness of women, are "deeply dependent on the structure of society to define [their] role."[17]

In short, women channel and confine the generalized male sexual desire in such a way as to protect themselves and their children, and in so doing teach men to subordinate their impulses to the long-term cycles of female sexuality and biology on which society has always been based. In order to avail himself of the intense and intimate sexual meaning a woman can give to his life, and the extension of himself into the future through children that only a woman can provide, a man must give something in return—and this must always be "the external realm of meaning, sustenance, and protection in which the child can be safely born."[18] And that's just the start. When you stop to consider deeply the complex, lifelong physical, emotional, and financial requirements of the average family (I have five children), the seriousness of this undertaking sinks in. It requires what the anthropologist Margaret Mead called a "commitment of permanence" from each sex, and a "deal" struck between the parties, the terms of which are supplied by the culture. We break the deal at our own—and especially at our children's—peril.

While one can always quibble with details, or find exceptions, it will remain difficult to argue with Gilder's main thesis because it is so overwhelmingly supported by anthropological studies around the world, in every culture studied, past and present. In view of this, we must ask why, in our present society, the state-financed radical feminist program has been so influential. Sex education classes now take the experience of very early fornication for granted,[19] male/female differences are downplayed or outright denied in textbooks, homosexuality is presented as just another normal "orientation," so-called "value-free" discussions and "self-esteem" codes of "ethics" (the word "morality" has completely dropped from usage) are promoted as primary, and the crucial importance of procreative marriage and the family is all but forgotten. But the question to which all citizens ought to demand an answer is this: Why does the State legitimize and finance only radical feminist advocacy groups, and not those that promote traditional family life? Why does it massively fund abortion on demand, but only token sexual abstinence programs for the young? Why has it funded extreme left-wing radical organizations like the National Action Committee on the Status of Women (NAC), but never conservative pro-family organizations such as REAL Women of Canada? If its interest was really equality, wouldn't the funding be more even-handed? At a minimum, readers of this chapter should begin to suspect that the sorts of programs introduced in order to achieve an ideologically asexual, anti-biological society with equal outcomes regardless of gender is destructive of our social fabric, to say the least.

# THE ANDROGYNY HOAX

*As of 1980, 72 percent of mental health professionals . . . described a*
*"healthy, mature, socially competent" adult as androgynous.*
—Allan Carlson, *Family Questions*

A major instrument in the feminist effort to equalize sex roles in society, still used by those who insist on the by-now-embarrassing sameness argument, is their assault on the whole idea of gender. "Androgyny" is a term referring to both genders as one, and the use of it follows from feminist ideology. They think that if all sex role behaviours are just a result of social conditioning rather than biology, then without such biologically determined "roles" authentic human beings must be . . . naturally androgynous (an equal mixture of male and female). Hence the distinction between male and female, they have argued, is a social myth. At the extreme, feminists even argue that God is both male and female, that "Holy Wisdom" is the female persona of God, and that human beings can attain "spiritual androgyny." Such ideas have ancient origins in mystical forms of thought in which, at the extreme, the human spirit is said to be one with the universe, and all distinctions whatsoever are held to be a falsification of our original unity. This sort of spiritual egalitarianism is a retreat not merely from biology, but from all social and material reality.

In his detailed, eloquent, and sobering work *Family Questions*, Allan Carlson was among the first to cite a bevy of serious scientists, some of them feminists of the honest type, who showed that the whole androgyny movement was and remains ideologically motivated, has never had any basis in fact, and has "elevated corrupted science to the level of public truth."[20]

Beginning in the 1960s, in reaction to the "natural complement" theory of gender most people still hold (that males and females are both incomplete, and thus are a natural complement for each other), radical feminists began to argue that women would never attain sex role equality unless a different model of gender was created. Shulamith Firestone (who, as Carlson pointed out, did humanity a service by pushing feminist logic to its perverse conclusions), argued that "Mom" must be eliminated, and replaced by a "socialist feminism"; that sex roles had to be eliminated, and replaced with her preferred "polymorphous perverse" sexuality (meaning anything goes); that the incest taboo had to be eliminated, and that parents should freely have sex with ready children. Bottle-feeding "technology" and daycare, she said, would end the need for natural mothering. This, she called "revolutionary feminism." Her peer, Anne Ferguson of the University of Massachusetts argued that "androgynes," the "superpersons" of the coming new society (the feminist utopia she imagined), would be freed from the need for children (here's that anti-child theme again, masquerading as a concern for overpopulation), by experiencing pure "bisexual love." Ferguson despised natural biological parenting because it produces "a debilitating heterosexual identity" in children. Her formula to bring about the socialist society organized on feminist principles was simply to equalize all social, economic, and political power outside the home (with affirmative action programs). All else would follow.

Edward Tiryakian, of Duke University (still a real hotbed of feminist and postmodern psychobabble), was out of the gate early too, insisting that androgyny is a "truly revolutionary" principle for overturning both the sexual division of labour and "the present prevalent form of the nuclear family which is the source of the reproduction of heterosexuality." He too advocated revolutionary change through the perfection of baby-bottle technology, and also a U.S. Supreme Court ruling declaring it unconstitutional to teach or reinforce heterosexuality in the schools. Ruth Bleier, another early soldier of fanatical feminism, argued that the nuclear family must be "crushed." The bitterly hostile Andrea Dworkin made a name for herself promoting homosexuality and even bestiality—or what she called "other-animal relationships," and the freeing of children to enjoy their "right" to "live out their erotic impulses." That's what Rousseau advocated, and what his bizarre compatriot the Marquis de Sade actually did. She called for a "new kind of human being, and a new kind of human community." At a Canadian feminist conference she notoriously advocated that battered women "should feel free to murder their husbands."[21] Today, that would get her dragged up for "hate speech," as well as for discrimination, for she did not advocate that battered males murder their wives, or sons their mothers.

In acceptance of this model for the new and healthier human being, Alexandra Kaplan actually argued that "social sickness" ought to be redefined as a society with "overly masculine" men and "overly feminine" women. This, too, followed the peculiar egalitarian illogic of radical feminism, and illustrates the attempt to alter the foundational concepts and language of our society. Another writer, Christabelle Sethna, of the Ontario Institute for Studies in Education (now as radical a leftist "education" school as one could find anywhere), argued that dead animals represent patriarchal society and war, whereas live animals represent women; therefore, "meat eating is misogyny" [woman-hating], and milk dairying (all those nasty men a-squeezin' them thar udders) is a rampant exploitation of the female sex.

Without our tax dollars, such people would be reading this drivel to the walls in some holding tank for losers; but with our considerable dollars, they have created a tax-funded audience. The State pays for their jobs, subsidizes their books, and funds their travel and their conventions. More's the pity. Angry, narrow-minded feminists have been extremely influential, despite the blatantly ideological nature of their program, their shoddy science, and perverse antisocial values. As American psychologist Paul C. Vitz of New York

University discovered after intensive scrutiny of more than a hundred high school social studies and history textbooks, "by far the most noticeable position in the textbooks was a feminist one. Not a single story or theme celebrated marriage or motherhood as a positive experience. Sex-role reversals and the mockery of masculine men were common." More on the origins of North American man-hating—or misandry—below.

As seen in the last few chapters, public (government) schools in North America have for more than three decades been furiously promoting lies about human nature. They began with the androgyny myth (the lie that both sexes are the same); then moved on to the notion that human sexuality is a diverse phenomenon, and normal heterosexual relations, marriages, and families no better or worse than any other kind; to the general "postmodern" lie that all gender is at bottom a matter of choice, and is "socially constructed." That's why today we see vote-grabbing mayors gliding through some of our largest cities on garish, tax-funded floats surrounded by genitalia-brandishing exponents of "LGBT," or the "lesbian, gay, bisexual, transgender"[22] lifestyle. Your gender is what you construct for yourself. *Human nature is not defined by your biology, but by your will.* It's all a kind of sexual fascism—the imposition of human will on reality; another expression of the eternal revolt against . . . human nature.

In public schools this amounts to a tax-funded brainwashing of society through children, despite the fact that there have always been a host of serious social scientists demonstrating that the androgyny notion has no basis in fact, and is a political hoax. So-called "androgynous" people are in fact far more dysfunctional, more neurotic, lower in self-esteem, and more confused than normal people. There is nothing "super" about them. Researchers have shown conclusively that normal sex-typed parents make by far the best parents (androgynous parents "perform dismally"); that masculinity in males is correlated most highly with positive mental health; that male psychopaths have low masculinity scores, and so on. Researcher Diana Baumrind summed it up long ago when she said that traditional sex-typing is healthy for society and for children, and that androgyny, as a positive concept, is a complete and utter failure.[23] Carlson lamented that in the United States (ditto for Canada) "a small band of ideologues . . . has succeeded in imposing a fraudulent, dangerous ideology, masquerading as science, on broad elements of our public life." A major concern for our future is that this fraud has succeeded in legalizing "misandry"— the hatred of men.

*WASP men are the only safe target [for abuse] in advertising . . .*
*you don't get a single letter of complaint.*
—Terry O'Reilly, host of CBC's *The Age of Persuasion* (2009)

# SNAPSHOT
Legalizing Misandry

(This is a guest Snapshot prepared by Dr. Katherine Young and Dr. Paul Nathanson of McGill University. It outlines the transformation from an egalitarian feminism to an anti-male feminism.)

At first, in the 1960s, feminism was an extension of egalitarianism and therefore a modern "liberal" movement. The goal was sexual equality in both public and private life. The big test came in the 1970s, during the campaign for an Equal Rights Amendment (ERA) to guarantee sexual equality. Passing the test with flying colours, the National Organization for Women officially supported an equal military draft (although the government changed nothing); if the country needed a draft at all, in other words, young women should share the burden equally with young men. By the end of that decade, however, things were changing rapidly. Just as the egalitarian civil rights movement was losing ground to the radical Black Power movement, egalitarian feminism was losing ground to radical feminism. We refer to "ideological" feminism instead of "radical" or "militant" feminism, however, for reasons that we explain in great detail.

Like other political ideologies on both the Left and the Right, ideological feminism is profoundly dualistic. It is no longer enough to argue that women should have just as many "opportunities" as men to establish careers in the world beyond home (and that men should have just as many opportunities as women to establish close relationships with their children at home). The new goal is revolution, not reform. Men have "all the power," according to ideological feminists, because they *deliberately stole* it from women in the remote past and have tried to cover it up ever since. As a result, men have both *hated* and *oppressed* women everywhere. This is what we call the "conspiracy theory of history." Because history is a titanic conspiracy of "them" against "us," in other words, it follows that "they" (men) are innately evil, in effect, and "we" (women) are innately good. To put this ideology into operation and free women from the tyranny of men, ideological feminists believe, requires something much more radical than the naive and "bourgeois" egalitarianism of early feminism. It requires what we call the "mobilization of resentment" through the "teaching of contempt." Borrowing not only the notion of "class" from Marxism, but also the rhetoric of "blood" and "nation" from romanticism, simply replacing those keywords with "gender," ideological feminists systematically attack every feature of daily life—from ads and commercials, to marriage and heterosexuality—as the sinister manifestation of an almost metaphysically evil force. This requires not merely the "deconstruction" of masculinity in its historic forms, but also what amounts to the deconstruction of *maleness itself* (and the corresponding glorification of *femaleness*).

Not all feminists have adopted this cynical mentality, to be sure, and the common understanding of political life in democratic societies remains egalitarian. But ideological feminists, who have produced the dominant "discourse" in most universities and especially in law schools, are by now much more influential than egalitarian feminists. Without abandoning the original rhetoric of equality (which has made openly gender-specific, or openly discriminatory, legislation almost unthinkable), they have nonetheless found ways of institutionalizing and legalizing all sorts of inequalities that favour women instead of men. Misogyny is wrong, according to this new double standard, but misandry is right or at least tolerable. Two wrongs, apparently, make a right.

At the explicit level of legislation, all Canadian laws are gender neutral. At the implicit level of interpretation, however, many now favour women. And this legal inequality begins at the top. Due mainly to the efforts of ideological feminists, Canada's Charter of Rights and Freedoms has institutionalized *systemic* discrimination against men. This document refers explicitly to the goal of equality *for all people* in one clause, but also to the goal of giving special legal protection to women (and three other groups) in another clause. To get around the obvious inequality of affirmative action, ideological feminists have managed to redefine "equality" to suit themselves. They demand not merely "formal equality" (of opportunity), but "substantive equality" (of result), a utopian standard that not even totalitarian regimes have attained. Status of Women Canada gets millions of dollars from taxpayers to monitor the needs and problems of women, not surprisingly, but the government provides no comparable department for men. Nonetheless, studies show that male suicide and school dropout rates (which could eventually produce an uneducated and therefore unemployable male underclass) are increasing much faster than female rates. Canadian politicians and officials routinely refer to "violence against women" (as if violence against men were either nonexistent or trivial) and spend millions of tax dollars to provide abused women with shelters and other services, but provide nothing for abused men (even though studies show that women are as likely as men to initiate domestic violence and often cause physical injuries).

Although some American jurisdictions are now moving toward equal joint custody for divorced parents, ideological feminists have found ways of stacking the deck in favour of mothers not only by attacking divorced fathers (and fathers in general) as molesters or abusers, but also by influencing government bureaucrats (including those who, behind closed doors, came up with "guidelines" for child support that favour mothers), and the social service agencies that *administer* gender-neutral laws (often failing to enforce the visitation rights of fathers). Police officers routinely remove men—but not women—from their homes without evidence of misconduct, and hand down harsher sentences to men than to women (a discrepancy that is not confined to cases of domestic violence). We now have laws and policies against sexual harassment that rely on very subjective standards. In fact, we now have rape-shield laws and reformed rules of evidence that not only encourage accusers to come forward, but also make it very hard for the accused to defend themselves.

In short, Canada tolerates laws and policies that make an ideological assumption: that every woman belongs to a *victim class* and every man to an *oppressor class* (unless someone can show that this or that woman or man is an exception). This adds up to systemic discrimination against men and therefore to systemic misandry.

So far, we have discussed these problems in three books from McGill-Queen's University Press: *Spreading Misandry: The Teaching of Contempt for Men in Popular Culture* (2001); *Legalizing Misandry: From Public Shame to Systemic Discrimination Against Men* (2006); and *Sanctifying Misandry: Goddess Ideology and the Fall of Man* (2010). A fourth volume will be entitled *Transcending Misandry: From Feminist Ideology to Intersexual Dialogue* (expected publication, 2011).

## WHAT IS THE RADICAL FEMINIST POLITICAL PROGRAM?

As we have seen, natural male-female differences, and the free choices that spring from them, are generally reflected in a free society, and in the marketplace of jobs, goods, and ideas. Even though many militant feminists have now given up in their effort to prove that innate differences are the result of "socialization," they have developed a more sinister approach to getting what they want. In short, if you can't prove male-female differences are learned, but you still want to eradicate the natural as well as freely chosen consequences of these differences, you need a lot of money, and changes in the laws.

Most radical feminist organizations in Canada (and elsewhere in the West) lobby aggressively for abortion on demand, legalized prostitution, lesbian rights, universal tax-funded daycare, the nationalization of banks and industry, the abolition of the common law right to private property, and withdrawal from NATO and NORAD. Hardly the Canadian woman's agenda. In Canada, it's the socialist NDP agenda—one with which some 80 percent of Canadians openly and repeatedly disagree. But despite the promotion by NAC of such unpopular values, successive Canadian governments, including Conservative ones, have continued to finance feminist left-leaning programs lavishly, even those committed to bringing the entire government down. Some examples from the start? The June 1987 issue of *World Marxist Review* carried an article by Nancy McDonald, a member of the Central Executive Committee of the Communist Party of Canada, in which she stated: "The Communist Party participates actively in NAC [since renamed] . . ." Judy Rebick, a former head of NAC, once described herself as "a former Marxist" (*Globe and Mail*, July 4,

1990); and Judy Darcy, formerly head of CUPE, Canada's half-million-strong Union of Public Employees was once described as "radically left wing" (*Globe and Mail*, August 17, 1991). Although the Women's Program was invented in 1973 to promote the status of *all* Canadian women, it quickly morphed into an organization run by a hard-core radical feminist group that uses government funds to implant radical values in Canadian society that have nothing whatsoever to do with Canadian women as a whole.

Such an attitude would be perfectly acceptable and unobjectionable from a self-supporting group claiming to represent Canadian women. After all, they can *claim* whatever they want. But from a department of government? Funded by tax dollars? Pushing an openly socialist, anti-freedom agenda so obviously out of step with the sentiments of the people of Canada? And more pointedly, with those of the women of Canada? Why, it's nothing short of a scandal made possible by tax plunder. Any thinking woman who does not share radical feminist views and who stops to consider how her country is being socially reshaped by such feminists in her name, without her blessing, but with her money, ought to be outraged. Without such funding, these women's organizations would be a backwater collection of toothless radicals. With it, they are a dangerous force for social change completely opposed to the values of most Canadian women. I say let them fight as hard as they like for their views with their own money, but don't give them my tax dollars to do it, nor the dollars of millions of men and women who deeply disagree with them.

The balance of this chapter is concerned with a critique of three topics: so-called "pay equity," government daycare, and tax-funded abortion on demand, each of which is a fundamentalist plank of the radical feminist program to achieve the "whole transformation of society," as Louise Dulude cheerfully described her social revolution. Each of these is a sad and terribly flawed notion. Let us drill right down and examine what they are really about.

## THE "PAY EQUITY" SCANDAL

Almost everyone misunderstands so-called "pay equity." They think it is a fair-sounding idea that basically says any two human beings, regardless of gender, should be paid the same if they do the same work. But pay equity is not about that at all. The principle of paying people the same wage for the *same work* has long since been accepted as fair by almost everyone (although some economists still say that even this custom limits the freedom of individuals to offer their services for less, if they so desire, and is thus a form of minimum wage legislation that discriminates against the very poor). But radical feminists are not satisfied with the rule that women and men must be paid the same wage for the same work. They want them to be paid the same for *different* work if they can show that different kinds of work have the same "*value.*"

For example, if a government consultant can show that a female computer operator's job has the same "value" as a male truck driver's job, then the government will order that the two must be paid the same. Presto—gender equality in the marketplace! But there's a twist, of course: this applies only to women. If he makes more than she does, she can complain to the government, get the "value" of her job assessed in her favour, and then force her boss to pay her the same as the truck driver. But if she makes more than he does, he cannot use the same argument to force his boss to pay him the same as her! But I'm getting ahead of myself. Let's backtrack for a minute.

As it turns out, even though men and women don't very often choose to *do* the same kinds of work, feminists insist that as a class they ought to have the same earnings in the free market as men. But they don't. Men in free economies, as a class, are paid more than women as a class. So radical feminists have decided that any difference between the pay of men and the pay of women must be due to "sex discrimination." Once having decided this, they quickly began stigmatizing the kinds of work women tend to prefer as "job ghettos," or "pink collar ghettos." They conveniently ignored the fact that dental hygienists and legal secretaries, for example, are 99 percent female occupations and have very high starting salaries; but these jobs do not qualify as ghettos. In other words, if you train and strive for a high-paying job, you are assumed to be free; but if you take a low-paying or part-time job, or simply don't wish to earn any more than you do now, you are assumed to be suffering exploitation and discrimination. Once radical feminists succeeded in selling the government on the idea that any difference was really due to discrimination, the course was clear. They then had to set about forcing a world of otherwise-free people to conform to their vision of fairness. Despite the insult to the intelligence of free working women everywhere that this attitude suggests, their approach was very effective.

Here's the radical feminist's economic formula so far: men and women are the same, but because they are not paid the same when doing work we believe to have the same value, sex discrimination must be operating; therefore evidence of discrimination is required; then a *program* for correcting it; and finally, someone to *implement, finance, and police* the program. So ... the *proof* was the invention of a so-called "wage-gap"; the *program* was so-called pay equity; the sugar daddy (as always) would be ... the State. Canada's pay police would monitor all this. And they have done so.

Truth to say, one could marvel at the implacable and devious cleverness of the whole thing—if it weren't so dishonest and such an assault on our free way of life. The unfortunate result, and the deception of the public required to bring it about (Canadians have never understood clearly what the term "pay equity" means) is that many jurisdictions in Canada and America have the dubious distinction of having passed into law the most draconian pay equity legislation in the free world, and have completely hoodwinked the paying public in the process. Why so? Because . . .

## THE "WAGE GAP" IS A RED HERRING—IT'S MARRIAGE THAT ACCOUNTS FOR THE DIFFERENCE

Feminists say that there is a wage gap between the earnings of men and women in Canada (which is true, and always has been), and that much of this difference is proof of wage discrimination based on sex. But this is a plainly misleading and dishonest thing to say because the biggest reason for the difference in male-female earnings today is marriage. That is because *marital status has an asymmetrical effect on earnings by sex*, as the economists say.

In plain English: let's suppose a man and a woman are working side by side and earning the same wage. They fall in love and decide to get married and raise a family. Suddenly something absolutely normal happens. Visions of children dance in their heads, along with simultaneous worries. If both think even the best daycare is impersonal—"there's no way a stranger's going to raise our kids!"—then they worry immediately about how in the world they are going to give their children personal attention and both work full-time as well. Will her boss still keep her on if she asks for part-time work? He worries about mortgages, university education, clothing, food, and thinks: "Good Lord—I'm going to need a better job." The result of this totally predictable equation is that she reduces her work hours, or quits altogether, or quits and then takes a part-time job. And he? Well, the pressure is on. He arranges an appointment with his boss and lets him know in no uncertain terms that the promotion he wasn't so sure about last month . . . well, he's had a serious change of heart. In fact, given a chance, he'd love to run the whole department. When this occurs millions of times over, and you average their respective earnings, you have the makings of a "wage gap." But the crucial factor is not sex discrimination. It's the laudable preferential choices made by both parties in favour of marriage and their children.

The ratios of earnings between *never*-married men and women, and *ever*-married men and women in Canada, have always been stable. As long ago as 1971 (when the feminist movement was in full delirium), a study compiled from census data for Statistics Canada[24] showed the following:

|        | Never Married | Ever Married |
|--------|---------------|--------------|
| Men    | $4,201        | $6,675       |
| Women  | $4,170        | $2,217       |

The excellent American economist Thomas Sowell tells us that the same picture was found from the start in the United States, that "as of 1971 single women in their thirties who had worked continuously since leaving school earned slightly *more* than single men of the same age, even though women as a group earned less than half as much as men as a group." Yet another study in the U.S. showed that "female academics who never married earned *more* than male academics who never married," even before affirmative action became mandatory in 1971. Sowell summed up this confusion by saying that most of the current income and occupational differences between males and females as gross categories turns out, on closer scrutiny, to be *differences between married women and all other categories.*[25]

Almost two decades into the radical feminist era, a 1987 Statistics Canada report called "Earnings of Men and Women" still showed that never-married women made the following percentages of the earnings of never-married men:

| | | |
|---|---|---|
| never-married women | 25–34 years of age: | 96.8 |
| never-married women | 35–44 years of age: | 101.4 |
| never-married women | 45–54 years of age: | 107.2 |
| never-married women | 55+ years of age: | 102.4 |

Astonishingly, the women made more than the men at *all* ages except the youngest studied. Fact is that if anti-female discrimination was at work, this would have been impossible.

Further, here's some economic logic to put the whole mess to shame: if women were truly supplying business with cheap labour, business owners would naturally hire as many women as possible and would let the overpaid men go. But this has not happened. One of the lowest-paying jobs around is that of an outdoor-parking-lot attendant in winter—but you could count on one hand the number of females doing that in this country. Is this therefore a male ghetto? Not likely.

Furthermore, if the feminist thesis were true, firms that are said to be "exploiting" low-paid women would be making large profits. But they are not. Most, in fact, are fighting tooth and nail to maintain competitive margins in the face of world competition, especially in clothing, footwear, and food processing—family staples industries.

Furthermore, women who have been widowed, divorced, or separated should not be averaged into the figures and used as proof for the lower pay of single women. Obviously, after years out of the job market, they cannot expect to return to the job market at high pay, unless they have some skill that is in high demand.

## THE BACHELOR "WAGE GAP"

There's further and rather dramatic evidence to support the effect of marriage on earnings: it turns out that *bachelors*, in both the United States and Canada, show the same 60 to 70 percent wage gap with married men, as do all women as a group.[26] The reason for this is the same: bachelors don't need tons of money for family and children, so they don't engage in as much income- and promotion-seeking behaviour. The result? They earn, on average, the same as married women. In fact, the Statistics Canada data referred to above showed that bachelors as a whole made 42.8 percent of the wages of married men as a whole in 1987. Is this discrimination against bachelors? Obviously not. And yet the same arguments can be applied. Will pay equity supervisors soon be forcing us to pay bachelors the same wages as married men? Don't hold your breath.

## CANADA'S PAY POLICE

What about the draconian program in use to bring about pay equity? If it weren't so sad and ridiculous, it would be funny. Suffice it to say that in the province of Ontario (much the same elsewhere) the plan for its implementation engendered a whole new class of paid bureaucrats, consultants, inspectors, and, let's face it, *pay police*. These ordinary folks are empowered: to hear complaints from employees; to enter an establishment and seize records without warning; and to haul employers before their "pay equity tribunal." Clearly, the many pay equity commissions dotting the landscape are kangaroo courts of the first order, empowered to "make final decisions of fact and law," made up mostly of unionists, feminists, and "experts" who make their money at the social policy trough. If the cook in your staff kitchen decides that she deserves the same pay for rustling up hamburgers as your maintenance man down in the basement fixing the boilers—watch out. The pay equity system is "complaint based," which means she merely has to pick up the phone and ask one of those friendly inspectors to drop in for a visit to your head office. These inspectors will evaluate her job—not her, but her job—in terms of four official categories: skill, effort, responsibility, and working conditions. They will then assign a "value" to each of these things, then run down to the basement, and do the same for the maintenance man's job. For this subtle science, they will use either the Hay Scale or the Willis Scale (two of the most-used scales for measuring social conditions).[27] The fact that there are hundreds of aspects to every job and they consider only four is, of course, passed over elegantly.

The witty Fabian socialist and elitist George Bernard Shaw, who criticized the market system because it paid so much to prizefighters, wrote: "To suppose that it could be changed by any possible calculation that an ounce of Archbishop or three ounces of judge is worth a pound of prizefighter, would be sillier still." Nevertheless, the Hay Study in San Jose, California, determined through "an objective point system" that a puppeteer's job was worth 124 points, the same as the jobs of an offset-print operator and a street sweeper. Of course, no one can objectively compare, say, the pay of a great teacher with the work of Oprah Winfrey. Such evaluations are possible only by *reduction*;

by reducing each job to aspects so common that you could walk an elephant through the subjective holes in the system. It's like saying that because a one-ounce diamond and a one-ounce piece of lead weigh the same, they are worth the same. The Canadian economist Morley Gunderson wrote that "while comparisons across quite dissimilar jobs are possible in theory . . . the results of evaluation procedures become more tenuous the more dissimilar the jobs."[28] And the ever-insightful Charles Krauthammer ridiculed the use of the Willis Scale in Washington State (where pay equity legislation was eventually thrown out as discriminatory and unconstitutional by three judges of the U.S. Court of Appeals), saying that the scale is a mandate for arbitrariness: every subjective determination, no matter how whimsically arrived at, is first enshrined in a number to give it an entirely specious solidity, then added to another number no less insubstantial, to yield a total entirely meaningless . . . everything is arbitrary: the categories, the rankings, even the choice of judges . . . there remains one factor wholly unaccounted for which permits the system to be skewed in any direction one wishes: the weight assigned to each category . . . Who is to say that a secretary's two years of college are equal in worth to and not half or double the worth of—the truck driver's risk of getting killed on the highway? Mr. Willis, that's who.[29]

But . . . we've left the inspectors in the basement! Suddenly, they dash breathless up the stairs and inform the president of the company that he (or she!) is guilty of wage discrimination based on sex. So the president is ordered to pay the cook the same wage as the maintenance man. Flabbergasted, the president cries out, "If I could find a maintenance man at her rate, I'd hire him!" ("Pay her!" is the response) "My hamburgers are three dollars. I'll have to raise the price to twelve dollars each, no one will buy them!" ("Pay her!") "If no one buys them we'll have to shut down the kitchen. It's losing money already!" ("Pay her!") "There're a hundred others who would love to have her job at what she's making now!" ("Pay her!") "I'm going to shut down the damn kitchen, it's always been a pain in the neck to the whole organization. She'll be out of a job, for all your bungling." ("We're sorry, we can't help that. Thank you. Goodbye. We'll send your records back sometime next year.")

In the riotous story "Pastry Cook Pay Angers 800 Nurses" (Toronto Star, May 18, 1990), the full idiocy of these situations is revealed. The pay police were called in to "evaluate" the work of nurses, and equate it to male work of equal value. They decided, after much precision and deliberation, that a nurse's job was equivalent to that of a male pastry chef. Well, the outrage! The scandal! The "unfairness!" Florence Nightingale, a mere pastry chef? Well, this was very funny. So-called pay equity was brought in to make pay more "fair" for certain groups of women who had voluntarily accepted their wages. But once the fairness judgment was rendered, these same women hit the streets, striking for "Fair Pay Equity" (Toronto Star, October 2, 1991). Jonathan Swift must be laughing in his grave. It has never occurred to these women that if hundreds of them line up eager to take a low-paying job, they will get low pay. In a free society, pay is a function of an employer's ability to produce a product for a price acceptable to consumers, and the worker's willingness to accept the wage required to make the product. How could it be otherwise? Next, we will see demands for "Fair, Fair Pay Equity"—but . . . the employers will all have left town.

The above scenarios illustrate the arbitrariness, confusion, and failure in principle of the whole pay equity scam. But this was inevitable as it was another male-style socialist idea, as are most of the radical feminists' ideas, and as such it could never provide any basis for economic calculation. For there is no way to establish economic value outside a voluntary market for goods and services. In other words, by its very nature, the value of anything can arise only from a cost-benefit transaction voluntarily entered into between free buyers and sellers. There can be *imposed prices* (that no one will voluntarily pay, or charge, except under duress). But there is no such thing as imposed economic *value*. In fact, nothing has any economic value outside a free market because any amount paid above the market price is immediately recognized as a kind of tax. Why? Because the "value" of a job is strictly related to the demand for the goods or services a job creates. And what's called the "market-clearing" price for a good (or the wage for a job) is always a result of how willing people are to exchange a specific sum of their own money for that good, or service, or job. You can pay the cook all you want, but if no one wants twelve-dollar hamburgers—goodbye, cook! If you keep the cook anyway, her cost to the economic unit, above what revenue she generates, will be a tax on the rest of the operation (or the industry, or the nation). After all, if the sale of hamburgers isn't paying for her keep, something else is, right? That's why I said feminists are ignorant of the principles of economics, in the same way socialists are. It hasn't worked for them, and it won't work for feminists, because it can't work. (In small ways, the Berlin Wall keeps on falling.) In the end, the pay equity idea makes feminists (of either gender) look pretty stupid.

Here's just a small sample of the kind of political jargon to which such pay police regimes must resort because their valuations are necessarily subjective and bureaucratic . . . and I've left out the myriad qualifications, exceptions, and caveats the Pay Equity Act in Ontario had to include in order to get around the obvious injustices and stupidities of this shabby program. It's hard not to giggle nervously when reading this offensive muddle. The language alone is a riot of confusion—but the pay police in Canada are very real. So read on, and weep:

"On definitions: The Act permits differences in compensation resulting from the use of gender-neutral formal seniority or merit systems, and from gender-neutral red-circling, temporary skills shortages, and temporary training or development assignments (see Section 8(1)). On job salaries: The midpoint and the reference point [of a salary scale] are two different things, which sometimes coincide and sometimes do not. In some salary ranges, the reference point might be two-thirds of the way up the scale, for example. The reference point is the point that employees performing at the levels their jobs require may be expected to reach."

At one stroke, the government of Ontario introduced a program that is as complete a model of the socialist process at work in a formerly free country as could ever be invented. As respected economist Thomas Sowell, who, as an African-American, has had lots of experience with discrimination, says, "If we buy the key assumption of [pay equity]—that third-party observers can tell what jobs are 'really' worth—then our whole economic system should be scrapped ... If somebody has this God-like ability, why restrict it to ... 'pay-equity'? ... why not rent equity, tuition equity, vacation equity, and all kinds of other equity?"

Take a look at the Snapshot below to see why all such forced-equity arguments are doomed. It shows that various ethnic groups in Canada have very different earnings. There are hundreds of "ethnic wage gaps." Some earn only half of what, say, Jews in Canada earn. So using the same fallacious tactics as feminists, can we argue that this is a result of *discrimination by Jews against non-Jews*? Either Jews earn more because they work harder and are better at earning good wages than others, or this is racial and religious discrimination against all non-Jews by a group that has itself suffered widespread discrimination.

## SNAPSHOT
Wage & Salary Differences in Canada, by Selected Ethnic Groups, 2005

| Ethnic Group | Average Male Employment Income |
|---|---|
| Jewish | $72,311 |
| Japanese | $51,988 |
| English | $48,088 |
| Greek | $45,612 |
| French | $42,142 |
| Chinese | $38,307 |
| West Indian | $37,261 |
| N.A. Indian | $31,681 |
| Inuit | $29,967 |

(Source: www.12.statcan.gc.ca/english/census06/data)

# DEFECTING MOTHERS:
# WHAT IS DAYCARE DOING TO CHILDREN?

> *Women want economic independence, to be able to go back*
> *to school, to get a real job, to be able to work.*
> —Carolyn Bennett, Liberal MP (*Hill Times*, March 22, 2010)

> *Working Parents want daycare. What children want . . . is their parent.*
> —Wendy Dreskin, *The Daycare Decision*

We now turn to the second program demanded by feminists. So-called "universal daycare" has been promoted by feminists from the start as an essential government service that would enable all women, regardless of income, to free themselves from the natural consequences of their own biology—the responsibilities (to many of them, the burdens) of homemaking and child-rearing. As men cannot bear children, feminists set themselves the target of equalizing the parental work of child-rearing. But they cannot force men to stay home and share that load. So instead, they seek to force all taxpayers to share it via tax-funded daycare. Then, liberated from their own children at last, feminists would be free to sally forth and compete with men as equals in the capitalist jungle. So this is at bottom a program of unknown expense—estimates range from $5 billion to $10 billion per year—designed not to give children the best care, as we shall see, but to level the gender playing field that radicals are convinced is stacked against women. So my immediate concern, once I understood the depth of the attack on traditional society such a program would mean, was to ask what it would mean for the nation's children? Right after the first edition of this book appeared I got busy researching, and published *The War Against the Family*.[30] What follows is a revised segment that addresses this very issue. I present it here as a critique, not of normal and reasonable use of good daycare, but of the feminist notion of long-term daycare as a tax-funded woman's "right." There was no need to update the alarming science because nothing has changed—the story has only worsened. Readers will find all the relevant references, and more, in *War*. And it's not as if radicals have given up, or that the ideological war against the family is over. Far from it. In the 2009 *Pink Book* of the Liberal Party of Canada's Women's Caucus, over which leader Michael Ignatieff gushed enthusiastically, a national tax-funded daycare program was once again promoted. They never give up. Such a plan may be a dream come true for radical feminists, or for androgynists, or for socialists, but . . . is it the best thing for the nation's children? Read on, and decide.

## WHAT'S BEST FOR YOU AND YOUR CHILDREN

We are in the midst of a terrible impasse, whereby in the pursuit of economic survival that is very real for some (the truly needy), a matter of economic comfort for most (yuppie daycare mothers), and endemic in a consumer society's pursuit of a flashier lifestyle, we are forcing children to pay a terrible price that will haunt us as long as they live. For as the old Jewish saying goes: "If you aren't there for children when they're young, you'll be there when they're old." That quote came from an article by Canadian psychiatrist Dr. Elliot Barker, who spent many decades working with angry psychopaths. I spoke with him. From his window he watches their anguished parents bent with sadness as they arrive to comfort their disturbed or criminal children, and says, "I cannot help wondering where they [the parents] were when it mattered most." He says that the psychopaths he treats invariably have the same history: shortly after birth the child is separated from its mother and given into the care of a multitude of surrogate parents. From Barker, from criminologist Stanton Samenow, from legions of researchers, the evidence has cascaded off the presses in a crescendo of damnation. It is a finger of shame pointed at a society that is rapidly breaking the bonds of the natural family, that has succumbed, encouraged by the shrill goading of tax-funded radicals, to an increasing abandonment of its children. What all honest researchers are rediscovering, however, is what the popular wisdom has always known: young children need an uninterrupted, intimate, continuous connection with their mothers, especially in the very early months and years of life. We all know that there are a lot of excellent daycare centres and dedicated childcare workers. What follows is not a critique of any particular facility or person. It is a critique of the notion of daycare as an adequate *substitute* for mom and dad, a report on some of the scientific findings concerning the effects of *extended* daycare on the behaviour and health of young children.

## BREAKING THE BONDS: WOMEN OPPRESSING CHILDREN

Quite contrary to the radical feminist insistence that "parenting" is a gender-free matter (either parent, or even a surrogate, will do), or that "mothering" is an oppressive role constructed to trap women and recruit them as slaves for a patriarchal society, highly respected social scientists such as John Bowlby have been tirelessly reiterating the obvious: that "the attachment relationship that a young child forms with its mother is the foundation stone of personality." We are discovering much too late that when this primal attachment is missing, or inadequate, children, especially young boys, develop into adults who lack any ability to form meaningful relationships with other people. In *Attachment and Loss*, and again in *A Secure Base*, Bowlby insists that "the young child's hunger for his mother's presence is as great as his hunger for food," and that "her absence inevitably generates a powerful sense of loss and anger." Woe betide us.

A veritable avalanche of "attachment" studies has shown that although fathers are crucially important to any child's development, attachment bonding is overwhelmingly a matter of the quality and continuance of the relationship between the mother and her children in the early stages of life. Through a variety of current experiments based on the "strange situation" used by psychologist

Mary Ainsworth in the 1960s, it is now devastatingly clear that when babies are placed in "other than mother" care during the first year of life—even very good-quality care—"about 50 percent are insecurely attached to their mothers." Ainsworth's technique of asking mothers to leave their children in a room with a total stranger abruptly and without explanation to the child (the strange situation), to reappear some minutes later, were decisive. During the mother's sudden absence, and on her reappearance, the children demonstrated clear differences in attachment, ranging from callous indifference and anger, to joy on reuniting. Penn State's Jay Belsky, who originally argued for the harmlessness of daycare, now says that daycare erodes a child's sense of trust and order in the world, and Belsky, Barglow, and others argue that when mothers leave children in daycare as infants, especially for more than twenty hours per week, *children read this as parental rejection.* Belsky argues that daycare weakens the father-child bond as well, because when full-time working mothers get home, they monopolize the child's attention during evenings and weekends.

Belsky says he has since been "smeared" by feminists for turning against daycare, but that his newly critical perspective is shared by many specialists who are reluctant to speak out for fear of incurring the wrath of daycare partisans. This truth, shared quietly by many Canadian specialists, is being hidden from Canadians through an academic and media blackout. Chillingly, Ainsworth has discovered that whereas only 30 percent of children demonstrated poor attachment in the 1960s, by 1990, 50 percent did so. She concluded that "it's very hard to become a sensitively responsive mother if you're away from your child ten hours a day, it really is." Recently, work by Mary Ainsworth, Mary Main, and Alan Stroufe, researchers from three major but different university research centres, has clearly and consistently shown that the pattern of attachment developed in infancy and early childhood is profoundly influenced by the mother's ready availability, her sensitivity to her child's signals, and her responsiveness to the child's need for comfort and protection.

Jay Belsky now calls extensive daycare in the twenty-plus-hours range a "risk condition" for children—and therefore, for society as a whole. Why? Because—there is near-professional unanimity on this point—*poorly attached children are sociopaths in the making.* They feel anger and aggression toward their parents and other children. Study after study shows that the ranks of the aggressive, of angry children, of dropouts, of detention centres, of welfare and unemployment rolls, of drug and drunk tanks, of the homeless hordes, and the jails, are increasingly occupied by those who missed out; mostly, who grew up, first without full-time mothers, then without a father model, or both. As young children they are less co-operative with adults, more aggressive in their play, fight more, cry more, hit more, cling more, are more rebellious, have far less tolerance for frustration, and are far more at risk for personality disorders in later life. Predictably, those in the lowest-quality daycare had the highest number of such disorders. And such profiles are very common in low-income strata. But even children from affluent homes, left with one-to-one nannies, showed significant attachment insecurity. Psychiatrist Graeme Taylor, of Mount Sinai Hospital in Toronto, concluded what all natural mothers already know by instinct, and can deny only by self-deception: that the infant-mother relationship is "an interactional system that organizes and regulates the infant's behaviour and physiology from birth," including such intimate and sensitive matters as heart-rate, enzyme levels of growth hormone, thermoregulation, responsiveness of the immune system, and upwards to psychological states of mind. This regulation comes about through the mother's direct and intimate attention and holding behaviour, and if it is lacking, can result in conditions of physical and personality inadequacy that endure for a lifetime. The point here, simply put, is that prolonged daycare serves to negatively restructure the mother-infant relationship, and thus may be dangerously restructuring society itself.

A clear sense of this can be grasped from the turnover rates of childcare workers—sometimes 40 to 60 percent per year. "Attachment" is impossible under such circumstances. Some Swedish researchers report that in Sweden the average Swedish child may have fifty to a hundred different "caregivers" by the age of ten (perhaps the word should be "caretakers"). Because of this, we can be sure that extensive daycare facilities will be matched by increases in the number of divorces, social violence, psychiatric beds, and jail cells. That's why Dr. Burton White, of Harvard University's Pre-school Project, once America's leading authority on the first three years of life, declared daycare to be "a disaster" for children, saying that it is impossible in daycare centres to manufacture "large doses of custom-made love." After more than thirty years of research on how children develop well, he said, "I would not think of putting an infant or toddler of mine into any substitute care program on a full-time basis, especially a center-based program . . . I urge you not to delegate the primary child-rearing task to anyone else during your child's first three years of life."

## BREAKING THEIR BODIES

As if the production of generations of children who grow up lacking empathic capacities were not enough, daycare facilities, by their very nature, are also hosts for all sorts of illnesses and diseases, some of them extremely dangerous to children and their families. Dr. Harrison Spencer, chief of Parasitic Diseases at the U.S. Centers for Disease Control (CDC), describes a fascinating Minnesota experiment in which researchers created a video showing how a disease organism can start in a child's diaper, and travel to other children and workers. They placed a tablespoon of tapioca pudding combined with a dye that becomes fluorescent under a black light in just one child's diaper. Eventually the diaper oozed. One child, then another, touched it, "and pretty soon it spread all over the whole room." They've got a video showing exactly how this happened. They took pictures at timed intervals which showed "a gradual progression as the dye spread onto the daycare worker's hands, the furniture, and so forth." Dr. Harrison said that daycare children "are at risk anywhere from two to eighteen times as much for certain infectious diseases that run the gamut from diarrheal diseases to respiratory and flu-like illnesses," and that "as many as 80 percent of children in daycare excrete cytomegalovirus (CMV) in their urine and saliva." Other studies show 100 percent for daycare children (compared to 50 percent for all children). Scandinavian children have higher rates than others, likely due to more widespread daycare there. CMV is a herpes-type viral infection that doesn't seem to bother young children much, but can cause a mononucleosis-type illness in older children and adults, and if contracted by a pregnant woman, can cause deafness, birth defects, mental retardation, and even death in her newborn.

Joanne Braithwaite, an infection expert with the City of Toronto Health Department, said daycare centres are "high risk institutions, just like hospitals"; they act as "a community reservoir" for infection—a place where bacteria and viruses are always present, ready to infect others. Winnipeg disease expert Dr. Ron Gold said the 200,000-plus Canadian children in daycare are twice as likely to get sick as those cared for at home (Canadian Press, February 2, 1988). And . . . there's a horrible litany of "daycare-related illnesses" (DCRIs), as they are called: over 70 percent of clinical cases of hepatitis A can be traced to a daycare setting, as can so many other fecal-oral enteric (bowel) diseases, including viral gastroenteritis, salmonellosis, shigellosis, giardiasis (found in 30 to 50 percent of daycare inmates, with an estimated 600 percent increased risk in centres with children under two), and pinworms, many of which have their highest "attack rates" for children under one year of age. It's the same story for respiratory diseases, the various forms of pneumonia, influenza B, the various pathogenic strep bacteria, and the deadly meningococcus diseases. In most cases it is useless to isolate such sick children in a daycare setting because they are often badly infected long before symptoms show up, and may well have already infected dozens of other children (and thus their families). Even worse, anxious mothers often resort to masking a child's illness with drugs so the sickness or fever will be undetected until after mom is at work. Studies show up to twelve times greater risk for such diseases in daycare children, and many of these bacterial and viral conditions can have sequelae like scarlet fever, nephritis (kidney inflammation), rheumatic fever (inflammation of heart), septicemia, meningitis, septic arthritis, and osteomyelitis.

Enough said. So alarmed are some authorities that even the cautious U.S. Centers for Disease Control has warned that "large, licenced daycare centers . . . are major transmission centers for hepatitis, severe diarrhea, and other diseases." Dr. Stanley Schuman, of the Medical University of South Carolina, blames daycare for the outbreak of all sorts of illnesses, saying that the situation "is reminiscent of the pre-sanitation days of the seventeenth century."

Daycare centres can also be magnets for certain types of workers: one study of sexual abuse in Michigan said 75 percent of the victims were daycare children (it didn't say whether the abuse occurred in the centres or not). U.S. senator Paula Hawkins described a daycare centre in Florida where "dozens of children were found to have gonorrhea of the mouth." The University of New Hampshire reported that from 1983 to 1985 there were 1,639 confirmed cases of sexual abuse of children in U.S. licensed daycare centres; in some cases, the children were used for the production of child pornography.

The current fear is that many unattached youngsters, utterly lacking in empathy, in a truly vicious social cycle, are becoming the angry radicals of tomorrow. Disappointed with the real world, they understandably become dependent on illusory utopian goals for the reformation of society, trying to force society to give them what they missed, and punishing their parental generation at the same time. Radical feminists, I'm afraid, are rather cornered, and will not succeed in negating or reconstituting human biology or gender or reforming society to their liking through daycare, no matter how many children they sacrifice to it. A nationwide *Globe and Mail*–CBC News Poll (November 5, 1991) revealed the deep feelings of the public on this issue: a huge majority of anxious Canadians (76 percent) said "children's well-being is being sacrificed" because both parents have to work. The poll indicated that "they have tremendous nostalgia for the way the family used to be run." So radicals would be better to reform themselves. In writing on this point for the *Harvard Business Review*, no-nonsense feminist Felice Schwartz said that some women are "career primary," but that following this urge "requires that they remain single or at least childless or, if they do have children, that they be satisfied to have others raise them." Pretty honest, even though she refrained from commenting on the satisfaction of the children. At any rate, we cannot prevent radicals from forcing their own children into heavy-duty daycare, but we ought to prevent them from restructuring society with our money in order to normalize this practice.

## ABORTION: HOW CANADA BECAME AN EVIL COUNTRY

I realize that abortion has for so long now been considered a woman's right that millions of ordinary women defend it passionately. But that is not my topic here. I am going to discuss the abortion right as the third fundamental plank of the radical feminist platform; which is to say, the so-called "right" to abortion as a tax-funded service of the State. All women understand that the work of birthing, suckling, and the early care of children fall disproportionately to them, and so no society can be "equal" in the gender sense unless this normal consequence of human biology is transformed into a manipulable consequence of a woman's will, rather than of her sexual behaviour. Abortion on demand achieves this result by enabling women to eliminate their unwanted children, leaving them only with wanted children, thus removing any grounds for complaint about unchosen inequality. The radical feminists of Canada have been extraordinarily successful in procuring this objective. Canada currently has no law whatsoever against abortion of any kind. Indeed, almost all Western nations allow abortion (though in most of them there are restrictions after twelve weeks' gestation). As the survival of a conceived child is now a matter completely dependent on its mother's will, Canadians are warned severely on wine bottles and cigarette packets not to drink or smoke, for fear of "harming the fetus," but thanks to feminist radicals, they may with impunity kill an unborn child in their womb at any time prior to the moment of natural birth and throw it in the garbage.

I include the "Three Questions on Abortion" below because although I was once in favour of abortion for hard cases (though never as a general or contraceptive right), both the facts of this grisly reality and what I believe is the inescapable logic of the arguments offered below, have convinced me that abortion as practiced in all modern democracies must be judged a distinct moral evil no different in character from the early programs of death by infanticide practiced by the Nazi regime in Germany.

Now, it grieves me to say this about my country, but all who doubt this statement are encouraged to read *The Nazi Doctors*, by Robert Jay Lifton, which details very precisely the amoral gradualism by which very highly educated German scientists and intellectuals developed arguments for the tax-funded liquidation of those having what they called "lives not worth living." The fundamental legal trick that enabled this for the Nazi regime is the same as that used by the Canadian Supreme Court: they simply invented what I call "category law" to redefine disabled children as non-persons or "not human beings." Canada has declared that an unborn child in Canada is not a person or human being until it is "born alive." It so happens that this was also, to the letter, the same legal trick used by all former slave-owning regimes in history (Canada was also a slave-owning society, as mentioned previously). They legally defined blacks and other slaves as property, or chattels, or non-persons, rather than as human beings.

Many libertarians and conservatives part company with me on this issue because they are staunch supporters of individual freedom. But I suggest they have not followed their own logic far enough to see what their liberty-licence has produced—a plain and obvious evil: the deaths, since 1988, of over two million perfectly healthy unborn children in Canada (averaging now around 90,000 per year, down from a peak of 113,000), and over 40 million in America (now at one million per year, down from a peak of 1.5 million).

I challenge all doubters, here and now, to read the following questions sincerely and honestly, and to face their own honest answers.

## THREE QUESTIONS ON ABORTION[31]

*All who support slavery are free; all who support abortion are alive*—Anonymous

Some time has passed since Canada disgraced itself by conferring its highest citizen honour upon Henry Morgentaler, a doctor who has devoted his entire adult life to legalizing abortion on demand at any stage of pregnancy as a political right. Ironically, at the press conference for this nefarious presentation he offered the opinion that abortion has helped to reduce violent crime because "there are people out there who would otherwise have been murdered." In the days that followed there were a few cries of moral outrage concerning who, exactly, was doing the murdering, and a number of distinguished citizens returned their Order of Canada pins in protest. But the spectacle of erudite leaders locked in passionate public debate, even courageously risking their political careers for profoundly held moral beliefs on this disturbing matter, was not to be.

What is true of our leaders is even more true of the citizenry. There is today such angry polarization on the question of abortion that consensus is considered impossible, and if Canadians share anything it is a sense of relief that this and similar morally difficult topics (gay "marriage" is another) are now routinely decided by the edicts of courts, the activities of which seem aimed precisely at deflecting genuine public debate.

And that is why we need to ask: What happened? How did we change from a people that once so valued human life that we criminalized abortion (with only a few exceptions having to do with rape, or a real medical threat to the life of the mother), to a people that now permits and publicly subsidizes the right to terminate human life in the womb at any stage of pregnancy up to the moment of birth? Some will immediately object to the phrase "human life" on the grounds that many courts have declared that a fetus is not a "person" or a "human being" until it is "born alive." That is true, but I think the facts will expose the bogus use of these terms for the following reasons.

Even if we all were to agree that what a pregnant woman is carrying is not a fully developed person, or "human being," we nevertheless cannot deny that in every case what she is carrying is *alive*, for if this were not so there would be no need for anyone to claim a right to "terminate" their pregnancy. In other words, we are talking about actual life, and not in any degree (as Justice Bertha Wilson so archly declared) a "potential life." And so now, once we have secured what must be unavoidable agreement on this point, we are then forced to agree that in every case, absolutely, the life a pregnant woman is carrying *is a human life*. No one believes she is carrying a developing puppy, or a swan.

So having come this far, and only once we decide to face this singular truth as honestly as possible, any reasonably informed person will be led to the ultimate question of whether or not it is morally acceptable for one person in full possession of his or her own human life to terminate another human life at any stage of development.

Reasonably informed? By any measure, most people who adamantly support abortion are grievously uninformed. They simply don't know how we arrived at the new *moral* ground we seem to be standing upon; what changes in the *law* have enabled such a strange about-face; or what the current *practices* of abortion are that this very recent thinking has permitted.

The answers, explored below, are each followed by a plain question that readers are challenged to think deeply about and to answer as honestly as possible.

### How we got this way—the change in our moral thinking

Until about the middle of the nineteenth century, all philosophers, and all religious and political leaders in the Western world accepted as obvious the idea that we live—and ought to live—under a common moral bubble, so to speak. Which is to say that moral standards were considered *public* by their very nature, rather than private. The mere idea that morality should be something sourced in a personal point of view aimed at serving the purposes of solitary individuals or, even more fickle, something constructed to suit the occasion, had always been considered absurd, if not a sign of moral sickness.

But with the advance of egalitarian democracy came an increasingly shrill demand for individual rights divorced from duties, and with this a weakening of shared moral consensus and an entirely new idea: that each human being lives under his or her own private moral bubble. The most famous articulation of this historically bizarre alteration in the public conception of morality was by J.S. Mill in his booklet *On Liberty* in 1859. Within certain confusing limits he basically argued that morality is a private matter and the only case for concern occurs when we directly harm someone else by our conduct. This is today called Mill's "harm principle" and it has rapidly become the most common ideal of what it means to live a free and moral life. Indeed, Canada's own Supreme Court, in *R. v. Labaye* (2005), in which a citizen complained that it was indecent and against community standards to allow a swingers' sex club in a residential neighbourhood, ruled in favour of the club, and in doing so wrote that "the philosophical underpinnings of the . . . harm-based approach are found in the liberal theories of J.S. Mill. This philosopher argued that the only purpose for which State power can be rightfully exercised over a member of the community is to prevent harm to others."

And so it has come to pass by edict of our highest court that there is no longer a common moral bubble; that we have no duty to be concerned for others, nor for the greater good, nor for society as something comprising real relationships that is far more than the sum of its individual parts.

### First Question:

How is it possible for a civilization to thrive and for a people to arrive at any consensus of the common good when the most fundamental questions of human life are to be decided solely by the will of self-interested individuals without regard to the common good?

### The flimsy legal right

Unfettered abortion in Canada has been possible since 1988 when the existing law placing minimal conditions on abortion was struck down as "unconstitutional." Several efforts were subsequently made to replace it with a compromise law that failed due to a tie vote in the Senate (where twenty-three senators did not bother to vote at all). The result is that Canadian law does not presently say that abortion is right or wrong. It says nothing at all—even though no poll has ever shown that a majority of Canadians accept unlimited abortion on demand. Quite the reverse. Strong majorities oppose exactly that.

The conjuring began the moment judges decided, mostly for radical feminist reasons having to do with the growing demand for individual freedom and moral autonomy (as explained above), that a woman ought to have a "right" to abort. This meant that all unborn human life had to be redefined as a valueless thing without humanity, or *personhood*, so as to remove it from legal and public concern. As it happened, the legal category of non-personhood was well-known; it is a very old device introduced throughout history whenever States, tribes, or courts want to justify the elimination of an enemy. As such, it was easy to adapt for the purpose of facilitating abortion.

For example, slave-holding regimes (Canada and the United States were no exception) have always defined their slaves as less than fully human to make enslavement morally acceptable. Jews and many other groups in the horrific Nazi and Soviet regimes were defined as non-persons, or more aggressively, as subhuman (if not as vermin, or some such despicable creature).

Such linguistic and moral contortionism and the official justifications for it have been almost exactly duplicated by the abortion regimes in all Western nations, and this parallel is far more than an analogy. *For with the sole distinction of the existence of the victim either inside or outside the womb, there is no difference between a declaration of non-personhood that creates a class of born-alive victims that enables, sustains, and makes invisible to its perpetrators a regime of chattel slavery, and a declaration of non-personhood that creates a class of alive but not-yet-born imminent victims, that enables, sustains, and makes invisible to its perpetrators the abortion regimes currently defended in the name of egalitarian democracy.*

The reasoning produced in Canada for granting a pregnant women a "right" to decide the life-or-death fate of her unborn child, *a right that has priority even over the will of society at large* (and, not incidentally, even over the will of the child's own father), is that if the mother does not want her child, then the "security" of the mother's person (which now means her psychological "health" as a self-flourishing and freely choosing individual) has been put at risk (ironically, also by her own will). She is therefore said to be justified in protecting herself from such a threat by demanding the tax-funded professional removal of the offending object, or enemy, from her womb.

The same sort of legal and verbal legerdemain was used in the United States where the justifying ground for this practice was not security of the mother's person, but her right to "privacy." There, if the life within is unwanted by its mother, it is considered a kind of enemy "occupying" the mother's womb without her consent, an illegal trespasser invading her privacy.

This is a very brief overview of the constitutional artifice required in both countries to justify ending human life in the womb. Note that in both cases, whether with respect to the artificial grounds of security, or privacy, what I have called a developing human life, once considered sacred and of the highest value in itself, *and without regard to the opinion of the moment of any other human being*, may now by the sole and godlike edict of its own mother be declared of no value whatsoever—or, of a supreme value, as she decides, calling, if necessary, upon the unlimited and heroic resources of the medical profession and the State (and the taxpayer) to save its life.

**Second Question:**
Can it be right and good for any civilization that the most fundamental question—whether or not another human life has value, and so whether it is to be protected or terminated—should be decided by the private and changeable will of a single individual?

**The practice of abortion**
Now let us ask what is actually being done to unwanted human life. How many unborn lives are ended? How large are they? What are the methods? Once abortion enthusiasts learn a little of the bald truth, many are horrified, back-pedal a lot, and start to suggest ways to severely restrict abortion, if not to end it entirely. This grisly aspect will only be touched upon here.

Suffice it to say that of the average of approximately 106,000 abortions performed annually in Canada over the past decade (that's about 290 per day, or 1,060,000 per decade, the vast majority of whom would have been perfectly healthy citizens), most are in the first trimester of pregnancy. The routine methods of abortion at this stage involve injecting saline solutions that burn and kill babies, to scraping the womb, and so on. Many people who don't know much about this subject say abortion is acceptable because they falsely believe all abortions take place during the first twelve weeks of pregnancy and that this involves getting rid of what they consider to be a microscopic cluster of valueless human cells.

But many are changing their minds because the debate surrounding abortion has been altering rapidly not, as we often think, due to religious or moral claims, but because of neonatal science, neurology, DNA studies, cell biology, CAT scanning, surgery on infants in the womb, and so on. We now know that a human heart starts beating at around twenty-one days, because we can see it and hear it; that a human life in the womb has a distinct and unique personal genetic endowment (and thus is, in every strictly biological sense, a genetically complete and unique, if undeveloped, human life); and studies with tiny digital cameras show clearly terrified second- and third-trimester babies trying desperately to escape the vacuum tube (or other devices) inserted into their mother's wombs to suck away their lives or tear off their limbs. And who has not seen the incredible photo of baby Samuel's tiny hand reaching out of a small incision in his mother's belly to grasp the surgeon's finger during an operation to save his life? This itself is a bizarre situation whereupon, once taken outside the womb for surgery, such a child is considered a full person with all normal human and civil rights (because "born alive"). But when put back in the womb to finish gestation, it again *disappears as a human being*, or person, and is without value, or any such defence or rights until eventually born alive once again (if mommy so wills).

These are simply facts. And so is the distressing reality that about 10 percent of all abortions in Canada and the United States (perhaps 100,000 annually there) take place in the second trimester. At this point, many unborn babies are about twelve inches long, and weigh up to a couple of pounds. At this five- to six-month stage of development (when the human life to be terminated looks in every way like a small human being), there are often "evacuation" problems, and so the most efficient and "safe" way to get a sizable baby out of an unripe womb is in pieces, by first ripping off its arms and legs and crushing its head with forceps for easy extraction, after which all the pieces are counted and thrown into a garbage pail. Those who want to read a viscerally upsetting description by an American physician of his real-life accidental encounter with recently aborted babies that fell out of a hospital garbage bag from a truck onto the street in front of him should read the essay "The Street of the Dead Fetuses" on my website. Be prepared. And those who want to see shocking photos of babies acid-burned to death or torn apart in this way can simply Google "abortion photos," and a lot of upsetting websites will pop up.

There is more. About forty U.S. states have restricted or banned third-trimester abortions because unborn children at this stage are very large—about twenty inches and between six and eight pounds. Canada has no law whatsoever against late-stage abortions, and it is true that even where they are allowed (or, not prohibited), many abortionists will refuse to perform them. But when it comes to women who want to get rid of their large second- or third-trimester babies, there is an especially gruesome practice called "partial-birth abortion" (formally called "intact dilation and extraction") that I am obliged to describe briefly here because although it has been successfully banned by President George W. Bush, President Bill Clinton before him refused outright to ban the method, and it may have come into use again under Barack Obama's presidency (Obama, as a senator, refused to vote against it on several occasions, and one of his first acts as president was to reverse Bush's ban on American funding of abortion in other countries). It is impossible to verify if, where, or when this method has been used or may now be in use in Canada. But there is nothing to stop it, and no one is telling. In the last year for which I have seen numbers for America, the National Coalition of Abortion Providers estimated that there were four thousand to five thousand partial-birth procedures in the United States (*New York Times*, February 26, 1997).

For this method, the unborn child's position in the womb is manipulated until it can be pulled out of the birth canal feet first. When the abortionist sees the back of the baby's head, he stops pulling, takes a pair of scissors and jabs them into the back of the baby's skull. Observers have said that at that moment the child startles, as if falling. The abortionist then inserts a vacuum hose and sucks out the brains. He must do this before the child leaves the birth canal alive and is transformed by law into a person, possibly exposing the medical staff to charges of murder. An alternative method is by "disarticulating at the neck," which means the abortionist manually breaks the baby's neck prior to extraction. Then home for supper goes the doctor.

**Third Question:**
Once a people is aware of such practices, which necessarily implicate all citizens morally because they are not forbidden by the laws of the people and (in Canada) are paid for through the tax system, is it possible for any reasonable person to say that these practices are right, and good, or that a country that sanctions them is right and good? And if they are evil, as they clearly seem to be, is not a country that refuses to forbid them, indeed, that promotes them, also evil?

In any civilization such questions must be asked. By our answers we shall be known.

# FEMINISM, EMPTY SCHOOLS, AND THE DEMOGRAPHIC WINTER: RESTORING THE PRO-FAMILY STATE

Canada, like most other Western democracies—and some Eastern ones like Japan—is heading for a "demographic winter" or a "birth dearth" in short order. Japan, which is already getting very cold, has produced a doll for lonely adults that has been programmed with 1,200 phrases such as "I love you," and also with questions for the senile a typical grandchild might ask. It is a toy for elderly children who never had children.

It takes what is called a total fertility rate (TFR) of 2.1 children per woman just to *replace* our existing population via natural increase. Canada's TFR has been around 1.5 for twenty-five years or more. When what I call the "Great Die-off" becomes evident over the next thirty years, there will be panic in the land. It is festering already. We are beginning to see more and more panicky newspaper reports demanding the closing of schools. In August 2009, the chairman of Toronto's public school board said: "Our biggest challenges is that we have too many schools and not enough students. We have 110 schools that are less than half full" (*National Post*, August 11, 2009). That is because there are not enough babies being made. So that is where we see the shrinking population first. Teachers' unions have panicked and, very hungry for votes, the province of Ontario has responded by legislating a $1 billion mandatory pre-kindergarten program for four-year-olds, to be started in those empty public schools. Ah, democracy! To hell with how this may affect our children!

After emptiness in the lower schools, we will see it in the high schools. Then in the universities. And then in the retail malls. Dropping sales of all goods connected with youth—that's a lot, as any parent knows. Then landlords will begin to have trouble finding tenants for their stores because there will be fewer businesses selling such goods, and fewer customers for them. Then it will be lights out for lots of office towers.

Eventually, governments will panic, too late as always, and then they will start calling for "emergency measures" to counteract the demographic winter. Quebec started this a decade ago or more, and so did France, by offering a lot of money for each newborn, and/or large tax breaks. That's just the start. When the panic comes, it will be serious. Feminism will be scorned and defunded (with retroactive apologies from supine politicians), and delisted in universities as a program of serious study (it never was); homosexuality will be considered very antisocial behaviour by selfish non-contributing citizens, and eventually recriminalized (say goodbye to gay marriage); textbooks will be furiously re-written and children vigorously schooled in the attractions of heterosexual marriage and family life. Anyone opting to have only two children will be informally stigmatized as unpatriotic. Posters in buses and subways and all public buildings will blazon the theme "The Survival of Canada: It's Up to You!," showing a smiling mother and father, hands linked, with four or five happy children surrounding them. Tax codes will discriminate positively in favour of marriage and fertility, and . . . well, it's all in the Snapshot below.

For the timid, some of these may seem aggressive notions. But get ready. When human beings panic, they can justify and normalize just about anything. In a democracy they will quickly adopt lazy-minded and very radical social policies if there are votes to be won; and if there is panic at the result (too few citizens born), they will as easily do the opposite. When that time comes, every leftist in the place will shout, "Discrimination!" And that is precisely the point. All true public policy, as I have argued, is intentionally discriminatory. It is meant to achieve a specified public purpose by application of the policy to some particular target group, but never to all groups (for this would defeat the policy). For example, a policy would not be designed both to encourage baby-making and discourage it at the same time; or to encourage and discourage enterprise all at once. And a "policy" that favours everyone will not change behaviour at all because the beneficiaries of the program (it is now no longer a policy) will reason they do not have to change any of their behaviours one bit to benefit.

So if we want to push back the State, restore a strong civil society, bolster procreation and the family, and mitigate the Great Die-off that is looming over the coming decades, we will need all of these ideas, or something like them. I am not a legal or taxation expert, and I know that to make any of these ideas work there would be a labyrinth of (hopefully better) laws and rejigged regulations. But the intent is clear, and where there is a will there is a way. To the objection that these are radical ideas, I answer, again: never underestimate the lengths to which a frightened population will go. These ideas are only as radical (in reverse) as the ideas that have already eroded our pro-family society. If you want to know what a family-friendly State's policies might look like, read on.

## SNAPSHOT
How Canadians Should React to the Coming Demographic Winter
(Here, LMH means "legally married heterosexual.")

Allow splitting of incomes for LMH couples only (a pretty strong incentive for home-rearing of children; for scaredy-cat common law couples to get off the pot and commit themselves to a real marriage; and to discourage homosexual unions. The French government currently permits income splitting between *all* family members for precisely this purpose. I have a friend who has five children and earning a high salary. He moved to France three years ago where he pays zero income tax because his income is divided as if earned by seven. The French government has also forbidden gay marriage and gay adoption due to the absence of what it calls "filiation" in such couples: the central focus on having children together as the foundation of marriage. Canada should have done the same.

1.  Increase dependent-child tax credits progressively, by the number of children, payable until each child reaches eighteen.
2.  Introduce a generous and progressively larger one-time maternity cash and tax-free bonus for each child in addition to 1), above.
3.  Allow mortgage-interest deductibility for LMH couples until the last child reaches eighteen (same motive as 1, above).
4.  Index incomes of LMH couples to counter "bracket-creep" (being taxed in a higher tax bracket solely due to inflation).
5.  Allow higher Registered Retirement Savings Plan (RRSP) contributions for LMH couples with children. The greater the number of children, the higher the contribution limit.
6.  Allow a generous tax credit for "same-home" care of each elder, by any family member.
7.  Disallow welfare for children of the wealthy. (This helps drive them back to their own families for support first, rather than into the arms of anon-

ymous taxpayers. Mostly it forces misbehaving rich kids to grow up fast if
they want to eat.)

8. Create business-loans insurance for LMH small-family enterprises.

9. Eliminate no-fault divorce on the grounds that no fault means no responsibility and also removes the contractual basis of the marital union (a true
   contract requires the consent of both parties to enter or to break the contract, and of both to end the contract, while breaches of contract must
   entail fault and a penalty).

10. Make divorce a lot tougher for families with young children; require, say,
    a minimum five-year cool-off period before a divorce is granted, or until
    the youngest child is fifteen.

11. Encourage LMH families to adopt Canadian children with generous tax
    credits for each adopted child. Like the French, do not allow gay couples
    to adopt children, on the grounds that the State has no moral right to
    dictate that any child be raised without a mother or father as a matter of
    State policy.

12. Define the traditional family as "a married mother and father living together
    with their dependent natural and/or adopted children." All other forms are
    less committed, and ought to be less favoured in law, policy, and taxation.

13. Rigorously enforce child and spousal payments from errant fathers (or
    mothers).

14. Consider mothers and fathers each legally, morally, and financially respon-
    sible for their own children from conception.

15. If we are too blinded to its pernicious effects to dump it entirely, and
    return to our common law basis, then we should at least restrict the use of
    the Charter of Rights and Freedoms to the protection of citizens against
    government force and infringement. End its use by citizens against each
    other, and especially against society as a whole (which would end such
    things as court-invented arguments against traditional marriage and all
    other such hallowed traditions).

16. Ban all abortion except for serious threat to the life of the mother. This
    would immediately and naturally produce 100,000 brand-new Canadian
    citizens per year. With a normal population growth gradient, this alone
    would mean 1,100,000 new citizens in ten years, and in one generation
    (twenty-five years) about 2,500,000 new citizens! All by doing nothing but
    saving the lives of citizens we have already created. This might balance the
    losses of the Great Die-off.

# 11: MEDICAL MEDIOCRITY
## AN AUTOPSY ON THE CANADIAN
## "HEALTH CARE" SYSTEM

*Metro wait for surgery forces 100 heart victims to US*

*Patients wait in line for hospital bed*

*Second heart patient dies, as surgery delayed nine times*

—Newspaper headlines that appeared in the 1990 edition of this book

For a country that spends so many billions on "health care" every year (we spent $84 billion in 1998, but 118 percent more—a cool $183.1 billion—in 2009, or $5,452 per capita) these headlines were alarming, to say the least, and should have provoked us to ask: What is really going on in this country?[1] Billions spent? Patients dying in hospital corridors, or lying at home in pain because they can't get a timely appointment with a specialist? Or spending their life savings to get treatment in the United Stated that they simply can't get, or are denied, in Canada?

Twenty years have passed, and . . . here are some very recent newspaper headlines: "Canada's Health Care System Heading for Demographic Blowout" (*Canadian Institute for Health Information*, November 14, 2008); "Obesity Patients Dying on Long Wait List"—twelve obese Canadians (of 6,783 waiting for surgery) died, while wait-listed for "just over five years" (*Canadian Journal of Surgery*, 2007); "Funding Lag Keeps Some Hospital Beds Empty" (*National Post*, June 8, 2009).

A little investigation tells a sad but predictable story: regular cost over-runs; very long waits for surgery; many of our very best medical scientists and specialists quietly leaving the country (my own specialist left Canada in 2007 to work at the Mayo Clinic); patients who die waiting for withheld treatment, outdated equipment (or simply no equipment); wage clashes and strikes between professional staff and hospitals, fee-schedule battles between physicians and the government; hospitals with whole wings shut down though patients line up; Charter challenges. And . . . who hasn't had that most distressing, but by now typical, Canadian Third World experience of waiting for many long hours in an overheated, overcrowded hospital "Emergency" Room? And . . . how many Canadians each year simply give up and head south for treatment they cannot get here or cannot get soon enough?

Now I state my caveats. I have been involved personally at the very highest level of medical science in Canada through a family foundation that gives international awards annually for the most prestigious achievements in various fields of medical science. Canada has some of the most devoted and skilled medical scientists and specialists to be found anywhere, some amazing family doctors, and some great hospitals. I am aware of how very good Canadian medical care and science *can* be. But for the $183 billion we spend on our system *every* year (an amount that has been climbing at a 6.5 percent rate annually—much faster than any other program of government), I expect no less. Neither should the reader.

Actually, I think all Canadians should demand a lot more. But I will explain how we are powerless to do that now because *we surrendered our freedom of medical choice* many decades ago when, like sleepwalkers, we accepted without much protest a top-down bureaucratic control of government-rationed medicine, and we and our physicians fell under the threat of criminal punishment for attempting to exchange our own money for the treatment of our own bodies, as we had always previously done.

The same citizens who would scream bloody murder if told that from now on they could buy or rent only a government-made home, or had to buy and wear only government-made pants, dresses, and shoes, or had to purchase and eat only government food, suddenly thought it quite normal to have politicians dictating, regulating, and rationing the quality and amount of health care they would be permitted to have for themselves, their failing parents, or their sick children.

## TRAPPED: WHY DID WE ALLOW POLITICIANS TO LIMIT OUR ACCESS TO HEALTH CARE?

Few Canadians pause to think about their health care "system," or how it got to be the way it is. Many are too young to remember, others too old to care (although they are the first shocked victims of rationing and cutbacks). But the long-term predictable breakdown that follows the socializing of anything, as night follows day, will eventually confront us all, some in the most heartbreaking way, as we watch a loved one deteriorate at home, or suffer lined up in the corridor of some drab hospital, or simply for lack of medical services, facilities, or equipment that have been available in other countries for years. You or I may have to listen in anguish as a doctor who says, "My hands are tied," explains that the treatment we need is reserved for certain categories of patient because of a lack of funding. We persist. We see empty hospital beds. We are told there are surgeons and nurses waiting for and wanting work; we are even willing to pay for the treatment ourselves. Then we learn that *it is illegal for our doctor privately to provide, and for us privately to pay, for any medical services "insured" by government in Canada.*

Lack of government funding? In Ontario, spending on health was about 12 percent of our provincial budget in 1970 when the State began moving to take over medical care. It climbed to 33 percent by 1997. By 2007–2008, it had reached 42.5 percent, and is projected to be 50 percent of spending by 2036!

What? "Health care" soon to be 50 percent of provincial spending?

Well, in a system offering unlimited "free" health care as a right, there is no reason why it shouldn't eventually climb to 75 percent or more. This trend is inevitable because as human nature and economic theory have always predicted, *the demand for an unlimited "free" commodity is infinite.* Of course, nothing in life is free. It is "pre-paid" via tax extraction and/or debt financing, and whenever there is unrestricted demand, it must be strictly rationed.

In this chapter I explain how our system came to be the way it is—how the State usurped and trapped an entire once-free profession and swept in to control the health freedom of millions of patients—and why it was always doomed to fail. Finally, I question the basic idea of having a "health care system" at all, because, while there is obviously some connection between the availability of physicians, facilities, and treatments—most are shocked to learn that *no government health care system has any necessary relationship to the status of a population's health,* even though politicians in their quest for votes present them as if they do. Japan, for example, which also has a universal public system, spends per capita about 40 percent less than Canada, but its population is far healthier than ours.

## HOW IT USED TO BE

Whenever someone asks what it was like in the 1960s before socialized medicine, I ask them what they do today when they need a dentist. Unless the treatment is being paid for by an employee dental plan, or through a private insurance plan they purchased for this purpose, they usually say that the doctor told them what the treatment would cost, and when the treatment was done, they wrote a cheque. That is exactly what we all did before Statists got a grip on medicine. Back then the core professional relationship between doctor and patient was direct, private, and unmediated. This was entirely in keeping with our Western way of life, with our law, morality, right to contract, the Hippocratic oath, and the individual freedom and responsibility of both patient and doctor.

Enter so-called medicare. The National Health Service (NHS) was introduced in Britain in 1948, and Canada (and the United States) soon began to flirt with the same idea. The Americans introduced a partly socialized system with Medicaid for the poor and Medicare for the elderly. Then Canada's prime minister, Lester Pearson, became powerfully attracted to the (vote-getting) image of the all-caring Nanny State promised by such a program. So Canada soon introduced its own far more total so-called "single-payer" system, which is actually more complex than this phrase suggests.[2]

The National Health Service—NHS—basically owns and *operates* public health facilities and hires doctors in Britain, whereas Canada's public system does not own most facilities, it *regulates and pays*. Unlike the Canadian system, however, Britain allows physicians who wish to do so to practice and to be paid privately outside the NHS, allows "pay beds" in public hospitals, and allows private companies to compete in the medical-insurance market. To lure physicians into the government plan they were assured they would finally be "freed from the money factor." Indeed, when they threatened to strike, the health minister promised "to stuff their mouths with gold." He did. Thirty years later, as John Goodman wrote in his book *National Health Care in Britain: Lessons for the USA*, "Doctors have discovered a great many reasons why the doctor-patient relationship should *not* be 'freed from the money factor.'"[3] For one thing, it was going to mean near-total State control of medicine in Britain. In 2004, over one million Britons in need of care were waiting for hospital admission, another 200,000 were waiting to get on *that* list, and each year, the NHS cancels over 100,000 surgeries.[4]

## THE CHOIRMASTER OF CANADA

In Canada, the chief architects of our national health insurance scheme were British immigrant Tom Kent, an avowed socialist adviser to Prime Minister Lester Pearson, and after him, Prime Minister Pierre Trudeau and his successive ministers of health. Monique Bégin, one of the most radical of these, and minister of health, from 1980 to 1984, during which time the Canada Health Act was made law, described her campaign to remove freedom of choice in health care from Canadians and impose a national regime of State-controlled and rationed health care in her 1987 book, *Medicare: Canada's Right to Health*.

In a review of Kent's own book, *A Public Purpose*, Peter Desbarats, then dean of the School of Journalism at the University of Western Ontario, wrote that "Kent was one of the two or three most influential men in Canada in the mid-1960s ... and at times he came close to running Canada single-handedly" (*Globe and Mail*, March 5, 1988). Kent, he explained, was "the choirmaster who orchestrated much of [the government's] production."

Now, how a single *unelected* individual can "orchestrate" the government of a supposedly democratic nation and in so doing eliminate many of the people's hard-won freedoms—in this case the historical freedom to decide upon, seek out, receive, and pay for any quality of health they needed and could find—is a question that does not seem to bother Canadians. Kent was "a fervent believer in Medicare" who said he "saw it as the jewel in the record of achievement on which the government might go to the people in the following election" (*Toronto Star*, February 20, 1988). In other words, he astutely saw that it would be a powerful election goodie. He based the whole of his moral fervour for medicare on this single proposition: "I regarded it as morally wrong that money in the bank, rather than severity of need, should determine who got what health care services." This is a sentiment with which most would agree. But as a man determined to shape Canada's distinctive brand of utopian socialism, Kent was hitting a fly with a sledgehammer. He intentionally ignored the ready, almost universal availability of a wide range of private insurance options, and also the creative option of combining such free-market solutions with a government program, as the Swiss and many others have done, to help those with insufficient "money in the bank."

The problems that might arise from such a clash of our historic and hardwon rights and freedoms with State compulsion were not unforeseen. Out of the gate, Ontario's 1970 Commission on the Healing Arts prophetically warned that "society would not regard as sufficient, the amount of health goods and services that could be produced, even if all society's resources were devoted to the provision of health care." Many of Canada's provinces can now forecast the day when 50 percent of revenues will be consumed by "health care." (I persist in putting this phrase in quotation marks for two reasons. First, because most of it is not health care, it is sickness or disease care. Second, because even if we keep the phrase, a large proportion of Canada's expenditures are for trivial health care.)

The economic trap, the lure of "free" medicine, was sufficient in itself to cause the decline of medical standards and services in Canada. But it was accompanied by a number of moral traps it will also be the burden of this chapter to explain. Indeed, a recurring thesis of this book is that *any political or economic system resting on immoral foundations must eventually crumble from within*. For starters, think of the corruption of the language. Our national "health insurance" program is no insurance at all. The very term is deceptive. For like many other government programs discussed in this book, it is a sort of pyramid, or Ponzi scheme, by which the working young at the bottom bear most of the burden for the old at the top. (Half of all lifetime health care is consumed after age sixty-five.) Canada does not have a single penny of medical "insurance" in a financial pool generating revenue to cover the costs of health care. The bills are paid directly from general tax revenue. In other words, our socialized medicine "plan" is yet another cradle-to-grave welfare scheme intended to relieve citizens of all their health worries (and personal responsibility for same), and not incidentally to buy vote support for politicians licking their chops at this prospect. For this reason, they simply rammed into public policy what honest health economists call an "open-ended scheme with closedend funding." That's a fancy way of saying they were floating a politically self-aggrandizing plan for financial and—as it would turn out—medical and moral bankruptcy.

The first moral clash was with the Hippocratic oath, once taken by all physicians, that *commands strict physician-patient privacy*.[5] For, to make good on its new political promise, the State had to hand itself the legal power to supervise and to ration; that is, a State right to *rupture the professional private relationship between physician and patient*, to *police* the work of hospitals, to examine, proscribe, and *dictate available services*, to *examine patient records without any knowledge of patients*, and so on. In short, so-called "health care" was a ready symbol for exploitation by the paternalistic State; a formerly free and very intimate realm of private human experience was soon a sitting duck for government takeover and control. Canadians didn't stop to think that very soon the personal medical records of themselves or their loved ones describing their vaginal warts, their alcoholism, their hysterectomy, or their psychiatric care would soon be spread out for purposes of "cost control" on the dining room table of Susie Q, the health ministry bureaucrat living down the street.[6]

Another moral consequence was that Canadians would henceforth be relieved of all personal awareness and responsibility for the true cost of the medical care they would be demanding as a right. Ask any Canadian: How much does it cost to have an appendix removed? To get a cast on a broken arm? They have no idea. And to this day, if you ask Canadians how much of their personal taxes is spent on their health care, you will get a blank stare (see below for this amount). This rupture is morally damaging in principle (separating consequences from personal actions). And although it is true that socialized health care is still very popular with the people (said to be part of our "identity" now), I suggest these very moral ruptures and economic disengagements from the consequences of personal actions are part of the reason. At any rate, my sense is that our system may not be so popular when it has run its full course of decline.

## CANADIAN HEALTH CARE AND THE "STOCKHOLM SYNDROME"

A possible explanation for why so many Canadians fiercely defend a medical system in which they are trapped, and which has such a high potential to harm them, is the so-called "Stockholm syndrome." This term was first used to describe the bewildering fact that a group of hostages held during a five-day bank holdup in Stockholm in 1973 slowly turned against the police trying to liberate them, and began defending their captors.

The term is now used for any situation in which people who are held hostage to anything—a bad situation or system they feel powerless to change, and that to an outsider is clearly not good for them, irrationally and quite emotionally begin defending it.

Socialized medicine as described in this chapter poses a clear potential danger, and sometimes significant pain and suffering for millions of people who nonetheless proudly defend it as something that "makes us Canadian." Why?

Psychiatrists have tried to explain this conundrum by saying that any-one—a child, say—in a difficult situation they know they cannot alter will (especially if they are frightened in any way) be deeply thankful for the slightest kindness shown and will tend to bond emotionally and express great loyalty to whoever they begin to see as their only relief and hope. In short, the hopeless situation causing the pain and suffering in the first place (horrific "emergency" waits, no hospital beds, rationing, long and painful waits for treatment, fear of possible death) becomes a general context or boundary within which the slightest relief produces a reaction of deep personal appreciation, an emotional bonding to the system that produces the relief and therefore (if the hope of a better alternative is lost) a strong defence of it. That is why so many Russians who lived under communism still defend it emotionally (even though there is no possible objective defence left), and it could be why so many Canadians subjectively defend a medical system that objectively has the potential to harm them or their loved ones at some point in their lives.

## ORGANIZING SCARCITY

*This policy of equalizing misery and organizing scarcity instead of allowing diligence, self-interest and ingenuity to produce abundance, has only to be prolonged to kill this British island stone dead.*
—British prime minister Winston Churchill, 1945

*If you think health care is expensive now, just wait until it's free!*
—P.J. O'Rourke, 2005

Governments know that for many of their humdrum programs in less personal-policy areas, they can always withdraw, alter legislation, cut budgets, or reverse the policy. But health care is different. People primordially fear illness and death, and physicians, from shaman to modern scientists, have always been perceived as holding a near-talismanic power over both. With the rise of modern wealth came the potential for enormous tax harvesting, and politicians were quick to see that this power over life and death could generate deep feelings of gratitude and loyalty. Could they take this power unto themselves? "Health care" provided innumerable situations and sound bites evoking public pity and concern—irresistible material as ripe for the front pages as it is was for takeover by politicians wanting to be thanked with votes. The title of the internationally renowned health economist Victor Fuchs's book *Who Shall Live?* poignantly addresses this power to dispense the very stuff of life. It was a power the State could hardly wait to assume.

## THE DICTATORSHIP OF WELL-BEING

The dynamics of this process—re-packaged as ObamaCare—have recently been played out in the United States, much of it as it was played out in Canada in the 1970s. On March 21, 2010, President Obama's Health Care Bill was passed by a narrow margin of Democrats, forever committing America to more socialized medicine. It is a sharp historical irony that so many Americans are calling for "a public option" just as Canadians, who are finally getting a serious whiff of the decay seeping through the floorboards of their socialized medical system are calling for a "private option." Meanwhile, Obama has split America into two camps concerned about serious moral and philosophical questions, of which his bill was an overt manifestation. One-half saw his legislation as a humanization of the American welfare state; the other, as America's dreaded final leap into the arms of the dehumanizing State. For this legislation is as close as anyone in a free nation has ever come to the dictatorship of well-being. Just one instance: it forces otherwise free citizens (and larger firms) by law to purchase health insurance, or suffer a hefty fine. And yet it is clearly unconstitutional for the U.S. government—it is immoral for any government—to force any citizen to purchase a good or service against his or her free will. If you choose to buy a car, the law requires you to acquire and pay for a licence to drive it. That is a normal legal consequence of your choice. But no government in history has ever imagined it could force you to buy a car in the first place. If Americans allow Obama to force them to buy health insurance, then why should he not force them to buy a home (great for the U.S. housing industry), an American car (great for the U.S. automobile industry), or a fishing rod (great for the fishing industry), or . . . life insurance, flood and hurricane insurance, valuable-possessions insurance, and so on. It is not certain Obama ever fully understood the furious nation-splitting resistance to his bill. The Snapshot below is an attempt to explain it.

---

## SNAPSHOT
The ObamaCare Scare

Most observers, right and left, were surprised at the summer 2009 spectacle of outraged citizens vociferously protesting President Obama's plan for socialized medicine. The bill is law now.

But what, exactly, in the politically quietest months of the year, could have compelled so many Americans to show up at those town hall meetings to shout down their political leaders? How could Obama's team have misread their reaction so badly?

This was no staged setup by Republicans, as spooked Democrats persisted in claiming. And anyone could see (until these meeting were cancelled in a panic), the citizen anger was quite genuine, bubbling up from a deeper source.

What source? From the 1960s, to be precise. They have grey hair, bellies, and grown-up kids now. But the hippies are back! If anything united Joan Baez, the flower children of the Left, the Students for a Democratic Society (SDS), and all the other protest groups of the hippie generation, it was the simple message they wanted to send to their elders, to big government, to the military, the media, to anyone who aimed to order them around:

"Get your foot off my neck!"

When it came to equality of external public goods such as education, welfare for the poor, affirmative action quotas for the disadvantaged, even subsidized medicine for the poor or the elderly, the cheers went up because all those things were publicly funded and had nothing to do with individual private choices.

But when it came to even a hint of messing with their own bodies or relationships, the sit-ins, marches, and window-breaking began.

Free love and marijuana? My choice, my body.

Whether or not to abort my baby? My choice, my body.

Homosexuality? My choice, my body.

Assisted suicide? My choice, my body.

Spend my money on my own health care? My choice, my body.

So how do we make sense of what seems to be a passionate concern for tax-supported public services—more government—alongside a concern just as passionate for personal freedom from government?

Just think of the private body as the boundary. Your skin. Anything outside it is fair game for the State. But anything from the skin inward is your own private business, including whether or not you want to spend your own money on another CT scan, buy organic carrots, or pay to see the specialist of your choice at the Mayo Clinic, or . . . buy a vacation instead of health insurance. My choice, my body.

What we witnessed was a resurgence of that old American revolutionary spirit of independence. When the Obama government wrapped itself in the symbols of Big-Brother-Provider of public goods, that was acceptable. But once it started talking seriously about getting under the people's skin, so to speak— to control and ration the quality and availability of what they will be allowed to do for their own bodies, or for their children's and parent's bodies—all hell broke loose.

I have described this seeming contradiction elsewhere in this book as "libertarian socialism," a political reality in which the State has all the public duties, and individuals have all the private rights. It's the legacy of the sixties.

It's who we are now. And don't mess with me is the message.

Except . . . with respect to the degree of State power over us, we are cowards compared to our immediate ancestors and all those whose legacy of freedom we were asked to uphold. Today we say: "Don't mess with my body."

Then, they said: "Don't mess with my life."

---

Alas, any State health care system must end by handicapping excellence and productivity and undermining personal responsibility in the ostensible interests of equality. Such systems are inevitably limited by, and in turn generate, the following general features: a real suppression of scientific initiative and reward; a parallel market in private services (ours is situated in the United States, and elsewhere, to which thousands of Canadians travel each year for services they cannot get in Canada); a substitution of political values, methods, and choices for free market and personal ones; a deterioration of medical capital stock and investment; a flight of the best medical talent; and a cynical populace.

## SCREWING THE SYSTEM

Critics of free-market systems say private physicians can "induce" demand for their services, thus putting at their personal disposal the purchasing power of their patients. For the small minority of traumatized or seriously ill and unaware patients, this is undoubtedly true, for in the hands of a physician determined to take advantage of someone in a weakened condition as a means to boost income, we have no recourse. We are as an animal in the hands of a veterinarian. (Worse, actually. At least the vet will first ask if the owner wants to try this or that expensive treatment to save Rover from dying.)

However, such manipulations are just as likely in a socialized system like ours when a physician knows an impersonal government is paying, rather than the patient. Some time ago, health economist Malcolm Brown warned us about such devious practices. In addition to the predicted increased patient demand for "free" services, he said some doctors, in an attempt to increase their incomes under medicare's fixed lower rates, may resort to: "time shuffling" (treating patients on overtime hours, to increase fees); "upgrading" (the paying agency is billed for a service that pays more than the one actually performed); "injury enlargement" (overstating the nature of the problem); "ping-ponging" (referring to other physicians or professionals without sufficient reason); "service splitting" (splitting the treatment into many smaller fee-paying parts); "phantom treatment" (billing for services not performed); and "assembly line" treatment (patients treated at too high a speed). Physicians may also refuse to take critically ill patients because they require too much time, and choose to perform better-paying procedures over low-paying ones. While no one can be sure how much of this is going on, suffice it to say that the perverse economic incentives built into any socialized system create a perfect environment for such activities. The physician doesn't care (because he or she is ripping off an impersonal government); the patient doesn't care (because "it's free").[7]

## GO OVER THE WALL OF STATE MEDICINE: DEMAND YOUR RIGHT TO "MEDICAL FREEDOM"

At any rate, it is wrong to assume that the average medical consumer is a dolt with no interest in health, or is incapable of saying "no thanks" to more treatment. That is especially true today because the Internet has vastly altered the former gatekeeper status of physicians. With only basic computer skills, a patient can easily surf the Net and then walk into a physician's office with a fat file of the latest studies downloaded from the best medical journals in the world. Obviously there is always a danger of seduction by flawed studies. And this our physician can always correct. But the sophisticated information modern patients have acquired about available medical procedures and treatments is so astonishing that the weak grip of the gatekeepers has been broken for good. A physician treating a patient today will often find him- or herself listening to an informed citation from a great medical journal along with the patient's complaints.

A far wider consequence of this new and widespread public knowledge, however, is a noticeably increased dissatisfaction with rationed, low-grade State medicine and especially with restrictions on personal medical freedom. Since the 1970s Canadians have been trapped by their politicians inside an invisible medical jail. There is no other word for it. And citizens with the means to break out do so with alacrity. An estimated 41,006 Canadians escaped the confines of Canadian socialized medicine in 2009 to get treatment they couldn't get, or were denied here, and this annual exodus constitutes a decisive judgment on the failure of our system.[8] Dropping, say, $5,000 to $10,000 each represents around 200 to 400 million exported dollars. Interestingly, this estimate was lower than the year previous because Canadian wait-times have improved a little. But it is still very likely a low number because many Canadians, like myself, do not report their medical trips abroad. As I explained earlier, I broke out and went to Minnesota, where I gladly spent $2,000 for diagnostic tests that I was denied in Canada. It is a sad reality that if our system were as entrepreneurially vigorous, inventive, and as scientifically and technologically up-to-date as it ought to be, those medical dollars would have been spent here.

Just so, a direct and very exciting result of the new planetary freedom of medical knowledge provided by the Internet and by the electronic transmission of diagnostic information, video-surgery-via-satellite connection, and the like, is the booming international phenomenon of "health tourism," or "medical tourism."[9] If you can't get the timely operation you need in Canada you travel to a fee-for-service private clinic where treatment is quicker and cheaper. Popular worldwide destinations include: Argentina, Brunei, Cuba, Colombia, Costa Rica, Hong Kong, Hungary, India, Jordan, Lithuania, Malaysia, the Philippines, Singapore, South Africa, Thailand, and recently, Saudi Arabia, the United Arab Emirates (UAE), South Korea, Tunisia, and New Zealand, where you are very likely to be treated promptly in a facility cleaner and better equipped than almost any here. South Africa is taking the term "medical tourism" very literally by promoting "medical safaris." And here's an embarrassing irony: communist Cuba has been a popular medical tourism destination for more than forty years. Thousands of patients travel to Cuba, particularly from Latin America and Europe, attracted by the "fine reputation of Cuban doctors, the low prices and nearby beaches on which to recuperate." In 2006, Cuba attracted nearly 20,000 health tourists. A flourishing Winnipeg-based company, Choice—Self Directed Healthcare, announces: "We are proud to partner with the Cuban medical system to provide real solutions for the healthcare issues here in North America" (http://www.choicemedicalservices.com/index.html).

This trend, of course, is not always positive. Patients risk contracting foreign diseases never seen here; there are few international medical standards governing procedures; medical insurance may not cover patients for medical problems encountered in politically risky countries; there is little likelihood of success in suing a foreign entity for malpractice (though some insurance companies offer policies for exactly this). However, it is clear that this "outsourcing" is an emerging international industry that despite its growing pains is really booming. Estimates are that 11 percent of private medical insurers in the United States happily cover medical tourism (because costs are lower abroad). Fifty years ago, a Japanese camera or car was a joke. Today, half of all American vehicles are imports because they are better and/or cheaper cars. More bang for the buck! It will be the same with all medical products and services. For an interesting analysis, see http://www.ncpa.org/pub/ba623#. Wake up, Canada.

According to Deloitte Consulting, an estimated 750,000 Americans went abroad for health care in 2007, and the report estimated that a million and a half people would seek health care outside the United States in 2008.[10] Double, in one year. Such growth in medical tourism has the potential to cost American health care providers billions of dollars in lost revenue (which, in a private medical market, should help drive prices down). But there is a lot of "reverse medical migration" happening, too. Thousands of medical tourists travel to the United States every year for the most advanced medical care in the world, and . . . even Canada has become a favourite destination for "immigration medicine." There are three million Canadian citizens who live abroad, many of whom have never lived principally in Canada, and have never intended to do so. They know if they take up residence for the required six months they will qualify for "free" medical care, heavily subsidized education, the lot. One fellow I knew personally was very clear about this: "My principal residence is not in Canada, but I live there long enough to get all my medical care free." He has never paid a dime into the system. He knew he was very ill before his last trip to Canada, so he got qualified in this manner, and leeched from our system for a decade before he died.

## SOME MORAL CONTRADICTIONS OF SOCIALIZED MEDICINE

But still, there is something fundamental that had never been violated before State medicine came along: *a physician or a patient in Canada, until the mid-1960s, was always a free person.* In a free country, no one is owned by another, and no one's income is dictated by another. Voluntary exchange is the rule. But if you cannot freely negotiate a price for your labour, you are not free. If as a patient you have no free choice either of an alternative, or of a better service, you may be free to choose, but have been deprived of meaningful choices. If as a medical provider the value (the price) of your work is dictated by another and you cannot change your paymaster without leaving your country, then you are not free. If you cannot protect the strict privacy of a professional relationship, you are not free either as doctor or patient.[11] How did thousands of Canadian doctors, and millions of their patients, who lost their medical privacy and freedom of choice to seek better care for themselves and their loved ones *inside* Canada, to pay more (or less) for better (or more cost-efficient) health care if they so choose, lose these fundamental freedoms?

## MORE OF THE RIGHTS ILLUSION

Basically, it was simple. Because medical care is designated as strictly a *provincial responsibility* under Canada's Constitution, the federal government, in its eagerness to take control of medical care for political gain, while at the same time avoiding a confrontation with the highest law of the land, settled on the clever method of *fiscal bribery.* The feds simply raised taxes on everyone, and then offered a "shared-cost" program to subsidize the medical expenses of any province that accepted its centralized "universal" medical standards.[12] Soon, without having broken the law of the land, or having to alter the Constitution to permit central control of a provincial matter, Canada's federal government got *virtual control* over each province's health program and subjected the medical behaviour of millions of citizens to possible fines and criminal penalties. The stage was now set for government rationing of all basic medical services in Canada, and for the misleading public perception of unlimited medical care as a right. Such rationing is accomplished in many ways, such as by restricting overall *supply* of medical goods and services, by restricting *access* to specialists, by restricting the *number of medical graduates*, by *closing* hospital beds and wards, by *limiting income* of physicians, by *delisting* formerly insured services, and by *denying purchase* of or access to technologically advanced equipment.

Politicians loved it. And that's why Monique Bégin entitled her book

*Medicare: Canada's Right to Health.* Few stopped to realize that the *rights* of some always imply the *obligations* of others (other taxpayers). Once the State proclaimed that Canadians had a "right" to health, and that as Bégin proudly said, echoing Tom Kent's moral belief, "no financial barrier should hinder access to health care,"[13] the irreversible process of professional, financial, and moral corrosion had begun. The State was on the hook. What the caretaker State *should* have said was that once the *truly needy* were guaranteed *basic* care and covered for "catastrophic" health insurance by the State, for hamburgers, not filet mignon, any citizen could purchase as much additional care, whether essential or elective, as personal resources would permit and professional advice suggest. Instead, the notion of medicine as a right opened up a moral and fiscal can of worms because now *all citizens could claim as a right whatever health care was available.* It only took about a day for governments to realize that *the secret to cost containment in a socialized system would have to centre on the word "available":* medical care would have to be strictly rationed.

Nevertheless, on April 9, 1984, the Canada Health Act with its five national conditions[14] received the support of all federal parties, effectively banning and criminalizing "extra billing" throughout the realm, completing the quasi socialization of medicine, and thoroughly extinguishing a fundamental freedom of all Canadians to secure their personal health with their own means. *Canada is the only Western nation to have criminalized the private purchase or sale of essential health care,* and the only one of twenty-seven of its partners in the Organisation for Economic Co-operation and Development (OECD) to ban a private option. In the beginning, private physicians were wary of any "third parties" making profits from the medical profession. But in the end, our once-free private physicians ended up with the worst "third party" master of all, with no freedom, and no profits (See Snapshot on Canada versus U.S. Health Care, below: the average income of the average Canadian GP is 40 percent that of the equivalent American GP).

## PRICING YOUR BODY PARTS

It takes some pondering to realize that in a socialized medical system patients always count as an *expense,* or a cost to "the system," and physicians under socialism represent "a huge cost-generating entity"[15] (whereas, in contrast, in a liberty-based system, patients always count as *revenue*), and so our ailing body parts are inevitably assigned a bureaucratic rank order for treatment that has little to do with ourselves, our pain and suffering, or with the professional treatment priorities of our physician. That is because in a fixed-budget system that criminalizes the use of additional private funds, patient demand is a drain on available public funds. Hence the need for rationing. A bureaucrat, somewhere, must always decide whether two gallbladder surgeries are worth one knee replacement, etc., and allocate health dollars accordingly. The main concern is not about alleviating your problems, but to make sure the budget stretches for the current budget year.

In contrast, in an open, liberty-based system meant to satisfy real demand, more spending from private sources is always considered better. You count as *revenue* (and so do your body parts). That is why a hospital that has a limited public budget will be eager to skimp on or delay services, and will kick you out of your bed as soon as possible; but a private hospital is happy to have you feeling better before you go home—"Stay another day!" The sour receptionist in the socialist hospital is not so happy to see you because you represent more damn work. "If you want that appointment six months from now, you'd better be nice," is the feeling we too often get (and that the decent ones struggle to suppress). But people in a private clinic will generally smile easily because you are another reason they will get paid well, keep the jobs they love, and help their enterprise grow. There is a legitimate worry you might be overtreated or that expensive care is being recommended just for the money. Very possible. But most people would rather have the option to decline a sophisticated treatment that is readily available than to be told they are being refused a treatment due to rationing, or that the technology or treatment just isn't available in Canada, so they will have to travel abroad to get treated.

## THE MEDICAL POLICE

Doctors in Canada are required by law to make available to government inspectors the once-confidential private details of any visit, diagnosis, treatment, lab test, or operation, which may then be registered on the medical computers of the State. Previously, the Hippocratic oath, once taken routinely by all graduating doctors, demanded the protection of the intimate details of medical care; but now the most intimate details on any patient in Canada are *public property*, courtesy of the health-audit provisions of each province. The computers that process this information in most provinces can then flag sensitive matters and send files to a medical review committee. Thereupon, a physician inspector working for the government—that's right, *medical police*—may pore over hundreds of seized patient records, make copies of a significant number of these and send them off to other members of the committee. *No patient in Canada has any power or right to disallow such an inspection or invasion of his or her private medical life by total strangers.* Our ancient right to bodily privacy and confidentiality has been legislated away. This process may occur even though the patient so invaded has never complained or been consulted, and *has never been notified that his or her private life is being reviewed by medical police.* If in any province a hundred doctors per year are reviewed at, say, a hundred charts each—that comes to ten thousand invasions of patient privacy per year. Ontario's Bill 147 allows medical police to inspect all health facilities and records, without a warrant.[16] When this medical spying process first got under way in Canada, Mr.

Justice Horace Krever was asked to examine it, and was "shocked . . . by the inadequate laws, the abuses of confidentiality, and the fact that so many people—*except the patient*—had access to medical records."[17]

## FROM ADULT-ADULT, TO PARENT-CHILD TREATMENT

Through an unsubtle transformation, all private doctor-patient relationships were transformed overnight into a three-party relationship consisting of doctor-government-patient. Which is to say that the State has made itself an uninvited partner—sometimes quite visible, but mostly invisible—in all your medical relationships and transactions.

Another way to say this is that if you are a grown-up, a genuine relationship with a physician is always adult-to-adult. But once a physician is constrained by law or any third party to control and dictate the treatment you are allowed to have for reasons that have nothing to do with you or with your physician (but with rationing and the State's budgets), then this relationship is converted into an adult-child one. You are then disempowered as an adult.

And because in any socialist system the dollars allocated for medical care must compete in "prioritization" with the dollars allocated to myriad other publicly funded programs, the pay of doctors and staff, and the spending on patients are always targets for government trimming. Doctors and medical facilities are then set against nosy bureaucrats, hospital administrators against patients, and patients against politicians. Doctors may even begin to see their own patients as cost-integers, or drains upon "the system": Will Dr. Jones readily recommend an expensive treatment for older patient Mary, when he has been warned there are limited funds, and maybe they ought to go to a seriously ill younger patient? Too often, Dr. Jones will go silent. That is another moral hazard of socialized medicine, and a natural product of the triangular relationship I describe. The same is true when the doctor knows a treatment is simply "not covered" in Canada, but may be available for a fee in the United States (or elsewhere): if the doctor senses Mary doesn't have the funds, he would be raising fruitless hopes to mention the existence of an option she cannot afford. *Professional silence* is a real moral hazard of Canadian medical rationing.

As the system weakens we see endless spending on commissions and committees to study "spiralling" costs (which are disconnected from true demand). Patients lose because a lot of excellent doctors leave Canada to go where they can practice free of government interference and control. It is a real concern that Canadians are getting left with second stringers. Medical students are alert to this, and that is why increasing numbers of them write American medical board exams in preparation for a possible exodus. Hundreds of our medical students whose high-tech education is highly subsidized by Canadians graduate on Monday and are on the plane to a lucrative job in the United States on Tuesday . . . while we suffer physician shortages.[18] In 1996 alone, some

713 doctors were graduated from Canadian universities, and that same year as many physicians left Canada to take U.S. jobs. Overall, about 11 percent of Canadians trained in our medical schools each year emigrate to the United States. In 2002, there were 8,990 Canadian-trained physicians working in the States (and 519 U.S.-trained physicians working in Canada the same year). It takes a generation or so, but when anything is socialized it will always produce the same result. Things slowly move from a condition in which there was an unequal distribution of blessings, to one in which there is an equal distribution of miseries. That is because on a quality scale from zero to ten, a socialist government will always prefer a situation in which everyone gets four, to one in which most get six, and some eight.

# THE TRANSITION FROM HUMAN TO VETERINARY MEDICINE

*Your dog or cat can get an MRI faster than us as humans.*
—Randy Valpy (of Petplan Insurance), in
"MRI's and Chemo—all for Fluffy," *Toronto Star*, June 4, 2008

*Canada is a country in which dogs can get a hip replacement in under a week, and in which humans can wait two or three years.*
—Dr, Brian Day, former president, Canadian Medical Association
(*New York Times*, February 26, 2008)

Positron emission tomography (PET) scans will discover hidden illnesses and cancers better than any other devices (such as MRI and CT scanners), but given the high cost—as much as $2,500 a scan—government agencies limit their use to patients who will benefit most. As it happens, Ontario is the most under-served province in Canada, and "remains the only part of the OECD that does not have routine access to PET services." Indeed, Dr. Jean-Luc Urbain, chief of nuclear medicine in London, Ontario, said, "I've never seen in twenty-five years of care so many advanced cancers because of the lack of access to this type of technology." In London, human patients are made to line up at hospitals for rationed treatment (Ontario has a PET. "steering committee" that decides if you are "eligible" for a scan or not). Forbidden to pay with their own cash, their cancers will grow while they wait, undetected, far too long.[19]

But if you are doing animal research, you can pay cash to have your animal scanned. No problem. Human scans are so tightly restricted at St. Joseph's Hospital in London that, as the director put it, "empty [human] patient slots are occasionally filled to do animal research so the machine does not go to waste." Well, hold on now. Veterinary researchers pay to have their animal patients scanned, but human patients who have figured out that their very lives are being thrown into a high-risk, scan-denied pool by bureaucrats, must then go to places like CareImaging in Mississauga to purchase a private PET scan—in an attempt to save their own lives? CareImaging will scan you for cash, as long as the scan you want is not on the government's insured PET scan list (in which case you cannot purchase that scan).

The natural conclusion of an egalitarian—but the wrong one—is to stop all animal research scans because it looks bad when an animal can be scanned, but humans can't. The correct conclusion, however, is to understand that we badly need more animal research, not less, to help us discover human cures. But we also need a lot more human scans to catch human diseases early enough to cure them. A PET scan, due to its much finer image resolution, will result in an accelerated treatment regime. In the London situation, the animal scans are helping to fund the machine, which otherwise could not have been purchased.

Clearly, the solution is to create the same sort of market situation for humans that vets and researchers have created for animals. Almost any vet of any consequence has a portable X-ray, and often also a portable CT scanner. You can pay to have your dog or cat scanned any day. Without waiting. Neurologica Corporation is just one of the world's companies specializing in "portable diagnostic scanners" (www.neurologica.com). I had my horse's ankle X-rayed for $175 and saw the results myself, on the spot, just after writing this chapter. Why shouldn't every GP in Canada have a similar small X-ray unit? I have read that some Swedes, distressed with denied service in their socialized system, are using veterinarians for human medical care.

So that was a little reality check on this topic, just to make the point that there is a free market in animal medicine, animal medical research, and pet health insurance, and it is booming. Actually, many animals in Canada get more rapid and better care than humans. And so now I might as well just say what's on my mind, though this terminology may seem strange to some: I think *a socialized medical system converts ordinary human medicine into veterinary medicine*—with the caveat that in Canada, outside of emergencies (which we tend to handle very well), animals will often have speedier access to good care than humans do.

The following reflection on the underlying ethic of veterinary medicine from Dr. Hans Truffer, of Switzerland, one of the early opponents of applying animal medicine policy (State medicine) to humans, helps us see why:

"The real danger of collectivized State medicine is that the patient becomes a tool in the hands of the holders of power, and is dispossessed of the protection afforded by the Hippocratic principle (which is to care for the patient according to the latter's specific requirements), in favour of a veterinary ethic, which consists in caring for the sick animal, not in accordance with its specific needs, but according to the dictates of its master and owner."

I live on a farm and keep horses and a few other animals, and it is clear as a bell that the health of my animals depends wholly on me, their master. I decide the quality and quantity of their feed, when to give or not to give them their annual shots, and . . . if one of them gets sick I decide how much or how little to spend on the treatments—or to spend nothing at all. When they look at me with their innocent eyes, I am keenly aware that I alone make these decisions. They have no say. So, as many of the illnesses, treatments, and drugs used for humans and animals are the same, it is clear that morally speaking, the main thing that makes animal medicine different from human medicine is that the sick animal *has no choice of, or control over, the available treatment options or budget.* A domesticated animal lives under a health care dictator. So I think we have to face the bald truth: if a human lives under a health care dictator, he or she is being treated just like an animal, but in our case, all too often, as a second-rate animal.

So the logic of this parallel leads me to say: Whenever the citizens of a country are free to buy whatever available medical services are on offer, are free from arbitrary legal prohibitions, cost controls, political ideologies, or imposed government rationing, they live in a medically free society in which *human medicine* is being practiced.

But if a medical regime change is imposed by politicians as a totalizing (or "universal") health care system, such that the choice of the type, quantity, and quality of medical care available is dictated, controlled, and rationed by a third party over whom the patient (whose income is being forcibly extracted for this purpose) has no control, then the patient lives under a system of animal, or veterinary, medicine, that is being applied to human beings. I don't see how it is possible to escape the logic of this charge.

## SNAPSHOT
A Story About the Canadian Medical System: Not As Funny As It Seems

Two patients limp into two different medical clinics with the same complaint. Both have trouble walking and appear to require a hip replacement.

The FIRST sees his family doctor after waiting three weeks for an appointment, then waits three months to see a specialist. Then he gets an X-ray, which isn't reviewed for another week. And finally has the surgery scheduled for six months later.

The SECOND patient is examined within the hour, is X-rayed the same day, and has an appointment booked for surgery the following week.

Why the different treatment for the two patients?

The FIRST is a Canadian citizen.

The SECOND is a golden retriever.

# DOES A GOVERNMENT "HEALTH" MONOPOLY IMPOSE POSSIBLE DEATH-BY-WAITING? ASK THE SUPREME COURT OF CANADA

> The evidence in this case shows that delays in the public
> health-care system are widespread, and that, in some serious cases,
> *patients die as a result of waiting lists for public health care.*
> —Supreme Court of Canada, in *Chaoulli v. Quebec*, June 9, 2005[20]

This is another hard truth for most people to swallow—at least it was for me when I first heard of it. But upon further thought, it seemed dead right, so to speak. In a country where the availability of all basic medical care is rationed by the State, and where individuals are forbidden by law to purchase such care for themselves, we indeed are able to trace the premature deaths of hundreds of individuals—usually those who cannot afford medical tourism—directly to the State's withholding of, or delay in, providing adequate medical care. In other words, death is often imposed as a result of State action.

In Ontario, seventy-one patients died waiting for coronary surgery in 1997. Another 121 became too sick for surgery while waiting, and so were sent home to die.[21] The headline about withheld surgery for obesity patients near the start of this chapter is another instance of death-by-rationing in 2007. Anyone could be next. We cannot escape the logic of the fact that any rationing by the queue and laws forbidding the use of personal funds to save one's own life that happen to lead to death constitute a deliberate form of anonymous *letting-die* by the State. Now, those are hard words. But when we think about them, what else could this be?

There are, as they say, sins of commission, and of omission. If you have the means to save and secure the life of a helpless child in a hospital by providing food and water, but decide to withhold these things, and the child dies, then you have surely caused the death of the child by a failure to act. As distinctly, if you have the financial means to purchase life-saving care, but are forbidden to do so by the State, then the State has caused your death just as surely as if it made a law to bar you from purchasing sufficient food and water.

How is such a thing possible? Here's how.

Each hospital receives enough money in its budget for, say, one hundred serious operations annually. If you are the hundred and first, you will simply have to wait, perhaps in pain, until the next budget allocation. Often a year or more. But, you complain, are there not eager surgeons, willing nurses, empty surgical theatres, empty hospital beds? The answer is yes to all these queries. So, because you are naturally afraid to suffer or die, you or your family offer to pay for the service yourself. But in Canada, as already stated, it is illegal for a physician to accept money from patients for "insured" health care. So if you are a poor Canadian, you will certainly suffer, and may even die waiting for your rationed treatment. But if you can dig up the money, you will probably fly to the United States or elsewhere for treatment.

Notable recent cases are such as Ontario's Lindsay McCreith who, suffering terrible headaches, faced a four-and-a-half-month wait for an MRI scan in January of 2006. He went to Buffalo instead for a same-day scan which revealed a brain tumour. He then learned he'd have to wait months for surgery in Ontario! So . . . back to Buffalo, where he had the tumour removed. He is now challenging Ontario's health insurance system on the grounds that it violated his right to life and security of the person by withholding care. In 2007, Ontario's Shona Holmes suffered a loss of vision, and after an MRI that showed a brain lesion, was told she'd have to wait months to see a Canadian specialist. So she went to the Mayo Clinic in Arizona, where the precise nature of the lesion was diagnosed. She came back to Canada for what ought to have been urgent surgery, only to be told there would again be an indefinite delay. Back to Mayo she went for immediate surgery, after which she got her sight back. Shona is co-operating with the Canadian Constitution Foundation to challenge the province of Ontario's health care monopoly. In Alberta, Bill Murray, fifty-seven, was in terrible pain due to a badly arthritic hip. He needed a "Birmingham procedure," but government bureaucrats told him he was "too old" for it. He was allowed to pay for the first hip, but not the second. So he is suing the Alberta government. I hope they all win.

## SICK IN CANADA? YOU HAVE MORE FREEDOM AS A FOREIGNER!

Perhaps to avoid just such court cases, OHIP in Ontario will substantially reimburse you if you are pre-cleared (expect a long delay) by the Ministry of Health for serious life-saving medical treatment in a foreign country that is not offered in a timely manner in Ontario (but not if you are doing this to "jump the queue" in Ontario). Indeed, this ministry is on record as preferring to pay far more for necessary medical treatment in a foreign country than to allow the same surgery to be performed in Ontario by a private clinic. In other words, the ministry is prepared to trigger considerable extra expense for purely ideological reasons. *However, if you are a foreigner who gets sick while visiting Canada and you offer to pay for treatment yourself, you may be treated right away for cash. No problem.* I asked David Jensen, media relations coordinator for the Ontario Ministry of Health, to shed light on this, and he basically verified the statement.[22]

Canadians must wait, while foreigners are served? Canadians may die, while foreigners live? It's a scandal! There is a lame argument that we could—or perhaps do—charge foreigners hefty fees to help fund our hospital programs. But no one knows what a medical service really "costs" in Canada, so it is impossible to know what more would mean. But even if we knew and were so inclined, why not charge more to Canadians who can afford it, too, and thus subsidize our own system by keeping the business in Canada? Canadians ought to be free to purchase whatever basic health services they need. We are a bright enough people to figure out how to make the same services available to the truly needy without handicapping everyone in the process. See the end of this chapter for some solutions.

## REMEMBER: THE POWER TO RATION IS THE POWER TO CONTROL!—TRIAGE AND *M\*A\*S\*H*

As the Canadian population ages we will see a great deal more imposed suffering and premature death. When performed openly, as in war, the practice of letting some of the badly wounded die is called "triage"—a French term describing the habit of dividing patients into three groups—those beyond help who shall be left untreated; those who may live but can wait for treatment; and those who will live only if treated immediately—and allocating available medical resources accordingly. I'm not sure it's possible to avoid some of this under any system, but even though we are not at war it's officially at work in Canada right now. When this book was first published, no one contemplated open triage in a Canadian hospital outside of wartime. Now, every hospital in the country has a "triage nurse." When I last spoke of this with a top physician at Ottawa General Hospital, he described his emergency room on most days as "a scene from *M\*A\*S\*H*."[23]

Of course there will always be scarcity if demand for a product or service is higher than supply. So the most serious question shouldn't be: How do we restrict, or ration, or outlaw the private procurement of something of which we don't have a sufficiency? But rather: How do we create a system that can service rising demand and remain financially healthy? How well does the political-economic system we rely upon to *produce* medical resources and new technology actually function? It seems clear that medical freedom and free markets are the clear winner when it comes to availability and extraordinary inventiveness, for medical care in socialist, or socializing, nations (at least once we see past the political show projects created to mislead) is a disaster; and there is a clear relationship between the scarcity of such resources and the degree of government control of medicine.[24]

But critics will answer: in free nations there is a problem of inequality. I respond that this is true, but that socialist systems have their own inequality problems, if more for political than financial reasons. They tend to operate at an even worse level of equality than do freer societies, at a much lower level of professional adequacy, and the moral and political price paid in loss of fundamental freedoms by all citizens is simply far too high. Meanwhile, Canada is the only nation among its twenty-eight OECD neighbours to have actually *criminalized* parallel private care,[25] while all the rest allow parallel private options and user fees in various degrees.

# RATIONING BY THE QUEUE AND OTHER MORAL HAZARDS

Because the level of medical resources available will always be lower than the level of demand in a system that tells everyone they have a "right" to the best, and can receive the care they want "free," scarcity is inherent in our delivery of medical services. This means that not everyone will be able to get what in a perfect world he or she might wish to have. American health economist John Goodman once calculated that if every single American demanded a right to all available blood tests in the same year, the cost would exceed the entire GDP of the United States. So there must always be some kind of *brake* (formerly the brake of personal finances, self-help, and insurance costs; now, of government budgets) on the amount of money spent on health care. In a free country— and assuming for the moment that the State always has the means to protect the truly needy from medical disasters—*the natural brake on spending is the patient's own resources, coping ability, financial priorities, and personal lifestyle.* In other words, the patient makes a judgment and balances the personal and family cost-benefit of purchasing increasing amounts of care or better insurance. The patient then chooses between a variety of medical services and imposes a form of self-rationing that is controlled by cash on hand, by the cost of an annual medical-insurance premium, and by self-discipline (whether or not to drink more, smoke more, or less, etc.). This is called "rationing by price"; and it does a very good job of ensuring that the costs arising from unhealthy personal choices are paid by those who incur them. On the new-medical-technology side, if a million people think they might benefit from some special kind of medical treatment and are willing to pay for it, a market for this treatment will be created by entrepreneurs, all financed and paid for by medical consumers, but without drawing a penny from the incomes of those who have no interest in or need for such treatment.

Furthermore, there are usually valuable entrepreneurial spinoffs from such investment that trickle down to the less well-off in the form of new drugs, technologies, and the like. In short, the price system generates solutions for all, fits in perfectly with the Freedom System outlined in this book, and creates incentives for success, rather than disincentives that produce failure. But a system based on egalitarianism produces resentment due to scarcity, in which a different, more insidious form of rationing arises of which the State is always the arch-practitioner, called "rationing by the queue." This is brought about by the State's budgetary restrictions.

After all, it's easy to keep costs down in a State-controlled medical system: you simply withhold service by rationing, or refuse to provide it altogether. But because socialist systems tend to reward inefficiency and to spend large amounts on bureaucratic control, expenses for the latter tend to grow within available budgets, increasingly crowding out funds for medical needs. When Canada was just launching itself down this road, a shocking example came from Great Britain, where by 1978 it was found there were five health administrators for *each* hospital bed.[26] There are no such figures available for Canada, but rest assured there are a great number of health administrators on handsome salaries or contracts crawling all over Canadian hospitals right now, obedient to their political bosses (who pay them), arrogant to medical professionals and patients (who "drain the system"), all the while searching desperately for ways to cut costs by more rationing of care. Socialism always results in a downward pressure on quality and an upward pressure on costs. Thus does the State itself consume resources that might otherwise have gone to patients, forcing them to wait for care, many of them in pain, some of whom will die.

In a survey of wait-times in Canada for 2009 drawn from data supplied by Canadian hospitals and specialists, it was estimated that nearly 695,000 Canadians were on waiting lists for medical treatment (I have been one of these for the past year). The median wait-time from visit with a GP to actual treatment by specialist (some provinces have longer waits than others; they are averaged here) grew from 9.3 weeks in 1993 to 16.1 weeks in 2009. That's a 73 percent longer wait-time in only sixteen years![27] As it happens, I have a severely osteoarthritic shoulder from an old athletic injury. The sharp pain has become debilitating to the extent that it is difficult sometimes even to wash my hands. I was researching this section on wait-times in Canada at the same time as I was looking for a good surgeon to do a total shoulder replacement. Two of the best work at hospitals within a half-hour from my home. I was shocked to hear that the first surgeon had a wait-list of two years *for a first consultation*; the second, eighteen months. I saw the second surgeon in March 2010 and was informed he could operate in six to eight months! The statistics had come alive for me in a very personal way.

## THE MYTH OF SINGLE-TIER MEDICINE IN CANADA

Politicians know there is a vast pool of latent citizen envy lurking in the bosom of every nation that is easily aroused with misleading equality talk. Just so, an unreflective Canadian public has swallowed the politically promoted belief that Canada has a "single-tier" medical system. This has become such a near-sacred myth that our governments loudly boast of the "prohibition of 'two-tier' medicine,"[28] and various provincial acts have threatened physicians and corporations with penalties of a $25,000 fine (more for corporations) and up to twelve months' imprisonment for offences[29] (though the Ontario Ministry of Health says it is "not aware of any individual or company to have been convicted or fined").

Two-tier has become a code-accusation of rich privilege. But the truth is, Canada has always had a multi-tier medical system. Here's why:

## SNAPSHOT

The Myth: Canada has a "single-tier" medical system

The Truth: Canada has always had a "multi-tier" medical system

*Tier One—Those Who Are Wealthy Enough for "Health Tourism"*
Clearly, if we did not have the best medical care in the world at our doorstep in America, socialized medicine would never have got off the ground here, because influential Canadians who get there what they can't get here would have screamed bloody murder and taken the entire system down. Instead, they quietly slip out of the country, get first-class care, and as quietly return. They are silent because they are privileged.* I suspect that most Canadian doctors, medical bureaucrats, and top medical scientists belong here financially, even if it is true that some of them are socialistically inclined, and will insist on waiting their turn.

*Tier Two—Those Who Live Far from Big Towns and Cities*
This tier comprises all those who cannot get medical treatment as conveniently as others because they live far away from big towns and cities. If they need complex surgery or diagnosis they will have to travel to get what city dwellers access with ease, and will likely incur considerable expenses for hotel, travel, and food in the process.

*Tier Three—Those Who Are Highly Educated and Articulate*
A further consequence of government medicine is the market it creates for various kinds of persuasion and influence. There is overlap with tier one folks here, but getting into a Canadian hospital quickly has a lot to do with who you may know, whether or not you are wealthy. Here's a view of this that still rings true from Quebec economist Pierre Lemieux: "In Québec, you can be relatively sure not to wait six hours with your sick child in an emergency room if you know how to talk to the hospital Director, or if one of your old classmates is a doctor, or if your children attend the same private school as your pediatrician's children, or if you deal with a medical clinic in the business district."[30]

*Tier Four—Those with Influence or Celebrity Status*
If you are a very well-known social figure, an important politician or government figure, or an idolized NHL, basketball, baseball, or football star, or a

medal-winning Olympian, you will already know who you have to call to jump the queue. Your adoring fans in the system will pave the way. In "Health Minister Tells Athletes to Get in Line" (*National Post*, November 6, 2009), we read about star Toronto Maple Leafs and Raptors athletes jumping the queue to get the H1N1 virus vaccine. The entire Calgary Flames hockey team did so. Medicine is a very close fraternity, and very few medical experts wait for treatment in the hallways of our hospitals. Criminals in Canada's prisons are also treated like celebrities. They go to the front of the queue, as do Workers Compensation cases. Until 1994, the National Defence Medical Centre (NDMC) in Ottawa saw lots of non-military patients in a hurry. Canada's Auditor General reported that at NDMC "patients include members of the RCMP, members of Parliament, and senior civil servants. In fact, 61 percent of NDMC's 1987/88 patient days were for non-military patients."" This means that the very people who passed legislation in Ottawa forcing Canadians to queue up for months, even years, to get government medicine, themselves walked down the street for immediate medical attention of the highest calibre whenever they wished.

There is a good argument that key people such as the prime minister, the premiers, perhaps a handful of other key government personnel, police, RCMP, and higher military folks should be able to jump the queue because they represent us or protect us and we need them to get well quickly. No argument there. That is a justifiable tier within a tier. But there is something very wrong when run-of-the-mill elected legislators place themselves and their staffs above the restrictions they place on the people who elected them.

*Tier Five—Those in General Triage Who Are Wait-Listed*
This is the Canadian "tier-in-waiting" comprising the 695,000 mentioned above who do not have either enough money, or smarts, or motivation, or influence to make it into a better tier. Many are older people with complex conditions. Many are in pain and suffering, and many wait with fear that each day of delay could mean a worsening of their condition. These are obviously not the same people every year. So how many Canadians have been members of this tier since 1970? About two million would be a good guess.

*Tier Six—Triage within Triage: The "Worst-Case" Wait-List*
A surgeon in British Columbia explained how this works. In that province, a surgeon is allotted six hours a week of surgery time in hospital. Easy cases (hernias, gallbladders, arthroscopies, and the like) and healthier patients (younger and low-risk) are easier to do. So the surgeon will naturally line his patients up in priority from easiest to toughest (most time-consuming) to get as many through in his six hours per week as possible. The tough cases go to the end of the line, end up waiting the longest for treatment, and get bumped

most often. Many patients report being prepped and readied for surgery many times over, only to get bumped yet again. Surgeons who want to help you get in quicker will advise you: "Go to Emergency when I'm on shift and start complaining about unbearable pain. I'll see you there."

*Tier Seven—All Who Suffer or Die in the System*
This is the smallest but saddest tier. Most have lived through the anguish of tiers five or six, but simply never get treated. An unknown number die because while waiting so long, their condition worsened and became untreatable. No one has a tally of how many have been dumped into this tier since the 1970s. But it is a significant number. As mentioned above, in 1988, six heart patients died waiting in a Manitoba hospital; in 1989, 24 British Columbians died waiting for surgery.[31] In Ontario, 71 patients died in 1997 while waiting for coronary surgery, and another 121 had become too sick for surgery while waiting and had to be sent home.[32] A government that promises equal and "accessible" health care for all should in such cases be held liable.

*Tier Eight—Those Who Cannot Find a Regular Physician*
Statistics Canada reported that in 2007, nearly 1.7 million Canadians over the age of twelve "could not find a regular physician." See *Canadian Community Health Survey, The Daily News* (June 18, 2008), at http://www.statcan.gc.ca/daily-quotidien/080618/dq080618a-eng.htm. Many of these people may have found walk-in clinic care, if such was available in their towns. But often it is not, and so in the best sense of the words "accessible" and "universal," how are they true if you cannot find a physician?

˙ Some I know of who have done this recently are: myself (for diagnostic tests at the Mayo Clinic, denied here); my daughter (who went to Buffalo to get a CT scan of a higher resolution than is available here); my mother-in-law, who went to Seattle for a similar scan not available in Vancouver; my surgeon at Mississauga Hospital (who went to Houston, Texas, for surgery not available in Canada); MP Belinda Stronach (who went to California for timely cancer care); Mike Dyon, president of Brooks Canada (for immediate heart surgery, after being told he would have to wait six months here). And ... Premier Danny Williams of Newfoundland, who went to the United States for heart surgery (to an undisclosed location) in the first week of February 2010.
˙˙ http://www.oag-bvg.gc.ca/internet/English/parl_oag_199011_23_e_8018.html

# ESCAPE! GET RESCUED!

*Access to a waiting list is not access to health care.*
—Statement by Beverley McLachlin, Chief Justice,
Supreme Court of Canada, (in Chaoulli v. Quebec)

*You can't force a citizen in a free and democratic society to
simply wait for health care, and outlaw their ability to
extricate themselves from a wait list.*
—Dr. Brian Day, former president, Canadian Medical Association

*You mention health care reform, and people's hair lights on fire!*
—Alberta premier Ralph Klein, 2000

In its *Chaoulli v. Quebec* ruling of 2005, the Supreme Court of Canada ruled (at last!) that the Canadian public health care system is causing pain and suffering by forcing Canadians to wait too long for treatment, and that a government monopoly on health care "*imposes a risk of death and irreparable harm to health.*"[33]

Due to this disastrous—and for many, *life-threatening*—situation, many medical entrepreneurs are coming out of the woodwork to answer the call for help of citizens trapped in Canada's single-tier system. This is especially so in British Columbia and Quebec (on a scale of medical freedom, from one to ten, Ontario gets only a one). In an October 1, 2009 item in the *Wall Street Journal*, "Escaping Canadian Health Care," we read: "Hoping to capitalize on patients who might otherwise go to the US for speedier care, a network of technically illegal private clinics and surgical centres has sprung up in British Columbia, echoing a trend in Québec . . . more than seventy private health providers in British Columbia now schedule simple surgeries and tests such as MRIs with waits as short as a week or two. . . ." In late 2008, a report by the Health Coalition said there were then 120 such private diagnostic and surgical clinics operating in Canada, 89 of which are in possible violation of the Canada Health Act.[34]

One such provider—there are many now—is Richard Baker, who started an organization based in Vancouver called Timely Medical Alternatives (www.timelymedical.ca) to help distressed citizens get served very fast in the United States and Canada. Here is Richard Baker at a recent conference on health care:

"Our organization was formed in 2003 to help Canadians from coast to coast, to leave the queue and take personal responsibility for their own private medical services. Since then we have helped hundreds of Canadians obtain second medical opinions, MRIs/CT scans/PET scans (within days) and surgery (within weeks). We have helped our clients to regain their mobility, to get relief from chronic pain, to get diagnoses of illnesses and we have, in some cases, helped to save the lives of a number of our fellow Canadians."

Rick and his organization (and others like it) are in rebellion against State medicine and are making a living by rescuing trapped Canadians. Let us cheer them on. If you want to hear how one Canadian was rescued by Rick, get the Kleenex box out, and watch a clip called "The Cheryl Baxter Story" at http://www.youtube.com/watch?v=-TettQFtNy8. Another is called "Hanging by a Thread," at http://www.timelymedical.ca/news-video-5.html. It's a sobering testimonial in which a Canadian physician and his counterpart in Bellingham, Washington, discuss the cross-border "medical escapees" heading south (I'm not sure if anyone flees the United States for medical care in Canada):

Here is Rick's price list for some standard procedures with wait-times compared to those in Canada. The longer government insists on outlawing medical freedom, the more of these organizations we will see. If any government-controlled medical system could perform this well, we would all be socialists:

| Procedure | Promised Wait Time | Rick's Price |
|---|---|---|
| Gall Bladder Removal | 3 weeks | $6,700 |
| Cardiac Bypass Surgery | 48 hours | $16,000 |
| MRI | 3 days | $750 |
| Spinal Discectomy | 3 weeks | $7,000 |

** The website also states: Wait times for clients of Timely Medical Alternatives depend only on: The urgency of your condition. As an example—we can arrange for cardiac consultations normally within one week. In emergencies, we can arrange for next-day consultations with the surgery/procedure to follow immediately.

## "HEALTH ADVOCATES" FOR HIRE

Another way to escape the worst of government medicine is to hire a private physician as a "health advocate." Just prior to writing these words I spoke with a Toronto man who did exactly this. He had so much trouble getting an appointment to see a specialist for a very complicated urological problems (the specialist eventually hung up the phone on him) that he hired a private physician to interface between him and the system. That got the job done. As long as a government monopoly on medical care exists in Canada this will be a prime area in future for enterprising young physicians. A new business, called something like "Health Advocates Canada," would do very well indeed. My wife spent most of five days in Lion's Gate Hospital in West Vancouver as an advocate for her eighty-year-old mother in the fall of 2009. Mom got stuffed into a room for two in which there were four beds—the three others were men—and in the stifling, poorly ventilated and crowded room my wife kept hearing repeated panic calls on the intercom: "Overflow on ward six; overflow on ward three," and so on.

Many physicians in Canada's provinces have formed associations such as the Ontario Physician's Alliance (OPA) to reverse State control of medicine. Article 3 of this organization states: "The OPA supports the view that the present government-funded health care system must be modernized by the creation of a parallel non-government health care system as exists in every other Western democracy. The present legislated government monopoly of physician services *has failed to deliver a reasonable standard of health care and is a violation of physicians' and patients' democratic rights.*" To this I would add: "... and a direct violation of an even more fundamental human right" (freedom to secure and protect one's own life and health).

## CANADA'S HEALTH SYSTEM AT THE CROSSROAD

> *Canada's provinces face "the health Pac Man" which is eating up everything else in their budgets.*
> —Derek Burleton, director of economic analysis,
> TD Bank Financial Group, 2009

When national populations are adjusted for age (older populations require much more health care), we find that Canada has one of the most expensive health care systems in the developed world; only Iceland spends more. Japan spends 38 percent less than we do for much better, queue-free access, with better health outcomes. In 2007–2008 health care spending in Canada at all three levels of government consumed 17.8 percent of *all* government revenues—and climbing. In the decade 1997–2007 health spending grew nationally at a provincial average of 7.3 percent, while average GDP was 5.6 percent. Obviously, this cannot be sustained. Ontario spent 43 percent of all its tax revenues on health care in 2008, and this figure is projected to reach 50 percent by 2035 in six of ten provinces. There is nothing except more and more severe rationing of public health care to prevent this figure from climbing higher every single year.

Because what they spend on personal health care is invisible (extracted in their taxes), Canadians often wonder: How much do I actually pay for my health "insurance"?[35]

For 2008, here's the picture:

| Your Income Category | Your Average Annual earnings | Cost of Your Medical "Insurance" |
|---|---|---|
| Lowest Earners | $11,309 | $389 |
| Unattached Individual | $35,600 | $3,484 |
| Family of 4 | $51,298 | $4,862 |
| Family of 4 | $96,217 | $9,873 |
| Family of 4 | $122,321 | $12,877 |
| Family of 4 | $232,739 | $29,575 |

How much do you cost the system per year, for life?

Here is the breakdown in averages per age-group, for 2006: Canadians younger than 1: $7,891 per child; 1 to 64: $3,700; 65–69: $5,369; 70–74: $7,382; 75–79: $9,987; and over 80: $17,121.

## HOW DO WE RANK IN MEDICAL TECHNOLOGY AND SERVICE?

In recent surveys of developed nations in terms of machines-per-million population, Canada ranked: 14th in MRI machines (and even lower in scans per 1,000 population[36]); 19th for CT scanners; 8th for mammograms; and tied for second-last of 21 nations for lithotripters (machines that pulverize gallbladder, liver, or kidney stones with sound waves, thus eliminating the need for surgery). In 1970, Canada ranked 2nd highest for the number of physicians per 1,000 population. But by 2006 Canada ranked 26th at just under 2 physicians per 1,000. To equal first-ranked Iceland (at 4.5 per 1,000, in 2005) we would have needed *another 65,817 doctors*. Instead, in 2007, according to Statistics Canada, 1.7 million Canadians over the age of 12 *could not find a regular physician*.[37] Of note is that all the nations that do better than us on measures of health care have "mixed" private-public systems. No one in the developed world outside Canada has ever been threatened with imprisonment for hiring a physician privately to supply core services. As mentioned, the greatest irony of all is that just as American Democrats are calling for a "public option" (though 50 percent of all American health care is already public), Canadians are increasingly calling for a "private option."

Canada spends 10 percent of GDP (2006) on health care, of which 7 percent is public, while the US spends 15 percent of GDP on health care, of which 7 percent is also public (see Snapshot, below). So both countries have the same level of *public* spending on health care. But total *private* spending in Canada is only 3 percent, while private spending in America is 8 percent. The reason for this difference is that Canada has banned so much basic private health care and insurance that we have ended up with a fiscally feeble health care sector, while America considers private health care to be one of its most vital and growing sectors.

It is an obvious error to smugly boast of our lower *overall* health spending as if this make us the winner, when in fact our lower private spending reflects our policing mentality more than it does our smarts with cost control (cost control is easy if you have the power to deny service). The main point is that for any private economic activity, whether housing, automobiles, computers, clothing, or health services, *more is always better*. In a free country, a lower percentage of GDP spent on medical care (or any of those other products and services) probably indicates a lacklustre sector, whereas in an unfree country it usually means taxpayers are getting the short end of the medical stick and are being forced against their will to suffer rationed health care by waiting (and other means).

Canada indeed has a lower level of spending on health care than the U.S. But so what? So does Nigeria. And a hundred other countries. However, if free people want to spend *all* their private resources on their own health care, we might say that's a little odd. But it should be a decision between them and their health care providers, not between them and their governments. The typical American family spends the same 5.4 percent of family income on clothing as it does on health care, but as Sally Pipes observes: "We don't hear politicians calling for sweeping legislation to put price controls on textiles because every American has a right to designer fashion."[38]

## HEALTH CARE IN CANADA AND AMERICA

Much is made in the media about the superiority of the Canadian system to that of the United States, where only half of all health care is state subsidized. Superior? America does not have the best medical *system* in the world simply because no one does. But there is no question it has the best *medicine* in the world. America delivers most of the world's best medical research, technology, and pharmacology, and about 75 percent of the best scientific articles in international medical journals. Astonishingly, each year, America produces more than half of the entire world's annual $175 billion worth of medical technology, and in 2004 alone funded $18.4 billion in medical research. The next closest was the far more populous European Union at $3.7 billion. Canada's health research budget for 2006 was $700 million.

Between 1999 and 2005, America produced 71 percent of the sales of the entire world's new pharmaceuticals (runners-up were Japan and Germany at 4 percent each).[39] America has also produced by far the most Nobel laureates for medicine/physiology and chemistry. Of its 270 winners in *all* categories, eighty-five were for medicine/physiology, and forty-five for chemistry. The next-closest country is the United Kingdom at one hundred for all categories. Canada has collected sixteen in all categories. Americans pay more and invest more in medical care because they want more and are getting more. And yet, although many thousands of Canadians travel to the United States every year and spend millions there annually for services and technology they can't get or have been denied here, critics of the American system continue to float misinformation into the mediasphere.

In 1990, when this book first appeared, American health analyst John Goodman gave a speech in Toronto exploding "ten myths" about medical care in the United States. I will mention those first because they are still valid, and then provide an update on them, and on "the myth of the 46 million uninsured Americans," of which so much has been made of late by American proponents of socialized medicine. This will be drawn from several sources, but mostly from two Canadian analysts, Dr. David Gratzer and Sally Pipes, president of the Pacific Research Institute (and now an American citizen). Both of them know a lot about both the American and Canadians systems, and both are critical of government medical systems.[40]

The poorest in the United States, according to Goodman, are totally covered by Medicare (but they have to enrol to get free care. Millions don't bother to enrol). The elderly, rich or poor, are totally covered by Medicaid once they hit sixty-five, regardless of income. By law, American hospitals are required to treat all who show up for a first treatment or emergency, insured or not (but they are not obliged to continue treating the uninsured). Government-mandated insurance laws (on average, there are thirty-eight such laws per state) force state insurance companies to cover up to 1,900 medical conditions, and in this way government regulations have priced inexpensive "no-frills" insurance out of the market. Some 90 percent of all *hospital* bills are paid for by insurance, and 70 percent of all *medical* care is paid by third-party insurance (usually under the policy held by the company that hired you). One-twentieth of one percent of American families suffer medical bankruptcy—most often because they neglected to buy, or chose not to buy, medical insurance. (How does this differ, I wonder, from the personal bankruptcy of people who neglected—or decided not—to insure their homes?) High infant mortality rates in the U.S. are due to ethnic heterogeneity, drug and alcohol abuse, and poor nutrition—it's a cultural problem. After age sixty-five, American citizens get the best care in the world.

U.S. health care did not explode in cost until 1965, when the federal government got involved. Then it went from 5.2 percent of GDP to 12 percent by 1988, to 15-plus percent by 2006. But as explained, *public* medicine in the U.S. only runs at 7 percent of GDP, same as Canada. The rest is not a *cost*, it is *private investment* by free people in their own health care and in the medical system that provides it. The U.S. does not have an unfettered free-market system, as we often think; it runs a "cost plus" system that, perversely, rewards cost increases. Readers will find substantial backup for John Goodman's analyses at his National Centre for Policy Analysis website (www.ncpa.org).

# SNAPSHOT
Canadian versus U.S. Medical Care

| Items (2006) | Canada | U.S. |
|---|---|---|
| Percent of GDP health spending that is public | 7 | 7 |
| Percent of GDP health spending that is private | 3 | 8 |
| Total percent GDP spent on health care (public + private) | 10 | 15 |
| Number of doctors per 1,000 pop. | 2.1 | 2.4 |
| Number of nurses per 1,000 pop. | 8.8 | 10.5 |
| Average Canadian doctor's salary as percent of American equivalent | 42 | 100 |
| Number of MRI scanners per million pop. (2006) | 6.2 | 26.5 |
| Number of MRI exams per 1 million pop. (2004–5) | 25,500 | 83,200 |
| Number of CT scanners per million pop. (2006) | 12 | 33.9 |
| Number of CT exams per 1 million pop. (2004–5) | 87,300 | 172,500 |
| Average age of hospital facilities | 40 yrs (Ontario) | 9 yrs |
| Life expectancy at birth | 80.8 | 77.8* |
| Percent who waited 4 months or longer for elective surgery | 27 | 5 |
| Percent who waited 2 months or longer for specialist app't. | 42 | 10 |
| Canada's net drain or gain of doctors leaving or returning to Canada | -215 per year** | note# |
| Percentage of pop. legally prohibited from buying private insurance for necessary medical services (1) | 89.9 | 0 |
| Percent total personal bankruptcies (*#) | 0.2 | 0.27 |
| Ranking of overall care among WHO member states*** | 30 | 37 |

Sources: OECD, WHO, Canadian Institute for Health Information, Canadian Health Services Research Foundation
* Racially mixed populations tend to have lower life expectancy than racially homogeneous ones. Experts cite the American drug and crime culture for this lower life-expectancy figure. After age 65, Americans have the highest-level care and longevity.
# the phrase "doctors leaving Canada" returned over 20,000 hits on Google, while "doctors leaving USA" returned 1 hit (October 6, 2009).
** The exodus of doctors from Canada is down considerably from the 1990s. The -215 is a net figure. In 1996, the Canadian Institute for Health Information reported that 713 doctors left Canada, *about the same number as were graduated from all Canadian medical schools that year!* (see Gratzer, *Code Blue*, p. 48). But Gratzer points out that the figure is understated because many Canadian medical graduates never practice in Canada at all. They get licensed and immediately leave for their first job, or if graduated from a foreign

school, do not return home. In 1995, fully 33 percent of the medical graduating classes at the Universities of Toronto and Alberta were "leaving the country." Over $150,000 dollars of their education is covered by Canadian taxpayers.
(*) From Brett Skinner, "Health Insurance and Bankruptcy Rates in Canada and the United States," see www.fraserinstitute.org/researchandpublications/publications/6765.aspx
*** such rankings are heavily influenced by the weight they give to an egalitarian provision of "free" care. Treating everyone exactly the same is ranked more highly than treating them well.
(1)Six out of 10 provinces accounting for 89.8 percent of the national population legally ban the purchase of private insurance for necessary medical services (provided in-province).

As mentioned, America has the best *medicine* in the world, but an inadequate medical *system*. But then ... every country has an inadequate system, in the sense that all systems, public or private, are plagued with all sorts of inadequacies, frauds, trivial medical demands, failures to deliver care, cost overruns, phony doctor billings, bureaucratic overload, inflated union demands, false promises, misleading language (like "free" medical care, or "insurance" that is simply no such thing), and rampant lawsuits against physicians for malpractice, against hospitals for terrible mistakes like removing the wrong breast, and against governments for death-by-rationing.

That is a frank litany of the sickness of medical systems in most countries. My personal reaction is to say: okay, if I am faced with an inadequate system of *any* kind, at least let it be one where I am free to find the best care if I and my loved ones need it and not one where I am denied this right by medical socialists. I agree with Sally Pipes, who, in the face of claims that socialized medicine is more humane, says: "The truth is exactly the reverse. It is government monopoly health care that is heartless and uncaring." She should know. Her own ailing mother was told by Canadian medical authorities that she was "too old and too sick" to merit the highest-quality care, so (this is a chilling statement) "she was hastened to her fate by actuarial calculations in what is truly a dehumanizing system of triage."

## THE POWER OF SYMBOLIC NUMBERS
One of the most effective sound bites, snatched from data originally published, with public reservation, by the U.S. Census Bureau, but soon widely and irresponsibly used to criticize the American health care system, was the belief that "46 million Americans are chronically uninsured." At first, you could find "the 46 million" factoid even on President Barack Obama's website where, like so many others, he made a very effective but dishonest use of it.

Was it ever true?

During the intense national marketing phase of Obama's bill this number was critiqued so heavily that it was quietly knocked down to "32 million uninsured," though no one ever explained what happened to the 14 million–people difference in these numbers. They simply evaporated. But was even that lower number true? Although, as anyone can see from the following Snapshot there are indeed about 8 million Americans who obviously need help—either financially to purchase basic medical insurance, or in qualifying and enrolling for free medical care to which they are already entitled—this Snapshot helps us understand the true background to one of the most successful political marketing events in recent history.

## SNAPSHOT
*The Facts on the Myth of the 46 Million Uninsured*

- Any poor person can walk into any hospital in America and be treated "free" for an accident, injury, or disease. Under the federal Emergency Medical Treatment and Active Labor Act, passed in 1986, hospitals are not allowed to deny treatment to patients with no health insurance. (Such costs are routinely absorbed into a hospital's operating costs.) However, hospitals are not obligated to continue free care after an emergency is treated.
- The U.S. Census Bureau states that more than *10 million* of the 46 million uninsured (1 in 4) *are not American citizens*. They are illegal immigrants. Which raises the question: Why should American taxpayers provide free medical care for the citizens of other countries?
- Another *14.7 million* (or one-third of the mythical 46-million number) "are fully eligible for generous government assistance programs like Medicare, Medicaid, and SCHIP [State Children's Health Insurance Program]. The problem is, they just *haven't bothered to enroll in these programs.*"
- A "whopping *70 percent of 'uninsured' children* are in fact eligible for either Medicaid, or SCHIP, or both programs." In other words, 5 million of the 8 million American children Barack Obama has said are uninsured are in the large group that simply hasn't bothered to enrol.
- Medicaid, set up only as a safety net in 1965, "has grown into an enormous welfare program serving 53 million [poor] Americans." Some $338 billion are spent annually to cover "15 million *more* people than the 37 million Americans estimated to be living in poverty."
- The Urban Institute says that "roughly 27 percent of non-elderly Americans who are eligible for Medicaid simply haven't enrolled, and live their lives without health insurance."
- So, health critic Sally Pipes asks: "Have we reached a stage where the government has to *force* people to show up for a free lunch?" [Pipes

320 11: MEDICAL MEDIOCRITY

wrote this a year before Obama passed a law forcing people to buy health insurance.]

- Many of the uninsured argue that if state insurance companies are mandated by government to cover them even if they are already sick, then why buy insurance *until* they are sick?

- Twenty-eight million of the 46 million earn more than $50,000 per year.

- The fastest-growing segment of the uninsured is households making over $75,000 per year.

- The "uninsured" are a churning number: fully half of all the people who lacked health insurance at a given time had full health insurance five months later (Gratzer, p. 86).

- Sixty percent of Americans get their medical insurance as a tax-free benefit from their employers. The median duration of unemployment (and of being uninsured due to unemployment or job change) is 7 weeks (Gratzer, p. 86).

- A full 93 percent of Americans are insured, or, if not, could afford to buy insurance if they so chose (Gratzer, p. 82).

- In a study of the uninsured in California earning twice poverty-level income, 40 percent owned their own homes, and more than half owned a personal computer. Sixty percent reported they were in excellent health, and almost half had not seen a single health professional in the previous year. Of this group, 57 percent *disagreed* with the statement "Health insurance ranks very high on my list of priorities for where to spend my money" (Gratzer, p. 88).

- About 15 percent of Americans are uninsured, a percentage that has remained constant over two decades or more (Gratzer, p. 86).

- Conclusion? America indeed has a problem: There are about 8 million "chronically uninsured" working poor who really do need help. They earn less than $50,000 per year, but have too much income to qualify as "poor" and get free government care. So they have "slipped between the cracks," and Pipes argues these should be the focus of any solution for the uninsured.

- Health economists from the Urban Institute published a study in *Health* stating that "no coverage" is not synonymous with "no care." In 2001, for example, the total spent on health care for the uninsured, from all private, public, and charitable sources, was $98.9 billion, which worked out to an average of $1,586 a year, compared to the $2,484 spent on each insured person (from all public and private insurance sources).

- Medicaid is already gobbling up state tax revenues in America at an unsustainable rate, estimated to be 60 percent of state expenditures in places like Florida (where there are lots of retirees) by 2015. (This is also the situation in Canada, where medicare will constitute 50 percent of Ontario's spending by 2036 or earlier.)

Quotations in this Snapshot are taken from Sally Pipes, *The Top Ten Myths of American Health Care: a Citizen's Guide* (San Francisco: Pacific Research Institute, 2008), Ch. 3. Facts or quotes from David Gratzer, *The Cure* (New York: Encounter Books, 2008) are as noted.

## THE EQUALITY MYTH AND THE CONFLICT OF MORALITIES

The original reason for the State's coercive humanitarianism in introducing compulsory national health care, taking over the medical profession, eliminating the fundamental freedoms of both patient and physician, transforming our former adult-adult (physician-patient) relationship into a parent-child (government-patient) one, and so on, was "equality." But why should a secondary moral imperative such as forced *equality* trump the primary moral imperatives of human *liberty, security of the person*, the *right to life*, and to personal *privacy*? The key historical truth to be faced here is that the law, even though with difficulty, has managed, more or less, to *guarantee* liberty, security of the person, a right to life, and personal privacy; but no country in the history of the world has ever been able to guarantee equality in substantive terms short of turning the subject nation into an administrative and regulatory prison. There are more, and even more, basic moral quandaries that arise as we look deeper that any Statist ought to be required to face.

## CHOOSING SICKNESS

Most of our health care dollars are spent on people who suffer from lifestyle diseases (not infectious diseases or trauma). In other words, much of their ill health is self-inflicted. So someone needs to explain why it is morally right to extract hard-earned money from those who take responsibility for their own health, and transfer it in the form of pre-paid medical services to those who intentionally do not? Well, you may ask, what percentage of health care problems fall into that category? My attention was first drawn to the enormous differences in individual health due to lifestyle choices by health economist Victor Fuchs's book *Who Shall Live?* in which he wrote: "Positive health can be achieved only through intelligent effort on the part of each individual . . . the notion that we *can spend our way to better health is a vast oversimplification*. At present there is very little that medical care can do for a lung that has been over-inflated by smoking, or a liver that has been scarred by too much alcohol, or a skull that has been crushed in a motor accident."[41]

His book has a fascinating section entitled "A Tale of Two States," which basically shows the results of comparing the health of citizens of Nevada and Utah, two neighbouring states with similar climate, incomes, demographics, and so on. While "the inhabitants of Utah are among the healthiest individuals in the United States, the residents of Nevada are at the opposite end of the spectrum." From birth until old age Nevadans have a death rate some 40 to 50 percent higher than those from Utah for all age groups! Fuchs asks what accounts for this discrepancy, and shows that the answer lies in the different lifestyles of the residents of the two states. Utah is inhabited primarily by Mormons, whose influence is strong throughout the state. "Devout Mormons do not use tobacco or alcohol, and in general lead stable, quiet lives," writes Fuchs. "Nevada, on the other hand, is a state with high rates of tobacco and alcohol consumption and very high indexes of marital and geographical instability ... The populations of these two states are, to a considerable extent, *self-selected* extremes from the continuum of lifestyles found in the United States." I include them here because they provide an object lesson in the demographics of health that is difficult to find in any other country.

The chart below shows the shockingly higher percentages of *diseases caused by tobacco and alcohol* in Nevada as compared with Utah. This does *not* include other self-inflicted illness arising from such variables as obesity, inactivity, drug use, consumption of fatty foods, and so on—only alcohol- and tobacco-related illness. Neither does it include the health and social catastrophe that results from the use of the much harder drugs that have become prevalent since his book appeared:

(Utah is the norm, at 100 percent)

| Age groups | Nevada males | Nevada females |
|---|---|---|
| 30–39 | 590 percent greater incidence | 443 percent greater |
| 40–49 | 111 percent | 296 percent |
| 50–59 | 206 percent | 205 percent |
| 60–69 | 117 percent | 227 percent |

A University of California study corroborated Fuchs's work: middle-aged Utah residents had only 34 percent of the normal U.S. death rate from cancer and 14 percent the normal U.S. death rate from heart and blood vessel disease.[42] This study examined only *one* aspect of lifestyle. But consider the enormous reduction in health expenditures if everyone were to manage personal health responsibly. A voluntary reduction of all behaviours known to cause self-inflicted "diseases of choice" by the total population could possibly cut "health" costs (they are mostly disease costs) by at least half.

The argument that costs would nevertheless equal out in the end because healthy people live longer (hence they use the system longer) doesn't hold weight simply because while that point is true, healthy people don't just tend to live longer; they also live *better* and more productive lives, see doctors less, recover from illness faster, and when they do see doctors, it's for less serious complaints, like strains or for knee surgery, not for terminal lung cancer from smoking. A business owner who employs a thousand people in a wealth-creating enterprise who dies at forty (though he or she thereby spends fewer lifetime health dollars) is a great loss to the nation. Also, the key point, as mentioned, is that someone in a free country *buying* more health care with their own funds or insurance is a boon to the medical system and the economy, a plus, an income, a growth factor. It is only under a rationed socialist system that human illness is registered as a net cost, or loss.

## GOVERNMENT HEALTH SYSTEMS DON'T MAKE PEOPLE HEALTHIER

When N.B. Belloc and L. Breslow studied American health habits in depth, they determined that those at seventy-five years of age who had followed their "seven rules" had the same health status as forty-year-olds.[43] Here are their now-famous rules: don't smoke cigarettes; get seven hours' sleep each night; eat breakfast each morning; keep your weight down; drink in moderation; exercise daily; don't eat between meals. That's a pretty simple and inexpensive formula for personal health care.

Here's another shocker: health economist Cotton Lindsay long ago demonstrated that "access to health care resources has little impact on the aggregate measures of health of a population," which, as mentioned, is more a function of lifestyle than of resources. On the Conference Board of Canada's health ranking of sixteen nations for 2009, Japan once again got an "A," as it has for decades, while Canada, which is a far bigger health spender, placed 10th with a low "B," and picked up a lot of "C's" along the way.

Here is the OECD's Canada–Japan comparison on a few key health variables

| | Per capita spending in $US, ppp* | Infant Mortality per 1,000 births | Longevity, both sexes | Cardio Deaths per 100,000 |
|---|---|---|---|---|
| Canada | $3,895 (2007) (Amount in 1974 was $412) | 5.0 (2006) | 80.7 (2007) | 41.5 (2004) |
| Japan | $2,581 (2007) (Amount in 1974 was $245) | 2.6 (2007) | 82.4 (2007) | 16.2 (2007) |
| (* ppp = purchasing power parity) | | | | |

So what's going on here? Why, despite huge increases in health spending over the past half century, has Canada *never rated higher than a "B"*? Check it out.[44] To put this in perspective: Canada spends 22 percent more than the average of all the other universal-health-access nations, but has median wait-times from first GP visit to treatment by a specialist of 17.3 weeks, while seven other universal-health-access nations (Austria, Belgium, France, Germany, Japan, Luxembourg, and Switzerland) deliver care without any wait-times. Panicked, Canada's federal government, after staring straight into the face of the medicare Pac-Man, introduced a "benchmark" wait-time program with a public target of . . . 182 days. Some consolation.

Lindsay adds that if we study only the cancer death rate, the heart death rate, and the infant mortality rate, the maternal mortality rate, the general death rate, and male and female life expectancy, we find that "no [national] plan has even a ripple of an effect on either male or female life expectancy. If government medicine is preferred on the grounds of better employing health resources, there is scant evidence for these effects in statistical measures of health."[45]

Such findings "are remarkably consistent," according to a recent report from Dartmouth University which states that "higher spending does not result in better quality of care, whether one looks at the technical quality and reliability of hospital or ambulatory care, or survival following such serious conditions as a heart attack or hip fracture." Patients in high-cost areas receive more procedures and tests, they see more specialists, and they spend more time in hospitals. *But they are no healthier.* Simply, the Dartmouth doctors report: "More isn't always better."[46] In its 2009 summary of a decade of health care, the Canadian Institute for Health Information announced that "internationally, the health status returns from increased per-capita spending drop off severely after about $1,000 to $1,500,"[47] and added a note that "many conditions are self-limiting—we get better regardless of whether [or not] we seek health care—and some [conditions] are impervious to health care [incurable]."

Such findings are underscored by the fact that "the vast proportion of a GP's work is concerned with the routine, the non-urgent, and often the non-medical."[48] Even long before Canada got as deeply involved in government health care, there were warnings: a 1966 study in Britain found that 25 percent of doctors felt their consultations were for "trivial, unnecessary, or inappropriate reasons . . . Fully 53 percent of these 'trivial' consultations were for such conditions as coughs, colds, morning sickness, dandruff, indigestion, and the like . . ."[49] A 1974 study "found that 28 percent of consultations were for non-medical services. Of the remaining 72 percent who actually sought treatment, in 43 percent of the cases, the doctor was *unable to diagnose any definite illness . . .*"

Various other studies have estimated that from 30 to 75 percent of consultations "are with patients displaying no objective evidence (either psychological or physical) for their attendance."[50] Striking testimony to the fact that a lot of "health care" is determined more by *demand* than by *need* is a British study covering a period of ten years that compared two groups: one that *never* saw their doctors, and one with an *average* number of attendances. The rather shocking conclusion of the study: *There was little obvious medical difference in the health of the two groups* (but a lot of difference in the money spent on them).

Finally, an enormous quarter-billion-dollar national study by the Rand Corporation, in 2004, found that when two groups of patients were compared, one that had a "free" health care plan, and the other a shared-cost plan (plus some form of "catastrophic" insurance for medical disasters), the people on the "free" plan ran up costs 40 percent higher than the latter group, *but were no healthier.*[51] These observations have to do with the triviality of complaints. My own excellent GP is certain that 15 percent of his patients are what he calls "the worried well." They are fine, but they come to see him because they don't think they are. He sends a bill for this to the government. Every time.

By now the gist of my argument should be clear. It is obvious that a great deal of health care spending is for conditions that cannot be helped: the known major diseases, inexplicable diseases, accidents, geriatric illnesses, and so on. But we also know that many of our health problems come from "diseases of choice"; that is, from diseases that people could prevent by an act of will: stop smoking, stop drinking excessive alcohol, stop imbibing so much caffeine, stop engaging in high-risk activities, reduce intake of fatty foods and calories, cut down or eliminate salt and most added sugar from the diet, and exercise regularly.

When the self-inflicted nature of many illnesses is considered, the picture is dramatically worse, and even more morally contorted. We know that 10 percent of the population of Canada consumes over 50 percent of all alcoholic beverages.[52] Yet the enormous health costs from alcoholism and its many associated illnesses, car accidents, property damage, and family and public violence are borne by all. How can that be just or fair? What is "equal" about that? We know now that up to 50 percent of all premature cardiovascular diseases and many cancers could be avoided by an act of will on the part of the affected individuals. But the costs are borne by all. How can that be just or fair, or equal?

Here are a few of Sally Pipes's observations on self-inflicted illnesses in America:

- Recent studies show that as much as 75 percent of what we spend on health care goes to treating conditions brought about by activities such as eating fatty foods and smoking (so states like California have passed laws requiring restaurants to disclose fat content of foods served).
- 10 percent of the nation's health care dollars are spent annually on diseases attributable to obesity, and an estimated $167 billion go to treat smoking-related illnesses.
- (So almost all modern states and municipalities now ban smoking in public places. Bill Gates has offered $500 million to the global anti-smoking campaign.)

- Expensive anti-smoking and anti-fats "education" programs are useless. No people in the history of the world has ever known as much about the evils of fats and smoking. But obesity continues to rise apace,[53] and people still choose to smoke [not certain if marijuana smoke is worse than tobacco, but the anti-weed campaign is also an expensive failure].

So again: Why is it morally right for the State to tax those who take personal responsibility for their own health care, to benefit mostly those who do not? I believe that morally backward policies such as rewarding the irresponsible create inequalities that are less defensible than any condition of financial "inequality" that Pearson, Trudeau, and Tom Kent imagined themselves to be curing when they introduced socialized medicine to Canada.

The following is the core argument personalized.

## HOW STATE MEDICINE CHEATS THOSE WHO LIVE HEALTHY LIVES

Let us imagine Mary, a forty-year-old who takes pride in the management of her own health. She weighs only ten pounds more than when she was twenty, eats a balanced, nutritious, low-fat diet, enjoys moderate exercise almost daily, practices relaxation techniques, sleeps well, avoids sunburn, doesn't smoke, and although she enjoys drinking, restricts herself to an occasional glass of wine, maybe two, with a meal. Even when she gets sick with an unavoidable flu, she rarely stays in bed. She hardly ever visits a doctor because she feels vibrant most of the time. But more to the point, she decided long ago that life's occasional physical discomforts and suffering—headaches, menstrual discomfort, mild allergies, occasional back pain, sore muscles, a twisted ankle, stomach upset, and so on—are a normal part of living that simply have to be cared for by oneself, or endured until they pass; one's body has an amazing way of healing itself. What she cannot abide, for herself or her family, is complaining and running to professionals for pills and soothing every time such situations arise.

Her neighbour Sally is also forty. However, she has smoked a pack a day since she was a teenager, likes to party a lot, and complains over the back fence of frequent hangovers. She is also thirty-five pounds overweight. In her house are lots of snack foods and soft drinks. Fast-food services are always driving up to her door. She has no interest in exercise, and even draws a good laugh when she mocks others for doing it. Her husband and three kids are all physically lazy and overweight. It is no secret—she herself lets everyone know—that over the past twenty years she has made innumerable visits to her GP for everything under the sun (she blames her frequent discomforts on everything but herself); she has had a tummy tuck (too fat), her gallbladder removed (too many fatty foods), surgery for varicose veins in her calves (too heavy and too sedentary), and has had a stern warning from her GP that she might be contracting liver problems associated with her drinking. She is on medication for high blood pressure (often controllable with exercise and diet), has a chronic sore back (most back pain is also manageable with weight loss and exercise), and uses a cough suppressant to sleep at night (constant cough, throat, and sinus irritations from tobacco use). Her medicine cabinet is overflowing with pre-scription drugs. Last week, after an extensive series of cardiovascular tests, her doctor informed her that she had dangerously narrowed coronary arteries and that if she didn't stop smoking, didn't exercise, and didn't change her diet, she might soon need a bypass. She told him that was a ridiculous suggestion—she was known to be a character, and her life wasn't worth living without a bit of fun.

Last week, the taxman came to inform everyone on the block that more money would be needed to cover "health" costs in Canada. Because so many like Sally are unwilling to change their ways, twenty years of heavier expenses have been projected by government health economists. Peering into the future, they see a high probability for the neighbour's bypass, perhaps also lung cancer or emphysema, and ever more frequent visits to doctors, both for her and the rest of her family, who are already following in her footsteps. By their calcula-tion, every family in this neighbourhood will have to deliver an additional $2,000 per year in taxes for the next twenty years, indexed for inflation.

The taxman remained silent when Mary and her husband told him an-grily that all those who look after themselves properly are paying crazy taxes for other people's bad habits, while *saving* the government money. The com-plaint that the illnesses he outlined are their neighbours' health problems, not theirs, and that if Sally had changed her ways they wouldn't have been brought on her, fell on deaf ears. The taxman said, "I don't make the policy, I just collect the money. We are required to treat everyone equally!"

## A CAVEAT ON "SAVINGS" FROM PREVENTIVE HEALTH CARE

Lots of perfectly healthy people contract unexpected diseases that have nothing to do with lifestyle, as we know. And from the discussion above it is clear that by some combination of public and/or private insurance most nations look after them. But one of the greatest ironies we face is that whereas it is indeed unfair and morally perverse to reward people who are smokers, slothful, glut-tonous, alcoholics, or who engage in high-risk behaviours, or use dangerous drugs (phew!) by offering them unlimited public funding of their more serious and more frequent health care needs, it is also erroneous to believe that "good living" and "preventive health care" will save the State health care dollars.

That is because people with healthier lifestyles tend to live much longer, and so they are the ones who will require more money for late-life health care than the ones who pop off sooner. The irony is that if governments only wanted

328 11: MEDICAL MEDIOCRITY

to cut health expenditures sharply in the long term, the best way would be to encourage us all to be physically lazy, eat lots of fatty foods, smoke at least a pack a day, use dangerous drugs, and drink as much alcohol as possible. Pipes cites an ironic fact of life: the medical expenses for a non-smoker who dies at eighty-four are about $100,000 more than for a seventy-seven-year-old smoker who dies (due to smoking) at seventy-seven.[54] As mentioned, however, this truth fails to take into account the economic and social contributions to our common life of the longer-lived healthier people. So . . . although we cannot save long-term health care dollars—mere fiscal capital—with preventive care, we can preserve our national investment in individual, family, social, and economic productivity, or human capital.

I rest my case. So now . . .

## WHAT IS TO BE DONE?

Government must pull out of medicare and the moral and financial mess it has created before disaster hits in the form of more budgetary crises and very severe rationing. We can protect the truly needy from medical disasters, restore the medical profession to its former status, and free up medicine—and all Canadians—from the health police, as follows:

1. Encourage all Canadians to carry "major medical and catastrophic insurance," which is relatively cheap. This can be provided on the free competitive insurance market, and can be provided partially subsidized by the State (in the same market) for those who can show by a means test they are among the truly needy.

2. Eliminate first-dollar insurance. In other words, bring in user fees (for all but the truly needy) to discourage the draining of medical resources for trivial reasons and to reduce the heavier taxation of those who manage their own health.

3. Continue a government service—a "public option"—with a user fee for all basic care for those people who prefer to have the government look after them (but don't expect public medicine to thrive in a competitive health market).

4. Make private patients, private hospitals, and private, competing basic medical insurance legal again, thus restoring the lost entrepreneurial aspect of medicine. Remove all laws threatening jail or fines for private care. Government may also mandate that all such private health policies be portable anywhere in Canada. However, government should not mandate specific illness coverage. This allows people who look after their health (don't smoke, don't drink, are not overweight, etc.) to purchase a policy suited for their lifestyle. A creative twist might also be that individuals could buy insurance against insurer default. Point: in a free market there

may be some insurance companies that try to deny coverage and/or delay payment for unacceptable reasons. There is a niche here for insurance against bad insurers (a similar situation is that of real estate lenders who buy insurance against lease default).

5. Support only the truly needy with "free" (pre-paid) health care and a smaller user fee (this likely comprises no more than 5 percent of the population).

6. Put the freedom and responsibility back where they belong by using patients as their own best caretakers and cost controllers. Patients should pay physicians directly, as in the past, and claim from their own public or private insurer.

7. Once the above is in place, the State must stop telling free citizens how much of their own resources they are allowed to spend on their own health, and must also stop blocking their access to better care.

8. Experiment with many more retail health or "walk-in" clinics, where basic medical services can be purchased from an advertised price list, and prescriptions can be filled on the spot. (Expect a fight on this one from physicians' associations attempting to restrict physician supply.)

9. End the "lawsuit lottery" by legislating a liability limit to sky-high malpractice suits launched by gouging lawyers.

10. Another good recommendation, a way in which government can help those who are likely to fall through the cracks in a free society's medical system, is to issue health insurance vouchers that could be used by the chronically ill and the truly needy to purchase health insurance from private insurers or from a public high-risk pool set up for this purpose.

11. We could try a made-in-Canada modified "Singapore Plan" in which citizens are urged to open their own special "Medical Savings Account" (MSA) or "Health Savings Account" (HSA) and place 6 percent of their income in it annually, thus spending their *own* funds on their *own* medical care. In Singapore, such plans are mandatory, and if a sick person uses more than the account contains, the State continues to withdraw to recover the medical cost. As a further creative twist, all contributions to such accounts would be tax sheltered for life, like an RRSP. Employers could match employee contributions. Governments eager to help the truly needy could match their contributions. Amounts contributed beyond 6 percent of income per annum could be loaned to a medical pool at low rates to help the medically needy, to contribute to medical science projects, and so on.

In these ways, and many others, we could begin to heal Canada's sick health care system.

# 12: THE CRIMINAL JUSTICE SYSTEM
## "HUG-A-THUG," AND
## PUBLIC SAFETY BE DAMNED

*There is only one thing crazier than me,*
*and that's the system that allows me to do what I do.*
—Allen George Foster, after sentencing
*for the murder of three women while on full parole*

*He's a highly sensitive and intelligent person—*
*one of the sanest people I have ever met.*
—Vasha Starrie, Foster's case management officer
at Agassiz Mountain prison, B.C., just before he was granted full parole

Crime rates in most Western nations have risen steadily for the past hundred years, but have declined from their peak rate in the early 1990s. But even these declining rates are four times higher than they were in the 1960s. That is why citizens correctly perceive that over time the ordinary peace and civility of daily life in Canada has been going down. Dramatically. In 1963, there were just a few companies in Toronto selling residential security systems. Today there are hundreds. As we will see below, according to the most authoritative UN international reports on crime, Canada has a rate of *police-reported criminal incidents* among the highest in the world, almost double the U.S. rate.

Twenty years ago, few had ever imagined their children might get kidnapped by a sex maniac on the way to school, or mugged or shot to death by another student while in a university classroom. No one ever imagined they might find themselves facing the business end of a shotgun from their car window, due to some stranger's road rage. Or that so many frail seniors would be raped, beaten, and robbed by brazen two-hundred-pound "youth" criminals who have no fear of the law. All parents today clutch the hands of their youngsters with an abnormal tightness, fearful that behind a mall pillar, in a parking lot, or a washroom, there might lurk a criminal on day parole. Though we are surrounded now by video cameras, women are increasingly anxious in ordinary buildings, on walkways, and in subway stations. Newspapers routinely describe terrible crimes by violent criminals who have extensive criminal records. Gated communities are much in demand by retirees. Many businesses now have employee-access cards and monitored or locked-down hallways. The surviving victims of crime in Canada live with broken hearts, smashed lives, and the haunting fear that what they think of as the "criminal injustice system" will soon send their nemesis back into society, to smash again. Because they often do.

In 1962, the Canadian *violent* crime rate—the rate that rightly frightens citizens the most—was 220 *convictions* per 100,000 citizens. By 1992, this had risen to its highest point ever at 1,100, and it has declined since to around 900. This seems like good news until we realize that this "decline" is still four times the 1962 rate. And crime has shown up even in places where it was once unthinkable: many Canadian schools today are plagued with drugs and illiteracy. Inner-city teachers need karate more than teaching skills, and they confiscate a lot more knives than cigarettes. Many Canadian public schools now have "School Resource Officers" (SROs). That is doubletalk for "Cops in Schools," the title of a column by Christie Blatchford, who informed the public that by mid-2009 Toronto schools had twenty-nine fully armed SROs on location. But by the end of 2009 that had risen to more than fifty schools. She reported that some 15 percent of students have been "threatened with weapons" at school, 20 percent "admitted bringing a gun to school," and 80 percent said they "would not report crime, even against themselves," likely for fear of reprisal (*Globe and Mail*, September 9, 2009). I have never heard of this in any of Canada's 1,400 private schools. When I was in high school in the late 1950s, you got a good strapping—six on each hand, and six on the rear end—for lying, swearing, smoking, fighting, and for many other offences overlooked as minor today. We have stopped strapping the kids. So now they are strapping us.

About 20 percent of killers on parole in Canada are returned to prison because they have committed new crimes (too often, another murder). Of all prisoners admitted to federal and provincial prisons in 1988, *more than 60 percent were repeat offenders*. The same year, 116 prisoners escaped. Little has changed. In 2006, 169 escaped—mostly by walking away from minimum-security facilities (seven escaped from medium-security facilities). In other words, they weren't locked up—so they walked away. Things may be improving. In 2008–2009, only twenty-four federal prisoners escaped, and twenty-one were soon recaptured. But as of March 31, 2009, there was a total of 130 federal escapees from prior years still on the loose, and 254 federal offenders who had violated parole conditions and were unlawfully at large.

The trouble with Canada, as a famous criminal lawyer once said, is that our criminal justice system "is great. Great—for the criminal!" Like so much else in Canada it is managed by a small, nearly invisible group of specialists who act often, as I shall argue, against the best interests of society. In this chapter, I will try to show how the values currently embedded in official thinking about criminality are philosophically naive and morally confused. From the top at Correctional Services Canada (CSC), with a budget of $1.87 billion in 2007, down to the ordinary staff that manage hundreds of community facilities for criminals, there are official misconceptions about human behaviour that in practice constitute terrible risks to all Canadians and to prisoners themselves (and their guards). In a moment you will read nightmarish examples of such risks. There are many, many more, all products of the same erroneous and misguided assumptions.

Before we move further, consider this: statistical reports on crime in general are based only on *reported* crimes and convictions. But the American Bar Association has estimated that the number of serious crimes *committed* is usually about *2.5* times greater than the number *reported*. Statistics Canada has reported that of all criminal incidents in Canada, only about 40 percent "become known to the police."[1] In other words, official data do not even begin to convey the seriousness of crime. Furthermore, only a small percentage of crimes result in convictions. Many criminals are released on technicalities, acquitted at trial, receive dramatically reduced sentences via plea bargaining, or serve their sentences in the community. This skews our public perception of crime because if, say, there are a hundred murders and half are plea bargained down to manslaughter, the statistics will show only fifty murders. It's a public lie.

Here are some gruesome stories of just a few of the "clients" (as they are now often called) that have gone through Canada's justice system. There are many more like these. All of them were released into society by the National Parole Board (NPB) after a lot of "successful" therapy sessions, human potential seminars on self-esteem, behaviour analysis, interviews with trained "facilitators," sessions with psychologists, and other criminology experts.

Consider the profiles of the following:

### The case of Clifford Olson

Clifford Olson was first arrested in 1957 at the age of seventeen for breaking and entering. In Canada, this crime still carries a maximum penalty of life imprisonment (Criminal Code, s.98.1). At age forty-two, he was "imprisoned for life" for the brutal rape and murder of eleven children. In the twenty-four years between, he had been in jail for twenty-one years. *But he escaped seven times.* By the time he was caught for what we hope is that last time, he had had ninety-four convictions. *He was convicted of twenty crimes while on parole,* including armed robbery, theft, breaking and entering, buggery, indecent assault, forgery, fraud, escape, possession of firearms, and drunk driving. Although, as mentioned above, breaking and entering a private residence carries a penalty of life imprisonment, Olson never received more than a three-year sentence for this repeated crime. *At no time was he ever labelled a habitual or dangerous offender. He was given supervised parole seven times, and full parole twice, and . . . four of his murders were committed while under police surveillance!* In 2006, he was denied parole. By 2008, Olson had sued the warden of Kingston penitentiary seventeen times. Since age sixty-five (he was seventy in 2010) he has been receiving $1,100 per month in Old Age Security and pension payments from the federal government.

### The case of Melvin Stanton

At the age of fourteen, Melvin Stanton escaped from a juvenile detention centre and raped a sixty-two-year-old woman. That same year (how did he get out?) he killed his own girlfriend. A few years later he raped another woman *while he was on day parole.* That same spring he escaped and raped a woman who was five months pregnant. Sentenced to a total of twenty-four years, he was on parole at a halfway house (in January 1988) when he walked out and eight hours later raped and brutally murdered Tema Conter, a total stranger, in her own apartment by stabbing her eleven times and smashing glass pop bottles over her head. Officials at the halfway house did not know Stanton's full name, date of birth, or convict number. His parole record did not mention that he had previously brutally raped three women, also *while on parole.*

### The case of John Finlayson

John Finlayson was labelled "dangerously insane" in 1973 for the sexual abuse and mutilation killing of nine-year-old Kirkland Deasley, and acquitted of murder on the grounds of insanity. He was committed to a mental institution for an indefinite period. Although in 1974 *three psychiatrists had labelled him "insane and extremely dangerous,"* Finlayson was released for good behaviour and for six months was living full-time away from the medium-security prison on a "loosened warrant," when he stabbed and killed a Brockville, Ontario, woman. The prosecutor in the original case was utterly shocked, and said, "I never wanted to see him out again. It was without doubt the most grisly murder that I've had the misfortune to prosecute." But after the Brockville murder the hospital handling him pleaded that "they could not have prevented the stabbing." (They failed to mention that if he had still been locked up he would not have had the opportunity.)

### The case of Michael Hector

In 1996, Ambi Chenniah wrote a glowing supervisory report about Michael Hector's "progress" while on parole serving a sentence for armed robbery with a restricted weapon. She effused about his upbeat spirit, and about his future plans to become a professional writer and semi-retire in Australia. Ambi and others had spent a lot of their time and a lot of our money trying to change

Hector's view that "nothing is a crime unless you get caught." But unknown to Ambi, eleven days prior to issuing her report, sweet-smiling Hector had brutally murdered two men in cold blood by shooting them in the face, below the right eye; one of them for refusing to sell him an ounce of cocaine for $2,000; the other, because he was a witness. Three weeks later he murdered a twenty-year-old gas station attendant from whom he had stolen $944, by shooting him, as he described proudly, "once in the head, once in the ear." At the time of all these murders he was on parole while serving an eight-and-a-half-year term for armed robbery. That robbery had itself been committed while he was on parole from a previous armed robbery sentence. Despite his three armed robberies and three brutal murders committed *while on parole* Hector was never once classified as a dangerous offender, nor as a vicious psychopath, but as "a medium-security model inmate." Sent back to prison, he got married and qualified for conjugal visits.[2] About his future freedom, we know nothing.

For most people, the basic purpose of a criminal justice system is to ensure the highest level of public safety through the administration of . . . a justice system; which is to say, a system that makes sure criminals don't "get away with it," keeps dangerous criminals away from the public as long as the law permits, and where possible, makes bad people into better people who are less likely to reoffend. The degree to which any of these objectives is successful depends a lot on the theory of human nature held by those in charge of the system.

## WARRING CONCEPTS OF HUMAN NATURE

It is difficult to understand the present climate of criminal justice in Canada without first understanding the warring concepts of human nature, personality, and punishment that created that climate. As with so many social issues in Canada, there is a radical polarization of views—few of which ever surface for public inspection—beneath a seemingly calm surface. The people who consciously or unconsciously hold these opposing views fight for control of the bureaucratic and political turf that constitutes the criminal justice system in Canada. Unfortunately, the laboratory for the experiments these people undertake is us: our families, our children, and the civility of our society. We are guinea pigs for social scientists, penologists, wardens, case management officers, parole board members, and the politicians who legislate criminal justice. In their classic book *Crime and Human Nature*,[3] Harvard professors James Wilson and Richard Herrnstein provide an overview of Man the Calculator, and Man the Naturally Good, the two principal, and radically opposed, views of human nature that have always divided criminologists.

## MAN THE CALCULATOR

In *Leviathan* (1651), Thomas Hobbes made famous the idea that our minds work somewhat like little cost-benefit calculators that help us decide what we want. Each of us is considered *quite capable of weighing the likely pain or pleasure to be obtained from our actions.* The object of the law is to ensure that the few do not get their pleasure from the pain of others, and that the community as a whole experiences the greatest pleasure and the least pain possible from the totality of social action. On this view, the justification for punishment is "to outweigh the profit from crime" obtained when some wish to gain by hurting others. Punishment prevents greater pain to the community and is meant to incapacitate, to deter, and to provide society with its just deserts—that is, to make society morally whole again. This is the aim of all retributive justice.

After their exhaustive survey of criminology, Wilson and Herrnstein say that "the view of human nature developed by Hobbes accords with much of what we have learned about the causes of crime." This view *places responsibility squarely in the hands of the knowing, calculating offender.* In this respect, it is harmonious with our understanding of moral agency and with the political, economic, and cultural institutions of a free society surveyed in Part One of this book.

## MAN THE NATURALLY GOOD

The opposite view is very old, but was sparked by the Swiss philosopher Jean-Jacques Rousseau who supplied the eighteenth-century Romantic movement in literature and the arts momentum by declaring that in our original state we were born innocent as "noble savages." It was the institution of private property, the class system and poverty, bad laws, acquisitiveness, social conventions, and inequality—in brief, *all the faulty institutions of civil society*—that set us against each other, thus spawning crime. He argued that only a healing education—a transformation of the person and of all society—could return us to our condition of natural goodness. Hardly an example of natural goodness himself, Rousseau and his mistress gave away all five of their newborn children to state orphanages, where they surely died. But despite the lie given by his personal life to his own ideas (many tried, unsuccessfully, to expose him), his writing had an enormous impact. In fact, much of modern criminology, directly or indirectly, draws from Rousseau: "It is indebted to him when it favors preventing crime through proper education and constructive social programs as well as when it prefers helping offenders by rehabilitation instead of preventing offenses by deterrence . . . the view that crime is caused by social forces . . . and that the individual is not fully to blame for his behavior is still widespread."[4]

The first thorough probe into the ills of the Canadian justice system was the three-hundred-page Daubney Committee Report to Parliament on sentencing, parole, and related matters in 1988.[5] Committee members heard solid evidence to the effect *that rehabilitation and parole do not work*, including evidence from the solicitor-general's report which said that "a large body of empirical research which has been extensively assessed . . . has shown a lack of evidence of positive effects on recidivism [repeat crime] from any correctional program, either in prison, or in the community." Nevertheless, even after evidence that some of these programs actually make criminals worse, we read: "*The committee believes that people can and do change; it rejects the notion that nothing works.*" Now, that was a stunning statement, because—presto!—the committee *believes*. Nothing more. It had no evidence. No expertise to support such a bald statement. In fact, it had contrary evidence.

So we stand warned: almost nothing in the Canadian justice system presented to the public as a "philosophy" or "policy" on crime and punishment is rooted in hard fact or impressive argument. More often than not it is a jumble of confused and contradictory theories of sentimental origin, combined with wishful thinking. Much of it strikes a reader as a kind of secular evangelism. By the time of the Trudeau era, Liberal solicitor general Jean Goyer announced that "rehabilitation rather than punishment must become the goal of our penal system." At the time, Trudeau was parading himself as the Great Forgiver (Rousseau, whom he often quoted, was one of his intellectual heroes), informing us that we must learn to see offenders as citizens and members of society rather than as felons. The 1977 MacGuigan Report was duly implemented, promoting "the three Ps"—probation, parole, and pardons—as a less costly and more humane way to deal with crime.

John Braithwaite, an influential writer on criminal justice, explicitly argued at the time that rather than pain and punishment, offenders must be shamed, then socially reintegrated in quick sequence (this step he called "reintegrative shaming") so that they will accept the social bonding offered by the community instead of rejecting the community for having rejected them. The basis of his theory is Rousseauian: the offender is good; it is the *behaviour* that is bad.[6] This in turn was a secular echo of the Christian stance that we should condemn the sin, but not the sinner. By 1988, this thinking was enshrined as our official "restorative justice" doctrine in Correctional Services Canada's mission statement presented at a conference in Banff, Alberta. More on "Jesus in the Jails" later in the chapter.

My objection to this view is that blame must be placed where it belongs—on the moral agent responsible for the choices that lead to crime. Why? Because a terrible action does not choose itself. An agent is always the cause of an act. So it is wrong to say blame the sin, not the sinner. It is the sinner's choosing the sin that makes the crime.

I will be making the case here that one of the troubles with Canada is that since the late 1960s, our parole and correctional establishment (except for the guards and the prisoners themselves, who know better) has been basing its public safety practices on incoherent and dangerous ideas, using Canadian society as a laboratory for what amounts to a criminal experiment with human nature. Many innocent citizens have already died, and many will continue to die in its name. Here's just one explicit example of Rousseauian psychology at work: In response to the charge that five young murderers sentenced to nine years in penitentiary in 1985 (but already out on parole) were recommended for release too soon, psychologist Stanley Newman, who authorized their parole, said, "The chief issue is how five apparently ordinary youths could end up with such vile thoughts. Average kids, average grades, involved in sports. They were very well liked. That's what makes it all the more chilling. *It's not innate, it's the environment. I really believe that.*"[7] Stanley had a passionate belief. That's all he had. The fact that these five killers came from a model environment deeply threatened his entire criminology education, his deepest belief system, and his sense of professional worthiness. So he had to reject the facts.

To this point, I have outlined the two warring concepts of human nature that underlie all conflicts over how we ought to deal with criminal behaviour. But we must go deeper still, for underneath each of these concepts are even more fundamental assumptions about how the human mind works. You won't find this discussed in official statistics or justifications for parole, but serious debate on the causes of crime must eventually lead to the watershed difference I am about to explain.

## WARRING CONCEPTS OF MIND
An anecdote about two genetically identical twin sons of a violent and alcoholic father, with exactly the same family upbringing, poignantly sums up this whole matter.

Question to first twin: "Why are you a drunken criminal?"
Answer: "With a father like mine, *who wouldn't be?*"
Question to second twin: "Why are you *not* a drunken criminal?"
Answer: "With a father like mine, who would *want* to be?"

### The Determinist View of Mind
In the scenario above, the first twin has a determinist view of the mind (that how our minds work is determined by, and can be predicted from, events in our environment). The second twin has the opposite view. Let us examine the first.

It goes as follows: If it is true that we are born naturally good, and it is society that creates evil in us, then there must be some direct causal link between the events of daily life and our behaviour. The model for this notion is Newtonian physics (for the first time a scientist had provided exact laws for the physical world): for every known action, there will be a known reaction. Physics, of course, produces very clean results compared with social life (where we are forced to use such phrases as "is likely to produce"). When behaviourists speak of "socialization," they mean that social life works on us just like a physical event, and that we will all have predictable reactions according to our circumstances. At the coroner's inquiry over the repeat crimes of the violent rapist-murderer Melvin Stanton (above), his social worker Dr. Khanna pleaded that Stanton had told her of "abuse and neglect by his family" (her assumption was that he would otherwise have been normal); she recommended that "his attempts at pro-social behaviour need to be rewarded so that such behaviour will be strengthened" (the assumption is that the right physical stimuli will cause a positive change). His psychologist, Maurice Klein, deplored how Stanton deteriorated "when community *stimuli* are encountered." There you have it: the patient as a physical entity, ruined by prior physical events, corrupted by the wrong "stimuli." Many of these theories are very clever. Nevertheless, what it boils down to is that they all *more or less eliminates the conscious, choosing, knowing-right-from-wrong subject from the formula.* The choosing person is theoretically superfluous because all life is said to unfold in a predictable way.

What Canadians must now face is this question: Why have we accepted the creation of a vast academic, political, and social bureaucracy for the determination of criminal justice based on such a theory—one manifestly at odds with the moral values by which normal people and their families attempt to live? Why have we accepted the twisted arguments of criminal defence lawyers eager to prove that some new pathology deprives people of responsibility for crime? For, in the end, what consistent connection could possibly exist between a mood, or a feeling, and a moral decision to act one way or the other? Moods and emotions, in themselves, have no *intent.* If anger "caused" murder, then half the world would be murdered. Rather, personal emotions are the instruments we deploy to authorize and gain our chosen ends; they are performances enacted in the dark theatre of the Self.

## The Moral Agency View of Mind

*Homines fere credunt libenter, id quod volunt.*
*(Men almost always believe freely whatever they want.)*
—Julius Caesar, *Commentaries on the Gallic Wars,* 55 BC

There has always been another, very serious view of how the mind works. This view, which has profound theological sources rooted in the belief that humans are rational moral agents, has been developed for modern secular consumption by philosophers like Martin Heidegger, Karl Jaspers, and Jean-Paul Sartre. It claims that the crucial difference between human beings and material beings is that all humans have an innate capacity to say no—to refuse to choose a certain path at any given moment, and thereby to constantly re-create themselves through free choice. This is a view that rejects all determinism by declaring that the glory of human existence, and the quality that makes us distinct from lower animals, is rational moral agency. Accordingly, theories that deny these powers remove our essential humanity by imagining us as unthinking robots. But because we are always free to negate whatever we are at any moment, and to choose a new beginning, however humble, to escape past forces by a new choice, we are free. Free! No social environment can *make* us do something any more than can a stone.

This free-choice model of the mind is radically different from the determinist model, *and cannot be reconciled with it*: societies that choose one view or the other, therefore, or mix them up, embark on a particular course. Whenever there is a grey area between them, they must decide in favour of their particular course, and individuals will sometimes be sacrificed to that course. In fact, I would argue that societies that opt for human freedom and responsibility have chosen to sacrifice criminals (by catching and punishing them) to the moral urgency of the Freedom System, whereas those that opt for determinism have chosen to sacrifice the victims of criminals, and society at large (by going soft on crime and endangering society) to the moral urgency of their Handicap System. Socialist and communist states officially take the determinist view. So does Canada now. So does the U.N. In its web discussions of crime we read platitudinous statements about "the etiological factors *producing* crime—poverty, racism, cultural/social values." There it is, in broad daylight.[8] Crime is "produced" by external factors.

Such thinking inevitably evolves into a materialistic idea of "personality," the notion that holds we have a good and true "Self" (like a thing) lurking deep in our core that we can "get in touch with," after the appropriate searching, therapy, and "transformation." When this Self is deemed to be damaged by social causes, therapeutic types aim to "rebuild" it. But the confusion in such a hope must be exposed. For how can I say I am searching for myself? Are there two selves inside each of us—the searcher and the searched? And if there are, how do we know which one of the two is the true Self? No, the Self is not a thing, but a construct of free will, and is sustained or altered by our ongoing free choices. Every moment of life. The fact that people may choose to act *as if* they are determined robotic selves gives the illusion of a changeless character. But even this is a choice. Even the crazy killer George Foster (in his statement at the head of this chapter) did not say he blamed the system "that *makes* me do what I do." He said he blamed "the system that *allows* me to do what I do." I do, too.

Now that we have looked at the roots of crime in human moral agency, let us examine, once again with the help of James Wilson and Richard Herrnstein, the warring concepts of incapacitation, deterrence, and retribution.

## Incapacitation

Prison (and of course, capital punishment, where it is used) protects the public by separating the offender from possible future victims, thus reducing the opportunities for crime. The question to what extent such punishment ought to be used is at the heart of the conflict between the judiciary and the parole powers in our society. Alas, a wise judge may decide on a certain sentence, only to see it undermined by social workers and parole boards. In fact, a judge in Canada today has no means of telling how much of the sentence he or she sweated over will in fact be served. This casts into disrepute the whole meaning of justice, and especially the authority of the law and of judges who agonize over appropriate sentences. Justice is as much a moral as a professional matter, and every citizen has the right to offer a sincere opinion on the meaning of justice. That's why we rely on juries (rather than on the opinion of one person), and that's how the community's sense of *equity* is arrived at in the first place. But once the *therapeutic* idea takes hold (based on the we-are-naturally-good-but-have-been-damaged-by-society model), the people's right to determine justice is stolen from them by "experts" who want a cure more than they want justice, and are prepared to erode the latter for the former. This substitution slowly dissolves the moral bonds of society. As the experts proceed (through various forms of early release) to reduce sentences held appropriate by courts and the community, they undermine public respect for the law. This unresolved conflict between opposing views of appropriate punishment (the judge's sentence) and therapy (how parole boards and therapists reduce those sentences) has arisen because many therapists believe that "if an act is not a choice but merely the inevitable product of a series of past experiences, a man can be no more guilty of a crime than he is guilty of an abscess."[9] The result is that the "Hug-a-Thug" mentality now operating in the Canadian justice system has eroded the free-choice-and-responsibility view of crime. This is bad for society, and especially bad for criminals.

### Deterrence and Moral Education

Another traditional justification for punishment is that it provides a deterrent while giving moral education to prospective criminals. Wrongdoers are punished and the public example of their fate provides a punishment rehearsal for those contemplating the same acts. For "if a connection has been established between action and aversive consequences, and if the aversive consequence is adequately intense . . . the action will be prevented or reduced in frequency." In Wilson's view, *all crime*, for that matter all human action, is *controlled by its probable consequences* (and not by prior stimuli); the reason punishment works is that it makes non-crime more attractive. Punishment also creates social sanctions, which are then incorporated within each individual as conscience, transferred from generation to generation through the family and in religious and civil law. Lectures from parents, teachers, pastors, coaches, the fines and parking tickets we pay, and reminders of the Ten Commandments do have an effect. Swift, sure punishment helps a society to internalize and thus clearly to express its prohibitions. But a "punishment" that causes no psychic pain in offenders (the likely result of converting punishment to therapy) will not have the desired effect of creating a broad social conscience. Society is thus weakened, and crime advances. Indeed, "a community which is too ready to forgive the wrongdoer may end by condoning the crime."[10]

### The Retributive Theory of Justice

An excellent writer on crime (and the history of law) is University of Ottawa professor David Paciocco. In his book *Getting Away With Murder*, he describes the call for retribution as a "primal stirring," an urge to return pain like the need for revenge, suggests that punishment is "often useless," and doubts that crime is prevented by sentencing offenders.[144] But I disagree. As described below, retributive justice is not a call for revenge; it is a call for moral rebalancing. There is nothing primal about it. It is the most noble—actually, the only—eternal standard of justice we have. It is expected, practiced, understood, and debated universally by individuals, parents, and nations worldwide, has been defended by every serious moral philosopher, and is enshrined in natural and international law, and in the law of just war.[11]

In his essay "The Humanitarian Theory of Punishment," C.S. Lewis complained that those who take the determinist, or Hug-a-Thug view that crime is caused by external forces and therefore punishment should be replaced by therapy, or "rehabilitation," miss the central point: such a theory removes from crime the concept of *just deserts* (getting what you deserve), which is a universal conception of justice operating everywhere, as when we say "the punishment must fit the crime."[12] Indeed, just deserts "is the only moral link between punishment and justice." In other words, once we remove the idea of just deserts from punishment, we remove justice itself, and then we debase society as a whole. And Wilson, agreeing, reminds us that "an offender has violated an implicit social contract that ties the members of a community together. . . . *Punishment as retribution balances the books.*"

Such retributive equity, or fairness, should never be called revenge, which is what results when vigilantes take the law into their own hands. Rather, punishment-as-equity restores the torn fabric of law and order by exacting what the community as a whole (not any one individual) thinks is a fair repayment for what has been lost. Interestingly, this is exactly the philosophy underlying tort law the world over: the redress of injustice. When the retributive equity that is society's due is debased by parole programs proffered on the therapy-instead-of-punishment model, however, society is diminished and cheated; law and order are rightly perceived to have failed. Justice is neither done, nor seen to be done. So crime is repeated and increases. This is not to say that we cannot seek justice and deter, as well as educate and try to reform, but that therapy or rehabilitation must never be—it cannot in principle ever be—a *substitute* for punishment. For as the criminologist Jeffrie Murphy once wrote, "*A retributive theory of punishment . . . is the only morally acceptable theory of punishment* . . . [and] the twentieth century's faddish movement toward a 'scientific' or therapeutic response to crime runs grave risks of undermining the foundations of justice."[13] In Canada, the foundations have been badly cracked for some time.

## THE CRIMINAL PROFILE

Here are a number of sobering observations from established criminologists that run counter to the concept of a therapy-oriented justice system. First, from *Crime and Human Nature* comes a picture of the typical criminal: overwhelmingly, the typical criminal is male. Males are from five to fifty times more likely to go to jail than females, and the male offence rates reach more than 90 percent in many crime categories. The typical criminal is also quite young. In Canada, some 55 percent of federal felons are between twenty and thirty-four years old (crime declines rapidly with age); he is also of somewhat below-average intelligence, generally has a muscular body, is inarticulate (verbal ability is highly correlated with intelligence), and most telling of all, is extremely impulsive and given to heavy "time-discounting." In other words, criminals have a very short time horizon. Also, most criminals show signs of trouble very early in life and most have never formed strong emotional attachments (the lack of "attachment" to mom in early childhood is a real worry here. See my comments on prolonged infant daycare in chapter 10[14]). Because they are very "present oriented," they generally refuse to postpone personal gratification. This trait may be thought of as: "I see it, I want it, I get it"—whether it is a woman, a car, or an item in a store. We should note, however, that this is a *calculated impulsiveness*, for a criminal who knows he is being watched by the police can easily control his criminal desires (indeed, he sees such strategic control as arch cleverness). What we typically see is an extreme reluctance to plan for the future, and a buck-passing, it-wasn't-my-fault mentality (reinforced by our therapy orientation). Criminals show a lack of anxiety over the things that generally create anxiety in others, and a complete lack of dependability. Of course, crime suits such individuals very well because it provides a means to short-circuit the normal reward pathways of society that require effort, time, and postponement of gratification. Punishment always seems remote to criminals—because it is. It is the homogeneity of the criminal-personality profile that is so striking, not the variation. Indeed, many criminals have been wholly seduced by crime, as we shall see.

# WHY WE CAN'T "BLAME SOCIETY"

One of the most striking chapters in Wilson and Hermstein's *Crime and Human Nature* deals with "Crime Across Cultures." There we learn that international cross-cultural assessments of the heinousness of various crimes are uncannily similar, but that crime *rates* are quite different between nations; that societies have a lot to do, not so much with shaping criminals as with shaping the morality and levels of sanction that permit the easy expression of criminality.

This is especially so for Japan, and tellingly, for Americans of Japanese origin, who have far lower crime rates than others. For the Japanese, as these authors put it, "have somehow managed to swim against the tide" of modern crime. Japan experienced a national crisis in 1982 when the number of murders in Tokyo rose to *thirteen* in one year (as many as New York City had at that time on an average weekend). By 2006, Japan had 565 murders—fewer than Canada's 606, even though Japan has a population four times as large as ours. Japan is even more densely populated than North America (with which it is mostly compared), poorer, and is 70 percent urban, with fewer police per capita. But once indicted and prosecuted, a Japanese person faces a 90 percent likelihood of conviction. The reasons for low crime in Japan have partly to do with ethnic and cultural unity (racially mixed countries tend to have far more crime), and the fact they have somehow preserved the village communal spirit even in their large cities. Japanese people are also far more concerned about their obligations than about their rights. The suggestion in all of this is that the cultural internalization of sanctions against crime and social and moral obligations (including just deserts and equity) leads to a stronger conscience in the people, who then self-limit crime.

# PUTTING THE RACISM AND POVERTY MYTHS TO BED

Social scientists are fond of saying that crime is primarily caused by social problems, racial discrimination, and poverty, but . . . "The experience of the Chinese and Japanese suggests that social isolation, substandard living conditions, and general poverty are not invariably associated with high rates of crime among racially distinct groups."[15] The same finding is true of desperately poor Jews who lived in ghettos—they were very law-abiding. At the time Wilson was researching for his book there were only five criminals of Chinese or Japanese origin in the entire California prison system. These examples should be a benchmark against which our own society's rush to blame things like poverty and race for crime ought to always be compared. Such theories are an insult to the honest and law-abiding poor (most of the world's people), who have made personal choices to live within the law.

Criminologist Stanton Samenow also rejects the modern pro-criminal ethos and clearly establishes a link between crime and psychopathy. He and Samuel Yochelson conducted a seminal fifteen-year study of criminals at St. Elizabeth's

Hospital, a psychiatric institution in Washington, D.C. The portrait they drew, summarized in Samenow's sobering book *Inside the Criminal Mind*, is strikingly similar to that of many other modern criminologists. His hands-on work with hundreds of criminals over many years bears more weight than the assumptions or beliefs of theorists. Samenow tells us that as most criminals will one day be out of jail, rehabilitation efforts must continue. But if we are looking to the environment for the cause of deviant behaviour, we've got it all wrong. The focus must be on moral responsibility, because

> [C]riminals cause crime—not bad neighborhoods, inadequate parents, television, schools, drugs, or unemployment. Crime resides within the minds of human beings and is not caused by social conditions. Once we as a society recognize this simple fact, we shall take measures radically different from current ones . . . Too long have the social sciences promulgated the view that a human organism comes into the world like a lump of clay to be shaped by external forces. This view renders us all victims! . . . Far from being a formless lump of clay, the criminal shapes others more than they do him . . . [and] criminals are remarkable in their capacity to size up their environment in order to pursue objectives important to them.[16]

It would be gratifying to see such insights in Canada's criminal justice system. But instead, we have been moved in the other direction entirely, as was made clear to the public in an article twenty years ago: "Correctional Services Canada has charted a future course that rejects the public's get tough attitude in favor of treatment programs and the integration of convicts into the community."[17]

## CANADA'S DECISION TO ADOPT A "HUG-A-THUG" THEORY

The same article introduced Canadians to Ole Ingstrup, a "reform-minded veteran of the Danish correctional system," who was fresh from two years' running of our National Parole Board and who was now to head up Correctional Services Canada. Ingstrup said, "The image of a group of people who are running in and out of prison is a myth. The majority go in and out but once."

Now, that was an astonishing statement, and a fib, to boot, because before Ingstrup (who came here from a peaceful country where one-fifth of all crimes reported are for bicycle thefts) even got started with his Danish reforms, a 1977 parliamentary report on the crisis in the Canadian justice system showed that an appalling 60 to 80 percent of Canada's criminals were repeat offenders. And about ten days after he resigned in August 2000, a Kingston police study of 1,378 inmates recorded a repeat-offender rate of 47 percent. To test this cheerful claim myself, I asked the Correctional Services Branch of the Ontario government to answer this question: Of all those admitted to Ontario prisons in 1988, how many had ever been in prison before? Here's what they told me: 44,692 were admitted; 31,242 had been in prison before (about 8,000 of these were double- or triple-dippers—they go in and out of prison more than once in the same year). That meant *a whopping 70 percent of admissions to prisons in Ontario were repeaters* that year. Nevertheless, despite such evidence, from 1988 until his resignation in 2000, Ingstrup single-handedly transformed the way we treat criminals in Canada.

Canadians had best beware, because Ingstrup may have resigned in 2000, but he left his stamp on Correctional Services Canada, an organization that for more than two decades has had every intention of loosing *more* criminals (um, "clients") into society. During his reign, while under budgetary pressure, he imposed a 50/50 in-jail/in-community target for our corrections system. He was an arch-reformer in the people-are-born-good-so-it's-society-that-makes-them-bad mould. His "mission" was shot through with philosophical confusion.

At the CSC administrators conference in 1988, his speech was filled with talk of "excellence," the need for "vision," "positive human potential," the "potential for growth in our offender population" (we only hope he didn't mean that literally!), and "partnership" between staff and offenders. He also wanted more money to hire more psychiatrists. And this was so even though another Ontario program for the treatment of anti-social criminals billed as "one of the most ambitious in the world" was announced as a dismal failure in August of that very year. Doctors reported that, overall, "the study sample [those treated] fared worse than offenders who had been sent to prison without any treatment." Research head Marnie Rice said, "There's almost no room to do any worse." These researchers also said that unlike other criminals, anti-social ones do not appear to get less violent with age, and that lifelong incarceration was the alternative to treatment.

Just as I was writing about Rice's remarks I was handed a new article, "Treatment Failing Sex Offenders" (*Toronto Star*, June 20, 1989):

A widely acclaimed treatment program for sex offenders at the Penetanguishene Mental Health Centre has produced dismal results . . . The study of 137 sex offenders . . . showed 29 percent were convicted of another sex offence within a six-year period and more than 40 percent committed a subsequent violent offence . . . [the research director said] if a less conservative definition of failure had been used . . . nearly 100 percent of the patients would have failed, adding: "It may be in fact that *the treatment isn't helpful, but harmful*" [emphasis mine].

In that article, University of Toronto law professor Bernard Dickens said our system "is allowing an unsuspecting society to be 'guinea pigs.'" Despite this evidence, however, Ingstrup insisted that Canadians needed to move parole decisions to the more local level (meaning, speed up the process, get more offenders out to establish "partnerships" with the public). He was a dyed-in-the-wool Danish flower child, and his brochures were filled with "protection of society" talk as a cover for Hug-A-Thug therapy notions he tried to sell as "opportunities" to protect ourselves.

The name that came to be used for what he was trying to sell is "restorative justice," an approach that amounts to a revolt against ordinary retributive justice. All this was extremely offensive, since obviously the best way to protect ourselves is to keep criminals away from us as long as legally possible. Further, he implored us to respect "the dignity of individuals"—a call to our humanity that is hard to resist. But the whole point of incarcerating a heinous murderer like Clifford Olson is that he forfeited all dignity and any right to ordinary respect with each of the eleven children he raped, murdered, and buried. Do we really believe he can ever earn it back, or that respect ought simply to be conferred upon him by decree of CSC? Most would say that basic human dignity is shared by all equally at birth. But after that, it's sustained, or lost, according to our behaviour. Sadly, in all of this we heard very little concern for the dignity of the larger society, the victims, and the families that these "dignified" criminals have decimated—though in the twenty-first century more room has been made for "victim input." The National Parole Board heard 244 victim-input statements at its hearings in 2007–2008.

As for the additional psychiatrists Ingstrup wanted? His legacy continues. Read the CSC web page and you will see lots of psychobabbling faith in "psychology." A continuation of the same old stuff that has never worked (except for the odd minor criminal already eager to change). In a *Science* magazine report that appeared when I was writing the original of this chapter, two researchers, both psychologists, David Faust and Jay Ziskin, showed that social workers, psychologists, and psychiatrists are batting zero when it comes to assessing the human mind and forecasting behaviour. In screening patients for brain damage, "professional psychologists performed no better than office secretaries"; in predicting violence, the experts "are wrong at least twice as often as they are correct," and "the amount of clinical training and experience are unrelated to judgemental accuracy."

## THE SEDUCTIONS OF CRIME

Anyone familiar with criminals knows that psychology in the healing sense is but another hopeful but dangerous wild goose chase simply because psychologists know less than zero about what author Jack Katz, in the subtitle of his chilling book *The Seductions of Crime*,[18] calls "Moral and Sensual Attractions in

Doing Evil." Among these are the powerful seductions of "righteous slaughter." For criminals, as writers such as Fyodor Dostoevsky and Friedrich Nietzsche knew better than most, are in fact preoccupied with moral questions, many of them riveted by "the primordial evil of senseless murder." But psychologists, as one observer put it, are "better with madness than with badness." They have trouble understanding, as one reviewer of Katz's book put it, that

[D]anger is thrilling. The unpredictable is better than its opposite. Difficulties have a pleasurable friction that is missing in over-lubricated courses of life. Both good and ill fortune are alluring, for our wonder is aroused by the prospects of death, wounds, long imprisonment, even disgrace ... Crime offers freedom of a high degree: freedom from the commandments of the state, from the burdensome customs of civil society, from the worrisome calculations of consequences, from the boring routines and humiliations of regular employment ... A crime is an adventure, and so is flight [said one escapee]: "I used to get a buzz out of being wanted, and outwitting them."

Added to this are: the criminal-stroking servile homage to the superiority of the assailant that is deeply embedded in the act of handing over your wallet or watch; the fact that resistance to their actions is taken as moral defiance and they retaliate morally as a matter of personal pride and principle; that in poor and disorganized communities law-abiding is perceived as a recipe for obscurity, and the life of crime the way to prestige; and above all, that most of the studies and numbers on crime are produced by bureaucrats and police, for whom such moral and mental perversities and sophistications are mysterious. Hence, we fester in misleading conclusions.[19] Canada had its own direct experience with this sort of amoral darkness when the Homolka-Bernardo killings were made public. Lawyer Ken Murray testified that when Karla was watching the sex killings, "she had a look of feral joy in her face." Given these realities, what could be driving the "psychology" at CSC and the NPB? Let's take a look at their public statements.

## RESTORATIVE JUSTICE—JESUS IN THE JAILS

*Love, when substituted for justice, may become an accomplice of tyranny.*
—Reinhold Neibuhr

The revolutionary concept of restorative justice, or RJ, has been energetically introduced to Canada as a replacement alternative for our system of retributive justice without any national public debate or real awareness. It was socially engineered as a thoroughgoing Hug-a-Thug regime change in Canadian penal ideology from behind tightly closed doors.

Readers can visit CSC's website at www.csc-scc.gc.ca where they will find the statements about RJ that are critiqued below. What these statements are telling us is that since the early 1990s we have been—still are—hostages to a sweet-sounding but soft-headed ideology of "corrections" that will continue to pose a danger to public safety until it is itself corrected.

Hundreds of innocent Canadians minding their own business have been murdered in cold blood over the past few decades by hardened criminals on the loose because well-meaning but misguided people running our system became enraptured by the ostensibly cost-saving notions of sentences to be served "in the community."

RJ has since its inception spread widely, and is now embraced enthusiastically by frustrated correctional theorists and social workers around the developed world, even at the highest levels of the U.N.[20] Canada now has more than four hundred restorative justice programs, and the United States more than seven hundred, most of them used for minor crimes and youth criminals—though the real ambition of RJ evangelicals is to work the "healing" of RJ on hardened criminals. Some critics of RJ argue it is a Pollyanna theory that privatizes justice and interferes with an independent application of the law and the workings of courts and juries; others that it amounts to a theory of "compulsory compassion" that is romantic and misses the point that justice and love cannot successfully be merged.[21] My own view is that there is nothing more rewarding than helping a lost soul find truth, honour, courage, responsibility, and the like, and this prospect alone makes restorative justice worth trying. However, there is serious concern that it amounts to yet another fancy justification for going soft on crime, and that it has helped make possible the sorts of horror stories you will read about below. Now let us scrutinize Canada's official statements about RJ. I have italicized the loaded words and phrases.[22]

> *Restorative justice* is a *non-adversarial, non-retributive approach to justice* that emphasizes *healing* in victims, meaningful *accountability of offenders*, and ... It gives all parties involved in *a conflict* the opportunity to take an active role in a safe and *respectful process* that allows *open dialogue* between the victim, offender and the community.

Okay. So then we ask: What, exactly, is "restorative justice"?

> Restorative Justice is a way of viewing justice that puts the emphasis on repairing harm caused by conflict and crime. In this approach crime is understood as a violation of people and relationships and a

disruption of the peace of the community. It is not simply an offence against the state. Restorative Justice is collaborative and inclusive.

When we wonder what this looks like in practice, we read:

> When people affected by *a harmful event,* both the one who is harmed and the one who caused harm, want to participate in a restorative justice process, they individually meet with *a trained facilitator who helps them define their unmet needs,* and identify *the tools* to meet those needs. Often, this involves working towards *a face-to-face conversation* about the harmful event, in which *the concerned individuals* talk about how they were *affected by the harm,* and *decide together* what needs to happen to *make things as right as possible.* Together they come to *an agreement* about how obligations created by the harm can be met, and people are supported through meeting those obligations.

Most of these terms are without credible philosophical or moral support. They are just sweet-sounding policy announcements of a change from a retribution-based corrections regime, to a "restorative" one. Let us reflect for a moment on the seductive language used in the above quotes.

### "Restorative Justice"? "Healing"? "Accountability"?

Justice is universally understood to be the core legal and moral principle of moral equity at the heart of all societies. Mercy in all properly functioning societies is also universally important in varying degrees, of course, but it is always secondary to justice, because while a society with little mercy may be thought cruel, a society with scant observance of justice, or with an arbitrary or inadequate understanding of it, cannot sustain the loyalty of the people. Indeed, a society without justice is a society without any basis in moral equity (a firm standard of what is deserved). It is therefore open to arbitrary power and tyranny.

Justice can only be sustained as an ideal when grounded in the concept of retribution—the repayment of a moral (and/or material) debt to society. A criminal can pay back such a debt only by receiving a fair legal punishment that society as a whole considers sufficient to equal the harm (the pain) suffered by the victim(s). Other forms of repayment, by way of money or community service, and the like, may indeed "restore" some of the material damage done, and may even "repair" relationships. But these ought never to be considered, or pawned off as, substitutes for moral and legal repayment, for although material things can be "restored" (because they are material things), justice is an abstract moral and legal principle or standard that cannot be restored any more than courage, or honour, or the concept of truth, or of the good, can be restored. They can be forgotten, neglected, and rediscovered. But in themselves they are not corruptible concepts. In short, we may speak of "restoring law and order," but we cannot improve or harm, deplete or restore, the principle of justice itself, which is the strict and eternal standard to which law and order must always appeal.

### "Respectful Process"? "Healing in Victims"? "Open dialogue"? The "Conflict"? "An Agreement"?

In choosing to make himself an enemy of the common good, a criminal forfeits all claims to the treatment due to law-abiding members of society. Therefore the "process" of exacting justice must be one-way, with two overriding aims: public safety and retribution—the first by way of preventing further harm as effectively as possible (usually incarceration); the second by way of a just punishment that fits the crime. This means there is no authentic "dialogue" possible because criminals have no right to debate their own punishment, and at any rate, an authentic "conversation" is impossible in principle between unequal power-holders. Neither is it acceptable to describe a criminal act as merely a "conflict" between parties, as if society and the offender could resolve their "unmet needs" by way of a mutual agreement or contract. A criminal has no such moral freedom or contractual right, and neither does an individual victim have a vigilante right personally to dictate the terms of justice. That is because the principle of justice itself has been attacked in a crime, so the just punishment must be decided by the people as a whole via their impartial moral and legal institutions. "Non-adversarial"? Nonsense. By his act, a criminal self-defines as someone who has voluntarily made himself an enemy of society by breaking the law and offending against the common good. A criminal by such an act makes himself an adversary both of the victim(s) of his crime, of the people as a whole, and of the law, and remains so until his moral and legal debt is repaid fully.

### "Non-retributive approach to justice"? "A way of viewing justice"? "Decide together"?

As mentioned, law and order can be eroded, or restored, but justice is an untouchable principle that is *served* via calculated equitable retribution—the only thing that links punishment with justice. We cannot simply "approach" justice, or "view" justice with some invented therapeutic puffery of the day, because justice is above all that—it's an immutable and universal concept of human moral and legal equity that demands a repayment be made by the offender in order to restore law and order (which is corruptible). Neither is it the main role of the defenders of public safety to "heal" victims, nor to seek a flaky admission of psychological "accountability" from a criminal, nor to posture heinous crime as a matter of "agreement" between criminals and victims, the restoration to be "decided together" as if both sides were active parties in the original "event." Such language is very objectionable, a smokescreen, a thinly disguised attempt to reconfigure crime as an unfortunate happenstance amenable by private justice.

RJ is best described as a career-bolstering mixture of secularized Christian compassion (if we can just get them to confess their crimes and repent, we can forgive, the victim and the community will forget, and everything will be better), and romantic moralizing (they are all potentially good; they became bad because their world was bad; so we need to facilitate getting them into supportive, understanding communities where they can heal), and budgetary pressure (let's dump them on the community where supervision costs a quarter of what prison costs). You won't find the word "God" in the Public Safety Canada (PSC) manual on restorative justice (heaven forbid!), but at the head of Module # 6, we read: "Forgiveness is 'a pilgrimage of the heart; it is to love one's enemy'—That's difficult!"

There is a lot of talk in RJ of healing, reparation, and reintegration, but no talk whatsoever of retribution in the context of ordinary justice and balancing the moral books. Indeed, in the PSC manual there is a scolding rejection of the latter: "The central focus of *traditional* justice is offenders getting what they deserve (there is a lot of scolding of those who want to make offenders suffer pain). The central focus of *restorative* justice is victim needs, and offender responsibility for repairing harm." The former asks: "What laws have been broken and what does the criminal deserve as retributive punishment?" The latter asks: "Who has been hurt? What are their needs? Whose obligations are these?" In many spots, the manual speaks of "the social causes of crime." Criminals are said to be socially "marginalized" (in the margins, not part of the main text of social life). RJ folks want to shift the whole system from one they believe is repressive and punitive to one that is reparative (repairing offenders, victims, and the damage done to their community).

We can see from this that in the RJ model the central question of justice as a transcendent universal principle held by all the people as their constant measure of proper law and order is not addressed. That is why I say that in RJ the question of true justice is not addressed, either. Clearly, in keeping with changes in the larger political world view of our times RJ has turned its back on the ideal of a common justice of all the people and has substituted for that a notion of local and personal *contractual* justice between the immediately affected parties only. To hell with the people as a whole. It is in this sense both a moral relativism, a return to tribal justice, and a repudiation of the role of the State both as an offended party and guardian of justice for all. There are realistic concerns that RJ "agreements" that may satisfy private individuals may not be in the larger public interest, and that criminal justice will thus deteriorate into "a publicly-funded private collection service."[23]

## WHERE DID RJ COME FROM?

The most influential short work on this movement is *The Little Book on Restorative Justice* by the American Mennonite author Howard Zehr,[24] whom a spokeswoman for CSC, in a conversation with me, described as "our guru." Zehr and his brethren see restorative justice as the emulation of Jesus' love, and accordingly, a vast improvement on what Zehr terms "the adversarial game" of retributive justice. "Respect" is the most important term for Zehr, "respect for all . . . even those who seem to be our enemies." Even John Braithwaite, an influential Canadian whose secular theories have formed a basis for Canada's RJ work, speaks of "the ritual of love," and of extending "unconditional love" to offenders as an essential aspect of RJ. So at first, and because the Jesus influence is not up front, this movement strikes one as a feel-good program adapted from the kitschy human potential movement, with a bit of postmodern lingo thrown in. There are lots of stories about "transformation," "healing," and "taking responsibility," but not much in the way of supportive practical results (especially the gold standard: proof of lower recidivism rates).

Public Safety Canada has produced its own gospel, *A Little Manual of Restorative Justice* (2008), prepared by Pierre Allard. You can download it from the PSC website.[25] It is a basic teaching manual for public consumption, the last section written by a prison chaplain. I can't resist saying here that it is rather ironic that Canada, a nation that has so assiduously chased God and Jesus from public schools and square, has in some desperation over its failures with crime, invited Jesus into the jails because, as Allard states, "Jesus is the great 'restorer.'" I think converting to Christianity (or, if you prefer, to Buddhism, Islam, Hinduism, or Taoism) would certainly help our prisoners worship something higher than themselves. And I am certain turning the other cheek is good for loving. But I don't think it has anything to do with true justice.

Ironically, it was around the fifteenth century when the Christian States first took over the rendering of justice from their local communities. Prior to that time local justice was mostly reparative of local harm done (you must give a new horse to the man whose horse you killed, or fix the house you damaged, as in modern tort law). But under the influence of Christian teachings, States grew more concerned about the quality of the soul than about the sins committed, and began punishing crime not only as a bad act to be repaired, but also as a moral sin in need of retribution and a deserved punishment. In short, material payback was not enough. You had to be punished for the sin of having chosen a crime. Even for thinking about doing evil! Jesus warned that to have lustful *thoughts* of adultery was to *commit* adultery. That is why in modern times, we punish even for *intent* to harm, such as for planning a murder or a failed conspiracy, where no actual harm may yet have been done. We are making sure to punish the inner state of mind.

At the time of the sixteenth-century Reformation, Protestants verily defined themselves as anti-institutional by pushing back against the established church, its dogmas, and its methods for dealing with sin and retribution (such as official definitions of the Seven Deadly Sins, mandatory Confession, reciting Hail Marys, etc.). In place of such institutionalized religious ritual, they called for the pure transformation of the individual spirit. Those first Protestants fought systemic Catholic notions of inherited sin; RJ evangelicals are fighting the same notions in our secular justice system. Restorative justice amounts to a kind of a Protestant Reformation in the prisons."[26]

There are other theoretical roots of RJ drawn from well-worn speculators in human psychology such as René Girard, Carl Jung, and Martin Buber. Girard wrote an excellent book, *Deceit, Desire & the Novel*, in 1976. I had the pleasure of teaching from that book and meeting with the author at York University when he lectured there. From these literary endeavours he turned his attention to anthropology with *Violence and the Sacred*, at the heart of which is his theory of the scapegoat. In a nutshell, the theory says that in their attempts to deal with their own evils, communities will search for a scapegoat upon whom they will unload unlimited punishments *as a means to cleanse themselves*. The accusation is that modern States have been doing this for a long time, and the implication is that criminals are unfairly treated victims of our deepest evils-cleansing processes. In the radical "anti-psychiatry" family-therapy work of R.D. Laing, we find the same groupthink, where the one "acting out" is said to be expressing the deeper pathology of the whole family. The most notorious treatments of this theme were by the late and determinedly dissolute postmodern French thinker Michel Foucault, who published intellectually suspect treatises claiming the West has for centuries been "constructing" both madness and criminality for its own social-cleansing purposes.[27] J.W. Mohr, a defender of RJ, actually attempts to criminalize justice itself when he argues that "there is little difference between the crime committed by offenders, and those we commit in the name of sentencing."[28] This is surely an attempt to neutralize criminal responsibility with the rather desperate argument that society (which, according to Zehr "has responsibilities for the situations that are causing or encouraging crime") is itself criminal, and because two wrongs don't make a right, the criminal is clean.

Mixed in with this theoretical brew is the Jungian theory of the personal "shadow" in which are hidden the emotional parts of ourselves that we have repressed but that may "leak out" and will even "begin to lead us into life situations which will give them a chance to emerge." There you see it again: but now it is not the tribal need for a scapegoat that will push you into criminality, it is your own internal shadow that will "lead" you. We all have a shadow! Beware! The message of this whitewashing theory is that any of us can become a criminal. Criminals are us.

354    12: THE CRIMINAL JUSTICE SYSTEM

Finally, there is the influence of Martin Buber, a Jewish mystic famous for extolling the primacy of human Subject-Subject ("I-Thou") relationships, over Subject-Object ("I-It") ones. RJ argues that we and our justice system convert criminals into objects, outsiders, enemies, and that crime and its wrongs can't be healed because offenders are excluded from our world at the start. Only by first establishing "right relations" (I-Thou) between ourselves and offenders can we arrive at authentic justice and repair harm.

RJ thinking more or less evolved along with cultural relativism, post-modernism, and the modern "diversity" and multicultural movements—all attempts to find answers tailored to the specific needs of different individuals, ethnicities, and groups, rather than according to coldly universal concepts of justice, morality, or retribution. All general, or "essentialist" or exclusivist categories came under fire as forms of "cultural imperialism." At bottom—and I think this is its Achilles heel—RJ has arisen as an attempt to use extremely personal means to deal with impersonal crime. Hence the incorporation of things like the Maori or Canadian native "healing circle," the "medicine wheel," the "sentencing circle," and the "healing lodge" models that inspired much of this new direction in Canada, and that have been part of a desperate attempt to address the atrocious aboriginal record for criminality. CSC currently has eight tax-funded "healing lodges" in operation, and RJ often models itself on supposed concepts of communal native justice. But many anthropologists say our notions of native justice are romantic. For while it may be true that in most primitive communities people tied by blood or marriage often in fact settled things communally (as we still do in families), those outside the immediate kin group were more often than not treated brutally and severely. As for other early forms of justice? In most primitive, as well as in frontier, societies justice was often pursued privately via personal vigilante action, scheming, feuding, assassination, the public stocks, the scarlet letter, kangaroo courts, and of course by that paradigm symbol of runaway "community justice"—the lynching tree. We also find a lot of "democratic" rhetoric in RJ programs, and of this we ought to be suspicious, as the term "democracy" may be used to justify all sorts of villainy. Then there is the reality that RJ sessions—some in America have had over a hundred participants—inflame the passions for justice as popular theatre, frequented by self-styled local justice preachers. In Northern Ireland this sort of informal justice included shootings, maimings, and the beating of offenders by the crowd.

What will this new direction do to our public sense of "justice"? This remains to be seen. But immediate problems have to do with questions such as: Why, for the same crime, does one criminal get to go to a healing lodge, while another gets jail time? My suspicion is that the multiplicity of (often racial) justice standards applied to the same crimes is already undermining respect for justice in Canada.

In the end, it is hard to get a factual assessment of the real value of RJ because of selection bias: supporters talk up only the good cases. Furthermore, because participation is voluntary, there are few bad cases included in this experiment. Critics also say RJ is biased in favour of offenders who know they will get something out of it (a lighter sentence), and of experienced criminals who are quite capable of "performances" of authenticity, faked "right-relations," and insincere love. Word is that RJ is also very expensive (contrary to the budget-reducing basis on which it was promoted). Personally, I am guessing RJ works very well for certain kinds of minor crimes, for youths from decent families who are not yet embittered by a life of crime and feel naturally repentant, and for small communities where offenders and victims already know each other. Watching someone go clean is inspiring. One writer tells of how moving it is to be in a mediation (now called "conferencing") after which a victim and an offender embrace each other, or when the victim offers the offender a job. I bet.

But I suspect it is a danger to public safety when attempted with deeply dangerous people who are arch-deceivers. Remember that every one of the criminals on parole or serving time "in the community" who has killed, wounded, or otherwise damaged the lives of innocent Canadians since our Hug-a-Thug policies got going in the 1960s was first declared harmless and "not a public danger." For the chilling truth is that some 70 to 80 percent of all violent criminals have been diagnosed with anti-social personality syndrome, and one of the key indicators of this condition is a combination of moral disconnection and silky-smooth skills in persuasion. Their most polished skill is an unfeeling manipulation of other human beings to achieve personal ends. Generous-spirited people are easy marks for this emotive display. But all the while, you, me, other offenders, other human beings in general are meaningless pieces on the offender's chessboard of life. In one RJ mediation over a car theft, the offender apologized sincerely (tears all 'round); the victim then forgave him sincerely (feeling so good). And then he asked the thief, "So, after all this healing, do you think you will ever steal a car again?" Without missing a beat, the thief said, "Well, I'm definitely not going to steal *your* car again."[29]

A final complaint is that RJ is a return to a kind of community vigilante justice as it was before the state got involved in order to guarantee uniform procedural safeguards and justice to all. Zehr complains that "when the state takes over in our name it undermines our sense of community." But modern States like Canada got involved in justice on opposing assumptions: it is the entire State, the whole nation—in our case, it is our highest authority, the Crown—which symbolizes the principle of justice itself, which has been offended by the criminal. It is Her Majesty the Queen who represents us all who is most damaged, and who is the legal plaintiff. That is why in Canada we have a "Crown attorney," and why criminal cases are described in terms of "the Queen" (*R.* or *Regina*) versus someone, as in *R. v. Joe Blow* (who harmed Rudy), and not *Rudy v. Joe Blow.*[30]

Up to this point, we have been looking mostly at the flashy concepts underlying our flimsy system. Now let us see what Canada's crime profile looks like.

## CANADA IN THE WORLD OF CRIME

First, a blunt fact that may surprise: Canada has one of the highest crime rates
in the developed world, with a medium incarceration rate, and a low number
of police personnel per capita. This evidence comes from the United Nations
Office on Drugs and Crime (UNODC) which compiles an exhaustive "Survey
of Crime Trends and Operations of Criminal Justice Systems." The "Tenth
Survey" covers crimes recorded in 2005–2006. Below is a table of some of the
countries that responded to the survey with their "Grand Total of Recorded
Crimes."

Crime rates are obviously a function of good policing and victims' willingness to report, but if we assume these things are more or less on par in developed
nations, it looks as if there is trouble with Canada in the crime department. In
2006, on this scale, Canada was a far more crime-ridden country than our
closest neighbour, though our tally has been declining for a while (along with
overall declines in most other Western nations). Canada's rate continued to
decline in 2007, which I show below (data for other nations was not available
for 2007). In reading this information, remember that this is a tally of crimes
reported to police, not of convictions. But it does give a sense of how disturbed
a nation is by crime.

| Nation | Reported Crimes per 100,000 population, 2006 |
|---|---|
| Sweden | 13,493 |
| England & Wales | 10,399 |
| New Zealand | 10,245 |
| Canada | 8,317   (6,984 for 2007) |
| Scotland | 8,200 |
| Germany | 7,628 |
| Netherlands | 7,439 |
| Italy | 4,715 |
| Switzerland | 3,865 |
| United States | 3,764 |
| Argentina | 3,128 |
| Spain | 2,397 |
| Greece | 2,167 |
| Japan | 1,602 |
| Costa Rica | 1,231 |
| Singapore | 900 |
| India | 443 |

* Note: 3,282,193 Canadians have a criminal record, and 377,477 of them (about 12 percent) have been granted a pardon—almost 25,000 in 2007–2008 (a pardon means their record has been sealed).

Canada's national figures for 2006 for "All Incidents" of reported crime per 100,000 population were as follows, by province and territory (regions above the national average are in bold). Readers will note that some of these Canadian regional rates are literally "off the scale" compared to other nations in the world (see above).

All Incidents of Crime—2006 (per 100,000)

| All Can. | NL | PE | NS | NB | QC | ON | MB |
|---|---|---|---|---|---|---|---|
| 8,269 | 6,571 | 7,468 | **8,698** | 6,781 | 6,626 | 6,251 | **12,325** |
| | SK | AB | BC | YT | NWT | NU | |
| | **15,276** | **10,336** | **12,564** | **22,197** | **44,074** | **32,831** | |

(Source: 2006 crime statistics for the provinces and territories as reported by Statistics Canada, last updated: February 28, 2007). Note: the difference between Canada's total here, and in the UN report, above, may be due to timing of reports.

Some International Incarceration Rates (per 100,000)

| | |
|---|---|
| USA | 762 |
| New Zealand | 185 |
| Scotland | 155 |
| England/Wales | 153 |
| Australia | 130 |
| Canada | 108 |
| France | 91 |
| Italy | 83 |
| Denmark | 63 |

# SOME FACTS ON CANADA'S CRIMINAL POPULATION

• The number of incarcerated federal offenders has been on the rise: from 12,413 in 2004, to 13,581 by 2008. The Harper government budget in 2010 called for construction of more prisons in a move to put more hardened criminals where they belong.

• Over 3,000 admissions each year are "revocations"—prisoners whose parole or conditional release is revoked for breaking their conditions (or for a new crime).

- Since 1998 the number of women admitted to federal prison has increased 32 percent.
- By race the federal prison population is: Caucasian: 67.5 percent; aboriginal: 17.2 percent (of which: NA Indian 11.9; Metis 4.7; Inuit 0.7); black, 6.9 percent; Asian: 4.7 percent (of which SE Asian and Arab West Asian are the largest groups).
- Sixty-eight percent of male federal prisoners are admitted for violent crimes (79.8 percent for aboriginals; 66 percent for non-aboriginal. For women it's 73.4 percent for aboriginals, and 48.1 percent for non-aboriginal).
- Each year there are about 100,000 offenders on probation, with another 14,000 on conditional sentences.
- Since 1978 there have been 455 criminals designated "Dangerous Offenders" (DO), of which 394 are alive and active, 377 are in prison, and others on community supervision. Some 24 percent of all DOs are aboriginal. There are no females designated DO.

(Source: Corrections and Conditional Release Statistical Overview, 2008.)

## INTERNATIONAL KILLING RATES: WHERE DOES CANADA STAND?

The United Nations survey above gives homicide rates per 100,000 population, by country. Here are a few countries with which Canada may be compared (leaving out the most murderous African and South American nations, among others). What Canadians ought to note, however, are the figures supplied by Statistics Canada for some of the highest-homicide Canadian jurisdictions for 2004 (keep in mind that a one-digit difference may represent a lot of dead bodies, depending on total population).

*UN Country Comparisons—Homicides per 100,000 (2006)*

| | | |
|---|---|---|
| El Salvador | 12.63 | |
| Mexico | 10.97 | |
| USA | 5.62 | |
| Canada | 1.86 | |
| England/Wales | 1.6 | (for 2005) |
| Sweden | 1.27 | |
| Switzerland | 0.80 | |
| Holland | 0.97 | |
| Italy | 1.06 | |
| Denmark | 0.53 | |
| Germany | 0.88 | |

THE TROUBLE WITH CANADA ... STILL!  359

| Greece | 0.98 |
|--------|------|
| Ireland | 1.59 |
| Japan | 0.44 |

*Canada's most homicidal regions (2004)*
BC: 2.7; AB: 2.6; SK: 3.9; MB: 4.2; NW: 9.2; NU: 13.4 YT: 22.2
(Source: Statcan)

## THE CRIME TREND DURING CANADA'S FIRST CENTURY

In 1998, Professors Stephen Easton and Paul Brantingham, of Simon Fraser University, showed the rising crime trend in Canada measured in rates of conviction per 100,000, from Confederation to the late 1960s (as calculated from Statistics Canada data, cat. 85–201).

Everything went up. Criminal *convictions* as a whole rose from a mere 75 per 100,000 in 1867, the time of Confederation, to 500 by the late 1960s. Property crimes rose from 44 to 304 per 100,000; violence against persons from 16 to 58 per 100,000; and violence against property from 6 to 118 per 100,000. Canadians have experienced a massive growth in crime rates in the form of waves—with peaks surrounding the 1914 and 1940 war eras, and the 1963 radical era, all followed by two more peaks: in 1981, and—at our highest level ever for violent crime—in early 1992—and falling since.

Easton and Brantingham comment that Canadian crime levels by 1981 in all three categories "were three times higher than they were in 1962." They add that although rates of crime have declined appreciably since their peak, they "remain at levels unimaginable thirty years ago" (back in 1968). They add that by 1998 there were "400 percent more violent crimes per person, and 300 percent more property crimes."

They also remark that private security guards in Canada now outnumber police more than two to one, and every year one in four Canadians report they have been victimized by some kind of criminal act. Alarmingly, only two-thirds of break-and-enter crimes, one-third of all assaults, and one-tenth of sexual assaults are reported to police.

Perhaps counterintuitively, we learn that the rate of property crime in a country is directly related to affluence, urbanization, and the number of women in the workforce (nobody home, fewer kids, less home activity?), while the rate of violent crimes is inversely related: the poorer a nation, the higher the rate of violent crime. Canada has relatively high property crime rates and lower violent crime rates. In 1998, Interpol ranked Canada 26th of 50 countries for highest number of murders (2.57 per 100,000), but 5th of 50 for theft (5,453 per 100,000). Typically, more than half of all Canadian crimes are property crimes (break and enter, theft, fraud, car theft, vandalism, possession of stolen goods). About 20 percent of Canadian households per year suffer one of these property crimes. Violent offences against persons comprise 11 to 13 percent of all crimes—a steady figure for recent decades.

Our professors also calculate that over a lifetime the average Canadian will suffer from at least one criminal act. As for gender? Crime in all categories except prostitution has over the centuries been overwhelmingly a male preserve. Two-thirds of all homicide victims are men, and men have far higher victimization rates for robbery and assault than women. Married persons have far less chance of suffering a homicide than do common law couples or singles. Young children, who "run a relatively high risk of being murdered in Canada," are far more likely to be killed by a stepparent or lover of a parent than by a parent.

As for alcohol? In 1996, 50 percent of those accused of homicide and 38 percent of their victims were intoxicated at the time of the crime by alcohol or related drugs. And . . . heavy drinkers are four times more likely to be victimized than non-drinkers. (This holds true for crime in all European countries as well—somewhere close to 50 percent of all offenders and their victims are high on something.)

Easton and Brantingham also calculate the costs of crime in terms of what a criminal may expect to pay in jail time when convicted. Deterrence from the threat of jail time in Canada, they concluded, is not great: serious sexual assault?—9 months in jail; serious non-sexual assault?—3 months; robbery?—2 months; assault with a weapon?—17 days; assault of a police officer?—8 days; fraud over $1,000?—2 weeks; break and enter?—1 week; theft and mischief over $1,000?—17 hours. (As for the question whether or not jail = pain? Many modern Canadian jails are more comfortable and homelike than the places criminals were living in.)

A 2004 CSC bulletin states that "approximately 36 percent of federal offenders on conditional release [relaxed "supervision" while free in the community] will be convicted of a new crime *within two years* of completing their sentences," and "11 percent of federal offenders return to federal custody" . . . of which almost half are for new violent offences.

As for the burdens crime imposes? In 2007–2008, Canada had 13,581 criminals in federal prisons and 8,434 on conditional release (day parole, full parole, or statutory release). There are another 20,000 in provincial jails. Total staff of Correctional Services Canada was about 15,000, of which just under 2,000 work at national headquarters in Ottawa. Overall, for federal and provincial systems we have about 1.3 inmates per staff member. The total cost of running Canada's justice and prison systems is over $10 billion annually, not counting the cost to victims and society (incalculable). More than half of all federal prisoners are aged twenty to thirty-four, and 5 percent of those are in for first-degree (intentional) murder, 13 percent for second-degree (non-intentional) murder, and 18 percent for violent sexual offences. In 1999, about 3,600 convicts were serving "life sentences," about a third of them "in the community."

That is, about 1,200 people convicted of killing someone are walking around free, every day. They enjoy juicy burgers and milkshakes, dance, party, smoke, have sex, and drink as they wish. But for their victims, all of life's pleasures came to a sudden end. There is something deeply wrong with this picture.

## RECENT DECLINES IN OVERALL CRIME RATES MASK DISTURBING TRENDS

Since the early 1990s crime in general has been declining in many Western nations, including Canada. This is most often attributed to better policing and crime technology, sophisticated forensics, electronic and GPS monitoring, video surveillance, satellite and Internet communications, cellphone-camera witnessing, retina and saliva testing, and so on. The decline, however, is most likely due to the fact that the populations of all Western democracies are aging fast, and producing fewer children, which means the highest-crime cohort— men aged fifteen to twenty-five, is shrinking, and so crime shrinks.

Here is a peek at the decline in Canada, though we note that this "decline" is occurring at an historically very high level of criminality.

Violent Crime in Canada

Rate per 100,000 population

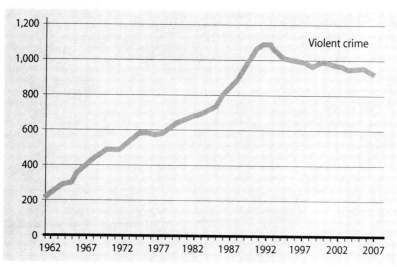

Rate for All Crimes, Property Crime, and Violent Crime (excluding vehicular traffic offences)

Rate per 100,000 population

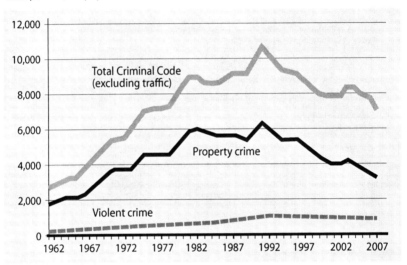

Rate of Violent Youth Crime (violent crime has risen dramatically among youth in the past decade or so)
Source: *The Daily*, Statcan, July 17, 2008.

Rate per 100,000 youth population (12 to 17 years)

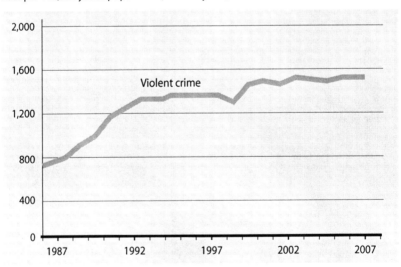

## A CONNECTION BETWEEN FALLING CRIME RATES AND ABORTION?

According to the Federal Bureau of Investigation's *Uniform Crime Reports*, the violent crime rate in the United States fell an astonishing 17.7 percent from 1998 to 2007, and the country's property crime rate fell 19.5 percent in one year, from 2006 to 2007. There is a possible and gruesome explanation for the steep decline in crime since the early 1990s. All Western democracies over the past four decades have embarked on what I have described in this book as the road to "libertarian socialism"—a condition in which a strident public philosophy of increased individual freedom has been combined with increasing claims to "rights" and benefits provided and funded by the State. Individuals are deemed to have more rights, and States more duties. A woman's legal "right" to abortion on demand is one of these things (tax-funded in Canada, but not in the United States). This is considered by radical feminists to be *the* banner achievement of modern women's liberation. No one knows for sure, but the following Snapshot explains the connection between abortion, crime, and its eugenic implications.

---

## SNAPSHOT

Abortion and Declining Crime Rates:
Is It Capital Punishment in the Womb?

What is the reason for the decline in crime in North America and many other Western democracies since the early 1990s? Here is a possible explanation.

At an estimated average rate for the past few decades of over 1,400,000 abortions per year for the United States (peak year was 1980 with 1,600,000), and a 100,000 per year average for Canada (with a peak year of about 113,000, the rate now declining slightly in both countries), it is clear that there are about 45 million *missing Americans*, aborted between 1973 and 2005 (Source: Alan Guttmacher Institute), and about 3 million *missing Canadians*. Fifty percent of these extinguished human lives were males.

This means there is *a missing cohort* of almost 25 million young males in North America who were simply not here to commit the millions of crimes a certain percentage of them would have committed during what would have been their highest crime-producing years, from age fifteen to twenty-five or so. There are also 25 million missing females, many of whom would have been teen mothers in poverty duplicating the irresponsible pregnancies and welfare habits of their own mothers. The effect of this would have been felt most sharply beginning in the early 1990s—which is exactly when we begin to see the sharp decline in crime in both countries. From a eugenics (cleansing populations) point of view, this has disturbing implications, for the following reasons:

About 37 percent of all U.S. abortions are performed on black women

(Source: Guttmacher Institute). And black men, at 6 percent of the U.S. population (half of the total of the 12 percent of all blacks in the U.S. population), are responsible for 50.4 percent of all murder and manslaughter charges in the United States (*World Almanac*, 2009), which is a rate *eight times higher* than their proportion of the U.S. population. So, millions fewer black male babies alive and maturing would have to mean proportionately less crime. Critics of eugenics refer to this abortion and lower crime rates result as "womb lynching."

We have a rough pointer to the continuation of the missing Canadian cohort in the *Canada Year Book* 2009, where we learn that whereas in 1971, 48 percent of the Canadian population was under age twenty-five, by 2006 only 31 percent were under twenty-five. That's a huge difference.

Someone will write a book someday about how the 1973 U.S. Supreme Court *Roe v. Wade* decision, which capitulated to the feminist demand for abortion on a number of complicated grounds, literally killed three birds with one stone: it calmed strident feminists by removing the biological penalty for unguarded fornication; it slowed natural population growth (deemed a matter of great panic at the time); and it reduced violent crime, especially crimes by black men.

In Canada, the aboriginal population, at about 3.8 percent of Canada's total (2006 census), accounts for about 22 percent of Canada's prison population, and about 23 percent of Canada's homicides (almost all by males). In other words, the male aboriginal 1.9 percent of Canada's population commits 23 percent of Canada's homicides. This is a homicide rate that is *thirteen times higher* than the male aboriginal proportion of Canada's population. There is no information on what percentage of Canadian abortions are performed on aboriginals. I suspect not very many. Indeed, aboriginal people are producing so many babies that Canada's aboriginal population is growing at the rate of 45 percent per decade. In contrast, Canada as a whole is growing at 8 percent per decade. But because the birth rate of Canadians more or less equals the death rate, this growth rate is mostly due to immigration.

Note: After I wrote this Snapshot I discovered chapter 4, "Where Have All the Criminals Gone?," in Steven D. Levitt and Stephen J. Dubner, *Freakonomics* (New York: Harper, 2005), which told this same story. There have been many clever efforts to dismiss the abortion-crime-rate thesis, presenting possible explanations, such as the rise and drop in cocaine epidemics, and other such culprits. However, they all assume that the 1973 pre-legalization abortion rates were about two-thirds the post-legalization rates, which is a gross exaggeration of the facts. The pre-legalization number in the United States was about 10 percent of the post-legalization rate (see Ian Gentles, "Good News for the Fetus: Two Fallacies in the Abortion Debate," in *Policy Review*, No. 40, Spring 1987, pp. 50–54).

# WHAT ABOUT MAJOR CRIME RATES?

For 2008, Statistics Canada reported declines in police-reported crime for the fifth year in a row (except PEI, which had a 7 percent increase). About one in five, or 20 percent of all reported crime in Canada is classified as violent, and of these, about 1 percent are homicides. Homicide was the only crime category to rise—about 2 percent—in 2008. Other crime increases were in driving offences (up 6 percent) and drug offences—a thirty-year high—with 102,000 offences, half of which were marijuana related. On a rather cheerful note, the Canadian Centre for Justice Statistics reported that Canada's crime rate for 2006 had "reached its lowest level in 25 years." However, in a Correctional Services Canada review of this report, we read that "this decrease was driven by declines in non-violent crime"[31] and that while the overall violent crime rate "remained relatively stable in 2006 . . . many other serious violent crimes increased in 2006." In other words, there was a slight increase in certain specific crimes, in a generally declining picture. Among them were:

- murders increased for the second year in a row
- aggravated assaults, the most serious form of assault, were up 5 percent—the second consecutive increase
- assault with a weapon or assault causing bodily harm increased for the seventh consecutive year, up 4 percent; now at the highest rate since the offence was introduced into the Criminal Code in 1983
- robberies increased for the second year in a row, up 6 percent
- robberies involving firearms rose 4 percent (accounting for one in eight robberies)
- kidnapping/forcible confinement continued to increase; over the past twenty years, the number of incidents reported to police *has increased sevenfold*, from about 500 in the mid-1980s, to over 4,000 in 2006
- youth crime increased by 3 percent, the first increase since 2003; the rate of youths accused of homicide was the highest since 1961
- drug crimes increased 2 percent; cannabis offences (which comprise 60 percent of all drug crimes) were down 4 percent, but cocaine offences were up 13 percent, and offences related to other drugs, including crystal meth (methamphetamine), rose 8 percent.

Note: The official facts on murder are misleading for Canada, and camouflage a deeper danger: Paciocco offers data showing that 30 percent of charges of first-degree murder end up in plea-bargained convictions for manslaughter, and 75 percent of second-degree-murder charges end up as manslaughter convictions. He adds that 90 percent of manslaughter charges draw custodial sentences of three years or less, and that in Ontario, only 53 percent of those convicted of manslaughter actually go to jail, whereas in Quebec almost all manslaughter offenders serve a median jail term of nine years.[32]

## CRIME—AND THE CRIMINALS—ARE DIFFERENT NOW

In the same report, CSC commissioner Keith Coulter warned that crime in Canada is changing its face, and speaking of criminals, said: "Roughly 9 out of 10 now have previous criminal convictions," with "more extensive histories of violence and violent offences in their criminal history, and far more are assessed as violence prone, hostile, impulsive, and aggressive. There has been an increase of more than 100 percent in the proportion of offenders who are classified as maximum security on admission [to prison]." Scary stuff. Coulter also announced that there has been a 33 percent increase in the number of criminals incarcerated with known gang affiliations, and that the number serving sentences for homicide has increased 14 percent, and now stands at one in every four male offenders [a.k.a. prisoners]. Also very worrisome is the number of offenders with "very serious mental health problems": 12 percent of male and 26 percent of females. And "four out of five offenders now arrive at a federal institution with a serious substance abuse problem, with one out of two having committed their crime under the influence of drugs, alcohol, or other intoxicants." He closed by remarking that CSC now has an offender population that is *more violent than ever*, requiring more interventions than ever, and that needs "to learn how to live as law-abiding citizens *for the first time*, as they have failed to learn the skills required to be productive members of society."

Under the Harper government, steps are being taken to address these faults, such as greater use of drug-detector dogs, improved perimeter surveillance, and better searches (to catch visitors who smuggle drugs to prisoners). There is also a move "to fix the problem in the parole system that allows early release of criminals."[33] From now on, criminals will have to "earn" parole. This government has also narrowed qualifications for house arrest (conditional release), ended sentence discounts for multiple murders, is phasing out the "faint hope" clause that allowed violent criminals to seek reduced parole conditions after fifteen years served, and has passed a Truth in Sentencing Act to ensure adequate sentences are actually served. All good, and hopefully a sign of more to come.

## INSIDE CANADA'S PRISONS

> *Canada's prison system is a place where criminal behaviour is rarely altered, true recidivism rates are hidden from the public, and the so-called "restorative justice model" is embraced with all the fanaticism of a cult so sure of its philosophy that it is openly hostile to criticism and reform.*
> —Michael Harris, *Con Game: The Truth About Canada's Prisons*

Correctional Services Canada has a published public policy of "Zero Tolerance for Alcohol in prison," "Zero Tolerance for Drugs in prison," and "Zero Tolerance for Sex in prison."

The following was largely derived from the must-read *Con Game: The Truth About Canada's Prisons*, by Irving Chair in Journalism Michael Harris, currently at St. Thomas University in New Brunswick.

On average, Canadian criminals serve 32 percent of their sentence before day parole, and just under 40 percent before full parole. Non-violent federal offenders who qualify for "accelerated parole review" may be paroled after serving only one-sixth of their sentence. For most of us who assumed that a sentence was handed down because it was deserved, the reality seems to be— justice defeated.

Some 64 percent of prisoners have not finished high school, 30 percent did not complete grade 8, and on standard literacy tests, the average prisoner scores at grade 7.5 level. Inmates retain all the rights of ordinary citizens (why is a mystery, as they have by their actions attacked society). At institutions like Fenbrook, in Gravenhurst, Ontario, inmates can buy their own TVs and for a small fee can watch restricted movies on HBO or Cinemac. They can also sub-scribe to over fifteen pornographic magazines. In 2000, 528 inmates at a Saskatchewan penitentiary were treated to a New Year's "pizza and porn" party organized by the unit managers, who organized the food and piped the porn over the prison's closed-circuit TV. There were 128 sex offenders in that prison enjoying all this. In 2002, the Sun newspaper chain reported a prison party that included tree-climbing and swimming naked while other inmates barbecued filet mignon.

All Canadian prisons have a very serious drug problem, and 80 percent of the drugs are taken "in the front door" by visitors, who due to Charter restrictions are difficult to search properly. A 2000 warden's memo recommended searching visitors in "a non-intrusive way." But drugs are smuggled in any available body cavity, even in baby diapers (children are never searched). One favourite is swallowing a condom filled with cocaine, tied with dental floss to a tooth. During the visit, it is pulled up and delivered. In 1999, guards seized 2.2 kilograms of cocaine, 164 grams of opiates, 5.4 kilograms of cannabis, and 1,916 gallons of "brew" (homemade alcohol). Visitors sue prisons at the first opportunity for personal-search infringements, and if from a minority, they sue for racial insult, too. One visitor was arrested for trying to smuggle in $51,000 worth of painkillers. Due to such Charter blockades, many drug dealers say they make more inside prisons than outside. At Joyceville Institution, in Ontario, 24 percent were intravenous-drug users, and a quarter of those started their drug habit in prison (guards are often pricked by infectious needles). Although official policy is zero tolerance for drugs—and sex—in Canada's prisons, Harris's book mentions many prison memos alerting inmates to the dangers of drugs, or that a cyanide-laced drug may be circulating, and about clean-needle policy. Prisons also distribute condoms and safe-sex guides (HIV/ AIDS levels in prison are ten times those outside), clean needles, and bleach kits. Two-thirds don't use condoms, and many share needles. If the drug use to which inmates are accustomed is threatened at all, they react with threats of major riots. One guard said that notwithstanding official policy, the real policy on drugs and alcohol is "tolerance and appeasement." In inmate surveys, 40 percent admitted to having used drugs in prison. (In 2009, violent offender Wade Gunoff, who was jailed for three years for beating and permanently disabling a sixty-one-year-old man, and who had already tested positive for drugs five times while in prison, told the parole board that he "won't quit smoking marijuana until he is freed from jail" [*National Post*, December 11, 2009].)

As for aboriginal offenders? The story is horrendous. Canada's justice system has responded to the aboriginal penal disaster by going aboriginal itself: there is now something akin to a separate system of justice for aboriginals in Canada that "ensures spiritual and cultural needs are addressed" during the criminal's "healing journey" [which is accomplished by means of the restorative justice methods described earlier]. Harris opines that Canada has never had a unified "aboriginal culture," however, so the correctional cocktail of native spirituality and customs actually "has corrupted native tribal traditions rather than incorporated them into correctional programs."

At any rate, along with all this special attention to presumed cultural roots (we really have no idea how genuine or nominal the "spirituality" of the average aboriginal is), there are infuriating instances of racial bias trickling down from the top: in April 1999, Canada's Supreme Court ruled that a lower court had not paid sufficient attention to the "nativeness" of killer Jamie Gladue, and suggested that natives should be judged in different ways from the rest of us. Result? Jamie served only six months for manslaughter. This has resulted in what Harris rightly calls "a racially based, two-tier justice system" [an extension of Canada's aboriginal apartheid system]. Some native reserves now sign custody contracts with CSC and take their criminals—even their first-degree murderers—home, even when they have first been sent to the white man's prison without any right of parole. In 1994, native offender Susanne Riley got herself into a healing circle and never served a single day in prison for murdering her common law husband.

As for that other special class of criminals—women? There are just under five hundred women in federal prisons, and just over five hundred serving time in the community. About 28 percent of female prisoners are serving sentences for murder. Harris reports that for the most part they are treated not as criminals but as "social victims." The trend has been to get women out of prison and into the community insofar as safely possible. Short of that, we have built them very expensive community-style minimum-security "living-unit" prisons where they enjoy group housing in cottages (as mentioned earlier, where they are called "clients" rather than prisoners) and do their own shopping, cooking, learning and laundry, and more or less decide on how their lives will be run while serving time. Karla Homolka cooked her own food, wore the clothes she liked (it is hard to tell guards, who do not wear uniforms at such prisons, from prisoners), wandered the grounds of her "prison" freely, and participated in fun-loving birthday parties. (When being transferred, she was flown more than once on private RCMP planes at a tag of $20,000 per flight.) This RJ approach, with its emphasis on rehabilitation rather than punishment, was a fiasco at the new Edmonton Institution for Women, where, in the first six months, there were assaults on staff, one inmate was murdered by another, suicide attempts, "and seven escapes of medium and maximum security inmates within eighteen days." Drug use and needle-sharing is rampant at Edmonton. In 2001, twelve of sixty-eight inmates tested positive for HIV/AIDS, and fifty for hepatitis C (as deadly).

As for human rights? They apply rigidly to all prisoners, under the U.N.'s Tokyo Rules, which mandate member nations to give prisoners all normal human rights. In 2002, Canada's Supreme Court, without authority of Parliament, granted prisoners the right to vote in federal elections, but as Harris points out, the judges "saw no contradiction in allowing the people who break the country's most serious laws to have a say in electing those who make them." Guards are another story. Their rights seem wholly ignored. They are routinely physically and verbally attacked and threatened. Inmates get away with a myriad of crimes against each other and against guards, which, Harris writes, "would be the subject of civil and criminal proceedings" if they happened anywhere else.

## VIOLENCE IN THE JAILS

In 2007–2008, there were fifteen major "disturbances" (a.k.a. riots), 3 hostage takings, 5 suicides, 49 assaults on inmates, and 33 escapes from minimum-security prisons. There were also 214 assaults on staff, 497 inmate assaults on each other, 45 staff injuries resulting, and 496 inmate injuries; 1,146 inmates drew new convictions while on supervision, of which 209 were for violent crimes. These latter are posted in CSC's *Annual Performance Report* for 2007–08 for inmate behaviour "*in the community*." Look at what these criminals, *released because they were judged no danger to public safety*, actually did. How can we avoid the basic question: *Why did you let them out?*

Here is the score:

|  | 2003–04 | 2004–05 | 2005–06 | 2006–07 | 2007–08 |
|---|---|---|---|---|---|
| Murders | 4 | 12˙ | 7 | 7 | 5 |
| Attempted Murder | 8 | 4 | 2 | 5 | 8 |
| Sexual Assaults | 14 | 15 | 15 | 26 | 21 |
| Major Assaults | 61 | 59 | 42 | 13 | 15 |
| Hostage Takings | 1 | 2 | 0 | 1 | 1 |
| Unlawful Confine. | 4 | 1 | 3 | 3 | 11 |
| Armed Robberies | – | – | – | 51 | 24 |
| Robberies | 124 | 94 | 112 | 65 | 90 |
| Other | 19 | 21 | 19 | 16 | 11 |
| ˙includes the murder of a CSC staff member | | | | | |

CSC makes light of this horrendous tally of crimes loosed upon the community by individuals already known to be violent. Are we to believe that CSC's "psychologists" had no inkling these incidents were very likely to occur? And if they did have an inkling, why were these people let out? Where's the "public safety"? In advising of these facts, CSC calmly writes that of the 16,500 or so "community flowthrough" of convicts they handle, these incidents occur at a 1.2 percent rate. So, suddenly, what is truly horrible, irresponsible, and unconscionable is . . . good performance? On March 31, 2009, there were 2,876 federal offenders who had been convicted of murder or Schedule 1 offences (violent offences), serving their sentences in the community on either day or full parole.[34]

## THEY SAY IMPRISONMENT IS TOO EXPENSIVE? BUT IS IT?

A protest often heard from the anti-punishment forces is that even if arguments such as those presented here are correct, it's just too expensive to keep criminals in jail. Parole, probation, rehabilitation, and supervision are much cheaper. The average annual cost of keeping a male convict in a Canadian federal prison in 2006–2007 was $90,744 (about $121,000 for a male maximum-security prisoner). The average federal female prisoner costs $166, 830. But it costs just under $23,076 a year to supervise a criminal on parole. So the "high cost" argument seems persuasive. Hence the big push for more RJ. At any rate, on this purely financial basis the pro-criminal lobby argues that we ought to jail fewer and parole more—and spend the difference on better programs. But wait! So far, the Canadian public has never been told the *true net costs of crime.* That is, not just the costs of the cell, food, guards, and so on, but the difference between this and the total costs arising from all the damage to all property and persons associated with each crime committed by criminals when they are *not* incarcerated. And we may never be told. But there are some clues.

In an important 1987 study that blew this argument up, conducted by the Rand Corporation for the U.S. Justice Department's National Institute of Justice, entitled "Making Confinement Decisions," Edwin Zedlewski, for the first time ever, attempted to estimate the *net cost* of crime to society. The study surveyed 2,190 prison inmates in California, Michigan, and Texas, and estimated that *the average felon out of prison commits 187 crimes a year,* costing society over $430,000 annually. (Ten percent of the group committed an estimated 600 crimes per year—exclusive of drug deals.) Zedlewski's study was savaged by the Hug-a-Thug lobby. But even if his estimates are halved, his argument was new and important: *Criminals cost us more free than when in jail.* This was echoed in a Metropolitan Toronto study that showed only 12 charges are brought for every 100 offences reported. For Canada, Peter McMurtry, a Toronto probation officer with thirty years' experience, said of his "clients" that many had committed numerous crimes, "maybe even thousands," before they got caught (*Toronto Star,* June 25, 1989).

## KILLERS ON THE LOOSE! PLAYING GOD AT THE NATIONAL PAROLE BOARD

*Canada's enduring commitment to conditional release [freeing prisoners, with supervisory conditions, before their sentence is up] reflects key values in Canadian society—tolerance, compassion, and the recognition that people can and do change . . . and the safe reintegration of offenders.*
—Vision and Strategic Plan 2000 and Beyond, National Parole Board

*Research has shown that criminal psychopaths who undergo cognitive and anger management training before release have an 82 percent recidivism rate compared with a rate of 59 percent for psychopaths who don't take the program. According to Dr. Robert Hare, the world's best-known expert on psychopaths, "These guys learn the words, but not the music."*
—Michael Harris, Con Game: The Truth About Canada's Prisons

"Safe reintegration"? Never mind the cozy, flattering self-congratulation about Canadian "tolerance" and "compassion." Tolerance may too often mean a lazy-minded acceptance of flabby moral standards and poor conduct, while compassion is often an easy emotion, accompanied, as it tends to be, by a false sense of emotional dignity that can blind us to deeper considerations. At any rate, no nation has cornered the market on these things, which are not "values" at all. They are human attitudes that historically have been quite malleable, are often manipulated for purposes of State, and even when they are properly dignified, they are the province of no nation or people in particular.

So what kind of psychobabble from on high are we being fed? What kind of "safe reintegration" do we see? I suggest mandatory reading for all parole board members should be Robert D. Hare, *Without Conscience: The Disturbing World of the Psychopaths Among Us*. The promotional material for the book gives the main conclusion:

Individuals with this personality disorder are fully aware of the consequences of their actions and know the difference between right and wrong, yet they are terrifyingly self-centered, remorseless, and unable to care about the feelings of others. Perhaps most frightening, they often seem completely normal to unsuspecting targets . . . Presenting a compelling portrait of these dangerous men and women based on 25 years of distinguished scientific research, Dr. Robert D. Hare vividly describes a world of con artists, hustlers, rapists, and other predators who charm, lie, and manipulate their way through life.[35]

Clearly, they are highly skilled at fooling parole boards, too. Dr. Hare has designed the Hare Psychopathy Checklist, which is now the world's most widely used screening system for detecting psychopathy in criminals. What is his professional and sobering conclusion? "On average, about 20 percent of male and female prison inmates are psychopaths," and . . . "psychopaths are responsible for more than 50 percent of the serious crimes committed," and . . . "the recidivism rate of psychopaths is about double that of other offenders," and . . . the recidivism rate for violent psychopathic criminals "is about triple that of other offenders."[36]

Hare also states not only that ordinary group therapy programs "do not work for psychopaths," but that psychopaths released from therapeutic community programs are four times more likely to commit a violent offence than other (non-psychopathic) participants; in other words, the therapy "may actually have made them worse!" And why? Because, Hare concludes, psychopaths "are perfectly happy with themselves, and so they see no need for treatment." Therapy just makes them more angry, and that's because, although their behaviour is obviously maladaptive for society . . . it is perfectly adaptive for them.

With this knowledge in mind, we read a 2009 parole board report informing the public about criminals who commit homicide "while serving the balance of their sentences in the community" under various forms of release or supervision, which had the following devastating things to tell us:

During a 33-year period from 1975 to 2008, some 508 criminals who, after extensive psychological testing and interviewing *were judged no danger to public safety* by the NPB, were released from prison and in that period *killed 557 perfectly innocent Canadians.* This is a horrifying and grievous tally, dropped on the page as if by happenstance.

It amounts to an utterly gratuitous homicide rate of 17 people per year over 33 years (perhaps another 17 between my first typing these words, and this book getting published). Three of these criminals were convicted of the multiple murders of a total of 37 people. The report cheerfully announces that these homicides accounted for "less than 3 percent of total homicides" in Canada in that 33 years (some 21,000—at about 600-plus per year). However, that is a misleading calculation. Officials are fiddling with the numbers.

Of the 508 killers mentioned, 10 percent were on day parole—they walked out and on the same day killed 49 Canadians. Thirty percent were full parolees who killed another 151 people. Sixty percent had served two-thirds of their sentence and therefore had been released by law. They proceeded to kill 302 innocent people. No one mentioned how many lives would have been spared if they had been kept in prison (the best public protection against crime other than jail is the aging of male criminals, which is what occurs while they are in prison).

As for the likelihood of reoffending? The NPB has this to say in its Performance Monitoring Report (2007–2008): In the period between 1996–1997 and 2006–2007, offenders on statutory release [who had to be released by law because they had served two-thirds of their sentences] were:

- Over six and a half times more likely to be convicted of a violent offence than offenders on full parole; and
- Over two times more likely to be convicted of a violent offence as offenders on day parole.
- For the decade 1997–2007, offenders on statutory release averaged 53 violent offence convictions per 1,000 offenders, per year, while full parole averaged 8 per 1,000, and day parole averaged 24 per 1,000.

### But Hold On! What are these numbers really telling us?

These "53 convictions per 1,000 offenders" (once put in international crime terms per 100,000 offenders) becomes 5,300 per 100,000. However, these are not merely police-reported *incidents*, they are *convictions!* This means that the violent offenders Canada releases into the population long before they have served the sentences meted out by our judges as their just deserts, which means justice was unfulfilled, are one of the most violent populations on earth! Why do I say this? Because although Canada has a rate for *all criminal incidents* of about 7,000 per 100,000 (UN figure above, for 2007), we know that about 12 percent of these are *violent crimes*, which equals 840 per 100,000 in Canada's general population. So if we compare the 5,300 to the 840 figure, we can say that the offenders we release back into society are over six times more likely to commit a violent crime than the rest of us.

*If we already know they are six times more violent, then why are we releasing them by law at two-thirds of their sentences?* "Public safety" cannot be the motive, because obviously if we keep them in until the end of their sentences, they cannot commit the new murders, assaults, sexual assaults, robberies and so on that we know with considerable certainty they are going to commit. Which means these crimes would be at least postponed for many years, and many lives saved. And *that* is sufficient reason not to release them until we absolutely have to.

There have been several suits instigated against—and many settled quietly by—CSC for having released dangerous criminals into society where they have wreaked havoc. Good. Canadians harmed by these soft-headed policies should sue the hell out of everyone responsible, from starry-eyed caseworkers, to parole board members, to the legislators who have made this travesty possible. That's tough though. NPB members cannot be sued for mistakes made in the pursuit of their duties (another example of the *droit administratif* described in chapter 1), and public knowledge of the numerous lawsuits by the families of those raped, assaulted, or killed by parolees is kept under lock and key. In *Con Game*, Harris mentions twenty such suits brought since 1989 and one $1.6 million lawsuit brought by Mark Turner, a reoffender who is suing because he claims he never should have been released!

Now, Canadians are supposedly against capital punishment, and one of the reasons given is that there have been innocent people executed by the State. Perhaps true, and if so, horrible. But in a sentence that rings with an equally horrible truth (in which I substitute updated numbers), Harris wrote: "If a court system in a jurisdiction with capital punishment ever executed 557 innocent victims in 33 years, it would be abolished. Yet CSC and the National Parole Board trivialize this horrific record behind heartless statistical percentages ... Their sin is not imperfection, as CSC executives sarcastically claim, but a deadly arrogance that is blind to the human misery their policies cause."[37]

So now I propose a thought experiment as a Snapshot.

---

## SNAPSHOT
The National Parole Board's Robots

Let us try to imagine what the public would think if the National Parole Board had lots of cute little mobile robot devices—you know, cuddly little fellers that are computer-programmed to do nothing at all most of the time.

But some of them are programmed to fire a bullet into a crowd at random and without warning at some unspecified time after they are set free. The NPB places hundreds of these robots "in the community"—in malls like the Eaton Centre, in Toronto, where they simply mosey around, gliding up and down the hallways, in and out of stores, minding their own business. We know statistically that at an unpredictable time in the future, a predictable number of these robots will fire their bullet into the crowd and a predictable number of innocent Canadians will die.

That is my thought experiment.

Now I ask: Could someone explain to the Canadian public how the National Parole Board releasing into the public previously identified violent criminals who have a known rate of repeat violent crime is different from sending random killing-robots to roam about in public? I suggest there is no difference whatsoever—except that the robot feels even less emotion about this than the criminal, and has no motive.

However, if our parole board did in fact send such robots into the public to kill with predictable certainty, there would be violent public fear and outrage. The NPB would be dragged before a public commission (a Canadian must), and those responsible for release decisions severely punished. Actually, they would be charged as accessories to murder.

But ... what is the difference between the predictable repeat offender and the predictable robot?

So is it not reasonable to suggest that whenever officials release criminals into society prior to the end of their sentences who assault and kill, those making such decisions should pay a price? If the threat of even minor punishment were held over them—lose their jobs, publish their names—I suggest they would never grant parole to a violent criminal of any kind. And that is because they are never 100 percent certain. And if is true they are never 100 percent certain, they must be uncertain, which means they are aware that some members of the public may be injured or die due to their decisions. But they do it anyway. Why? Clearly, if we are reluctant to punish our parole officials for their fatal decisions, then we ought to eliminate parole and early release altogether.

On the very day I was writing this passage, I read of Justice of the Peace Fraser Hodge, of Kamloops, British Columbia, who, against the pleas of police officers that Allan Schoenborn, who had a lengthy criminal record and had already been arrested two times that same week, ordered his release. He said he was "prepared to give the man a break." Schoenborn showed remorse, and said "God bless you" to Justice Hodge. Then he returned to his trailer home and murdered his three children. He stabbed his ten-year-old daughter to death and smothered his two sons, eight and five. I don't know how Justice Hodge can live with the knowledge that those murders would not have happened if he had not released their father.

National Parole Board members (presently they number thirty-seven) have traditionally needed no special training for their jobs (though selection is now more demanding), and they have a large number of reviews or hearings per year. Federal day parole is granted 71 percent of the time, and full parole 43 percent. Day parole fails 17 percent of the time, and full parole, 27 percent, because convicts breach the conditions of release. In Canada, by law, most federal prisoners must be released automatically after serving two-thirds of their sentence (this "statutory release" is not applicable to violent criminals serving life sentences or indeterminate sentences).

But so-called "accelerated parole" gets a lot of criminals out after serving only one-sixth of their sentence, full parole after one-third. "The National Parole Board is powerless to stop the [legally mandated] release of a criminal, *even when they believe the criminal will offend again*" (National Parole Board media release, October 26, 2009). The board also prides itself on issuing "pardons" to former prisoners. But why they do this is not explained. As others have remarked, if you are going to take the view that crime cannot be helped, that it is some kind of determined or socially caused event, then what is there to pardon? Clearly, the mere performance of granting pardons implies a standard of direct moral culpability that is not officially endorsed by the folks at CSC. Some 350,000 pardons have been issued since 1970.

At any rate, even though there is no board accountability or repercussion for personal decisions that have led to the harm or death of innocent victims, many families of murdered Canadians have successfully sued CSC for terrible release decisions. The board itself has immunity from all prosecution, and obviously is another government institution where there is no penalty for gross incompetence. I was astonished when working on the first edition of this book to read of one board member *who insisted that even his mistakes were "correct"*! In defending himself against charges that Melvin Stanton and Daniel Gingras should never have been released (because both murdered again while on parole), Chairman Fred Gibson said: "I'm not prepared to characterize those two particular decisions as bad decisions" (*Toronto Star*, June 21, 1989).

I submit that, when a paroled killer murders again, then by definition his early release was not only a bad decision but a tragic one. But here we have a public officer *defending* decisions that clearly led directly to death. He sent a killing-robot into society. As I said, such a system is structured to weaken public protection. In response to all this, the Canadian Sentencing Commission recommended in 1987 that parole be abolished so that "truth in sentencing" could be restored. We are now more than two decades along and the Harper government is about to do just that.[38] But the commission's price was too high: it wanted to eliminate parole, but in its place to set maximum sentencing at twelve years—surely a bad joke. Alas, parole has continued in Canada, even though the same Daubney Committee mentioned above had already tabled yet another analysis of the faults of the system, underlining its earlier report that "there is no very accurate system for predicting violence," and that with present criteria, parole predictions would "more often be wrong." This committee studied 52,484 releases between 1975 and 1986 and found that fully 130 had resulted in convictions for murder or manslaughter, 5 of them by paroled murderers. These 130 homicides, we are told, were "only" 2 percent of the more than 7,000 in the eleven-year period. But the rate works out to 1 killing per 400 parolees. In other words, *as a group these parolees were ten times as likely to kill.* The committee then had the temerity to say: "Even if we were prepared and could afford to [keep all such violent offenders in jail], *these homicides might only have been delayed*" [emphasis added]. This is an astonishing statement, as if 130 irreplaceable human lives were some kind of disposable inventory, or grist for the great parole experiment; that we might as well expose your son or daughter, or mine, to a bit more violence now, while they're children, because they have the same chances of getting nailed later anyway.

This is extremely offensive reasoning and false, to boot. First, we have seen that we *save* money in society at large by keeping such offenders in prison; second, perhaps the most powerful predictor of violence is age. As mentioned earlier in the chapter, as most criminals age, they get less violent. That's a strong argument for keeping them in until the end of their sentences. Then, if society is unhappy with the result, we can always lengthen sentences. But *postponement of an evil act is always a good*, and the committee had no right to play statistical executioner and decide on our behalf that 130 more murdered today is the same as 130 murdered ten years from now. It is not. First of all, those (if we accept the board's argument) who might be killed anyway got ten extra years of living. Those in charge of public safety are absolutely obligated to use any legal means at their disposal to spare society a present life-threatening danger, for a danger withheld from society now is always better than a danger released into it now, even if we could prove that the same danger might occur years later (though it is less likely if the culprit is twenty years older).

## HOW THE CHARTER ENDANGERS US ALL

We have been led to think of our Charter of Rights and Freedoms as our friend and protector. But in the case of criminal justice, we have also slowly become aware that since 1982, when the Charter became law, it has too often been used to protect the criminal—often endangering society ("Charter Bolsters Rise in Prison Litigation," *Globe and Mail*, June 24, 1989). Here's why. Before the Charter came along, evidence presented in a criminal trial, *even if illegally procured* (the bloodied knife, say) was admitted *if relevant to the case* (*Regina v. Wray*). Suppose a police officer stopped someone for drunk driving and when the driver aroused suspicion searched the trunk of the car without a warrant, finding a severed limb and a bloodied knife. Before the Charter came along, the knife and the limb, even though obtained without a warrant, could be admitted as evidence in the subsequent trial for murder because they were relevant.

But no longer. Today, the Charter (sec. 24.2) says that such evidence "shall be excluded" *if* admission of it "would bring the administration of justice into disrepute." There is no talk of *relevance* any longer, and the judge alone decides on the "if." So, if the judge is a pro-criminal determinist, he just ignores the knife and the limb, and the murderer goes free or gets off with a lesser charge, and the police are scolded publicly for improper policing. Thus are obviously guilty murderers and other violent criminals getting away with murder under the Charter, not because they are innocent, nor because their trial was unfair, but because some technical detail in properly procuring evidence was overlooked. It's fine to discipline the police severely for abridgement of procedures. But it is not acceptable to release violent criminals we know are guilty into society when all the evidence clearly convicts them, on the grounds that some of the procedures used to obtain the evidence were technically improper.

After all, *evidence may sometimes be unfairly procured. But this does not mean that the trial in which it is used is unfair.* Our *Charter* does not make this distinction, but we can and should, because section 24.2 is being used to free clearly guilty criminals, thus endangering society, and there is nothing, absolutely nothing, that brings justice into disrepute with greater speed and certainty than this. Paciocco teaches the distinction between a *rule utilitarian* (someone who says you have to procure evidence strictly by the rules, or its not admissible), and a *case utilitarian* (it's too bad if there were mistakes made, but we cannot let a guilty criminal go free just because police didn't have a warrant, etc.). The first type believes justice is brought into disrepute by flouting the rules of evidence. The second type thinks justice is brought into disrepute when clearly guilty criminals are let go. Paciocco is the first type. I am in the middle. We can't allow any storm trooper police to maraud over society to get their evidence. On the other hand, guilty people should not be allowed to go free, for any reason.

So perhaps there is a middle way? What about allowing the improperly procured evidence *if it is relevant*, as we always used to do, but reducing the sentence by a fixed amount (just as we do when plea bargaining) as a way to punish the justice system, so to speak. This way, the criminal gets punished (convicted) for his or her wrongdoing, and the justice system gets punished, too.

# WHAT IS TO BE DONE?

## 1. Too Many in Jail?

Many committees and commissions on crime have said that Canada incarcerates too many people for petty crimes (our incarceration rate is 108 per 100,000—not that high). For such crimes most Canadians would probably support a penalty *and* repayment by the criminal of some kind, instead of a jail term. However, it is not morally sufficient simply to apologize sincerely and replace something stolen or damaged. A society that believes in freedom and responsibility must have the damage repaired and *also* exact a just punishment, or a price, for the crime itself. This can be accomplished by a combination of repayment and community work to help the needy, ordinary public works like public construction, or by work for the victims themselves if they want that. Some RJ would fit here. Most of us would be happy to know that first-time minor offenders were making restitution and "working it off," so to speak. But if they become repeaters—it's off to prison.

## 2. Minimum Determinate Sentencing.

The deplorable situation must end whereby judges are forced to second-guess parole boards and social workers, thereby handing down longer than normal sentences in some tortured estimate of what the real time served might eventually be. We must move to a system of minimum determinate sentencing so that everyone—especially prospective criminals—becomes aware of the minimum jail term carried by each crime. In this way, society's prohibitions will be inculcated and the proper moral climate restored. Then, if society feels that public danger is increasing (or decreasing), it can with confidence legislate sentences up or down. But it will no longer legislate its penalties only to have them overturned by social workers and corrections officials with an ideological or therapeutic axe to grind. If society wants to "rehabilitate" criminals it can do so *within* the sentence period, and afterwards. (Rather, we should say "habilitate" them: as criminology expert Stanton Samenow says: "You can rehabilitate an old house. You can rehabilitate a stroke victim. But there is nothing to rehabilitate in a criminal because he never acquired moral values or concepts of responsible living." In a phrase acquiring increasing currency among criminologists, many criminals are simply not fixable because they are "moral imbeciles.") Or, a judge could always *add* rehabilitation time to the basic sentence. Such sentencing would be a "cost plus" system, whereby rehabilitation programs would be part of, or an addition to, incarceration, not substitutes for it.

## 3. Early Release.

All forms of parole and early release should be eliminated entirely for many of the above reasons. The former undermines justice, demoralizes and endangers society, undermines sentencing, is based on extremely tenuous assessment

THE CRIMINAL JUSTICE SYSTEM

procedures no better than fortune-telling, and creates inequities between the sentences of different criminals, thus heaping more scorn on the system from criminals themselves and accentuating one of their problems—disrespect for the fairness of society. We must also end day parole—except for emergency medical treatment. Thousands of violent criminals are getting out on day passes to party with friends, celebrate their own birthdays, do shopping trips, go to sporting events, you name it. For there are sometimes grisly consequences when day parole goes wrong. Even though prison guards had warned the warden not to give Daniel Gingras escorted day parole, he was granted a "birthday pass" to West Edmonton Mall in 1987. Then, as feared, Gingras overpowered his guard and escaped. He remained at large for fifty-seven days and killed two innocent people. Harris writes that CSC "censored the official report of this bloody fiasco." Enough, we say. Finally, Canadian provinces must stop issuing welfare cheques, as they presently do, to criminals at large who are wanted by the police.

**4. The Moral Life of Society.**
Principles of justice and equity must be restored to the system. Politicians and legislators, from top to bottom, must understand that moral life and decisions are utterly independent of how good or bad someone is feeling, or how poor or rich their family was; that one man in the vilest of circumstances who feels disgusted with society may decide to do charitable work, while another just as disgusted may decide to murder a total stranger. Nothing in their equally deprived situations dictates these choices. We must eradicate the slave psychology (the criminal as slave to his circumstance and emotions) permeating the justice system in Canada.

**5. The Young.**
The mere idea that under the 1984 Young Offenders Act a person under eighteen could violently kill an innocent person and suffer only three years in prison was a moral scandal and a severe public danger. As an experienced criminal court judge remarked to me, "People think young offenders are rosy-cheeked innocents. But most of them are strong, aggressive, pumped-up males in their physical prime. They're violent, and scary, and they know the score. They know they can't get hurt much by the law. So crime pays handsomely for them. In fact, older criminals are using them to do crime for them. Having a record doesn't mean anything to them. They're proud of it." The newer Youth Criminal Justice Bill of 2001 now lets a province send a violent criminal as young as fourteen to adult court. But our chart on youth crime, above (see page 362) shows that we have been doing something wrong, because violent youth crime has been on the rise.

## 6. How about Capital Imprisonment?

The Canadian public has long and often expressed its wish to restore capital punishment for heinous capital offences accompanied by a clear confession and conviction. But Parliament voted (in a secret ballot) against the wishes of the people—a strange but not uncommon practice in Canada. I think what matters is not so much that criminals do or do not get executed (for justice is imperfect, and some innocent persons have been wrongly executed, which is a terrible miscarriage), even though execution is a certain deterrent for the person executed—but that retribution and public safety can be equally well served by keeping offenders away from society for life. Just deserts and public safety are the main issues, not an all-or-nothing position on execution. Thus, all can be satisfied and the public protected by a system of "capital imprisonment." Such a sentence would mean you never get out and will die in prison. Societies wealthy enough to be squeamish about execution for heinous crimes are wealthy enough to afford this moral luxury.

# 13: MULTICULTURALISM, IMMIGRATION, AND TERRORISM
## THE LINKS

*Things fall apart; the center cannot hold.*
—W.B. Yeats, "The Second Coming"

We fear expressing our honest views on multiculturalism because we don't want to be labelled a racist or bigot. But a dislike for a multiculturalism policy has nothing to do with disliking other cultures or ethnic groups. For, multiculturalism is not a culture. It is a clever government policy invented to respond both to the continuing weakening of Canada's own cultural heritage and to the resulting growth in potential for clashes between strong foreign cultures within our borders. My objective is to expose the danger to Canadian unity posed by this policy. So let us begin with a bald truth about a bald lie to be found, of all places, in Canada's Constitution.

Section 27 of the Canadian Charter of Rights and Freedoms states that the Charter shall be interpreted "in a manner consistent with the preservation and enhancement of the multicultural heritage of Canadians." That's the bald lie.

Here's the bald truth: Canada has always been a *multi-ethnic* nation. But it has never been a *multicultural* nation.

Shortly, we will examine this important distinction.

Not so long ago, after centuries of "normal" ethnic frictions, Canada was arguably becoming a more colour-blind and race-blind nation, primarily because we were the very fortunate historical beneficiaries of a unique and complete cultural heritage that worked very well and that I defend in this chapter. Immigrants came to Canada to be part of that heritage. They fully expected their host country would expect them to *assimilate*. They came expecting to embrace Canada's culture wholeheartedly, and to the extent they wished, maintain their old ways privately at their own expense. They wanted their kids to respect the best of their former homeland, but to become "Canadian"—with no hyphens. Most Western nations operated this way until after World War II. Whenever ethnic troubles arose, the typical reactions were tighter policing and controlling of borders, outlawing or controlling immigration of this or that kind (Quebec, for example, has its own immigration controls), enforcing national language laws (Quebec, again), mandatory civics and national history classes, public schooling that induces specific cultural beliefs, ritual anthem singing, prayers, and national celebrations and religious holidays.

But by the mid-1960s things began to change as a new postwar radicalism began to infect all Western nations, much of which was expressed by university students attacking Western universalizing values and culture.[1] It's hard to blame the young for wanting a better world, for the disaster of two world wars had not left them much faith that there was *any* superior culture in all of human history. So the new thinking gravitated away from all oppressive or dominating moral regimes, and toward a peculiarly new individualistic *moral* relativism. Expressions such as "You do your thing, and I'll do mine," and books with titles such as *I'm OK, you're OK*, appeared. Even when it came to statements of fact, we began to hear strange utterances such as, "Well, it may be true for you, but it's not true for me." No one bothered to ask how any certain fact can be true and false at the same time.

Neither did anyone bother to ask: "Is it possible for an individual to sub-scribe to a *moral system* that includes no one else?" Nevertheless, the felt-liberation provided by these new attitudes—now I can do whatever I want without so much fear of being judged—led naturally to the *cultural*-relativism bandwagon: all cultures are unique, so don't judge my culture. This idea had been taught in anthropology classes for some time as a liberal antidote to political oppression. But it was now to assume the status of scripture. In a nutshell, it was the belief that all cultures are equal, relative, and sovereign in their own domains, and (as President Obama recently stated—"no one culture is superior to any other"). I disagree with Obama on that score, and I will explain why below.

At any rate, this postwar cultural-relativism dogma came along at the same time as there was growing pressure from people living in Third World countries to leave their politically and economically unstable homes and seek a better life in a superior country like Canada. Indeed, I would say that if noth-ing else, the simple fact of immigration is a foot-vote for cultural superiority. At a minimum, many of the countries they were leaving were clearly undevel-oped and politically oppressive, if not violent societies floundering in hopeless cultural, legal, and economic backwaters. Plainly, they were inferior cultures that in many instances frightened their own citizens. A lot of them were what more honest anthropologists would by the end of the twentieth century call "sick societies."[2]

Simultaneously, Canada was experiencing its own "Quiet Revolution" during which a previously quiescent Quebec population was agitating for a more prominent place in the national sun. So Prime Minister Lester Pearson struck the "Bi & Bi" Commission (Bilingualism and Biculturalism) to study that situation, and then in 1970, just two years into Pierre Trudeau's first term, we got violence and murder in the name of ethnic separatism during the FLQ (Front de libération du Québec) crisis. Meanwhile, other cultural groups led by Canada's Ukrainian community grew alarmed that they were going to be left out of what looked like an official redefinition of Canada. So an alarmed government soon ditched the Bi & Bi Commission for something to be called "multiculturalism."

## CANADA'S NEW, OFFICIALLY EMPTY CULTURE

Here was a new concept—a kind of Big Multi-culture Tent—that was going to be erected by the State over all citizens. It was to be *inclusive* (all Canada's "cultures" would be in the tent); *egalitarian* (all cultures would be treated equally); and culturally and morally *relativist* (no one culture would be deemed superior to another, nor be allowed to judge another negatively). This was to be the new, but empty, Canadian national "culture" declaring that we are united . . . by our differences. What? Few perceived the lie (mentioned above) or the inherent logical and practical flaws in this equation. But politicians saw its advantages immediately. As Peter Brimelow pointed out, leaning on Gordon Tulloch's now-famous "public choice" theory: "Individuals tend to act rationally to maximize their self-interest"; and "When political parties are in competition with each other, [they] *will seek to segment the undifferentiated electorate.* They will appeal to it on the basis of whatever salient characteristics they can identify, offering programs with benefits concentrated on the special interest group, and costs dispersed across all taxpayers."[3] Brimelow acutely described the result of this: "A frantic *auction* develops between the political parties on the one hand, and the ethnic groups with their newly-subsidized professional leaders," fundraisers, and grant-seekers, on the other. As a result, the new policy went largely unchallenged. It was simply enshrined as a lie in Canada's Charter of Rights and Freedoms in 1982, and not long after, Canada went international with full-page announcements coast to coast that we were "the world's first multicultural society." There was little serious objection, and little notice of the obvious contradictions.

## CONTRADICTIONS IN CANADA'S MULTICULTURAL POLICY

When the government of Canada proudly invited Canadians to "Celebrate the World's First Multiculturalism Act" in 1988—an act supported by all parties—it advertised eight principles on which the act was based. Not surprisingly, many of these principles were in conflict with each other. The principles were:

- Multiculturalism for all Canadians
- Advancement of multiculturalism within a bilingual framework
- Equality of opportunity
- Preservation and enhancement of cultural diversity
- Elimination of discrimination
- Establishment of affirmative measures
- Enhancement of heritage languages
- Support for immigrant integration

It all sounded good, except . . . how could "immigrant *integration*" be achieved at the same time as "enhancement of cultural *diversity*"? Integration to what? By "integration," our leaders avoided the term "assimilation" (to gradually lose your old ways, and adopt new ones). But if we believe, as I do, that real citizenship is about sharing a common home, rather than living in a motel; about a kind of national friendship, a bonding with fellow citizens in common principles and values—what one observer has called "patriotic assimilation"—then to what beliefs and deep-culture bonds were newcomers to be integrated? Their own? Those of Canada's inherited deep culture the policy was now subordinating? With the State's manipulative egalitarianism? How was "*equality* of opportunity" to mesh with "affirmative measures" (tax-funded *reverse discrimination*)? Would government get "advancement" of its bilingual framework by *forcing* some immigrants to use French (as Quebec subsequently decided to do)? There are more than six thousand languages spoken in the world. So how many of the hundreds of "heritage" languages would be *enhanced*? Whose heritage? At whose expense? What would the Ministry of Citizenship, Immigration and Multiculturalism have to say when the soon to be publicly subsidized core traditions, religions, and ethics of each different culture came into conflict with English- or French-Canadian culture? There was no mention of this possibility because the committee simply had no idea. It was gambling that its expensive effort to present a Coca-Cola image of one big happy Canadian family all singing the same culture-lite song would suffice. Superficially, it sounded sweet.

But the act was the first step, not toward, but away from Canadian unity in the name of a self-contradictory policy that has made us a more race-conscious, race-sensitive, and culturally divided people than ever before.[4] As Canadian author Salim Mansur (a Muslim and professor at the University of Western Ontario) has written, the policy of multiculturalism "was an invitation to newcomers to maintain their own respective religious-cultural values, while embracing cultural relativism—the belief that all cultures are equal." As Mansur points out, what we have really been promoting is not "multiculturalism," but rather "a *plural mono-culturalism* that allows cultural groups to withdraw into their own spaces." In the process, multiculturalism had introduced a pan-Canadian disrespect for Canada's historical national "culture"—a term that calls for examination.

## WHAT DOES "CULTURE" MEAN?

There are three levels of "culture," in descending order of importance that ought to concern us: deep culture, skin-deep culture, and folk culture.

*Deep culture* has to do with the most important components of culture. These are the things that bind and unify a people, that most of us are born into, but that can also be adopted or rejected at will, such as a common language and thought (including the literature, poetry, history, and foundational ideas of a culture); a common religion (core theological beliefs, myths, symbols, and traditions); and common political and legal institutions (including the laws, rights, freedoms and duties held in common by a people). These are things a unified "people" has inherited or *learned*, will go to war to defend—or to propagate—and for which they are usually prepared to die. However, a deep culture cannot be claimed as something that belongs by right to any one race or ethnicity—even though it is a fact of life that many people of the same ethnicity tend to share a deep culture.

*Skin-deep culture.* This is the second component of a culture, which comprises the superficial (literally, "on the surface") unwilled things that are part of us all, such as our ethnicity, colour, and physical features—things over which we have no control. We are born that way. However, there is no such thing as a black or yellow or brown culture, because "culture" is not normally defined by such unchangeable things.[5] People of any ethnicity can choose to participate in, or to share, or sustain (or neglect) a deep culture. But no one can share their skin-deep culture or ethnicity. We may choose to band together solely for reasons of skin-deep culture if we have nothing else in common. But deep culture is usually the stronger force, and that is why two fellows with, say, common Asian features, or a common colour, but with different languages or strongly opposed political philosophies or religious beliefs, will find they do not have much in common except—features and colour. That is not enough to bind people deeply. A Japanese-American from Hawaii, for example, may have little feeling for Japanese culture, and vice versa. Conversely, people of very different colours and features may share everything else. A close black friend and I have different colour and features, but we are culturally almost identical–same religion, language, literature, sports, work ethic, and so on. I submit that what is dangerous and disorienting about our new multicultural regime is its tendency to suppress the real significance of important deep cultural differences, and to equate these with race and ethnicity. These two terms, "race" and "ethnicity," are often used interchangeably, but may be different. For example, an ethnic German and an ethnic Pole may racially both be Caucasians.

*Folk culture.* This is the most recognizable, most aggressively marketed, and sometimes the most evocative aspect of culture. But it may also be the weakest, most casual aspect, having to do with the externals of dress, foods, folk songs, folk dances, folklore, and so on. Anyone can *effortlessly* share in them. At costume parties, for example, people enjoy doing just that. Folk culture has to do with cultural externals, adopted, sustained, or shucked at will. I have good friends who love Scottish dancing, though they are not Scots. Of course, tourists the world over often imagine they are genuinely part of a foreign culture for a time when they eat their biftek frites in Paris, hear Mexican serenades, drink their latte in Florence, or ride a camel in Egypt. They may feel such experiences with deep intensity. But there are lots of Indians who do not like curry, Scots who have never worn a kilt, and blacks who do not listen to reggae. Keeping these things as an expression of our identity, or making them such, preserving or forgetting them, is up to us. There are also many powerful folk symbols that all nations strive to maintain, such as the works and reputations of their great artists, coins and stamps carrying the images and words of great political leaders and warriors; national anthems; national sports, natural wonders, animals, trees, maple leaves, and so on. Such symbols are concrete, but the ideals and feelings they evoke are emotional. Ice hockey is considered the national sport in Canada, and raises us up when we win. But if you look around the arena, you will see mostly white faces and white players, just as when you look around a Canadian pro basketball team you will see mostly black players (and many American ones). Same with pro baseball. We love them when they are winning. But if they lose consistently, or go on strike (as did the Toronto Blue Jays baseball team), the ardour cools. We love folk culture with a conditional passion. Few will die for it.

## THE "SOFT" AND THE "HARD" MULTICULTURALIST

It is important to distinguish between what may be called the soft and hard varieties of multiculturalist. The *soft* type is generally somebody who loves folk culture, eats frequently at ethnic restaurants, likes endearing national, religious, and ethnic customs—"they make Canada *so neat!*"—and mostly wants everyone to get along. This type is a kind-hearted peacemaker who will downplay deep-culture differences, is on the lookout to squelch every ism in sight: racism, sexism, lookism, ageism, and so on, wherever they may surface—and feels that cultural and moral relativism are badges of open-mindedness. If, say, you defend Canada's deep culture and don't like seeing it watered down, this type will by reflex consider you intolerant, a bigot, or both. By showing a preference for your own deep culture, you must be oppressing someone!

However, a genuine concern is that many of the sincere people who promote this kind of tolerance, inclusiveness, and diversity (these are their buzzwords) are simply unaware they are behaving as unwitting instruments in the weakening of Canada's deep culture, of the real ties that bind. They see the tree, but not the roots. They either assume there is no meaningful deep culture, or if there is, it is best to keep it private (itself a contradiction, because what would an unshared culture be?), and to leave behind any non-inclusive divisions the deep culture may cause. So what they are in fact practicing is a form of reverse bigotry, for they insist you support an untruth—the myth that all cultures are equal and compatible. You are forbidden to favour a real culture (especially if it is the dominant Western one). You are to favour only an empty, administrative "multi"-culture. But this dogma is itself very oppressive.

The *hard* multiculturalist is another type altogether. Easily inflamed ideologically, this person may be actively engaged in an attitudinal or even an activist-style war against Western civilization. The enemy is any religion that dictates morality, any kind of colonialism or imperialism, the military-industrial complex, and the entire economic, corporate, and private property system of the West—especially of America with its supposed political philosophy of acquisitiveness and me-first individualism (though America has always been a far more community-based society than most of us grant). Many of the hardest multiculturalists are closet Marxists by another name. Such persons will resist the idea that America or Canada have ever had any core culture or people, and so will speak only of *cultures* and of *peoples*, plural, rather than singular. The famous American motto *E pluribus unum* (Out of many, one), they reverse, to "Out of one, many." For them, all talk of assimilation is deemed a form of "cultural genocide."

Canada has lots of this latter type teaching courses on topics like native rights. A few years ago I helped a black male high school student write a paper recommending native assimilation and the ending of Canada's aboriginal apartheid system. When we went to see his teacher, her desk was covered with books promoting native rights and revolution in Canada. She disagreed with his position, and tried to soothe him by saying: "It's all about *identity*." He responded: "Ma'am, I'm a black man. We were slaves. But we got Magic Johnson, Bill Cosby, and Oprah. We got *identity*, and we didn't need tax-free reservations and $8 billion a year to create it." She all but ran us out of her office. Here was a Canadian public-school teacher calling for more race identity, not less; less unity, not more.

## THE MULTICULTURAL INVERSION: HOW DEEP CULTURE GOT REDUCED TO YOUR BLOOD, OR YOUR T-SHIRT

One of the damaging—but quite intentional—effects of modern multicultural policy is that it seeks to weaken deep culture by reducing it to the skin-deep or folk-culture level. Identity politics (as for the teacher above) then tends to form around your blood and/or your T-shirt. It is considered either a permanent part of you that ought to be exalted (your blood and race), or a set of folk customs you ought to identify deeply with, or both. So-called "race-consciousness" is formed around these things. You are encouraged to be more authentically black (not an "Oreo"), or more native, rather than less, and so on. In February 2010, a Kahnawake native band south of Montreal issued an order to evict two dozen residents on their reserve because they had insufficient native blood, and "were running around with red hair or blond hair." The band press attaché, Joe Delaronde, worried that "we sound like a bunch of Nazis here," then went on to justify acting like a Nazi. Just so, Canada is now more race-conscious than ever. The covers of Bell telephone directories, public transport ads, and most corporate ads these days will often show a handful of ultra-happy people doing something very ordinary, proud of their skin-deep selves, and wearing their folk-culture regalia as they talk on the phone, use computers, walk to the subway. Who doesn't feel the explicit manipulation? The formula is one Black, one Asian, one Woman, one Muslim, one Native, one Child, one White guy, one fellow with coffee-coloured skin, one white-haired Senior, one Disabled, and so on. The multicult presented in these images is all externals, all skin colour, or gender, with some T-shirt-type paraphernalia—a sari, a toque, some African silks thrown in to tip us off—a professional image-fashioning of seemingly harmless and equal culture-lite differences. Deep culture is gone. Poof!

## IS IT MULTICULTURALISM OR SOFT MULTI-FASCISM?

Even to use a word such as "fascism" to describe what is happening in Canada is to invite charges of extremism. But if it is true, we should not avoid it, for I am quite concerned that Canada, along with many other democracies, is walking slowly in that direction. So let us ask first of all: What is it? In Roman times, the *fasces* was a widely recognized ceremonial bundle of sticks strapped together by a rope with an axe blade protruding. It was carried proudly in Roman parades as a symbol of authority and unity. "Don't mess with us Romans," was the message. Today, people wrongly believe that modern "fascism" as practiced by European "national socialists" was a right-wing political movement. But that is an intentionally misleading accusation invented to escape the charge of authoritarianism that is inherent in all forms of socialism. The term described exactly what was being promoted: a national socialism, with an emphasis on the mystical uniqueness of a specific, unique people, culture, and history—and the superiority of same—as in German or Italian fascism.[6] Unlike Mussolini, who was not officially anti-Semitic, Hitler added racial identity to this volatile brew, which he saw as one with cultural identity, thus producing the first modern "identity politics." One of the troubles with Canada is that our lazy-minded multicultural policy, by teaching identification mostly with unchosen externals, leads us to believe that culture is something indelible, like race, even that it includes a kind of mystical *inherited blood consciousness*. Soon this leads to the sorts of ridiculous race and gender-based claims we have all heard of late, such as: only a black person can teach black history, or slave history, or a novel by a black writer; or only men can teach a male writer; or only women can teach gynecology; or only fat people can teach about obesity; or only natives can teach native culture; or only Nazis can teach about the Third Reich.[7]

This kind of thinking is very human, distinctly tribal, and perfect for a lazy-minded, materialistic people happy to dwell on things primitive while avoiding sophisticated mental effort. Civilizations that do not guard against it succumb to it. We could say that but for the extraordinary combined influence of the classical Greek and Roman philosophies, which were always on the hunt for universal truths,[8] and Christian theology, which still embraces all humanity, the West might well have fallen to its own divisive tribal instincts long ago, as became the case with most of the world. As it happened, however, even as the Christian influence waned, this powerful Western expression of universalism continued during the so-called "Age of Reason" and included the impressive rise of science. This period endured for a couple of centuries, losing its ideological (but certainly not its technological) force only by the middle of the eighteenth century, when there began a general revolt against cold rationalism and all universalist thinking, that found expression as European Romanticism.

## ROMANTICISM—THE ROOT OF FASCISM

Romanticism began to surface in the late eighteenth century, most noticeably in all the arts by favouring emotion over cold reason, and in political matters by favouring particular local and national identity and experience over universal experience. It was especially keen to repudiate the sort of French rationalism that was being imposed on most European nations as a political and even a snobbish cultural pattern. Napoleon had invaded the hundreds of loosely allied principalities of what is now Germany and consolidated them politically and geographically along rationalist lines. Perhaps the most easily visible symbol of this trend, this rationalist domination, was the imposition of standard weights and measures and metrication. Rationalists hated the myriad illogical local measuring systems of Europe—Pounds? Feet? Yards? Chains? Ells? They would eliminate them and impose the universal logical perfection of the metric system. But it was precisely this sort of rationalist homogenization, this threat to local identity, that made local citizens very angry. For what could be more human and organic, they said—more us!—than measurement by a foot, a thumb, an arm, a chain? They thought of *culture* as local, warm, organic, and human, in contrast to *civilization*, which was rationalist, universalist, cold, and inhuman. Most of all, they correctly perceived metrication and all other such administrative tools as aids to far more State control, taxation, and conscription.[9]

In reaction to this homogenization, thinkers everywhere began repudiating all foreign models of universal human perfection that they had for too long been expected to *mirror* in their manners, thought, and arts. An entire generation of poets and artists began to adopt a more inward model, the metaphor for which was the *lamp*—the burning inner light of personal identity, and therefore of local, national, and above all, racially authentic feeling. It was thus the European Romantic movement that set the tenor for all modern national fascist systems. It was there the distant die was cast even for Canada's multicultural identity politics. Since the 1960s we have been living in a Neo-Romantic age.

The German Johannes Herder was Romanticism's most notorious racial/ cultural philosopher. Nearing the end of the eighteenth century he was meditating upon the clash of cultures in the Baltic and came to the conclusion "that every tribe and people was unfathomably and indestructibly unique." What made them unique were mysterious "primary forces deep in the collective soul ... each Nation represented a truth of its own, which was a compound of blood, soil, climate, environment, experience—in brief, race, geography and history. There was no universal criterion by which to judge nations ... Men did not create a nation; a nation brought forth men."[10] Implicit in this aspect and in all forms of socialism (whether national or international) is an attack on Western individualism and self-reliance, for socialism and fascism are one in conceiving of the individual as a *product* of unique social forces. Hence, all socialists and fascists attack the very notion of "individual rights," believing that "if the culture is at the root of the individual's identity and meaning, then the culture must acquire a mystical, even a God-like status."[11]

Richard Wagner, the most notorious musician of this movement, invoked triumphalist German folk-life and warrior lore in his operatic extravaganzas. The most influential recent philosophical giant evoking this lore was the brooding philosopher from the Black Forest, Martin Heidegger. His wife sounded like one of our contemporary multiculturalists when she said that fascists like herself and Martin had not committed "the fatal error" of believing in the equality of all human beings (because for them, all races are uniquely different); rather, their whole struggle was "*to recognize the diversity of peoples and races.*"[12] These seekers of inner truth were arguing passionately that human identity burns with a profoundly local, racial, tribal, and national flame, and that the enemy of true identity is the philosophy of the French type of universalism and internationalism. This, Herder had described with disgust as "the slime of the Seine." It was a reaction feeding the flames of national socialism and the Nazi program: Heidegger was for a time rector of Freiberg University and the unofficial philosopher of the Nazi Party. The party slogan intended to sum up "identity," was *Blut und Boden*—"blood and soil." I have developed arguments elsewhere that trace the course of this Romantic passion as it was shaped by the German philosophical reaction to Western universalizing thought, and how in politics it developed into fascism.[13]

Without stretching the point, it now seems clear that the recent, if now fading, postmodern movement (which also repudiates all universal thought), and the moral and cultural relativism that accompanies it (which rejects all

universal moral and cultural standards), found a confused—and confusing—
home in Canada. In a 2006 Library of Parliament research report on Canadian
multiculturalism, the authors say that: "As fact, 'multiculturalism' in Canada
refers to the presence and persistence of diverse racial and ethnic minorities
*who define themselves as different and who wish to remain so.*"[14] To this official
extent, Canadian multiculturalism officially identifies and promotes separate
racial and ethnic identities, and as such, it must be understood as a clearly
expressed nationalistic form of soft *multi-fascism*—a fascism not of a single
race (as in wartime Germany), but of many races, or tribes. The history of
classical political and moral liberalism in Canada is still, and will likely always
be, strong enough to inhibit any unitary fascism of the type seen in Europe.
But if I am correct that soft multi-fascism is already present, then we have begun a journey down a potentially dangerous road. At the least, we can now say
that *Canadian multiculturalism is an official multi-racial doctrine.*

A recent social study by the University of Toronto confirms this predictable
trend: compared with their parents, the second generation of visible minority
immigrants now feels less, not more, Canadian.[15] Professor Zheng Wu of the
University of Victoria found that the higher the concentration of people from
their own ethnic group in the neighbourhood, the less adult immigrants feel
like they belong to Canada.[16] The prestigious Harvard sociologist Robert
Putnam has vigorously underscored the fact that immigration and diversity are
reducing social solidarity and social capital."[17] In 2004, a Statistics Canada
report revealed that whereas Canada had six "visible minority neighbourhoods" in 1981, by 2001 there were 254. Some time ago, the American senator
Huey Long warned, "When fascism comes to America, it will come in the name
of democracy." People will vote for it. Well, we voted, and it is here now, in a soft
form. It is everywhere in the West under names like multiculturalism and
diversity. Soft, but here, nonetheless.[18]

## THE TRUTH ABOUT THE UNIVERSAL VALUES
## OF OUR DEEP CULTURE

The main objection to multicultural relativism is that to anyone who thinks
deeply about the matter it is obvious there are indeed such things as superior
cultures, political and economic systems, literatures, legal systems, philosophies, and theologies. As mentioned, it is these deeper things—not their
borscht, their kilts, or their bagels—that people are normally willing to die
defending. That's why our multicultural policy is so unsettling. It is a national
expression of retreat from defence of the distinctive deep culture that made
Canada a great nation. In removing or minimizing the crucial importance and
value of the things for which Canadians were once willing to die, the policy
also removes our deepest motive for living together. I don't mean living in the
same neighbourhood or city. I mean living in and sharing the same mental

space and furniture. Oh, I know, it's great to see everyone "getting along" in their "diversity," but a people that neglects to be vigilant about the deepest sources of its own civilizational truth and strength, a people that accepts the political conversion of a once-unified home into a multicultural motel, will soon be vulnerable to those who have made no such mistake. Winston Churchill warned us long ago: "A nation that forgets its own history will have no future." There are many Canadians who fear that one of the most deleterious consequences of official multiculturalism is the sense it creates that Canada has no specifically Canadian culture. Indeed, in 1977, Canada's prime minister Pierre Trudeau publicly declared: "There are no official cultures in Canada."[19] He meant there is no deep culture the Canadian government was prepared to articulate and defend. Yet he said this as a direct personal and political beneficiary of our British parliamentary procedures, our common law, habeas corpus rights, our independent judicial system, and more. Clever Quebec has made no such mistake. Quebec does not promote multiculturalism. It promotes "interculturalism," which is to say, diversity is tolerated there, but only as subservient to a framework that establishes the unquestioned supremacy of French language and culture in Quebec. Bravo.

Am I now arguing for a revival of a specifically Canadian particularism, a kind of icy northern fascism? It would seem this way, except . . . the deep-culture values and principles I defend, the culture that I believe is distinctively Western, and distinctly superior, so far, to all others, and to which I think all Canadian immigrants *ought* to assimilate are largely tried-and-tested universalizable principles and practices elaborated only by the West, but that may be appropriated and enjoyed by all who care to adopt them. Here they are.

## OUR GREAT POLITICAL SYSTEM

I have many complaints about it, and out of my love for my country have aired these in writing, as in this book. But I defend the historical fact that almost no other political system in history—and few for such a length of time—has produced such peace and prosperity combined, when it comes to influence over rulers, with the right of the people "to throw the bastards out." That is a most lovely right that did not spring from whole cloth. It is a dear gift of our ancestors, to be venerated. Nor has any other system but ours defended to the death the most revolutionary idea of all: that all people everywhere *have rights (and duties) that are independent of the culture in which they happen to find themselves.* They are rights grounded, it is argued, in human nature, and not in any one culture. This was a claim and ideal of ancient Greek and Roman "natural law," as can be clearly seen in the works of such writers and thinkers as Cicero. It was later a Christian claim and ideal spread by the Gospels (and most clearly articulated philosophically by Saint Thomas Aquinas), and it has found a vulnerable success wherever Western values have spread. Further, and despite all that may be reproached of our unique limited representative democratic system embedded in a constitutional monarchy, our right to express our individual views through elected parliamentarians who in turn are checked by a *loyal* Opposition and a region-based Senate system (so as not to trample minority regions)—the whole jumble is a superior crowning glory! Included are our many other inherited checks and balances on raw power. And so much of this we owe to Mother England. I defend all this as a superior system because no other people has ever produced anything as good. The oft-vaunted Greek and Roman democracies were slave-infested systems. Even the American republican system is not as good, as our founders well knew, because the Americans hold elections in which they castigate, vilify, and ridicule each other—and then one of them is elected. Whereupon all those who voted for the loser—sometimes more than half of all the people—find themselves unrepresented. But Canadians have a non-political monarch who represents and symbolizes them as a united people, always, for our prime minister represents only the government of the people, but not the people themselves. It is a superior and noble thing indeed to have a symbol of high decency representing all the people that cannot be touched by partisan politics. So do not pretend other systems are as good . . . or you may soon find yourself living under one of them!

## OUR GREAT FREEDOM SYSTEM

Much of the first part of this book explains and praises what I have called "the tools of freedom and wealth creation." To confess, I do not like much of what raw capitalism has produced. Ugly commercial sprawl, grating and incessant advertising, the sexualization of all human life, pornography for sale even in the swankiest hotels, a population taught that the best man is the one who dies with the most toys, and so on. On the other hand, compared to all the other systems—communism, socialism, fascism, the various dictatorships, and the mixed and mixed-up systems of most other nations—ours is amazing. It supplies the ordinary citizen with largely unrestricted free choice in daily commercial life with respect to how to spend the fruits of personal labour. It is indeed a form of democratic capitalism, or what I have called a "dollar democracy" under which ordinary people make or break those who serve them well or poorly. Okay, we are half slaves to the State because we are forced to surrender up to half our earnings every year. Nevertheless, what I have called our Freedom System is exactly that. It is a superior system of private property rights, contractual rights, legal justice, protection against force and fraud, and investment opportunities large and small that enable the vast majority of people freely to guide their own lives economically, to their own ends, by their own means, in a culture more or less free of normative corruption. That is a unique, superior, universally duplicable system that we owe to our unique history. We forget this at our peril.

## OUR GREAT LEGAL SYSTEM

It needs criticism and ongoing improvement, as much in this book suggests. But compared to the legal systems of other cultures? No contest! To Mother England, once again, we owe most of the freedoms and the common law rights that we too often take for granted. Superior is the British-based right to private property we have known since the twelfth century. Superior are the individual freedoms and rights to protection from Statism that were enshrined in Magna Carta in 1215, and improved and defended ever since (well, until 1982 in Canada). Superior is the right to be presumed innocent until proved guilty before a jury of peers or an independent judge. Superior are the rights of citizens to legal appeal to higher courts. Superior is the right of the poor to free counsel. Other than Rome at the height of her glory (from whence also we have drawn much in the way of legal practice), no other system has ever provided its people with such a cultural fabric of superior legal rights and freedoms. Indeed, one of the supporting ribs of this book is the nation-defining contrast between the British-based common law system and the French-based code law system, arguing for the superiority of the former. The practical reality that all who have thrown in their lot with the English bottom-up common law system are *free to do anything that is not prohibited by the law* is an extraordinary inheritance of the English people. We are presumed free by birth and by inherited right. This stands in stark opposition to the dictates found in so many top-down nations of history where citizens are permitted to do only what is specified—or altered by judges—in a written code. In chapter 15 I describe how Canada's Charter of Rights and Freedoms has seriously undermined our proud legal tradition.

## OUR GREAT PHILOSOPHICAL, LITERARY, AND AESTHETIC TRADITION

Here, I beg indulgence. I was trained as a professor of English and comparative literature, and I enjoy most the study of the History of Ideas, as it is called. The contributions to human life, understanding, and enrichment by many other cultures have of course been impressive in their own right. But my preferences are clear. The cumulative human search for goodness, truth, and beauty in the Western tradition is unique, something to marvel at and defend, and the recent root and branch attack on it—mostly by egalitarian, postmodern radicals—to be energetically rebuffed. For there simply is no other culture that has produced works of the mind and heart, of philosophy, literature, music and art, as grand and fruitful as those of the Western tradition. From Socrates, Plato, and Aristotle, to Augustine and Aquinas; from the insight and beauty of the King James Bible, to the soaring cathedrals—Westminster, Winchester, Chartres— angelic choir voices descending; to the glorious music of Bach, Beethoven, Mozart, Handel, Tchaikovsky—and countless others; to our great literature from *Beowulf* to the *Canterbury Tales*—and yes, all that very fine French and German and Spanish literature, old and new—to virtually all of Shakespeare, to the great tradition of the novel from Fielding to Dickens, Tolstoy, and Dostoevsky, to Joyce and Faulkner, to the ringing songs of our poets, and yes, all those gorgeous visual forms, and paintings—the *Winged Victory*, *Venus de Milo*, all of Rembrandt, Turner, much of Van Gogh, almost all the French Impressionists, our own fine Group of Seven—whole continents of stunning modern painting and sculpture . . . Rodin's *Burghers of Calais*, oh, my heart.

And of course our lofty English—of all languages, the most ample, most flexible, the most free and open to innovation—has, precisely because of this adaptive freedom, become the new lingua franca, as they say. Open and ample? A famous professor of French, Alphonse Juilland, boasted to us in a Stanford lecture that he could find all or part of every word of the French language somewhere in the English language. Flexible? Resourceful? No language has, over the last millennium, taken over and absorbed as its own so many words from other peoples. It is now the universal language. The *Oxford English Dictionary* is still the largest and most astonishing glory of all the world's dictionaries, the miraculous endeavour of its assembly after a century of labour a signal tribute to the English people's love of their language.

## OUR GREAT THEOLOGICAL TRADITION

Here I only state that despite all its faults and wrong turns, the Judeo-Christian theology of Western civilization seems to me quite superior as a basis of a national culture and morality (at the root of all moral systems, a distinct theology may be discovered). Superior is its insistence on the sacredness of all human life (though in recent times, for adult sexual convenience, almost all nominally Christian nations have denied this to the unborn), the essential goodness of creation, its teachings on the equal moral agency of all, and the need for universal love between all people. Christianity is also uniquely rooted in a belief in discoverable absolutes; that is, in the existence of accessible universal truth, the conviction that we live in a universe with meaning. This belief in turn has unleashed a cornucopia of near-miraculous scientific and technological development—for the reason that no people searches for absolute truth if they believe there is none to be found—and it explains why in so many other cultures with other theologies, science and technology have either never developed or have lain dormant for centuries, only now awakening through vibrant Western methods. Notwithstanding the errors and evils, pogroms and crusades that people enjoy citing as the fault of religion, those were minor compared to its glories. Christendom was responsible for the creation of the first universities, beginning in the eleventh century[20] (and for so many great ones since), for most of the great hospitals, and of course for countless of the world's charitable organizations, still. Almost all the private charitable organizations helping the poor of the world are of Christian origin. To this must be added, as above, the soaring arts, music, and architecture of Christendom, and the moral urgency that underlies the Western legal tradition (where even intent to commit a crime is a criminal offence). In these, as in so many things, the West has never had an equal. It still doesn't.

## THE CULTURAL COMMON DENOMINATORS OF CANADA

It also bears noting that according to our own official documents such as the *Canada Year Book* 2009, and official census data, Canada's big cities may look multicultural and "diverse"—because they are—but Canada does not. In terms of ethnicity, language, religion, political system, and law, Canada looks like this:

*   Canada is still overwhelmingly a white country (census data show about 16 percent visible minorities, and this figure includes our more than one million aboriginal citizens). We are 84 percent a white nation, just as China is overwhelmingly a yellow nation, and Jamaica is overwhelmingly black (90 percent).
*   Canada's national language of home and business usage is overwhelmingly English. Almost 68 percent say English is the language of home, and English is 90 percent Canada's national and international language of trade (80 percent of Canada's trade is with the United States).
*   An overwhelming majority of Canadians—nearly 80 percent—say they are Christian, nominal or otherwise.
*   Canadians are overwhelmingly supportive of their representative-democratic political system.
*   Canadians want only one law for all and equal provincial rights. Recent aboriginal legal exceptions and calls for sharia (Islamic) law are aberrations. Canadians don't want people like Afghan-Canadian Hasibullah Sadiqi, who in 2006 murdered his own sister and her boyfriend in an honour killing.
*   In 2007, a national SES Canada Research poll conducted for the Montreal Institute for Research on Public Policy on citizen acceptance of "reasonable accommodation" for multiculturalism in Canada, only 18 percent said it was reasonable to accommodate religious and cultural minorities. Fifty-three percent thought immigrants should "adapt fully to culture in Canada" (for Quebec, the result was 77 percent). Interestingly, some 49 percent of Canadians polled in a Léger Marketing study considered themselves "somewhat racist" (59 percent in Quebec).

Much of the above is the reason why, in 2009, our minister of multiculturalism, Jason Kenney, released a refreshing new citizenship guide entitled *Discover Canada: The Rights and Responsibilities of Canadian Citizenship*. It is surely a matter for national celebration to realize this is the first and most definitive statement in fifty years from any level of Canadian government to insist that rights and responsibilities are two sides of the same coin. There is no such thing as a right that does not trigger responsibilities at the same time. But astonishingly, Canada's Charter of Rights and Freedoms, the "Supreme Law" of Canada, does not mention the word "responsibilities." Not once.

I have offered a brief defence of Canada's deep-culture heritage. These are realities of which I am deeply proud. I am willing to share them with everyone. All they have to do is come on board. My complaint is simply that because we do not adequately articulate and defend our Canadian deep culture, we are stumbling into a national darkness, well on the way to cultural separatism and soft fascism. This begins as people of different ethnic and cultural backgrounds insist on affiliation with their old identities, choose to live only in their own ethnic communities, call for their own types of dispute mechanisms and laws, for different criminal justice treatment (many aboriginals already often get sentenced to healing and sentencing circles, rather than to jail, like non-native prisoners), and for race-based schools. Ironically, the broad and initially sincere effort of multicultural thinkers to end exclusionism is going to end instead with most ethnic groups hunkering down only with their own kind, each promoting their own ways, their ethnic pride, and yes . . . their superiority to all others. Just outside Paris, France, there are immigrants, who are mostly Muslims, living in "lawless zones" where French authorities dare not enter.

So in what follows, a lot of questions must be raised, such as: Do Canadians want Canada to stay the way it is, or to change? And if the answer is "to change" (which citizens ought to be free to choose), then in what direction? Should we simply accept random change, imposed by external forces, by the immigration wishes of other nationalities? Or changes from the top imposed by elite politicians, left or right? Or change engineered by entrenched political radicals and intellectuals? Seems to me no one is asking. I think we should ask.

### Cultural Relativism, Immigration, and Falling Fertility

By the mid-twentieth century we became the first civilization in history to define ourselves and our future by the methods, controls, and consequences of sexual behaviour severed by technology from human biology; that is, by contraception and abortion. This was also the first century during which the West caught a glimpse of itself heading into a "demographic winter." The United States is now the only nation in the Western world still replacing itself via natural increase (the Total Fertility Rate [TFR] of a nation must be at least 2.1 children per woman to maintain population level). Canada has been trucking along at a TFR of 1.6 or less for thirty years.

As a policy consequence of this negative TFR, slow population growth, and labour shortages, many Western borders were gradually opened to mass immigration. There were labour shortages in Germany and Switzerland. France had the same situation (plus a moral obligation to Muslim allies after the Algerian War). For Canada and the United States the most common reason given is economic growth (a bad motive, as we shall see below). As it happened, this recent mass immigration began during the same post-1960s period of radicalism in which the entire Western world came under leftist attack for "imperialism," "cultural hegemony," "capitalist greed," "oppression," "environmental rape," "eurocentrism," and many other "crimes" against humanity.

Much of that attack was—is still—carried forward under the banner of a supposed culturally and morally liberating "relativism"; the idea, still taught in virtually all anthropology classes that *all the world's cultures are equal*, none is superior to any other, and so no single culture's values, ideals, laws, or customs can be judged good or bad by another culture.[21] This mostly anti-Western cultural relativism inevitably spawned a rejection of the old, and a yearning for a new "global" society. However, it was immediately clear that this new world was to be of a strictly egalitarian nature: if we could embrace all cultures equally, no one nation would oppress another, and human conflict would come to an end.

Liberal politicians of the early 1960s such as Prime Minister Pearson's sidekick Tom Kent (see chapter 11) saw the Toronto-Ontario WASP power axis as an expression of the democratic-capitalist ideology that progressives the world over had wanted to change for a long time, and he figured the quickest way to dilute it was to flood cities with immigrants who were not white, Anglo-Saxon, or Protestant. Not long afterwards, Pierre Trudeau burbled: "It doesn't matter where the immigrants come from" (March 15, 1979, in Vancouver). Well, that was a flaky thing to say, because it's true it doesn't matter if all you are concerned about is folk culture. *But it matters a lot if you want to preserve the deep culture that made your country great in the first place.* For if there are only nine seats on your town council or local school board, and a decision must be made whether to dedicate the only land available to a secular, a Christian, or an Islamic school, the vote will be based on the deep-culture values of the majority on the board. That's where the rubber hits the road.

**White Guilt, Self-Loathing, and the Therapeutic State**
Most dominant cultures do not end up in self-hate. They fight hard to maintain the authority and control that flow from their deep culture. That is what Rome did for a thousand years. One of the very large questions that historians will soon be trying to answer during what appears to be the clear and present decline of Western civilization, is: Why did the West turn against itself? One plausible explanation is so-called "white guilt."

In an interesting treatment, Paul Gottfried argues that we have recently travelled from the managerial welfare state of the first half of the twentieth century, to the behaviour-and-attitude-controlling therapeutic state of the present. This may be seen as a secular expression of our earlier Christian-based search for purity of soul and atonement for original sin. Due to the pervasive psychological weight of the latter, some have described all Christian societies as a "guilt culture" (in contrast to the prevalent description of Islamic societies as a "blame culture").

The process began with the Protestant Reformation in the early sixteenth century. People often think the Reformation was a cry for release from religious oppression. But it was the opposite. It was a puritanical protest against religious laxity and corruption. People began turning their backs on church authority. They wanted an individual relationship with God and spiritual salvation. No sooner was this right won, when a call went out for individual political rights, too. In that sense, modern democracy has been recognized by many historians as "a child of the Reformation." For as soon as it was realized that Protestant religious fragmentation was producing a multiplicity of new sects, a call for toleration arose, and it was not long before the right to an individual relationship with God was translated into an individual right to vote. Over time, as Western society became more secular and religion weakened, the emphasis fell on various human rights crusades. Our present stage of attitude control and "political correctness" is enabled by an increasingly therapeutic state complete with purity-of-behaviour and re-education courses, sensitivity-adjustment units such as Human Rights Commissions and Tribunals (which seek to control, purge, and punish even internal attitudes or impure private thought and speech), and a politicized judiciary that sees its role as the purification of democracy (see chapter 15 for statements from Canadian judges to this effect).

In short, almost overnight the notion of sin as *spiritual* bad attitude gave way to *political* and *cultural* insensitivity as bad attitude. The ancient search for religious purity and salvation slowly gave way to a yearning for psychic and even bodily purity, for "a mind cleansed of pathological thoughts." Accompanying all this, we see an almost fanatical modern emphasis on bodily health, on pure "organic" foods, along with strident calls for environmental-recycling behaviour in all citizens. In no small way, the worldwide concern for cleaning up the garbage in the streets has replaced the prior need to clean up the garbage in the soul. This latter point needs emphasis, for due to their Romanticism, their love of *Blut und Boden*, modern fascists lashed out at all forms of alienating urban technology, such as polluting factory systems that separated people from their organic physical, social, and cultural roots. The deepest desire was to reconnect man with the purity of the land, nature, and national race history. Indeed, "fascism was possibly the first environmentalist ideology of the [twentieth] century," for its "emphasis on health and fitness was part of the Nazis' back-to-nature movement."[22] Radical environmentalism—so influenced as it has been by the Martin Heidegger's critique of the alienation and uprooting caused by Western technology—has often been described as "eco-fascism"—a violent movement that conceives of human beings as "a mistake," a blight on the original and sinless purity of nature.[23]

In this way, a line is easily drawn from the longed-for pure heart and transformed consciousness of original Protestantism, to our modern "politics of sensitivity."[24] It's a different focal point, but it has the same psychological wiring. The original Protestant strain was extremely egalitarian and anti-hierarchical, shunned all religious authority, and sought atonement for personal sins. Our new purity radicals, however (most of them now aging hippies entrenched in media and academic institutions), having abandoned the notion of *personal* sin, latched onto the concept of *group* and *racial* or *national* sin, expressed as an historical "white guilt." Atonement therefore comes to mean the rejection of, detachment from, and revolt against one's own evil national history and culture. This deformed and secularized Protestantism, Gottfried writes, eventually merged with the therapeutic state, whereupon "individual sensitivity, social guilt, and the personal overcoming of one's depraved ancestral society" forms the core of modern white guilt.

Indeed, modern Westerners are periodically called upon to remember and to feel apologetic for the sins of their predecessors (for earlier slavery, racism, sexism, etc), as if such acts were biologically inherited. Such concepts of inherited group sin have resulted in the strange spectacle of a generation of Canadians who have done no wrong, apologizing publicly, and in certain cases making payments to a generation of people who have suffered no harm. Although we increasingly reject any notion of personal sin (we imagine ourselves born pure), we believe passionately in the notion of inherited racial and cultural sin. To take seriously the idea that our blood, our identities, and racial histories are actors in history is another sign of our turn toward soft fascism. Just so, liberal leader Michael Ignatieff recently encouraged Canadians to reject their entire national history as a very troublesome heritage, in favour of newer, untainted "shared understandings."[25]

## Relativism and Tyranny

As mentioned, the popular cultural relativism of the West quickly led to moral relativism. But this, as Noam Chomsky once warned, "is a dictator's dream." For if there is no commonly held truth, then whoever controls the levers of power can make up their own truth. Then, power, or the will of the leaders, becomes the only truth. In 2008, in *The Book of Absolutes*, I laid out a refutation of the relativist idea in general by showing that there are in fact countless universals of nature, and human nature. That is irrefutable. I was arguing that all people are the same underneath (so it shouldn't matter where they come from). So now, as I take up the defence of my own deep-culture superiority, am I arguing against myself? Not necessarily. For deep culture is everywhere a willed phenomenon, and so the most cherished values of different peoples may indeed clash, and when they clash on the same soil, national unity is threatened, because—just to take one example—you cannot be a democracy and a dictatorship at the same time. You cannot uphold an ideal of free speech and unfree speech at the same time (though Canada has lately been trying this). Furthermore, the cultural values I uphold are a concrete, tried-and-tested, rather than an abstract or theoretical form of Western universalism.

As it happened, Canada's first—and ongoing—demonstration of how cultures may clash at the deepest level on national soil was also our first and ongoing experiment with multiculturalism: our long struggle with French Quebec, which brought Canada very close to national chaos during the 1995 "referendum" on separation.[26] Many Quebecers continue to yearn for independence. And former Quebec premier Jacques Parizeau continues to foment what he calls "artificial crises" in order to spark sovereignty agitation. Indeed: in a poll published by *La Presse*, June 9, 2009, 58 percent thought Quebec should "have greater autonomy, or separate," and in a protest against a decision by Canada's Supreme Court criticizing Quebec's language-police regime, a Quebec official anguished that "the Supreme Court—a court appointed by another nation—has just butchered once again a fundamental instrument of the Québec nation." Another nation! You see, it's all in the lingo. They want only ethnically pure Quebecers, *"pur laine."* In an upcoming chapter I will present some thoughts on the illegality of any unilateral separatism in a legally constituted federation. Suffice it to say that our long and unsettling experience with Quebec more than makes my entire argument against multiculturalism-as-multi-fascism. Canada has been a fragile bicultural regime (no real unity) since 1867. Why do we think we can ever be a successful multicultural one?

## A PARADOX: DEEP CULTURE IS ALWAYS ILLIBERAL

> *Community love always requires aggression against non-members.*
> —Sigmund Freud, *Civilization and its Discontents*

For thousands of years, rulers, kingdoms, and States—governments large and small—have understood very well how human social bonding works (affiliation to the maximum number of common cultural denominators). So they have strived to ensure their people share a common deep culture, and have struggled against all threats to the unity this produces. They have understood that you can enjoy lots of *ethnic* diversity within an existing deep cultural unity, but *you cannot derive cultural unity from diversity.* That's why for most nations in history, *assimilation* has been the key to unity: get newcomers to forget their old ways and adopt the new host culture.

Arguably, the five-hundred-year-old rule of the Roman Republic, which continued as the Roman Empire (with the ascension of Julius Caesar to perpetual emperor in 44 BC), for an additional five hundred years in the West, was the first, most successful, and most ethnically diverse state in history. But it lasted so long mainly because it insisted on conformity to a common official language, and common legal, political, and religious standards and symbols. You used Latin in all official discourse and documents (some Greek for high culture); if a citizen, you obeyed and were protected equally by Roman law; you shared common political citizen rights in all Roman provinces; you worshipped whatever gods you wanted, but if you attacked the gods of Rome you would be crucified. Above all, the rule was: When in Rome, do as the Romans do.

So it seems that the most central logical and historical reality without which there can never be a "people" is the sense of *inclusiveness*—what Freud called "community love"—that arises from bonding to *the same deep culture*, and this inclusiveness is necessarily and by definition also *exclusive*: you are either for us or against us (and our culture), an insider or an outsider. That is what creates the bonds and privileges of membership in any social group. This is simply a fact of human history, the way the world has always worked, and this natural process of inclusion/exclusion is the only thing that produces social bonding in any group. Whether in sport teams, families, churches, or nations, all human social bonding—which is a universal cultural phenomenon—demands sacrifice to group ideals, subordination to group authority, commitment to group purposes, and then and only then do members get group privileges.

For a very long time Canada offered its deep culture to all immigrants, and expected a national social bonding to take place naturally; in effect, the private property rights, rule of law, individual freedom, our many legal and political rights, as outlined above, comprised a real-world practical universalizing culture that worked very well to assimilate and unify foreigners. The trouble with Canada is that in embracing multiculturalism as an official policy—the absurd idea that differences unite—we have turned our backs on what really unites: our own deep-culture inheritance (however filtered or enriched by other skin-deep cultural experiences).

In addition to these distortions of value and truth, these trivializations of deep culture, perhaps the most insidious effect of "diversity" is that it is no diversity at all. It has produced a strict and unrelenting, extremely narrow-minded, and very radical anti-Western orthodoxy of a kind rarely seen before. The diversity in question is in fact a diversity of the like-minded, and the like-minded are primarily radical secular leftists of a bitterly anti-Western type operating in lockstep attitudinal conformity who employ all the techniques of modern Statism to shut down opposing views via what author Camille Paglia, herself a leftist, has called "fascism of the left." Another astute critic from the

Left who saw this scam long ago was Christopher Lasch, who said that "in prac-tice, diversity turns out to legitimize a new dogmatism in which rival minorities take shelter behind a set of beliefs impervious to rational discussion."[27]

So much is this true that one of the newly rarefied meanings of "racism" includes a charge of *failure to recognize* racial differences, special racial identi-ties, and the unique perspectives of racial minorities (in the unique sensibili-ties of which you may be genetically barred from sharing, due to your different race). Toronto opened an all-black school in 2009 (but a school especially for whites would be considered racially discriminatory). Authorities are now dis-cussing the need for all-aboriginal schools. There is nothing "diverse" about all this. It is our new orthodoxy.

To close this section, I offer now the shocking results of the "great experi-ment" in multiculturalism and diversity that was set up at my alma mater, Stanford University, California, for all the world to see. The conviction was that if this program did not work at Stanford—a community of forty thousand enlight-ened souls committed to making it work—then it would not work anywhere.

---

## SNAPSHOT
A Model for the World?
The Diversity Myth at Stanford University

*Hey, Hey, Ho, Ho! Western culture's gotta go!*
—multiculturalist chant at Stanford

Beautiful Stanford University, flush with sun and palm trees, is a case of special interest for anyone watching the onset and confusion of the multicultural ex-periment in the West. Boosters and critics were watching very closely. Saddened, and intrigued, with what I saw on campus during a visit in 2000, I decided to read David Sacks and Peter Thiels's *The Diversity Myth: Multiculturalism and Political Intolerance on Campus*. This book gives a blow-by-blow description of how from the mid-1980s onward Stanford became a sociological testing ground for what then president Donald Kennedy called the "great experiment." Stanford prided itself on elaborating the fine points of this experiment for all Americans in a noble application to every imaginable aspect of campus life. Diversity was to be the new basis for unity, a "constructive pluralism." But as Sacks and Thiels pointedly asked: "What could 'unity' possibly mean in the context of multi-racial/multi-ethnic diversity?"

It rapidly became clear that multiculturalism and diversity at Stanford had nothing to do with true culture, but everything to do with the uniformity of anti-Western radical leftist politics, and was producing results distinctly nondiverse.

*Economic diversity* was out the window because Stanford, already an elite university, was soon burdened by so may new expenses and staff in its attempt to convert the university to a multicultural utopia that it was becoming what its own president described as "a mini-welfare state."

*Political diversity* became almost non-existent on campus. Stanford's faculty went even further left, soon reaching a self-reported level of 80 percent of faculty who were left, or far-left Democrats (while the 3 or 4 percent of "conservative" faculty were mostly centrists or moderates).

*Racial diversity* also went in the opposite direction, toward racial uniformity and segregation: Stanford, along with many other universities, began putting students into very non-diverse Asian-American, African-American, and Native-American "race dormitories," offered race-based graduation ceremonies, and lots of race- and gender-based courses. Much of this new teaching on race inevitably leaned toward its own fascistic kind of racism ("Black is Beautiful," etc.). Black professor Leonard Jeffries is cited as declaring that melanin in the skin of black people "allows us to receive the vibrations of the universe."

*Intellectual diversity*, too, has suffered, due to political correctness, severe speech restrictions (which Canada also now suffers greatly), political grading (for a decade hardly any student at Stanford received less than a B grade), and severe ostracism of nonconformists (Sacks and Thiels's book relates a bizarre but true incident of multicultural hysteria over a white student's denial of a claim that Beethoven was a black man), open denunciation of the West, and "a curricular obsession with oppression theory and victimology."

*Sexual diversity?* It is non-existent. LBGTI (lesbian/bisexual/gay/transgender/intersex) thinking is the norm, and students are hounded mercilessly for defending or espousing the normalcy of heterosexual family life or procreative biology. Many men's washrooms at Stanford have "glory holes" bored through toilet privacy panels by homosexuals for the purposes of anonymous fellatio (whatever). Anxious about squelching diversity, the administration refused to repair them.

*Cultural diversity?* It became immediately clear that multicult boosters had no interest in learning about the deep cultures of others. Indeed, pressures were soon applied to drop all foreign and classical language requirements for higher degrees, while enrolment in courses on Roman, Greek, Slavic, and Asian cultures declined precipitously. Stanford then shut down several of its overseas campuses.

All of this has made it very clear that in a single decade, Stanford University fully transitioned from the very open and free, intellectually diverse university it had been for a century, to a very closed institution with strict rules of correct intellectual orthodoxy, racist codes of conduct, and even "multicultural educators" (campus thought-police) to "inculcate ideas" in all who "resist educational efforts."

In the end, as the great experiment faltered, Stanford's president was charged by a U.S. Senate subcommittee for misuse of federal research funds, and summarily dismissed. Money earmarked for research had been used for such as: repair of the university's yacht; a Lake Tahoe retreat for trustees and their families and friends; tuition for faculty children; $400 worth of flowers for the dedication of the Stanford horse stables; and $7,000 in bedsheets and linens, and $10,000 worth of silverware for Donald Kennedy's campus home.

## IMMIGRATION: WHAT IS IT? WHY DO WE HAVE IT?

> *It doesn't matter where the immigrants come from.*
> —Prime Minister Pierre Trudeau, March 15, 1979, in Vancouver

> *Q: Should the size and content of immigration*
> *be permitted to change our ethnic and cultural balance?*
> *A: No.*
> —response of 78 percent of Canadians in a Gallup poll, June 15, 1987

Most of us are very moved by the experiences of immigrants who come to this country and work incredibly hard to advance themselves and their families. Especially when we read of native-born people whining about unemployment, only to discover many of them have either made themselves unemployable or have refused hard physical jobs that immigrants gladly take, or for which we import temporary foreign labour (though as we shall see—not so temporary). I am not for a moment criticizing hard-working immigrants who came to Canada to be Canadian. I am criticizing a deeply flawed immigration policy that was set up—and is continued—by self-serving politicians craving votes, and sustained by a huge immigration lobby, most of whom care a lot more about their own careers than about the future of Canada and its deep culture. One immigration officer told Stewart Bell, author of *Cold Terror*, that he "works all day at trying to get terrorists out of this country, and then watches as politicians court these same violent organizations for votes."[28]

Canada's original policy was designed to ensure that the bulk of Canada's children would grow up among parents and people more or less similar to themselves, who spoke French or English, and who were more or less rooted in the same Judeo-Christian religious tradition, Graeco-Roman philosophical and legal tradition, and European culture. Was it all that unreasonable to want to provide future generations with the same deep-culture environment that made the nation strong? And if not, why did we change a system that was working?

Naturally enough, all peoples of the world have a fear of losing their deep culture, a threat normally posed only by foreign forces. But if governing elites impose an immigration ideology that differs radically from that of the people, and are aware it is going to change the country beyond recognition, and if they nevertheless strive to impose it against the expressed will of the people, or without sincerely engaging them in a genuine choice about such change, *then the foreign threat exists internally*, and the idea of the voice of the people is upended.

## IMMIGRATION AND ... DEMOCRACY?

In the beginning, when Trudeau's government turned toward multicultural-ism as yet another Statist innovation, the question Does it matter, or not, where immigrants come from? gave a sense of the tension between Canada's smug elite opinion and the popular wisdom for which the latter felt only scorn. The American situation was not much different, as evidenced in "Elite vs. Public Opinion," a press release issued December 2002 by the U.S. Center for Immigration Studies[29] that spoke with some alarm of the "enormous gap" between American elites and the public on immigration. Sixty percent of the American public found their present levels of immigration (which propor-tionally are one-third of the Canadian level) "a critical threat to the vital inter-ests of the United States." But only 14 percent of the nation's leadership—well-off opinion-setters—agreed: a gap of 46 percent. Much of this difference had to do with working people being anxious about their jobs, whereas educated people are less vulnerable to immigrant job-seekers. Nevertheless, the analysis made it clear that *politicians get their opinions on immigration policy from elites, not from ordinary people.*

This truth constitutes a sharp challenge to whatever democratic founda-tion may exist in Western nations, for given that *any* kind of immigration is either going to maintain, strengthen, or weaken a nation's identifiable deep-culture profile—its historical identity (a reality distinct from race identity)—there are reasonable questions we ought to be asking. Such as: Do we want to *maintain* our national deep-culture profile (as described above) or *change* it? If we say change is okay, then we have to ask: What kind of change? And . . . Should we accept *random* change imposed externally by foreigners demanding a "right" to come to Canada? Or should we *manage* the direction of change ourselves, insisting that immigration to Canada is not a right but a privilege *to be controlled only by Canadians*? If, having decided the latter, we want to man-age future change ourselves, then we have to ask: *Who* in Canada—elites or the people—should make the decision to change, and in what direction?

Clearly, any decision about the future cultural profile of Canada may turn out to be a good or a bad one, regardless of who makes it. However, I submit that on decisions of such importance that have the potential to alter the ethno-cultural fabric of an entire nation—especially in any nation with a meaningful degree of democracy—*it is the people who ought to decide on their own future cultural profile*, for better or worse. In other words, *all nations have the right to defend themselves against demographic capture, or, if you prefer, against passive ethnic or cultural takeover.* Either elected representatives should affirm what the ethos and fabric of society is to become after extensive and sincere consultation with all the people, or—my preference—after the same in-depth process, a question of such importance ought to be put directly to the people in a referendum, and subject to a special majority of, say, two-thirds. Alas, by now, the entire subject of immigration has become so politicized, the average Canadian so frightened of expressing an honest opinion (such are only whispered), and our lopsided leftist media so ready to pounce with charges of bigotry (whereas they themselves ought to be charged with anti-Canadianism), that reasonable dialogue does seem impossible. This attests to the attitude-control powers of governments and elites, and the intellectual infantilization of the nation. But it does not reflect the appropriate responsibility and self-direction of a free people.

## WHAT ARE THE FACTS? HOW HAS OUR IMMIGRATION PATTERN CHANGED?[30]

Below is a Table showing the flip from traditional European/American sources to non-traditional immigration from the Rest of the World (ROW), from 1981 to 2031.

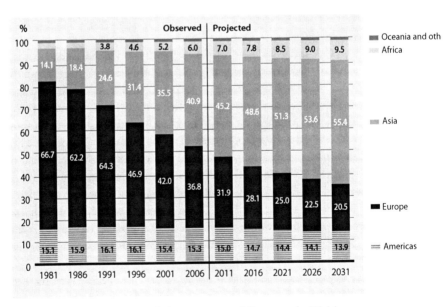

Sources: Statistics Canada, population censuses and Demography Division

As a result of this altered pattern, a Statistics Canada Ethnic Diversity Survey showed that by 2003, only 21 percent of Canada's over-age-fifteen population was of British-only ancestry, while only 10 percent were of French-only ancestry. About 8 percent said they were "Canadian" (impossible to say what this means in ethnic terms), and 7 percent were a mix of all three. Visible minorities rose to 13.4 percent by 2001 (including aboriginal peoples), and by 2009 we had over 5 million, or 16 percent, visible minorities. However, these visible minority immigrants are not so much coming to Canada, as coming to Canada's largest cities. Some 60 percent of those 5 million immigrants live in Toronto and Vancouver. Metro Toronto's foreign-born population has already reached 46 percent and Vancouver's almost 40 percent. Our 2006 census verified that some 82 percent of all immigrants who arrived in Canada after 2001 settled in three provinces: Ontario (where 50 percent of all recent immigrants settled); Quebec (which has 13.8 percent foreign-born population, and received 17.5 percent of all recent immigrants, and going down); and British Columbia, which received 16 percent of recent immigrants. The implications of this reality for a country whose major cities are ethnically dominated by visible minorities subsidized and encouraged to cleave to their old cultures, but whose suburban and vast rural areas are overwhelmingly populated by whites who cleave to Canada's historical deep culture (if to any), are unsettling. As James Bissett, former executive director of the Canadian Immigration Service, has asked: "At what point does diversity mutate into a form of [internal] colonization?"

## CANADA'S IMMIGRATION: RATES AND TYPES
Per capita, for the past quarter century, Canada has been taking in more immigrants annually than any other Western nation: over 250,000 per year, or about three-quarters of 1 percent of our total population annually (depending on the year). So, about a million people every four years. Our rate is twice that of the U.K. and the United States on a per capita basis. Yet Canada's Liberal and NDP parties have pushed for 1 percent or 330,000 per year. They smell the vote potential. One of our greatest problems is that our immigration legislation essentially requires us to issue a visa to anyone who pays the application fee and meets our selection criteria, no matter how many choose to apply. As a result, in recent years Canada has been so overwhelmed by applicants that we have effectively lost control of our own borders and of the future ethnic and cultural profile of our nation. By June 2008, Canada had a backlog of almost a million immigrants lined up for entry (estimated to be a 1.5 million backlog by 2012 if no reforms are made), and about 70,000 "refugee" claimants. Each claimant going through the system (which includes the right to appeal at three separate stages, right up to the Supreme Court) "costs Canadian taxpayers an estimated $29,000" according to the minister of immigration. Some rejected refugees are able to resist deportation for up to fifteen years.

Canada's Immigration Annual Report stated that 112,658 foreign temporary workers were brought into Canada in 2006, supposedly for labour
market shortages. Surely it is a mystery why Canadian taxpayers are forced to
hand over wads of their income each year to support workers on "unemployment," many of whom have refused low-paying work, only to find that government turns around and imports hundreds of thousands of temporary workers
over the years from foreign countries for a work program also subsidized by
our taxes. Due to recent rule changes, many of these temporary workers are
now allowed to apply for citizenship from within Canada (in a legal queue
jump).

Most Canadians have been led to believe that the majority of immigrants
are brought into Canada for economic reasons. They have been sold the song
that we need immigrants to "grow." But the truth is that fewer than 20 percent
of all our immigrants are selected on the basis of their qualifications. Most
come in as immediate family members—"family class" immigrants sponsored
by "relatives," or for "humanitarian" reasons. None of these people are required
to satisfy any criteria whatsoever under Canada's point system for immigrant
selection. They just have to be alive when they enter. This lack of marketable
skills may explain why 50 percent of them are living below the poverty line.
And I put the word "relatives" in quotes because some countries, for example,
the United States, have found that many sponsors who say they are relatives of
immigrants are lying. After carrying out DNA tests on sponsors in the U.S. and
their "relatives" from Africa, it was discovered that "more than 80 percent of
the latter were not, in fact, related to the sponsors at all. They were trying to
enter the USA under false pretenses."[31] Canada has many of its own experiences with immigrant identity fraud, and in 1991 had to announce that most
Somali passports were bogus. Canada sees up to a 50 percent rate in fraudulent
documents from some parts of China, and up to 80 percent from the Indian
state of Punjab. Close them down, I say. We don't need cheaters here (we have
enough of our own!).

## PHONY REFUGEE CLAIMANTS
The UN estimates that over four million human beings are smuggled into
various countries each year, most of them by criminal organizations that reap
more than $7 billion from this enterprise. They are told: If you want to get into
Canada fast, just lie. Tell the border officials you will be persecuted or tortured if you are forced to return home.

In 1987, according to our immigration authorities, more than 26,000 people claimed refugee status[32] in Canada. Based on the standard used by the
United Nations Convention on Refugees, *nearly 85 percent of the claims were
found to be false.* Such scandals have been known for a long time: in 1981, even
our very liberal immigration minister Lloyd Axworthy complained of the

75,000 refugees we took in that year that "a lot of them are claiming they left for political reasons, but in fact it's economic."

Nothing has changed. In 2002, *citizens from 152 different nations*, many of which no other nation in the world but Canada would consider to be refugee-producing, claimed homeland persecution and therefore a right of asylum in Canada. How can this be? How can people who enter Canada illegally get away with naming almost every nation on earth as a place dangerous to life and limb? How soft-headed are we? Very: a Canadian federal court judge recently declared the United States of America "unsafe" for refugees! And . . . in December 2004, Canada's government passed a law enabling *anyone charged with a capital offence* in another country to seek legal asylum in Canada. In this way, as former Canadian ambassador James Bissett put it, we "laid out the welcome mat for murderers."

I would say Canada is now in a tight spot on this score. We have signed UN treaties against torture, which prevent us from deporting phony asylum seekers claiming homeland persecution, and we have passed laws saying that all "individuals" in Canada automatically have the full Charter rights and freedoms of citizens. Now, there are obviously some very unsafe countries in the world, and we must always be open to helping genuine refugees *according to our own capacities*, as long as they do not overwhelm us. But the vast majority of asylum seekers are economic refugees out "immigration shopping," which means they are hunting for the country with the slackest entry conditions, the greatest number of free benefits, and the least likelihood of sending them back home. Having chosen Canada, they then choose to lie, break the rules, and jump the immigration queue under false pretenses. How false? Hard to say. Martin Collacott, former Canadian high commissioner to Sri Lanka, informs us that "in one year alone, 8,600 Sri Lankans with refugee claims pending in Canada, applied to the Sri Lankan High Commission in Ottawa for travel documents so they could go back to Sri Lanka for visits." Most European nations now avoid this problem by refusing all refugee claimants from "safe" countries (those with a democratic system, a rule of law, etc.). Canada proposed this idea as recently as 1989, but it was opposed by a self-interested immigration lobby (there is no other kind, it seems). At any rate, this is how Canada has become "a home away from home" for millions of people whom we subsidize to ensure their deepest identities here are still rooted in their countries of origin.

Since 1985, over 700,000 asylum seekers have entered Canada without proper scrutiny. Actually, with no scrutiny whatsoever. Many of them are brought here with false documents by clever smugglers of human beings, for large fees. Smugglers guarantee them at least a few years here, fully paid by Canada's government until their case reaches the front of the refugee-hearing lineup. But after a few years (if they get married and have a baby or two), it is unlikely they will get tossed out. Their offspring are automatically entitled to Canadian citizenship, and they are granted a full hearing, given tax-paid legal services, rights to appeal if denied entry, full medicare, dental, and social services, the lot. Canada remains the only Western nation without any preliminary screening process for sorting out potentially deserving claims from those that are manifestly unfounded. At a cost of $10,000 to $12,000 per year per claimant, estimates are that we spend a billion dollars per year dealing with this mess. One step we could take is to change the rules: Canadian citizenship should not be granted to immigrant children unless their parents are already Canadian citizens.

More shocking is the fact that although many thousands of phony refugee claimants are *ordered to leave Canada* each year . . . most of them don't. In May 2008, Canada's Auditor General reported that there were 41,000 *warrants of arrest* outstanding on illegal immigrants. They are somewhere in Canada, but authorities do not know where. We do not know how many of them have communicable diseases, or criminal records, or are terrorists. Canada's most notorious asylum seeker was the Millennium Bomber, Ahmed Ressam, who in reality was an al-Qaeda operative. He lied when he showed up in Canada, but was admitted as a refugee, and was then caught crossing the border into the United States with a truckload of high explosives. He was on his way to blow up the Los Angeles airport.

## IS THE ECONOMY A GOOD REASON FOR MORE IMMIGRATION?

Many argue that because we have an aging society, a changing ratio of retirees to workers, and falling fertility rates, we need lots of immigrants or the economy will eventually go into a tailspin. This argument seems plausible at first because without sufficient bodies, who will buy the food, rent the offices and retail spaces, buy the diapers, and so on? The prospect of a rapidly falling population is scary, and the looming demographic winter seems real. Canada's own Annual Report on Immigration notes that immigration will be "a key source of workforce growth in the future." But bad thinking has produced what looks like a false assumption.

Canada's first serious study of this question was carried out in 1985 by the Royal Commission on the Economic Union and Development Prospects for Canada (known as the Macdonald Commission). Its conclusion was that "immigration did not contribute to economic growth, but in fact caused a decline in per capita income and real wages in Canada."[33]

In July 2009, the C.D. Howe Institute warned: "For Canadians to expect more, younger immigrants to counteract the effects of low past fertility on workforce growth and aging would be a serious mistake."[34] The institute's sophisticated projections tell us that "only improbably huge increases" in "net" immigration rates (after subtracting all those who return home) of "more than 2.5 times" recent rates (600,000 to 700,000 new immigrants per year) have any

THE TROUBLE WITH CANADA ... STILL! 413

chance to offset the consequences of lower past fertility. Even when "age filters" favouring much younger immigrants were plugged into the projections, they showed the need for a future Canadian population ranging between 60 and 200 million people before the current aging and falling fertility factors were neutralized. Projections relying on immigration flows to improve the economy tended "to produce explosive population growth, with ludicrous terminal numbers. . . ." In the year 2050, Canada would need 7 million immigrants.

The conclusion was that better and faster results could be achieved by raising the age of retirement from sixty-five to seventy, boosting natural fertility rates from the current 1.5 children per woman to 2.1, and increasing productivity (real output per worker) by 1 percent. The authors also cite a major 2004 study of the European situation by the RAND Corporation. It concluded that "immigration could do little to mitigate the challenges created by low fertility in the European Union" because, as in the numerous Canadian studies cited, "the momentum of the resident population largely overwhelms immigration's influence." More sobering: the United Nations Population Division has concluded that for Europe to rebalance its own demographic mixture to avoid eventual collapse, it would require over 700 *million* immigrants by 2050—more than the present population of the whole of Europe![35]

In his survey of Canadian immigration research, Martin Collacott points out that "the government's own research" indicates that immigration plays a minor role in boosting the economy. "Overall economic performance of newcomers," he writes, "has fallen below that of earlier immigrants and people born in Canada. A major reason for this is the priority given to family-class immigrants," none of whom is required to bring any marketable skills to Canada, nor to speak either official language.[36] Underlining the problem of immigrant illiteracy, Frank McKenna of the TD Bank Financial Group said that the immigrant illiteracy issue is "sort of like boiling a frog, it's not . . . something that would alarm people, because it's not all that evident; we just gradually become poorer as a nation as a result of this loss of potential."[37] Adding to the complexity is the fact that immigrants to Canada increasingly are coming from areas such as Asia where English and French are not native tongues (up to 40 percent of Canada's new immigrants speak neither English nor French). The concern is that the economic well-being of newcomers has been deteriorating over the past twenty-five years, with unemployment and poverty levels significantly higher among immigrants than among Canadian-born citizens.

In sum, too many immigrants arrive with no skills, no common language with which to engage with their host country, and immediately demand free social, medical, dental, and unemployment benefits. This phenomenon is all but international now and is causing some panic in many established welfare states because, as European analyst Martin Paldam found, "the traditions of protection of the weak *cause adverse selection of immigrants*, so that most are unskilled."

However, welfare states, he warns, only survive if they stand on an implicit compact: we all give, in order, if necessary, to receive. People will accept high levels of taxation if they believe recipients of welfare are like themselves: if they "have made the same effort to be self-supporting and will not take advantage." However, "if values become extremely diverse in a diversified population, then it becomes difficult to sustain the legitimacy of a risk-pooling welfare State."[38] In plainer words, if you set your country up to attract freeloaders, they will come.

George Borjas of Harvard University (himself an immigrant and perhaps the world's most acknowledged authority on this question) echoes the findings of other major studies done since the mid-1980s by mainstream economists in Canada, the United States, Australia, and the UK: *the only significant economic impact of immigration is to reduce the wages of native workers.*[39]

In 2007, a Statistics Canada study, "Chronic Low Income, and Low Income Dynamics Among Recent Immigrants," revealed that notwithstanding the emphasis on education in the "skilled worker" category of immigrants, "their earnings in relation to native Canadians were significantly lower and continue to deteriorate."[40] Professor Alan Green of Queen's University has stated categorically that "the current political posture of using immigrants to solve economic problems is no longer valid."[41]

To conclude: a recent study by economist Herbert Grubel of Simon Fraser University revealed that the 2.5 million immigrants who came to Canada between 1990 and 2002 *received $18.3 billion more in government services and benefits in the year 2002 alone than they paid in taxes for that year!* Grubel states that this amount was more than the federal government contributed to health care in 2000–2001, and more than twice what it spent on defence.

And finally, let us bash the "Bigger is Better" myth. A bigger economy is not necessarily a stronger one. China, for example, has a huge economy because it has more than a billion people. But in per capita earnings it is around 100th in the world—whereas Canada is in the top ten. As long as a strong economy of any size continues to produce sufficient numbers of babies to maintain viable age-to-dependency ratios (ratio of born to dying, and workers to retirees), a country will remain stable. Small but strong stable economies such as those of Switzerland, Finland, the Netherlands, Austria, Singapore, and Hong Kong do not have to be big. Neither does Canada.

## COMING OR GOING? HOW COMMITTED ARE THEY TO CANADA?

A 2006 Statistics Canada study revealed something rather astonishing. Many thousands of immigrants do not come here to become Canadian or make Canada their home: more than *one-sixth* of all immigrants who come to Canada return to their native countries within a year, and *one-third* within twenty years! So if over twenty years we took in 5 million immigrants, some 1,666,000 went back home. Any citizen forking over tax dollars to screen, interview, educate, and supply free government medical, legal, language training, and subsidized education services to admit millions of people to Canada as citizens in the first place might be forgiven for getting a little angry at learning they take what they want from us and then go back home, not to mention the amounts of cash they send out of Canada while they are here. The bulk of the returnee-immigrants in the twenty-five to forty-five age group are people who entered Canada in the "skilled worker" or "business" category; some 40 percent of all professional male immigrants leave Canada for good within a decade. Readers will be forgiven for thinking many of the immigrants who come are "citizens of convenience." But do these immigrants know much about Canada's deep culture? Would they die to defend Canada? Don't hold your breath. If our own government tells us so many skilled workers and professionals are leaving, who stays?

Canada is at war just now, and we have had a very proud history of immigrant warriors willing to fight and die to defend us. But is this true since multiculturalism took hold, that is, since we began subsidizing and encouraging immigrants to maintain their original identities? In "Who Fights and Dies for Canada?"[42] Douglas Bland, chairman of Queen's University's Defence Studies Program, answers the question bluntly: "Young white men, that's who fights." Of the 133 Canadian who died in the recent war against terror (as of January 2010), there were six soldiers from visible minorities. Despite significant efforts since 1982 to attract military personnel from all social groups, visible minorities—now at 16 percent of Canada's total population—make up only 3.4 percent of Canada's armed forces. But then, how many of Canada's soldiers, visible or not, are from big cities? Either way, this race divide further underlines the urban-rural civil war of values to be discussed below. Here is a more interesting question: If Canada went into a direct, war today against, say, an Islamic country, and began to draft citizens for war, would our immigrant-citizens from that country fight with Canada, or against? In the past, when we insisted on assimilation and patriotic allegiance, we knew the answer. Today, it remains a question mark. I think all immigrants to Canada should be required to sign a Vow of Citizenship that among many other things would include a statement to the effect that in the case of a conflict or war with their country of origin, they would, if required, unhesitatingly defend and fight for Canada.

## IMMIGRATION: THE TROJAN HORSE OF TERRORISM?[43]

*We've got Sikh and Tamil organized criminals from India, Vietnamese gangs and the very sinister Big Circle Triad from China, Yakuza from Japan, networks of Nigerian fraud artists, criminal networks from Lebanon, Armenia, Albania/Kosovo, Mafiya from the former Soviet Union, Yardies from Jamaica and Trinidad, criminal gangs from Iran, Colombia, El Salvador, Mexico, Roma [Gypsy] pickpockets, Warriors and Posses from our own aboriginal communities—and we still have the old Mafia, the Bikers and the traditional Triads. . . .*
—Mackenzie Institute (Toronto, 2009)

*With perhaps the singular exception of the United States, there are more international terrorist groups active here [in Canada] than in any other country in the world.*
—Ward Elcock, director, Canadian Security and
Intelligence Service (CSIS), 1998

In the eagerness of too many to vie for ethnic votes, politicians of the successive governments of Canada have conveniently ignored the historical fact that many of the cultures we now encourage and subsidize to maintain their old ways on Canadian soil have been at each other's throats, either attitudinally or in periodic armed conflicts, from time immemorial. Jews with Arabs, Greeks with Armenians (and both with Turks), French with English, Spaniards with Basques and Moors, African tribes with other African tribes, Iranians with Iraqis, Chinese with Vietnamese, Sikhs with Hindus (and both with Muslims), Japanese with Koreans, and . . . English with French! Given the truth of this, how has the Canadian government deluded itself into believing that by promoting and subsidizing each group's ethnic and cultural *differences* such hostilities will ever disappear?

If the argument were still the original one that governed Canadian immigration for centuries—They will get along because we will encourage them to assimilate to Canada's deep culture, which is a set of universally workable and time-tested practices, values, and political institutions grounded in respect for compromise, love of law, and of British liberty, etc., and in doing so they will become one with us—that would make sense. But in our age of cultural and moral relativism, that national confidence is gone. Too bad.

Faced with our own cultural decay, we grew timid. Politicians (there were few statesmen) saw the potential votes that could be theirs if they catered to cultural differences and multi-exclusionism—a kind of unity of differences—rather than to concrete historical, tried-and-true Canadian unity. But even before this, Canada had a sorry history of ethnic violence.

Consider the following:

---

## SNAPSHOT
Some Historical Examples of Canadian Inter-Cultural Violence Prior to 9/11

- In April 1868, Thomas D'Arcy Mcgee was assassinated in Montreal by an *Irish terrorist* who was continuing the Irish Fenian conflict on *Canadian* soil.
- In the 1920s, the first organized *terror threats against Canada* came from the Sons of Freedom, a minority sect of the Doukhobors, a Russian religious community dedicated to non-violence. Over four decades this sect was responsible for "over a thousand arson and bomb attacks" (Bell, *Cold Terror*, p. 21). They burnt many Doukhobor villages, planted dynamite bombs, attacked schools, and paraded naked. In October 1924, they blew up a train, killing six people including the main Doukhobor leader. Canadian police stopped them only by the early 1960s.
- Beginning in the early 1960s, Cuban exiles from Fidel Castro's island socialism *attacked Cuban interests in Canada*, mostly in Montreal; Serbs and Croats, angry over ethnic tensions in what was then Yugoslavia, *attacked each other in Canada*; and the Arab-Israeli conflict (ongoing) became violent in the 1970s (then mostly aimed at diplomats in Canada).
- On October 5, 1970, British diplomat James Cross was kidnapped, and on October 17, Vice-Premier of Quebec Pierre Laporte *was murdered* by *French-Canadian terrorists* of the Front de libération du Québec (FLQ). They were fighting to *separate Quebec from Canada* and form a new French nation. Beginning in the late 1970s, *Armenian terrorists* bent on revenge for what Turkey had done to their grandparents in World War I, *targeted the Air Canada baggage centre* for bombing, *murdered* a Turkish military attaché *(Colonel Atilla Altikat) on an Ottawa street*, then *murdered a Canadian security guard (Claude Brunelle) during an arme*d takeover of the Turkish embassy in Ottawa.
- In 1982, the Squamish Five *bombed a hydroelectric station in British Columbia and a Litton Industries building in Toronto*. They were protesting the "American War Machine." They were eventually caught and jailed.
- A videotape of dozens of turbaned *Sikhs at the Toronto airport* on July 6, 1984, shows them all standing with their swords raised in the air, chanting, "Death to Indira Gandhi!" On October 31 of that year, she was assassinated by her own Sikh bodyguard. Hindus retaliated. CSIS warned that this would lead to "serious animosity *between the two groups in Canada.*"
- In 1985, *Sikh terrorists* belonging to the *Canadian branch* of Babbar Khalsa, a radical group fighting for their own Sikh state (Khalistan), succeeded in

blowing up Air India flight 182, killing all 329 passengers, of which *280 were Canadian citizens*. They were also behind the attempted destruction of another Air India flight that failed, when the bomb they planted exploded in Narita International Airport, *killing* two Japanese baggage handlers. The court case over this attack took more than twenty years to conclude at a cost of $130 million. Neither of the *two Sikh-Canadians charged* was ever convicted. One witness prepared to testify against them was murdered. Only one man, Inderjit Singh Reyat, was convicted—for making the Narita bombs. He received a five-year sentence in 2003. In 2003, Babbar Khalsa was finally listed as a terrorist organization, eighteen years after the Air India tragedy. Prior to this it was given charitable status and provided Canadian tax receipts for its blood money until 1996, when this status was revoked. Canada's Air India terrorism attack was the *largest mass murder in Canadian history*, the largest attack in history prior to 9/11, and for Canada was proportional to the American 9/11 attack in which around three thousand innocents died. But in contrast to the American public reaction, neither the Canadian reaction was muted—perhaps for racial reasons: the victims, though all Canadian citizens, were ethnic Indians. Prime Minister Mulroney embarrassed himself publicly by expressing his condolences to India. The separatist Khalistan movement has mostly fizzled in India, but "maintains a small but loud presence here in Canada." (*National Post*, October 28, 2009).

- In 1997, *Canadian Sikh radicals attacked* Sikh moderates with knives and swords over matters of policy and control at the Ross Street Temple, Surrey, B.C.

- In 1998, the publisher of the *Indo-Canadian Times*, Tara Singh Hayer, was attacked and left paralyzed from the waist down; later the same year, he was murdered. While no one has ever been charged, it is widely believed that this crime was carried out by Sikh extremists since he was prepared to provide incriminating evidence in connection with the Air India case.

- *Canadian terrorists* are known to have taken part in: the 1993 World Trade Center bombing; bombings in Israel; political killings in India; the murder of tourists in Egypt; the 1995 bombing of the Egyptian embassy in Islamabad that killed seventeen; a 1996 truck bombing in Sri Lanka that killed almost a hundred civilians.

# INSIDE THE TROJAN HORSE: DOES IMMIGRATION FOSTER TERRORISM?

*I find it very alarming that people who are Canadians who grew up in this country [would] turn against their country.*
—Peter Van Loan, Canadian minister of public safety, March 28, 2009

There is some persuasive evidence, here and elsewhere, that immigration does indeed foster terrorism. Consider that a study of forty-eight foreign-born al-Qaeda terrorists who committed crimes in the United States between 1993 and 2001 (including the 9/11 hijackers) found that they had penetrated almost every part of the U.S. immigration system. They were either legal residents, naturalized citizens, illegal aliens, or asylum seekers. Almost half had violated ordinary immigration laws.[44] Another study found that the immigration visa application of every single 9/11 terrorist ought to have been rejected on ordinary, non-security grounds. This is appalling but not surprising: a 2006 U.S. study revealed that at least four million people whose "temporary" visas to the United States had expired, simply stayed on as illegal aliens. For most modern nations the problem is the same: they cannot seem to prevent questionable people from entering their territory, and cannot seem to remove them once they are there. But the international community is reacting: the terrorist bombings in London, Madrid, and Mumbai, the murder of Theo Van Gogh in Amsterdam, the international protests over the Danish cartoons ridiculing Mohamed, and the riots in France, among other events, are persuading confused authorities that *mass immigration and national security are incompatible objectives.*

As for Canada? Ever since the mid-1980s, Canada has been easily entered by extremists who have plotted against and often attacked their historical enemies on our soil. Let us examine a few of these internal situations before looking at the matter of external Islamic attacks on the West, and homegrown Islamic terrorism.

---

## SNAPSHOT
More Recent Facts and Examples of Inter-Cultural Terrorism in Canada

- In 1998, the Canadian Security Intelligence Service (our version of the FBI, created July 16, 1984) reported to Parliament that there were "*more than 50 terrorist organizations* operating in Canada."
- In 1999, Fateh Kamel, alias Moustapha, an Algerian-born *Canadian Muslim citizen*, was arrested by French authorities for his alleged role in *plotting international jihadist attacks* on the West. After serving his sentence in France, Kamel returned to Canada in January 2005. He has never been charged as a terrorist in Canada. He wanders freely here, and is presently suing the federal government for infringing on his Charter rights by refusing him a new Canadian passport.
- In 1999, Ahmad Ressam, an Algerian who asked for *asylum status in Canada* (even though France had warned us he was a terrorist!) took over Kamel's Montreal cell (now defunct). The members were planning to bomb a Jewish section of Montreal and the Montreal subway system, but

they wanted a bigger target. Ressam (who used a false identity to get *a Canadian passport*) was stopped at the U.S. border with a truck full of explosives. He was on his way with his *made-in-Canada bomb* to blow up the Los Angeles airport. Ressam was a member of a Montreal cell of the Algerian Armed Islamic Group (which has strong links to al-Qaeda). On February 3, 2010, a U.S. appeals court quashed his twenty-two-year jail sentence and increased it to forty-five years.

- In 2002, U.S. attorney general John Ashcroft identified two former *Montreal residents* as being on the U.S. Most Wanted list of al-Qaeda terrorists.

- An Iranian assassin who was *ordered deported from Canada* in 1991 is still here! If his most recent appeal is successful, it will be the third time he will have appeared before Canada's Supreme Court.

- As of 2009, there were at least *eight individual asylum seekers* with clear al-Qaeda links, all either convicted or alleged terrorists, *fighting deportation from Canada.* All entered Canada with forged papers.

- From September 2001 to January 2002, over 2,500 "asylum seekers" entered Canada from "terrorist-producing" nations (all these nations are now on the U.S. priority-screening list).

- From the 1990s forward, the World Tamil Movement, an organization *based in Toronto*, has according to the RCMP sent multimillions of dollars raised in Canada to overseas accounts, much of it "to finance weapons" (*National Post*, May 5, 2009).

- In 2006, the *"war taxes" collected coercively from peaceful Canadian Tamil citizens* by rebel Tamil Tigers to fund the recently ended war in Sri Lanka were estimated at a million a month. Canada refused, despite strong recommendations from CSIS, to put the Tamil Tigers (or Hamas, or Hezbollah) on the Canadian banned-terrorist-organizations list until the Harper government did so in January 2006.

- There are about 225,000 Tamils living around Toronto and they form a powerful "exile community" here. We saw their influence when without resistance from police they blocked major Toronto traffic arteries in the summer of 2009. "The RCMP and Toronto police believe that as many as *8,000 Tamil Guerrillas with military weapons training* are now living in the Toronto area alone." (Bell, p. 48).

- A Tamil Tigers speaker addressing a Tamil rally in Toronto in 1997 told them: "Your support should be converted into money. That money should be converted into *arms for the movement*" ("Public Funding for Private Wars," Mackenzie Institute).

- FINTRAC, a government program for tracking financial transactions, revealed that in 2003–2004, some $700 million in Canadians funds was transferred for purposes of criminal activity, and 10 percent of that ($70 million) was for terrorist activities. By 2005–2006, the amount identified by FINTRAC as going to suspected terrorist activities causes had risen to $256 million.

- On January 25, 2010, *two Canadian Tamils were sentenced in a U.S. court to twenty-five years in prison* for attempting to buy Russian SA-18 missiles and AK-47 rifles for Tamil Tiger rebels.

- On April 17, 2009, Canadian newspapers reported that *a Toronto man, Mahmoud Yadegari, was charged with trying to send nuclear devices* (pressure transducers) to Iran from Canada.

- Until December 2001, it was perfectly legal to raise money in Canada for foreign terrorist causes.

- A 2003 Library of Congress report noted that as of that date Canada had banned *fewer than half* the international terrorist organizations banned by the United States. It concluded that for terrorists, *Canada is "a favoured destination . . . a safe haven, transit point, and place to raise funds."*

- By 2004, the United States had charged 310 suspected terrorists and successfully prosecuted 179. Canada had charged 5, and prosecuted only 1.

- On Wednesday, October 28, 2009, U.S. authorities raided a Michigan warehouse and discovered a Sunni Muslim Brotherhood with cells across the United States. The ambition of this primarily Afro-American group is the violent overthrow of the U.S. government and the creation of a new sharia-law nation called "Ummah" in America to be ruled over by H. Rap Brown, former leader of the Black Panthers (now in jail for shooting police officers in Georgia). Police said the group's leader and his thirty-year-old son, *a Canadian* named Mujahid Carswell (arrested on October 29 in Windsor, Ontario), "viewed themselves as soldiers at war against the United States Government and against non-Muslims." *Two other Canadians* in this group fled, and are still at large.

- On January 15, 2010, a U.S. Grand Jury indicted *Pakistani-Canadian* Tahawwur Rana for his *alleged role in the Mumbai, India, bombing that killed 160* (he had already been charged with plotting to attack a Danish newspaper for printing unflattering cartoons of Muhammad). Rana owns a home in Ottawa.

- In April 2010, Sikhs in Brampton, Ontario, savaged each other with weapons in a battle for temple control. One was stabbed with a kirpan (a ceremonial dagger). Five were hospitalized. There was "blood all around" after this temple melee (*National Post*, April 20, 2010).

## THE QUESTION OF ISLAM: TERRORISM AGAINST THE WEST, AND DEMOGRAPHIC TAKEOVER

*Virtually all of the most notorious international terrorist organizations are known to maintain a network presence in Canada.*
—Canadian Security Intelligence Service, 2003

*Osama bin Laden has publicly identified Canada as a country he believes his followers should attack . . . He ranked Canada fifth out of seven countries, and every other country on that list has already been attacked.*
—Robert Wright, national security adviser to the Canadian prime minister, in a security speech, October 2004

*[Islamic] leaders have always thought globally, viewing their struggles as part of a broader War against the West.*
—Clifford May, president, Foundation for Defense of Democracies, and former *New York Times* foreign correspondent, October 31, 2009

*We have to establish Islam in Canada. I wanna see Islam in every single corner of the city; I would like to see niqabis and hijabis [women wearing face masks and head coverings] everywhere in the city. I want to see "brothers" [Muslim men] in beards everywhere in the city. Because when they see more of us, they will have more respect for us. They will say, 'Look, they are everywhere . . . we cannot go against them."*
—Said Rageah, Muslim cleric, Toronto, 2009

Picture a map with two colours, red for Islam, blue for Christendom. If we ran maps of the past 1,400 years at high speed, we would see these two colours advancing and retreating across the entire Mediterranean basin, parts of middle Europe as far north as Vienna, all of North Africa, the Middle East, not to mention the vast regions north of, and including, chunks of India, and to the far east, south to Indonesia. We would notice immediately that there is never any white space between the two colours. To freeze this map at any point in history since the sixth century would show the labile boundaries between these two theological kingdoms. Anyone visiting the beautiful Alhambra in Grenada, that stunning aesthetic and horticultural tribute to Islamic culture and thought, will sense the beauty and confidence that once was there. In such places—throughout Spain and in other southern European countries—we find plentiful physical evidence of the map: mosques built over churches; then churches built over mosques; or inversely, a veritable warfare of art and theology, ideas and stones. I will come back to this war momentarily. But first, let's look at the slow transformation of the West's own spiritual and ideological foundations that began during the Protestant Reformation in the sixteenth century, and that has made us vulnerable to attack from within and without.

## WE BEGAN BY ATTACKING OUR OWN FOUNDATIONS

As mentioned earlier, the modern democratic spirit that mutated into radical individualism was born a child of the Reformation. It did not take long, however, due to the influence of materialistic science and the dreadful experience of two world wars to abandon this spiritual origin altogether, turning in the end against all public belief in spiritual transcendence (the idea that there might be a spiritual reality that transcends the physical world). This was a fateful turning, as we shall see shortly, that has weakened us considerably, simply because when a materialistic people for whom the universe has lost all higher meaning is faced with a people infused with such spiritual confidence they will blow themselves up as martyrs for God, they stand a good chance of losing.

At any rate, under our new secular paradigm, the communal concept of democracy that began in the faith communities of the West as *Vox populi, Vox dei* ("the voice of the people is the voice of God") also began mutating. From the idea that majorities with a common belief system could—and would— arrive at a common truth by voting, we mutated to a people who believe that democratic rights are most properly expressed by individuals, often as "democratic rights" asserted (via courts) against the larger community itself. Secular scientists were breaking down the physical world into constituent parts in a hunt for the ultimate material truth of the universe; secular philosophers were promoting radical—and very relative—moral individualism. Quantum particles; moral particles. One man, one vote. Atomistic Man. Soon, morality too would be considered a matter of pure individual truth, rather than a truth held in common. These two forms of individuation—one physical, the other political and moral—have produced the disunited, atomized, secular, and materialistic regimes of the West, wherein even the suggestion that morality is a public good to be held in common is now considered offensive.

Raw materialism, however, has always been empty with respect to the "ultimate" questions. It tells us a great deal about the What, but nothing about the Why of existence. Moral relativism is an advance surrender of any possibility of locating a single Why. However, all humans seem to have a spiritual hunger, so the quest for the Why doesn't go away. In the West, even as we mistook the What for the Why and summarily dropped God from the entire question, the hard-wiring of the quest remained. By then, the unspoken logic was: If there really is no spiritual Kingdom of Heaven, well, then let's damn well create a secular one. So in the twentieth century the Western world went to war against itself, twice. The aging, spiritually weakened liberal democracies, living off the rapidly depleting moral surplus of the Judeo-Christian belief system, found themselves waging war against secular totalitarian systems that had become, of all things, political religions! They were attempting to engineer never-before-seen societies of human perfection on earth, in the name of . . . humanity. Across the blasted face of Europe, in a truly fateful historical apocalypse, the old spiritual armies, fighting to defend and preserve the residue of their worn-out religious tradition—self-reliance, the sacredness of human life, equality before the law, and so on—managed to win once again for what may have been the last time. After the atomic bomb, the young found it hard to believe there was much worth fighting for.

What was left? Only demands for equal rights from the State, moral relativism, and its necessary corollary—a mindless "tolerance" of all personal truths. This is now the reductive and unshakable foundation of the Western political and secular orthodoxy. In its name the Western world embarked on a vast and self-contradictory egalitarian program of legal discrimination demanding wall-to-wall equality in social and economic outcomes. All would be good if all were *made* good by law. At last, we would have our Earthly Kingdom. To achieve this, all traditional forms of life rooted in spiritual belief in a fixed natural moral law and in the realities and distinctions of natural human biology were deemed exclusionist and discriminatory. The new orthodoxy teaches that religions discriminate (against all secular norms); that the heterosexual (or "heteronormative") family discriminates against individuals due to its economic, tax, and legal privileges; that traditional sexual morality is oppressive, and so on. It soon became apparent that once aimed at society in this way, democratic equality had become *a universal solvent* because the practical result for all post-Christian regimes has been ever more aggressive attacks on all social, sexual, and economic privileges and laws intended precisely to protect and ensure the success of our traditional regimes. So wherever enforced, equality rights have produced the atomization and decay of traditional morality, and of the common forms of life once based upon them.

This process has produced bizarre ideological consequences—or clashes—*within* all Western societies, to the extent that all those still attempting to live according to our once-spiritual norms (or the moral surplus of them), principles that were the foundation of the Western world for millennia, began to realize they were being drawn in to a radical "civil war of values" within their own countries. Samuel Huntington's insightful study *The Clash of Civilizations* told only half the story. He argued persuasively that many civilizations—such as Islam and Christianity—are rooted in clashing ideologies that will not, and cannot, be melded.

But the deeper story of the Western democracies is that there is a more serious clash *within* each of them. For, having repudiated natural law and human nature, and replaced these foundational premises with a simplistic egalitarian dictate, they proceeded to eviscerate marriage with laws granting individuals unilateral no-fault-divorce rights (to hell with the contractual rights of the observant spouse); laws granting individual women abortion rights (to hell with the rights of the fathers, and of the unborn children); laws granting individuals gay-marriage rights and benefits (to hell with civilization's procreative objective); and then ... they begin fining and jailing citizens for resisting this regime change (to hell with free speech and open debate). This new orthodoxy was to bring about our utopia.

But other segments within Western populations—very often immigrant populations—have rejected this regime utterly. They saw, they continue to see, all these liberations—quite correctly, I believe—as signs of a profoundly demoralized civilization. Thus has the West been engaged in its own civil war of values for a very long time, especially rapidly since the 1970s. Moderate Muslims, however, have made no such mistake. Their spiritual logic has proceeded differently. It is similar to the logic that supported all of Christendom until very recently.

## THE SPIRITUAL LOGIC

The secular Westerner looks at the universe and says: "Because there is no God, the universe must have created itself by purely physical means, so there is no ultimate truth, no answer to Why."

But the Westerner of faith (and the Muslim) says: "As nothing can come from nothing, the universe cannot have created itself, because *for anything to create itself, it would have to precede itself in existence*—which is clearly an impossibility. Hence, the universe must have had a beginning and an eternal or uncreated creator. So absolute truth must exist somewhere, and therefore I must humble myself before this reality and strive to know the truth in whatever way I can."

Anyone can follow the logic embedded in this spiritual conclusion without necessarily belonging to an organized religion. As a purely logical conclusion it has served as the foundation of the Judeo-Christian world for two millennia, and of the Islamic world view for 1,400 years. I was going to say the modern democratic world has rejected it. But that would be wrong. It has never been rejected, because it cannot be refuted. Rather, it has simply been ignored by preference for the weaker self-serving delights of personal liberation promised by secular individualism. It was precisely this choice to abandon our original spiritual logic that divided the West against itself. As a result, within every Western nation today we can see at least a three-way split of the population. To understand the relationship between these parts is to understand why and how Islam, both moderate and radical, fits into the picture.

# THE WEST AGAINST ITSELF:
# OUR HOMEMADE "CIVIL WAR OF VALUES"

*The modern world is full of old Christian virtues gone mad.*
—G.K. Chesterton

**Cohort 1: Our Secular Liberal Population**

This is the largest segment in each Western democracy. Modern liberals are almost uniformly progressive, Statist, materialistic and secular, rarely religious (or if so, only nominally). They believe in the separation of church and state, support egalitarian policies and affirmative action, support moral relativism and "toleration" (are "non-judgmental"), and consider religious morality old-fashioned, Victorian, oppressive (though many will say they are good, with "spiritual" values). They support homosexual rights, abortion rights, and much of radical feminism as a badge of their open-mindedness, and have flexible notions of families (plural), are easy on divorce, soft on crime, okay with pornography. These people live mostly in the big cities of the West, make good money in the free-market system, with which they have few complaints. They are people of low fertility (way below replacement level), and at least in urban settings are often high livers, do plenty of partying, enjoy alcohol, sample recreational drugs, and so on. They find the attitudes expressed by people in Cohort 2 to be ignorant, bigoted, and behind the times. Theirs is the prevailing secular orthodoxy of the modern State. When Muslims and our own faith communities say the West is decadent, they are talking about Cohort 1.

**Cohort 2: Our Faith Population**

This cohort comprises all people of faith who accept the spiritual logic, above, and work that out each in their own way in their own faith communities or simply as individuals. They tend to oppose just about everything Cohort 1 supports, though there is some overlap (such as churches that support gay rights, etc.). They tend toward tradition in all family, moral, and sexual matters. They drink less, smoke less, do less drugs, divorce less, and have a lot more kids than Cohort 1. They also tend to live in outlying suburbs, small towns, and rural areas, with one exception: the immigrant faith population that shares most of these values tends to live in big cities, where they can be with others of their cultural or ethnic kind and keep the faith traditions of their country of origin alive.

The moderate Muslim population fits in here. They are "against the West" only in the sense that they are against all the values—especially the anti-family policies and the moral relativism—promoted and practiced by Cohorts 1 and 3. They consider the values of Cohort 1 immoral and unnatural, and the values of Cohort 3 fascist (whether left or right), or at best utopian, but without moral roots in any set of permanent principles or natural law.

I have direct experience with this moral cleavage myself. In the middle of the night, in the summer of 2008, I received a phone call from a Muslim woman in Iran informing me that her pro-family women's rights group had translated my book *The War Against the Family* into Farsi (Persian). That book was a full-on assault against the anti-family program in the Western world. She was in complete sympathy. I am no Muslim. But I applauded her Cohort 2 pro-family and pro-children values. I still do. Every sociological or psychological study ever done on this cohort tells us these people have stronger and bigger families, less divorce, happier children, less alcoholism, suffer fewer illnesses (including smoking-related diseases) and neuroses, almost none are in poverty or on welfare, they have very respectable educational and occupational levels, and on it goes.

## Cohort 3: Our Radical-Leftist Population

Let us dismiss as disturbing, but to be watched, the small number of right-wing radicals, skinheads, and the like. That done, we can say that Cohort 3 consists mostly of well-to-do educated radicals, many of an alienated, extremist anti-Western nature who are uniformly leftist in their politics, if not openly Marxist, socialist, or anarchist. They are also libertarian (anti-authoritarian) in their morals. They can be found employed by the thousands in the universities and media outlets of the West, where they exercise a powerful influence. They oppose the values held by both Cohorts 1 and 2: the first, because they see them as complacent well-fed, undiscerning materialists (okay, capitalist pigs); the second, because they hold to a holier-than-thou oppressive religious morality (fundamentalist rednecks).

Although they are against capitalist society as a whole and prefer an egalitarian socialist utopia, they live very well themselves. The vast majority of radicals in this cohort have higher pay, drive better cars, and live in more affluent neighbourhoods than the populations they seek to educate and radicalize. Even though they do not share Islamist theology, they are often sufficiently anti-Western to be openly sympathetic with radical Islamist attacks on the West. Radical Islamists want to destroy the West because it is run by "unholy infidels". Our homegrown radicals want to destroy the West in order to build a secular-socialist Kingdom of Heaven on Earth. They are secularized radicals who happen to have a lot in common with . . . Muslim hatred of the West. That is why Osama bin Laden said: "*The interests of Muslims* [he meant his kind of radical Islamist] *and the interests of the socialists* [he meant these Cohort 3 folks] *coincide in the war against the crusaders.*" For him, "crusaders" means all those in Cohort 1, the cozy liberals who have brought the world today's brand of secular capitalist democracy. This analysis tells us that smack dab in the middle of all Western nations today we have *two powerful cohorts that are partly or wholly in sympathy with the Muslim (if not the Islamist) revolt against the West.*

First, we have radicals of our own making who want to bring Western society down through revolution or anarchy. Here are some of the heartless things they said just *after the mass murder of their own fellow citizens* by Islamists on 9/11.[45] Keep in mind that in most nations throughout history, these people would have been prosecuted and jailed for sedition for saying such things in public:

- Professor Robin Kelly, of New York University, said: "We need a civil war, class war, whatever, to put an end to U.S. politics that endanger us all."
- Professor Ward Churchill, then of the University of Colorado, blamed the murdered victims themselves, whom he described publicly as "little Eichmanns."
- Author Norman Mailer said the suicide attackers were "brilliant" and that "everything wrong with America led to the point where the country built that tower of Babel which consequently had to be destroyed."

Second, we have a very large faith population, which, although without such revolutionary motives, is in strong passive sympathy with Muslim disapproval of sexual licence, homosexuality, gay-rights parades, abortion rights, pornography, social saturation with drugs and alcohol, violence in film, TV, and advertising, anti-family legislation, court rulings against religion by secularizing judges, and more. By the same token, most Muslims express strong support for devout Christians (as distinct from nominal ones) because of this sharing of the same moral views.

To summarize: A weakened Western civilization has become so divided against itself that we now fail even to recognize, much less defend, our own deep culture. More often than not, we attack it ourselves. This has exposed us to Islamists who have no such doubts about their own foundations, and who are prepared to use terrorism to replace Western culture.

## ISLAM IN THE WEST: SOME DEMOGRAPHIC FACTS

In the space of a mere half century, as the West has divided against itself in this fashion, it has imploded demographically even as the Islamic world has exploded. Western women (except for Americans) have been reproducing at a Total Fertility Rate (TFR) far below the Population Replacement Rate of 2.1 children per woman since the 1970s. Canadian women now average around 1.5 children each, or fewer, from a high of 3.91 in 1957. But Islamic women everywhere are still averaging 3.4 children each (though their fertility seems to decline rapidly once they are Westernized). At 1.8, a country will be at 80 percent of its current size in a century; at 1.3, it will be at one-quarter. Canada has close to a half-million Muslim females. Demography is the future, and we are witnessing what the French call *la revanche des berceaux*—the revenge of the cradles, an expression coined by French-Canadians when they became aware that the long-term demographic victory over their British masters had to begin between the sheets (a program since defeated by abortion and the pill). In exactly this way, the victory for Islam, as Muslims say, "will be won in the wombs of our women." Western civilization is in the throes of fornicating to death within a regime of contraceptive (and abortive) sterility, while Islam is breeding new life.

In the mid-twentieth century there were almost no Muslims in Western Europe. By the end of the century there were about 16 million—of which, 5 million in France, 4 in Germany, 2 in Britain. Canada's 1981 census listed 98,000 Muslims in Canada—a third the number of Jews, their historical enemy. By 2006, we had 783,700 Muslims (over 2.2 percent of Canadians), and Statistics Canada released estimates in March 2010, that at current immigration rates, Canada will have 2,870,000 Muslims by 2031—seven times the expected size of the Jewish community. Expect trouble. America currently has about 2 million Muslims (excluding Black Muslims). But this type of immigration, as Christopher Caldwell puts it, "is not enhancing or validating European culture; *it is supplanting it*."[46] This supplanting is taking place in racial ghettos all over Europe. And in Canadian cities, too. The City of Vaughan already has one dedicated Muslim housing development—Peace Village—with Islamic schools, mosque, shopping and bank.[47] Accordingly, sociologists remark that many new immigrant groups have no more than a material and pragmatic connection to their new country; they are internal colonists who express only "neighbourhood nationalism." Some immigrant-overwhelmed nations (really, their cities), at a loss for solutions to this ghettoization, are beginning to use the weak argument that this is normal "integration." The mayor of Gothenburg, Sweden, says: "I don't care if you respect our culture; you just have to obey the law." But, as Caldwell observes, this was to demand nothing at all from newcomers, for their notions of excellence and virtue had nothing whatsoever to do with European notions.

Result? Only 50 percent of British Muslims see Britain as "my country" (they identify most strongly with Muslims elsewhere); only 5 percent of Germany's Turkish immigrants say they want to be buried in Germany. Meanwhile, an estimated 50,000 Italians have converted to Islam, and Germany has perhaps 4,000 converts a year. And . . . 37 percent of British Muslims favour executing all Muslims who convert to Christianity. Integration? . . . Ninety percent of Europe's Muslims choose spouses from their home countries. As Caldwell puts it, their marriages alone "are evidence of a collective choice against assimilation." Some 53 percent of Turkish women would not consider marrying a German "under any circumstances," and Germans felt the same. In Britain, only 1 percent of Pakistanis have white partners. Observers say today's immigrants want "a Third World life at a European standard of living."

How are Western secular liberals fighting back? With "compulsory liberation": Holland requires new immigrants to watch a video of Dutch life that includes homosexuals embracing and bare-breasted women on Dutch beaches. All of which is a bizarre turn of events because (Caldwell again): What today's secular Europeans call "Islamic values" are clearly "a set of values that Dante and Erasmus would recognize as their own," whereas the "core principles" of the modern secular West, whether of the European Union or Canada, they would not recognize. Islam is filling a spiritual vacuum we have created ourselves.

## WHAT KIND OF ISLAM IS IT?

*[Jihadists] say that they are committed to the destruction of the entire secular world because they believe this is a necessary first step to create an Islamic utopia on earth.*
—Mary Habeck, professor, School of Advanced International Studies, The Johns Hopkins University[48]

An Environics poll of February 2007 gave this result: about 80 percent of Canada's Muslims said they were satisfied with their new life in Canada, and 73 percent thought the 9/11 terrorist attacks were completely unjustified. But more sinister responses in the poll were buried. Namely, the fact that *an alarming 12 percent of Canadian Muslims questioned in this poll thought the planned attacks for which "the Toronto 18" were arrested, were justified* (Licia Corbella, *Calgary Sun*, February 18, 2007).[49] In other words, by extrapolation, we may have anywhere from 50,000 to 85,000 Canadian Muslims who believe that blowing up our Parliament Buildings (presumably with all MPs inside) and beheading the Canadian prime minister is a great idea. They have lots of European company. Immediately after the 9/11 attacks there was much Muslim dancing and cheering in Belgium and England. In Holland, *Contrast* magazine found that 50 percent of Dutch Muslims were "in complete sympathy" with the attacks.[50] On the second "anniversary" of the 9/11 attacks, radical British Muslims put up posters honouring the terrorists as "*the Magnificent 19.*" Who *are* these people? Why was there no public outcry?

## WHY ARE *WE* THE ENEMY?
The brand of Islam we ought to fear most, the one that is at the root of modern Islamic terrorism, is called Wahhabism. It is at the root of modern jihadism (a term that originally referred to personal spiritual struggle, but which, for radicals, now also means struggle against all non-believers: us). Wahhabism is the spiritual foundation of al-Qaeda.

Its main radical theorists, ancient and modern, have been three: Ibn Taymiyah (1263–1328), who told his followers, "prescribed to you is fighting";

Abdullah Azzam (1941–1989), who advocated "Jihad and the rifle alone. No negotiations, no conferences, and no dialogue"; and Sayyid Qutb (1906–1966), the most cited, and most influential, who declared. "It is the duty of Islam to annihilate all other systems." Like Azzam, Qutb advocated global domination by Islam. All these theorists are united in the singular view that the decline of Islam is not due to the internal weaknesses of the faith, but "is the deliberate policy of an external religious enemy whom jihadis can—and do—blame for all the evils suffered by Muslims around the world."[51] Hence, the term "blame culture."

Wahhabi Muslims have been encouraged "to think for themselves," and to reject the accumulated wisdom of Islam handed down by their clerics, and to favour instead a jihadist interpretation of Islamic teachings (the *hadith*) and of the Qur'an, and to disregard those parts that preach tolerance and peace, and ignore the peaceful Islamic mystics.[52] Their underlying conviction is that true human liberation comes from serving God alone, and that all man-made institutions rooted in beliefs such as democratic sovereignty and materialism are false beliefs that entrap and enslave us. We must be slaves to God, but never to each other, or to false beliefs. For this reason, "jihadis today have made a critique of democracy the centerpiece of their ideology."[53] Democracy is false because it teaches that we can arrive at truth by majority voting, whereas only God knows the truth. So we must strive to know and obey only God's will. Democratic voting enslaves us to false human truth by majority rule and through a secularizing process of spiritual disarmament. Hence, all secular regimes must be either converted, or ended. "Islamism," a term created by the Muslim Brotherhood in the 1920s, describes the belief that Islam is "the complete, obligatory, and virtually non-negotiable guide to human existence,"[54] the foundation for which is sharia law. For Islamists, this means ending even Islamic regimes that are not truly Islamic: estimates are that 100,000 moderate Muslims have been slain by militant Islamists aiming for control of Algeria. It is a pattern repeated in many Muslim nations oppressed by their own radicals. Less than purely Islamic regimes are considered despicable "*jahiliyya*"—places of darkness and ignorance. They complain of modern Christians and Jews that, once secularized, banished religion from public life, and in so doing (as members of Cohort 1, above) they "destroyed the only source of ethics and morality, and therefore have no aim in life except to seek benefit and enjoyment."[55] So, for true believers, the United States and the West (yes, Canada too) are regimes of darkness, modern *jahiliyya*. To see this belief in action in Canada, go to the website of the Institute of Contemporary Islamic Thought, which has an office in Toronto, and which "publicly supports armed struggle against the unbelievers."[56] Follow the threads. Although Wahhabist radical thinking has not found deep support in the world's wider Muslim movements, it nevertheless exists as a powerful force devoted to the use of terrorism both within and against the West to achieve its utopia. After 9/11, Swiss police raided the

Lugano, Switzerland, home of a key Muslim Brotherhood organizer, Youseff Nada, and found a fourteen-page manifesto entitled "The Project," written in Arabic in 1982 by Wahhabi luminaries. It outlines a twelve-point strategy to *"establish an Islamic government on earth."*

---

## SNAPSHOT
Islamic Terrorism in Canada, Against Canada, and Against the West

- Canada is the only country left on Osama bin Laden's seven-country hit list, still to be bombed.
- The bomb that killed or injured more than 1,400 people in Sri Lanka's capital city, Colombo, in 1996 was paid for from a Canadian bank account (Source: Paul Collier, *The Bottom Billion*).
- At a terrorism conference in May 2004, the U.S. Attorney General and the FBI revealed that Abderraouf Jdey, found with a martyrdom video, and Amer El-Maati, a licensed pilot who wanted to crash a plane into a U.S. building ... were both Canadians.
- In 1997, U.S. intelligence awoke to the fact that Canada nurtures and exports terrorism when Gazi Mezer crossed our border into the United States to blow up the Atlantic Avenue subway in Brooklyn.
- One of Osama bin Laden's confidants is nicknamed "El Kanadi"—the Canadian.
- The Mississauga-based Al-Fauz Institute, just outside Toronto, has featured Azzam Tamimi as a lecturer. He has proclaimeds: "I don't believe in democracy anymore," explicitly praises suicide bombers, and says he is willing to blow himself up in Israel.
- In March 2009, Canadian Momin Khawaja was sentenced to 10.5 years in jail for financing and building explosive detonators for use in terrorist attacks.
- In a 2009 Quebec case, Sid Namouth was pronounced guilty of planning terrorist attacks.
- Zakaria Amara, leader of the Toronto 18, who pleaded guilty on October 8, 2009, confessed that his plan for U-Haul trucks loaded with explosives (and metal chips to cause more civilian casualties) were meant "to cripple Canada" and to be detonated mid-November at the Toronto Stock Exchange, at the CSIS office, and at a military base between Toronto and Kingston. In January 2010, Amara was sentenced to life in prison (which in Canada can mean out in fifteen).
- In February 2010, Said Namouth, a Moroccan living in Canada since 2003 who spread hatred from his Montreal apartment, was also sentenced to life in prison. On his blog he wrote: "Terrorism is in our blood, and with it we will drown the unjust."

- The ritual Islamic prayer, says Tarek Fatah, former head of the Muslim Canadian Congress, an anti-extremist Muslim group, "asking for the defeat of Christians and Jews, and the Victory of Islam, is not unique"; it is uttered by many imams across Canada, and is "spreading hate instead of harmony."
- In May 2009, the CBC quoted an anonymous source who claimed that Al-Shabab, a Somali Taliban-style terrorist organization, has recruited twenty to thirty young Canadian men.
- On March 8, 2010, Canada added Al-Shabab to its list of banned terrorist organizations.
- On January 3, 2009, al-Qaeda called on Muslims "to kill every Western diplomat on the Arabian Peninsula." There are Canadian diplomats there.
- In December 2001, the *National Post* listed sixteen Islamic terrorists who had been living in Canada, most of whom had previously been convicted of terrorism by other countries. They were never charged in Canada.
- Among defendants in the $1 trillion lawsuit against 9/11 attackers are Muslim groups such as the Benevolence International Fund, the Islamic Relief Organization, the Muslim World League, the International Islamic Relief Organization, and the SAAR Foundation, all of which have a presence in Canada, several with offices in Ottawa.
- As of 2006, Canada, acting on a British tip, laid its first charge of terrorism, against Mohammad Khawaja, for involvement in a London bombing plot.
- On his Saudi-based Web portal *Islam Q & A*, Muslim cleric Al-Munajjid, who has a large Canadian following, has (quoting the supposed words of Muhammad) "urged Muslim youth not to live among the non-Muslims, unless the objective of living in the West was to convert the non-Muslim to Islam" (*National Post*, November 9, 2009).
- On Christmas Day 2009, Umar Abdulmutallab was prevented by passengers on a flight from Europe to Detroit from igniting explosives hidden in his underwear. In a speech reported in March 2009, warning the United States to think more proactively about terrorist possibilities, Israeli agent Juval Aviv said he was now just "waiting for some suicidal maniac to pour liquid explosives on his underwear." Prophetic, what?
- Conversion from Islam to Christianity (or any other religion) is punishable by beheading.
- As of 2008, "Muslim countries or groups are either at war or in a hostile truce with every civilization that Islam abuts, from Nigeria to Xinjiang [China]" (Caldwell, *Reflections on the Revolution in Europe*, p. 163).

## WHO PAYS TOR TERRORISM?

We do. We buy billions of dollars' worth of oil from Wahhabist countries, and a lot of that money is used to fund the Islamist attack on the West. In his interesting study *Energy Victory: Winning the War on Terror by Breaking Free of Oil*,[57] Victor Zubrin argues that if it had not been for the massive quantities of oil needed every year by the West, the Wahhabism now so energetically exported by Arab countries would have only their hungry goats for an audience—which is all they had prior to the oil-guzzling twentieth century. Zubrin goes on to offer "biofuels" as the solution he is convinced would kill two birds with one stone: biofuel agriculture would employ billions of the world's poor by creating huge demand for bio-crops, cutting off the dollar drain to Arabic countries at the same time.

Since the first oil embargo that jacked up prices 700 percent in 1973, Saudi Arabia has hauled in more than $2 *trillion*, and Western petrodollars still constitute 91 percent of all Saudi Arabia's national income. Meanwhile, 70 percent of all Saudi jobs are performed by Westerners, and only one in six Saudis does real work. After all the mansions, yachts, and white-elephant display projects have been purchased, the leftover money is spent on their passion: spreading Wahhabism throughout the world.

In his chapter "Terrorism: Your Gas Dollars at Work," Zubrin outlines some of the places to which this money goes, including the Muslim World League (MWL) which "functions as the world headquarters for Extremist Islamic networks" (it funded bin Laden's teachers). With gobs of money, the MWL has funded thousands of Islamic teaching schools (madrassas) in other countries like Pakistan, and "hundreds of thousands of graduates of these madrassas soon developed into a fanatical terrorist movement that virtually destroyed civil society in much of Pakistan . . . [and] on the Afghan border, they grouped together to create the horrific totalitarian force known as the Taliban" (of which Azzam, above, was leader until his assassination in 1989, to be replaced by bin Laden). The World Assembly of Muslim Youth (WAMY), also Saudi funded, was established in 1972 by the Saudi Ministry of Education to spread Wahhabism—and its texts—globally. These books, which include manuals for bomb-making, have been found in raids on Canadian Muslim terrorist organizations. WAMY controls 450 youth organizations in thirty-four countries, including the United States. In the 1990s, its president was Abdullah bin Laden, Osama's brother. In 1996, WAMY was listed by the FBI as "an organization suspected of terrorism." Its Washington office was raided in 2004 for suspected contacts with four of the 9/11 bombers. Another item is the International Islamic Relief Organization (IIRO), the financial arm of the MWL (feeling surrounded yet?). It is fully funded by the Saudi government (that is, by our money). It has been the conduit for the funding of radical Islamist organizations in many other countries. Then we come to the al-Haramain Islamic Foundation (also funded by Saudis), which "employs billions of [petro]dollars every year to promote religious extremism and terrorism around the world." It operates in over ninety countries, and in forty of them operates out of the Saudi embassy.

NATO documents of 2002 showed this organization was diverting funds to al-Qaeda and to its Somali contacts. The U.S. government subsequently froze these accounts. After his detailed examination, Zubrin concludes that all these organizations "have spent several hundred billion [petro]dollars over the past thirty years promoting terrorist ideology." He adds that these amounts are more than the totals spent by the Soviet and Chinese communists combined in spreading international communism. Saudis have also built and funded 1,500 mosques worldwide and staffed them with Wahhabist clerics, and an estimated 20,000 madrassas which graduate hundreds of thousands of anti-Western students who are taught that the only certain way to heaven lies in killing unbelievers. And then there are the billions spent building and funding Islamist universities, radio stations, newspapers and TV, and the . . . 210 Wahhabist centres around the world, among which are those in Toronto, Calgary, and Ottawa.

The long and short of this story is that a lot of Middle Easterners who used to herd goats are rich now. The next time you fill up at the gas pump, think about how your petrodollars are making their assault on Western civilization possible.

# WHAT IS TO BE DONE?
## Multiculturalism:

*Stop funding "multiculturalism"*
Ethnic groups lobbying for money from the State are like any other lobby group. They use the money to circumvent the political process. The government must stop funding all of them—left, right, business, radical, ethnic, all of them. Let them fight for what they want through their democratically elected representatives, or through privately funded groups. Canada's government should reconstitute, publicize, and require schools to inculcate the key symbols of Canada's deep culture before they are totally forgotten.

*Require instruction in Canada's deep culture*
Immigrants to Canada should be instructed in the core heritage and culture of this nation, which is Judeo-Christian, Graeco-Roman, and Anglo-European. And they should be expected to assimilate to that culture. This does not mean losing their own, which they are free to promote and protect, using their own resources, if they so desire. But it does mean their own culture is secondary.

*End the contradictions and unrest of multicultural policy*
The government must recognize that its "multicultural" policy is self-contradictory and that it is currently funding long-term social unrest by rewarding the development of cultural differences within Canada. Unity cannot be derived from "diversity." Just as deep cultural differences lead to strife between nations, they lead, and have led, to strife between the "nations-within-Canada."

## Immigration:

*The people must set the immigration agenda*
Government must consult the people through a democratic referendum on immigration to find out what they want their country to become. That should set the government's immigration agenda. During the period of the referendum discussion—say, two years—all immigration should be halted: visitors' permits only. If the country belongs to Canadians, then let them decide on their own future.

*Stimulate homegrown population*
If there is concern over zero growth, Canada should aggressively examine ways to stimulate growth in the Canadian family before resorting to costly and culturally dislocating immigration.

*Make immigrants sign a Vow of Citizenship*
All immigrants should be required to sign a Vow of Citizenship that among many other things would include a statement to the effect that in the case of a conflict or war with their country of origin, they would, if required, unhesitatingly defend and fight for Canada. This is expected of all citizens born here, and it ought to be explicitly required of all immigrants who become citizens.

*End dual citizenship*
Dual citizenship should be banned. If you want the rights and freedoms of Canadian citizenship, you must surrender those of all other nationalities. No cherry-picking. You cannot defend or fight for Canada if in terms of patriotism you live in a divided house. Split national loyalties and "citizens of convenience" are not wanted in Canada.

A government that imposes a multicultural policy and non-traditional immigration on any nation in a calculated attempt to neutralize its deep culture is guilty of subverting the ethos of the nation. Such programs are a veneer disguising cynical vote-grabbing. They have had the effect of transforming Canada, in the space of two decades, into a nation that is eradicating its own past. Unless we learn the lessons of history, this can end, at best, in long-term erosion of our civilizational greatness, and at worst in intra-ethnic strife and militancy on our own soil (such as we have seen already, and will likely see again, in Quebec, and are now seeing among other ethnic groups on our soil).

# 14: FRENCH-FRIED
## OFFICIAL BILINGUALISM, SEPARATISM, AND THE POLITICS OF LANGUAGE AND CULTURE

*It is possible to lead astray an entire generation, to strike it blind. . . .*
—Alexander Herzen

If I had to live in another country, I would probably choose France. I speak and read the language fluently, love the food, and I know a little of the history, literature, and philosophies of the French (and of Quebec, if less so). But a discussion of the politics of language has nothing to do with that. It has to do with cultural domination and submission, and therefore with national politics. For language is like a second skin in which we live, think, and feel. So patriotism and language are almost inseparable, and depending what they are, language rights can over time achieve more than an army on the ground. Indeed, for most nations in history the imposition of an official language is far more than a convenience for the people: it is a tool enabling State penetration, organization, and control of their lives and ways, for a State that cannot "read" the doings of these lives and ways is blind, not in control (if not out of control).[1]

## "OFFICIAL BILINGUALISM": CANADA'S FIRST EXPERIMENT WITH MULTICULTURALISM

The French-Canadian population of Canada is now about 23.2 percent of the total, and of these, about half—or 12 percent, almost 4 million citizens—are unilingual francophones (they speak only French). But the story of Canada's historical experience with the French language does not reflect the 12 percent interest of this minority. It has been a story of the steady advance from no status at all, to an official and mandatory fifty-fifty status equal to that of the English language, from sea unto sea.

Canada's politicians at first wanted either to limit severely, or abolish altogether, the use of French in Canada, to assimilate all French Canadians so that they would lose their original language and we would be one national linguistic community. By the Act of Union of 1840, the use of French in the Canadian legislature was abolished. But there was significant protest, and by 1848 that law was abolished. Then, in 1849, a law was passed that all Canadian laws must be adopted in French as well as English. With Confederation, Section 133 of the BNA Act, 1867, specified that "*Either* the English or the French Language *may* be used by any Person in the Debates of the Houses of the Parliament of Canada, and of the Houses of the Legislature of Québec; and both those Languages *shall* be used in the Records and Journals of those Houses." It also specified that *either* language *may* be used in any court in Canada, and that the legislative Acts of Parliament and of Quebec's legislature *shall* be printed and published in both languages. That's the way it was for Canada's first century.

By the 1960s, however, as a kind of extension of the rising call for identity politics examined in the last chapter, Quebec radicals began stridently demanding more French language rights and protections. So, as discussed in an earlier chapter, the Royal Commission on Bilingualism and Biculturalism (the Bi & Bi Commission) was struck in 1963 to examine this problem, and by 1969 Canada got its first Official Languages Act (OLA), which for the first time proclaimed French and English to be the "official languages" of Canada for all matters under federal jurisdiction. This meant that far beyond the legislatures and courts of Canada, both French and English languages were now mandatory for the work and communications of all departments of the federal government, of all Crown corporations, and for any private companies in Canada receiving federal assistance. Then, with Section 16 of the Canadian Charter of Rights and Freedoms of 1982, French and English were declared the official languages of Canada for *all* purposes (now including all provincial purposes). In 1988, the OLA of 1969 was further amended to ensure that all Canada's laws reflected the reality of the new "official bilingualism." A strange irony of logic: Canada's language regime has never been a truly "bilingual" one; rather, it is official "two-language-ism," for if Canada were truly a bilingual nation, then either language would do, and we would need only one for official purposes. However, even if we leave this paradox aside, the practical fact is that "the continued decline of French outside Quebec and of English inside the province [of Quebec] serves as proof that efforts to build a bilingual nation have been an exercise in futility."[2]

At any rate, at the time, Canada looked at other countries such as Switzerland and Belgium and learned that . . . we had a choice. A bilingual (or multilingual) national language policy could be based on the *person* principle, or the *territorial* principle. Language rights could be vested in each individual person, and would thus be portable; or, language rights could be defined by such as provincial geographical boundaries. Under the first principle, you could demand the right to be served in French or English no matter where you happened to be in Canada. Under the second, Quebec, say, could declare that French was its official language (which it had done), while Ontario might declare English, Italian, and Chinese to be its official languages, and then your language rights would change at the border between these two territories.

Switzerland has five language groups within its national borders, and twenty-four cantons, or provinces. So Switzerland went with the territorial principle. In this canton the official language is German, in that canton, it is Italian (or French), and so on.

For purely political reasons, as we shall see, Canada chose the person (or "personality") principle, instead. The reason was that Quebec separatists were agitating for (and they murdered Pierre Laporte in an attempt to achieve) their dream of a separate French-Canadian state. But Pierre Trudeau famously and powerfully pushed back with the argument that Quebecers would never become an influential part of the Canadian or world community by going inward. Instead, they should come out and become part of this nation and of the world. They could best achieve this under a personality language principle of official bilingualism that gave them the right to be served by their government in French in Toronto, Iqaluit, or Flin Flon. No matter where. Trudeau wanted English people to have the same rights in Quebec, and his Charter specified this right (which Quebec subsequently overrode, trampling on English language rights there). But that notion was both a political sop for French Canadians, and an essential tool for the construction of national socialism à la Canada. For only by ensuring French-Canadian language rights from sea to sea could he credibly diminish the temptation festering within Quebec to break up Canada and build a separate Québécois welfare state (which they have since done anyway).

However, the Quebec legislature (which, irritatingly, they call their National Assembly) fought back. They passed provincial Bill 101 declaring French to be their only official language. So whereas Canada adopted the personality principle as a means to exercise political control over Quebec, the latter reacted by adopting the territorial principle to better control itself. The result is that official bilingualism now exists in all provinces and territories of Canada—except Quebec, the very province for which the policy was designed (and for which Canada was bent out of linguistic shape) in the first place. It is important for Canadians to get a feel for the political forces underlying the present linguistic realities of their nation, and the extent to which language policy is also a political power and culture-domination policy. Examples?

Here are startlingly honest words in a letter to *Alberta Report* (August 1, 1980) by Robert S. Matheson, Q.C., describing his meeting with then dean of law at the University of Alberta, Gérard La Forest, principal draftsman of the Liberal proposals for constitutional change: "I was dismayed to learn how bitterly anti-British La Forest was and how clearly he stated his position that *he would do everything possible to advance the position of French-speaking Canadians over English-speaking Canadians*" [my emphasis]. Here are more startling words from Canadian prime minister Brian Mulroney: "It is the French dimension of our national personality that constitutes the soul of Canada" (interview with *Le Figaro*, 1989). That's news to Albertans! And in his official capacity, Canada's

1982 secretary of state Serge Joyal said, "Everything we undertake and *everything we are doing to make Canada a French state* is part of a venture I have shared for many years with a number of people . . . The idea, the challenge, of making Canada a French country both inside and outside Quebec . . . is something a little beyond the ordinary imagination"[3] [my emphasis].

## THE REVENGE OF MONTCALM—ONCE AGAIN?

The crucial national factor in this story was that Canada's history of blandishments to French Canadians, once in the hands of the master politician Pierre Trudeau, became a key tool in the creation of his dream: *a more socialist nation, from sea unto sea, along French rationalist lines.* His dream was itself an extension of Saint-Simon's theories of the unitary State (as explained in chapter 5), with a bit of Rousseau's mystical bumph mixed in for good measure. What Trudeau's Charter would eventually achieve legally, his 1969 OLA achieved culturally. But his game plan went unnoticed by most English Canadians, who still see the learning of French simply as a fine (even a snobbish) cultural achievement. Of course, learning any additional language is indeed a fine achievement. But Trudeau's official bilingualism was not primarily about language. It was about national political power and unity. What Trudeau wanted most—disliking intensely what he considered irrational English-style checkerboard federalism in general, and free-market capitalism in particular—was a strong socialist nation governed by uniform national regulations, standards, and funding, coast to coast. He wanted to convert our bottom-up, common law–based, piecemeal—and yes, *intentionally* checkerboard Confederation— into as unitary a State as possible in the monistic French style. So he did. Or at least, he got as close as he could. He never deeply understood, or if he did he nevertheless passionately resisted, the theory of personal and constitutional liberalism latent in our founding: the idea that a checkerboard Confederation with a separation of powers (even if not complete) and distinct constitutional freedoms and responsibilities divided between general (federal) and local (provincial) jurisdictions was the best, perhaps the only certain, protection we had against the very tyranny of State powers he preferred. Our once-British liberty was constitutionally wholly poised, not against all State power, but against unlimited, unchecked, unbridled State power.

In short, in Trudeau's mind, our sloppy system of British liberty had to be sacrificed to as much French-style rationalism as was required for the imposition of a uniform constitutional regime. Official language policy was an essential tool for the job. In *Seeing Like a State*, Yale professor James C. Scott details the reasoning behind this, and many other such Statist tools, which, he argues compellingly, are essential to provide powerful regimes with "legibility." This is a term meaning that no State can control its population—conscript, tax, regulate, document, or police the people—if it cannot "read" the population. To follow his metaphor: a country may have gotten along just fine with a myriad of languages and local documents when there was no pressing need or ambition for national control. The affairs of villagers and farmers, even their languages and dialects, may have differed from one town or region to the next. Indeed, before the modern period most of today's nations had hundreds of different dialects, systems of weights and measures, land-use documents, deeds, contract formats, and methods of local taxation, all according to which prince was controlling what. Everything local was quite legible—to locals. But it was illegible to elites, and locals very much liked it that way, for no one then imagined—indeed, they vitally resisted—the demands of the regulatory State. But once modern nationalism reared its head, legibility was immediately an issue, and official language policy became the key instrument for providing the State with the needed legibility. For different languages are effective barriers both for insulating insiders and isolating outsiders (especially elites of the State). Scott writes that in France (the first paradigm case, and the locus of the most insanely egalitarian revolution in history), imposition of an official language was part of a process of "domestic colonization" in which "various foreign provinces are linguistically subdued and culturally incorporated."[4] French officials insisted that every legal document be drawn up in French, and this "campaign of linguistic centralization was assured of some success, since it went hand-in-hand with an expansion of state power." Hear, hear, Canadians! He then adds that "one can hardly imagine a more effective formula for immediately devaluing local knowledge and privileging all those who had mastered the official linguistic code. It was a gigantic shift in power." In the case of Canada, as we shall see below, it has been a question of mastering the official bilingual code. Scott then cites historian Eugen Weber, who remarked that for revolutionary France, "there can be no clearer expression of imperialistic sentiment . . . *whose first conquests were to be right at home*" [emphasis mine]. In Canada's case, imperialism never died, for to the extent possible, the Charter has subjugated the provinces and made them internal colonies of Ottawa. Official language policy played a large role in that transformative process.

For to make his socialist dream a reality Trudeau *had to suppress the desire of Quebecers to become a separate nation*, because a broken country would mean no national socialism. The defeat of Statism in Canada. A broken dream. His solution to the problem was to force official bilingualism on the Rest of Canada (ROC), thus neutralizing the old French complaint that they were second-class. All he had to do was *to confer upon a small minority the same language status and rights as the far larger majority*. Because Quebec tends to vote as a bloc in its own interests, and thus a federal party is unlikely to win an election without Quebec's support, this clever policy amounted to simultaneous *appeasement* and *control* of the French fact in Canada. It was simple. And it was also a recipe for a very successful program to discriminate against English

Canadians and at the same time subordinate to the French style what was to him an intellectually unsavoury English form of constitution. It was "a gigantic shift in power," both from the English to the French governing style in Canadian life, and from the periphery to the centre.

While English Canada slept, Trudeau did something insidiously clever that was—and still is—invisible to parents trundling their children off to French-immersion classes (English-immersion classes for francophones remain illegal in Quebec). With his Charter, he made the minority and the majority culture politically equal in law, and perpetuated the long-standing myth that Canada had two founding peoples. But as one of Canada's constitutional experts, the late Eugene Forsey had long since made quite clear in his 1966 lecture entitled "Seven Devils of Pseudo-History" the idea of Canada as a Confederation of two founding peoples, with two linguistic groups relatively evenly balanced, has always been a fairy tale: "It was certainly not intended to be two political nations. This is unmistakably plain. Over and over again the 'Canadian' Fathers of Confederation, French, English, Irish and Scots, declared emphatically that they were creating a *new* nation."[5]

In short, the experience of the French and the English in Canada is a sharp illustration of my argument against official multiculturalism: once you give official equality status to minority cultural identities you are then forced to provide "rights," *which each different group will then use to dismember the common social fabric through lobbying for cash and power to protect its own interests.* How, otherwise, could a minority French population in a vast land like Canada have succeeded in exercising such political clout over the linguistic, cultural, and constitutional framework of this nation? Part of the answer is that since 1969 we have shelled out a great deal of money to promote official bilingualism.

In a study by François Vaillancourt and Olivier Coche, the costs of official bilingualism for the year 2006—which included all direct and indirect costs, subsidies, transfer payments, translation services, language training, $800 annual "bilingualism bonuses" for all 71,269 civil servants holding federal "bilingual positions" (there's $57 million a year in bonuses alone!), mandated bilingual printing, and more—were conservatively estimated to lie between $1.6 and $1.8 *billion* annually.[6] This means that for the forty years during which official bilingualism has existed—a policy, recall, that only makes a positive language difference to 4 million unilingual francophones, or one-eighth of Canada's population who live in Quebec (and do not require services in English)—an estimated average (assuming the costs started lower, and grew) of, say, $1 billion per year for forty years would bring the total governmental compliance costs of bilingualism since 1969 to . . . $40 billion.

However, this does not include all private sector costs, with which many thousands of corporations across Canada (where there are virtually zero unilingual French-speaking citizens) are forced to comply in their hiring, advertising, bilingual labelling, services, and so on. (After English, the second-largest language group in British Columbia is Chinese. But 100 miles deep in the mountains you may come across a public-park sign in English and . . . French.) The private sector cost has been estimated at between ten and twenty times the public cost (no one can say for certain). If this is true, and we take a low multiple of twelve, it means that publicly and privately over forty years we have spent almost as much to satisfy a legislated national bilingualism policy ($480 billion) as the principal amount of Canada's entire federal debt (as of 2010 heading over $500 billion again—a sum that does not include provincial or municipal debt). To this amount annual interest payments must be added. At a low estimated average from the start of, say, 6 percent per year on a forty-year average annual federal debt of, say, $350 billion per year, this would come to about $20 billion per year, times forty years—or $800 billion! Now all private spending on bilingualism is a deductible expense to corporations. But if those expenses had not been mandated by government the amount would likely have remained in the taxable economy, producing tax revenue in amounts sufficient to pay down Canada's entire federal debt! In sum, if we suppose Canada had not had a powerful prime minister with national socialist ambitions (Quebec has had only provincial socialist ambitions), and if we had instead chosen a reasonable territorial language policy such as did Switzerland—and Quebec—then these costs would have been avoided. Result? Federally at least, Canada would today be a debt-free nation!

## THE EFFECT OF BILINGUALISM ON POWER

As of 2006, Canada had just over 4,100,000 unilingual francophones, almost every one of them living in Quebec. This means that for every unilingual francophone in Quebec there is about one bilingual (speaks French and English). But for every anglophone in the rest of Canada who is bilingual in French, there are *fifteen* who speak English only. As Peter Brimelow acutely points out, in an understatement, "They [unilingual anglophones] constitute an improbably large bloc . . . to be permanently reduced to the status of second-class citizens." He continues: "That the children of the majority should be required to bear the brunt of acculturation, particularly when their language is that of the entire continent, is a measure of the extent to which the [French] minority has the moral [and political] initiative in Canada."[7]

So here's the picture: we have a situation in which full and free language rights have been legally suppressed for English speakers living in Quebec, at the same time as all other Canadians are being told their public and commercial world must by law become increasingly bilingual. The result is that since the 1970s unilingual Canadians have had a much harder time gaining public or private employment wherever bilingualism is required. The government of Canada is our largest employer by far, and as we have seen, offers very cushy jobs with wages above the private sector equivalent (see chapter 7) with dream pensions. But as journalist Richard Gwyn put it, those in the majority were destined "to be disadvantaged in life, through no fault of their own. . . . The central inescapable fact of bilingualism [is] clear: it mean[s] loss of power for unilingual English Canadians."[8]

## A LOPSIDED FRENCH INFLUENCE?

Here are the facts: the federal government is the single largest employer in Canada, with a lot of plum civil service positions to fill. Every year, of all federal public servants who fail the Language Knowledge Examination, about two-thirds are anglophones. They have trouble passing because they were not raised as minorities in a bilingual context, so most of them have never had occasion to use French regularly. In an effort to get the facts on this situation— is federal employment biased against English Canadians?—in January 2010, I asked Canada's Treasury Board: "What percentage of our federal government's 71,290 'bilingual positions' are held by people whose mother tongue is French?" The answer was that 63 percent (44,909 employees) declared French as their first official language. Only 37 percent declared English.[9] This means that French Canadians have a 200 percent advantage over English Canadians in securing a federal bilingual job. That is "a gigantic shift in power." And that does not take into consideration the many "bilingual positions" in other provinces. It seems pretty obvious that Canada has institutionalized a form of national linguistic racism. Indeed, this form of racism is now hereditary in Quebec: you may not send your children to an English school unless you were yourself educated in an English school. All other ethnicities or language groups are barred from sending their children to English schools.

As for French influence at the top? I couldn't find a good study of French influence in Canadian public life as of 2010. But when Trudeau was at the height of his power, 44 percent of his cabinet comprised francophones, including twelve of his top eighteen ministers. Ever since 1969 and the first OLA, the percentage of francophones in the federal civil service has been well beyond any "quota" percentage in most important departments. In 1989, at Elections Canada, francophones represented 82 percent of staff; of the House of Commons staff, 65 percent; of the Public Service Commission, 62 percent; of the Canadian International Development Agency (CIDA), 57 percent; of the Governor General's staff, 68 percent; of the Secretary of State staff, 68 percent; and (wouldn't you know it!) of the Office of the Commissioner of Official Languages, 71 percent.[10] And still, the one part of the country where bilingualism is *not* officially promoted is the province of Quebec. For the English there have been under direct "legislative attack," which is why so many have left Quebec in recent decades.[11] It is also the biggest reason why so few immigrants choose Quebec as their new home.

The upshot of all this? The Supreme Court attempted to sustain the Trudeau game plan by declaring Quebec's Bill 101 unconstitutional because it suppressed fundamental language freedoms of the English and other minorities there. In response, Quebec used the Charter's "notwithstanding" clause to maintain its bill in force. The irony is that as a result of the imposition of a code law Charter, the million or so English then living in Quebec got their language rights mangled, and the 29 million Canadians who are not unilingual francophones have been forced to accept federal and provincial language policing of their public and private businesses and employments, and second-rate status when it comes to government jobs. Some ask: Do we really have language police in Canada?

## THE CREATION OF CANADA'S LANGUAGE POLICE

The ostensible purpose of Bill C-72 (July 7, 1988) was to extend Canadian laws relating to both official languages, and to ensure respect for both. But as the late Kenneth McDonald wrote in his study *A Solution to the Problem of Quebec*, "It's clear that the purpose of the Bill was to expand the use of French far beyond the provisions of the Official Languages Act, which themselves went far beyond those of the British North America Act." The two languages were now mandated to be "the language of work" in "all federal institutions," and officers and employees would henceforth have the *right* to use either. Thenceforth, "all Crown corporations, courts, boards, commissions, councils or departments of the federal government, the armed forces, the RCMP," fell under Bill C-72. Thenceforth, language skill, rather than professional merit, would be the key to employment and promotion.

Here are just a few of the draconian provisions of Quebec's Bill 101, and Ottawa's Bill C-72, both prototypical instruments in Canada's regime change. The latter was enthusiastically supported by all three federal parties. After reading this, you will not wonder that Amnesty International, an organization that serves as a watchdog on political repression around the world, vowed to "keep an eye" on Canada after it saw these bills. Here are some of the things variously found in them that worried this international freedom watchdog: French was declared the only official language of Quebec, and in many important public and commercial respects English was declared illegal by diktat for almost a million anglophone Canadian citizens; immigrants to Quebec are forbidden to send their children to English schools (Section 81 of Bill 101 explicitly demands that immigrants sacrifice their personal well-being for the sake of the well-being of the French language); only the French text of statutes and regulations is official; all private company names, business publications, signs, and advertising are to be in French; English on signage and advertising must appear in regulated lesser font sizes and inferior positioning; Quebec language officers cannot be prosecuted in the line of duty (and the Quebec people, and their language police, are encouraged to spy upon and report illegal English language usage); the identity of someone complaining about a language infraction cannot be revealed; those who contravene the act are liable, in addition to costs, for fines of up to $500 (payable by persons), or $1,000 (payable by corporations) on a first offence, and $1,000 to $5,000, respectively, thereafter. For carrying on business without a "francization certificate," a firm is liable for fines of up to $2,000 a day. Canada's official languages commissioner and staff are not compellable witnesses, nor can they be pursued in the courts or sued for libel or slander (more French-style *droit administratif*). That such language police provisions have survived court challenges in Canada is a sign of the present debasement of the Canadian people, of how we have lost our founding dedication to British liberty.

## POSTSCRIPT ON THE PROBLEMS OF SEPARATION—FOR QUEBEC, OR ANY OTHER PROVINCE

The 1995 Quebec referendum on "sovereignty association" almost shattered the unity of Canada forever. One percentage point more in favour of separation would have certainly led to a messy and violent skirmish. The Rest of Canada (ROC) is of course tired of this endless and perilous exercise, and Western Canada's eagerness to remain in Confederation under such conditions has been strained to the breaking point. Curious people will be able to find lots of online information on Western Canadian separatist movements. I have included the following because there is widespread misunderstanding in Canada on the whole question of separation. For example, in a recent *Edmonton Journal* article concerning Quebec's perennially resurgent agitation for separation, columnist Lorne Gunter wrote: "Let them stay or let them go, it's their decision" (*National Post*, February 19, 2010). However, I submit there can be no such unilateral decision in a duly constituted nation.

To the contrary: there can be no greater vandalization of a nation's Constitution than an illegal attempt by a part to destroy the whole. Quebec has tried to destroy Canada a number of times, and may do so again. Although the current opinion is that Quebec separation is now impossible (former Quebec premier Lucien Bouchard stated this publicly, to the dismay of radical Quebec separatists, in February 2010), the future is long. In a *La Presse* poll of June 9, 2009, a majority of 58 percent said Quebec "ought to have greater autonomy, or separate." A year later, Gilles Duceppe, leader of the Bloc Québécois, sent out a letter to 1,600 elected officials in the United States, Central and South America and Europe and Asia warning the whole world "to brace for a referendum." As many of the older pro-Canada Quebecers are dying off, are they leaving the field open to a younger, more separatist crowd?

If as a nation we wish to escape strife and more possible bloodshed in the future, over the separatist ambitions of Quebec or any other province, if we wish to avoid the fate of Ireland, Yugoslavia, and other divided nations that have devoured themselves over lines on the map, then we have at the very least a duty to ask the right questions. Then, if any of us end up as patriotic Canadians abandoned in Alberta, or if we suddenly discover our shipments to eastern customers can no longer pass freely to Newfoundland through Quebec, or if our sons and daughters are conscripted to defend Canadian citizens or a federal airport inside a separating province—we will not be able to say we never dreamed it could happen.

## THE BIG LIE

To focus for the moment on Quebec: the official Big Lie, relentlessly spoon-fed to Canadians by their own governments since 1960, says that Canada was a nation "created by two founding peoples," the English and the French, and that Canada is "an equal partnership between two founding races." We saw what the distinguished constitutional historian Eugene Forsey said, above: from the start, Canada was intended to be a new nation, not two nations. In "The Myth of Biculturalism, or the Great French-Canadian Sales Campaign" (*Saturday Night*, September 1966), historian Donald Creighton wrote that no one at any of the three conferences called to create Canadian Confederation "would have dreamed . . . of constituting such a meeting along ethnic or cultural lines." And further, "there was nothing that remotely approached a general declaration of principle that Canada was to be a bilingual or bicultural nation." In fact, all the fathers of Confederation, English, French, Scots, Irish, wanted only a single nation. And the French Canadians? Keenly aware of French continental despotism, and of American civil war, they mostly welcomed the stability of English rule. In fact, when the Quebec legislature was completed in 1883, carved into its coat of arms were the words "*Je Me Souviens.*" That phrase is today inscribed on Quebec licence plates and is taken to imply a longing for former French rule. On the contrary. The words are from a short verse composed by Eugène Taché, architect of the building and deputy minister of public works. The verse reads:

> *Je me souviens,/Que né sous le lys/Je fleuris sous la rose.*
> (I remember/That born under the [French] lily/
> I flourish under the [English] rose.)

That was a great sentiment. It was earlier quite passionately supported by another Taché—this time the French-Canadian founding father Sir Etienne-Paschal Taché who, so cognizant of the historical stability of British institutions and British liberty—as contrasted to the fragility and fanaticism of a long series of French experiments in Statist rule—swore that "the last cannon which is shot on this continent in defence of Great Britain, will be fired by the hand of a French-Canadian![12]" Ah, such sweet words . . .

But in 1963, less than a hundred years later, on the cusp of the centralizing welfare state that he initiated, Liberal prime minister Lester B. Pearson directed his Bi & Bi commissioners to find ways to build Canada not as our own founders had wished, as a blending of a single people in a single nation, but as an *equal biracial partnership* between two founding peoples, despite the obvious numerical difference in what were rapidly becoming "two solitudes."[13]

In short, Pearson specifically directed his commissioners to change the basic character of this *single* nation and establish it in the public mind as a nation of *two* nations. That is why Secretary of State Serge Joyal spoke so euphorically of "making Canada a French country both inside and outside Quebec," adding that in Canada's Charter can be found "the real foundation of French." Before him, in the 1970s, academic and politician Jean-Luc Pépin had often told the press that he himself, as well as Trudeau, Gérard Pelletier, Jean Marchand, Marc Lalonde, and Jean Chrétien, were "a well-organized group of revolutionaries." He told the CBC with evident delight: "We were making the civil service, kicking and screaming all the way, bilingual."

## A CLASH OF CENTRALISMS

But this strategy was doomed from the start for one simple reason. The main pressure felt by the French minority, itself possessed of a distinctively French-derived centralizing mentality all but contained within Quebec, was the imposition on it of the much larger and even more centralizing and interventionist Canadian welfare state. In other words, the essence, not of French-Canadian discontent (which will always be with us), but of the growing populist appeal of separation, flowed from a clash of two centralizing forces within the bosom of a single nation, *neither of which could succeed if the other did*. The homogeneous reality of a Quebec *determined either to succeed in preserving and strengthening her French culture, or else to separate from Canada* was obviously about to be penetrated and diluted by the much larger and more powerful centralizing forces of Canada's rising federal welfare state. It was a small circle inside a very large one. The ancients referred to this as the problem of "*Imperium in imperio*"—a power within a power. They knew from experience that the larger power will always wear down and take over the smaller by encroaching on its rights.

Key also during the 1960s and afterwards was the serious international threat to Canadian federation posed by the efforts of France, which under Charles de Gaulle was eager to strengthen the failing French presence in the entire world. As York University historian J.L. Granatstein pointed out: in the 1960s and thereafter, France devoted large sums of money to the Quebec separatist cause, sent three thousand military conscripts to Quebec to work as secret agents, teachers, and revolutionaries, and gave many other forms of assistance which were intended, as an angry Trudeau put it, "to demolish the unity of Canada."

So the combination of three realities—the presence of a large bloc of French-Canadian voters who had to be kept happy in the war of political and economic spoils ("the bidding war"), external interference from France, and the Liberal government's persistent vision of a distinctively Canadian national socialism—meant that the only solution (for a committed socialist) was *to make Canada more French in its political, economic, and linguistic structure*; which is to say, more bureaucratically controlled, regulated, and standardized. So they had to create the Big Lie. *Equal* founding partners? This meant there was going to be a struggle to the death between two top-down French-style socialist polities on the same turf, one federal, the other provincial. The Charter would be the key instrument for the implementation of this dominating master plan throughout Canada, and for the subordination—the "domestic colonization"—of Quebec's own brand of socialism by means of Canada's much larger national variant. Once the Charter was in place in 1982, the continuation of the domestic struggle to achieve a rational and a national internal colonization in the French style was going to mean a confrontation between two radically opposing systems: between Montcalm and Wolfe, the French versus the English style of government, from sea unto sea. As between Canada and Quebec, however, in the manner of matryoshka (those Russian dolls nesting within dolls), it would mean a war of attrition between Montcalm Sr. and Montcalm Jr.; in the sense that Quebec's own internal Statist demands deeply influence the direction of Canadian Statism as a whole, we have been *francized*.

The predictable result was that as of October 1993, Canada had two large minority parties in Parliament, each determined to end the Big Lie: one, the Bloc Québécois wishing to separate from Confederation altogether; and the other, the Reform Party of Canada, wishing to refederalize the nation on equal terms for all provinces—to return more or less to the original British structure of Confederation, or else to negotiate the separation of Quebec. Here were two opposed and elected parties symbolizing in their very existence the historical clash between the French and English styles—Montcalm and Wolfe—facing off in a Parliament foolish enough to have accepted as legitimate a political party dedicated to national destruction.

In the next chapter we will see that in an effort to address the problem of separatism, Canada's Supreme Court judges—once again without authority of Parliament—amended our Constitution's amending formula. Clearly, they had fallen under the sway of the modern democratic conceit (the idea that a majority vote is sufficient to solve everything) in constructing a formula of sorts permitting any province of Canada to separate. I fear that in doing this, however, they demonstrated a misunderstanding of the true constitutional basis of Confederation. What is the truth? Who's calling the shots? Does any province have a right to break up Canada?

## CONFEDERATION IS A CO-OP

Try to imagine that you and nine of your friends (together making up the ten provinces) have all seen a ten-room apartment building you wish to purchase. Together, you enter into an agreement to purchase it based on equal ownership. It's a co-op. By written agreement, each of you has a share of a certain amount of living space, benefits, and costs, depending on the size of your family, but nothing prevents anyone from relocating within the building, and nothing prevents you as a group from agreeing to reshape the interior. But you all own the whole building equally.

One day, nine of you arrive home from work to find François, chainsaw in hand, attempting to cut his apartment away from the building. He is angry. He says he wants to leave and "take what I own." Imagine the justifiable and spontaneous outrage from the rest: "We all own this building together. You have no right to reconfigure the building without our permission. We all got into this deal together, and no one can change it without unanimous consent. Anyway, you owe us a lot of money. We subsidized you from the start. Even if we decide that we will let you out of this deal, you will have to settle up with us for what you owe, and maybe even pay damages for devaluing our building, too."

So there it is. A confederation of provinces is not like a condo building. It is like a co-op apartment building in which citizens can live in any of the spaces they want. In other words, all Canadian citizens, regardless of where they live for the moment, own Canada equally. The lines on the map for each province (like each apartment wall) are there for administrative and political convenience but do not confer ownership of geographic real assets on the citizens of any province. So if the Québécois, or any other group of citizens in any province attempt to saw off a province and cart it away, they are really trying to take what is owned in common away from all of us without permission. They are breaking their contract.

Based on this understanding, I suggest there are three huge issues, each of them likely irresolvable on the basis of the democratic conceit, around which the dialogue must revolve. They are the issues of *permission, partition,* and *duplication.*

### 1. Permission—Or, Who Says You Can Leave?

Can a province just walk away from Confederation? Does any province have the legal right to leave? The answer is a flat no. Canada's Supreme Court has declared as much. But then the court stumbled blindly into political territory when it said that if a clear question on separation had a clear majority in favour, Canada would have an obligation to negotiate. But that is not true.

Absent real persecution, there is no right for a province to secede unilaterally, and any international court would agree. Why is this so? Legally speaking, if any province of Canada wishes to separate, it must get permission from other

Canadians through consent of their legislatures. Obviously, any such permission must be on terms and conditions that satisfy not only the province wishing to secede, but also all the others from whom it is attempting to secede. That's a recipe for a massive fight.

But what if a province says, "To hell with your permission, I'm getting out!" and starts up the chainsaw? Well, that's what's called a Unilateral Declaration of Independence. A UDI, a form of democratic "self-determination" gets a certain amount of sympathy from freedom lovers around the world (let it be said: they often confuse democracy with liberty) who are eager to see oppressed people free themselves. But, in fact, by declaring a UDI, a province would be appealing not to other Canadians, whom they would spite by such a tactic, but to the international community. After all, in the long run, it's the international community that confers sovereignty on a nation through official recognition. If no one recognizes your declaration of independence, you haven't got a separate country. But let us pause here.

Arguably, far from being oppressed, Quebec is one of the freest and wealthiest territories in the world—in part because it has also been massively subsidized by the rest of us for a very long time, enjoying a standard of living higher than if it had been left on its own. Much higher. More dangerous than any referendum on separation, however, is the decision criterion. Quebec nationalists would insist that a simple majority of 51 percent plus one is sufficient. But many experts argue that for a matter so serious, a special majority of two-thirds, or even 75 percent, ought to be required. Our Supreme Court has called for "a clear majority." After all, the simple-majority basis means that one-half of all the citizens of Quebec—more than three and a half million Canadian citizens!—who have paid taxes and sworn allegiance to Canada all their lives and who clearly prefer to live in their own ancestral homes as Canadian citizens would be forced to live in a separate country. What about their livelihoods, citizenship, passports, properties, investments, rights to Canadian services, and so on? They would scream for protection, and Ottawa would be morally and legally bound to help them. That means federal intervention and force necessary to protect loyal Canadians would be used to enter any province that tried this. By now, the idea of a UDI ought to be looking awfully messy.

**2. Partition—Or, What Came In Goes Out**
Well, here's another problem. As I said, the lines on the map, like the partitions inside a building, are just there by common agreement for administrative and political convenience. The lines do not bestow a right of ownership on anyone. If on Monday you move to Quebec, you cannot say on the first day there that you own part of Quebec. Just as if, on Tuesday, should you move back to Ontario, you cannot then say you own part of Ontario and have surrendered whatever it was you owned of the province of Quebec on Monday. Just try to

imagine the "ownership" of each province switching around every time hundreds of thousands of Canadians decide to migrate internally each year. Anyway, figure it out. Who, other than the people as a whole could possibly own Canada? Their governments, right? But democratic governments represent the people. And governments come and go. So we are left with the people as owners of the whole. And make no mistake—the taxes you pay every year on Canada's federal debt are not earmarked by province. You're paying off debt for the whole nation. So even if Quebec or any other province got nasty and tried to declare a UDI, the battle would quickly shift from lines on the map to arguments over what property could by law be taken out of Confederation as real assets, and what debts had to be paid to Canada.

In the case of Quebec, this takes us straight into treaty law to find out what portions of the province were actually ceded or transferred to Quebec; the real question, in other words, is not about separation, but about partition, a distinction we don't hear much about. But our various governments know this distinction very well, and they consider the whole topic too volatile for our poor little heads. And the media, typically, are silent.

There are many books and articles on the subject of what actually belongs with Quebec. You can search them online. What it boils down to is that Quebec came into Confederation as a much smaller province than it is now. About two-thirds of that province—a vast cornucopia of future extractable wealth—used to be called Rupert's Land, and it was ceded by Britain to Canada, then by Canada to Quebec in two parcels in 1898 and 1912, to be administered by Quebec *as a province of Canada*—not by Quebec as a separate nation. In effect, Rupert's Land was given to Canada, then transferred to Quebec under the Crown, in trusteeship. Strictly speaking, if Quebec attempted to separate, that land would by rights transfer back to Britain. Now, that's bizarre. Such a result could be legally avoided only if Quebec seceded peaceably as an independent monarchy, thus retaining those lands. That's even more bizarre.

But the underlying argument over partition is that if Quebec (or any other province or territory) were granted the right to separate, it would be allowed to take out of Confederation only what was brought into it in 1867 (or thereafter). When push comes to shove, as they say, the French-Canadian "people" (make no mistake, in the Quebec case, this is not just a conflict over territory, but over culture and race) could only lay a bona fide legal treaty claim to a strip of land running from west of Montreal, north about a hundred miles, then east to Labrador. Other "peoples"—including a lot of English people—were involved in settling the rest of Quebec.

### 3. Duplication—What's Good for the Goose is Good for the Gander
In the extremely unlikely event that Quebec were to succeed with the argument of self-determination, why should that same argument not be duplicated for

the many enclaves of English Canadians, and other non-French minorities within Quebec? Why should they not use the same self-determination arguments to separate from the newly partitioned Quebec? Separatists attempt to argue that these minority groups are not a "people," or that in the case of the English, they already have their own "people" in the Rest of Canada. Now, that's a stretch. Just think of some densely populated enclaves within Quebec such as West Island of Montreal with its 220,000 citizens of various languages and cultures, of whom the largest group (43 percent, 2001 census) is English-speaking. They, too, will likely demand to be partitioned out of Quebec as a Canadian enclave, and will want protected travel corridors by land and water, and so on, just like West Berliners had in East Germany. Along with several other enclaves that would vote to stay in Canada, the new Quebec nation would look like a piece of Swiss cheese. Having said this, if Canada ever decided to deal with the French fact it could indeed come up with a cantonal system on the Swiss model, whereby enclaves or legitimate cantons within what is now Quebec territory would exist with ties either to a new Quebec state, or to Canada.

And what about Canada's natives and Inuit? They are obviously a "people" in any sense of the term who, in addition to language and culture, also have racial distinctiveness, which is not the case for all francophones. And . . . aboriginals in *la belle province* have already laid serious treaty land claims to over 75 percent of the province of Quebec. Some 15,000 Cree who occupy most of northern Quebec have made it very clear that they want no part of any separation from Canada, and have publicly declared their intent to separate from Quebec if such an effort were to be successful. We can be certain that all native peoples currently under the jurisdiction of Ottawa and enjoying its considerable largesse (about $8 billion per year spent by Ottawa alone on Canada's aboriginals) will want to continue this way.

## WHAT'S NEXT?

Just as the normal tensions of the French-Canadian minority within Confederation were grossly exacerbated by the rise of the interventionist federal Canadian welfare state, the solution, if we wish to keep Quebec in Confederation (some say let's expel her on our own terms!), is to reverse this process. Canada must return to a condition of true federalism, which, contrary to public perception, means a return to our original pre-Trudeau decentralization: more or less a sovereign nation of sovereign provinces, the central government and the provinces each with well-defined rights and obligations according to general or local matters, accordingly. And just let 'er fly, so to speak. That is exactly what Canada's original Constitution—the 1867 BNA Act—prescribed. That was our founding British vision. I know—England is a unitary state. So it seems more true to say that Canada was modelled on American federalism. But that is not wholly true, either. The Canadian founders created a new

Canadian-type of polity they called Confederation. They wanted to avoid American-style republicanism in favour of the British model, and so democracy was to play a role only in the House of Commons, but never directly. Canada was to begin with more central constitutional powers than the American model, but was also to have a specified and marked (though not complete) division of powers—laid out in principle, if not always followed in practice *in order to check the growth of despotism from the centre*—and allow each province to grow as each might choose. Montesquieu, in his *Spirit of the Laws*, had famously extolled the British model exactly because of these checks and balances, while allowing that a country of huge expanse would have to arrange this in a federal form. We did.

But to return to the vision of our founders, to that original freedom and independence from all-pervasive Statism, we would need to scrap the Charter; return to our common law roots; stop all socialist transfer payments to provinces (and regions); live within our means both provincially and nationally, withdraw central government from all provinces in all areas from which the general government is barred by the BNA Act. Then Quebec, like every other province, could live in peace and tolerably run its own affairs. Quebec could continue as a French-style welfare state within Canada all on its own, but without taking money from the rest of us to do that. For, ironically—an extreme irony, actually—in order to preserve its unique culture while trying to build a provincial welfare state inside Quebec with our generous help, Quebec alone, of all the provinces, has insisted most strongly on its provincial rights under the BNA Act to conduct its own affairs. In other words, in order to become a provincial French-style welfare state, Quebec has aggressively resisted Canada's much larger welfare state, mostly *by insisting on the specified provincial rights and legal terms of our original British-style Constitution*. The other provinces should follow suit.

Alas, our current regime, as argued throughout this book, has resulted from a defilement of the foundations and spirit of our original Constitution (a constitution that was more about rules than deals), and thus our once-free nation has been changed into a radically egalitarian and far less free one. In effect, the people's Constitution was used against the people.

# 15: HERE COMES THE JUDGE!
## HOW CANADIANS LOST THEIR REAL
## RIGHTS AND FREEDOMS

*Canada is free, and freedom is its nationality.*
—Sir Wilfrid Laurier, seventh prime minister of Canada, 1896–1911

*Mesmerized by human rights rhetoric and the blandishments of
lawyers and law professors, Canadians have stood by quietly and
meekly while the judges hijacked their country.*
—Robert Ivan Martin, *The Most Dangerous Branch: How the Supreme Court of
Canada Has Undermined Our Law and Our Democracy*

### A JUDICIAL CIVIL WAR

After 115 years as a free nation guided by elected representatives of her people
enjoying a British-based *parliamentary sovereignty*, Canada's legislators succumbed to rights fever, and under the sway of their ever-forceful prime minister Pierre Trudeau and eight fawning premiers, had the Charter of Rights and
Freedoms stuffed down their throats in 1982.[1] This addition to Canada's
Constitution, as law professor Robert Martin put it, became "the foundation
for the most unabashed aggressive and blatantly political judicial foray into
every aspect of Canadian politics and public policy."[2]

Let us clear up a confusing matter at the start. A "constitution" or body of
law serving as a legal framework for the governance of a people may be written
out as a document, or acknowledged in an unwritten form as are legal rites or
traditions. But it is most often a combination of both, as in Canada. As discussed in an earlier chapter, Canada's written constitution prior to 1982 was
called the British North America Act. Most of the document was about "rules"
governing the structure of government and the division of powers between
Parliament and the provincial legislatures. In general, Parliament was to look
after things common to all Canadians while provincial legislatures were to
look after local matters within their provinces. There was no bill of rights in
our original constitution and no mention of "equality" or "disadvantage" of
persons or regions. The unspoken (because presumed) foundation of Canada's
first written constitution was a common understanding of British liberty. The

*real* rights and freedom of citizens were understood as derived from and defended according to the principles of the customary common law of England, and were from the twelfth century so long established as to be considered more nuanced and higher in value and deeper in meaning and importance than any possible—and by its nature, any restrictive—written code or charter. Other than administratively, the only notion of "equality" assumed in our constitution as an ancient English principle was equality before the law: a prince or a pauper were to be dealt with in the same manner for stealing a loaf of bread, and so on. After Trudeau succeeded in entrenching his Charter of Rights and Freedoms in the BNA Act in 1982, the whole business was consolidated as the Constitution Acts, 1867 to 1982.

In this chapter, the terms "code law" and "charter law" are used generally to distinguish the top-down written type of constitutional law consisting of abstract principles, of which the French are so fond,[3] from the evolved common law, bottom-up type typical of England and her colonies. The word "Charter" here refers to Canada's 1982 code law document. In that year, Canada underwent a constitutional regime change at the hands of Pierre Trudeau and his revolutionary colleagues. It was a regime change that imposed a written French-style code law constitution as "supreme law" on our historical English written constitution, as well as on our written and unwritten common law. That is why I have described it as "the revenge of Montcalm."

Alas, just like other democratic nations that have invented code law instruments, Canada is slowly learning that abstract legal terminology set up as supreme law has had the unfortunate effect of weakening parliaments by passing the legislative torch to judges—whether or not this was the intent. Below I will argue that such charters are the greatest menace not only to individual freedoms, but most worrisome to the vital protective shield against State power normally provided for individuals by the strength of a free civil society.

This is particularly true if the terms of a charter are devoted to egalitarian ends (usually their main ideological purpose). If so, the right of interpretation of such instruments is soon captured by a collection of activist individuals and groups whom two of the best and earliest critics of this tendency described as "the court party."[4] Then the charter is typically used as a legal battering ram to break down the most important social, legal, and economic privileges—whether those granted by public policy or by private organizations—as crucial protections essential to the very health and survival of society's most important institutions such as families, churches, clubs, sports teams, charities, and so on. All such entities—whether publicly protected or privately formed—attract the powerful affiliation of their members through the process of human social bonding and privileging that I will describe in detail below—a process which *intentionally excludes non-conforming individuals and behaviours*, and thus constitutes a challenge to the egalitarian State.

Indeed, it is precisely the privileging features of public policies and private rules that are the key means by which both States and private associations try to nudge human behaviour this way or that. Even very small changes in something such as a tax rate can have very widespread and immediate behavioural consequences. The point is that all true policies and rules of group association are *intentionally discriminatory* in a positive way. They extend privileges only to individuals (or groups of same) who qualify for them for some reason of public (or private) policy, but not to others. However, if under egalitarian pressure a government policy is altered so that it then applies to all without distinction, if there are no inclusive/exclusive qualifications attached as a condition for receiving benefits, then it has been converted into a general handout, and by this alteration loses its power as a policy. For example, in Canada, only war veterans qualify for generous veteran's benefits and pensions; only the poor qualify for welfare cheques; only families with children qualify for child bonuses; and until recently, only legally married heterosexuals qualified for the legal protections and myriad social and economic benefits granted since time immemorial to married couples. Indeed, gay marriage is a particularly clear example of how this egalitarian process—the battering ram—works. For, until very recently, a homosexual person could not meet the first of the four traditional qualifying conditions for marriage in Western nations, which are: you must marry someone of the opposite sex; you can only marry one person at a time; it cannot be someone under a specified age; it cannot be a close blood relative. As in Canada, several activist American courts ruled that the exclusion of homosexuals inherent in traditional marriage was discriminatory (which, of course, it was, as I say, and intentionally so, for positive procreative and child-protective reasons). But unlike in Canada, where the Supreme Court can direct the battering ram at traditional marriage federally, in America the law of each state is the deciding factor. So, in the good old USA, the people took action. To date, some forty-one American states have firmly pushed judges back in their chairs by enacting laws or amending state constitutions to reaffirm the traditional, common law definition of marriage as a union between one man and one woman. The general point, however, is that anything that smacks of a social or policy exclusion today, even for the very best of reasons, has become a target for egalitarian activists, and this means that, Charter in hand, Canada's courts have too often been active agents poised against the natural social bonding and intentional exclusive privileging provided by traditional public policy as well as by the most important institutions of civil society. Alas, the moment an abstract charter or code is introduced as the "supreme law" of the land into a country whose legal system was previously based on *parliamentary sovereignty* and the concrete common law, the transformation begins. For all new laws must now either pass the test of egalitarian conformity, or they will meet the battering ram and get thrown out. After all, Canada's Charter stresses terms like "rights and freedoms," but it cannot hope to describe the many possible meanings of rights and freedoms. That is why we say that charters are not self-interpreting. For, the fact is, most of the key terms of code law documents are expressed in nouns and verbs. When someone says, "Did you see my *dog?*" (a noun), we naturally ask, "What *kind* of dog is it?" (we are asking for an adjective). Just so, when the word "right" or "freedom" comes up, the qualifying adjectives and adverbs—the precise meanings in each case—must be supplied by judges. If they are *restrained* legal professionals, then in doing so they will stick to legal precedent and principle and the original intent of the laws when framed. But if they are *social activist* judges they will ignore all that and attribute meanings that reflect their personal idea of what they believe social reality *ought to be.* Indeed, Canada's Charter specifies in Section 1 that the rights and freedoms guaranteed in it "are subject to such *reasonable limits* prescribed by law as can be demonstrably justified in a free and democratic society." And the plain truth is that activist judges have wasted no time in *claiming for themselves* (starting with *R. v. Oakes*, 1986), the right to say what "reasonable limits" are, rather than *reserving this right for Parliament and the provincial legislatures.* In so doing they have usurped the legislative powers of the elected representatives of the people in Parliament and in all provincial legislatures of Canada.

In all historically common law countries, however, the accepted meanings of abstract legal terms arise from the wisdom of actual case law decisions accumulated over long periods of time. For a common law judge does not try to define freedom in the abstract, in a personal fashion. Instead, the observation is made that when your neighbour blocked your driveway last week with his oversized truck, he diminished your freedom. This case decision then becomes a precedent for all future driveway-blocking cases. But as there is no case law defining the abstract terms of a newly minted charter, then in order to say what any term in a charter means, a judge has only two choices: either the recognized legal principles and original understandings of the term as used in framing the charter can be relied upon, and the judge then proceeds to argue in a politically neutral way to a decision; or, the judge may simply disregard the intended meanings of those who created the charter, ignore the restraining interpretive principles of law, and attribute to the term a personal moral or political meaning. The first method is the only clearly legal option and is styled *original intent* because in following this standard the judge will limit interpretation to the intended meanings of the framers. The formidable logic of this approach is that *unless original intent is the standard of interpretation, there is no reason to have a charter in the first place.* You might as well just let the judges make it up as they go (which, as we will see below, many activist judges have done).

The second method is called *living tree* interpretation because it conceives the law as but a flexible guide to novel judicial interpretations.[5] This interpretive temptation is so compelling and flattering to the judicial ego that many judges soon talk themselves into the notion that they have a high moral duty to "improve" or "refine" democracy—to make sure it is working properly—by "reading in" personal meanings to the abstract terms of the charter that they are perfectly aware were never intended by its framers.[6] This is the method used by far too many judges. Chief Justice Antonio Lamer rode the revisionist legal horse so hard he galloped through our Charter all but shouting, "Down with democracy!" He stated publicly that he preferred a benevolent monarchy (which, minus the benevolence, is how he often behaved on the bench).[7]

## "CHARTER CHILL"

*Parliament would not presume to intrude upon the powers of the judiciary by trying a man for murder, yet the Supreme Court of Canada has no compunction about systematically intruding upon the powers of the legislative branch of government by presuming to change rather than to uphold the law and the Constitution as written and originally understood.*
—Rory Leishman, *Against Judicial Activism: The Decline of Freedom and Democracy in Canada*, 2006

After the dust settles behind the horse, startled legislators soon begin to think: "Why bother to make a law for the people if it will not pass the test of the Charter, or if judges will just trample it, amend it themselves, or declare it unacceptable?" Even worse, they go on snooze control: "Why bother to scrutinize the most important moral issues of human life at all? Let's wait and see what the judges think, then we will not have to take the heat from constituents for actually having an opinion, one way or the other." Suddenly judges (many at first unwillingly, it is true) are transformed into social activists. Suddenly we have *judicial sovereignty*. Canada's chief justice Beverley McLachlin as much as said so when, in writing for herself and Madame L'Heureux-Dubé—the latter a justice so radically feminist that Professor Martin described her as "a major national disgrace"—she stated that "the common law *must reflect the values enshrined in the Charter*."[8] Well, that is a circular argument because the "values" enshrined in the Charter are largely the ones attributed to it, or "read into" it, by the opinions—legal and personal—of judges. Aware of this, L'Heureux-Dubé herself wrote in 1994 that it was "no longer acceptable for courts to foist the entire responsibility of law-making upon the legislature." That was an astonishing and twisted thing to say in a country that struggled for two centuries to get its own legislature! But such is the manner in which an ancient framework of law that once reflected the concrete lives of the people and their values was transformed into an instrument for the propagation of the personal values of activist judges. Let it be said here that not all judges are activists. Some of them are bona fide judges under the law, and themselves deplore all judicial activism. But they are in a near-silent (or silenced) minority in Canada. And that is why in democracies governed under code law constitutions, competing political parties strive to "load" the courts with judges favourable to their political and social views. A loaded court then becomes an instrument of policy for government.

## HAVE WE LOST RESPONSIBLE GOVERNMENT?

Has this strange process affected political legitimacy in Canada? Consider that with Confederation in 1867 Canadians finally succeeded in escaping the rule of English parliamentarians and British governors in Canada who were appointed by and responsible to the English Parliament, rather than to Canadians. We did not elect the legislators who ruled us then, and they could not be removed from power by us. But 1867 changed all that definitively. We became free at last of direct colonial rule (though until 1949 we remained subject to English judges sitting in the Judicial Committee of the Privy Council). The point, however, is that until Confederation, we had foreign political masters. When with Confederation we got full "responsible government" it meant that our government would be responsible to our own elected Parliament (to us). We, the people, could then control our legislators from the bottom by electing someone else in their place—in effect, by firing them. We enjoyed this independence from foreign lawmakers for over a century. Then suddenly, in 1982, we fell back into a quasi pre-Confederation condition once again. Below we will see many examples of how our democratic law-making rights have been usurped by activist judges who are not responsible to us, whom we did not elect, and who cannot be removed from power. My conclusion, therefore, is that we Canadians have been colonized, once again.

## THE SWITCH TO POSITIVE RIGHTS

Slowly, in place of the negative rights common to the English system since the thirteenth century, new "positive rights" (thus termed because they have specific objects in mind) are invented and quickly organized by individuals belonging to a whole variety of interest groups, into claims against the State for goods and services that the government promises to provide (the better to get itself re-elected). Such positive rights are claimed without regard to effort or merit— only with regard to an ever greater equality. And because they can only be provided by the State's first taking from some to give to others, or by abolishing policy privileges that were originally created only to fortify social institutions, these new rights, again "found" by judges—though unmentioned—in abstract charters, soon form the ideological and legal basis for the Handicap System, just as the concrete common law formed the basis for the Freedom System. Indeed, in a speech she gave in 1998, L'Heureux-Dubé stated that *"equality"* should be preferred over our fundamental freedoms, and even "*must permeate our thinking*"![9] From this point on, the State begins to turn its back on freedom and instead of telling us what we cannot do, uses the law imperatively to force us to behave, and to speak, and to think only in certain prescribed ways, for which techniques such as fining and compulsory "re-education" classes—at one time associated only with the most totalitarian regimes—become standard instruments for compelling conformity. Indeed, a number of Canada's mayors have been heavily fined for publicly expressing personal conscientious moral objection, or for refusing to undertake a morally objectionable public function. From this point on, public and private moral and legal confusion generally increase because absolute equality requires absolute control.

However, not even a Solomon would be wise enough to balance so many conflicting rights and freedoms. So whose viewpoint rules? Justice Bertha Wilson, a self-admitted socialist, a radical feminist, and a white woman, once declared publicly that neither a *white*, nor a *masculine*, nor a *heterosexual* view of the world could be neutral. So then, why do we have judges at all (whom we presume ought to strive for legal and professional objectivity and neutrality), especially brainwashed radicals who actually admit they cannot be neutral?[10] If there can be no neutrality as she says, then let's get rid of these activist courts altogether! Canada's widespread use of official Charter-supported discrimination and "quotas" to "rebalance" racial, gender, sex, age, and other purported discriminations, its coercive language laws, its systemic nationwide programs for economic redistribution, and in particular its use of draconian, guilty-until-proven-innocent Human Rights Tribunals wherein "truth is no defence," are just a few embarrassing examples of the moral confusion at work in contemporary Canada.

## THE DIFFERENCE BETWEEN EARNED FREEDOM AND CONFERRED FREEDOM

*[Under the English system] every Canadian has every right and freedom in the world except those abridged by law . . . Under the [French system] one has no rights unless one can point to a piece of paper.*
—J.P. Nowlan, Commons Debates, *Hansard*, October 10, 1980

So how, then, did the State acquire a right to *confer* rights and freedoms on people who already had them? It was by judicial rape. The State simply decided to *appropriate* the rights and freedoms we already had by *declaration*, then to turn around and publicly *bestow* them upon us, while promising to *guarantee* them. Such manipulations of public attitude are dangerous, for as the great English constitutional scholar A.V. Dicey put it, they make the claim that "personal liberty is a special privilege insured . . . by some power above the ordinary laws of the land. This is an idea utterly alien to English modes of thought, since with us, freedom of person is not a special privilege but the outcome of the ordinary law of the land. . . ."[11] Nevertheless, in this sneaky way, presto! A personal right or freedom fought for, defended to the death over centuries, and inherited as a concrete product of lots of wise common law decisions rooted in real life is suddenly subordinated to the supreme law of a new-invented code, then handed down to the people as a gift from their masters. At this point all common law is vulnerable to redefinition, limitation, or even possible abolition . . . by the highest courts of the State—the very entity *against* which we historically struggled to win so many of our actual rights and freedoms. Thus did the inclusion of the Charter in Canada's Constitution "cast the Canadian people in the role of supplicants, supplicants at the feet of judges."[12]

And why did we allow it? We would consider it insanity to surrender control over our ancient rights and freedoms to re-interpretations by the Ford Motor Company or by the executives of Microsoft. So why did we surrender them to re-interpretation by the State? Because the State has courts to enforce them, you say? I answer that we had a thousand years of restrained common law decisions under which we developed and defended our concrete rights and freedoms, whence we embedded them in all the documents, deeds, contracts, and legal precedents of what Dicey called "the ordinary law of the land." So why, then, do so many now seem to feel that their rights and freedoms are somehow more valuable because blessed by unelected public servants? Can they not see the danger: that *a freedom or right officially granted by the high court of the State is a freedom that may just as officially be amended, suspended, or abolished entirely*?

D.H. Lawrence famously argued that we fall victim to the need for worship. People everywhere are simply not satisfied with Earthly bread. They want Heavenly bread. So they work hard to get their Earthly bread and then hand it over to the Priest, who blesses it and hands it back as Heavenly bread. Then they are happy. Just so, we sweat to earn Earthly bread as paper money, and hand it over to the State in taxes, which then hands it back to us as Heavenly bread in the form of State-subsidized goods and services and judge-sanctioned rights and freedoms. Alas, once we agree that the State can "grant" us what was always ours by right and inheritance, we have already surrendered. So now, since the advent of the Charter, we have a specific, limited number of judge-defined abstract rights and freedoms that form our fetters, for to travel outside their boundaries we must ask unelected judges whether, in doing so, we will still be free. Will we be? Are we?

## CAN THESE CONFLICTING STYLES MIX?

General Wolfe must be rolling in his grave. Trudeau was well aware that his Charter would be in immediate and inherent conflict with our English common law system—which, as mentioned, he mocked snidely as our British checkerboard federalism—and that the common law of Canada would henceforth be subjected to a slow process of judge-made legal uniformity imposed from the top. For his amended Constitution (now including the Charter) was from henceforth to be the "supreme law" of Canada (sec. 52.1), and "any law that is inconsistent" with it, "of no force and effect." That section is the legal battering ram to which I referred above. What did Trudeau hope to see the Charter produce? It bears repeating. When asked "What society would you choose to make Canada?," Trudeau answered, "Labour party socialist—or Cuban socialism, or Chinese socialism." (He seemed to believe, as an American pundit put it, that when the Berlin Wall was torn down, all the Germans ran to the East!)

In legal terms, this was the top-down code law system smothering the bottom-up common law system. It was in far too many cases the replacement of the people as lawmaker by the court as lawmaker. Although Canada's Charter ostensibly defends the individual *against* the State, it in fact presupposes the huge controlling State required to satisfy all the uniform rights to equal goods, services, and affirmative fiscal and social rebalancing guaranteed by the Charter itself, the disheartening economic and Statist effects of which on this formerly free nation can be seen graphically in most of the charts in chapter 7. As Professor Martin so aptly observes, the point of a charter is to protect the citizens against the State. But Charter-based cases today seldom involve individuals protecting themselves against the State. They mostly involve State-created and State-subsidized organizations locked in battle with the State itself in pursuit of more advantage. Thus has evolved the hard-core egalitarian or socialist vision Trudeau and his "liberals" worked so hard to fashion for Canada. They were not and are not real liberals. They began—and they continue—to impose a form of soft national socialism on Canada. This was barely resisted and in many respects has been perpetuated by the nation's "conservatives." It is a growing trend that has been visible in most Western democracies for more than a century. On this point, as Fareed Zakaria observed in his excellent book *The Future of Freedom*: everywhere in the world today we have more democracy, but less freedom.[13] He laments the loss of our original "constitutional liberalism," the highest indication of which was "the impartial judge."

## DOES A CONSTITUTION BELONG TO THE PEOPLE, OR TO THE GOVERNMENT?

It is true that if the elected representatives of the people create a constitution, then it is made legally and "democratically," even though the citizens as a whole did not themselves create it or vote directly on it. The BNA Act was made this way. It was cobbled together by our colonial politicians and blessed as an Act of the British Parliament. And a darn good Constitution it was! Indeed, I would vote in a moment to return to it because, as I said, it was fundamentally an administrative document detailing key matters of constitutional self-governance in this Confederation, such as the division of powers as between central and provincial governments. It was Canada's version of "constitutional liberalism." At the time, the very idea of all the people making or having a voice in a constitution was considered heretical because democracy had a very poor reputation. The French Revolution was a memorably disastrous and bloody experiment in radical democracy, and the Americans had just finished killing each other in a democratic fratricide. But perhaps most important, Canadians then had a socially binding common religious and moral ethos that united them and made an arm's-length constitution created by politicians the acceptable norm. But that time has long since passed. The bonds have been broken since, and so everything is far more political now. Our once-common ethos has fragmented, the people have become correspondingly less trusting of politicians, and accordingly are demanding a say in the constitutional changes that are going to rule their lives, especially after the flawed constitutional exercises from the 1980s forward. Those schemes were carried out in an undemocratic way for the last time, and there is even a serious case that due to the dishonourable strategies employed, Canada is today *without a legitimate Constitution.*[14] Strictly speaking, however, that is not the case. We do have a legitimate Constitution in *law,* but, it can be argued, perhaps not in *spirit.* Premier Clyde Wells summed up the new spirit of all this when he shot down the Meech Lake Accord in 1990.[15]

As for the 1992 Charlottetown Accord experience, that was, well, a little different. With a loud crashing noise, Canada's elites, from out-of-touch politicians, to half-educated media (most of them), to snooty academics, got their comeuppance when, in October 1992, Canadians issued a bracing repudiation by national referendum of the government's Charlottetown Accord (by then mockingly relabelled by many "the Charlatan Accord"). That important exercise in direct democracy finally told the governments of Canada at every level: "The Constitution belongs to the people. We will decide, thank you very much." On this note, the pathetic October 1995 spectacle on national television of a weepy prime minister Jean Chrétien beseeching Canadians in Quebec to reject a provincial "referendum" on sovereignty association was remarkable. For that was not a legal referendum. It was a unilateral, non-binding plebiscite, resting on a complete misunderstanding (or dismissal) of Canada's Constitution. But most Canadians did not know the difference.

The truth is that at no time prior to 1992 had the Canadian people ever been asked to create or accept or amend a proposed constitution, unlike, say, the Swiss, or Australians, or Americans, who have had plenty of say on the terms of their most cherished legal documents. We had a different and very British tradition. In 1867, when citizens more or less trusted their politicians to create a constitution in their interests, governments had not yet become overwhelmingly Statist. But now they are, and citizens are now rightly suspicious of the State. This suggests that eventually, and even though they are democratic instruments that conflict with our representative system,[16] we will at some point need limited instruments of direct democracy such as recall, binding referendums, and citizen initiatives, enjoyed with particular energy by the Swiss, to discourage the political class—especially the courts—from structuring society against the legal or moral interests of the people, from taxing them to death, and from spending their money in irresponsible ways, or from changing the ethos of the nation unilaterally from the bench. A vivid example of this push-back, mentioned above, is the recent "defence of marriage" enactments by forty-one American states. In chapter 16 I will briefly discuss the Swiss system.

In any elitist government, every effort is of course made to avoid such instruments. Instead, Inquiries are held, Royal Commissions, Standing Committees and Task Forces established. But none of these constitutes a device with any legal power over the government, which, with predictable regularity, shelves, forgets, or simply dismisses the findings. Poor fools that we are. Such devices are in reality the opposite of democratic: they are bureaucratic strategies for diffusing popular dissent. I am no fool for democracy as such, however. It can produce evil as well as good results, for the democratic principle allows even the election of despots, and it has happened plenty of times (think of the election of the terrorist Palestinian party Hamas in 2006). But as compared to all other systems that are beyond the reach of the people, a democratic system has three main virtues: you can throw your leaders out; the laws have the consent of the people they govern; and there is opportunity to correct legislative mistakes.

# HOW CANADA'S JUDGES, WITHOUT ANY AUTHORITY, HAVE CHANGED THE LAWS OF CANADA

*The task of . . . we in the justice system, is to solve people's problems.*
—Chief Justice Beverley McLachlin, speech to the
Ontario Bar Association, January 2002

Is it? Most people with an understanding of the proper function of the law in a free society have always assumed that the task of the courts is to interpret and apply the laws made by the people according to the meanings the people intended when they made the laws. Otherwise, why would the people have made the laws in the way they did in the first place? And if judges are going to make laws, rather than apply them as made, then why have a court at all? We don't need two Parliaments!

Let us examine a handful of Canadian cases to understand just how very far our judges have roamed at will.

## Our Judges, Without Authority of Parliament, Changed Canada's Law on Abortion

In *R. v. Morgentaler* (SCC, 1988), in a chaotic ruling featuring four separate opinions, the Supreme Court of Canada struck down a law made by Parliament restricting abortion (Criminal Code, Section 251) on the grounds that it offended Sections 7 and 15 of the Charter guaranteeing everyone "the right to life, liberty, and security of the person," and "equality before and under the law." What was their justifying reason? That all Canadian women did not have equal access to abortion. This decision, however, did not establish a constitutional right to abortion. It went beyond that. It abolished the existing law and left Canada with no law on abortion whatsoever. We are now the only country in the world that is silent, that has *no law, on the crucial question of the value of unborn human life.* Justice William McIntyre, in his dissenting opinion, correctly rebuked the majority of the Court for usurping the authority of Parliament: "The solution [to the question of abortion] in this country must be left to Parliament," he said. "It is for Parliament to pronounce on, and to direct, social policy."

Worse, the decision was grievously flawed because it relied on flimsy technical arguments (security of the person, and lack of equal access) to achieve an ideological result that happened to be favoured by the judges: unlimited tax-funded access to abortion at any stage of pregnancy prior to the moment of birth. But it was not favoured *by the people.* There is not now, nor has there ever been, a national opinion poll in Canada on the question of abortion that yielded a majority in favour of unlimited abortion. Worse, the grounds of equality and security of the person relied upon by the Court were utterly inappropriate. Parliament had already considered unrestricted abortion a crime, and had said so in law. But now the Court was arguing perversely that the lack of equal access to a crime was a justification for abolishing a law against it. The Court thus produced a judicial decriminalization of a crime. Security of the person is not a viable ground either, because abortion concerns two human lives, not just one. No Court has ever given a credible reason why the right to life of an unborn child should be sacrificed for the security of the person of its mother. Courts get around this moral dilemma by denying that the unborn human life is a "person" until "born alive." But this is a sad and transparently ideological opinion invoked by judges to achieve their political objective. It has nothing to do with the principles of fundamental justice, and it does not and cannot erase the fact that even if we agree the unborn child is not a legal "person," a pregnant woman is indubitably carrying a human life.

## Our Judges, Without Authority of Parliament, Made Their Own Pay a Constitutional Right

In *Manitoba Provincial Judges Association v. Manitoba (Minister of Justice)* (1997), the Supreme Court of Canada "went so far as to concoct a constitutional provision giving the judges of Canada unprecedented authority to determine their own pay."[17] Chief Justice Antonio Lamer, a man guilty of multiple fanciful distortions of the law, argued that the independence of judges was compromised unless they could determine their own pay. Professor Martin Friedland of the University of Toronto Faculty of Law observed, however, that by this ruling judges are "in a real sense determining their own pay—particularly with respect to federally appointed judges," and added that when a judge is caught pleading a personal cause in this manner it is normally grounds to overturn their judgment.[18] Not least, Lamer was unilaterally and without leave of the people, amending Canada's Constitution which in Section 100 clearly states that the pay of Canada's federally appointed judges "shall be fixed and provided by the Parliament of Canada." Though never a member of Parliament, Lamer was also responsible for instigating two anti-constitutional pieces of legislation, neither of which succeeded in making it past Senate scrutiny. One was actually called "the Lamer Amendment." It was created by him to provide special pension benefits for himself and his wife (also a judge), equivalent to his full annual salary. Another he created became known as "the judges' harem law," which would have enabled a judge to confer pension benefits on both a legal spouse and a former mistress at the same time.[19]

## Our Judges, Without Authority of Parliament, Decided to Amend Our Amending Formula

After a disastrous and phony Quebec "referendum" in which Quebec attempted a "unilateral secession" on October 30, 1995, Canada's Supreme Court judges (Lamer, McLachlin, et al.) were asked by the Government of Canada if unilateral secession from Canada was permitted under our Constitution. The Court properly answered: "*There is no right, under the Constitution, or at international law, to unilateral secession.*" Great. They did their job. But then, in what we must suppose was a fit of democratic passion, the judges decided once again that they were not merely judges, but also politicians. So they offered us their unsolicited political opinion by way of inventing, out of the blue, a new Constitutional Amending Formula for Canada. They stated that "a clear majority vote in Quebec on a clear question in favour of secession would confer democratic legitimacy on the secession initiative which all the other participants in Confederation would have to recognize." In doing this, the judges went far beyond the law of the Constitution in Canada where there has never been any mention of "democratic legitimacy" in order to allow secession for Quebec, or for any other province of Canada. Instead of shutting up at the right point, the judges decided, with zero legislative authority, to enrobe their mundane—and, as I argued in the last chapter, erroneous—political opinion with constitutional clothing. By what right?

## Our Judges, Without Authority of Parliament, Decided to Give Killers Voting Rights

*If anyone had said to [the first ministers] in 1981 that*
*the Charter would be used to win voting rights for prison*
*inmates, we never would have believed it!*
—Sterling Lyon, premier of Manitoba at the time of the
Charter's adoption, and later a judge on the Manitoba Court of Appeal

In *Sauvé v. Canada* (2002), after a lower court had ruled against giving prison-ers voting rights, Canada's Supreme Court, against all precedent in Canadian legal history, against the examples of many other Western democracies that continue to ban prisoner voting, and even against the recommendation of Canada's own expensive Lortie Commission (1989) set up to examine voting rights,[20] overturned the *Sauvé* judgment (Richard Sauvé was a convicted murderer who sued for the right to vote) and gave Canada's convicted rapists, murderers, thieves, burglars, wife beaters, drug addicts, fraud artists, break-and-enter thugs, pickpockets, and the like the right to vote. Parliament never had the chance to make that decision. In other words, without the people being asked, the Court simply decide it would be nice if violent criminals convicted of breaking our laws got to vote on what our laws should be! Once again, judg-es behaved as if they were legislators standing in for Parliament. In a February 2010 newspaper article, Ontario justice David Cole held forth about judges who, like him, disagree with Parliament's latest get-tough-on-crime stance. He complained that "draconian sentencing policies have been forced upon the judiciary." He then revealed that "judges are skilled at devising creative ways to fight back against laws they believe may skew the system."[21] Fire him, I say!

## Our Judges, Without Authority of Parliament, Decided to Change the Definition of Marriage

In *Halpern v. Canada* (2003), a three-judge tribunal of the Ontario Court of Appeal decided that marriage, as restricted traditionally and throughout English, Canadian, and all of Western history to the union of one man and one woman, is a discriminatory institution because it does not include same-sex "partners." One of the judges was Ontario's Roy McMurtry, whose daughter was living with a lesbian lover at the time. He did not disclose his daughter's circumstances, nor did he offer to excuse (the legal term is "recuse") himself from this case on the normal grounds of personal bias (unlike Justice Albert Rosenblatt of New York who, at the same time, in the same circumstances, did recuse himself). Rather haughtily, and without the slightest authority, McMurtry simply declared: "*We reformulate the common-law definition of marriage* as 'The voluntary union for life of two persons, to the exclusion of all others.'" In *Egan v. Canada* (1995), the Supreme Court of Canada, against the clear intent of the framers of Canada's Charter who had specifically considered and *rejected* the inclusion of homosexual rights, and also after Parliament voted in 1999 by a majority of 216 to 55 to protect traditional marriage, decided that "sexual orientation" is an "analogous" ground[22] of discrimination and therefore must be included in Section 15(1) mandating equal rights. Citing this lawless and foundationless ruling, the Court, in the *Reference Re Same-Sex Marriage, 2004*, simply declared, uttered, announced, held forth, then constitutionalized the completely unjustified personal and political opinion that same-sex marriage in Canada is guaranteed under Canada's Charter. It is not.

### Our Judges, Without Authority of Parliament, Decided to Change Our Standard of Decency

In *Regina v. Labaye* (2005), otherwise known as "the swingers' case" in which Mr. Jean-Paul Labaye pleaded his right to operate a swingers' fee-for service sex club in his Montreal community where for a fee "members" have sex with groups of total strangers, our Supremes once again decided against Canadian moral opinion. Without the slightest authority, evidential proof, moral or historical insight, prudence, or concern for the quality of public life in Canada, they declared that the traditional centuries-long principle of community moral tolerance is no longer to be our standard of decency. In its place, the Court offered, and directly cited what is called the "harm principle" developed by the famous English libertarian thinker J.S. Mill in his 1859 tract, *On Liberty*. It is likely they picked up their knowledge of this principle in a first-year humanities class, where it is often sold as veritable holy writ to unsophisticated students. The essence of the "principle" is that we are all free to do whatever we like as long as we do not harm someone else. It is an impoverished and entirely selfish individualist principle of human conduct that utterly disregards any concern for the quality of life of the larger community. I have critiqued this principle thoroughly in a separate article as the basis of much modern malaise, and the foundation of our modern "libertarian socialism."[23]

At any rate, Michel Bastarache and Louis LeBel, the dissenting justices in *Labaye*, were very alarmed by this utterly unwarranted judicial demolition of community standards, and even if to no avail, said so, as follows: "The application of the appropriate test leads to the conclusion that the impugned acts were indecent and that the accused's establishment was a common bawdy-house within the meaning of s.210 (1) of the Criminal Code. The new approach to indecency proposed by the majority is neither desirable nor workable. Not only does it constitute an unwarranted break with the most important principles of our past decisions regarding indecency, *but it also replaces the community standard of tolerance with a harm-based test*. [But] whether or not serious social harm is sustained has never been the determinative test for indecency. . . . This new harm-based approach also *strips of all relevance the social values that the Canadian community as a whole believes should be protected.* The existence of harm is not a prerequisite for exercising the state's power to criminalize certain conduct: *the existence of fundamental social and ethical considerations is sufficient"* [emphasis added].

This case illustrates well the fact that judges (the majority in this case), when they behave as social activists more than as experts in law, simply use the egalitarian imperatives of the Charter to attack the traditions, customs, and moral certainties of the people, whereas judges who are of a more conservative inclination (the minority in this case) tend to restrain themselves and adhere to the original intent of the law and the known customs and traditions of the people.

## A FEW MORE EXAMPLES OF JUDICIAL REVOLT AGAINST THE PEOPLE

In *R. v. Big M Drug Mart* (1985), the Supreme Court of Canada amended the Constitution of Canada by striking down the Lord's Day Act legislating Sunday-closing laws in Canada on the grounds that they offended the "freedom of conscience and religion" provisions of the Charter. Again, that was for Parliament alone to decide. In *Re B.C. Motor Vehicle Act* (1985), the Supreme Court amended Canada's Constitution by deciding that the words ". . . with the principles of fundamental justice" in Section 7 of the Charter, actually mean "with due process of law." With this decision they handed themselves a carte blanche right to amend the Charter. Indeed, in his judgment on the meaning of Section 7, Chief Justice Lamer held that *Section 7 confers a broad mandate upon the judiciary to strike down laws that conflict with a judge's perception of sound public policy!* In *Halm v. Canada* (1995), the Supreme Court decided that as the age of consent for heterosexual intercourse was fourteen and for anal intercourse eighteen, homosexuals suffered discrimination. So the Court lowered the age for both classes of sexual intercourse to fourteen, thereby nullifying Parliament's concern, as expressed in this law, for the dangers of older homosexuals preying on young boys. Madam Justice Barbara Reed exposed the Court's disdain for parliamentary law in this case when she wrote: *"I am not persuaded that in a free and democratic society that it is justifiable to make an activity criminal merely because a segment— indeed maybe a majority—of the citizenry consider it to be immoral"* [emphasis mine]. Wow. If that is not a statement in support of judicial oligarchy, and a condemnation of the will of the people, what is? Would she be fine with making an activity criminal if only she thought it was so? In *Regina v. Rosenberg* (1998), a case of the Ontario Court of Appeal, the court amended the Income Tax Act by concluding that lesbian partners can be registered as "spouses" even though the wording of the act specifically restricted registration to a husband and wife of the opposite sex. Meanwhile, notoriously feminist justice Rosalie Abella wrote that with respect to "public attitudes," governments may have to wait around for

them to change, but the courts don't. She said that "public confidence and institutional credibility *argue in favour of courts being free to make independent judgments notwithstanding those same attitudes.*" She was saying that judges will point
the way to the good life for all of us poor fools who believe in parliamentary
democracy. In *M and H* (SCC, 1999), the Supremes again used the equality provisions of the Charter—on the grounds, once again, of "discrimination"—to
attack the privileges of family benefits traditionally accorded only to heterosexual
couples. And they did this as if nations have no right to discriminate positively
in favour of procreative unions. This was a notorious radical feminist decision
out of synch entirely with countries such as France, which rejected the legalization of homosexual marriage outright, and with forty-one of our neighbouring
American states. Here's another: in the "spanking case"—*The Canadian
Foundation for Children, Youth and the Law v. Canada* (2004), Chief Justice
Beverley McLachlin unilaterally amended Canada's Criminal Code without leave
of the people by ruling that Section 43, which provides for corporal punishment
of children if "reasonable under the circumstances," could henceforth (just because she said so) be used only for "educative" or "corrective" purposes designed
to restrain or express disapproval of a child's behaviour, and only for children
between the ages of two and twelve. The chief justice was amending the law and
also telling us how to raise our children. In *Egan v. Canada* (1995), and even
though (again) a Joint Committee of the Senate and the House of Commons
voted 22 to 2 against including gay rights in the Charter, the Supremes decided
that "sexual orientation" (itself not a scientific, but rather a loaded political term)
should be read into the Charter's equality section on "analogous" grounds. In
other words, the term "equality" may be applied to anything a judge thinks is
analogous. Then, in *Vriend v. Alberta* (1998), and even though the Alberta provincial legislature had resoundingly voted *twice* to exclude sexual orientation
from its human rights legislation, the Supreme Court *ordered* the legislature of
Alberta to amend its laws to include homosexuals. Judges in Canada are not shy
about ordering legislatures to spend money, either. In *Schacter v. Canada* (1992),
the Court decided, with no legislative authority whatsoever, to extend pricey tax-
funded postnatal maternal benefits to all fathers. In other cases, judges have ordered hospitals in Canada to offer free sign-language interpretation, and governments to provide pension benefits to same-sex common law couples.

Regardless of what a reader may think about any of these decisions, what
they all have in common is just one thing: the illegitimate usurpation of legislative powers of the people by judges who represent nobody.

## THE MICRO-DYNAMICS OF THE
## CONSTITUTIONAL BATTERING RAM

Now we have to drill down. For most people, to style a constitution as a battering
ram seems backward. They fervently believe that a constitution is meant not to

destroy, but to protect society. But if we wish to understand the decline of many modern democratic states, we must distinguish clearly between the intent and the consequences of modern egalitarian constitutions, for as I shall try to explain—and as the above discussion on the courts illustrates—they unleash an unforeseen process that strengthens the State in inverse proportion as it undermines civil society.

## THE POLITICAL SANDWICH, AGAIN

The simplest way to understand how this destructive process works is first to imagine that all nations can be divided into three parts, or levels, with respect to how they control themselves, as follows:

- *The State* relies on formal, involuntary control
- *Voluntary associations* rely on informal, voluntary control
- *Individuals* rely on personal control

The uppermost level in all nations is the apparatus of the State. It is coercive by nature, enjoying a legal monopoly on power such that our most meaningful political freedom is the ability to change our masters from time to time. Plainly, this form of authority is formal and involuntary, in the sense that individuals cannot influence it. In modern welfare states, in which maintenance of power and the thirst for more can be satisfied only by more votes, ostensible dedication to equality and the public good obligates such states to make larger and ever more widespread and costly public promises. To fulfill these, ever more tax dollars are needed. Because tyrannical power is not a viable democratic option, every effort of government must be directed toward the cultivation of loyalty to the State and its egalitarian values, and any competition for that loyalty must be diminished, if not entirely eliminated. Accordingly, a successful strategy for producing loyalty by marketing the State and its programs to the people will be characterized in the code law of the State and in its courts by *a commitment to end various kinds of legal, social, and economic privilege* that present as affronts—in the optics, if not in reality—to the official egalitarian orthodoxy. These may be privileges embedded in public policies, or part of the social structure of private organizations (as explained below). No matter. For under regimes that justify their power by substituting equality for freedom, the more equal the citizens become in reality, the more intensely are their minute differences felt—and the more intensely challenged and targeted for eradication. At the bottom of this structure is a huge mass of individuals, each walking around with the approved set of enumerated State-sanctioned rights and freedoms in their heads, wondering what's in it for them. But we must be clear: a mass of individuals is not a society. It has no concentrated purpose, form, or being. It's just a mob. Each person is an autonomous individual, or, as I like to put it, a purpose looking for a cause. The State at the top? Millions of aimless individuals at the bottom? So where is what we call "civil society"?

Well, here's the rub.

The middle, or intermediate level, is civil society. It is made up of all the voluntary associations or groups to which all those autonomous individuals already either belong, or strive to belong, to bind themselves. Here is where we find the many millions of families, corporations, charitable organizations, sports teams, clubs, academic groups, scientific groups, children's organizations, arts groups, self-help groups, and so on, each made vital and dynamic by virtue of its inherent purposes, relationships, loyalties, and activities. Free societies are a complex matrix of millions of such groups, many interactive, all of which *sustain themselves by a voluntary four-stage dynamic of social bonding* not found at the other two levels. As we are increasingly discovering, these four characteristics are not only profoundly essential and emblematic of all human social life, they are also, and just as profoundly, *anti-egalitarian*, because they grant their privileges and protections to members only. My family confers family rights and obligations only on our family; my company on its employees only; my ski club on club members only, and so on. This process even occurs at the heart of the State itself, of course. Canada only confers the benefits of its passport on citizens. It excludes all others. There is a good argument—I am arguing—that what all powerful modern States try to do is to hijack the human desire for social bonding they realize is so widely expressed in civil society and by transferring this emotional allegiance to themselves, turn the State into a national "family." But they can only do this by first weakening, if not entirely ending, the most powerful forms of social bonding with which the State is in competition for citizen loyalty. Now let us see how the process under attack actually works.

As mentioned above, there are four stages in the process of social bonding. Whether we are speaking of the Boy Scouts, a marriage, or membership in a bridge club or a social fraternity, we will usually find some expression, formal or informal, actual or symbolic (or both), of *sacrifice, subordination, commitment,* and *privilege*.

*Sacrifice* refers to the requirement of all groups that individuals aspiring to join must voluntarily agree to place the common will of the group above personal needs. From this flows loyalty to the group. The motto of common organizations like Rotary International is: "Service Above Self." Individual members who can't make the sacrifice of self required will usually leave or be forced out.

*Subordination* refers to the requirement that all members submit to the authority and rules of the group, however derived, formal or informal, as an expression of group discipline. Insubordination normally triggers some internal process for dismissing, disowning, or firing, and all members carry around an internal understanding of the rules by which they feel bound and are proudly distinguished from non-members. The important process of social *exclusion* of non-members (who are not bound by nor expected to obey the rules) begins here.

*Commitment* is the process whereby, the first two requirements having been met, a new member is asked formally to make a vow, or public commitment, to the group. Boy Scouts, marriage partners, and club members make their commitments in words, written contracts, or deeds, to the ideals, activities, and undertakings they agree to shoulder and share. No vow will mean no membership, or the end of membership.

*Privilege* is the last stage—and the red flag for egalitarians—whereby the group approves and bestows privileges, benefits and protections, small or large, secret or open, on each full member. This is often accompanied by a significant ceremony in which the commitment or vow of loyalty is made, and by special symbols, hats, ties, rings, or costume and the like, intended to distinguish members from non-members. It is a rite of passage. Boy Scouts and Shriners get to wear their caps and kerchiefs, and say secret things; marital partners sign covenants, wear rings, pins, get lawful and exclusive access to each other, and become eligible for certain legal, tax, and social privileges at one time available only to married heterosexual couples. Signed-up club members are expected to be loyal, carry cards, be dutiful, observe their vows, pay their dues, do required club work, abide by rules, and so on.

You can see what I'm getting at by now.

All successful human social bonding is *intentionally exclusionist*, or non-inclusive. It is characterized by an eagerness to *distinguish*, that is, *to discriminate*, not in any negative, but in a very positive sense between members and non-members, between those who qualify for group status and privileges, and those who don't. Society, you might say, is a vast organism for the conferral of positive benefits and status on those who voluntarily opt into its preferred social forms. It has no wish to harm those who refuse to opt in. Their freedoms and rights as autonomous individuals remain intact. But by this four-step process, civil society seeks to encourage, even to lure, the undifferentiated mass of autonomous individuals into its own far more difficult and challenging forms of social life, the crowning mark of which is *privilege*.

For egalitarians, however, that is a dreaded word, because the modern welfare or therapeutic state is defined by its eagerness to *equalize* outcomes for everyone. Just so, the most radical project of the State is to circumvent this four-step process, either by eliminating such forms of privilege, or (the preferred method) by dumbing-down or legally changing the qualifications for membership so as to enable the State to shower the formerly exclusive benefits on all individuals alike as a general handout. In order to bestow marital benefits, for example, on "any two persons" who decide they want the privileges and considerable benefits that traditionally accompany marriage, the State did not

eliminate the institution; it simply eliminated one of the four traditional qualifications for marriage in the Western world: the opposite-gender qualification.
Presto—marriage is undermined, and the State looks *so* generous.

Alas, at the heart of the matter is the fact that the modern egalitarian State
and civil society have opposing objectives because *the social bonding that
humans crave and that alone creates true community, is exclusionist and illiberal*
by its very nature. Hence the civil war of values between traditional society and
the State. What is before us is a deadly conflict between the deepest social dynamic of a living society, and the aims of the power-hungry State. For in order
to spread equality, the State must actively seek to diminish the multifarious
forms of social bonding that individuals naturally seek, and to graft these loyalties onto itself through the technique of supplying tax-funded goods and services as substitutes for the same things once supplied privately. In other words,
the State must steal its customers from the living society, which, inevitably, in
time, will produce a dead society and an all-controlling State.

Thus do powerful States consume their own societies.

This process of social breakdown is particularly well advanced in North
America, where egalitarian codes, laws, or interpretations of same are being
used by individuals and interest groups in the name of rights to break down all
once-privileged exclusions, public or private, whether of the heterosexual
family, of spousal rights, of gender privacy in male or female locker rooms or
on sports teams, or to create novel maternity/paternity benefits, pension inclu-
sions, force a banishment of religion, and so on—nothing is sacrosanct.
Wherever even one angry individual can be found willing to mount a court
challenge to a legal, social, or tax privilege from which that individual (or a
group of same) has been excluded (or for which they have refused to qualify),
they will invoke what one critic has called the "universal solvent"—equality—to
charge that the State is not fulfilling its democratic mandate.

Modern written charters and constitutions, with their entrenched egalitarianism, positive rights, and arbitrary law, are now the central weapon in this
struggle against all social distinction and privilege, and when there is no meaningful society left, we will have only one "family": the all-powerful State, culti-
vating allegiance from its millions of autonomous children. And we will have
brought this upon ourselves in the name of rights and freedoms.

Alas, our current regime has resulted from a defilement of the essence of our
original Constitution (a Constitution that was more about rules than deals),
and thus a once-free *nation* was changed into a radically egalitarian one. In
effect, the people's Constitution was used against the people. So, as law professor Robert Martin put it: If Canadians want their democracy back, they will
have to stage a counter-revolution—"a democratic struggle against the judges."
The last chapter of this book includes a discussion of how to do just that.

Fortunately, there is some good news. Since the Conservative Harper government has been in power, it has recognized these judicial travesties, and, as Professor Martin recommended, has ended the tax-funded Court Challenges Program that provided much of the funding for ultra-feminist causes through such groups as the Women's Legal Action and Education Fund (LEAF). It has always been a scandal and an offence against democracy that taxpayers have been forced to cough up hard-earned money to fund radical sectarian causes of any kind, right or left. But Canada can do more. If we don't have the moxie to scrap the Charter, then we could start by reducing judges' terms from retirement at age seventy-five, to a ten-year maximum. We could also de-fang our judges by eliminating Section 52, which says that all Canadian law that is "inconsistent" with the provisions of the Constitution (of which the Charter has been a part since 1982) is of "no force and effect." That is the section which is the most Statist of all, and which wholly subordinates the future of Canada to activist judicial interpretation.

We could also establish a citizens' legal panel—I call it "CourtWatch Canada"—which would be mandated to research and publish corrective legal opinions that would serve to discipline the judges of Canada by example. CourtWatch Canada would be staffed by the very best legal scholars devoted to the highest principles of the law and dedicated to the discipline of restraint and original intent in interpretation. CourtWatch would be funded privately by concerned citizens to research and publish opinions on major upcoming cases *before* Supreme Court of Canada opinion is published. In effect, this would establish a de facto dialogue between the opinions of our too-activist courts, and high scholarly legal opinion dedicated to law, and to the understanding that it is the role of the people to make the law, and not of judges.

Finally, if all else fails, and if the people want to reassert themselves as the true voice of their country, they may wish to recall that the Supreme Court of Canada was created by an Act of Parliament (the Supreme Court Act of 1875). If we, the people, cannot figure out how to discipline our courts—especially the Supreme Court—forcing a return to their proper legal foundations, then the first step in the struggle to get back our "constitutional liberalism" and the right to the legal direction of our country would be to enact legislation to abolish the Supreme Court, and then amend our Constitution to eliminate the Charter.

Then, we would have fully responsible government, once again.

# 16: GOING FORTH BOLDLY
## A CALL TO ACTION

Enough of the trouble with Canada. At the end of each chapter of this book there are specific suggestions for positive remedies. This chapter offers some broader suggestions, both general and particular. In the 1990 original I was so upset with what I considered a betrayal by our leaders of our original British liberties that I called for the use of "direct democracy" as a potential solution, a way to enable the people to push back the top-down regime change we have suffered since the mid-1960s. At the time I did not fully understand the clash in political philosophies between direct democracy and our parliamentary system. In a nutshell: in the former system, citizens may either vote on a law they want directly, as in the case of a town hall meeting, or they may elect a representative as a legislator to whom they can give instructions. It is a situation in which the will of the majority rules. Its weakness is that the will of the losing 49 percent will often get trampled (unless there is a provision requiring a "special majority," such as for constitutional matters).

In a parliamentary system such as Canada's, however, a representative is forbidden to take instructions or mandates from voters, but rather is expected to deliberate and to make laws, not only for his or her electors, but for the benefit of the whole people. The idea here, passionately defended by our own first prime minister, John A. Macdonald, is that pure democracy of the direct type is uncivilized, for "in all countries the rights of the majority take care of themselves, but it is only in countries like England, enjoying constitutional liberty, and safe from the tyranny of a single despot or of an unbridled democracy, that the rights of minorities are regarded."[1] Under English constitutional liberty, full and keen deliberation in Parliament with other legislators is expected to produce better and more nuanced laws for the whole people than any of the partisan proposals tabled prior to a full discussion. Above all it avoids the trampling of minorities that occurs under direct democracy.

In a nation unified by a single moral, political, and religious ethos in which there remains a lot of trust in the stewardship of politicians, a system of representative constitutional liberty—rule by experts, really—can work very well, because legislators will generally make laws more or less in keeping with the common good. But in a nation like Canada that since the 1960s has suffered considerable moral dislocation, cultural weakening and fragmentation; where a common ethos is no longer so apparent; where a top-down radical regime change has, to all intents and purposes, been imposed on the people; when the direction of their country is all too often steered by judges who represent no one; then we need tools to fight back by way of a counter-revolution from the bottom. Here's how . . .

## HOW TO FIGHT THE MONSTER OF OLIGARCHY WITH DEMOCRATIC TOOLS

We the people—particularly when the three major parties are all singing from the same Statist songbook—need political and legal weapons to fight back; to regain control of our national destiny. We must once again (as we did in our long struggle for responsible government) figure out how to force government to be responsible to our legislators, and our legislators responsible to us. In order to achieve this state of affairs, we have to muster the resolve to introduce a very careful use of the tools of popular democracy. Along the way, we need a means to force judges to abide by the laws we have made, according to our intent when we made them, as expressed through our legislators. Isn't this what our democracy, however restrained and checked, is supposed to be? Am I guilty of spinning unattainable dreams, just like Statists?

Not at all. For there is a real, live, warm-blooded successful example at work in the world today. No untried theories are necessary. I am referring to the tools of direct democracy as used variously in Switzerland, the United States, and Australia, and I heartily recommend we hasten to adopt them, however modified to suit the Canadian situation. Many historians have observed that oligarchy (despotic power exercised by a small clique) is the inevitable result of all political systems. If true, then Canada's "executive federalism" is just a kinder name for oligarchy.

Below, we will see how the Swiss, and others, have managed to bring the monster of oligarchy to heel in their own countries, forcing politicians to serve the people. It's inspiring. We have a system that delegates all law-making to representatives. But it is time to introduce some popular influence over those representatives, for two main reasons: first, to prevent parliamentarians from making laws *against* the will of the people who sent them there; second, to force our judges to abide by the intent of the laws as and when we made them, rather than making laws themselves, which, as we saw in chapter 15, they often do. Let's look at how the Swiss do both of these things.

## DEMOCRACY IN SWITZERLAND

Switzerland is a small country of fewer than seven and a half million people with very few natural resources, a harsh winter, and a quarter of its land area covered by lots of impassable mountains. It has four official language groups, many ethnic subgroups, and large regional economic disparities. It's rather like a compressed Canada. But what sort of country is it? The Swiss enjoy:

- A very high standard of living over the past century
- Very low unemployment
- Extensive high-quality health and educational services (health services provided mostly through private insurance and user fees)
- Generous social services for the truly needy, especially the handicapped
- World-class public transportation—the trains are clean and on time!

In proportion to population, Switzerland has a very *small* federal bureaucracy, *low* tax rates, and a *small* per capita national budget. Sometimes people object that it is unfair to compare such a small nation with a large one like Canada. Well, there are problems unique to all countries. But government-to-population ratios are ratios; it doesn't matter if a country is huge or of middling size. Ten to one of anything is still ten to one. If we want to see two different countries with comparable quality of life and services, but with huge differences in operating costs and in the degree of private versus public control, and personal rights and freedoms, just compare anything you wish in Switzerland to the same thing in Sweden (or Canada). The Swiss do it all with a much lower tax burden than Swedes (or Canadians) and, I would argue, do it better. Here's how:

### Self-Governing Cantons

Switzerland is divided into twenty-six smaller states or provinces (called cantons) which have exactly equal rights and are largely independent in operation, handling their own education, health care, cultural affairs, and many other local matters themselves *without interference from the federal government.* Not incidentally, this is what Canada's BNA Act specified for the same sorts of functions in Canada (a wise prohibition long since overridden by federal fiscal bribery, and by the egalitarian mandates of the Charter). Each canton has up to a six-member government, its own laws, courts, constitution, parliament, medical systems, schools, welfare and other government services, distinctness, culture, and, of course, official language(s). Swiss cantons are basically self-governing and look after *everything* except for certain national functions dealt with by only seven federal ministries.

### Like the Swiss, We Need a Constitutional Limit on Government

In Canada, by contrast, the functions of our federal government are *without sufficient constitutional limit.* Here's a snippet from the website of Public Works and Government Services Canada: "PWGSC provides office space for 105 federal departments and agencies. We're currently providing office space for over 241,000 federal employees in over 1,800 locations across Canada." Wow. And that's only half of it. Counting Crown corporations, Canada has over 450,000 full-time federal employees. In 1990, our federal cabinet had thirty-nine members (not seven) overseeing twenty-eight full departments, with fifteen "sub-departments." In addition, there were twenty-eight "parliamentary secretaries" to assist in these machinations. Nothing much has changed. Canada is a small country with a *very* large government. The Swiss have one full-time federal employee for every 250 citizens. We have one for every eighty. Their ratio of feds to citizens is one-third ours.

Here's what the Swiss people *allow* their federal government to do (just to say those words feels good). The seven ministries (plus one chancellor) are: Justice and Police; National Defence; Interior; Finance; Economic Affairs; Transport and Energy; and Foreign Affairs. That's it. So, seven ministries; seven ministers. If Canada had this eminently sensible system, we would be able to shut down more than twenty ministries and reduce the size of our federal government by perhaps a hundred thousand civil servants, or more. Just multiply that number times the average salary and . . . that's right, it's billions of dollars per year—and I haven't included rent for office space, indexed pensions, travel, perks, and so on. (True, the provinces would pick up some of these costs—but not all, for they would control them better, each in its own way, and our costly federal-provincial duplication of ministries would be eliminated.) Okay, Canada has Fisheries and Oceans, and Switzerland does not. But if they did, they would include it under Economic Affairs.

### The Swiss Cabinet, Referendums, and Citizen Initiatives

The Swiss vote on average four times per year and on four or five "issues" each time. In other words, *they vote directly on all important matters.* Indeed, the Swiss Constitution emphasizes the fact that the people are the supreme authority, and not the cabinet, nor the courts, nor even the written Constitution itself. Indeed, each member of the seven-member cabinet is elected separately by Parliament to serve a four-year term. They run the government together as a kind of executive committee of Parliament. They are usually from different parties, but are pledged to operate on a collegial basis as a kind of permanent coalition of government. On key issues they negotiate a position in private, but then all stick to their decision as a team. Hardly anyone in the world can say who the president of the Swiss cabinet is, because that person is elected as a "first among equals" from among cabinet members to serve only a one-year term, and is then replaced by another elected member of the cabinet. Hence, there is no "political personality contest" possible in the Swiss system. Now, wouldn't that be a relief?

*Optional Referendums* enable Swiss citizens to pass judgment on federal, cantonal, and municipal legislation, and even on certain international treaties—*after* the event. If government passes a law they do not like, they just have to collect 50,000 signatures protesting it within a hundred days of publication of the law. This measure is considered a *brake* the people may apply to any new legislation, and it ensures Swiss legislators will not bother to pass a law they know will likely be struck down by the people.

*Popular Initiatives* may be used by the people to force government to amend the Constitution. Initiatives are considered the driving force of direct democracy, the real "people power." If we had such a thing, we could, for example, include a private property right in our Constitution, even if the government and courts resisted this (which they have); we could get rid of discriminatory clauses; we could insist on an amendment to clarify our traditional definition of marriage. No matter on what issue, the people, rather than manipulative activists or judges, consciously make the laws.

*Mandatory Referendums* are yet another great instrument. By law, these must be used *to approve* all constitutional amendments by a double majority (a majority of the people nationally, and also a majority of the cantons). Canada already has this sort of amendment formula called the "7/50 rule": to amend our Constitution (that is, when our judges are not taking it upon themselves to do that for us), we need the approval of seven provincial legislatures *representing* at least 50 percent of the population. However, there is no requirement for the *direct* approval by a majority of the Canadian people. There should be. The purpose of such a change would be to make sure that any constitutional change is openly supported by a significant majority of the people; that they have "ownership" of their own constitution. In contrast, Canada's Charter "deal"—this is really embarrassing—was made by a furtive coffee klatch of plotting politicians in a kitchen somewhere, where Trudeau and his henchmen connived to exclude Quebec.

In short, you could never have a situation in Switzerland where, say, perhaps 80 percent of the people want less government spending, but Parliament votes it up; or the people don't want to dish out money to radical interest groups, but the government does it anyway; or the people do not want gay marriage, but the government (or the Court) votes for it anyway. Unthinkable for the Swiss; for they go to the polls *specifically to control their politicians.* To block oligarchy. This procedure acts as a powerful brake on the ambitions of social engineers, and the Swiss are proud that they generally say no. In Switzerland, the people *are* the government, and the referendum is the key.[2]

### Recall—To Get Rid of Bad Politicians

An instrument called "recall" is used in some countries to fire politicians at any time who have been elected on a specific political platform, but who once in office betray the trust of those who sent them to Parliament. Critics say that is not a good idea because voters will think more deeply about their choices if they know they have to live with them for four or five years. But I like the idea, if it can be structured conservatively, for it is not a tool to be used frivolously. But in cases of malfeasance, lying to electors, betraying election promises, and the like, voters, with sufficient justification and popular support by way of legal signatures, and so on, ought to be able to fire a politician at any time for cause, just as they are able to fire someone they employ.

482 16: GOING FORTH BOLDLY

Recall procedures are used today in a small number of countries. Some thirty-six American states allow recall votes for regional or city officials, and eighteen have provisions to recall state legislators or governors (recall is not used for U.S. federal offices). Only two U.S. governors have ever been recalled, the most recent being Gray Davis of California, who was removed from office in 2003 and replaced by Arnold Schwarzenegger. American voters used recall thousands of times throughout the twentieth century. Six of Switzerland's cantons have recall provisions, as do Venezuela and the Philippines. Canada's British Columbia also has recall provisions. Premier William Aberhart's Social Credit government brought recall legislation to the province of Alberta in 1936, and then a year later, when he discovered he was about to be the target of a recall petition, he had the legislation rescinded. In 2009, a British House of Commons expenses scandal tarnished the reputation of many members of Parliament, and led to demands that recall mechanisms be introduced. I recommend that Canada introduce recall provisions because to hold the threat of legitimate recall over the head of a politician, even in a system of representative democracy such as ours, is a constant reminder that the power to rule is a grant of the people, and it flows up, not down.

## SOME GENERAL RECOMMENDATIONS

### What About Ending Ottawa's Direct Taxing Power? Let's Pay a Fixed Percentage of GPP to Ottawa, instead. Or a Rate Keyed to Population.

Let's have a real revolution. Something more than mere words. Perhaps the strongest underlying reason for the development of auction politics and the Statism it aids and abets is direct taxing power. The federal government decides on the level of federal taxation then taxes each citizen individually. But then, money in hand, Ottawa offers "shared-cost" promises (or huge block grants) to *bribe* provincial consent to federal regulation in areas that under our own Constitution have always been solely a provincial right. How? Simple. Ottawa says: "If you accept our *national* rules for this program, we will pay half (or a give a block grant for) your *provincial* costs." So, why not modify the federal government's power to tax individuals directly? But . . . if we removed Ottawa's direct taxing power, but kept the other forms of federal taxation, such as trade taxes, tariffs, and so on, how would Ottawa get the money required to fund federal obligations?

One way would be for the provinces to constitutionally bind themselves to transfer to the federal government *an equal percentage of annual Gross Provincial Product*. Or, alternatively, they could each transfer to Ottawa a fixed fee per capita of provincial population, to be raised by the provinces as they see fit. For any government, more money means more control, and less money means less control. As a nation, just like so many other democracies, Canada has failed miserably to control its own spending under the system we have used. The report card shows an F. So it is time for a structural change that will discipline federal government spending by controlling it at the source. Something like this would overturn the top-down control of provinces and people, and substitute a bottom-up control of runaway central spending.

### End Our Socialist Redistribution Programs

We should block the power of the federal government to subsidize one province at the expense of others, which is exactly what our own BNA Act, 1867, mandated before our home-bred socialists (from all parties) did an end run around it. Each province was meant to stand on its own merits, and to borrow only on its "sole credit." If we went back to that wise provision, would some regions be different—less, or more, well off than others? Of course. But because political, economic, and cultural freedoms would be preserved for all equally, people could move and live anywhere they wished. The Swiss don't believe it is the government's function to equalize outcomes for everybody, because all individuals are different, as are all regions and communities. They are aware that if you subsidize something (like unemployment), you will get more of it, and if you tax something (like hard work and success), you will get less.

### End Government's Immunity from the Law

Let's enshrine in the Constitution a sanction against government's doing anything that a citizen is not allowed to do. That is, make sure all government is subject to the rule of law, and not above it, as it often is now. (Examples are official discrimination measures under Section 15, the *droit administratif* in Quebec, and elsewhere, such as the privileged immunities of language police, etc.) It is only through insistence on submission to the rule of law by all citizens equally, and the corresponding insistence on individual freedom and therefore responsibility for one's own actions, that makes a free civil society possible.

### Let's Impose a Fiscal Guillotine on Government

Above, I suggested an alternative way to fund our federal government. But we would still need a constitutional limitation or brake on out-of-control fiscal gluttony and borrowing. Political leaders are presently unaccountable to the people during their term of office (our only recourse is to turf them out every five years—or sooner, if we get the chance). They regularly plunge us and our offspring into unconscionable long-term debt and then, instead of going to jail, they walk away on handsome pensions for life. A solution would be a rule such as the following: *Any provincial or federal government that runs a deficit two years in a row may automatically be put to an election by the Opposition in Parliament, or by the people in a citizens' initiative.* In short, the Auditor General's report on the government's fiscal performance could trigger an election. The United States had somewhat the equivalent in the Gramm-Rudman Act.

Other American states have Tax and Expenditure Limitation laws (TELs) that seem to be effective. It's time we had them, too.

### What About Annual Tax Bills Only?

If we must keep the present system of unchecked tax harvesting of individual (and corporate) incomes, then let's disallow tax deduction at source from paycheques. Especially despicable are automatic "withholding" deductions from paycheques, and "tax instalments." These devices conceal what government intends to do with your money. The laws ought to be challenged. Instead, all taxes should be visible. Citizens should get a clearly marked tax bill once per year indicating where their money will go. Also, all income taxes should be indexed for inflation, to prevent the "bracket creep" that artificially forces people into higher tax brackets (alternatively, a "flat tax" removes this problem—see below). Such changes would bring transparency to taxation and drive home to Canadians the hidden cost of their welfare state. As an added twist on this for Canada, such a bill could include a line showing exactly how much of the total national debt is owed and will have to be paid by each taxpayer and family. In France, for example, no income tax is deducted at source. You take home your gross earnings and are responsible for paying the applicable tax when you get your annual tax bill. There is a cost to switching systems, of course (the financing costs of the one-time postponement of monthly cash flow), but this is not as great as the cost of not switching.

### Let's Sunset All Government Contracts and Corporations

Sell off Crown corporations at an even faster rate than we have done since the 1990s through a broad share-distribution to employees and the general public (thus making it difficult for any government to take them back). Such a program does not prevent a government from rightly setting the *terms of contract* for a public service company. For example, if Canada Post were to be put on the block, a legitimate fear is that unprofitable routes would be folded. Government could simply contractually include the servicing of such routes in the sale. Government should legislate such terms for certain "public good" companies, but not operate them. The result would be better service at half the cost. Sunset clauses would mean that all government corporations potentially could be wound up under a five-year sunset clause (or be publicly inspected for ongoing viability before being allowed to continue).

### Let's Ban All Public Unions

It is plainly wrong to allow public employees to strike against citizens who are forced to pay their wages. As government is created only to serve and defend the people, it is a moral contradiction to allow anyone who has agreed to serve the people to refuse to serve them (except by personally withdrawing from such work). Public administration work is today notoriously soft, inefficient, and high-paying in comparison to equivalent private sector employment. Such work is very close to tenured, as few are ever laid off or fired. Public unions have inordinate control over government services, and public pensions are grotesquely generous (especially for MPs). We should also strike down the "Rand Formula," which allows unions to deduct dues from employees who choose not to join a union. Canada is dangerously close to being a tripartite society in which one-third do productive wealth-creating work, one-third work for government, and one-third depend on government in some substantial way. It doesn't take an economist to see that the last two segments can easily gang up on the first.

### End Tax Discrimination: Let's Try a Flat Tax

It is no less than an enormous scandal that an average intelligent citizen (not an oxymoron) with mildly complicated affairs cannot hope to complete a personal income tax form in a way that protects him or her from tax plunder. Our so-called "progressive" income tax system is a discriminatory mess that unjustifiably favours some over others, and discourages hard work. It is a residue of an age of class envy, and is Marxist in origin. Its purpose is to redistribute wealth earned by some, to others who have not earned it, and who have no moral right to it. In addition, we have seen that a huge dollop of government largesse in all socialist nations is actually being redistributed to middle- and upper-income citizens as well, in what is called a tax-and-redistribute "churning" process. We should switch to a principled "flat tax," as the Americans call it (often called a "single tax" here—not as apt a term). Research, especially by Robert Hall and Alvin Rabushka of Stanford University has long since shown that a flat tax (meaning that all taxpayers pay the same percentage of their income), in addition to its obvious simplicity, actually *creates more revenue for government*, or, at the least, is neutral. A sure sign of its success is that it makes tax planners, tax lawyers, and tax supervisors more or less obsolete, freeing them to do productive work. With the flat tax, there are no "loopholes" or "tax shelters" allowed for individuals or corporations. A flat tax system would mean: no more income discrimination. No need for a GST or HST, and so on. Just basic fairness for everyone, equally. Any citizen who can read could prepare his or her own tax return on the back of a postcard. Finally, all citizens ought to pay something (even if just a pittance by the truly needy), on the grounds that paying something creates an "ownership" in the country, an interest in how the country is run, and removes the misleading idea that we have a right to something "free."

### Eliminate Corporate and Capital Gains Taxes

We should eliminate the so-called "corporate tax," for this is in reality a disguised form of double taxation. It is also another envy-based tax that deceives the public into thinking that "greedy corporations" whose only interests are profits are finally being made to pay. However, a moment's reflection will tell us that in order to stay in business—to maintain an acceptable margin of income above expenses—a corporation must raise the price of its goods and services sufficiently to preserve a normal operating margin after accounting for the taxes to be paid. So a tax on a corporation is really just a pass-through, invisible consumer tax. We should eliminate the capital gains tax with the aim of turning Canada into the most investment-friendly place on earth. The creation, operation, and buy-sell decisions with respect to corporations and property should not have to be made mostly for tax-efficient purposes, but rather for the purposes of production and investment success.

### Give the People the Last Word, Not the Courts

In a free society the Constitution must ensure that Parliament—the people—retain sovereignty over the courts. A constitutional amendment is needed to the effect that by a super-majority of both houses of Parliament (or in the case of provincial courts, by a provincial legislature), any court ruling may be overturned by legislative veto. In effect, Parliament, rather than a bench of politically appointed judges (whether leftists or rightists) who cannot be removed, must be the supreme shaper of the nation's laws.

### Screen Judges for Legal Suitability

No judge should be appointed to any court in Canada who rejects (or whose work and rulings can be shown to have rejected) the concept of a rule of law, the doctrine of legal restraint and original intent, and the fundamental principles of our common law tradition. Our judges must publicly swear to uphold these standards of the law, in addition to our constitutional division of powers, the strict political and ideological neutrality of the courts, and the legislative supremacy of Parliament. All tribunals, such as so-called Human Rights Tribunals and Commissions, where truth is no defence, and there is no standard of evidential proof, are an international scandal and an affront to what was once a proud tradition of freedom under law. They must be abolished immediately.

### Forbid All Social Engineering

A constitution must forbid all Charter-style discrimination and social engineering designed to equalize citizens, economies, or regions; for equality and freedom are inversely related, and more of one always and automatically means less of the other. Citizens have the right to migrate to any region of Canada, there to express their personal or economic aspirations and differences in any fashion they choose within the law. There should be no constitutional promises of transfer payments or equalization of benefits to any person or region, nor recognition of any citizen's claims for equal substantive goods, benefits, or services.

## Demand Equality of Provinces

Eliminate all provincial or regional favouritism and "distinct society" clauses (or, in the breech, declare all provinces and regions distinct). There must be complete freedom of movement, culture, trade, etc., as between provinces. Quebec, the province most troubled by federal intrusions (and rightly so), would love that freedom, and so would love its place in Canada. The only "deals" to be kept would be those of the original BNA Act, 1867.

## Let's Demand Language Freedom

A free country ought to aim for a free market in languages, without restraint or coercion by the State. Provinces that wish to have one or more "official languages" for public affairs may regulate this matter internally, and territorially, by referendum. There ought to be no such thing as a portable language right carried by citizens personally, wherever they may choose to travel in the country. Nationally, and for international affairs, Canada only needs one official language—English. It is the official language of the free world. French-speaking citizens should have the language rights promised in the BNA Act, and all provinces as many official languages within their own boundaries as they think reasonable. Language policy in Switzerland is a territorial right, and not a personal one. If you don't like living in the language of your canton, you just up and move to the one you prefer.

## End the Government Monopoly on Schooling.
## Let's have "Choice in Education." Bust the Teachers' Unions!

No private school in Canada's history has ever needed a Ministry of Education to turn out the most impressively accomplished young men and women. Indeed, Canada has never had a crisis in education. It has had an ongoing crisis in public, or government-run, education. Thomas Jefferson got it right: "The philosophy of the schoolroom in one generation will be the philosophy of the government in the next." Radicals agree. The Ontario Institute for Studies in Education (OISE) in Toronto, for example, has been a soft-headed factory for leftist radicalism for decades, churning out six hundred new "change agents" every year.

We should invoke anti-trust legislation to bust all public teachers' unions, and the grip of the leftist orthodoxy on teaching and on the minds of our children. A "voucher system" such as the Dutch (and recently Sweden, and also many U.S. school districts) have used successfully for almost a century would enable all parents to spend the educational portion of their taxes on any independent school of their choice, anywhere. The struggle to end the grip of Statists on education ended in Holland with an amendment to the country's constitution, passed in 1917, that guaranteed equal funding for public and independent schools. Within a few years, close to 70 percent of students were attending independent schools. The Dutch education system thereby changed from a state-organized monopoly into a system that gave priority to parental choice and freedom of education. It continues to flourish today. Such a change in Canada would introduce competition between schools by changing the paymaster of the teachers and administrators from government, to parents, thus making teachers and schools responsive to the parents and communities that pay them. At the same time, we should strip all ideological courses from our schools, from radical feminism (that, among other things, teaches misandry), to sex-ed courses (that teach primarily sexual liberation, abortion rights, and gay rights), to scientifically bogus environmentalism courses, and the like. Readers interested in this topic may want to read my book, *The War Against the Family*. Be sure you are sitting down. It is a book that will radicalize you in a good way.

## THE CONSTITUTION AND THE CHARTER

It is not likely Canadians will return to the intensive constitutional rounds of the 1990s any time soon. But we never know. And if we do, it might help to think about what a new Constitution ought to include. Here is one man's view.

### Return the Priority of Common Law

If we want to fight for our original rights and freedom—for British liberty—the first step is to amend the present Constitution by removing Section 52.1, which basically says that the Charter rules (that is, judges rule) over all other forms of law in Canada that are "inconsistent" with the Charter. Let's end that at once, and get our judges out of politics. Then, our amended Constitution would be back in balance with our common law heritage. We then make it official by referendum. No more backroom constitutional deal-making. No more leaving out one-quarter of all citizens!

### Only Negative Rights

A good constitution will specify that the State must refrain from interference with the inherited common law rights and freedoms of individuals. It will specifically say that it is the role of government to guarantee equality before the law only, which, for example, shall treat a rich man and a poor one with the same severity—but not to guarantee any "substantive" or material equality. There shall be no guaranteed "positive" rights to meals, homes, jobs, clothing, medical care, income, insurance, or anything at all. The minimum standard for adulthood in the real world is looking after oneself and one's family. That old founding Canadian self-reliance! If any government welfare is established for those proven to be truly needy, it should be offered as a privilege—a gift of some to others—but never as a right, or claim against others (because that is legal plunder). All welfare states are known to dry up the wellspring of private charity. We must make it a national objective to reverse this sorry truth.

## Restraint

A good constitution must be a viable instrument for the protection of the people, their freedoms, families, and enterprises—indeed, of civil society itself—from the depredations and interventions of the State. In it we must carefully enunciate the need for controls on Statism, spelling out specific systems for dividing, restraining, balancing, and checking the powers of government (because too many judges don't get it), which in turn must be thoroughly characterized as the servant of the people, obedient to their expressed legislative will. That is part of the meaning of the term "public servant."

## Subsidiarity

This is an ancient term meaning that in a free society all emphasis shall be on localism, not centralism, for the glory of free societies arises from the moral agency of citizens, and the self-help of all, in freedom from State oppression. Our political environment must encourage the maximum use of moral agency in all personal, family, and community life, and desist from policies designed to relieve human beings from the necessity to solve their own problems. Under the rule of subsidiarity, all problems must be solved at the level where they originate, and a higher level of government invoked only if a lower fails, and then only if invited. This is a principle enunciated in the Swiss constitution, and is to be emulated.

## Property Rights and a Takings Clause

Canada's Constitution does not specifically protect the right of citizens to own and enjoy private property—although our common law does. However, we have seen that the Charter makes all common law subordinate to itself. So the justified fear is that unless the Constitution supports this ancient right—without which the whole concept of freedom becomes almost meaningless—it will increasingly be eroded in any test under the Charter. Actually, it has been so eroded, since 1982. That is because, as history shows, even many States that permitted a right to own property have nevertheless so heavily regulated its use that ownership becomes almost a burden—there is no "enjoyment" of property. That trend must be reversed in Canada. And for certain, a good constitution must contain a "takings" clause that guarantees full and fair-market compensation for any property taken by the State. Ours does not.

## Economic Rights

Economic rights flow from the secure protection of individual freedom and of property, because property rights without freedom are void, and freedom without control of one's own property is close to empty. Canadian courts have been reluctant to admit even our inherited common law property and economic rights as certainties. Indeed, in the 2005 *Chaoulli* case, the Court said "the argument that 'liberty' includes freedom of contract . . . is novel in Canada, where economic rights are not included in the Canadian Charter."[3] But that was a nonsensical thing to say, because human beings make contracts every day, and the very word "contract" implies the liberty of the parties. Indeed, English (and Canadian) law has for a long time firmly argued that where there is no "meeting of the minds," there can be no contract, and minds cannot meet, or be in agreement, except freely. At any rate, Canadians should fight hard to articulate in the law of the nation the basic economic rights to own, trade, sell, buy, and contract for all legal goods and services, because through excessive taxation, regulation, zoning, and environmental laws, it is clear that any State can preserve these rights on paper, but nullify them in practice. Also, the economic right of all citizens to trade their goods and services voluntarily between themselves and their regions, without undue impediment or tariff, ought to be guaranteed. Canada is awash with barriers and regulations, union and product-favouritism laws, and the like. Down with it all.

**Let Us Speak only of "Citizens"**
A constitution should be blind to any differences between individuals or groups. It must speak only of "citizens," without qualification. Canada's current Charter fails this test, for it contains numerous sections which were specifically included to permit the State to treat *groups* of citizens differently, according to language, sex, religion, ability, or ethnicity—a surefire recipe for inter-group squabbling over who has the highest victim status, what is the correct pecking order of rights, and so on. Homosexuals were added as one of these groups by the Supreme Court (though that inclusion was specifically and *repeatedly rejected* by various Canadian legislatures and by the framers of the Charter itself). Most national constitutions contain some "deals" that made them possible in the first place. Canada's gave deals to the French and to religious schooling. America's gave deals to the southern states. But such deals should in principle be eliminated or kept to an absolute minimum.

**No Constitutional Favouritism**
Canada's Constitution has "ranks" granting special treatment and privileges to some citizens according to language, race, disadvantage, religion, and a few other categories, too. Section 15 of the Charter has provided our philosopher Kings and Queens on the Bench an open door to admit any group of citizens they please for special treatment on "analogous" grounds. This conflicts with the principle that a constitution should speak only of "citizens," without qualification. We want the same rules for all citizens and provinces, not deals for some but not others.

## Free Speech

... is the right of citizens to express and publish their ideas freely. In its origins "free speech" referred mostly to intellectual, philosophical, and religious matters—public debate. It has never included a right to breach local moral standards; to walk naked in the street, for example (although a benighted Canadian judge did manage to amend our Constitution to allow women legally to walk bare-breasted), or to yell "fire" in a crowded theatre. Common law protections against libel, slander, misrepresentation, and the like have always been sufficient to protect people from real (in contrast to flimsy "politically incorrect") speech abuse.

Over all moral matters, citizens ought to have meaningfully defined local and provincial control, which they do not, rather *cannot*, possibly have under our Charter because one specific effect and object of all charters is to overrule local citizen control by judge-edicts from the centre. A community's desire to ban pornography at a local milk store, for example, is controlled by urban legal libertines in Ottawa. Just so, we saw in chapter 15 that Canada's Supreme Court, without authority, has amended the country's standard of community morals and reduced it to a pathetic individual harm principle. More than anything, this gives the sense of Canada as an internal empire of provincial and municipal colonies controlled by a morally alien centrist culture.

## A Modified Elected Senate

In 1990, and due to the blatant patronage surrounding Senate appointments, I wrote that we should "ensure that all political bodies, including the Senate, are elected." But I have reconsidered. Direct election of senators would just expose us all to even more political party power, but in two houses instead of just one. The result? More oligarchy. Also, if both houses were elected, then in the case of a conflict between Senate and House of Commons, the immediate questions would be: Which should rule? Which would *really* represent the will of the people? With two directly elected houses, that would be an undecidable.

However, if we want to end the obvious cronyism and patronage of our prime ministers, we could allow provinces to present their own slates of elected (or appointed) candidates for appointment to the Senate. This could be achieved without changing the Constitution. Indeed, after drafting these suggestions I saw that the government has been proposing something like this.

## The Notwithstanding Clause (Section 33)

In 1990, I wrote: "If the people want to keep a *Charter*, then let's get rid of the 'notwithstanding' clause, thus preventing government from skirting Constitutional provisions, as Premier Bourassa did recently." I was upset by Quebec's use of the clause to stomp on English language rights in Quebec. But that was just an unfortunate use of the clause. Now I would say that Section 33 is the last and only measure of legislative supremacy by which a provincial government in Canada can escape domination by federal legislators in Ottawa, or by which any government in Canada can override a bad court judgment. We should keep it, and as mentioned above, strike down Section 52.1, thus making Canada's code law subordinate to the democratic will of the people and their inherited common law.

**Let's End All Foreign Control of Canada**
Various governments, liberal as well as conservative, have signed international treaties enabling international leftists to reach into Canada for control of our national life. These treaties attempt to control many types of domestic policy on matters we have never voted upon: such things as the generosity of our welfare system and foreign aid (because domestic welfare and foreign aid are conceived by leftists as international rights), and our childcare and parental rights laws (via treaties on the "rights" of the child). But to dictate so-called children's rights to Canada is especially nosy and pernicious, because children are too young to exercise rights; they must be exercised for them by third parties. This usually means some busybody will exert pressure on Canada to pass laws against the traditional rights of Canadian parents. Canada should reject and/or abandon any and all treaties that purport to control the lives of free citizens inside our own borders by constraining the will of our elected politicians (who should be obeying *our* will, our customs, our traditions, and not dictates from a radicalized UN). Especially annoying, too, are the myriad treaties and attempted treaties concocted by radical feminists in Canada and elsewhere that promote international "sex-ed," contraception, and abortion as the "rights" of underage children, or as a tax-funded obligation of all nations.

Canada has been blindly self-righteous, seeking to impose a failed liberal sexual ideology on an international scale, through a process that undermines the local moral codes and family and sexual ways of other peoples. To support feminist causes in foreign lands, during the period 1999 to 2006 alone, Canada extracted from taxpayers, and then forked over to other nations through CIDA, $792,800,000. More than *three-quarters of a billion dollars*. That's enough money to build a decent indoor multi-sport facility for youth in every urban centre in Canada with a population over 50,000 (there are only sixty such). But that's such a sensible use of public funds, we are never likely to see it. So I would say that if we insist on tax plundering for sexual purposes, perhaps using the money to teach our own young people less about condoms, pills, and abortion rights, and more about the importance of private sexual restraint and public modesty, would be a good idea. But come to think of it . . . that's what all parents used to do, and it didn't cost a penny.

## The "Four F's"

Canada is a nation culturally and historically based on Freedom, Family, Free Enterprise, and Faith: on the importance of the exercise of personal freedom and responsibility by each citizen (as opposed to a life lived by State-regulated orthodoxies); on the recognition and protection of the natural family (a married mother and father living together with their dependent children) as our most important social institution; on the right of individuals and families to voluntary economic exchange (as opposed to excessive and growing State control, taxation, and regulation of the economy); and finally, on the important role of faith in a free society, whereby individuals may choose to shape their lives by moral values higher than the dreary and community-fracturing secular orthodoxies of the State. The Four F's, and everything they imply, are the true unwritten constitution of a free society.

# WHAT CAN THE ORDINARY CITIZEN DO?

1.  Write to your member of Parliament, at the House of Commons, Ottawa, Ontario K1A 0A6 (no stamp required).
2.  Write to your member of the provincial legislature (stamp required).
3.  Write to your local newspaper(s), with copies to a goodly list of influential citizens and local politicians. You can build your list gradually. This really concerns politicians, who will wonder what others are thinking of your point of view. Short letters are more likely to be published. Even if your letter is not published, you can be sure it is being read, and thus is contributing to a body of opinion, making it easier for the next letter to get printed. Media and political types sometimes *do* listen (mostly because they are afraid of becoming unpopular and/or losing perks if they don't).
4.  Participate in radio call-in shows—these are a form of "street democracy."
5.  Be brave. Be sure to express your sincere opinions carefully to friends and acquaintances—this has a domino effect. If you give your opponent an argument from a higher principle than the Statist one they are likely relying upon, they will generally calm down and eventually come onside.
6.  When you hear of some new proposal to tax the people and spend more government money, ask yourself why the thing proposed couldn't be done by individuals and their families, or by local communities, or contracted out, or insured privately. Most of all, ask whether it is good for Canada. And remember: nothing is "free." It is just pre-paid—more than likely by you.
7.  When you send in cheques for property taxes, always send a letter (with distributed copies) to the mayor, councillors, and so on, asking the municipality to economize by eliminating redundant wasteful services, or by contracting out inefficient government services to the private sector.

8. When you receive fundraising letters from political parties, write back and tell them your views.

9. Campaign personally in small and large ways for the Freedom System as described in this book, and for reasonable tools of direct democracy, which, while they ought never to replace our system, would discipline it considerably. A politician who knows he or she can be recalled for misleading the electors, for example, is a cautious politician.

10. In every way possible, argue to rid Canada of its present top-down system, one that regards the people like children, incapable of making important decisions in their own best interests, and for the creation of a more bottom-up system of controls in which the input of the people in the creation of their own democracy is encouraged, respected, and protected by law.

Great nations spring from great principles. My fondest hope for this book is that it will help Canadians understand that those principles can work only if they arise from the hearts and minds of each individual. To surrender our destiny to others, even if they appear to have the best of intentions, is to be controlled by them.

It is time for us to take back our country.

# NOTES

## PREFACE TO THE 2010 EDITION

1   Throughout this book terms with a special meaning specific to my argument are capitalized. The word "State," for example, refers not to the concept of the state in general, but to the uniquely modern high-tax, pervasively regulatory welfare states distinctive of all modern democracies (with the possible exception of Switzerland).

## INTRODUCTION

1   On this topic, see William D. Gairdner, *The Book of Absolutes: A Critique of Relativism and a Defence of Universals* (Montreal: McGill-Queen's University Press, 2009).

2   Fareed Zakaria, *The Future of Freedom: Illiberal Democracy at Home and Abroad* (New York: W.W. Norton, 2004).

## 1: CANADA'S REGIME CHANGE

1   The main influences shaping the French style were such as Henri Saint-Simon and Jean-Jacques Rousseau, especially in the latter's *The Social Contract*. There is a long British and Scottish history and legal tradition in defence of individual liberty, property rights, preference for common law, economic rights, free markets, and so on, best articulated by such as John Locke, David Hume, Adam Smith, Adam Ferguson, Bernard Mandeville, and Edmund Burke. A short primer on this latter tradition is Ronald Hamowy, *The Scottish Enlightenment and the Theory of Spontaneous Order* (Carbondale, IL.: Southern Illinois University Press, 1987). There is much scholarship on the cross-fertilization of these two styles as seen in the influence of Montesquieu on the American founders, and such as Auguste Comte on John Stuart Mill, who was an important progenitor of both styles.

2   Louis-Joseph de Montcalm-Gozon, Marquis de Saint-Veran, was commander of the French forces in North America and was killed at the Battle of the Plains of Abraham at Quebec on September 14, 1759, when attacked by England's General James Wolfe (who was killed in the same battle).

3   See Paul A. Rahe, *Soft Despotism, Democracy's Drift* (New Haven, CT: Yale University Press, 2009): ". . . the narrow elite constituting [France's] political class is drawn from the roughly one hundred individuals who

graduate each year from the *Ecole national d'administration* founded by Charles de Gaulle, in 1945." This elite corps, nicknamed the *énarques*, "form an aristocracy of a sort." They lead lives of great privilege at public expense, and "as recent scandals have repeatedly made clear, in practice, to a very considerable extent, *they are above the law*" (p. 232) [emphasis added]. They run most of the great (publicly assisted) corporations and ministries, and dominate the civil service and the political parties.

4   A helpful essay on this contrast is in Irving Kristol, *Reflections of a Neoconservative* (New York: Basic Books, 1983), Ch. 12, pp. 139–76.

5   Trudeau was suckled on the intellectual teats of Descartes (among others) and was determined to uproot Canada from its historical Anglo-Saxon ways. His personal, and very Cartesian, motto was "Reason before Passion." In French, "*la raison avant la passion*" was woven into a quilt made by Canadian artist Joyce Wieland that he hung on the wall of his official residence at 24 Sussex Drive, Ottawa. At any rate, Trudeau all but imposed the idea that human societies can be successfully formulated, planned, and then engineered like some kind of simple math problem from the top by philosopher kings and queens. To hell with "the people"; we will force the rational good life on them with our superior ideas, was the mood. U.S. president Barack Obama has just tried this with his financial and health legislation: the State will heavily fine all those who do not purchase health insurance, aims to direct major corporations and financial interests, and so on.

    To be fair, in 1968, Trudeau warned us all he was setting out to do this in his first book, *Federalism and the French Canadians*. But hardly anyone read it. All his life, at least with respect to the role of government, he resorted to Rousseau's concept of the General Will, especially in his chapter "Federalism, Nationalism, and Reason" in that book. When he spoke against the Meech Lake Accord in *Trudeau Speaks Out* (1990), he seemed more obsessed than ever with Rousseau's notion of a collective will, and wrote that from 1927 until his Charter in 1982 Canadian federalism had strived "to create a national will . . . or '*une volonté générale*' as Rousseau had called it" (p. 45). Then we read, like a drumroll, that "the foundation of the nation is will" (p. 187); "for there is no power without will" (p. 187). "Self-determination is based on will," he writes (p. 184), and any international order would be founded on "the free will of the people . . . willing their way toward Statehood." On page 195, Trudeau repeats the phrase "will of the people" four times in one paragraph, then complains that "with [the] Meech Lake [Accord] there is no national will left" (p. 66), and so on.

6   On the theme of totalitarian democracy, see J.L. Talmon, *The Origins of Totalitarian Democracy* (1952), and for an in-depth analysis of the role of

gnosticism in the formation of modern political religions, see William D. Gairdner, *The Trouble With Democracy* (Toronto: Stoddart, 2001, BPS Books, 2008).

7   As this book was being prepared for publication, the conservative American political commentator Ann Coulter was officially warned in a letter from François Houle, vice-president and provost of the University of Ottawa, where she was to speak March 23, 2010, to be careful in her remarks or she could be charged for uttering "hate speech."

8   Paule A. Rahe, *Soft Despotism, Democracy's Drift*, Ch. 3.

9   In Canada, the French style—a "*code civil*"—is used in Quebec for all except criminal matters. The English-style common law survives in the other nine provinces, but has been subordinated to the code law of Canada's Charter of Rights and Freedoms since 1982.

10  The Magna Carta, or Great Charter of 1215, was a summary protest against abuses of power by King John of England who, with his seal at Runnymede, acquiesced to the demands of English barons as set forth in the Charter. The form of it that has entered into British law was reissued in 1225.

11  Alan Macfarlane, *The Origins of English Individualism* (Oxford: Basil Blackwell, 1978), p. 5.

12  In the first edition of this book, I used the term "Bonus System" because rewards are the natural consequence of such a system. But the term "Freedom System" is better because without the underlying freedom there can be no rewards.

13  Since the French Revolution of 1789, France has had five republics, two monarchies, two empires, and a postwar dictatorship. In this period France has also lived under sixteen different "constitutions." More than one-quarter of the entire French labour force works for the State—close to the Canadian figure.

14  Paul Johnson, *A History of the English People* (London: Weidenfeld and Nicolson, 1972), p. 9.

15  See Thorsten Beck, and Ross Levine, "Legal Institutions and Financial Development," prepared for the World Bank under the title *Handbook of New Institutional Economics*, World Bank Policy Research Working Paper 3136, September 2003, p. 6. See also, P. Mahoney, "The Common Law and Economic Growth: Hayek Might Be Right," in *Journal of Legal Studies*, 2001, No. 30, pp. 503–25, and J.H. Merryman, "The French Deviation," in the *American Journal of Comparative Law*, 1996, No. 44, pp. 109–19.

16  Beck and Levine, p. 6.

17  Ibid., p. 10.

18  Brian Lee Crowley, *Fearful Symmetry: the Fall and Rise of Canada's Founding Values* (Toronto: Key Porter Books, 2009).

19  It is seldom mentioned that Trudeau's ambition in steering the Canadian ship of state to the left was facilitated by the pervasive influence of some 100,000 well-educated leftist American draft dodgers who settled in Canada between 1967 and 1974 and who took so many positions of influence in our universities and media. (Of the original 100,000, half returned to the United States after President Carter's 1974 amnesty.)

20  Richard Gwyn, *The Northern Magus* (Toronto: McClelland & Stewart, 1980), p. 28.

21  Pierre Elliott Trudeau, *Federalism and the French Canadians* (Toronto: Macmillan, 1968), pp. 126ff. [Italics mine.]

22  Spoken by Trudeau at a private dinner at Rob Prichard's home in Toronto and cited by William Thorsell, editor, in the *Globe and Mail*, on March 23, 1991. Prichard is an influential citizen who became president of the University of Toronto, then CEO of Torstar, and is now president and CEO of Metrolinx.

23  Barrington Moore Jr., *Authority and Inequality under Capitalism and Socialism: USA, USSR & China* (Clarendon Press: Oxford, 1987).

24  For a rendering of this, see Peter H. Russell, *Constitutional Odyssey: Can Canada Become a Sovereign People?*, 3rd ed. (Toronto: University of Toronto Press, 2004), Chap 8. See also Janet Ajzenstat, *The Once and Future Canadian Democracy* (Montreal & Kingston: McGill-Queen's University Press, 2003). The latter argues that Canadians were fully and legally constituted as "a sovereign people" with the BNA Act of 1867. Very true. My view, however, is that although we were indeed properly constituted as a people in 1867—it was a very good constitution—Trudeau and the first ministers imposed an illegitimate regime change on us in 1982. They did it under the letter of the law, but not under its spirit, for the reasons explained in this book [Italics mine].

25  In December 1973, Trudeau told a TV audience: "Nine-tenths of politics appeals ... to emotion rather than to reason. I'm a bit sorry about that, but this is the world we are living in, and therefore I've had to change." Cited in Richard Gwyn, *Pierre Elliott Trudeau* (Toronto: Fitzhenry and Whiteside, 2006, p. 24).

**2: EIGHT POPULAR ILLUSIONS: OBSTACLES TO CLEAR THINKING**

1  Max Singer, *Passage to a Human World* (Indianapolis: Hudson Institute, 1987), p. 59.

2  "Racing Toward Riches, Together." From a *Newsweek/Washington Post* online discussion, January 22, 2008.

3  Charles Murray, *In Pursuit of Happiness and Good Government* (New York: Simon & Schuster, 1988), and *Losing Ground* (New York: Basic Books, 1984).

4    Charles Murray, *Losing Ground*, p. 273.

5    Henry Hazlitt, *Man vs. the Welfare State* (New York: University Press of America, 1983), p. 107.

6    Figures taken from Milagros Palacios, Niels Veldhuis, Michael Walker, *Tax Facts 15* (Vancouver: Fraser Institute, 2008), Ch. 5.

7    Cited in Brian Lee Crowley, *Fearful Symmetry: The Fall and Rise of Canada's Founding Values* (Toronto: Key Porter Books, 2009), p. 309n49.

## 3: DEMOCRATIC CAPITALISM: BREAKING THE CHAINS OF ECONOMIC STAGNATION

1    William Easterly, *The White Man's Burden* (New York: Penguin Books, 2006), p. 119.

2    See R.J. Rummel, *Death by Government* (New Brunswick, NJ: Transaction Books, 1996). Rummel provides evidence that whereas some 50 million combatants were killed in all the wars of the twentieth century, more than 150 million people, all of whom were legal citizens of their countries, were killed by their own governments.

3    Nathan Rosenberg and L.E. Birdzell Jr., *How the West Grew Rich: The Economic Transformation of the Western World* (New York: Basic Books, 1986). A good source on early and developing capitalism.

4    Michael Novak, *The Spirit of Democratic Capitalism* (New York: Simon & Schuster, 1982).

5    The Anti-Slavery Society and its many branches (see www.anti-slavery. addr.com) has been in existence since 1839. It documents and publicizes the incidence of "slavery" around the world. Its findings clearly show that many countries currently practice a variety of forms of child labour, child and adult labour-bondage (in India in particular), and the selling, trading, and kidnapping of children. In 1988, UNICEF estimated that there are currently more than 80 million known child workers between ages ten and fourteen, and probably double that when clandestine child labour is included. In 2007, UNICEF estimated about 1.2 million children are trafficked every year for a variety of purposes, from camel jockeying, to bonded labour, to the sex trade.

6    Cited in W.H. Hutt, "The Factory System of the Early Nineteenth Century," in Friedrich Hayek, ed. *Capitalism and the Historians* (Chicago: University of Chicago Press, 1954), p. 168.

7    Novak, *The Spirit of Democratic Capitalism*, p. 17.

8    Ludwig von Mises, *Human Action* (Chicago: Contemporary Books, 1966), p. 617ff.

9    Peter L. Berger, *The Capitalist Revolution* (New York, Basic Books, 1986).

10   Sven Rydenfelt, *A Pattern for Failure: Socialist Economies in Crisis* (New York: Harcourt Brace Jovanovich, 1984).

## 4: THE FREEDOM SYSTEM: HOW IT WORKS

1   Max Singer, *Passage to a Human World* (Indianapolis: Hudson Institute, 1987).

2   In 1985, the *Los Angeles Times* conducted one of the most extensive surveys of journalists in history. Using the same questionnaire they had used to poll the public, the *Times* polled 2,700 journalists at 621 newspapers across the country. The survey asked sixteen questions involving foreign affairs and social and economic issues. *On fifteen of sixteen questions, the journalists gave answers to the left of those given by the public.* A key finding was that *self-identified liberals outnumbered conservatives in the newsroom by more than three to one,* 55 to 17 percent. This compared to only one-fourth of the public (23 percent) that identified themselves as liberal. In the same year, Peter Desbarats, dean of the Graduate School of Journalism at the University of Western Ontario, publicly lamented "the leftism" of Canadian media (*Financial Post*, July 13, 1985).

3   Julian Simon, *The Ultimate Resource* (New Jersey: Princeton University Press, 1981). Simon's work was also among the first seriously to question the work of environmentalists and their anti-capitalist campaign.

4   See Jonah Goldberg's bestseller, *Liberal Fascism: The Secret History of the American Left from Mussolini to the Politics of Meaning* (New York: Doubleday, 2007). Goldberg was savaged by the Left for this study of the Statism of the Left, even though he exerted himself to distinguish smiling American liberal fascism from the brutal European varieties.

5   Alan Macfarlane, *The Origins of English Individualism* (London: Basil Blackwell, 1978).

6   On this note, see Barry Shain, *The Myth of American Individualism* (Princeton, NJ: Princeton University Press, 1994).

7   Rydenfelt, *A Pattern for Failure: Socialist Economies in Crisis* (New York: Harcourt Brace Jovanovich, 1984) p. 38.

8   James C. Scott, *Seeing Like a State: How Certain Schemes to Improve the Human Condition Have Failed* (New Haven, CT: Yale University Press, 2009).

9   I have relied on Robert Hessen, *In Defense of the Corporation* (Stanford: Hoover Institute Press, 1979).

10  Freedom House is a "voice for democracy and freedom around the world." They give a ranking of nations by degrees of freedom, including civil rights, political rights, social progress, voting rights, and elections, at www.freedomhouse.org. See also James Gwartney and Robert Lawson, "Economic Freedom of the World" (Vancouver: Fraser Institute, 2008 Annual Report), which uses 42 components to measure 141 countries. Canada ranks 7th overall.

11  See Burton H. Kellock and Sylvia LeRoy, "Questioning the Legality of the Federal Spending Power," *Public Policy Sources*, Fraser Institute, No. 89,

October 2007. Also, Burt H. Kellock, "Federal/Provincial Fiscal Transfers: the Abuse of Governmental Power in Canada," Draft paper, June 15, 2009.

12  Don Lavoie, *National Economic Planning: What Is Left?* (Cambridge, MA: Ballinger Press, 1985).

13  In Peter L. Berger, *The Capitalist Revolution*, p. 109. [Emphasis added].

14  Paul Johnson, *Modern Times: The World from the Twenties to the Eighties* (New York: Harper & Row, 1983), p. 14.

15  Michael Novak, *The Spirit of Democratic Capitalism*, p. 64.

16  Ibid., p. 64.

17  F.A. Hayek, *The Counter-Revolution of Science* (Indianapolis: Liberty Press, 1952), p. 249.

18  Even though newly capitalist Asian societies would seem to contradict this view, there is, as Peter Berger suggests, evidence of ever-greater individuation with the increasing influence of Western ideas in all economically successful Asian nations. (See Berger, *The Capitalist Revolution*, pp. 168–69.)

19  See William D. Gairdner, *The War Against the Family* (Toronto: Stoddart, 1992) for a full treatment of this theme.

20  Roland Huntford, *The New Totalitarians* (New York: Stein and Day, 1972), p. 279. See also David Popenoe, *Disturbing the Nest: Family Change and Decline in Modern Societies* (New York: Aldine de Gruyter, 1988).

21  Bryce Christensen, "The Costly Retreat from Marriage," in *The Public Interest*, No. 91, Spring 1988, p. 59.

22  George Gilder, *Men and Marriage* (Louisiana: Graetna, 1986), p. 92.

23  The British (and Canadian) systems of parliamentary democracy have divided their powers, rather than separating them as thoroughly as in American republicanism. Many argue that Canadian executive and legislative powers are fused rather than separated. In many respects, Canada's executive does direct the legislature, but it is the latter that can vote out the government, not the former. And while Canada's courts have in many respects usurped legislative and constitutional power, it is the legislature that made this possible, and it is the legislature that can reverse it to get more division and less fusion. For a clear discussion, see Dennis Baker, *Not Quite Supreme* (Montreal-Kingston: McGill-Queen's University Press, 2010).

24  Boethius, *The Consolation of Philosophy* (New York: Bobbs-Merrill, 1962), Book II, Prose 5, p. 31.

25  Igor Shafarevich, *The Socialist Phenomenon* (New York: Harper & Row, 1980), pp. 262–63.

26  See M. James C. Crabbe, "Challenges for Sustainability in Cultures Where Regard for the Future May Not Be Present," at http://ejournal.nbii.org/archives/vol2iss2/communityessay.crabbe.pdf.

## 5: THE HANDICAP SYSTEM: THE SOCIALIST REACTION TO DEMOCRATIC CAPITALISM

1 When Leacock wrote this, government spending in Canada was 11 percent of GDP: one quarter of what it was in 2010. The highest level was over 50 percent in 1992.

2 The Socialist International was founded in London in 1864 by Karl Marx (called "The First International"). It has suffered a series of dissolutions and rebirths, most recently in 1951, in Frankfurt, Germany. By its own description, its "ideology is based on the principles of democratic socialism, expressed in the Declaration of Principles formulated in the Frankfurt Program of 1951, and revised in Oslo in 1962." This "ideology" is clearly contradictory because socialism is a top-down *dirigiste* phenomenon, and real democracy is a bottom-up process with no commitment to any pre-established direction (except perhaps to avoid all totalitarian regimes—such as socialism).

3 Joseph A. Schumpeter, *Capitalism, Socialism and Democracy* (New York: Harper & Row, 1942), p. 168.

4 Thomas Sowell, *Marxism* (New York: William Morrow, 1985), p. 156.

5 G.D.H. Cole, spoken when he became chairman of the Fabian Society in 1941 (*Encyclopaedia Britannica*, 1946, Vol. 20), p. 890.

6 Don Lavoie, *National Economic Planning*, p. 216.

7 Ibid.

8 Lavoie, p. 217.

9 F.A. Hayek, *The Counter-Revolution of Science* (Indianapolis: Liberty Press, 1952), p. 249.

10 Colin Campbell, *Governments Under Stress* (Toronto: University of Toronto Press, 1983).

11 Cansim 183-0002 and others, summarized in Herb Grubel, Fraser Institute Digital Publication, November 2007.

12 Robert Owen, *A New View of Society* (New York: Everyman's Library, 1963), p. 24.

13 F.A. Hayek, *The Counter-Revolution of Science*, p. 311.

14 These remarks on Saint-Simon by Kolakowski, Halévy, and J.S. Mill are from Lavoie, op. cit., p. 242n5.

15 William D. Gairdner, *The War Against the Family* (Toronto: BPS Books, 2007), originally published by Stoddart in 1993, this book ended up on many bestseller lists in Canada despite the fact that it was banned by some major bookstore chains such as Duthies Books in Vancouver. That caused a one-day debate over free speech that ended up on the front page of the *Globe and Mail*. My publisher immediately ordered an additional print run.

16 *Time*, April 8, 1996.

17 For an in-depth treatment of this "secularization" thesis, see William D. Gairdner, *The Trouble With Democracy* (Toronto: Stoddart, 2001, BPS Books, 2008), esp. Chap. 4 ff.

18 Marx's best try was his infamous theory of the surplus value of labour. He thought capitalists enriched themselves by paying workers less than fair value for their labour and kept the difference between this and the amount for which they could sell their products. This theory was demolished long ago in a devastating critique of Marx by Eugen von Böhm-Bawerk in *Karl Marx and the Close of His System* (1896).

19 A number of Canadian companies that were Crown corporations when the first edition of this book was published are now privatized, examples being: Air Canada, Alberta Government Telephones (now Telus Communications), British Columbia Electric Railway, BC Ferries,* BCRail, BCTel, Cameco Corporation, Canadian National Railway, Eldorado Mining and Refining Limited (part of Cameco Corporation), Intercolonial Railway, Manitoba Telephone System, Nova Scotia Power, Petro-Canada, Polymer Corporation, Potash Corporation of Saskatchewan (PCS), Saskatchewan Government Airways, Saskatchewan Mining Development Corporation (part of Cameco Corporation), Teleglobe, Wascana Energy. *Organized as a privately held corporation, but still owned by the provincial government.

20 Tax Freedom Day is calculated by province and nationally every year by the Fraser Institute in Canada, and is available at www.fraserinstitute.org, where individuals may calculate their personal tax freedom day. A similar calculation is published for the United States by Tax Foundation Inc.

21 John Metcalf, "Freedom from Culture," in *Fraser Forum* (Vancouver: Fraser Institute, January 1988), p. 6.

22 Lavoie, *National Economic Planning*, p. 52. This, and all subsequent quotes, are derived from the same chapter of Lavoie's book.

23 John Kenneth Galbraith is a well-known Canadian-born economist who was always arguing for Statism and who lived in America at the time.

24 Milton Friedman, *Friedman on Galbraith, and on Curing the British Disease* (Vancouver: Fraser Institute, 1977), p. 57.

25 Sven Rydenfelt, *A Pattern for Failure*, p. 44.

26 Jacobs, *Cities and the Wealth of Nations*, p. 191.

27 Ibid., p. 192.

28 Jacobs, *Cities and the Wealth of Nations*, p. 194.

29 Ibid., p. 202.

30 Gunnar Myrdal, *Asian Drama*, abridged by Seth King (New York: Vintage Books, 1972), p. 11.

31 Sherwin Rosen, "Public employment and the Welfare State in Sweden," *Journal of Economic Literature*, Vol. XXXIV, No. 2, June 1996, pp. 734–75.

[Italics mine]. I have translated into English a French version of this passage found in Gérard Bélanger, *Économie du Québec, Mythes et Réalité*, Ch.9 (Montreal: Les Éditions Varia, 2007).

## 6: THE POLITICAL PARTIES: WHERE THEY ONCE STOOD—WHERE THEY STAND NOW—AND WHERE YOU STAND

1   Peter Brimelow, *The Patriot Game* (Toronto: Key Porter Books, 1986), p. 49.
2   R. Rummel, *Death by Government* (New Brunswick, USA: Transaction Publishers, 1996), and see also his website at www.hawaii.edu/powerkills/ Rummel illustrates beyond any doubt that government is bad for your health. Example: In all the wars of the ghastly twentieth century, some 50 million armed combatants killed each other. But then we learn that the number of fully legal citizens murdered, slaughtered, quartered, drowned, shot, beaten, or starved to death *by their own governments* was a verifiable 167 million! He calls this "democide"—or "murder by government"—and he is certain the true (but unverifiable) number is closer to 300 million.
3   Peter Brimelow, *The Patriot Game*, p. 18. See also Nicole Morgan, *Implosion: An Analysis of the Growth of the Federal Public Service in Canada, 1945–1985* (Montreal: Institute for Research on Public Policy, 1986).
4   Peter Foster, *Other People's Money* (Toronto: Collins, 1983), p. 91.
5   "Resolutions Reference: Convention 1987 Supplement," subtitled "Taking the Future On." Available from the New Democratic Party of Canada.
6   Edmund Burke. *Reflections on the Revolution in France* (London: Penguin Classics 1982) is still considered the seminal work of modern conservatism.

## 8: THE GREAT WELFARE RIP-OFF: SOAKING EVERYONE, TO PAY EVERYONE

1   This figure, calculated by a Canadian senator, was trumpeted in the *Globe and Mail* (January 5, 1989).
2   A government-funded committee established to advise the federal government on poverty.
3   George Gilder, *Wealth and Poverty* (New York: Basic Books, 1981), p. 111.
4   Ibid., p. 110.
5   Ibid., p. 111.
6   Murray, *Losing Ground* (New York: Basic Books, 1984), p. 111 [my emphasis].
7   At the end of this book I discuss the pernicious trend of Canada's judges to read into the law meanings and rights that were never intended by lawmakers.
8   Murray, *Losing Ground*, p. 46.

9   Gertrude Himmelfarb, *The Idea of Poverty* (New York: Vintage, 1985), p. 399.

10  Murray, *Losing Ground*, p. 182.

11  *Welfare in Canada* (Ottawa: National Council of Welfare, 1987).

12  Murray, *Losing Ground*, p. 191. [Emphasis mine].

13  Ibid., p. 146.

14  *Canada Year Book*, 1988, p. 224–25.

15  *Canada Year Book*, 2008, p. 224.

16  "Low Income Cut-Offs for 2008 and Low Income Measures for 2007," Income Statistics Division, Statistics Canada, cat. no. 75F0002M— No.002 [emphasis added]. Note: Statscan was originally using gross before-tax income, but since the mid-1990s has been using after-tax income for determining these cut-off lines.

17  A "mean" figure (commonly called an "average") is the result of adding all cases together and dividing by the number of cases. A "median" figure is the middle case in a series of cases ranked from lowest to highest. So, for example, if we had the series 2, 4, 6, 8, 30, 50, 100, the mean (average of all cases) would be 28.6, but the median (the middle case) would be 8.

18  Sarlo, *Poverty in Canada*, p. 15.

19  Ibid., p. 27.

20  Ibid., p. 28.

21  Ibid., 1994, p. 12.

22  Sarlo, "What is Poverty? Providing Clarity for Canada," Fraser Institute Digital Publication, May 2008.

23  For pro and con discussions of international ethics (what we owe or do not owe the world's poor), see Thomas Pogge, "Priorities of Global Justice," *Metaphilosophy*, Vol. 32, Nos. 1/2, January 2001, and for a rebuttal, see Alan Patten, "Should We Stop Thinking about Poverty in Terms of Helping the Poor?," available at www.princeton.edu/~apatten/ poverty-ethics-internationalaffairs.pdf.

24  From Chris Sarlo, *Poverty in Canada*, 2nd ed., and 1999 figures from Sarlo, "The Economic Well-being of Canadians—Is there a Growing Gap?" (May 2009).

25  Barrington Moore Jr., *Authority and Inequality Under Capitalism and Socialism* (Oxford: Clarendon Press, 1987), p. 9. [Italics mine.]

26  Harmon Zeigler and Thomas R. Dye, "Freedom vs. Equality," in *Critical Review*, Vol. 2, Nos. 2 & 3, Spring-Summer 1988, p. 190. [Italics mine.]

27  Charles Murray, *Losing Ground*, p. 149.

**9: FOREIGN AID: HOW MUCH? TO WHOM? AND WHY?**

1   "The Group of 77 is the largest intergovernmental organization of developing states in the United Nations, which provides the means for

the countries of the South to articulate and promote their collective economic interests and enhance their joint negotiating capacity on all major international economic issues within the United Nations system, and promote South-South cooperation for development." The South Summit is the supreme decision-making body of the Group of 77. Its ambition is couched in the following language: "The attempt by the developing countries to persuate [sic] the developed contries [sic] to undertake joint measures aimed at promoting the sustainable development of the global economy and to enable the devoloping [sic] countries to become an integral part of this development process constitutes the essence of what has come to be known as the 'North-South dialogue.'" (from Vol. 3, North-South Dialogue, 2008). Perhaps some of the money they extort from the First World should be used for spelling lessons. See http://www.g77.org/doc/

2   The main tenets of the NIEO and the Charter of Economic Rights and Duties of States promoted by UNCTAD in the 1970s were: 1) Developing countries must be entitled to regulate and control the activities of multinational corporations operating within their territory; 2) They must be free to nationalize or expropriate foreign property on conditions favourable to them; 3) They must be free to set up associations of primary commodities producers similar to OPEC; all other States must recognize this right and refrain from taking economic, military, or political measures calculated to restrict it; 4) International trade should be based on the need to ensure stable, equitable, and remunerative prices for raw materials, generalized non-reciprocal and non-discriminatory tariff preferences, as well as transfer of technology to developing countries and should provide economic and technical assistance without any strings attached. Although this Charter was never accepted by developed countries and is now dead, the political, economic, and social concerns that inspired it are still present. The Charter *called for restitution for the economic and social costs of colonialism, racial discrimination, and foreign domination.*

3   Cited in Karl Brunner, ed., *The First World and the Third World* (Rochester: University of Rochester Policy Center, 1978), p. 8.

4   Brunner, p. 193.

5   Ibid., p. 26.

6   See Peter T. Bauer, *Equality, the Third World, and Economic Delusion* (Cambridge, MA.: Harvard University Press, 1981), as well as *Reality and Rhetoric: Studies in the Economics of Development* (Cambridge, MA.: Harvard University Press, 1984).

7   James C. Scott, "Compulsory Villagization in Tanzania," Ch. 7, in *Seeing Like a State* (New Haven, CT.: Yale University Press, 1998), p. 234ff.

8    Brunner, p. 140.

9    See Bonny Ibhawoh and J.I. Dibua, "Deconstructing Ujamaa: The Legacy of Julius Nyerere in the Quest for Social and Economic Development in Africa," in *African Journal of Political Science*, 2003, Vol. 8, No. 1.

10   Bauer, *Reality and Rhetoric*, p. 46.

11   Ibid., pp. 49–50.

12   Ibid., p. 51.

13   Brunner, *The First World*, p. 143.

14   Bauer, *Equality*, p. 70.

15   Ibid., p. 100.

16   Bauer, p. 113.

17   Ibid., p. 100.

18   Rydenfeldt, *A Pattern for Failure*, p. 94.

19   Dambisa Moyo, *Dead Aid: Why Aid Is Not Working, and How There Is a Better Way for Africa* (New York: Farrar, Straus and Giroux, 2009); Paul Collier, *The Bottom Billion: Why the Poorest Countries Are Failing, and What Can Be Done About It* (Oxford: Oxford University Press, 2007); William Easterly, *The White Man's Burden: Why the West's Efforts to Aid the Rest Have Done So Much Ill and So Little Good* (New York: Penguin Books, 2006).

20   Moyo cites an interesting study to the effect that "a democracy can be expected to last an average of about 8.5 years in a country with a per-capita income under US$1,000 per annum, sixteen years in one with income between US$1,000 and $2,000, thirty-three years between US$2,000 and US$4,000 and a hundred years between US$4,000 and US$6,000 ... above US$6,000 democracies are impregnable ... [they are] certain to survive, come hell or high water." p. 43.

21   The UN Millennium Development Goals (MDGs) are: eradicate extreme poverty and hunger; achieve universal primary education; promote gender equality and empower women; reduce child mortality; improve maternal health; combat HIV/AIDS, malaria, and other diseases; ensure environmental sustainability; and develop a global partnership for development—all by 2015.

22   See Canada's International Policy Statement: A Role of Pride and Influence in the World (April 2005).

23   The non-binding "Blueprint for Aboriginal Health" was entered into in November 2005 by the federal, provincial, territorial governments and national aboriginal organizations. It provides $1.3 billion to reduce the rates of suicide, infant mortality, obesity, and diabetes.

## 10: RADICAL FEMINISM: ATTACKING TRADITIONAL SOCIETY

1    On the concept and history of the "family wage," see Bryce Christensen, ed., *The Family Wage: Work, Gender, and Children in the Modern Economy*

(Rockford, IL: Rockford Institute, 1988); and David Popenoe, *Disturbing the Nest: Family Change and Decline in Modern Societies* (New York: Aldine de Gruyter, 1988). The latter traces the origins and changes in the family from medieval times to the present, then uses Sweden as the bellwether nation that went down the path of family destruction further and sooner than the rest of us. In my book *The War Against the Family* (Toronto: Stoddart, 1993), I summarized Popenoe's findings on Sweden, and also presented a thorough examination of modern anti-family policies and practices. See also Allan C. Carlson, *Family Questions* (New Brunswick, NJ: Transaction Books, 1988) for penetrating remarks on feminism and the demise of the natural family in modern times.

2    Everyone knows that a good daycare facility may provide *reasonably* good care, *equally*, to all the children in the centre. But a parent will almost always give *unreasonably* good care to his or her own child; and it will be *unequal*, which is to say always better than what this parent would give to anyone else's children. Whereas a daycare centre must operate on an egalitarian basis, to the extent that a childcare worker will be scolded for giving better care, or more love, to one child than to another, a parent at home will always give the most possible care and love—will always favour—his or her own children. Children who grow up with that kind of unconditional love (that will not reasonably be proffered by a stranger, because that would be unreasonable) never forget it.

3    Michael Levin, *Feminism and Freedom* (New Jersey: Transaction Books, 1987), p. 12. Readers will find this book remains a rigorous treatment and exposure of the philosophical and moral inadequacies of radical feminism.

4    Levin, *Feminism and Freedom*, p. 26.

5    Ibid., p. 20.

6    Eleanor Maccoby and Carol Jacklin, *The Psychology of Sex Differences* (Stanford, CA: Stanford University Press, 1974), Vol. 1. This was at the time a thorough survey of the entire field of sex-differences research. Despite the authors' expressed hypothesis that there would be no inherent differences between males and females, scholarly objectivity won out: both scholars conclude that there are indeed inherent, genetically and hormonally produced differences.

7    Levin, *Feminism and Freedom*, p. 70.

8    William D. Gairdner, *The Book of Absolutes: A Critique of Relativism and a Defence of Universals* (Montreal-Kingston: McGill-Queen's University Press, 2008), pp. 157–62.

9    References to universal (insofar as these have been cross-culturally examined) human sex differences abound in several books. See Eleanor Maccoby and Carol Jacklin, *The Psychology of Sex Differences* (Stanford, CA: Stanford University Press, 1974), for a survey of the then existing

literature. Moir and Jessel, *Brain Sex*, is an early popular display of this reality. Glenn Wilson, *The Great Sex Divide* (Washington, DC: Scott-Townsend Publishers, 1992), is a very readable treatment of the biochemical and experimental evidence for innate sex differences. Robert L. Nadeau, *S/He Brain* (Westport, CT: Praeger, 1996), is a review of the underlying biochemical and neuroscientific findings about sex differences, nested in some appropriately targeted political objections to feminist ideology. Doreen Kimura, *Sex and Cognition* (Cambridge, MA,: MIT Press, 2000), is a careful review of the findings to date, somewhat apprehensively expressed. David C. Geary, *Male, Female: the Evolution of Human Sex Differences* (Washington, DC: American Psychological Association, 1998), is the most detailed survey of studies on sex differences thought to be rooted in evolutionary theory. Steven Pinker, *The Blank Slate: The Modern Denial of Human Nature* (New York: Viking Penguin, 2002), is another of Pinker's long, cheerfully confident, and informative books, in which he summarizes much evidence for innate sex differences.

10  George Gilder, *Men and Marriage* (Gretna, LA: Pelican Books, 1986), p. 20.

11  Ibid., p. 26.

12  Levin, *Feminism and Freedom*, p. 91.

13  Gilder, *Men and Marriage*, p. 77. Polygamy, a general term, refers to having multiple opposite sex mates. Polygyny means having more than one female mate at the same time. Polyandry means having more than one male mate at the same time.

14  Allan Carlson, "Charity Begins at Home," in *Chronicles* (Rockford, IL: Rockford Institute), August 1988, pp. 12–15.

15  Gilder, *Men and Marriage*, p. 78.

16  Ibid., p. 5.

17  Gilder, *Men and Marriage*, p. 10.

18  Ibid., p. 14.

19  In and around Toronto where I live, the current rage among many teenage girls is oral sex, offered quite freely by many of them, even on school buses, and often for a fee. Twenty to fifty dollars is the going rate, and many teenage schoolgirls see this is as a much easier way to afford a new dress than working at a regular job, and they are happy they don't need to "have sex" to earn this kind of money. This is reported to me by credible teenage boys.

20  Allan Carlson, *Family Questions* (New Brunswick, NJ.: Transaction Books, 1988), p. 44.

21  *Alberta Report*, May 27, 1991.

22  From Wikipedia: In use since the 1990s, the term "LGBT" is an adaptation of "LGB" which itself started replacing the phrase "gay community" which many within LGBT communities felt did not represent accurately all those

to whom it referred. In modern usage, the term LGBT is intended to emphasize a diversity of "sexuality and gender-identity based cultures" and is sometimes used to refer to anyone who is non-heterosexual instead of exclusively to people who are homosexual, bisexual, or transgender. To recognize this inclusion, a popular variant adds the letter Q for queer and questioning (e.g., "LGBTQ") for those not explicitly denoted by LGBT, such as pansexuality, intersex, etc. The acronym has become mainstream as a self-designation and has been adopted by the majority of LGBT community centres and LGBT media in many English-speaking countries. These acronyms are not agreeable to everyone that they literally encompass. Some intersex people want to be included in LGBT groups and would prefer the term "LGBTI." Some argue that transgender and transsexual causes are not the same as that of LGB people. A correlate to these ideas is evident in the belief of "lesbian & gay separatism," which holds that lesbians and gay men should form a community distinct and separate from other groups normally included. Other people also do not care for the term as they feel the lettering comes across as being too politically-correct, an attempt to categorize various groups of people into one grey area, and that it implies that the issues and priorities of the main groups represented are given equal consideration. [Such are the contradictions and confusions of postmodern sexual fascism.]

23  Diana Baumrind, "Are Androgynous Individuals More Effective Persons and Parents?" in *Child Development* 53 (January 1982), pp. 45–66, cited in Carlson, *Family Questions*, p. 42.

24  Data from Walter Block, "Economic Intervention, Discrimination, and Unforeseen Consequences," in *Discrimination, Affirmative Action, and Equal Opportunity* (Vancouver: Fraser Institute, 1982), p. 112.

25  Block, p. 50.

26  See Gilder, *Wealth and Poverty*, p. 279n8, for Canada, see "Earnings of Men and Women," in Statistics Canada report, 1987.

27  The still-popular Hay and Willis scales, developed in the 1950s and refined since were developed by American social scientists E.N. Hay and John O. Willis.

28  Morley Gunderson, "Discrimination, Equal Pay, and Equal Opportunities in the Labour Market," in *Work and Pay: The Canadian Labour Market* (Ottawa: Ministry of Supply and Services, 1985), p. 238.

29  Charles Krauthammer, "From Bad to Comparable Worth," in *Regulation* (Washington, D.C.: American Enterprise Institute, 1984), pp. 32–33.

30  William D. Gairdner, *The War Against the Family* (Toronto: BPS Books, 2008). The book is available directly from www.williamgairdner.com.

31  "Three Questions on Abortion" was published in *The Interim* newspaper, February 2009.

## 11: MEDICAL MEDIOCRITY: AN AUTOPSY ON THE CANADIAN "HEALTH CARE" SYSTEM

1   In 2008, that was made up of: hospitals, $48 billion; drugs, $30 billion; physicians, $23 billion; other professionals, $19 billion; capital expenditures, $7 billion; and $45 billion for all other associated costs, such as long-term care, public health services, home care, and administration (Health Council of Canada, as reported in a Special Feature to the *National Post*, March 31, 2009).

2   Here is a description in Elizabeth C. Robertson, "Health Legislation Trends in Canada, 2001–2005," of how Canada's so-called "single-payer" system actually operates, with my comments in square brackets: "Medicare has often been described as a single-payer system which suggests that all health care is publicly funded. In reality, the system might be better described as a series of 'concentric circles.' Core services are publicly funded. These services comprise 'medically necessary' hospital and 'medically required' physician services. In the next circle, there are services, like prescription drugs and home care, in which the level of public funding varies across the provinces. The outer circle consists of services which attract no public support. For these services, the patient either pays out of pocket or through private health insurance. The scope of unfunded services varies from province to province and may include items such as: dental care; vision care; long-term care; ambulance services; psychological services; chiropractic services; physiotherapy and prescription drugs outside a hospital setting. At present, approximately 30 percent of health care spending in Canada is privately financed. The private sector *delivers* most health services [but the government *pays* for it].

"The majority of hospitals are private non-profit operations and most physicians are in private practice [but again, most physicians are paid by government]. Also, Canadian hospitals, although originally structured as private-not-for-profit, are today no such thing. [They are capitalized by the State, are compelled to employ union workers, are overseen by regional authorities, and can even be forcibly merged or closed by provincial order]. Many ancillary services, such as laundries, meal preparation services, laboratories, and diagnostic clinics are private, for-profit businesses. All these entities are compensated for their services by the public insurance scheme."

3   John Goodman, *National Health Care in Great Britain: Lessons for the USA* (Dallas: Fisher Institute, 1982), p. 16.

4   British figures are from studies cited in Sally Pipes, *The Top Ten Myths of American Health Care: A Citizen's Guide* (San Francisco: Pacific Research Institute, 2008), p. 129. For some time now the free market has been

alleviating some of the defects of the British NHS. There, private health insurance was never legally prohibited, private hospitals are thriving, and more than five million people are covered by private insurance, including members of many of the trade unions, who insist that government medicine is "just not good enough for our people."

5    The Hippocratic oath, which was once proudly considered a true oath to be taken by all physicians as part of their graduation ceremony, has been eliminated at most universities, or altered to remove its ancient prohibition against doing intentional harm to human life ... in order to make abortion on demand and very likely, as we shall soon see, euthanasia, possible.

6    Personal health information is "protected" in various ways by provincial legislation, and federally by the Personal Information Protection and Electronic Documents Act (PIPEDA) of 2004. But as never was the case prior to socialized medicine, all personal and private medical information in the public system in Canada is available to government for the purposes of monitoring and evaluation.

7    Malcolm C. Brown, *Caring for Profit: Economic Dimensions of Canada's Health Industry* (Vancouver: Fraser Institute, 1987).

8    See Nadeem Esmail, "Leaving Canada for Medical Care," *Fraser Forum*, February 2009. The institute's annual survey, "Waiting Your Turn," asks all participating physicians this question: "Approximately what percentage of your patients *received* non-emergency medical treatment in the past 12 months outside Canada?" For 2009, the averaged answer was 1.0 percent of all patients in Canada, or an estimated 41,000 people.

9    See Wikipedia, "medical tourism" for more international information on this topic.

10    Linda A. Johnson, "Americans look abroad to save on health care: Medical tourism could jump tenfold in next decade," *San Francisco Chronicle*, August 3, 2008.

11    Privacy? Canada's recent billion-dollar-plus eHealth program managed by a non-profit federal-provincial corporation called Canada Health Infoway, is an Electronic Health Records (EHR) project which aimed to have the health records of 50 percent of the Canadian population digitized in a uniform national format by 2009. But by 2009 only 17 percent was input. Electronic conversion of a single physician office is estimated to cost $45,000, accompanied by a 30 percent drop in service during the upgrade. Articles critical of *likely privacy invasions to come for research and commercial purposes, are such as*: Glenn Griener, "Electronic Health Records as a Threat to Privacy" (2005) 14:1, *Health Law Review* 14; Nola M. Ries and Geoff Moysa, "Legal Protections of Electronic Health Records: Issues of Consent and Security" (2005) 14:1, *Health Law Review* 18. This whole project is destined to be yet another central

planning nightmare already plagued by management scandals and waste (see Auditor General of Ontario report). It is what financial columnist Terence Corcoran aptly described as a project "with all the makings of an IT fantasy being converted into a bureaucratic nightmare" (*Financial Post*, October 10, 2009).

12 Due to the fact that sharing provincial costs did nothing to limit or make predictable the demand on the federal government for such sharing, the system was switched to a block-grant basis in the late 1990s. But that does not alter the fact that the State is in control in all provinces.

13 Monique Bégin, *Medicare: Canada's Right to Health* (Montreal: Optimum Publishing, 1987), p. 25.

14 The act is rooted in five conditions: Public Administration (to be government run), Comprehensiveness (to cover all basic health matters), Universality (to be available to all), Portability (provincial borders are not a block), and Accessibility (within the practical reach of all). None of these promises is strictly kept: many public facilities contract some of their work to private providers; some formerly insured services are delisted for budgetary reasons; Quebec does not have an agreement with the other nine provinces for portability; some provinces charge a small tax—an MSP tax in B.C., a "health premium" tax in Ontario, to cover health expenses; there are gaping differences in quality of care and available technology by region, and in terms of the urban-rural divide.

15 This was the central theme of cost-control studies by Canadian "health economists" in the 1990s, and it was used to justify reducing the number of physicians produced annually.

16 Making all health records electronic simply multiplies the opportunity for invasions of privacy. Recently, the Alberta Auditor General noted that Alberta had already spent $615 million on an ambitious EHR (Electronic Health Records) scheme that is not even close to complete. The audit found that due to poor user-access management, 158 terminated (fired?) health workers still had live passwords they could use to tap into the province's NetCare health database. The Edmonton computer for NetCare was hit with a virus in May 2009 that scrambled the medical records of up to 11,582 patients.

17 *Toronto Star*, April 29, 1989.

18 The Alberta Medical Association estimates the province has a shortage of a thousand physicians, and similar shortages of other health profession-als. (*Access to Doctors. Access to Care*, March 2006).

19 See "Patients wait as PET scans used in animal experiments" (*Globe and Mail*, November 23, 2006).

20 See the entire decision at http://csc.lexum.umontreal.ca/en/2005/2005scc35/2005scc35.html. This is the case that is quietly

overturning socialized medicine in Canada. Importantly, the court also held that "the evidence on the experience of other Western democracies with public health care systems that permit access to private health care refutes the government's theory that a prohibition on private health insurance is connected to maintaining quality public health care. It *does not appear that private participation leads to the eventual demise of public health care*" [emphasis added, both here, and above]. On the Law and the Constitution chapter in this book I severely critique Canada's courts for amending our Constitution, rather than leaving this function to Parliament. However, I do not believe the Court amended our Constitution by striking down a government prohibition on private health care. It did not, as a friend states, thereby "impose" two-tiered health care on Canadians. On the contrary, the imposition was the State's unconstitutional restriction on private care in the first place.

21   Richard F. Davies, "Waiting Lists for Health Care: A Necessary Evil?" *Canadian Medical Association Journal* 160, no. 10 (May 18, 1999): 1469–70.

22   By email communication, October 22, 2009: "Only residents of Ontario who are insured persons under the Health Insurance Act are entitled to OHIP coverage for insured physician, hospital and practitioner services. If a person who is not a Canadian resident is provided with such services in Ontario, *there is no prohibition against the person being charged by the provider for the services.* The ministry does not regulate the provision of services to uninsured persons—it is up to the providers to determine if and when they will provide services to uninsured persons." [Italics mine.]

23   A popular TV serial featuring the medical staff of an American hospital in Korea during the war there; blood and broken bones everywhere, staff coping with inadequacies on all fronts.

24   John Goodman, "Rationing Health Care: An International Perspective," in *Policies and Prescriptions: Current Directions in Health Policies* (New South Wales, Australia: Centre for Independent Studies, 1987), p. 89. Goodman remains one of the most astute critics of government health care. Visitors to the website of his National Centre for Policy Analysis will not be disappointed. Canadians will be informed by the centre's critiques of Canadian-style "single-payer" health insurance and other health matters at www.ncpa.org.

25   Ontario's Health Care Accessibility Act (replaced in 2004 by the Commitment to the Future of Medicare Act, with softer penalties) contained provisions for $25,000 fines of physicians and up to twelve months' imprisonment for infractions.

26   A.F. Gonzales, "Britain's NHS: a Sick Joke?" in *Canadian Doctor*, 44: 1978, p. 36.

27   The Fraser Institute is the only Canadian organization to have published

a close estimate of this figure annually since 1993. The estimate is not a hard number, but is nevertheless gathered from medical professionals themselves who have voluntarily co-operated in the survey. Some critics say physicians will inflate their wait numbers for such surveys because they want more government funding. Undoubtedly some have done this. But even if we reduce the numbers by a quarter for this inflation, it's still a lot of waiting human beings! There are also a dozen other professional estimates to be found in David Gratzer, *Code Blue* (Toronto: ECW Press, 1999), pp. 29ff., one of the few detailed book-length critiques of the Canadian system. This section gives the details of many institutional studies and medical journals reporting unconscionably long wait-times. His latest book, as good, is *The Cure* (New York: Encounter Books, 2008), which has more emphasis on the American health system. Here are two other studies of wait-times: Canadian Institute for Health Information, *Waiting for Health Care in Canada: What We Know and What We Don't Know* (Ottawa: Canadian Institute for Health Information, 2006); Pauline Comeau, "Wait-time benchmarks fall short" (2006) 174:3 *CMAJ* 299. If anything, it would appear the Fraser Institute study may be underestimating wait-times.

28 Ontario's Ministry of Health and Long-Term Care writes on its website, www.health.gov.on.ca/english/public/legislation/bill_8/hu_medicare. html, that one of the purposes of Ontario's Commitment to the Future of Medicare Act (which became law on June 17, 2004), and which has removed the imprisonment penalty and lowered the fines in the Health Care Accessibility Act it replaced, is "*strengthening the prohibition of 'two-tier' medicine by closing legislative loopholes that allow queue-jumping and extra billing.*" The ministry's website gives telephone numbers encouraging citizens to spy on and report physicians for infractions (charging a supplement to the allowable government fee).

29 These penalties were part of Ontario's original Health Care Accessibility Act, in force until 2004.

30 Pierre Lemieux, "Socialized Medicine: The Canadian Experience," in *The Freeman* (Irvington-on-Hudson, NY: Foundation for Economic Education), March 1988, p. 99.

31 See David Gratzer, *Code Blue*, p. 46.

32 Richard F. Davies, "Waiting Lists for Health Care: A Necessary Evil?" *Canadian Medical Association Journal* 160, No. 10 (May 18, 1999): 1469–70.

33 A clear description of the impact of the Chaoulli decision is in Elizabeth C. Robertson, "Health Legislation Trends in Canada, 2001–2005": "The most recent decision of the Supreme Court in *Chaoulli v. Quebec* has potentially removed the ability of provincial governments to prohibit

private health insurance for publicly funded services. The case was brought by a patient who had waited one year for hip replacement surgery under Medicare and a physician who wished to open a private hospital offering a private alternative to publicly funded services. The Court struck down a Quebec law which prohibited Quebec residents from purchasing private health insurance for services covered under the provincial health care system. The majority of Justices found that the legislation was a violation of a patient's right to security under s.1 of the Quebec *Charter of Rights and Freedoms*. The decision concluded that there was insufficient evidence to show that allowing a parallel private health care would affect the integrity of the medicare system" (p. 8).

34  For this trend, see Alexandra Shimo, "The rise of private care in Canada" *Maclean's* (April 25, 2006), and at http://www.Macleans.ca/topstories/health/article.jsp?content=20060501 125881_125881. And this overview from Elizabeth C. Robertson, "Health Legislation Trends in Canada, 2001–2005": "There has been a reported increase in the number of private clinics and surgical facilities operating in Canada. A number of provinces have legislation allowing private clinics to offer various medical services. For example, in Ontario, some of the services currently available in independent health facilities are anesthesia, induced abortion, cosmetic and plastic surgery, nuclear medicine, gynecologic procedures, ophthalmologic procedures, radiology, ultrasounds, magnetic resonance imaging [MRI], and computerized axial tomography [CT] scans. An area of current concern is the increase in the number of private MRI clinics. These facilities have been criticized as they allow patients to circumvent waiting lists for MRIs under Medicare. It is commonplace to hear reports of patients having had an MRI done privately to avoid the lengthy wait time for the procedure under Medicare. In 2005, the Federal Minister of Health wrote to four provinces to express concern about private MRI clinics and possible non-compliance with the Canada Health Act in terms of user charges and queue jumping" (p. 10).

35  See Esmail and Palacios, "How Much do We Really Pay?" in *Fraser Forum*, September 2008.

36  CIHI reported in February 2006 that the US performed more than three times the number of exams, reporting 83.2 MRI exams per 1,000 population in 2004–2005, compared to 25.5 in Canada and 19.0 in England's NHS.

37  See http://www.statcan.gc.ca/daily-quotidien/080618/dq080618a-eng.htm.

38  See David Gratzer, *Code Blue* (Toronto: ECW Press, 1999), as well his more recent *The Cure* (New York: Encounter Books, 2006), and Sally

Pipes, *The Top Ten Myths of American Health Care: a Citizen's Guide* (San Francisco: Pacific Research Institute, 2008), p. 28.

39 Sally Pipes *The Top Ten Myths of American Health Care: A Citizen's Guide* (San Francisco: Pacific Research Institute, 2008) p. 136.

40 Sally Pipes, *The Top Ten Myths*, and David Gratzer, *The Cure* (New York: Encounter Books, 2008).

41 Victor Fuchs, *Who Shall Live? Health and Economics and Social Choice* (New York: Basic Books, 1983), p. 28.

42 Reported in the *Toronto Star*, December 6, 1989.

43 Cited in Goodman, *Policies and Prescriptions*, p. 8.

44 See the sobering overview at http://www.conferenceboard.ca/hcp/details/health.aspx#

45 Goodman, *Policies and Prescriptions*, p. 18.

46 See Dartmouth Atlas Project, published February 26, 2009, in the *New England Journal of Medicine*.

47 See CIHI Health Care in Canada 2009: A Decade in Review, Ch. 3, p. 54.

48 John Goodman, *National Health Care in Great Britain*, p. 57.

49 Ibid., p. 58.

50 Goodman, *Policies and Prescriptions*, p. 57.

51 See David Gratzer, *The Cure* (New York: Encounter Books, 2006), p. 70.

52 Reported by the University of Victoria's Centre for Addiction Research (April 15, 2009). The centre added that this figure was likely substantially underreported.

53 Canada is experiencing what the World Health Organization has called a "global epidemic of obesity." The prevalence of obesity is rising not only in Western countries such as the U.S., the United Kingdom, Australia, Germany, the Netherlands, Sweden, and Finland, but also in countries such as Brazil, China, and Israel. According to the OECD, the U.S. has the highest proportion of adults considered overweight or obese, followed by Mexico, the United Kingdom, and Australia. (OECD, *Health Data 2006: Statistics and Indicators for 30 Countries*). In 2004, 20 percent of residents of Census Metropolitan Areas (CMAs) aged eighteen or older were obese, compared with 29 percent of those who lived outside a CMA. Furthermore, as the size of the city increased, the likelihood of being obese fell. In CMAs with a population of at least 2 million (Toronto, Montreal, and Vancouver), only 17 percent of adults were obese. The comparable figure for CMAs with a population of 100,000 to 2 million was 24 percent. In urban centres with populations of 10,000 to 100,000, *30 percent of adults were obese*. (Statistics Canada, *The Daily*, August 22, 2006).

54 Pipes, *The Top Ten Myths of American Health Care*, p. 89.

## 12: THE CRIMINAL JUSTICE SYSTEM: "HUG-A-THUG," AND PUBLIC SAFETY BE DAMNED

1   Criminologists get a close estimate of the number of unreported crimes from in-depth interviews with representative communities about their actual experiences with crime. Many citizens do not report crime because (among other things) they do not want police in their lives, do not want to incriminate friends, family, co-workers or employers, because they are protecting someone or because they are illegal immigrants.

2   The Hector case is adapted from Harris, *Con Game: The Truth About Canada's Prisons* (Toronto: McClelland & Stewart, 2003), p. 310ff.

3   James W. Wilson and Richard Herrnstein, *Crime and Human Nature: A Definitive Study of the Causes of Crime* (New York: Simon & Schuster, 1985). In my opinion, this is still the best overview of modern crime.

4   Wilson and Herrnstein, p. 519.

5   David Daubney, and M.R. Chairman, "Report of the Standing Committee on Justice and Solicitor General on Its Review of Sentencing, Conditional Release and Related Aspects of Correction" (Ottawa: House of Commons, August, 17, 1988). Emphasis added.

6   The remarks on Goyer, Trudeau, and Braithwaite were gleaned from Michael Harris, *Con Game: The Truth About Canada's Prisons* (Toronto: McClelland & Stewart, 2003), p. 152ff.

7   *Globe and Mail*, July 12, 1988 [emphasis mine].

8   http://74.125.95.132/search?q=cache:nbdATyFgMiQJ:www.iirp.org/pdf/beth06_mccold.pdf+percent22group+of+experts+on+restorative+justicepercent22+declaration+of+basic+principles&cd=1&hl=en&ct=clnk&gl=ca.

9   Wilson and Herrnstein, p. 492.

10   Ibid., p. 495.

11   For an overview of natural law and international law, see William D. Gairdner, *The Book of Absolutes: A Critique of Relativism and a Defence of Universals* (Montreal-Kingston: McGill-Queen's University Press, 2008), Ch. 8 and 9.

12   C.S. Lewis, "The Humanitarian Theory of Punishment," *Res Judicatae*, Vol. 6, 1956, pp. 224–30.

13   Cited in Wilson and Herrnstein, p. 498 [emphasis mine].

14   It may seem I am arguing against myself by suggesting that prolonged daycare causes crime. Rather, I think it may predispose individuals to crime due to a lack of capacity for emotional attachment. Nevertheless, it remains that no "predisposition" can command a specific behaviour of any kind. The conditions precedent for such a link are a widespread "psychology of excuse" such as we now promote.

15   Wilson and Herrnstein, *Crime and Human Nature*, p. 473.

16   Stanton Samenow, *Inside the Criminal Mind* (New York and Toronto: Random House, 1984). These excerpts are taken from Ch. 2: "Basic Myths About Criminals."

17   *Globe and Mail*, March 31, 1989.

18   Jack Katz, *Seductions of Crime: Moral and Sensual Attractions in Doing Evil* (New York: Basic Books, 1988).

19   These remarks and the quotation above are taken from a review of Katz's book by Gerald Owen, "The Pleasures of Crime," in *The Idler*, No. 23, May and June 1989.

20   In July 2002, the United Nations Economic and Social Council adopted a resolution containing guidance for member states on restorative justice policy and practice. Canada has played a key role in establishing these principles, and continues to share its experiences and expertise at the international level. "Basic principles on the use of restorative justice programmes in criminal matters" is available on the United Nations Economic and Social Council website (document E/2002/INF/2/Add.2, pp. 54–59). The report notes *"with appreciation*, the work of the Group of Experts on Restorative Justice at their meeting in Ottawa, from 29 October to 1 November 2001." The definition of restorative justice currently favoured is the "Marshall definition," as follows: "Restorative justice is a process whereby all the parties with a stake in a particular offence come together to resolve collectively how to deal with the aftermath of the offence and its implications for the future."

21   A moving and honest book on this theme is Annalise Acorn, *Compulsory Compassion: A Critique of Restorative Justice* (Vancouver: UBC Press, 2004).

22   Readers will find a longer description of CSC's take on this at http://www.csc-scc.gc.ca/text/rj/litrvw-eng.shtml.

23   Paciocco, *Getting Away With Murder*, p. 374.

24   Howard Zehr, *The Little Book on Restorative Justice* (Intercourse, PA.: Good Books, 2002).

25   http://www.publicsafety.gc.ca/prg/cor/res_justice-eng.aspx#about.

26   I am indebted to Paciocco, *Getting Away With Murder*, for many of these historical and legal remarks.

27   For a brief discussion of Foucault and his shoddy scholarship, see William D. Gairdner, *The Book of Absolutes*, p. 258ff.

28   Paciocco, *Getting Away With Murder*, p. 38.

29   Declan Roche, "The Rise and Risks of Restorative Justice," in Accountability in Restorative Justice (Oxford: Oxford University Press, 2003), p. 12n14.

30   Paciocco, *Getting Away With Murder*.

31   See Correctional Services Canada Review Panel—A Roadmap to Strengthening Public Safety, at www.publicsafety.gc.ca/csc-scc/

report-rapport/background-eng.aspx.

32   Paciocco, *Getting Away With Murder*, p. 51ff.

33   Public Safety Canada news release, October 26, 2009.

34   Email from Sheila Ouellete, senior performance measurement officer, National Parole Board, February 3, 2010.

35   Hare's book can be ordered from www.hare.org, and recent developments followed in Hare's research on psychopathy.

36   Robert D. Hare, *Without Conscience: The Disturbing World of the Psychopaths Among Us* (New York: Guildford Press, 1993), p. 87.

37   Facts derived from Michael Harris, *Con Game*, p. 4, and quotation from p. 5.

38   But because of similar problems in the United States, sixteen states have abolished parole, with four more pending, and the U.S. federal government has abolished parole entirely for all federal crimes, whether violent or not.

## 13: MULTICULTURALISM, IMMIGRATION, AND TERRORISM: THE LINKS

1   Two things were at play here with respect to universalism. There was a growing general resistance from the Left to a century of attempts to "Westernize" and modernize foreign nations and colonies, and to particular Western values in themselves—such as rule of law, equality of persons, sanctity of contract, property rights, free markets, and so on—which were criticized by the Left as falsely universal values that were in reality a cover for oppressive and "hegemonic" capitalist and imperialist activity. I argue in this chapter that Western values as they have evolved from their Judeo-Christian and Greco-Roman roots in the West are the closest approximation to pragmatic universal values of freedom and order that have ever been available to humanity. Whether or not they are transferable or adoptable by nations theologically or ideologically opposed to them is another question entirely.

2   See Robert B. Edgerton, *Sick Societies: Challenging the Myth of Primitive Harmony* (New York: Free Press, 1992).

3   Peter Brimelow, *The Patriot Game* (Toronto: Key Porter Books, 1986), p. 142–43 [my emphasis].

4   For this chapter, the following have been helpful overviews: Alvin J. Schmidt, *The Menace of Multiculturalism: Trojan Horse in America* (Westport, CT: Praeger, 1997); Paul Edward Gottfried, *Multiculturalism and the Politics of Guilt: Toward a Secular Theocracy* (Columbia: University of Missouri, 2002); and David O. Sacks and Peter A. Thiel, *The Diversity Myth: Multiculturalism and the Political Intolerance on Campus* (Oakland, CA: Independent Institute, 1998).

5   We do hear terms such as "black culture." But a culture has no colour.

Most "African-American" blacks are not culturally African. The majority
share a Caribbean culture, though there are also many different
Caribbean cultures (Jamaicans and Bajans may not even talk to each
other). There are hundreds of different African cultures.

6   It is true that most conservative political philosophers—such as Edmund
Burke and Joseph de Maistre—promoted the appeal of particular
cultural and historical identities. But that does not make them fascists in
practice or temperament, for their love of local community, family,
private property, and so on is inherently anti-Statist. What turns such
preferences into fascism is the insistence on the absorption of all citizens
into a unitary State, the cultivation of a national cult—often an ethnic
one—surrounding the leader, *führer*, or *duce*, the insistence on a
wholesale replacement of the myriad local functions of normal civil life
with government programs, and, in general, a pervasive State regulation
of a formerly free society.

7   This complaint was made by Professor Sidney Hook of Stanford
University, whose comments are in David O. Sacks and Peter A. Thiel,
*The Diversity Myth: Multiculturalism and the Political Intolerance on
Campus* (Oakland, CA: Independent Institute, 1998). Stanford was the
nesting place for multicultural theory in the mid-1980s, and its
reputation was almost ruined by it. This book is a must-read for an
understanding of how multicultural theory developed, unfolded, and
collapsed in America.

8   An objection might be that because Greece and Rome were slave-holding
societies we cannot say they were truly interested in universal truths of a
moral kind, and therefore our modern Western values were not inherited
from them. However, the influence of Greece and Rome on Western
civilization as a whole, its law, culture, and philosophical and religious
tradition (I think of our tradition of natural law and of Christian
Neoplatonism as just two examples), is incalculable. Finally, the ancients
simply did not consider chattel slavery immoral. Most of it was war
slavery and was considered justifiable retribution for past aggressions.
Slavery was only made possible by the legal redefinition of human beings
as non-persons (i.e., as property). Elsewhere in this book I make the
argument that all the modern democracies of the West, despite their
Christian roots, are de facto invisible slave societies because this same
legal redefinition of human life as non-human when in utero has alone
enabled the killing of countless millions.

9   On this, see the fascinating work by James C. Scott, *Seeing Like a State:
How Certain Schemes to Improve the Human Condition Have Failed* (New
Haven, CT: Yale University Press, 1998).

10   J.L. Talmon, *Romanticism and Revolt: Europe 1815–1848* (New York:

W.W. Norton & Co., 1967), p. 96ff.

11  Gene Edward Veith Jr., *Modern Fascism: Liquidating the Judeo-Christian Worldview* (St. Louis: Concordia, 1993), p. 37.

12  Cited in Gene Edward Veith Jr., *Modern Fascism*, p. 134 [emphasis added].

13  William D. Gairdner, *The Book of Absolutes: A Critique of Relativism and a Defence of Universals* (Montreal-Kingston: McGill-Queen's University Press, 2008), esp. ch. 11, "German Philosophy and the Relativist Revolt Against Western Civilization."

14  See Michael Dewing, Marc Leman, Political and Social Affairs Division, Parliamentary Research Branch, *Current Issue Review*, "Canadian Multiculturalism," revised March 16, 2006. This report is weakened by spurious assumptions with respect to Canada's constitutional founding. For example, on p. 2, the authors state that Canada's English and French founders "appointed themselves the official founders of Canada."

15  Jeffrey G. Reitz, Rupa Banerjee, Mai Phan, and Jordan Thompson, "Race, Religion, and the Social Integration of New Immigrant Minorities in Canada," Munk Centre for International Studies, University of Toronto, September 2008 (contact: Jeffrey.reitz@utoronto.ca).

16  "Ethnic Enclaves Weak Link, Study Finds" (*National Post*, June 2, 2010).

17  See Robert Putnam, *E Pluribus Unum: Diversity and Community in the 21st Century*, cited in Herbert Grubel, *The Effects of Mass Immigration on Canadian Living Standards and Society* (Vancouver: Fraser Institute, 2009).

18  A fascinating treatment of this historical and political trend is Jonah Goldberg, *Liberal Fascism: The Secret History of the American Left from Mussolini to the Politics of Meaning* (New York: Doubleday, 2007).

19  Spoken during his presentation on the Fourth Report of the Bilingualism and Biculturalism Commission to the House of Commons, October 8, 1971.

20  The word "university" is derived from the Latin term *universitas magistrorum et scholarium*, roughly meaning "community of teachers and scholars." The term was created by the Italian University of Bologna, which, with a traditional founding date of 1088, is the oldest university in the world. Note that many medieval universities were run for hundreds of years before their formal establishment as Christian episcopal or monastic schools, evidence of which appears as early as AD 501–600.

21  For a book-length critique of this notion, see Gairdner, *The Book of Absolutes*.

22  Gene Edward Veith Jr., *Modern Fascism: Liquidating the Judeo-Christian Worldview* (St. Louis: Concordia, 1993), p. 39ff.

23  Here are some of the anti-humanist sentiments I found in my files, from when all this was getting revved up around 1993. Here is David Bower,

anti-population spokesman for Friends of the Earth: "Childbearing should be a punishable crime against society, unless the parent holds a government licence." And here is Carol Amery from the German Green Party who says that she and her pro-nature colleagues "aspire to a cultural model in which the killing of a forest will be considered more contemptible and more criminal than the sale of six-year-old children to Asian brothels." Hear also Stephanie Mills, co-author of the book *Whatever Happened to Ecology?*, who insists that "humanity is debased protoplasm." Paul Watson, of the *Sea Shepherd* operation, told the press that "humanity is the AIDS of the earth." And finally, and perhaps the most rabidly anti-human of them all, was this bit from David Graber, a research biologist with the American National Parks Service: "Human happiness [is] not as important as a wild and healthy planet. We have become a plague upon ourselves and upon the earth. Until such time as *homo sapiens* should decide to rejoin nature, some of us can only hope for the right virus to come along." David seems to imagine himself surviving the virus he is wishing on the rest of us.

24  Gottfried, *Multiculturalism and the Politics of Guilt*, especially Introduction, and ch. 2.

25  See Michael Ignatieff, "Do We Need Canadian History?" *National Post*, September 4, 1999, cited in Gottfried.

26  It was not a true and legally binding referendum; it was a provincial plebiscite.

27  Cited in Robert Martin, *The Most Dangerous Branch: How the Supreme Court of Canada Has Undermined Our Law and Our Democracy* (Montreal-Kingston: McGill-Queen's University Press, 2003), p. 20.

28  Stewart Bell, *Cold Terror: How Canada Nurtures and Exports Terrorism Around the World* (Toronto: John Wiley & Sons, 2005), p. 11.

29  The report was based on a national poll performed by the Chicago Council on Foreign Relations, May to July 2002.

30  For much of what follows on immigration and on terrorism, I am indebted to and draw freely from the tireless work of James Bissett, a former ambassador and executive director of the Canadian Immigration Service, and of Martin Collacott, who has had thirty years of distinguished service in Canada's Department of External Affairs, including acting as director general for Security Services. I have also drawn liberally from Stewart Bell, *Cold Terror: How Canada Nurtures and Exports Terrorism Around the World* (Toronto: John Wiley & Sons, 2005), and also from Christopher Caldwell, *Reflection on the Revolution in Europe: Immigration, Islam, and the West* (New York: Doubleday, 2009).

31  *National Post*, October 15, 2009.

32  The terminology, as explained by Martin Collacott, is as follows: Canada

is the only country in the world that uses the term "refugee-claimant" as an exact equivalent of the term "asylum-seeker" used by other countries (i.e., someone who arrives on your soil and asks to be accepted as a refugee for permanent resettlement). When it comes to the general term "refugee," our usage is the same as that of other countries: it refers to people who have fled their own country and are living somewhere else until they can either return home or are accepted for permanent resettlement somewhere else—usually with the help of the United Nations High Commission for Refugees.

33   From James Bissett, "The Current State of Canadian Immigration Policy," p. 6, 2008.

34   Robin Banerjee and William B.P. Robson, "*Faster, Younger, Richer?: The Fond Hope and Sobering Reality of Immigration's Impact on Canada's Demographic and Economic Future*," C.D. Howe Institute Commentary, no. 291, July 2009.

35   See Christopher Caldwell, *Reflection on the Revolution in Europe: Immigration, Islam, and the West* (New York: Doubleday, 2009), p. 47.

36   Martin Collacott, "Canada's Immigration Policy: The Need for Major Reform," in *Public Policy Sources*, Fraser Institute, no. 64, 2003.

37   He is referring to the story of how, if you drop a frog into a pan of boiling water, it will immediately leap out. But if you start with cold water and gradually raise the temperature, the frog will sit until it dies (*National Post*, September 28, 2009).

38   Martin Paldam, cited in Herbert Grubel, "Immigration and the Welfare State in Canada: Growing Conflicts, Constructive Solutions," *Public Policy Sources*, no. 84 (Vancouver: Fraser Institute, September 2005), p. 24ff.

39   See George Borjas, *Heaven's Gate: Immigration Policy and the American Economy* (Princeton University Press, paperback, 2001).

40   James Bissett, "The Current State of Canadian Immigration Policy," p. 7, 2008. From Statistics Canada Cat No. 11F009MIE—2007198.

41   Cited in Herbert Grubel, ed., *The Effects of Mass Immigration on Canadian Living Standards and Society* (Vancouver: Fraser Institute, 2009), p. 9.

42   *National Post*, November 7, 2009.

43   The factual materials in this section are variously taken from works by James Bissett, Martin Collacott, Stewart Bell, *Cold Terror: How Canada Nurtures and Exports Terrorism Around the World* (Toronto: John Wiley & Sons, 2005); from materials on the website of the Mackenzie Institute, Toronto; and from various file and Internet sources.

44   See Mark Krikorian, "Mass Immigration Defeats Homeland Security," in *Immigration Policy and the Terrorist Threat* (Vancouver: Fraser Institute,

2008), p. 39.

45   From Jamie Glazov, "From the Left With Hate," *National Post*, April 21, 2009, excerpted from his book *United in Hate: The Left's Romance With Tyranny and Terror* (Los Angeles: WND Books, 2009).

46   For this, and many of the other facts, insights, and quotes in this segment, I am indebted to Christopher Caldwell, *Reflections on the Revolution in Europe* (New York: Doubleday, 2009). [Emphasis mine].

47   Here is a paragraph describing Peace Village: "Canada's first Islamic subdivision, where all 260 homes belong to members of the Ahmadiyya sect, who flooded to Canada in the 1980s after persecution in Pakistan. It looks ordinary, with basketball nets and minivans in the driveways, until you notice the street signs: Mahmood Crescent, Ahmadiyya Avenue and Noor-Ud-Din Court." You can Google "Peace Village" in Vaughan, Ontario, to read more.

48   From Mary Habeck, *Knowing the Enemy: Jihadist Ideology and the War on Terror* (New Haven, CN,: Yale University Press, 2006), p. 7.

49   As reported in Daniel Stoffman, "Truths and Myths About Immigration," in *Immigration Policy and the Terrorist Threat* (Vancouver: Fraser Institute, 2008), p. 14. The papers in this book were gathered from a conference on terrorism held in Toronto, June 2007.

50   Caldwell, p. 256.

51   Habeck, p. 12. Habeck explains that all Jihadists share five understandings: Islam is the one true faith that will dominate the world; Muslim rulers must govern by the Shari'a alone; that their Holy Books contain the whole truth for living a righteous life; that there can be no separation between religion and life; and . . . that all true Muslims are in a state of conflict with unbelievers (p. 17).

52   On this note, a man I assume was my forebear, William Henry Temple Gairdner (1873–1928), a former British Anglican canon of Cairo (referred to by his followers as "Temple Gairdner of Cairo"—which is also the title of the moving biography of his life by his secretary, Constance Padwick), published a then very successful book *The Reproach of Islam* (London: Church Missionary Society, 1909). That book sold over 20,000 copies, and was devoted to describing the contrast between Christianity and Islam. Gairdner's main thesis was that Christianity had failed to do its job, and so Islam arose to fill the spiritual vacuum. He was also the founder of a very long-lived journal, *Occident and Orient*, which attempted to bring the two worlds together.

53   Habeck, p. 72.

54   Andrew McCarthy, "Islam and the Left," in the *New Criterion*, January 2010, p. 18.

55   Habeck, p. 72.

56 Ibid., p. 193n31.

57 Victor Zubrin, *Energy Victory: Winning the War on Terror by Breaking Free of Oil* (New York: Prometheus Books, 2007).

## 14: FRENCH-FRIED: OFFICIAL BILINGUALISM, SEPARATISM, AND THE POLITICS OF LANGUAGE AND CULTURE

1 On this matter of the enhanced "legibility" of a people provided to the State by an official language, see especially James C. Scott, *Seeing Like a State: How Certain Schemes to Improve the Human Condition Have Failed* (New Haven, CT,: Yale University Press, 1998).

2 Scott Reid, *Lament For A Notion: The Life and Death of Canada's Bilingual Dream* (Vancouver: Arsenal Pulp Press, 1993), p. 101. This remains one of the few thorough critiques of Canadian bilingual policy.

3 In Peter Brimelow, *The Patriot Game* (Toronto: Key Porter Books, 1986), p. 95.

4 James C. Scott, *Seeing Like a State*, pp. 72–73.

5 See also Eugene Forsey, "Canada: Two Nations or One?" in *Canadian Journal of Economics and Political Science* XXVI, 4, November 1962. [Emphasis mine].

6 François Vaillancourt and Olivier Coche, *Official Language Policies at the Federal Level in Canada*, 2006 (Vancouver: Fraser Institute, May 2009).

7 Brimelow, *The Patriot Game*, p. 82.

8 Cited in Brimelow, *The Patriot Game*, p. 85.

9 Communicated by email from Monique Cheff, statistical adviser, Media Relations, Office of the Chief Human Resources Officer, Ottawa, January 5, 2010.

10 "Can Canada Survive Its Language Crisis?," an address by Nicholas J. Patterson, the Canadian Development Institute, to the third annual meeting of a group named US English, in Washington, DC, April 15, 1989.

11 The net immigration-emigration numbers for Quebec since 1971, supplied by economist Jean-Luc Migué, January 7, 2010, are: from 1971 to 2001, 812,500 moved from Quebec to other provinces, consisting of 454,400 (55.9 percent) anglophones. But 248,200 (30.5 percent) francophones also left the province and 110,000 (13.6 percent) "other." At the same time, some people moved to Quebec from other provinces. Net migrations (outmigration minus immigration) amounted to 387,100, of whom 276,000 (71.3 percent) were anglos, 37,500 (9.7 percent) were francos and 73,600 (19.0 percent) were "other."

12 See more on Taché in Janet Ajzenstat, Paul Romney, Ian Gentles, and William D. Gairdner, *Canada's Founding Debates* (Toronto: Stoddart Publishing, 1999; and in paperback, University of Toronto Press, 2003).

This quotation is on p. 334.

13 The phrase is from the iconic novel *Two Solitudes*, by Hugh MacLennan, my English professor at McGill in 1959–1960. The plot centres on the growing and isolating French-English difference in Canada.

## 15: HERE COMES THE JUDGE! HOW CANADIANS LOST THEIR REAL RIGHTS AND FREEDOMS

1 I have been assisted by the works and comments of colleagues Rory Leishman, author of *Against Judicial Activism: The Decline of Freedom and Democracy in Canada* (Montreal-Kingston: McGill-Queen's University Press, 2006); Rainer Knopff, author with F.L. Morton of *The Charter Revolution and the Court Party* (Peterborough, ON: Broadview Press, 2000); and Gwen Landolt, Canadian lawyer, founder of R.E.A.L. Women of Canada, and indefatigable warrior in defence of a civil society.

2 Robert Martin, *The Most Dangerous Branch: How the Supreme Court of Canada has Undermined Our Law and Our Democracy* (Montreal-Kingston: McGill-Queen's University Press, 2003), p. xii. Martin argues that Canada is in the grip of a theocratic "orthodoxy"—a "secular state religion" which has three main aspects: it is rooted in ideological beliefs that operate just like a faith; it is imposed on citizens (mostly by courts) and enforced by the State; it is secular in that it aggressively denies the existence of God and banishes other religions (other than secularism) from the public square.

3 Quebecers, unlike all other Canadians, live under a "*code civil*" that governs all except criminal matters.

4 Rainer Knopff and F.L. Morton, *The Charter Revolution and the Court Party* (Peterborough, ON: Broadview Press, 2000).

5 The phrase "living tree" was first used by Lord Sankey of the Judicial Committee of the Privy Council of England in its ruling in *Edwards v. Canada (A.G.)*, 1929, the so-called "Persons Case." This case was brought to establish that women were also "persons" under the law for the purposes of eligibility for appointment to the Senate of Canada, even though the plain words and original understanding of Section 24 of the BNA Act, 1867, clearly specified that only men (with significant property, wealth, and status in Canada) were to be appointed. As his justification for this judicial amendment of Canada's Constitution, Lord Sankey stated that "the British North America Act planted in Canada a living tree capable of growth and expansion within its natural limits." That was a rationale for judicial usurpation of legislatures that has been cited by activists ever since. We may agree that Parliament should have amended the Constitution to include women as potential senators, while deploring Sankey's usurpation.

6    Justice Lamer invented the Canadian term and technique of "reading in" in *Schacter v. Canada* (1992).

7    At the graduation ceremony for the law school of the University of Toronto, 1992, Lamer expressed his distaste for democracy because, according to him, it did not sufficiently encourage "human flourishing." For this, he suggested an absolute benevolent monarchy would be preferable. See Robert Martin, *The Most Dangerous Branch: How the Supreme Court of Canada has Undermined Our Law and Our Democracy* (Montreal-Kingston: McGill-Queen's University Press, 2003), p. 83.

8    Cited in Martin, p. 28. [Emphasis added].

9    Ibid., pp. 78, 85, 90. [Emphasis added].

10   In a shocking example of Wilson's overheated feminism, she wrote in chapter 1 of her tax-funded $10 million Panel on Violence Against Women Report, 1993, that "everyday in this country women are maligned, humiliated, shunned, screamed at, pushed, kicked, punched, assaulted, beaten, raped, physically disfigured, tortured, threatened with weapons and murdered." She managed to overlook the plain fact that although women may get the worst of it because they are physically weaker, sociologists have long established that responsibility for the initiation of male/female violence is about fifty-fifty; that in over half of such cases both participants are drunk or on drugs, or both; and that in all countries of the world violence is overwhelmingly directed at males, by other males. In Canada, men are about 50 percent more likely than women to be victims of violent crimes of all types, except for sexual assault (obviously).

11   See A.V. Dicey, *Introduction to the Study of the Law of the Constitution* (Indianapolis: Liberty Classics, 1982), p. 142.

12   Martin, *The Most Dangerous Branch*, p. 179.

13   Fareed Zakaria, *The Future of Freedom: Illiberal Democracy at Home and Abroad* (New York: W.W. Norton & Co., 2003). Readers who want a more detailed examination of the transformation of classical, or constitutional, liberalism into its modern welfare state variant in the twentieth century, from Mussolini to Roosevelt to Obama, will find it in Jonah Goldberg, *Liberal Fascism* (New York: Doubleday, 2007).

14   On this theme, see Peter H. Russell, *Constitutional Odyssey: Can Canadians Become a Sovereign People?* (Toronto: University of Toronto Press, 2004). Russell argues that "Canadians have never squarely faced the question whether they share enough in common to form a single people consenting to a common constitution."

15   Premier Clyde Wells of Newfoundland said of this process: "We must never again implement this process for Constitutional reform. It is impossible for the eleven first ministers to do justice to the matters they

have to consider, and it is grossly unfair to the 26 million people of this nation to have their first minister closeted and making decisions in a secret way without letting them know what was at stake, and the basis of the decisions were made."

16  The clash between representative democracy in the Westminster tradition, and the instruments of direct democracy, is this: representatives of the people in the Westminster system are required once elected to Parliament to serve the common good of *all the people*, and not merely the good only of the electors who sent them there (for the local good may conflict with the national good). They are not permitted to receive instructions from or obey mandates of the electors. In a system of direct democracy it is the opposite: representatives must specifically carry out such mandates.

17  Leishman, *Against Judicial Activism*, p. 146.

18  Ibid., p. 147.

19  Martin, *The Most Dangerous Branch*, p. 100.

20  The Lortie Commission argued for the disqualification of anyone convicted of an "offence punishable by a maximum of life imprisonment and a minimum sentence of 10 years or more to be disqualified from voting during the time they are in prison."

21  Cited in "Stephen Harper's Robed Opposition" (*National Post*, December 17, 2009).

22  The Supreme Court invented "analogous grounds" in *Andrews v. Law Society of British Columbia* (1989), and the definition of these grounds (detailed in Martin, p. 122) is so limitless it "allows courts to determine that almost any conceivable distinction is 'discriminatory' and, therefore, illegitimate."

23  William D. Gairdner, "Poetry and the Mystique of the Self in John Stuart Mill: Sources of Libertarian Socialism," in *Humanitas*, Vol. XXI, 2008. The article can also be obtained from the archive of my website at www.Williamgairdner.com

## 16: GOING FORTH BOLDLY: A CALL TO ACTION

1  Speech by John A. Macdonald, Legislative Assembly of Canada, February 6, 1865. The full and rousing speech appears in Janet Ajzenstat, Paul Romney, Ian Gentles, and William D. Gairdner, *Canada's Founding Debates* (Toronto: University of Toronto Press, 2003; Stoddart Publishing, 1999), p. 203ff.

2  On this question of control, André Carrel, a Canadian of Swiss origin, shared this insight: "All the issues you raise in your chapter under the heading 'Some General Recommendations' are issues that you could raise under a Swiss-style constitution. You might form a new political party with candidates who support your philosophy. You might initiate a

petition on taxation, public unions, corporate law, or anything, and if you could convince enough people, it would come to a vote, and the people would decide. Of course, changing the national constitution requires a national referendum. But a change of anything within the sphere of a local government is dealt with and decided by referendum at the level of the local governments. The other fundamental difference, linked to bottom-up sovereignty, is the relationship between the legislative, executive, and judiciary. Switzerland does not have the equivalent of a prime minister or president. Members of the Executive (the Swiss cabinet) are not members of the legislature. Can you imagine question period in Canada's Parliament if ministers were elected individually by Parliament? Can you imagine such as a minister of defence elected by Parliament, accountable to Parliament, and subject to re-election by Parliament, taking marching orders from a prime minister!"

3    Cited in Karen Selick, "The Right that Dares Not Speak its Name," a brief of the Canadian Constitution Foundation, January 2010.

# INDEX

groups, 47
and subsidized arts/culture, 125
and welfare, 182, 184, 185, 187, 414
annual bill, 484
charts/graphs, 159–60
corporations, 159–60, 203
increase in, 65
of middle class, 64
statistics, 64, 65
top marginal rate, 61
(See also corporate tax; consumption tax; flat tax; income tax; progressive taxation)
Taylor, Graeme, 271
terrorism, 13, 22, 227, 406, 412, 415–35
Thatcher, Margaret, 94, 210–11
theft, 359, 360
Thiels, Peter, 404, 405
Third World, 92, 207, 217–218, 208–13, 383 (See also foreign aid; poverty)
Thoreau, Henry David, 84, 85
Tibet, 218
tied labour, 221
Timely Medical Alternatives, 311–12
Tiryakian, Edward, 255
tobacco-related illnesses, 322, 323, 325, 326, 327
top-down style. See French style; Handicap System
Toronto 18, the, 430, 432
Total Fertility Rate (TFR), 280, 398–99, 428
totalitarianism, 83, 85, 91, 94–95, 96, 97, 98–99, 101, 116, 120, 209, 225, 258, 399, 423–24, 434, 461
transactions of decline, 22, 101, 121, 132–34, 168, 214
transgenderism, 43, 239, 256, 405
transgenerational borrowing, 165–66
Trinidad, 416
Trudeau, Pierre Elliott, 11–12, 18, 21, 29, 34,

39–47, 81, 82, 85, 113, 114, 119, 134, 145, 160, 184, 212, 219, 239, 326, 336, 384, 393, 399, 406, 407, 416, 441–42, 439, 440, 444, 448, 455, 457–58, 462–63, 496n5, 498n24
truth in sentencing, 366, 376
Tulloch, Gordon, 384
Turkey, 134, 417, 429
Turner, Mark, 374
Tutu, Archbishop Desmond, 208
Twinkie defence, 60

U.S. Court of Appeals, 265
U.S. Declaration of Feminism, 237
U.S. Office of Economic Opportunity, 201–2
U.S. Supreme Court, 102, 255
Uganda, 232
Ujamaa, 82, 213
UN Convention for the Elimination of All Forms of Discrimination Against Women (CEDAW), 240
UN Millennium Project, 230
underground economy, 63, 64, 101, 193
unemployment insurance, 87, 183, 185, 244
unemployment, 74, 202, 217, 270, 320, 410
unfunded liabilities, 18–19, 164, 170, 203–4
Unilateral Declaration of Independence (UDI), 451, 452
unions, 37, 80, 104, 484–85, 487–88
United Kingdom, 94, 124, 307, 315, 356, 357, 358, 409, 429, 430
United Nations Committee on Trade and Development (UNCTAD 1), 209
United Nations, 208–12, 226, 239, 348, 492
United States
crime rate, 356, 363, 364

family trends, 136
fertility, 398
health care, 291–93, 308, 310, 314, 315–21, 319, 496n5
homicides ranking immigration, 407, 409, 410, 419
incarceration rate, 357
justice system, 348
marriage laws, 457
wealth ranking, 78
welfare, 182–84, 201
universal day care, 39, 241, 245, 259, 260, 268–73
Universal Declaration of Human Rights, 54
universalism, 123–24, 390, 391, 402
universities, 76, 77, 86, 114, 115, 213, 214, 281, 258, 383, 396, 427, 401, 404–6
usage/exchange value conflict, 87–88
utopianism, 28, 108, 110, 112, 115–17, 120, 140, 143, 144, 152, 210, 229, 230, 249, 258, 273, 288, 425, 427

value, economic, 260–67
value, objective measure of, 90
value, subjective, 86
Van Gogh, Theo, 419
Van Loan, Peter, 418
victim class/oppression class, 259
Vietnam, 95, 209, 231
visible minorities, 397, 409, 415
Vitz, Paul C., 255–56
Voltaire, 34
voluntary exchange concept, 81
von Mises, Ludwig, 74, 153
vote-grabs, 164, 369, 416, 436, 441, 449, 468
voting rights, 139
Vow of Citizenship, 415, 436

wage and price control, 90, 91, 122

CPSIA information can be obtained at www.ICGtesting.com
Printed in the USA
LVOW080711130911

245967LV00003B/20/P

9 781926 645667